Volume III

The Van de Walle Professional Mathematics Series

Teaching Student-Centered Mathematics

Developmentally Appropriate Instruction for Grades 6–8

Second Edition

John A. Van de Walle
Late of Virginia Commonwealth University

Jennifer M. Bay-Williams
University of Louisville

Karen S. Karp
University of Louisville

LouAnn H. Lovin
James Madison University

PEARSON

Boston   Columbus   Indianapolis   New York   San Francisco   Upper Saddle River
Amsterdam   Cape Town   Dubai   London   Madrid   Milan   Munich   Paris   Montréal   Toronto
Delhi   Mexico City   São Paulo   Sydney   Hong Kong   Seoul   Singapore   Taipei   Tokyo

Editor-in-Chief: Jeffery Johnston
Vice President, Editor in Chief: Aurora Martínez Ramos
Executive Editor: Linda Bishop
Senior Development Editor: Christina Robb
Editorial Assistant: Laura White
Marketing Manager: Christine Gatchell
Production Editor: Karen Mason / Cynthia DeRocco
Editorial Production Service: Electronic Publishing Services Inc.
Manufacturing Buyer: Megan Cochran
Electronic Composition: Jouve
Interior Design: Electronic Publishing Services Inc.
Cover Designer: Laura Gardner

Image Credits: Chapter Opener Images: Left blocks, J. McPhail/Shutterstock; Middle tangrams, David Crehner/Fotolia; Right blocks, Sergey Galushko/Fotolia. Teaching Tip Icon: Koya79/Fotolia. Standards for Mathematical Practice Icon: Xuejun Li/Fotolia

Cover Image: Paulrommer/Shutterstock

Credits and acknowledgments borrowed from other sources and reproduced, with permission, in this textbook appear on the appropriate page within text.

Many of the designations used by manufacturers and sellers to distinguish their products are claimed as trademarks. Where those designations appear in this book, and Allyn and Bacon was aware of a trademark claim, the designations have been printed in initial or all caps.

Library of Congress Cataloging-in-Publication Data

Van de Walle, John A.
[Teaching student-centered mathematics. Grades 5–8]
Teaching student-centered mathematics: developmentally appropriate instruction for grades 6–8—Second edition / John A. Van de Walle, Virginia Commonwealth University, Jennifer M. Bay-Williams, University of Louisville, Karen S. Karp, University of Louisville, LouAnn H. Lovin, James Madison University.
     pages cm.
   Volume III of the Van de Walle professional mathematics series
   Revision of: Teaching student-centered mathematics. Grade 5–8 / John Van de Walle, LouAnn H. Lovin. c2006.
   Includes bibliographical references and index.
   ISBN-13: 978-0-13-282486-6
   ISBN-10: 0-13-282486-8
   1. Mathematics—Study and teaching (Elementary)—United States. I. Karp, Karen S. II. Bay-Williams, Jennifer M. III. Lovin, LouAnn H. IV. Title.
   QA13.V35 2014
   372.7—dc23.   2012040021

10 9 8 7 6 5

ISBN 10: 0-13-282486-8
ISBN 13: 978-0-13-282486-6

About the Authors

The late **John A. Van de Walle** was a professor emeritus at Virginia Commonwealth University. He was a mathematics education consultant who regularly gave professional development workshops for K–8 teachers in the United States and Canada. He visited and taught in elementary school classrooms and worked with teachers to implement student-centered math lessons. He co-authored the Scott Foresman-Addison Wesley *Mathematics K-6* series and contributed to the Pearson School mathematics program, enVisionMATH. In addition, he wrote numerous chapters and articles for the National Council of Teachers of Mathematics (NCTM) books and journals and was very active in NCTM, including serving on the Board of Directors, as the chair of the Educational Materials Committee, and as a frequent speaker at national and regional meetings.

Jennifer M. Bay-Williams is a professor of mathematics education at the University of Louisville (Kentucky). Jennifer has published many articles on teaching and learning in NCTM journals. She has also coauthored numerous books, including *Mathematics Coaching: Resources and Tools for Coaches and Leaders, K–12*; *Developing Essential Understanding of Addition and Subtraction for Teaching Mathematics in Pre-K–Grade 2*; *Math and Literature: Grades 6–8*; *Math and Nonfiction: Grades 6–8*; and *Navigating through Connections in Grades 6–8*. Jennifer taught elementary, middle, and high school in Missouri and in Peru, and continues to work in classrooms at all levels with students and with teachers. Jennifer served as member of Board of Directors for TODOS: Equity for All, as president of the Association of Mathematics Teacher Educators (AMTE), and as editor for the 2012 NCTM Yearbook.

Karen S. Karp is a professor of mathematics education at the University of Louisville (Kentucky). Prior to entering the field of teacher education she was an elementary school teacher. She is also co-author of *Elementary and Middle School Mathematics: Teaching Developmentally, Growing Professionally: Readings from NCTM Publications for Grades K–8; Developing Essential Understanding of Addition and Subtraction for Teaching Mathematics in Pre-K–Grade 2*; and numerous book chapters and articles. She is a former member of the Board of Directors of NCTM and a former president of AMTE. She continues to work in classrooms to support teachers of students with disabilities in their mathematics instruction.

LouAnn H. Lovin is a professor of mathematics education at James Madison University (Virginia). She co-authored the first edition of the *Teaching Student-Centered Mathematics* Professional Development Series with John A. Van deWalle, as well as *Teaching Mathematics Meaningfully: Solutions for Reaching Struggling Learners* with special educators David Allsopp and Maggie Kyger. LouAnn taught mathematics to middle and high school students before transitioning to pre-K–8. Over the last 15 years, she has worked in pre-K–grade 8 classrooms and engaged with teachers in professional development as they implement a student-centered approach to teaching mathematics. She has published articles in NCTM's *Teaching Children Mathematics* and *Mathematics Teaching in the Middle School* and has served on NCTM's Educational Materials Committee. LouAnn's research interest is investigating ways to develop teachers' mathematical knowledge needed to teach for understanding.

Brief Contents

Contents

Part II: Teaching Student-Centered Mathematics

10 The Number System   169

15 Working with Data and Doing Statistics   325

16 Investigating Concepts of Probability   354

Engaging

Most of the disciplinary issues in a classroom are a because of students being bored or because a student finds little relevance in the task.

The best way to engage the students is to involve them in activities that they enjoy and being allowed to solve problems that make sense to them.

Students enjoy the various creative ways of problem solving and sharing how they figured out.

With respect to math and science, students learn mathematics through real contexts, problems, situations & models that allow them

to build meaning for
their concepts
(Hiebert, Carpenter, fennema,
fuson, wearne, Murray,
Olivier & Human, 1997)
So teaching through
problem solving helps
student develop skills
& ideas that emerge from
working with the problem

Preface

All students can learn mathematics with understanding! It is through the teacher's actions that every student, in his or her own way, can come to believe this important truth. We believe that teachers must create an environment in which students are trusted to solve problems and work together using their ideas to do so. Instruction involves posing tasks that will engage students in the mathematics they are expected to learn. Then, by allowing students to interact with and struggle with the mathematics using *their* ideas and *their* strategies—a student-centered approach—the mathematics they learn will be connected to other mathematics and to their world. Students will see the value of mathematics and feel empowered to use it. The title of this book, *Teaching Student-Centered Mathematics: Developmentally Appropriate Instruction for Grades 6–8*, reflects this vision. This vision is so critical to the learning of mathematics that, in this second edition, we start the book with a new Part I that addresses how to build a student-centered environment in which students can become mathematically proficient.

 ## What Are Our Goals for the Professional Math Series?

Creating a classroom in which students design their solution pathways, engage in productive struggle, and connect mathematical ideas is complex. Questions arise, such as, "How do I get students to wrestle with problems if they just want me to show them how? What kinds of tasks lend themselves to this type of engagement? Where can I learn the mathematics content I need in order to be able to teach in this way?" With these and other questions firmly in mind, we have three main objectives for the series:

1. Illustrate what it means to teach mathematics in a student-centered, problem-based manner.

2. Serve as a reference for all of the mathematics content suggested for grades pre-K–2, 3–5, and 6–8 as recommended in the *Common Core State Standards* and the *Curriculum Focal Points* (CCSSO, 2010; NCTM, 2006), as well as research-based strategies concerning how students learn this content.

3. Present a practical resource of robust, problem-based activities and tasks that can engage students in the mathematics that is important for them to learn.

These are also goals of *Elementary and Middle School Mathematics: Teaching Developmentally*, a comprehensive resource for teachers in grades K–8, which has been widely used in universities and in schools.

There is some overlap of both the text and activities between the comprehensive K–8 book and this Professional Series. However, we have adapted the Professional Series to be more useful for a practicing classroom teacher by focusing the content on specific grade bands and adding additional information on creating an effective classroom environment, engaging families, and aligning teaching to the new standards. We've also included more activities and lessons. We hope you will find that this is a valuable resource for teaching and learning mathematics!

Why Revise the Professional Math Series?

Since the writing of the first edition of this book began nearly a decade ago, many developments in mathematics education have occurred—from the publication of NCTM's *Curriculum Focal Points* (2006) to the development and implementation of the *Common Core State Standards* (CCSSO, 2010). Research has provided new information about how children learn particular mathematical ideas. We have also received great feedback from readers about what they *liked* about the first edition and what they *wished* would be in the second edition. It was time to incorporate these ideas into the book to ensure classroom teachers had access to strong support aligned with the latest developments in mathematics education.

 What's New to the Second Edition of the Professional Math Series?

We made numerous significant changes to the Professional Series. They include:

- **A New Part I: Establishing a Student-Centered Environment.** The second edition is divided into *two* parts. Part I consists of seven chapters (all new) that address important ideas for creating a classroom environment in which all students can succeed. Part I focuses on what it means to teach mathematics *through* problem solving and how to differentiate instruction to meet the needs of *all* students. The final chapter in Part I expands the focus of mathematics education beyond the classroom, offering ideas for working with families, principals, and the community. These chapters focus on important "hot" topics that teachers and reviewers requested and that are important in making mathematics accessible to all learners. They are, by design, shorter in length than the content chapters in Part II, but are full of effective strategies and ideas. The intent is that these chapters can be used in professional development workshops, book study, or professional learning community (PLC) discussions. This new part replaces Chapter 1 in the first edition, which provided briefer attention to some of these topics. Part I includes:

  - A more in-depth definition of what we mean by *understanding*, using the eight mathematical practices identified in the *Common Core State Standards* (CCSSO, 2010), the five strands of mathematical proficiency from *Adding It Up* (NCTM, 2001), and NCTM's process standards (2000) (Chapter 1).

  - A discussion of what it means to teach mathematics *through* problem solving (as compared to teaching mathematics *for* problem solving). We include a discussion about criteria to use in the selection of problem-based tasks, and we present a set of recommendations for facilitating effective classroom discourse (Chapter 2).

  - Information on various formative assessment strategies, including observations, diagnostic interviews, and tasks, as well as creating and using rubrics (Chapter 3).

  - Strategies to support the diverse range of learners in your classroom (Chapters 4–6).

  - Concrete ideas about how to communicate and engage with a variety of stakeholders to ensure students receive the support they need to be successful in mathematics (Chapter 7).

- **Connections to the *Common Core State Standards*.** A priority in preparing the second edition was to align the material to the *Common Core State Standards*. This has resulted in important changes:

- Connections to the eight Standards for Mathematical Practice, critical components of the CCSSO recommendations, are highlighted in the text through margin notes that focus readers' attention on examples in the nearby text of what these eight practices look like across content areas and grade levels.

- Chapters have been reorganized and updated to reflect the CCSSO recommendations and present a more coherent progression of mathematical ideas and student learning. Explicit and specific attention is given to grade-level positioning of content throughout the discussion within each content chapter.

- **Increased Attention to Student Diversity.** A new emphasis on diversity can be seen with the addition of chapters on differentiating instruction (Chapter 4) as well as planning, teaching, and assessing culturally and linguistically diverse students (Chapter 5) and students with exceptionalities (Chapter 6). Additional strategies for supporting students with special needs and English language learners are included in Part II chapters, are highlighted in several activities in each chapter (noted with icons), and are incorporated into the revised expanded lessons at the end of each Part II chapter.

- **Coverage of Technology.** Since the first edition was published, technology has changed drastically. Now there is an increased availability of high-quality websites, applets, freeware, and so on. Throughout each chapter we identify effective, free technology that can help make content more visible, relevant, and interesting to students. To locate these examples, look for the Technology Notes in Part II.

- **Revised, Updated Expanded Lessons.** Every Part II chapter still has a lesson at the end, but they have all been revised. Lessons have been added or revised to explicitly focus on concepts central to middle school mathematics. All lessons now include (1) NCTM and CCSSO grade-level recommendations, (2) adaptation suggestions for English language learners and students with special needs, and (3) formative assessment suggestions for what to observe and what questions to ask students.

 ## What's New to Volume III?

The most obvious change to Volume III (*Developmentally Appropriate Instruction for Grades 6–8*) might be the missing grade. We moved grade 5 to Volume II and focused this book on grades 6–8. This allowed us to explicitly focus on content covered in middle school. The recent *Common Core State Standards* have resulted in major shifts in what is taught in middle school. There is a considerable emphasis on functions and algebra. Statistics and probability require much more advanced and abstract reasoning than has traditionally been the case, and students in elementary school are spending less time on these topics. Geometry requires reasoning at much higher levels. Because of these changes, major revisions to this book's contents focus on the following topics:

- **Fractions.** In middle school, students primarily focus on fraction operations, in which they must develop fluency. This requires understanding fundamentals of fractions such as fraction constructs, partitioning, and iteration, as well as knowing why the algorithms work. Chapter 8 now includes attention to these conceptual foundations, an effective process for teaching fraction operations, as well as common student misconceptions across concepts and operations.

- **Decimal Fractions.** Chapter 9 offers an increased focus on decimal operations and how to teach them conceptually (and use appropriate terminology). Each decimal operation section includes more attention to estimation and developing the algorithm. In addition, length models (bar diagrams) are now emphasized. As with fractions, more discussion of common student misconceptions is included.

- **Number System.** A major focus in Chapter 10 is positive and negative numbers (including integers). There are new lists of contexts to connect this content to real life, which resulted in an increased emphasis on the number line. The number of activities in this chapter grew from 6 to 14, and many more example tasks are included, too. This is indicative of the increased curricular expectation to conceptually develop concepts like exponents, irrational numbers, order of operations, and scientific notation.

- **Ratios and Proportions.** It can be said that nothing is more important to success in algebra and beyond than strong proportional reasoning. This topic receives significant attention in the *Common Core State Standards*, and so revised Chapter 11 has grown to include more support for teachers. Specifically, students should learn to apply various reasoning strategies, and each is now discussed in this chapter: mental strategies, ratio tables, double line (strip), comparison, percents, and cross-products. Also new is explicit attention to additive and multiplicative reasoning, as well as covariation.

- **Algebra.** Chapter 12 may be the most unrecognizable from the first edition. It merges two chapters from the first edition to better connect the concepts. It is now organized by three important areas of algebra, as described in recent literature on teaching algebraic thinking. The chapter includes significantly more attention to content described in the *Common Core State Standards* (CCSS), including generalization, inequalities, meaning of variables, understanding and using properties of addition and multiplication, functions, and mathematical modeling.

- **Geometry.** Chapter 13 includes a condensed section on van Hiele's levels, but increased focus on moving to Level 2 thinking within each topic discussion. There are many new geometry topics in the CCSS for middle school, and those topics have all been added. They include: Pythagorean triples, finding distances on the coordinate plane nets, and composition of transformations.

- **Measurement.** The structure of Chapter 14 is the same, but within each section the content has changed to reflect the CCSS. For example, the section on angles measures now focuses on supplementary, complementary, vertical, and adjacent angles. Each of the measurement formulas addressed in the standards for middle school are now included in this chapter and other formulas and topics have been removed.

- **Data and Statistics.** Chapter 15 also has undergone dramatic change. It now is organized around the process of doing statistics as described in the *Guidelines for Assessment and Instruction in Statistical Education (GAISE) Report* (American Statistical Association, 2005). Changes include new and revised sections on posing questions, data collection, data analysis, and interpreting results, as well as an emphasis on the shape of data and variability. The chapter includes terminology shifts consistent with new standards (e.g., dot plot, box plots, bivariate graphs). In addition, new content includes sampling and variability, including mean absolute variation.

- **Probability.** Chapter 16 includes a comprehensive look at probability, including common student misconceptions, because it is no longer in the elementary curriculum. Many more real and engaging contexts for exploring probability are included (beyond dice and cards), and the activities have grown from 5 to 13. Finally, there is an increased focus on the important concepts of sample size and variability.

What Special Features Appear in the Professional Series?

Throughout the Book

New! Teaching Tips. Teaching Tips identify practical take-away ideas that can support the teaching and learning of specific chapter content being addressed. These might be an instructional suggestion, a particular point about language use, a common student misconception, or a suggestion about a resource.

Stop and Reflect.   Reflective thinking is the key to effective learning. This is true not only for your students but also for ourselves as we continue to learn more about effective mathematics teaching. Keep your eye out for these sections that ask you to solve a problem or reflect on some aspect of what you have read. These Stop and Reflect sections do not signal every important idea, but we have tried to place them where it seemed natural and helpful for you to slow down a bit and think. In addition, every chapter in Part I ends with a Stop and Reflect section. Use these for discussions in professional learning communities or on your own.

Blackline Master Icons.   Blackline Masters are used in some of the activities and Expanded Lessons. Look for the icon in the margin alerting you to the Blackline Masters. In Appendix C, you will find a thumbnail version of all Blackline Masters. A PDF version of each full-sized Blackline Master is available on the PDToolkit site.

Additional Features in Part II

Big Ideas.   Much of the research and literature espousing a developmental approach suggests that teachers plan their instruction around "big ideas" rather than isolated skills or concepts. At the beginning of each chapter, you will find a list of the key mathematical ideas associated with the chapter. These lists of learning targets can help you get a snapshot of the mathematics you are teaching.

Activities.   Numerous problem-based tasks are presented in activity boxes. Additional ideas are described directly in the text or in the illustrations. They are designed to engage your students in *doing* mathematics (as described in Chapter 2). Most of these activities are presented in the numbered activity boxes and many have new adaptation and accommodation suggestions for English language learners and students with special needs. These are denoted with icons for easy reference. Following this Preface, you will find the Activities at a Glance table, which lists all the named and numbered activities with a short statement of the mathematical goal for each.

It is important that you see these activities as an integral part of the text that surrounds them. The activities are inserted as examples to support the development of the mathematics being discussed and how your students can be supported in learning that content. Therefore, we hope that you will not use any activity for instruction without reading carefully the full text in which it is embedded.

Formative Assessment Notes.   Assessment should be an integral part of instruction. As you read, we want you to think about what to listen and look for (assess) in different areas of content development. Therefore you will find Formative Assessment Notes that describe ways to assess your students' developing knowledge and understanding. These Formative Assessment Notes can also help improve your understanding about how to help your students through targeted instruction.

New! Technology Notes.   Integrated throughout the book are Technology Notes, which provide practical information about how technology can be used to help your students learn the content in that section. Descriptions include open-source software, interactive applets, and other Web-based resources—all of which are free.

New! Standards for Mathematical Practice Notes.   Connections to the eight Standards for Mathematical Practice from the *Common Core State Standards* are highlighted in the margins. The location of the note indicates an example of the identified practice in the nearby text.

Expanded Lessons.   The activities in the book are written in a brief format so as to provide many activities for the content without detracting from the flow of ideas. At the end of each Part II chapter, we selected one activity and expanded it into a complete lesson plan, following the *Before, During, After* structure described in Chapter 2. These Expanded Lessons provide a model for converting an activity description into a full lesson that can engage students in developing a strong understanding of the related concept. In this new edition, all lessons are now aligned with NCTM and CCSS grade-level recommendations and include adaptation suggestions for English language learners and students with disabilities.

New! Common Core State Standards Appendixes.   The *Common Core State Standards* outline eight Standards for Mathematical Practice (Appendix A) that help students develop and demonstrate a deep understanding of and capacity to do mathematics. We initially describe these practices in Chapter 1 and highlight examples of the mathematical practices throughout the content chapters in Part II. We used the *Common Core State Standards* (CCSSO, 2010) as a guide to determine the content emphasis in each volume of the series. Appendix B provides a list of the critical content areas for each grade level discussed in this volume.

New! PDToolkit.   The PDToolkit for *Teaching Student-Centered Mathematics: Developmentally Appropriate Instruction*, Second Edition (Volumes I, II, and III), together with the book, offers the tools you need to teach student-centered, problem-based mathematics.

The following resources are currently available:

- Video examples
- Virtual manipulatives
- Full-size, printable versions of the Blackline Masters from Volumes I, II, and III

In the future, we will continue to add additional resources.

To access the PDToolkit, go to http://pdtoolkit.pearson.com and enter the following code: PDTOOL-CLONK-LOSSY-SAVVY-HIGHS-LINES

 # Acknowledgments

We would like to begin by acknowledging *you:* the reader, the teacher, the leader, and the advocate for your students. The strong commitment of teachers and teacher leaders to always strive to improve how we teach mathematics is the reason this book was written in the first place. And, because of ongoing input and feedback, we endeavored to revise this edition to meet your changing needs. We have received input from so many teachers and reviewers, and all of it has informed the development of this substantially revised second edition!

In preparing the second edition, we benefited from the thoughtful input of the following educators who offered comments on the first edition or on the manuscript for the second: David J. Carrejo, University of Texas at El Paso; Adam Hile, Klein ISD; and Janis J. Parks, Tucson Unified School District. The reviewers' comments helped push our thinking on many important topics and many specific suggestions offered by these reviewers found their way into this book. We offer our sincere appreciation to these individuals for their suggestions and constructive feedback.

As we reviewed standards, research, and teaching articles; visited classrooms; and collected students' work samples, we were continually reminded of the amazing mathematics instruction going on in our profession. From the mathematics educators and mathematicians working on standards documents to the mathematics discussions occurring in pre-K–grade 8 classrooms that are then shared with others, we see great hope and vision in preparing all students to be mathematically proficient. It is for this broad commitment to mathematics education on the part of so many that we are so grateful, as well as the particular teachers with whom we have worked in recent years.

As authors, we also want to acknowledge the strong support of our editorial team throughout the process, from the first discussions about what a second edition might include, through the tedious editing at later stages in the development. Without their support, the final product would not be the quality resource we hope you find it to be. Specifically, we thank Kelly Villella-Canton for helping us envision our work, Linda Bishop for seeing this vision through, and both of them for their words of encouragement and wisdom. Working on three volumes of a book simultaneously is quite an undertaking! Christina Robb found a way to keep us organized and provided timely and much-needed feedback throughout our writing. We are grateful for Dana Weightman and the team at Pearson who patiently walked us through the permissions process. We also wish to thank Karla Walsh and the rest of the production and editing team at Electronic Publishing Services Inc.

Even with the support of so many, researching and writing take time. Simple words cannot express the gratitude we have to our families for their support, patience, and contributions to the production of these books. Briefly we recognize them by name here: Jennifer thanks her husband, Mitch, and her children, MacKenna and Nicolas. LouAnn thanks her husband, Ramsey, and her two sons, Nathan and Jacob. Karen thanks her husband, Bob Ronau, and her children and grandchildren, Matthew, Tammy, Josh, Misty, Matt, Christine, Jeff, Pamela, Jessica, Zane, Madeline, Jack, and Emma.

The origin of this book began many years ago with the development of *Elementary and Middle School Mathematics: Teaching Developmentally* by John A. Van de Walle. What began as a methods book spread to the teaching community because it offered content support, activities, and up-to-date best practices for teaching mathematics. The series was developed as a way to focus on and expand the specific grade-level topics. John was adamant that all children can learn to reason and make sense of mathematics. We acknowledge his enduring vision, his commitment, and his significant contributions to the field of mathematics education. His ideas continue to inspire the work you see in this new edition.

The response to the first edition has been amazing. We hope the second edition will be received with as much interest and enthusiasm as the first and continue to be a valuable support to your mathematics teaching and your students' learning.

Activities at a Glance

This table lists the numbered activities in Part II of the book. In addition to providing an easy way to find an activity, the table provides the main mathematical goal or objective for each activity, stated as succinctly as possible. You should see the table only as a listing of the named activities, and not as an index of instructional ideas.

Rather than a book of activities, this is a book about teaching mathematics. Many practical and effective activities are used as examples. Every activity should be seen as an integral part of the text that surrounds it. Therefore, it is extremely important not to take any activity as a suggestion for instruction without reading carefully the full text in which it is embedded.

Activity	Mathematical Goal	Page Number
Chapter 9, Decimal Concepts and Computation		
9.1 Calculator Decimal Counting	Explore the 10 to 1 relationship of decimal notation	144
9.2 Shifting Units	Explore the relative size of units when the whole shifts	148
9.3 Build It, Name It	Use base-ten blocks to show fraction–decimal equivalencies	149
9.4 Familiar Fractions to Decimals	Shade fraction of a 10 × 10 grid to find decimal fraction	149
9.5 Rational Number Wheel: Estimate and Verify	Estimate equivalent decimal fractions for given fractions	150
9.6 Decimals Lineup	Locate decimals on a number line and determine equivalent fractions	151
9.7 Close to a Familiar Fraction	Estimate fractions close to given decimal numbers	152
9.8 Best Match	Game to match decimal fractions with fractions	153
9.9 Line 'Em Up	Compare and order decimal fractions	155
9.10 Close Decimals	Find decimals between two numbers	155
9.11 Represent and Review	Represent decimal computation problems different ways	157
9.12 Where Does the Decimal Go? Multiplication	Use estimation to place the decimal point in multiplication	160
9.13 Where Does the Decimal Go? Division	Use estimation to place the decimal point in division	162
9.14 Percent Memory Match	Connect percent values with shaded portion of a circle	163
Chapter 10, The Number System		
10.1 Stacks of Coins	Explore the order of operations conceptually	172
10.2 Guess My Number	Write expressions to indicate order of operations	173
10.3 True or False Equations	Explore order of operations	173
10.4 Entering Expressions	Use calculators to explore order of operations	175
10.5 Find the Error	Identify errors that involve order of operations	177
10.6 How Far Away from the Sun?	Explore scientific notation and relative size of numbers	178
10.7 At a Snail's Pace	Explore scientific notation of very small numbers in context	179
10.8 Exploring Powers of Ten	Use calculator to explore scientific notation and powers of 10	179
10.9 What Is Her Net Worth?	Develop the concept of integers in context	181
10.10 (American) Football Statistics	Explore integers in a linear model	183
10.11 Find the Zero	Solve integer addition using opposites	185
10.12 Repeater or Terminator?	Analyze division that results in repeating or terminating decimals	193
10.13 Edges of Squares and Cubes	Develop the concepts of square roots and cube roots	194
10.14 Wheel of Theodorus	Explore irrational numbers through classic art project	195

1

Teaching Mathematics for Understanding

An understanding can never be "covered" if it is to be understood.

Wiggins and McTighe (2005, p. 229)

Teachers generally agree that teaching for understanding is a good thing. But this statement begs the question: What is understanding? Understanding is being able to think and act flexibly with a topic or concept. It goes beyond knowing; it is more than a collection of information, facts, or data. It is more than being able to follow steps in a procedure. One hallmark of mathematical understanding is a student's ability to justify why a given mathematical claim or answer is true or why a mathematical rule makes sense (Council of Chief State School Officers [CCSSO], 2010). Although students might know their basic multiplication facts and be able to give you quick answers to questions about these given facts, they might not understand multiplication. They might not be able to justify how they know an answer is correct or provide an example of when it would make sense to use this basic fact. These tasks go beyond simply knowing mathematical facts and procedures. Understanding must be a primary goal for all of the mathematics you teach.

 ## Understanding and Doing Mathematics

Procedural proficiency, a main focus of mathematics instruction in the past, remains important today, but conceptual understanding is an equally important goal (National Council of Teachers of Mathematics [NCTM], 2000; National Research Council, 2001; CCSSO, 2010). Numerous reports and standards emphasize the need to address skills and understanding in an integrated manner; among these are the *Common Core State Standards* (CCSSO, 2010), a state-led effort coordinated by the National Governors Association Center for Best Practices (NGA Center)

and CCSSO, which has been adopted by nearly every state and the District of Columbia. This effort has resulted in attention to *how* mathematics is taught, not just *what* is taught.

The National Council of Teachers of Mathematics (NCTM, 2000) identifies the process standards of problem solving, reasoning and proof, representation, communication, and connections as ways to think about how students should engage in learning the content as they develop both procedural fluency and conceptual understanding. Students engaged in the process of *problem solving* build mathematical knowledge and understanding by grappling with and solving genuine problems, as opposed to completing routine exercises. They use *reasoning and proof* to make sense of mathematical tasks and concepts and to develop, justify, and evaluate mathematical arguments and solutions. Students create and use *representations* (e.g., diagrams, graphs, symbols, and manipulatives) to reason through problems. They also engage in *communication* as they explain their ideas and reasoning verbally, in writing, and through representations. Students develop and use *connections* between mathematical ideas as they learn new mathematical concepts and procedures. They also build *connections* between mathematics and other disciplines through applying mathematics to real-world situations. By engaging in these processes, students are learning mathematics by *doing* mathematics. Consequently, the process standards should not be taught separately from but in conjunction with mathematics as ways of learning mathematics.

Adding It Up (National Research Council, 2001), an influential research review on how students learn mathematics, identifies the following five strands of mathematical proficiency as indicators that someone understands (and can do) mathematics.

- *Conceptual understanding:* Comprehension of mathematical concepts, operations, and relations

- *Procedural fluency:* Skill in carrying out procedures flexibly, accurately, efficiently, and appropriately

- *Strategic competence:* Ability to formulate, represent, and solve mathematical problems

- *Adaptive reasoning:* Capacity for logical thought, reflection, explanation, and justification

- *Productive disposition:* Habitual inclination to see mathematics as sensible, useful, and worthwhile, coupled with a belief in diligence and one's own efficacy (Reprinted with permission from p. 116 of *Adding It Up: Helping Children Learn Mathematics*, 2001 by the National Academy of Sciences, Courtesy of the National Academies Press, Washington, D.C.)

This report maintains that the strands of mathematical proficiency are interwoven and interdependent—the development of one strand aids the development of others (Figure 1.1).

Building on the NCTM process standards and the five strands of mathematical proficiency, the *Common Core State Standards* (CCSSO, 2010) outline the following eight Standards for Mathematical Practice (see Appendix A) as ways in which students can develop and demonstrate a deep understanding of and capacity to do mathematics. Keep in mind that you, the teacher, have a responsibility in helping students develop these practices. Here we provide a brief discussion about each mathematical practice.

Figure 1.1

Interrelated and intertwined strands of mathematical proficiency.

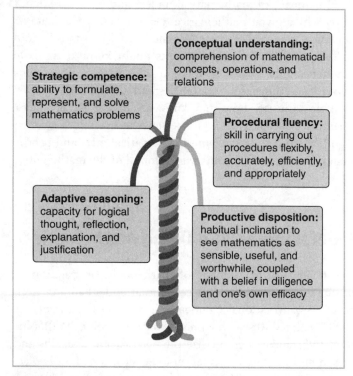

Strategic competence: ability to formulate, represent, and solve mathematics problems

Conceptual understanding: comprehension of mathematical concepts, operations, and relations

Procedural fluency: skill in carrying out procedures flexibly, accurately, efficiently, and appropriately

Adaptive reasoning: capacity for logical thought, reflection, explanation, and justification

Productive disposition: habitual inclination to see mathematics as sensible, useful, and worthwhile, coupled with a belief in diligence and one's own efficacy

Source: Reprinted with permission from Kilpatrick, J., Swafford, J., & Findell, B. (Eds.), *Adding It Up: Helping Children Learn Mathematics.* Copyright 2001 by the National Academy of Sciences. Courtesy of the National Academies Press, Washington, D.C.

1. *Make sense of problems and persevere in solving them.* To make sense of problems, students need to learn how to analyze the given information, parameters, and relationships in a problem so that they can understand the situation and identify possible ways to solve it. One way to help students analyze problems is to have them create proportional drawings to make sense of the quantities and relationships involved. Once students learn various strategies for making sense of problems, encourage them to remain committed to solving them. As they learn to monitor and assess their progress and change course as needed, they will solve the problems they set out to solve!

2. *Reason abstractly and quantitatively.* This practice involves students reasoning with quantities and their relationships in problem situations. You can support students' development of this practice by helping them create representations that correspond to the meanings of the quantities and the units involved. Also, a significant aspect of this practice is to be able to represent and manipulate the situation symbolically. Encourage students to find connections between the abstract symbols and the representation that illustrates the quantities and their relationships. For example, suppose students are generalizing a situation in which they are trying to determine what their earnings at the local ice-cream store will be if they earn $8.00 for each hour they work but spend $2.50 every two hours for their own ice-cream cones. They may represent the relationship symbolically as $y = 8x - 2.5(\frac{x}{2})$ or as $y = (8 - 1.25)x$ or as $y = 6.75x$. Ultimately, students should be able to reason how these equations are equal and relate the equations to the situation.

3. *Construct viable arguments and critique the reasoning of others.* This practice emphasizes the importance of students using mathematical reasoning as the basis for justifying their ideas and solutions, including being able to recognize and use counterexamples. Encourage students to examine each others' arguments to determine whether they make sense and to identify ways to clarify or improve the arguments. This practice emphasizes that mathematics is based on reasoning and should be examined in a community—not carried out in isolation. Tips for supporting students as they learn to justify their ideas can be found in Chapter 2.

4. *Model with mathematics.* This practice encourages students to use the mathematics they know to solve problems in everyday life, and to be able to represent them symbolically (i.e., the equation serves as a model of the situation). The equations given above for the ice-cream shop are models for describing the students' earnings. The equation (model) can then be used to predict and find earnings for any number of hours worked. Be sure to encourage students to determine whether the mathematical model is the generalization of the situation.

5. *Use appropriate tools strategically.* Students should become familiar with a variety of visuals and tools that can be used to solve a problem and they should learn to choose which ones are most appropriate for a given situation. For example, suppose students have used the following tools to investigate probability: coins, spinners, number cubes, and computerized simulations. If students are asked to create a simulation with two outcomes, one outcome twice as likely as the second outcome, they should consider which of these tools can best support their simulation. If the number cubes are six-sided cubes, the students might define one outcome as rolling a 1, 2, 3, or 4 and the second outcome as rolling a 5 or 6. However, a coin, because it is two-sided, would not be an appropriate tool for this particular investigation because the outcomes could not be modified to model the given situation.

Research suggests that students, in particular girls, may tend to continue to use the same tools because they feel comfortable with the tools and are afraid to take risks (Ambrose, 2002). Look for students who tend to use the same tool or strategy every time they work on tasks. Encourage all students to take risks and try new tools and strategies.

6. *Attend to precision.* In communicating ideas to others, it is imperative that students learn to be explicit about their reasoning. For example, they need to be clear about the meanings of the operations and symbols they use, to indicate the units involved in a problem, and to clearly label the diagrams they provide in their explanations. As students share their ideas, make this expectation clear and ask clarifying questions that help make the details of their reasoning more apparent. Teachers can further encourage students' attention to precision by introducing, highlighting, and encouraging the use of accurate mathematical terminology in explanations and diagrams.

7. *Look for and make use of structure.* Students who look for and recognize a pattern or structure can experience a shift in their perspective or understanding. Therefore, set the expectation that students will look for patterns and structure, and help them reflect on their significance. For example, when students begin to write rational numbers in decimal form, they learn that the decimal either terminates or repeats. Look for opportunities to help students notice that the denominator of any simplified rational number whose decimal form terminates can be rewritten as a power of ten—which provides insight into why the decimal terminates.

8. *Look for and express regularity in repeated reasoning.* Encourage students to step back and reflect on any regularity that occurs in an effort to help them develop a general idea or method to identify shortcuts. For example, as students begin adding signed numbers, they will encounter situations such as $5 - 3$ and $5 + (-3)$. Over time, help them reflect on the results of these situations. Eventually they should be able to express that subtracting a positive number is equivalent to adding the opposite (or negative) of the number.

Like the process standards, the Standards for Mathematical Practice should not be taught separately from the mathematics, but should instead be incorporated as ways for students to learn and do mathematics. Students who learn to use these eight mathematical practices as they engage with mathematical concepts and skills have a greater chance of developing conceptual understanding. Note that learning these mathematical practices, and consequently developing understanding, takes time. So the common notion of simply and quickly "covering the material" is problematic. The opening quotation states it well: "An understanding can never be 'covered' if it is to be understood" (Wiggins & McTighe, 2005, p. 229). Understanding is an end goal—that is, it is developed over time by incorporating the process standards and mathematical practices and striving toward mathematical proficiency.

 ## How Do Students Learn?

Let's look at a couple of research-based theories that can illustrate how students learn in general: constructivism and sociocultural theory. Although one theory focuses on the individual learner while the other emphasizes the social and cultural aspects of the classroom, these theories are not competing; they are actually compatible (Norton & D'Ambrosio, 2008).

 ### Constructivism

At the heart of constructivism is the notion that learners are not blank slates but rather creators (constructors) of their own learning. All people, all of the time, construct or give meaning to things they perceive or think about. Whether you are listening passively to a lecture or actively engaging in synthesizing findings in a project, your brain is applying prior knowledge (existing schemas) to make sense of the new information.

Constructing something in the physical world requires tools, materials, and effort. The tools you use to build understanding are your existing ideas and knowledge. Your materials might be things you see, hear, or touch, or they might be your own thoughts and ideas. The effort required to construct knowledge and understanding is reflective thought.

Through reflective thought, people connect existing ideas to new information and thus modify their existing schemas or background knowledge to incorporate new ideas. Making these connections can happen in either of two ways—*assimilation* or *accommodation*. Assimilation occurs when a new concept "fits" with prior knowledge and the new information expands an existing mental network. Accommodation takes place when the new concept does not "fit" with the existing network, thus creating a cognitive conflict or state of confusion that causes what theorists call *disequilibrium*. As an example, consider what happens when students start learning about variables. They begin in elementary school by using variables as unknowns, as in $2 + ? = 5$ or $4 \times ? = 24$, in which their goal is to determine what the question mark represents. Consequently, some students come to see a variable as a placeholder or missing number. So, when students encounter equations such as $y = 4x + 5$, the variable does not represent a single missing number (assimilation), but rather many values. Students must adapt their mental image of what a variable means (accommodation). It is through the struggle to resolve the disequilibrium that the brain modifies or replaces the existing schema so that the new concept fits and makes sense, resulting in a revision of thought and a deepening of the learner's understanding.

For an illustration of what it means to construct an idea, consider Figure 1.2. The gray and white dots represent ideas, and the lines joining the ideas represent the logical connections or relationships that develop between ideas. The white dot is an emerging idea, one that is being constructed. Whatever existing ideas (gray dots) are used in the construction are connected to the new idea (white dot) because those are the ideas that give meaning to the new idea. The more existing ideas that are used to give meaning to the new one, the more connections will be made.

Each student's unique collection of ideas is connected in different ways. Some ideas are well understood and well formed (i.e., connected), and others are less so as they emerge and students build connections. Students' experiences help them develop connections and ideas about whatever they are learning.

Understanding exists along a continuum (Figure 1.3) from an instrumental understanding—knowing something by rote or without meaning (Skemp, 1978)—to a relational understanding—knowing what to do and why. Instrumental understanding, at the left end of the continuum, shows that ideas (e.g., concepts and procedures) are learned, but in isolation (or nearly so) to other ideas. Here you find ideas that have been memorized. Due to their isolation, poorly understood ideas are easily forgotten and are unlikely to be useful for constructing new ideas. At the right end of the continuum is relational understanding. Relational understanding means that each new concept or procedure (white dot) is not only learned, but is also connected to many existing ideas (gray dots), so there is a rich set of connections.

Figure 1.2

How someone constructs a new idea.

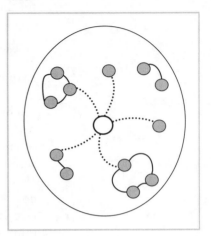

Figure 1.3 Continuum of understanding.

A primary goal of teaching for understanding is to help students develop a relational understanding of mathematical ideas. Because relational understanding develops over time and becomes more complex as a person makes more connections between ideas, teaching for this kind of understanding takes time and must be a goal of daily instruction.

◆ Sociocultural Theory

Like constructivism, sociocultural theory not only positions the learner as actively engaged in seeking meaning during the learning process, but it also suggests that the learner can be assisted by working with others who are "more knowledgeable." Sociocultural theory proposes that learners have their own zone of proximal development, which is a range of knowledge that may be out of reach for the individuals to learn on their own but is accessible if learners have the support of peers or more knowledgeable others (Vygotsky, 1978). For example, when students are learning about experimental probability, they do not necessarily recognize the significance of sample size. Teachers often have students collect data to explore the probability of two events, such flipping two coins. Students may think that HH, TT, and HT (H=Heads; T=Tails) are equally likely and therefore each has a probability of $\frac{1}{3}$. A more knowledgeable person (a peer or teacher) will know that if the students explore a large number of trials, the data will suggest that HT actually has a 50 percent probability, and that creating a list of possible outcomes will help to understand why the probabilities are $\frac{1}{4}, \frac{1}{4},$ *and* $\frac{1}{2}$, respectively. The more knowledgeable person can draw students' attention to this critical idea of how possible outcomes connect to probability.

The best learning for any given student will occur when the conversation of the classroom is within his or her zone of proximal development. Targeting that zone helps teachers provide students with the right amount of challenge while avoiding boredom on the one hand and anxiety on the other when the challenge is beyond the student's current capability. Consequently, classroom discussions based on students' own ideas and solutions to problems are absolutely "foundational to children's learning" (Wood & Turner-Vorbeck, 2001, p. 186).

Teaching for Understanding

◆ Teaching toward Relational Understanding

To explore the notion of understanding further, let's look into a learner-centered sixth-grade classroom. In learner-centered classrooms, teachers begin *where the students are—* with *the students'* ideas. Students are allowed to solve problems or to approach tasks in ways that make sense to them. They develop their understanding of mathematics because they are at the center of explaining, providing evidence or justification, finding or creating examples, generalizing, analyzing, making predictions, applying concepts, representing ideas in different ways, and articulating connections or relationships between the given topic and other ideas.

For example, in this sixth-grade classroom, the students are going to explore division of fractions by fractions. They have recently investigated multiplication of fractions and division of fractions by whole numbers and have used real contexts, manipulatives, and diagrams to make sense of the operations. Their work with multiplication of fractions has emphasized identifying the whole that is being used, an important idea in working with fractions and fraction computation. They also have revisited the different meanings of division: sharing or partitive division, and repeated subtraction or measurement division. The students have had previous experiences dividing fractions by whole numbers and have not been taught the standard algorithm for division of fractions.

The teacher sets the following instructional objectives for the students:

1. Solve word problems involving the division of fractions by fractions by using diagrams.

2. Interpret and compute the quotients of fractions.

The lesson begins with a task that is designed to set the stage for the main part of the lesson. As is often the case, this class begins with a story problem to provide context and relevance to the mathematics. The teacher displays this problem on the board:

How much chocolate will each person get if 4 people share $\frac{1}{2}$ pound of chocolate equally?

Stop and Reflect

Which operation is being described in this situation? Before reading further, try to solve this problem without using the standard algorithm. As a hint, can you act it out? ■

Before students start working on the task, the teacher asks them to think about what operation is being used in the situation. After some wait time, some of the students explain that because the chocolate is being shared or divided equally among four people, fair sharing or partitive division is being used. Students are then given a few minutes to work on the problem with a partner, share their ideas with another group, and prepare to share their ideas and answers with the class. The following two ideas were most prominent among the strategies used:

- We cut the half of a pound into four equal pieces so that each person would have an equal share. But then we needed to figure out what those pieces were, so we extended our drawing to make the whole pound. Since there are eight equal pieces in the whole pound, one piece would be one-eighth. So each person would get one-eighth pound of chocolate (Figure 1.4).

- We pretended we had one pound of chocolate. Then each person would get one-fourth of a pound. But each person really gets only half of that since we started with one-half pound. We knew that one-fourth is the same as two-eighths. So one-eighth is half of one-fourth or two-eighths. So each person gets one-eighth pound of chocolate.

As students share their ideas, the teacher highlights the notion of sharing that is going on in each of the solutions as well as the attention given to the whole or the pound of chocolate.

Because the teacher wants to extend students' thinking to division of fractions by fractions, she poses the following problem, which involves a fractional amount of money.

Dan paid $2\frac{1}{4}$ dollars for a $\frac{3}{5}$-pound box of candy. How much money is that per pound?

She uses money because she has found that students can easily think about partitioning money in a variety of ways. As is the norm in the class, students are told that they should be prepared to explain their reasoning with words and numbers as well as a drawing to support their explanation.

Figure 1.4
One solution for $\frac{1}{2} \div 4$.

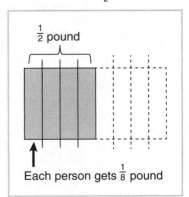

Stop and Reflect

Before reading further, how many different ways can you think of to solve the problem $2\frac{1}{4} \div \frac{3}{5}$? ◼

Figure 1.5

One solution for $2\frac{1}{4}$ dollars $\div \frac{3}{5}$.

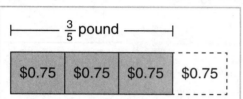

The students work in pairs for about 15 minutes. The teacher listens to different students talk about the task and offers a hint to a few who are stuck. For example, she asks, "Did Dan buy an entire pound of candy? What ways can you partition the whole (the box of candy that Dan bought) to help you think about this problem?" Soon, the teacher begins a discussion by having students share their ideas and answers. As the students report, the teacher records their ideas on the board. Sometimes, the teacher asks questions to help clarify ideas for others. She makes no evaluative comments, although she asks the students who are listening if they understand or have any questions to ask the presenters. The following solution strategies are common in classes where students are regularly asked to generate their own approaches. Figure 1.5 shows a sketch for the first method shared below.

Group 1: Since we had $\frac{3}{5}$ pound, we drew three rectangles. We know that in $2\frac{1}{4}$ dollars we had nine fourths, so we put three-fourths of a dollar in each rectangle. Then, the whole pound would be two more three-fourths, or a total of $3\frac{3}{4}$ dollars or $3.75.

Teacher: What do the three rectangles represent in the problem?

Group 1: Each of the rectangles is $\frac{1}{5}$ pound. Since we had $\frac{3}{5}$ pound, we had to show three rectangles.

Teacher: And how did you get $3\frac{3}{4}$ dollars?

Group 1: We knew each rectangle or $\frac{1}{5}$ pound was seventy-five cents or three-fourths of a dollar. Since there are five $\frac{1}{5}$ pounds in one pound, we multiplied $\frac{3}{4}$ by 5.

Group 2: We used a circle and divided it into five parts but used only three of them since we only had $\frac{3}{5}$ pound of candy. We knew we could not put $1 in each part because we did not have $3, so we started with $0.50 (one-half dollar). That left $0.75 (or three-fourths of a dollar) to share, and we knew 75 divided by 3 is 25. So that meant there was $0.50 plus $0.25 or $0.75 in each section. To figure out how much the whole pound would be, we just added $0.75 to $2.25 to get $3.00 and then added $0.75 to $3.00 to get $3.75 or $3\frac{3}{4}$ dollars.

Stop and Reflect

The invert-and-multiply algorithm plays out in this kind of division problem (partitive or fair sharing). Can you find in the explanations above where the calculation $2\frac{1}{4} \times \frac{5}{3}$ occurs? (Hint: Think of $\frac{5}{3}$ as $\frac{1}{3} \times 5$.) ◼

This vignette illustrates that when students are encouraged to solve a problem in their own way (using their own particular set of gray dots or ideas), they are able to make sense of their solution strategies and explain their reasoning. This is evidence of their development of mathematical proficiency.

During the discussion periods in classes such as this one, ideas continue to grow. The students may hear and immediately understand a clever strategy that they could have used but that did not occur to them. Others may begin to create new ideas to use that build from thinking about their classmates' strategies over multiple discussions. Some in the class may hear excellent ideas from their peers that do not make sense to them. These students are simply not ready or do not have the prerequisite concepts (gray dots) to understand these new ideas. On subsequent days there will be similar opportunities for all students to grow at their own pace based on their own understandings.

♦ Teaching toward Instrumental Understanding

In contrast to the lesson just described, in which students are developing concepts (understanding of fraction division) and procedures (ability to flexibly divide) and seeing the relationships between these ideas, let's consider how a lesson with the same basic objective (fraction division) might look if the focus is on instrumental understanding.

In this classroom, the teacher distributes coins to all students. The teacher reads to the class the same problem that was used in the first classroom about a $\frac{3}{5}$-pound box of candy costing $2.25 or $2\frac{1}{4}$ dollars. She explains that this means that they will be dividing $2\frac{1}{4}$ by $\frac{3}{5}$ and that this is the same as flipping the second fraction and multiplying so that the problem becomes $2\frac{1}{4} \times \frac{5}{3}$. The teacher directs the students to count out $2\frac{1}{4}$ dollars from the coins (nine quarters). The discussion continues:

T: What is $2\frac{1}{4}$ divided by 3? Use your coins to help you find this amount.

S: [Students take some time to partition their coins] $0.75.

T: So $2\frac{1}{4}$ dollars divided by 3 is $0.75 or $\frac{3}{4}$ of a dollar. This means that each $\frac{1}{5}$ pound is worth $0.75 or $\frac{3}{4}$ of a dollar. Can you see with our manipulatives that $\frac{3}{5}$ pound of candy costs $2\frac{1}{4}$ dollars or $2.25 because we have three groups of $0.75?

T: [pause] Now we need to find out how much one pound costs, and that's where we multiply the $0.75 or $\frac{3}{4}$ of a dollar by 5. *One*-fifth of a pound is $0.75, but there are *five* fifths in a whole pound, so we need to multiply $0.75 by 5 to get $3.75.

Next, the students are given three other similar problems to solve with manipulatives. They work in pairs and record their answers on their papers. The teacher circulates and helps anyone having difficulty by guiding them to use manipulatives and connect them to the steps in the standard algorithm.

In this lesson, the teacher and students are using manipulatives to illustrate the invert-and-multiply algorithm for fraction division. After engaging in several lessons similar to this one, most students are likely to remember, and possibly understand, how to divide fractions with the standard algorithm. Using manipulatives to illustrate the invert-and-multiply algorithm can build toward relational understanding. However, when the expectation is for all students to use one method, students do not have opportunities to apply other strategies that may help them build connections between subtraction and division, multiplication and division, or sharing (partitive) and repeated subtraction (measurement) concepts of division; these connections are fundamental characteristics of relational understanding. It is important to note that this lesson on the standard algorithm, in combination with other lessons that reinforce other approaches, *can* build a relational understanding, as it adds to students' repertoire of strategies. But if this lesson represents the sole approach to fraction division, then students are more likely to develop an instrumental understanding of mathematics.

♦ The Importance of Students' Ideas

Let's take a minute to compare these two classrooms. By examining them more closely, you can see several important differences. These differences affect what is learned and who learns. Let's consider the first difference: Who determines the procedure to use?

In the first classroom, the students think about the meaning of division in the situation and the relationships between the numbers involved. Using this information, they generate a drawing of the situation to help them make sense of and solve the problem. So they *choose* a strategy that is based on *their* ideas, using what they know about subtraction, multiplication, and division. The students in the first classroom are being taught mathematics for understanding—*relational* understanding—and are developing the kinds of mathematical proficiency described earlier.

In the second classroom, the teacher provides one strategy for how to divide fractions—the standard algorithm. Although the standard algorithm is a valid strategy, the entire focus of the lesson is on the steps and procedures that the teacher has outlined. The teacher solicits no ideas from individual students about how to partition the numbers and instead is only able to find out who has or has not been able to follow directions.

When students have more choice in determining which strategies to use, as in the first classroom, they can learn more content and make more connections. In addition, if teachers do not seek out and value students' ideas, students may come to believe that mathematics is a body of rules and procedures that are learned by waiting for the teacher to tell them what to do. This view of mathematics—and what is involved in learning it—is inconsistent with mathematics as a discipline and with the learning theories described previously. Therefore, it is a worthwhile goal to transform your classroom into a mathematical community of learners who interact with each other and with the teacher as they share ideas and results, compare and evaluate strategies, challenge results, determine the validity of answers, and negotiate ideas. The rich interaction in such a classroom increases opportunities for productive engagement and reflective thinking about relevant mathematical ideas, resulting in students developing a relational understanding of mathematics.

A second difference between the two classrooms is the learning goals. Both teachers might write "understand fraction division" as the objective for the day. However, what is captured in the word "understand" is very different in each setting. In the first classroom, the teacher's goal is for students to connect fractions and division to what they already know. In the second classroom, understanding is connected to being able to carry out the standard algorithm. The learning goals, and more specifically how the teacher interprets the meaning behind the learning goals, affect what students learn.

These lessons also differ in terms of how accessible they are—and this, in turn, affects who learns the mathematics. The first lesson is differentiated in that it meets students where they are in their current understanding. When a task is presented as "solve this in your own way," it has multiple entry points, meaning it can be approached in a variety of ways. Consequently, students with different prior knowledge or learning strategies can figure out a way to solve the problem. This makes the task accessible to more learners. Then, as students observe strategies that are more efficient than their own, they develop new and better ways to solve the problem.

In the second classroom, everyone has to do the problem in the same way. Students do not have the opportunity to apply their own ideas or to see that there are numerous ways to solve the problem. This may deprive students who need to continue working on the development of basic ideas of fractions or division, as well as students who could easily find one or more ways to do the problem if only they were asked to do so. The students in the second classroom are also likely to use the same method to divide all fractions instead of looking for more efficient ways to divide based on the meanings of division and relationships between numbers. For example, they are likely to divide $\frac{2}{3}$ by 2 using the standard algorithm instead of thinking that $\frac{2}{3} \div 2$ means that you divide $\frac{2}{3}$ into two equal parts, each of which is $\frac{1}{3}$. Recall in the discussion of learning theory the importance of building on prior knowledge and learning from others. In the first classroom, student-generated strategies, multiple approaches, and discussion about the problem represent the kinds of strategies that enhance learning for a range of learners.

Students in both classrooms will eventually succeed at dividing fractions, but what they learn about fractions and division—and about doing mathematics—is quite different. Understanding and doing mathematics involves generating strategies for solving problems, applying those approaches, seeing if they lead to solutions, and checking to see whether answers make sense. These activities were all present in the first classroom, but not in the second. Consequently, students in the first classroom, in addition to successfully dividing fractions, will develop richer mathematical understanding, become more flexible thinkers and better problem solvers, remain more engaged in learning, and develop more positive attitudes toward learning mathematics.

Mathematics Classrooms That Promote Understanding

Three of the most common types of teaching are direct instruction, facilitative methods (also called a *constructivist approach*), and coaching (Wiggins & McTighe, 2005). With direct instruction, the teacher usually demonstrates or models, lectures, and asks questions that are convergent or closed-ended in nature. With facilitative methods, the teacher might use investigations and inquiry, cooperative learning, discussion, and questions that are more open-ended. In coaching, the teacher provides students with guided practice and feedback that highlights ways to improve their performances.

You might be wondering which type of teaching is most appropriate if the goal is to teach mathematics for understanding. Unfortunately, there is no definitive answer because there are times when it is appropriate to engage in each of these types of teaching. Your approach depends on your instructional goals, the learners, and the situation. Some people believe that all direct instruction is ineffective because it ignores the learner's ideas and removes the productive struggle or opportunity to learn. This is not necessarily true. A teacher who is striving to teach for understanding can share information by using direct instruction as long as that information does not remove the need for students to reflect on and productively struggle with the situation at hand. In other words, regardless of instructional design, the teacher should not be doing the thinking, reasoning, and connection building—it must be the students who are engaged in these activities.

Regarding facilitative or constructivist methods, remember that constructivism is a theory of learning, not a theory of teaching. Constructivism helps explain how students learn—by developing and modifying ideas (schemas) and by making connections between these ideas. Students can learn as a result of different kinds of instruction. The instructional approach chosen should depend on the ideas and relationships students have already constructed. Sometimes students readily make connections by listening to a lecture (direct instruction). Sometimes they need time to investigate a situation so they can become aware of the different ideas at play and how those ideas relate to one another (facilitative). Sometimes they need to practice a skill and receive feedback on their performance to become more accurate (coaching). No matter which type of teaching is used, constructivism and sociocultural theories remind us as teachers to continually wonder whether our students have truly developed the given concept or skill, connecting it to what they already know. By shedding light on what and how our students understand, assessment can help us determine which teaching approach may be the most appropriate at a given time.

The essence of developing relational understanding is to keep the students' ideas at the forefront of classroom activities by emphasizing the process standards, mathematical proficiencies, and the Standards for Mathematical Practice. This requires that the teacher create a classroom culture in which students can learn from one another. Consider the following features of a mathematics classroom that promote understanding (Chapin, O'Conner, & Anderson, 2009; Hiebert, Carpenter, Fennema, Fuson, Wearne, Murray, Olivier, & Human, 1997; Hoffman, Breyfogle, & Dressler, 2007). In particular, notice who is doing the thinking, the talking, and the mathematics—the students.

- *Students' ideas are key.* Mathematical ideas expressed by students are important and have the potential to contribute to everyone's learning. Learning mathematics is about coming to understand the ideas of the mathematical community.

Teaching Tip

> Listen carefully to students as they talk about what they are thinking and doing as they engage in a mathematical task. If they respond in an unexpected way, try to avoid imposing *your* ideas onto their ideas. Ask clarifying questions to try to make sense of the sense your students are making!

- *Opportunities for students to talk about mathematics are common.* Learning is enhanced when students are engaged with others who are working on the same ideas. Encouraging student-to-student dialogue can help students think of themselves as capable of making sense of mathematics. Students are also more likely to question each other's ideas than the teacher's ideas.

- *Multiple approaches are encouraged.* Students must recognize that there is often a variety of methods that will lead to a solution. Respect for the ideas shared by others is critical if real discussion is to take place.

- *Mistakes are good opportunities for learning.* Students must come to realize that errors provide opportunities for growth as they are uncovered and explained. Trust must be established with an understanding that it is all right to make mistakes. Without this trust, many ideas will never be shared.

- *Math makes sense.* Students must come to understand that mathematics makes sense. Teachers should resist always evaluating students' answers. In fact, when teachers routinely respond, "Yes, that's correct" or "No, that's wrong," students will stop trying to make sense of ideas in the classroom and discussion, and learning will be curtailed.

To create a climate that encourages mathematics understanding, teachers must first provide explicit instruction on the ground rules for classroom discussions. Second, teachers may need to model the type of questioning and interaction that they expect from their students. Direct instruction would be appropriate in such a situation. The crucial point in teaching for understanding is to highlight and use students' ideas to promote mathematical proficiency.

Most people go into teaching because they want to help students learn. It is hard to think of allowing—much less planning for—the students in your classroom to struggle. Not to show them a solution when they are experiencing difficulty seems almost counterintuitive. If our goal is relational understanding, however, the struggle is part of the learning and teaching becomes less about the teacher and more about what the students are doing and thinking.

Keep in mind that you too are a learner. Some ideas in this book may make more sense to you than others. Others may even create dissonance for you. Embrace this feeling of disequilibrium and unease as an opportunity to learn—to revise your perspectives on mathematics and on the teaching and learning of mathematics as you deepen your understanding so that you can, in turn, help your students deepen theirs.

Stop and Reflect

> Look back at the chapter and identify any ideas that make you uncomfortable or that challenge your current thinking about mathematics or about teaching and learning mathematics. Try to determine why these ideas challenge you or raise questions for you. Write these ideas down and revisit them later as you read and reflect further. ■

2

Teaching Mathematics through Problem Solving

As it turns out, understanding is supported best through a delicate balance among engaging students in solving challenging problems, examining increasingly better solution methods, and providing information for students at just the right times.

Hiebert and Wearne (2003, p. 5)*

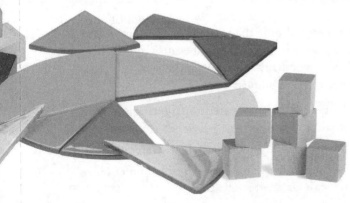

Teaching mathematics *through* problem solving is a method of teaching mathematics that helps students develop relational understanding. With this approach, problem solving is completely interwoven with learning. As students *do* mathematics—make sense of cognitively demanding tasks, provide evidence or justification for strategies and solutions, find examples and connections, and receive and provide feedback about ideas—they are simultaneously engaged in the activities of problem solving and learning. Teaching mathematics through problem solving requires you to think about the types of tasks you pose to students, how you facilitate discourse in your classroom, and how you support students' use of a variety of representations as tools for problem solving, reasoning, and communication.

Teaching through Problem Solving: An Upside-Down Approach

For many years and continuing today, mathematics has been taught using a teaching-*for*-problem-solving approach: The teacher presents the mathematics, the students practice the skill, and finally, the students solve word problems that require using that skill. Unfortunately, this "do-as-I-show-you" approach to mathematics teaching has not been successful for helping many students understand or remember mathematics concepts (e.g., Pesek & Kirshner, 2002; Philipp & Vincent, 2003).

Teaching mathematics *through* problem solving generally means that students solve problems to learn new mathematics rather than just apply mathematics after it has been learned. Students learn mathematics through real contexts, problems, situations, and models that allow them to build meaning for the concepts (Hiebert, Carpenter, Fennema, Fuson, Wearne, Murray, Olivier, & Human, 1997). So teaching *through* problem solving might be described as "upside-down" from the traditional approach of teaching *for* problem solving because the problem is presented at the beginning of a lesson and skills and ideas emerge from working with the problem. An example of teaching through problem solving might have students explore the following situation before they are taught how to set up proportions and solve for the unknown.

Tatyana has a coupon for 4 pizzas for $10. If the restaurant will give her the same rate for multiple pizzas, how much will 18 pizzas cost?

The teacher would explain to the class that there is more than one correct strategy to solve this problem and that they are to find as many different strategies as they can. Students might use counters, create a drawing, make an organized list, or solve through a series of operations.

Stop and Reflect

Find a way to determine how much money 18 pizzas will cost without using the standard algorithm of setting up proportions and solving for the unknown. ■

Through this context and exploration, students could see how to use ratio tables, which can be used to solve other real-world problems involving proportions. The pizza problem generates opportunities for students to improve their multiplicative reasoning as they find ways to relate numbers whose multiplicative relationship is not readily apparent. Using the standard algorithm of setting up proportions and solving for the unknown can take away the opportunity for students to develop multiplicative and proportional reasoning.

Teaching *through* problem solving requires a paradigm shift, which means that teachers are doing more than just tweaking a few things about their teaching; they are changing their philosophy of how they think students learn best and how they can best help them learn. At first glance, it may seem that the teacher's role is less demanding because the students are doing the mathematics, but the teacher's role is actually more demanding in such classrooms. Here are some of the important teacher responsibilities:

- Select high-quality tasks that allow students to learn the content by figuring out their own strategies and solutions.

- Ask high-quality questions that allow students to verify and relate their strategies.

- Listen to students' responses and examine their work, determining in the moment how to extend and formalize their thinking through targeted feedback.

There is no doubt that teaching mathematics through problem solving can be challenging, but the results are worth the effort! It promises to be a better approach if our ultimate goal is deep (relational) understanding because teaching through problem solving accomplishes these goals:

- *Focuses students' attention on ideas and sense making.* When solving problems, students are necessarily reflecting on the concepts inherent in the problems. Emerging concepts are more likely to be integrated with existing ones, thereby improving understanding.

- *Emphasizes mathematical processes and practices.* Students who are solving problems will engage in all five of the processes of doing mathematics—problem solving, reasoning, communication, connections, and representation (NCTM, 2000), as well as the eight mathematical practices outlined in the *Common Core State Standards*, resulting in mathematics that is more accessible, more interesting, and more meaningful. Note that the first Standard for Mathematical Practice is "Make sense of problems and persevere in solving them" (CCSSO, 2010).

- *Develops students' confidence and identities.* Every time teachers pose a problem-based task and expect a solution, they implicitly say to students, "I believe you can do this." When students are engaged in problem solving and discourse in which the correctness of the solution lies in the justification of the process, they begin to see themselves as capable of doing mathematics and that mathematics makes sense.

- *Provides a context to help students build meaning for the concept.* Using a context facilitates mathematical understanding, especially when the context is grounded in an experience familiar to students and when the context uses purposeful constraints that potentially highlight the significant mathematical ideas (Fosnot & Dolk, 2001).

- *Allows entry and exit points for a wide range of students.* Good problem-based tasks have multiple paths to the solution, so each student can make sense of and solve the task by using his or her own ideas. Furthermore, students expand their ideas and grow in their understanding as they hear, critique, and reflect on the solution strategies of others.

- *Allows for extensions and elaborations.* Extensions and "what-if" questions can motivate advanced learners or quick finishers, resulting in increased learning and enthusiasm for doing mathematics.

- *Engages students so that there are fewer discipline problems.* Many discipline issues in a classroom are the result of students becoming bored, not understanding the teacher directions, or simply finding little relevance in the task. Most students like to be challenged and enjoy being permitted to solve problems in ways that make sense to them, giving them less reason to act out or cause trouble.

- *Provides formative assessment data.* As students discuss ideas, draw diagrams, or use manipulatives, defend their solutions and evaluate those of others, and write reports or explanations, they provide the teacher with a steady stream of valuable information that can be used to inform subsequent instruction.

- *Is a lot of fun!* Students enjoy the creative process of problem solving and sharing how they figured something out. After seeing the surprising and inventive ways that students think and how engaged students become in mathematics, very few teachers stop using a teaching-*through*-problem-solving approach.

 ## Using Problems to Teach

When teachers teach mathematics through problem solving, students learn the desired content through problems (tasks or activities). A *problem* is defined here as any task or activity for which students have no prescribed or memorized rules or methods, and for which they do not have a perception that there is a specific "correct" solution method (Hiebert et al., 1997). In other words, the task or activity is a genuine problem.

◆ Features of a Problem

Problems that can serve as effective tasks or activities for students to solve have common features. Use the following points as a guide to assess whether a task or an activity has the potential to be a genuine problem.

- *The problem should engage students where they are in their current understanding.* Students should have the appropriate ideas to begin engaging with the problem and to solve the problem, yet still find it challenging and interesting.

- *The problematic or engaging aspect of the problem must be a result of the mathematics that the students are to learn.* In solving the problem or doing the activity, students should be concerned primarily with making sense of and developing their understanding of the mathematics involved. Any context or motivation used should not overshadow the mathematics to be learned.

- *The problem must require justifications and explanations for answers and methods.* In a high-quality problem, neither the process nor the answer is straightforward, so justification is central to the task. Students should understand that the responsibility for determining whether answers are correct and why they are correct rests on their mathematical reasoning, not on the teacher telling them that they are correct.

◆ Examples of Problems

Problems can be used to develop both concepts and procedures, and the connection between concepts and procedures. In the following examples, the first two problems focus on concepts, and the third problem focuses on a procedure.

CONCEPT: Comparing Ratios and Proportional Reasoning

Jack and Jill were at the same spot at the bottom of a hill, hoping to fetch a pail of water. They both begin walking up the hill, Jack walking 5 yards every 25 seconds and Jill walking 3 yards every 10 seconds. Assuming a constant walking rate, who will get to the pail of water first?

CONCEPT: Equality

$$64 \div 16 = 32 \div b$$

Find a number for *b* so that the equation is true. Is there more than one number that will make the equation true? Why or why not? Can you find more than one way to find a number for *b* so that the equation is true?

Note that a task in the form of a story problem does not automatically make the task a problem. A story problem can be "routine" if students read it and know right away that it is a division problem and divide to answer it. Conversely, an equation with no words, as in the second example above, is not necessarily routine and can actually be a rich problem to investigate.

PROCEDURE: Dividing Two Fractions

Solve this problem in two different ways: $\frac{3}{4} \div \frac{1}{2} = $ _____.

For each way, explain how you solved it.

The third example, although focused on a procedure, is a problem because students must figure out *how* they are going to approach the task (assuming they have not been taught the standard algorithm at this point). Students are also challenged to find more than one way to solve the problem. Implicit is the challenge to determine how the two solution strategies are different. The third example is important because it illustrates that virtually all mathematics—concepts and procedures—can be taught through problem solving.

◆ Selecting Worthwhile Tasks

As noted earlier in the three features of a problem, a task must engage students where they currently are in their understanding and simultaneously must be problematic for the students. In selecting such a task, consider the level of cognitive demand, the potential of the task to have multiple entry and exit points, and the relevancy of the task to students.

Level of Cognitive Demand

Research supports the practice of engaging students in productive struggle to develop understanding (Bay-Williams, 2010; Hiebert & Grouws, 2007). Both words in the phrase "productive struggle" are important. Students must have the tools and prior knowledge to solve a problem and not be given a problem that is out of reach because otherwise they will struggle without being productive; however, students should not be given tasks that are straightforward and trivial because they will not struggle with mathematical ideas and further develop their understanding. When students know that struggle is an expected part of the process of doing mathematics, they embrace the struggle and feel success when they reach a solution (Carter, 2008).

Figure 2.1 shows a useful framework for determining whether a task has the potential to challenge students (Smith & Stein, 1998). The framework distinguishes between tasks that require low levels and high levels of cognitive demand. Tasks that have low-level cognitive demand are routine and straightforward and do not engage students in productive struggle. Tasks with a high level of cognitive demand not only engage students in productive struggle but also challenge students to make connections between concepts and to other relevant knowledge. Although there are appropriate times to use low-level cognitive demand tasks, a heavy or sole emphasis on tasks of this type will not lead to a relational understanding of mathematics. As an example of different levels of tasks, consider the degree of reasoning required if you ask students to find the average of five given numbers versus if you ask them to find five numbers whose average is 35. The first task only requires students to find the average of five numbers. The second task requires them to use number sense and their understanding of average to generate five reasonable numbers that will result in a given average. As a consequence of working on this second task, students have potential opportunities to think about and use number relationships while they work on their computational skills for finding averages.

Multiple Entry and Exit Points

A problem or task that has multiple entry points has varying degrees of challenge within it or can be approached in a variety of ways. One of the advantages of a problem-based approach is that it can help accommodate the diversity of learners in every classroom because students are encouraged to use a strategy that makes sense to them instead of using a predetermined strategy that they may or may not be ready to use successfully. Some students may initially use less efficient approaches, such as guess and check or counting, but they will develop more advanced strategies through effective questioning by the teacher and by reflecting on other students' approaches. For example, for the task of finding five numbers whose average is 35, one student may use a guess-and-check approach, using five random numbers to see if their average is 35, while another student may use a more systematic

Figure 2.1 Levels of cognitive demand.

Low-Level Cognitive Demand Tasks	High-Level Cognitive Demand Tasks
Memorization • Involve producing previously learned facts, rules, formulas, or definitions or memorizing • Are routine, in that they involve exact reproduction of previously learned procedures • Have no connection to related concepts	**Procedures with Connections** • Focus students' attention on the use of procedures for the purpose of developing deeper levels of understanding of mathematical concepts and ideas • Suggest general procedures that have close connections to underlying conceptual ideas • Are usually represented in multiple ways (e.g., visuals, manipulatives, symbols, problem situations) • Require that students engage with the conceptual ideas that underlie the procedures in order to successfully complete the task
Procedures without Connections • Use procedures specifically called for • Are straightforward, with little ambiguity about what needs to be done and how to do it • Have no connection to related concepts • Are focused on producing correct answers rather than developing mathematical understanding • Require no explanations or explanations that focus on the procedure only	***Doing* Mathematics** • Require complex and nonalgorithmic thinking (i.e., nonroutine—without a predictable, known approach) • Require students to explore and to understand the nature of mathematical concepts, processes, or relationships • Demand self-monitoring or self-regulation of students' own cognitive processes • Require students to access relevant knowledge in working through the task • Require students to analyze the task and actively examine task constraints • Require considerable cognitive effort

Source: Reprinted with permission from Stein, M. K., Smith, M. S., Henningsen, M. A., and Silver, E. A. *Implementing Standards-Based Mathematics Instruction: A Case for Professional Development.* Copyright 2009 by the National Council of Teachers of Mathematics. All rights reserved.

approach, such as starting with five 35s and then moving part of one 35 to another 35 until he or she has five different numbers. Still another child may reason that if the five numbers were all 35s, then their sum would be 5×35, or 175, so partitioning 175 into five different parts would result in five numbers whose sum is 35.

Tasks should also have multiple exit points, or various ways that students can demonstrate an understanding of the learning goals. For example, students might draw a diagram, write an equation, use manipulatives, or act out a problem to demonstrate their understanding.

Consider the opportunities for multiple entry and exit points in the following tasks.

TASK 1:

If there are 1 red tile, 2 yellow tiles, and 1 blue tile in a bag, what is the probability of pulling out a red tile?

TASK 2:

The probability of an event is $\frac{1}{4}$. Describe what the event (situation) might be. Explain how you might use dice, a spinner, or some other tool to simulate the situation.

Stop and Reflect

To what degree do these tasks offer opportunities for multiple entry and exit points? ■

In the first task, students will gain some experience in thinking about the probability of one event in one situation, but they will miss any opportunity to think deeply about what a probability of $\frac{1}{4}$ means and how it can represent various situations. The second task offers more opportunity for students to engage with the task in a variety of ways, which also offers the teacher more information about each student's level of understanding. For example, do students select examples with more than four objects (e.g., drawing hearts from a deck of cards)? Do students create tree diagrams to help them reason through the situation? Do students create events that are all equally likely, or do they create events that are more likely than others? Can students think about compound events that result in a probability of $\frac{1}{4}$? Clearly, the second task offers many more opportunities for all students to engage in the task in a variety of ways.

Before giving a selected task to your class, anticipate several possible responses to the task, including possible misconceptions, and think about how you might address these responses. Anticipating the responses gives you time to consider how you will respond to various approaches, and it also helps you to quickly recognize different strategies and misconceptions when students are working on the task.

Relevant and Well-Designed Contexts

One of the most powerful aspects of teaching through problem solving is that the problem that begins the lesson can get students excited about learning mathematics. Compare the following two sixth-grade introductory tasks on ratios. Which one do you think would be more interesting to students?

Classroom A: "Today we are going to explore ratios and see how ratios can be used to compare amounts."

Classroom B: "In a minute, I am going to read to you a passage from *Harry Potter* about how big Hagrid is. We are going to use ratios to compare our heights and widths to Hagrid's height and width."

Your goal as a teacher is to design problems that provide specific parameters, constraints, or structure that will support the development of the mathematical ideas you want students to learn. But possibly even more important, familiar and interesting contexts increase students' engagement. In this example, literature was used to engage students. Contexts can also be used to learn about cultures, such as those of the students in your classroom, and can also be used to link to other disciplines (e.g., science, social studies).

◭ Orchestrating Classroom Discourse

Classroom discourse refers to the interactions among all the participants that occur throughout a lesson—in a whole-class setting, in small groups, between pairs of students, and with the teacher. The purpose of discourse is not for students to state their answers and get validation from the teacher but to engage all learners and keep the cognitive demand high (Breyfogle & Williams, 2008–2009; Kilic, Cross, Ersoz, Mewborn, Swanagan, & Kim, 2010; Smith, Hughes, Engle, & Stein, 2009).

◆ Classroom Discussions

The value of student talk throughout a mathematics lesson cannot be overemphasized. As students describe and evaluate solutions to tasks, share approaches, and make conjectures, learning will occur in ways that are otherwise unlikely to take place. As they listen to other students' ideas, they come to see the varied approaches in how problems can be solved and see mathematics as something that they can do. Questions such as those that ask students whether they would do it differently next time, which strategy made sense to them (and why), and what caused problems for them (and how they overcame them) are critical in developing mathematically proficient students. Orchestrating discourse after students have worked on problem(s) is particularly important as it is this type of discussion that helps students connect the problem to more general or formal mathematics and make connections to other ideas.

Implementing effective discourse in the classroom can be challenging. Finding ways to encourage students to share their ideas and to engage with others about their ideas is essential to productive discussions. Consider the following research-based recommendations that can be useful in a whole-class setting, in small groups, and in peer-to-peer discussions (Chapin, O'Connor, & Anderson, 2009; Rasmussen, Yackel, & King, 2003; Stephan & Whitenack, 2003; Wood, Williams, & McNeal, 2006; Yackel & Cobb, 1996).

- *Clarify students' ideas in a variety of ways.* You can restate students' ideas as questions in order to verify what they did as well as what they meant to confirm what you've heard or observed. You can also apply precise language and make significant ideas more apparent. Paying attention to students' ideas sends the message that their ideas are valued, and therefore this is a key step to encouraging participation of individual students. In addition, modeling how to ask clarifying questions demonstrates to students that it is all right to be unsure and that asking questions is appropriate. It is important to keep in mind that although you may understand a student's ideas and reasoning, there may be students in the class who do not. So look for opportunities to ask clarifying questions even if you do not need clarification. You can also ask students to restate someone else's ideas in their own words in order to ensure that ideas are stated in a variety of ways and to encourage students to listen to one another. This strategy of clarification is important for English language learners (ELLs) because it reinforces language and enhances comprehension.

- *Emphasize reasoning.* Ask follow-up questions whether the answer is right or wrong to place an emphasis on the reasoning process. Your role is to understand students' thinking (not to lead them to the correct answer and move on). So, follow up with probes to learn more about their answers and their reasoning. Sometimes, you will find that what you assumed they were thinking is not correct. Also, if you follow up only on wrong answers, students quickly figure this out and get nervous when you ask them to explain their thinking. In addition, move students to more conceptually based explanations when appropriate. For example, if a student says that he knows 4.17 is more than 4.1638, ask him (or another student) to explain why this is so. You can also ask students what they think of the idea proposed by another student, or ask if they see a connection between two classmates' ideas or between a classmate's idea and a concept previously discussed.

- *Encourage student–student dialogue.* You want students to think of themselves as capable of making sense of mathematics so that they do not always rely on the teacher to verify the correctness of their ideas. Encouraging student-to-student dialogue can help build this sense of self. Students are also more likely to question one another's ideas than the teacher's ideas. When students have different solutions, ask them to discuss one another's solutions. Or ask someone to rephrase another student's ideas or to add something further to someone else's ideas. Provide opportunities that allow students to share their ideas in small groups or with a peer. This will ensure that all students are able to participate in sharing because not all students will be able to share during every whole-class discussion. Before a whole-class discussion, students can

$\mathcal{F}igure\ 2.2$ Examples of teacher prompts for supporting classroom discussions.

Clarify Students' Ideas	"You used a unit ratio to find the price for 15 pounds?" "So, first you recorded your measurements in a table?" "What parts of your drawing relate to the numbers from the story problem?" "Who can share what Ricardo just said, but using your own words?"
Emphasize Reasoning	"Why does it make sense to start with that particular number?" "Explain how you know that your answer is correct." "Can you give an example?" "Do you see a connection between Julio's idea and Rhonda's idea?" "What if . . .?" "Do you agree or disagree with Johanna? Why?"
Encourage Student– Student Dialogue	"Who has a question for Vivian?" "Turn to your partner and explain why you agree or disagree with Edwin." "Talk with Yerin about how your strategy relates to hers."

practice their explanations with a peer, which is one way to support ELLs and other students with special needs during mathematical discussions. See Chapters 5 and 6 for other ideas about how to support these particular groups of students with mathematical discussions. Figure 2.2 offers examples of teacher prompts that can support classroom discussions.

Be sure to explain to students that after they hear a question or a prompt they will have time to think so that silence in the classroom does not feel uncomfortable. For example, you can say, "This question is important. Let's take some time to think about it." There will be times when no one responds to your question or prompt. If the situation gets awkward, make sure students understand the question or prompt, then ask them to talk with a partner and try the discussion again.

◆ How Much to Tell and Not to Tell

When teachers teach mathematics *through* problem solving, one of the most perplexing dilemmas is how much, if anything, to tell. On one hand, telling can diminish what is learned and lower the level of challenge in a lesson. On the other hand, telling too little can sometimes leave students floundering, or not productively struggling. Following are suggestions about three things that you need to tell students:

- *Introduce mathematical conventions.* Symbols, such as $\sqrt{}$ and x^3, and notations, such as $(1,\bar{}2)$, are conventions. Terminology is also a convention. As a rule of thumb, symbolism and terminology should be introduced *after* concepts have been developed and then specifically as a means of expressing or labeling ideas.

- *Discuss alternative methods.* If an important strategy does not emerge naturally from students, then you should propose the strategy, being careful to identify it as "another" way, not the only or the preferred way.

- *Clarify students' methods and make connections.* You should help students clarify or interpret their ideas and point out related concepts. A student may divide $\frac{5}{6}$ by $\frac{1}{3}$ by thinking about how many one-thirds can be measured out or subtracted from $\frac{5}{6}$. This strategy can be related to measurement division with whole numbers, such as thinking of $12 \div 3$ as how many 3s can be measured out or subtracted from 12. Drawing everyone's attention to this connection can help other students see the connection while also building the confidence of the student who originally proposed the strategy (Hiebert et al., 1997).

Representations: Tools for Problem Solving, Reasoning, and Communication

A representation can be thought of as a kind of tool, such as a diagram, graph, symbol, or manipulative, that expresses a mathematical idea or concept. Representations are not ends in themselves to be learned for the sake of learning but are valuable tools in problem solving, reasoning, and communicating about mathematical ideas. Representations can help you think through a problem and better communicate your ideas to another person. How you represent the ideas in the problem will likely influence your solution process. In fact, the representations that students choose to use can provide valuable insight into their ways of interpreting and thinking about the mathematical ideas at hand.

Models or representations give learners something with which they can explore, reason, and communicate as they engage in problem-based tasks. The goal of using representations is so that students can manipulate ideas, not manipulate symbols in a rote manner. By using personally meaningful representations to manipulate and communicate about mathematical ideas, students will make connections among mathematical ideas (relational understanding) and move toward mathematical proficiency.

◆ Tips for Using Representations in the Classroom

Because different representations can illuminate different aspects of a mathematical idea, multiple representations should be explored and encouraged. The more ways that students are given to think about and test an emerging idea, the better they will correctly form and integrate it into a rich web of concepts and thereby develop a relational understanding. Figure 2.3 illustrates various representations for demonstrating an understanding of any topic. Students who have difficulty translating a concept from one representation to another also have difficulty solving problems and understanding computations (Clement, 2004; Lesh, Cramer, Doerr, Post, & Zawojewski, 2003; NCTM, 2000). Strengthening the ability to move between and among representations improves students' understanding and retention of ideas.

The following are rules of thumb for using representations or models in the classroom:

- Introduce new representations or tools by showing how they can represent the *ideas* for which they are intended. But keep in mind that because the representations are not the concepts, some students may not "see" what you see.
- Allow students (in most instances) to select freely from available tools to use in solving problems.
- Encourage students to create their own representations. Look for opportunities to connect these student-created representations to more conventional representations.
- Encourage the use of a particular representation when you believe it would be helpful to a student having difficulty.

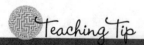
Teaching Tip

Pay attention to students' choices of representations, and use those representations as starting points for dialogues with them about their thinking. What they find important may be surprising and informative at the same time.

Figure 2.3

Mathematical understanding can be demonstrated through these different representations of mathematical ideas. Translations between each can help students develop new concepts and demonstrate a richer understanding.

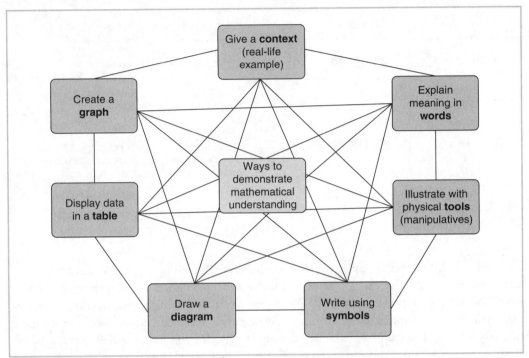

- Ask students to use representations, such as diagrams and manipulatives, when they explain their thinking. This will help you gather information about students' understanding of the idea and also their understanding of the representations that have been used in the classroom. It can also be helpful to other students in the classroom who may be struggling with the idea or the explanation being offered.

- In creating tasks and when facilitating classroom discussions, focus on making connections among the different representations used (and make sure each is understood). Helping students make these connections is very important to their learning.

Note that problems can start with one representation (e.g., a story problem) and ask the student to translate the information to another representation (e.g., an equation); yet a student might get to the final representation by working through other representations (e.g., creating a table or drawing a picture to get to an equation). These representations, whether student-created or more conventional, are critical in supporting students' reasoning and actually progressing toward more abstract symbolic representations.

◆ Manipulatives

Let's turn to one kind of representation that is commonly used to support students' learning of mathematics—manipulatives, or concrete objects. Any time a concept is new, regardless of the ages of the students, manipulatives can be a positive factor in students' learning. However, just using manipulatives, particularly in a rote manner, does not ensure that students will understand. It is important to consider how manipulatives can help, or fail to help, students construct mathematical knowledge.

Figure 2.4

Objects and names of objects are not the same as mathematical ideas and relationships between objects.

Names	Models	Relationships
Positive 3	● ● ●	3 chips that are black represent ⁺3
Negative 3	○ ○ ○	3 chips that are white represent ⁻3
Positive 3	● ● ● ●　]Equals ○　]zero	4 black chips and 1 white chip result in 3 black chips when a black and white chip equal a net gain/loss of 0

First of all, manipulatives alone have no inherent meaning. A person has to impose meaning onto them. The manipulative is not the concept. Figure 2.4 shows colored chips commonly used to represent integers. We define one color to represent positive numbers (usually black) and another color to represent negative numbers (usually red, but we have used white here). If a student is able to identify the black chips as "positive" and the white chips as "negative," does this mean the student has constructed the concepts of positive and negative numbers and can operate with them in meaningful ways? No, all you know for sure is that the student has learned the names typically assigned to the manipulatives. In fact, there is evidence across a range of grades that students struggle with negative numbers (Mukhopadhyay, 1997; Vlassis, 2004). Calculating with integers can become a lesson in memorization when students are rushed to follow rules such as "two like signs become a positive" and "two unlike signs become a negative." Consequently, teachers attempt to support students' work by using manipulatives such as colored chips. However, the concept of "negative" must be created by students in their own minds and imposed on the manipulative used to represent the concept (connecting money to the chips using a profit/loss context can help students construct this meaning). Through discussions that explicitly focus on the mathematical concepts over time, the connections between manipulatives and related concepts are developed.

Teaching Tip

It is incorrect to say that a manipulative or object "illustrates" or shows a concept. Manipulatives can help students visualize relationships and talk about them, but what they see are the manipulatives, not concepts.

Second, the most widespread misuse of manipulatives occurs when teachers tell students, "Do exactly as I do." There is a natural temptation to get out the materials and show students exactly *how to use them*. Students mimic the teacher's directions, and it may even look as if they understand, but they may just be following what they see. A rote procedure with a manipulative is still just that—a rote procedure.

A third and related misuse of manipulatives occurs when teachers always tell students which manipulative to use for a given problem. Students need opportunities to choose their own representations to use when reasoning through a problem (Mathematical Practice 5: Use appropriate tools strategically) and when communicating their ideas to others.

◆ Visuals and Other Tools

There are other ways for students to represent and illustrate mathematical concepts. Drawings are one option and are important for a number of reasons. First, when students draw, you learn more about what they do or do not understand. For example, if students are showing the part–part ratio 2:3 with their own drawings, you can observe whether they understand that the whole has five parts, with the first quantity making up $\frac{2}{5}$ of the whole and the second quantity making up $\frac{3}{5}$ of the whole. Second, manipulatives can sometimes restrict how students can model a problem, whereas a drawing allows students to use any strategy they want. Figure 2.5 shows an example of a seventh grader's solution for solving a ratio problem. Look for opportunities to use students' representations during classroom discussions to help them make sense of the more abstract mathematical symbols and computational procedures. Third, when students create a drawing you tend to get different representations, providing an excellent opportunity to compare and contrast the various approaches and visuals.

Representations generated and manipulated through technology can also support students as they reason about and communicate their mathematical ideas. Changes can usually be made to situations more quickly by using a computer than by using physical manipulatives or student-generated drawings, leaving more time for exploration. For example, using interactive graphing software, students can quickly make changes to graphs to help them analyze and interpret how situations change as variables change (see, for example, www.nctm.org/standards/content.aspx?id=25092). As another example, simulation software allows students to perform several trials in just a few seconds, as opposed to having to complete the actual experiment multiple times, again allowing more time for analysis and interpretation of the situation (e.g., go to http://nlvm.usu.edu/en/nav/grade_g_3.html and select "Coin Toss"). Plus, virtual manipulatives can help students link manipulatives to symbols. For example, some websites display decimals with numerals and computerized base-ten blocks, and as changes are made to the base-ten blocks, students can see the results

Figure 2.5   A seventh grader shows her thinking about a ratio problem.

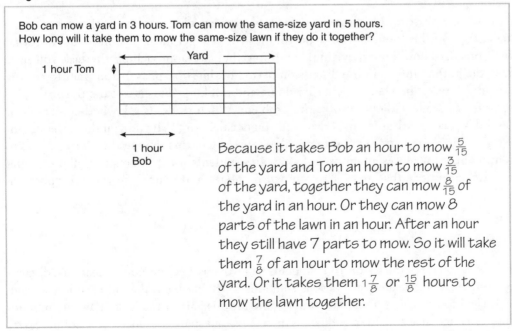

Bob can mow a yard in 3 hours. Tom can mow the same-size yard in 5 hours. How long will it take them to mow the same-size lawn if they do it together?

Because it takes Bob an hour to mow $\frac{5}{15}$ of the yard and Tom an hour to mow $\frac{3}{15}$ of the yard, together they can mow $\frac{8}{15}$ of the yard in an hour. Or they can mow 8 parts of the lawn in an hour. After an hour they still have 7 parts to mow. So it will take them $\frac{7}{8}$ of an hour to mow the rest of the yard. Or it takes them $1\frac{7}{8}$ or $\frac{15}{8}$ hours to mow the lawn together.

of the actions they take on the numeral representation of the decimal (e.g., go to http://nlvm.usu.edu/en/nav/grade_g_3.html and click on "Base Blocks—Decimals"). The dynamic link between these two representations helps students make sense of their activity as well as the numbers. An added bonus with technology is that sometimes the language displayed on the computer program can be changed for ELLs.

Meaningful contexts help students make sense of mathematical ideas. Using real objects, pictures, drawings, and virtual manipulatives can help students relate to and better understand a context, especially one that is unfamiliar. This is particularly important in supporting ELLs or students with disabilities.

 # A Three-Phase Lesson Format

A three-phase lesson format (*Before, During, After*) provides a structure for teaching mathematics through problem solving (Table 2.1). *Before* refers to the time before students start work on the problem; *During* refers to the time during which students work on the problem; and *After* refers to the discussion that takes place after students work on the problem. The lesson may take one or more class sessions, but the three-phase structure can also be applied to shorter tasks, resulting in a 10- to 20-minute minilesson.

Before

In the *Before* phase of the lesson, you are preparing students to work on the problem. As you plan for the *Before* part of the lesson, analyze the problem you will give to students in order to anticipate students' approaches and possible misinterpretations or misconceptions (Wallace, 2007). This can inform the questions you ask in the *Before* phase of the lesson to clarify students' understanding of the problem (i.e., knowing what it means rather than how they will solve it).

During

In the *During* phase of the lesson, students explore the problem (alone, with partners, or in small groups). This is one of two opportunities you will get in the lesson to find out what your students know, how they think, and how they are approaching the task you have given them (the other is in the discussion period of the *After* phase). You want to convey a genuine interest in what students are doing and thinking. This is not the time to evaluate or to tell students how to solve the problem. When students ask whether a result or method is correct, ask students, "How can you decide?" or "Why do you think that might be right?" or "How can we tell if that makes sense?" Use this time in the *During* phase to identify different representations and strategies students used, interesting solutions, and any misconceptions that arise that you will highlight and address in the *After* phase of the lesson.

After

In the *After* phase of the lesson your students will work as a community of learners, discussing, justifying, and challenging various solutions to the problem that all have just worked on. It is critical to plan for and save ample time for this part of the lesson. Twenty minutes is not at all unreasonable for a good class discussion and sharing of ideas. It is not necessary

Table 2.1 Teaching Mathematics through Problem Solving Lends Itself to a Three-Phase Structure for Lessons

Lesson Phase		Teacher Actions in a Teaching Mathematics through Problem-Solving Lesson
Before	Activate prior knowledge.	Begin with a simple version of the task; connect to students' experiences; brainstorm approaches or solution strategies; estimate or predict whether tasks involve a single computation or are aimed at the development of a computational procedure.
	Be sure the problem is understood.	Have students explain to you what the problem is asking. Go over vocabulary that may be troubling. Caution: This does *not* mean that you are explaining how to *do* the problem—just that students should understand what the problem is about.
	Establish clear expectations.	Tell students whether they will work individually, in pairs, or small groups, or if they will have a choice. Tell them how they will share their solutions and reasoning.
During	Let go!	Although it is tempting to want to step in and "help," hold back and enjoy observing and learning from students.
	Notice students' mathematical thinking.	Base your questions on students' work and their responses to you. Use questions like "Tell me what you are doing"; "I see you have started to [multiply] these numbers. Can you tell me why you are [multiplying]?" [substitute any process/strategy]; "Can you tell me more about…?"; "Why did you…?"; "How does your diagram connect to the problem?"
	Provide appropriate support.	Look for ways to support students' thinking and avoid telling them how to solve the problem: Ensure that students understand the problem (e.g., "What do you know about the problem?"); ask the student what he or she has already tried (e.g., "Where did you get stuck?"); suggest that the student use a different strategy (e.g., "Can you draw a diagram?"; "What if you used cubes to act out this problem?"; "Is this like another problem we have solved?"); create a parallel problem with simpler values (Jacobs & Ambrose, 2008).
	Provide worthwhile extensions.	Challenge early finishers in some manner that is related to the problem just solved. Possible questions to ask are "I see you found one way to do this. Are there any other solutions? Are any of the solutions different or more interesting than others?" Some good questions for extending thinking are, "What if…?" or "Would that same idea work for…?"
After	Promote a community of learners.	You must teach students about your expectations for this time and how to interact respectfully with their peers. Role-play appropriate (and inappropriate) ways of responding to each other. The "Orchestrating Discourse" section provides strategies and recommendations for how to facilitate discussions that help create a community of learners.
	Listen actively without evaluation.	The goal here is noticing students' mathematical thinking and making that thinking visible to other students. Avoid judging the correctness of an answer so that students are more willing to share their ideas. Support students' thinking without evaluation by simply asking what others think about a student's response.
	Summarize main ideas and identify future problems.	Formalize the main ideas of the lesson, helping to highlight connections among strategies or different mathematical ideas. In addition, this is the time to reinforce appropriate terminology, definitions, and symbols. You may also want to lay the groundwork for future tasks and activities.

to wait for every student to finish. Here is where much of the learning will occur as students reflect individually and collectively on the ideas they have explored. This is the time to reinforce precise terminology, definitions, or symbols. After students have shared their ideas, formalize the main ideas of the lesson, highlighting connections among strategies or different mathematical ideas.

What Do I Do When a Task Doesn't Work?

Sometimes students may not know what to do with a problem you pose, no matter how many hints and suggestions you offer. Do not give in to the temptation to "tell them." But when you sense that a task is not moving forward, don't spend days just hoping that something wonderful may happen. You may need to regroup and offer students a simpler but related task that gets them prepared for the one that proved too difficult. If that does not work, set it aside for the moment. Ask yourself why it didn't work well. Did the students have the prior knowledge they needed? Was the task too advanced? Consider what might be a way to step back or step forward in the content in order to support and challenge students. Nonetheless, trust that teaching mathematics *through* problem solving offers students the productive struggle that will allow them to develop understanding and become mathematically proficient.

Stop and Reflect

Describe what is (and isn't) meant by "teaching mathematics *through* problem solving." What do you foresee to be some opportunities and challenges to implementing problem-based mathematics tasks effectively in your classroom? ■

3

Assessing for Learning

I realize how valuable a well-designed, research-based probe can be in finding evidence of student understanding. Also how this awareness of children's thinking helped me decide what they (students) actually knew versus what I thought they knew.

A teacher from the Vermont Mathematics Partnership*

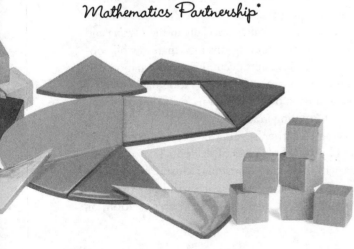

 Assessment That Supports Instruction

In a problem-based approach, teachers often ask, "How do I assess?" The assessment principle in *Principles and Standards for School Mathematics* (NCTM, 2000) stresses two main ideas: (1) Assessment should enhance students' learning, and (2) assessment is a valuable tool for making instructional decisions.

Assessment is not separate from instruction and in fact should include the mathematical practices (CCSSO, 2010) and processes (NCTM, 2000) that occur in the course of effective problem-based instructional approaches. The typical approach of an end-of-chapter test of skills may have value, but it rarely reveals the type of data that can fine-tune instruction so that it is tailored to improving the performance of individual students. In fact, Daro, Mosher, and Corcoran (2011) state that "the starting point is the mathematics and thinking the student brings to the lesson, not the deficit of mathematics they do not bring" (p. 48). Stiggins (2009) goes further to suggest that students in the upper elementary grades and beyond should be informed partners in understanding their progress in learning and how to enhance their growth in understanding concepts. They should begin to use their own assessment results to move forward as learners as they see that "success is always within reach" (Stiggins, 2009, p. 420). Using carefully selected assessment tasks allows you to integrate assessment into instruction and make it part of the learning process.

Assessments usually fall into one of two major categories: summative or formative. A *summative assessment* is a cumulative evaluation that may generate a single score, such as an end-of-unit test or a standardized test that is used in your state or school district. Although the scores are important for schools and teachers, used individually they often do not help shape specific teaching decisions on particular topics or identify misunderstandings that may hinder students' future growth.

A *formative assessment* is used to determine the point-in-time status of students' understanding, to preassess, or to attempt to identify students' naïve understandings or misconceptions so that the information is interpreted and used to provide feedback and make decisions about next instructional steps (Wiliam, 2010). Wiliam (2010) goes on to note three key processes in formative assessment: "1) Establishing where the learners are in their learning, 2) Establishing where they are going and 3) Working out how to get there" (p. 45). As Wiliam (2010) states, "To be formative, assessment must include a recipe for future action" (slide 41).

For example, a formative assessment for a sixth-grade class could pose the following proportional reasoning problem:

Jeff and Pamela are painting fences. Jeff's fence is 8 sections long, and he has 4 sections painted. Pamela's fence is 9 sections long, and she has 5 sections painted. Who is closer to finishing the painting project? Explain how you know.

Students then individually work to complete this task on paper, as a written record of their process and responses. After students have worked, the task is discussed. One student states, "They are the same. They both need to paint four more sections." Another student draws two lines on a paper and says, "Pamela. She is one-half of a section more than halfway done. Jeff is only halfway done."

The information gathered from observing and listening to these two students reveals different "paths" for instructional next steps. As the first step in Wiliam's three key processes, the teacher notes where students are in their learning. Moving into the second step, she notes that the first student is still thinking additively, and will need to develop proportional reasoning through more targeted instruction, while the latter student is thinking multiplicatively, and is therefore ready to move to more challenging proportional tasks.

If summative assessment could be described as a digital snapshot, formative assessment is like streaming video. One is a picture of what a student knows that is captured in a single moment of time, and the other is a moving picture that demonstrates active student thinking and reasoning. In the following pages and throughout Part II of this book in the "Formative Assessment Notes" feature, various formative assessment approaches are presented, including Piaget's three broad categories of formative assessments: observations, interviews, and tasks (Piaget, 1976).

Observations

All teachers learn useful bits of information about their students every day. When the three-phase lesson format (*Before, During,* and *After* phases) (suggested in Chapter 2) is followed, the flow of evidence about student performance increases dramatically, especially in the *During* and *After* portions of lessons. If you have a systematic plan for gathering this information while observing and listening to students, at least two very valuable results occur. First, information that may have gone unnoticed is suddenly visible and important. Second, observation data gathered systematically can be combined with other data and used in planning lessons, providing feedback to students, conducting parent conferences, and determining grades.

Depending on the information you are trying to gather, several days to two weeks may be required to complete a single observation of how a whole class of students is progressing on a standard. Shorter periods of observation will focus on a particular cluster of concepts or skills or on particular students. Over longer periods, you can note growth in mathematical processes or practices, such as the development of problem solving, representation, or reasoning. To use observation effectively, you should take seriously the following maxim: Only try to collect data on a reasonable number of students in a single class period.

Anecdotal Notes

One system for recording observations is to write short notes, either during or immediately after a lesson, in a brief narrative. A possibility is to have a card for each student in the class arranged and taped on a clipboard (see Figure 3.1). Another option is to write anecdotal notes on an electronic tablet and store them in a spreadsheet. Importantly, the notes need to provide insights into what each student does or does not know related to the unit goals. For example, you will probably find the comment "is beginning to estimate answers to multiplication of decimals to locate the proper placement of the decimal" more helpful than "cannot multiply decimals."

Checklists

To cut down on writing and help focus your attention, a checklist duplicated for each student with several specific processes or content objectives can be devised (see Figure 3.2). As you build

Figure 3.1

Preprinted cards for observation notes can be taped to a clipboard or folder for quick access.

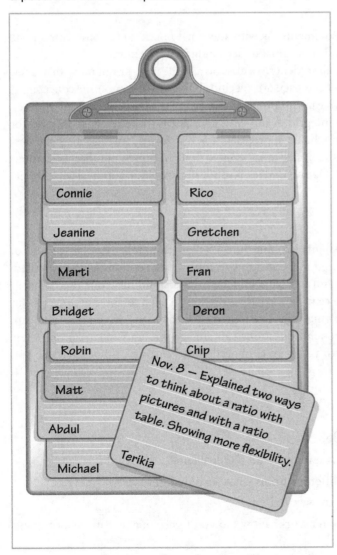

Figure 3.2

Example of a sixth-grade checklist and rubric (aligned to *Common Core State Standards* content and practices) that can be printed for each student.

NAME: **Sharon V.**

DIVISION OF FRACTIONS	NOT THERE YET	ON TARGET	ABOVE AND BEYOND	COMMENTS
Uses measurement interpretation		✓		
Uses partitive interpretation		✓		
Set models	✓			*Used two color counters to show* $1\frac{1}{4} \div 3 =$
Answers that are not whole numbers	✓			
Understands standard algorithm		✓		*Showing greater reasonableness*
MATHEMATICAL PRACTICES				
Makes sense of problems and perseveres		✓		*Stated problem in own words*
Models with mathematics	✓			*Reluctant to use abstract models*
Uses appropriate tools		✓		

Figure 3.3

A full-class observation checklist can be used for long-term objectives or for several days to cover a short-term objective.

Transformations *Mental computation adding 2-digit numbers* **Names**	Not There Yet *Can't do mentally*	On Target *Has at least one strategy*	Above and Beyond *Uses different methods with different numbers*	Comments
Lalie		✓ *3-18-2013* *3-21-2013*		
Pete	✓ *3-20-2013*	✓ *3-24-2013*		*Difficulty with any problems using rotation*
Sid			✓+ *3-20-2013*	*Can do dilations on grid*
Lakeshia		✓		*Struggles with reflections on a coordinate grid*
George		✓		
Pam	✓			*Beginning to use slides and reflections*
Maria		✓ *3-24-2013*		

your checklist, include a place for comments. As with anecdotal notes, these comments should be specific and focus on big ideas and conceptual understanding for the unit.

Another format involves listing all students in a class on a single page or not more than a few pages (Figure 3.3). Across the top of the page are specific abilities or common misconceptions to look for. (These can be based on learning progressions or trajectories.) Pluses and minuses, checks, or codes can be entered in the grid. A full-class checklist is more likely to be used for long-term objectives. Topics that might be appropriate for this format include mathematical practices, communication skills, and such skill areas as basic factorization of numbers or computational estimation with decimals. Dating entries and noting specifics about observed performance are also helpful.

Questioning

Observations do not have to be silent. Probing into student thinking through the use of questions can provide better data and more insights to inform instruction. As you circulate around the classroom to observe and evaluate students' understanding, your use of questions is one of the most important ways to formatively assess in each lesson phase. Write an open-ended question for each learning objective and ask it to as many students as you can. In addition, the following more general questions can engage students in explaining their thinking. Carry your questions with you on a clipboard, index cards, or a bookmark as you move about the classroom:

- What can you tell me about [today's topic]?
- Explain your process to me.
- How did you decide what to do?
- What did you do that helped you understand the problem?
- How is this problem like (or different from) what we did yesterday?
- How can you prove that your answer is right?
- Did you try something that didn't work? How did you figure out that it was not going to work?

Getting the students used to responding to these questions (as well as accustomed to asking questions about their thinking and the thinking of others) helps prepare them for the more intensive questioning used in diagnostic interviews.

◈ Diagnostic Interviews

A diagnostic interview uses what we know about students' cognition to design an assessment (Huff & Goodman, 2007). The interview is usually a one-on-one investigation of a student's thinking about a particular concept or the processes that are being used to solve problems. Aim for about 10 minutes for each interview as you design questions. A single task can be the basis of an interview. The challenge of diagnostic interviews is that they are assessment opportunities, not teaching opportunities. It is hard to listen when students are making errors and not respond immediately. Instead, the interviews are used to listen and probe and to discover both strengths and gaps in understanding, which will lead to more targeted instruction.

Tasks should be aligned to recent work or your attempts to pinpoint underlying foundational gaps in understanding. Middle-school diagnostic interviews might include tasks similar to those on quizzes or tests, such as these:

What is the unit rate (cost per cap) if we paid $102.00 for 17 caps?

Solve $6\frac{1}{4} \times 2\frac{3}{4} =$ _____ . Draw a picture to illustrate the solution.

[Student is given an isosceles right triangle drawn on cm grid paper, where the sides are 8 cm.] Find the length of the hypotenuse of this triangle.

As the student solves a task, the teacher is able to watch and listen. Diagnostic interviews have the potential to provide information that you simply cannot get in any other way.

Think of interviews as a formative assessment tool to be used for only a few selected students—not for every student in the class. You can briefly interview a single student while the rest of the class is working on a task. For example, if the whole class is working in groups, you can explain that you will be interviewing some of them while they work in order to better understand their thinking. Or, you can find additional time in the school day, possibly during the homeroom period or a study period, and make arrangements for a few students to meet with you to talk through a few mathematics problems.

An important reason to consider an interview is that you need more information concerning a particular student and how he or she is constructing concepts or using a procedure. These dialogues can be considered intense error analysis. Remediation will be more successful if you can pinpoint *why* a student is having difficulty before you try to fix the problem.

A second reason for conducting a set of interviews (i.e., interview a sampling of your students) is to gather information to plan your next instructional steps or to assess the effectiveness of your instruction. In an examination of hundreds of research studies, Hattie (2009) found that the feedback that teachers received from students on what they knew and did not know was critical in improving students' performance. That is precisely what diagnostic interviews are designed to do!

For example, are you sure that your students have a good understanding of operations with integers, or are they just doing the exercises according to poorly understood procedures? Let's look at an actual classroom situation.

Mr. Jergens noticed Jeremy was displaying difficulty with subtracting integers. Jeremy gave unreasonable estimates and was not able to state whether the result would be negative or positive. To better understand Jeremy's thinking in terms of what he

Figure 3.4

Student's work on a diagnostic interview task.

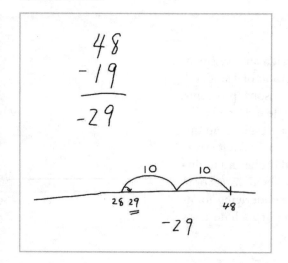

understood and where some gaps might be, Mr. Jergens planned a diagnostic interview. Using an adaptation of a problem he read in a journal (Tillema, 2012), he asked the student to write the answer to $(^{+}48) - (^{-}19) =$. The student wrote the problem vertically, subtracted, and quickly answered $(^{-}29)$. Mr. Jergens resisted the temptation to immediately correct the student, and instead probed further asking the student to talk about his thinking. Jeremy said that he needed to take away the 19 from the 48 and, because there was a negative sign, needed to show the "opposite" as the answer, so it was "negative 29." Second, Mr. Jergens asked Jeremy to show the computation on a number line, trying to stimulate some of the ideas discussed in a previous math period. Showing fluency with the "jump" movements on an open-number line, Jeremy used a "take-away" approach and reached the same answer (see Figure 3.4). Third, Mr. Jergens asked Jeremy to tell a story to go with the problem. Jeremy responded that it was 48 degrees one day and 19 degrees below zero the next. What was the difference in temperatures? Mr. Jergens asked Jeremy to compare his story to the number line jumps he has just illus- trated, asking where those temperatures would be located on the number line and what the difference was between them. The student said, "67? I am not sure." Mr. Jergens asked why he thought he had gotten two different answers and which answer he thought was correct. The student quietly pondered and then pointed to the original equation and said, "This one is right."

Although this interview revealed that the student had a good grasp of the use of a num- ber line for whole-number subtraction, it did reveal gaps in his full understanding of sub- traction of negative numbers. In the first two questions, Jeremy focused on a "take-away" model of subtraction, but in his story used a "difference" model (what is the difference or distance between these two numbers?). Notice that Mr. Jergens used one problem, but asked for the student to do three different tasks with the same problem. Importantly, he asked for Jeremy to relate his thinking from one representation (story) to another (number line). The cognitive dissonance caused by getting two different answers provided more insights into Jeremy's thinking, in particular showing that Jeremy has more confidence in an algorithm approach to get the "right" answer. Planning could then begin for future instruction based on actual evidence from the student.

There is no one right way to plan or structure a diagnostic interview. Flexibility is a key ingredient. In general, however, an interview includes an easier task and a more challenging task in case you have misjudged your starting point. Also, did you notice that Mr. Jergens had a suggestion of a model ready for the student to use? He selected the number line, a more difficult model perhaps, but one that addresses *difference* as distance, which was important in assessing the student's conceptual understanding of subtraction. His choice reflected an understanding of the content (both conceptual and procedural), as well as likely student mis- conceptions. Be sure you have thought about possible representations (see Figure 2.3 for seven different possible representations) and have materials available that match those students have used during instruction and that will provide insights into what the students understand.

Begin by explaining the purpose of the interview to the student, expressing your desire to learn more about his or her thinking. Then ask the student to complete the first task you have planned. When the opening task has been completed, ask the student to explain what was done. "How would you explain this to a sixth grader (or your younger sister)?" "What does this (point to something on the paper) stand for?" "Tell me why you did this that way." You may want to ask, "Can you show me what you are thinking with the materials?" If the student gets two different answers, as in the preceding scenario, ask, "Why do you think you got two different answers? Which one do you think is correct? If you tried to do this problem again which approach would you try first?" In each case, it is important to explore whether the student (1) understands what he or she did, and (2) can describe connections between approaches and/or representations.

Consider the following suggestions as you implement your diagnostic interview:

- *Avoid revealing whether the student's answer is right or wrong.* Often, your facial expressions, tone of voice, or body language can give a student clues that the answer he or she gave is correct or incorrect. Instead, use a response such as, "Can you tell me more?" or "I think I know what you are thinking." If the student asks whether the answer is right, you can say, "That's interesting," or "I see what you are doing."

- *Avoid asking leading questions.* Comments such as "Are you sure about that?" or "Wait. Is that what you mean?" may indicate to students that they have made a mistake and cause them to reconsider their answer. This can hinder your ability to discover what they know and understand.

- *Wait silently for the student to give an answer.* Give ample time to allow the student to think and respond. Only then should you move to rephrase the question or probe for a better understanding of the student's thoughts. After the student gives a response (whether it is accurate or not), wait again! This second wait time is even more important because it encourages the student to elaborate on his or her initial thought and provide more information. Waiting can also provide you with more time to think about the direction you want the interview to take.

- *Remember that you should not interject clues or teach.* The temptation to do so is sometimes overwhelming. Watch and listen. Your goal is to use the interview not to teach but to find out where the student is in terms of conceptual understanding and procedural fluency.

- *Let students share their thinking freely without interruption.* Encourage students to use their own words and ways of writing things down. Interjecting questions or correcting language can be distracting to the flow of students' thinking and explanations.

- *Ask students to demonstrate their understanding in multiple ways.* For example, ask "Can you show me that with the materials?" "Can a diagram help you think about this problem?" "Can you write a word problem to go with that equation?" or "Can you explain what you just did?"

The benefits of the diagnostic interview become evident as you plan instruction that capitalizes on a student's strengths while recognizing possible weaknesses and confusion. Also, you can always ask another question to find out more when the student is taking an incorrect or unexpected path. These insights are invaluable in moving students to mathematical proficiency.

Tasks

The category of tasks refers to written products and can include performance-based tasks, writing (e.g., journal entries, student self-assessments), and tests. Good assessment tasks for either instructional or formative assessment purposes should permit every student in the class, regardless of mathematical ability, to demonstrate his or her knowledge, skill, or understanding.

Problem-Based Tasks

When problem-based tasks are used for assessment and evaluation, the intent is to find what students *do* know (e.g., students can solve linear equations when given in a context), rather than just identify what they *do not* know (e.g., students can't analyze and solve linear equations). The result is a broad description of the ideas and skills that students possess—for example, "Adam can write a linear equation given a graph of several different functions but has difficulty calculating the slope."

Problem-based tasks have several critical components that make them good tasks for assessment. They do the following:

- Focus on a central mathematics concept or skill aligned to valued learning targets
- Stimulate the connection of content a student knows to new content
- Allow multiple solution methods or approaches with a variety of tools
- Offer opportunities along the way for students to correct themselves
- Confront common student misconceptions
- Encourage students to use reasoning and explain their thinking
- Create opportunities for observing students' use of mathematical processes and practices
- Generate data for instructional decision making as you "listen" to your students' thinking

Problem-based tasks can be written products (e.g., journal entries, student self-assessments, tests), or they can be performance-based tasks. Notice that the following examples of performance-based tasks are not elaborate, yet when followed by a discussion, each can engage students for most of a class period. What mathematical ideas and practices are required to successfully respond to each of these tasks? Will the task help you determine how well students understand these ideas?

TWO TRIANGLES (GRADE 8):

Learning targets: (1) Classify two-dimensional shapes into categories based on their properties. (2) Attend to precision by clearly applying definitions to define categories.

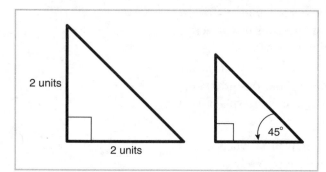

Task: Part A. Tell everything you can about these two triangles.

Part B. Given what you wrote about the two triangles, determine which of the following statements are true and explain your reasoning:

- The large triangle is an isosceles triangle; the small triangle is an isosceles triangle.
- The big triangle has an area of 2 square units.
- The small triangle has an area of 1 square unit.
- The large triangle has at least one angle that measures 45 degrees.
- The small triangle has at least one angle that measures 30 degrees.
- The two triangles are similar.

ALGEBRA GRAPHING FUNCTIONS (GRADE 7):

Learning targets: (1) Compare and analyze linear equations related to parallel and intersecting lines. (2) Use reasoning to build a logical argument for a conjecture.

Task: Part A. Does the graph of $y = x + 2$ ever intersect the graph of $y = x + 3$? Make a conjecture and provide a justification.

Part B. Would your conjecture hold true for other equations in the form of $y = x + b$?

Part C. Compare a line of this form with $y = 2x + 2$ and with $y = 2x + 3$. What do you notice about these lines in comparison with the lines $y = x + 2$ and $y = x + 3$? Write a statement to describe how these two pairs of lines are the same and how they are different from each other.

Translation Tasks

One important option for a task is what we refer to as a translation task. Using the seven representations for concepts (see Figure 2.3), students are asked to use more than one representation (e.g., words, tools, and numbers) to demonstrate understanding of a single problem. As students move between these representations, there is a better chance that a concept will be formed correctly and integrated into a rich web of ideas.

So, what is a good way of structuring a translation task? Using an adaptation of a template for assessing concept mastery from Frayer, Fredrick, and Klauseier (1969) (Figure 3.5), students can be given a computational equation and be asked to:

- Write a word problem that matches the equation
- Illustrate the equation with materials or drawings
- Explain their process of arriving at an answer

Figure 3.5 Translation task template with example task and student work.

Numbers in Chart/Equation	Word Problem/Real-World Situation
	One cell phone plan (A) costs $20.00 a month with an additional charge of $.05 for each minute. Another (B) costs $35.00 a month with an additional charge of $.02 for each minute. Show the relationship between the number of minutes and the total costs of the two cell phone plans.

Number of Minutes	Total Cost Plan A	Total Cost Plan B
100	25	37
200	30	39
300	35	41
400	40	43
500	45	45
600	50	47

Model/Illustation/Graph	Explanation
	I started with 100 min because it made the cents easy. I had to Go all the way to 600 min to see the PLAN A catch up with PLAN B Id choose plan A because I would NOT be Allowed to use 600 min in my FAmily

In particular, students' ability to communicate how they solved a problem is critical for responding to open-response questions on state assessments (Parker & Breyfogle, 2011).

Translation tasks can be used for whole-class lessons or for individual or small-group diagnosis. For example, seventh-grade students might be given a situation about the cost of cell phone plans in the section titled "Word Problem/Real-World Situation," as in Figure 3.5. Their task could be to create a table of values for different numbers of minutes in the "Numbers in Charts/Equations" area, use the values in the "Models/Illustrations/Graphs" area to draw a graph, and explain to another person in writing what plan would be the best under what circumstances (for which number of minutes a month is each plan best?) in the "Explanation" area. They could also be asked to write the function that goes with each of the plans (translating to written symbols) in the "Numbers in Charts/Equations" area.

Think about translation tasks when you want to find out more about a student's thinking. If a student represents ideas in various forms and can explain why these representations are similar or different, you can use this valuable information to recognize misconceptions he or she may have and then identify the type of activity you can provide to advance the student's learning. Here are two other options for tasks that can be used with the translation template to assess student understanding. Remember that a translation task may start in any quadrant of the template, and then the student proceeds to fill in the other three sections. Consider the following two "starters":

- In the "Equation" box, write this:

$3x + 2 = 11$. Solve for x.

Students then make a corresponding model, create a word problem, and explain how they solved the problem in the three other areas.

- In the section for "Real-World Situation" write this:

Seven soccer teams are playing in a tournament. Each team will play all the others only once. How many games will be played?

Students should write a corresponding equation, make an illustration or model to demonstrate the solution to this problem, and in the last section explain to a friend how they would approach the problem.

In some instances, the real value of a task is in what it can reveal about students' understanding, which will come primarily through discussion in the *After* phase of your lesson. It is important that you help your students develop the habits of adding justifications to their answers, and of listening to and evaluating the explanations of others. Importantly, as illustrated here, do not always start with the same section—sometimes, students can translate one way, but not in reverse.

 # Rubrics and Their Uses

Appropriate assessment tasks yield an enormous amount of information that must be evaluated by examining more than a simple count of correct answers. A *rubric* is a scale based on predetermined criteria with two important functions: (1) It permits the student to see what is central to excellent performance, and (2) it provides the teacher with scoring guidelines that support analysis of students' work. In teaching through a problem-solving approach, you will often want to include criteria and performance indicators such as whether the student did the following:

- Solve the problem(s) accurately and effectively
- Justify and explain strategy
- Use logical reasoning
- Express a grasp of numerical relationships and structure
- Incorporate multiple representations and/or multiple strategies
- Demonstrate an ability to appropriately select and use tools and manipulatives
- Communicate with precise language and accurate units
- Identify general patterns of ideas that repeat, making connections from one big idea to another

Rubrics are usually built from the highest possible score. By describing what an outstanding performance would be on a given standard or learning target, you are then able to set the benchmarks for the other levels.

Generic Rubrics

Generic rubrics identify general categories of performance instead of specific criteria for a particular task and therefore can fit multiple assignments. The generic rubric allows a teacher to score performances by first sorting them into two broad categories, as illustrated in the four-point rubric shown in Figure 3.6. The scale then allows you to separate each category into two additional levels. Note that a rating of 0 is given for no response or effort or for responses that are completely off task. The advantage of the four-point scale is the relatively easy initial sort into "Got It" or "Not There Yet." Another possibility is using

Figure 3.6

With a four-point rubric, performances are first sorted into two categories. Each performance is then considered again and assigned to a point on the scale.

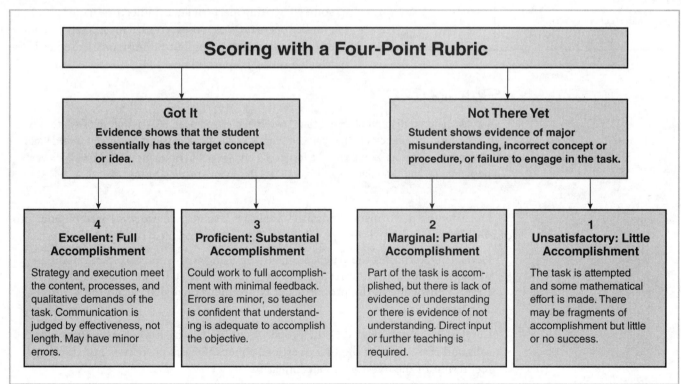

Figure 3.7

Record names in a rubric during an activity or for a single topic over a period of several days.

Observation Rubric Probability (3/17)	
Above and Beyond Clear understanding. Communicates concept in multiple representations. Shows evidence of using idea without prompting. *Finds probability of two events (independent and dependent). Explains reasoning.*	Sally Latania Greg · · · · · · · · Zal
On Target Understands or is developing well. Uses designated models. *Finds probability of two independent events. Needs prompts to describe reasoning.*	Lavant · · · · · · · Tanisha Julie · · · · · · · · · Lee George · · · · · · · J.B. Maria · · · · · · · · John H.
Not There Yet Some confusion or misunderstands. Only models idea with help. *Models idea only with help.*	John S. · · · · · · · Mary

a three- or four-point generic rubric on a reusable form, as in Figure 3.7. Include space for content-specific indicators and another column for jotting down the names of students. A quick note or comment may be added to a name. This method is especially useful for planning purposes.

◆ Task-Specific Rubrics

Task-specific rubrics include specific statements, also known as *indicators*, that describe what performance looks like at each level of the rubric. In so doing, they establish criteria for acceptable performance. Initially, when you create a task-specific rubric, it may be difficult to predict what student performance at different levels will or should look like. Your decision about performance levels will depend on several criteria: your own knowledge and experience with students at that grade level, the students who are working on the same task, and your own insights about the task or mathematical concept. One important part of setting performance levels is predicting students' common misconceptions, or the expected thinking or approaches to the same or similar problems.

To facilitate writing performance levels, write out indicators of "proficient" or "on-target" performances before you use the task in class. This excellent self-check will ensure that the task is likely to accomplish the purpose for which you selected it in the first place. Think about how students are likely to approach the activity. If you find yourself writing performance indicators in terms of the number of correct responses, you are most likely looking at drill or practice exercises, not performance-based tasks for which a rubric is appropriate.

Stop and Reflect

Consider the preceding problem entitled "Two Triangles" on page 36. Assume you wish to write performance indicators that you can share with your students in a four-point rubric. What task-specific indicators would you use for level 3 and level 4 performances? Start with a level 4 performance, and then think about level 3. Try this before reading further. ■

Determining performance indicators is always a subjective process based on your professional judgment. Here is one possible set of indicators for the "Two Triangles" task:

Level 4: Determines the true statements by using words, pictures, and numbers to explain and justify the results and describe how they were obtained. Demonstrates knowledge of the properties of two-dimensional shapes and the relationship to similarity.

Level 3: Accurately describes the properties of the two triangles. Gives correct results and reasoning for the first questions about the basic properties but an incorrect result for the question about similarity.

Indicators such as these should be shared ahead of time with students. Sharing indicators before working on a task conveys clearly what is valued and expected.

What about level 1 and level 2 performances? Here are suggestions for the same task:

> Level 2: Uses some reasoning about the properties of triangles but fails to identify all true statements and an understanding of similarity.

> Level 1: Shows some effort to describe the triangle but demonstrates little or no understanding of all of the properties of triangles and the connections to similarity.

Unexpected methods and solutions happen. Such occurrences can help you revise or refine your rubric for future use.

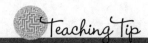

> **Teaching Tip**
>
> When you return papers, review the indicators with students, including examples of correct answers and successful responses. This will help students understand how they might have done better. Often, it is useful to show work from another class period. Let students decide on the score for the anonymous student. Importantly, students need to see examples of what a level 4 performance looks like.

◆ Student Self-Assessment with Rubrics

In the beginning of the year, post your rubric prominently and discuss it with the class. In your discussion, let students know that as they do activities and solve problems, you will sometimes look at their work and listen to their explanations and provide them with feedback in the form of a rubric, rather than as a letter grade or a percentage.

Make it a habit to discuss students' performance on tasks in terms of the rubric. You may have students use the rubric to self-assess their work, giving reasons for the rating. You can have class discussions about a completed task by talking about what might constitute "on-target" and "above-and-beyond" performance. Also, share student work from anonymous students as a way to highlight excellent responses as well as responses that need more detail or work shown. Use these work samples to get students to talk about what could make an answer stronger and better aligned with the rubric. This process of critiquing others' work is included in the Standards for Mathematical Practice (*Common Core State Standards*) and as such is recognized as an essential element to becoming mathematically proficient.

A rubric reveals much more than a grade. It is a meaningful way to communicate feedback to students (and parents). It should let students know how well they are doing and encourage them to work harder by giving specific areas for improvement. When their performance is not progressing satisfactorily, students should understand that there are specific things they can work on. Give them an opportunity to respond to your feedback by revising their work. Your task is to target the follow-up instruction in response to their gaps and misunderstandings as well as their identified strengths.

You do not need to use rubrics with every task. Nor is it necessary to reserve rubrics for assessments that you want to grade. If you are using the four-point rubric just described, the language of the rubric can be used informally with your students. "Maggie, the rubric states that to get a 4 you need to solve the problem with two different methods and explain your thinking. Is that what you did?"

The rubric scale can also be used in recording observations of student performance. If you describe the task across the top of a class checklist and list the students' names down the left side, then it is useful to record a 1, 2, 3, or 4 next to each name. You may want to leave space for writing detailed comments for some students so that they can be grouped in follow-up instruction according to common misunderstandings.

Plan for Assessment

"An assessment system designed to help steer the instruction system must give good information about direction as well as distance to travel. A system that keeps telling us we are not there yet is like a kid in the back seat whining 'are we there yet?'" (Daro, Mosher, & Corcoran, 2011, p. 51). Instead, we need a system in which teachers do the following:

- Establish where students are in their learning
- Identify the learning destination
- Carefully plan a route
- Begin the learning journey
- Make regular checks of progress on the way
- Make adjustments to the course as conditions dictate (Wiliam, 2010)

Then, assessments can more easily be translated into tools that inform instruction and support students' growth.

Stop and Reflect

How can sharing samples of students' work (both strong and weak responses) support all students' ability to generate more in-depth responses? ■

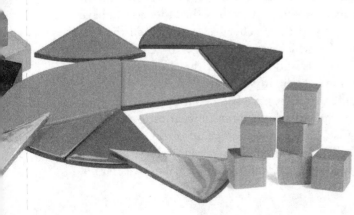

4

Differentiating Instruction

All seventh graders do not learn the same thing in the same way and at the same rate. In fact, every classroom at every grade level contains a range of students with varying abilities and backgrounds. Perhaps the most important work of teachers today is to be able to plan (and teach) lessons that support and challenge *all* students to learn important mathematics.

 ## Differentiation and Teaching Mathematics through Problem Solving

Teachers have for some time embraced the notion that students vary in reading ability, but the idea that students can and do vary in mathematical development may be new. Mathematics education research reveals a great deal of evidence demonstrating that students vary in their understanding of specific mathematical ideas. Attending to these differences in students' mathematical development is key to differentiating mathematics instruction for your students.

Interestingly, the problem-based approach to teaching is the best way to teach mathematics while attending to the range of students in your classroom. In a traditional, highly directed lesson, it is often assumed that all students will understand and use the same approach and the same ideas as determined by the teacher. Students not ready to understand the ideas presented by the teacher must focus their attention on following rules or directions without developing a conceptual or relational understanding (Skemp, 1978). This, of course, leads to endless difficulties and can leave students with misunderstandings or in need of significant remediation. In contrast, in a problem-based classroom, students are expected to approach problems in a variety of ways that make sense to *them*, bringing to each problem the skills and ideas that they own. So, with a problem-based approach to teaching mathematics, differentiation is already built in to some degree.

To illustrate, let's consider a sixth-grade classroom in which the teacher posed the following task to students:

Suppose you and a friend are making a drink from a powder mix. You use 3 tablespoons of the mix with every 2 cups of water, while your friend uses 4 tablespoons of mix with every 3 cups of water. Which mixture will be stronger, or will both mixtures be the same strength?

The teacher asked the students to be ready to explain how they knew. Below are some of the students' explanations:

Sam: I made it so each mixture had 6 cups of water. I knew I could do that because the first ratio used 2 cups and the second ratio used 3 cups, and 6 is a multiple of both 2 and 3. So I multiplied the first ratio by 3 to get 9 tablespoons to 6 cups, and I multiplied the second ratio by 2 to get 8 tablespoons to 6 cups. They now have the same amount of water, but the first ratio has more powder (9 tablespoons), so it has to be stronger.

Carmen: I did something similar, but I changed the ratios so that each has 1 cup of water. The first ratio was 3 tablespoons to 2 cups. Dividing both amounts by 2, the ratio became $\frac{3}{2}$ tablespoons to 1 cup. The second ratio was 4 tablespoons to 3 cups, and after I divided the amounts by 3, it became $\frac{4}{3}$ tablespoons to 1 cup. So now, I can compare how much mix there is because the amount of water is the same. Because $\frac{3}{2} > \frac{4}{3}$, there is more mix in the first ratio, so the first ratio will be a stronger drink.

Nora: Mine is like Sam's, but I used pictures because just thinking about the numbers confused me (Figure 4.1). But I used the same ideas Sam did, so that each ratio had 6 cups of water. Then I knew by looking at my picture that the first mixture had more powder, so it must be stronger.

Edwin: I changed the ratios so that they had the same amount of powder. So I divided the first ratio by 3 to get 1 tablespoon to $\frac{2}{3}$ cup, and I divided the second ratio by 4 to get 1 tablespoon to $\frac{3}{4}$ cup. Now they have the same amount of powder, but the second ratio has more water because $\frac{3}{4} > \frac{2}{3}$, so the second mixture dilutes the powder more than the first mixture. So the first mixture has to be stronger.

It makes sense to some students to rewrite the ratios so that the amounts of water are equivalent, while to other students, it makes sense to make the amounts of powder equivalent. One student had to use a diagram to help her understand the relationships in the problem. If the teacher had expected all students to use diagrams, then many of the students might have been using a less-efficient method than they would have used independently. If the teacher had expected all the students to recognize which ratio was larger by changing the amounts to decimals and comparing the decimals (a procedure sometimes taught to solve problems like this one), then some students might have been confused because they still needed to explicitly think about unit ratios to make the comparison. Also, the cognitive demand of the task would have been lowered! Instead, the teacher allowed the students to use their own ideas to determine which ratio was larger.

Figure 4.1

Nora's solution showing that one mixture is stronger than another.

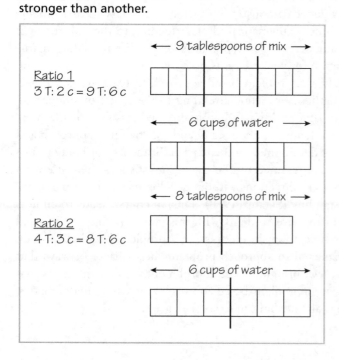

Ratio 1
3 T : 2 c = 9 T : 6 c

← 9 tablespoons of mix →

← 6 cups of water →

Ratio 2
4 T : 3 c = 8 T : 6 c

← 8 tablespoons of mix →

← 6 cups of water →

This expectation and the recognition that different students will approach and solve the same problem in various ways honors students' varying mathematical development and sets the stage for differentiated mathematics instruction. In addition, by listening to how different students approached the task, the teacher has acquired important information that can be used to plan subsequent instruction that meets a variety of students' needs.

The Nuts and Bolts of Differentiating Instruction

Differentiation is an instructional approach that requires a shift from focusing on the "middle-of-the-road" student to attending to all students. As overwhelming as this may sound, differentiation does not require a teacher to create individualized lessons for each and every student in the classroom. Rather, it requires emphasizing three basic ideas (Sousa & Tomlinson, 2011):

- Planning lessons around meaningful content, grounded in authenticity
- Recognizing each student's readiness, interest, and approach to learning
- Connecting content and learners by modifying content, process, product, and the learning environment

Planning Meaningful Content, Grounded in Authenticity

Before you begin to think about differentiation, you first need to know where you want students to "be" at the end of the learning experience. You must be explicitly aware of the content that students should know, understand, and be able to do after engaging in a given lesson or sequence of lessons. This awareness enables you to effectively guide students' learning by varying or differentiating instruction. If you do not have a clear idea about the specific learning outcomes, identifying how and when to differentiate can be difficult. In fact, Tomlinson (1999) claims that "If the 'stuff' [content] is ill conceived, the 'how' [differentiation] is doomed" (p. 16).

Note that the content must be authentic and grounded in important mathematics that emphasizes the big ideas in ways that require students to develop relational understanding. Authentic content engages students in the heart of mathematics by requiring them to be problem solvers and creators of knowledge. Through this kind of engagement, students also develop a productive disposition toward mathematics and see it as sensible, useful, and worthwhile.

Recognizing Students as Learners

Knowing each student in the context of learning requires finding out who he or she is as an individual on traits such as readiness, interests, and learning profile. *Readiness* refers to a student's proficiency with the knowledge, understanding, and skills embedded in specific learning goals. *Interest* means a student's attraction to particular topics, ideas, and events. Using contexts that are interesting and familiar to students enhances their attention and motivation to engage and achieve (Sousa & Tomlinson, 2011). A *learning profile* identifies how a student is learning—how each student prefers to learn (e.g., in groups, alone); process and reason about information (e.g., by listening, observing, participating, or through talking; by thinking about details first and then the big picture or vice versa; by doing one task at a time or multitasking); and use or demonstrate what has been learned (e.g., writing, verbalizing, drawing). By using students' preferences for learning to structure the environment, tasks, and assessments, you are greatly facilitating the learning process.

Figure 4.2 Learning profile inventory.

When working on a task, I like to . . .	I like to work . . .	When working, I like the room to be . . .	When working, I like . . .	When learning about a new idea, I like to . . .	When sharing information, I like to . . .
☐ sit at my desk.	☐ with a partner.	☐ warm.	☐ quiet.	☐ hear about it.	☐ talk.
☐ sit somewhere other than at my desk.	☐ in a small group.	☐ cool.	☐ noise.	☐ read about it.	☐ show.
☐ stand.	☐ alone.	☐ dim, with the lights off.	☐ music.	☐ see visuals about it.	☐ write.
☐ lie on the floor.	☐ other	☐ bright.	☐ other	☐ use materials to explore it.	☐ other
☐ other		☐ other		☐ talk about it.	
				☐ other	

Information about your students' traits can inform how you might modify different elements of the classroom (e.g., Sousa & Tomlinson, 2011; Tomlinson, 2003). You can gather information pertaining to students' readiness by using preassessments several days before a given unit so that you have time to analyze the evidence and assess each student's readiness for the unit. You can also use surveys, typically at the beginning and midpoint of the year, to gather information about students' interests and learning profiles. Interest surveys give students opportunities to share personal interests (e.g., what they like to do after school, on the weekends, and during the summer; what school subjects they find most interesting and why) and information about pets, siblings, and extracurricular activities. Use your students' interests to provide contexts for the mathematics they are learning to increase their motivation and engagement. Learning profile surveys or questionnaires also help students think about what helps them learn and what does not, such as preferring to work in pairs versus alone, being able to work with background noise, and needing to process ideas verbally (Figure 4.2). Teacher observation can also provide valuable insights into student learning profiles. By recording students' information on index cards, you can quickly refresh your memory by looking through the cards as you plan lessons. You can also sort the cards to help you create groups based on interests or learning profiles.

◆ Connecting Content and Learners

A critical component of differentiated lesson planning is determining how to modify four classroom elements to help the learner better connect with the content (Tomlinson, 2003). These four classroom elements are content, process, product, and the learning environment.

Content: What You Want Each Student to Learn

Generally, what is learned (the big ideas) should be relatively the same for all students. However, content can still be differentiated in terms of depth (level of complexity) and breadth (connecting across different topics) (Murray & Jorgensen, 2007; Small, 2009). Students' readiness typically informs the level of complexity or depth at which the content is initially presented for different groups of students. Interest and learning profiles tend to inform differentiation geared toward breadth.

An example of a depth adaptation for developing understanding and skill with organizing, representing, and interpreting data is a minilesson in which all students organize and represent data and answer questions based on the data. However, some students may have a smaller set of data to deal with, or they may be asked to answer given questions about the data, while others, who are ready for more sophisticated content, are asked to generate their own questions about the data. An example of a breadth adaptation for the same objective is to allow students a choice in terms of the kind of data with which to work. For example, based on their interests, students might choose to work with data pertaining to sports, books, science, gaming, or pets. By working with data from various contexts, students not only learn something about those contexts, but also can begin to see the broader applications of organizing, representing, and interpreting data.

Process: How Students Engage in Thinking about Content

Although the big ideas of a learning experience remain relatively stable when differentiating, how students engage with and make sense of the content—the process—changes. Tomlinson (1999) described the process as students "taking different roads to the same destination" (p. 12). You can use different strategies or encourage students to take different "roads" to increase access to the essential information, ideas, and skills embedded in a lesson (Cassone, 2009; Tomlinson, 2003). For example, the use of manipulatives, games, and relevant and interesting contextual problems provides different ways for students to process their ideas while engaging with content.

Teaching Tip

Be sure that the tasks you ask students to do are closely aligned with the learning objectives of the lesson.

The process standards in the *Principles and Standards for School Mathematics* (NCTM, 2000), which served as a basis for the Standards for Mathematical Practice in the *Common Core State Standards* (CCSSO, 2010), lend themselves well to differentiating how students engage with and make sense of content. In particular, the process standard of representation emphasizes the need to think about and use different ways to represent mathematical ideas, which can help students make connections between concepts and skills. With the process standard of communication, students can use verbal or written communication as they share their reasoning, depending on their strengths. In addition, the process standard of problem solving allows for differentiation because of the myriad of strategies that students can use—from drawing a diagram or using manipulatives to solving a simpler problem and looking for patterns.

Because of different levels of readiness, it is imperative that students be allowed to use a variety of strategies and representations that are grounded in their own ideas to solve problems. You can facilitate students' engagement in thinking about the content through a variety of methods. For example, teachers may

- Use visuals or graphic organizers to help students connect ideas and build a structure for the information in the lesson.
- Provide manipulatives to support students' development of a concept.
- Provide manipulatives other than those previously used for the same content.
- Use an appropriate context that helps students build meaning for the concept and that employs purposeful constraints that can highlight the significant mathematical ideas.
- Share examples and nonexamples to help students develop a better understanding of a concept.
- Gather a small group of students to develop foundational knowledge for a new concept.
- Provide text or supplementary material in a student's native language to aid understanding of materials written or delivered in English.
- Set up learning centers or a tiered lesson (a lesson that offer learners different pathways to reach a specific learning goal).

Product: How Students Demonstrate What They Know, Understand, and Are Able to Do after the Lesson Is Over

The term *product* can refer to what a student produces as a result of completing a single task or to a major assessment after an extended learning experience. The products related to a single task would be consistent with the ways students share their ideas in the *After* portion of a lesson (described in Chapter 2), which could include explaining their ideas with manipulatives, through a drawing, in writing, or verbally. The products related to an extended experience can take the form of a project, portfolio, test, write-up of solutions to several problem-based inquiries, and so on. An important feature of any product is that it allows a variety of ways for students to demonstrate their understanding of essential content.

Learning Environment: The Logistics, Physical Configuration, and Tone of the Classroom

Consider how the physical learning environment might be adapted to meet students' needs. Do you have a student who prefers to work alone? Who prefers to work in a group? Who can or cannot work with background noise? Who prefers to work in a setting with brighter or dimmer lighting? Attending to these students' needs can affect the seating arrangement, specific grouping strategies, access to materials, and other aspects of the classroom environment. In addition to the physical learning space, establishing a classroom culture in which students' ideas and solutions are respected as they explain and justify them is an important aspect of a differentiated classroom. Refer to the recommendations provided in Chapter 2 pertaining to facilitating effective classroom discussions and establishing a supportive and respectful learning environment.

 ## Examples of Differentiated Instruction

 ### Differentiated Tasks for Whole-Class Instruction

One challenge of differentiation is planning a task focused on a target mathematical concept or skill that can be used for whole-class instruction while a variety of students' needs are met. Let's consider two different kinds of tasks that can meet this challenge: parallel tasks and open questions (Murray & Jorgensen, 2007; Small, 2009).

Parallel Tasks

Parallel tasks are two or three tasks that focus on the same big idea but offer different levels of difficulty. The tasks should be created so that all students can meaningfully participate in a follow-up discussion with the whole class. You can assign tasks to students based on their readiness, or students can choose which task to work on. If they choose a task that is too difficult, they can always move to another task. Consider how the following parallel tasks emphasize the big ideas of volume and surface area (and the relationship between them), but at different levels of difficulty.

TASK 1:

A cube has a volume of 729 cubic units. What are the dimensions and the surface area?

TASK 2:

A prism has a volume of 90 cubic units and a surface area of 146 square units. What could the dimensions be?

Stop and Reflect

Which of the two tasks do you think would be more difficult, and why? ■

Both tasks provide opportunities for students to work with volume and surface area, but the use of a prism instead of a cube in the second task increases the level of difficulty for a number of reasons. First, because the dimensions of a cube are all the same, students are looking for one number that when cubed equals 729, whereas in the latter task because the dimensions can vary, students must consider different factor trios for 90. Second, task 2 has an added constraint in determining the dimensions because the surface area is given.

You can facilitate a whole-class discussion by asking questions that are relevant to both tasks. For example, with respect to the previous two tasks, you could ask the whole class the following questions:

- In general, what does your object look like?
- What is the relationship between the object's dimensions and the object's volume?
- What is the relationship between the object's dimensions and the object's surface area?
- How do you know the dimensions you have identified are correct?
- How are surface area and volume different?
- When would you want to know the surface area of a box? When would you want to know its volume?

Although the students work on different tasks, because the tasks are focused on the same big idea, these questions allow them to extend their thinking as they hear others' strategies and ideas.

For many problems involving computation, you can simply insert multiple sets of numbers to vary the difficulty. In the following problem, students are permitted to select the first, second, or third number in each set of brackets. Giving a choice increases motivation and helps students become more self-directed learners (Bray, 2009; Gilbert & Musu, 2008).

LEARNING OBJECTIVE: Compute fluently with multi-digit numbers (Grade 6)

It costs [$1.50, $1.65, $2.25] to play a game at the county fair. Mark played the game [9, 16, 43] times while the fair was in town. How much money did Mark spend on playing the game?

The following parallel tasks for seventh graders focus on the big idea of measures of center in statistics.

TASK 1:

A data set has a mean of 50 and a median of 20. If there are 10 pieces of data, what could the values of the data be?

TASK 2:

A data set has a mean of 30 and a median of 20. If there are 5 pieces of data, what could the values of the data be?

With the first task, the teacher provides a task for students who are ready to work with a larger set of data. Requiring them to use an even number of data also increases the challenge when finding the median. The parallel task still offers an opportunity for students to work with mean and median but lowers the difficulty by using fewer pieces of data, an odd number of data, and a mean that is closer to the median.

In thinking about how to create parallel tasks, once you have identified the big idea you wish to focus on, consider how students might differ in reasoning about that idea. The size of the numbers involved, the operations students can use, and the type of measurement with which students are most familiar are just a few differences to consider. Start with a task from your textbook and then modify it to make it suitable for a different developmental level. The original task and the modified task will serve as the parallel tasks offered simultaneously to your students. If you number the parallel tasks and allow students to choose the task they will work on, sometimes let the first task be the more difficult task. This randomness will ensure that the students consider both options before they choose their task.

Open Questions

A question is open when it can be solved in a variety of ways or when it can have different answers. Following are two examples of open questions. Both questions can have different answers and can also be solved in a variety of ways.

- The probability of an event is $\frac{1}{5}$. What could the event be?
- The product of three numbers is $^-120$. What could the three numbers be?

Stop and Reflect

How would you solve each of these tasks? Can you think of at least two different strategies or answers for each task? ◼

Open questions have a high level of cognitive demand, as described in Chapter 2, because students must use more than recall or do more than merely follow steps in a procedure. There are ample opportunities for them to approach the problems at their own level, which means open questions automatically accommodate student readiness. Consequently, when given an open question, most students can find something appropriate to contribute, which helps to increase their confidence in doing mathematics and can inform you of their level of understanding.

A variety of strategies can be used to create open questions (Small, 2009; Sullivan & Lilburn, 2002), including the following:

- Give the answer and ask for the problem.
- Replace a number in a given problem with a blank or a question mark.
- Offer two situations or examples and ask for similarities and differences.
- Create a question in which students have to make choices.

The two preceding examples illustrate the first strategy of giving an answer and asking for the problem. Below are examples that show how to use the other strategies to convert standard questions to open questions.

Strategy: Replace a number in a given problem with a blank or a question mark.

Standard Question	Open Question
2.3 × 0.68	Fill in the ? with values so that the result is greater than 1 and less than 2 [$1 < a < 2$]. ?.3 × 0.6? ————— *a*

Strategy: Offer two situations or examples, and ask for similarities and differences.

Standard Question	Open Question
Graph $4y = 2x + 8$.	Describe similarities and differences between these linear equations: $4y = 2x + 8$ and $3y = -6x + 6$.

Strategy: Create a question that can generate a range of possible answers so that students have to make choices.

Standard Question	Open Question
Use a tree diagram to show the outcomes of rolling a six-sided die and flipping a coin.	Use a tree diagram to show the possible outcomes of an experiment. Your solution should describe the experiment that your tree diagram is illustrating.

Facilitating follow-up discussions is also important when you use open questions. While students work on an open question, walk around and observe the variety of strategies and answers students are finding. During this time, plan which students you will ask to share their ideas during the follow-up discussion to ensure that multiple strategies and answers are examined. During the discussion, look for opportunities to help students make connections between different ideas that are shared. For instance, suppose for the second task above, one student explains that he graphed both equations by creating a table of values and noticed that both lines intersected the y-axis at $(0,2)$. Another student explains that she divided each equation by the coefficient of the variable y before she created a table of values so that she could use smaller numbers in her computations. You could ask the class to look at the second student's modified equations in light of the first student's comment that both lines intersected the y-axis at $(0,2)$ and see whether the class could make a conjecture about the equation of a line and its y-intercept. Asking questions that help students build connections can support those who need additional help and can also challenge students to extend their understanding. You could also do a gallery walk during which students posted their solutions for others to view. With the open question related to creating tree diagrams, students could go on a gallery walk and use sticky notes to write questions or comments to give feedback to their peers about their examples and the related illustration or explanations.

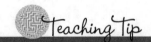
Teaching Tip

> Make sure students understand the vocabulary used in tasks before they begin working independently. For example, before students start working on the task asking them to use a tree diagram, have a discussion about the meaning of the terms *tree diagram*, *outcomes*, and *experiment*.

◆ Learning Centers

Sometimes a mathematical concept or topic can be explored by having students work on different tasks at various classroom locations called *learning centers*. Students can work on concepts or topics in learning centers as an initial introduction, as a midway exploration, or as a follow-up task that provides practice or allows extension. Because you can decide which students will be assigned to which centers, you can differentiate the content at each center. For example, each center can use a different representation of the concept, require students to use a different approach to solve a problem, or vary in terms of the difficulty of the task (e.g., different centers can use different numbers that change the level of difficulty).

A good task for a learning center is one that can be repeated multiple times during one visit. This allows students to remain engaged until you are ready for them to transition to another center or activity. For example, at one center, students might play a "game" in which they explore the probability of rolling particular sums. In this game, each student has a game board that shows a row of squares numbered 1 to 12 and, say, seven chips. Each student places his or her chips on numbers of their choice. The students can place all of their chips on one number or place single chips on different numbers. It is their choice. Once players have placed their chips, they take turns rolling two dice. At each turn, if the student has a chip on the number that is the sum of the dice, he or she can remove the chip. If the student has multiple chips on that number, he or she can remove only one chip at a time. The goal is to be the first one to remove all the chips from the board. Have students discuss what they notice about which sums seem to occur more often and less often than others. Students can play this game multiple times as they reflect on what is happening across each game and why.

Technology-enhanced tasks on the computer or interactive whiteboard that can be repeated can provide the focus of a center, but these tasks must be carefully selected. Among other aspects, you will want to choose technology-based tasks that require students to engage in reflective thought. For example, "Visualizing Transformations," in the National Council of Teachers of Mathematics online resources (www.nctm.org/standards/content .aspx?id=26772), offers students opportunities to explore geometric transformations with dynamic software. The dynamic nature of the software allows students to choose a particular transformation and then observe the results of the transformation on a given object. Students can change the orientation of a shape by dragging a vertex, change the distance of a translation and the distance between an object and its reflected image, and change the point as well as the angle of a rotation. As they engage in this interactive environment, they are enhancing their understanding of the results of various transformations.

You may want students to work at centers in small groups or individually. Therefore, for a given topic, you might prepare four to eight different activities (you can also use the same activity at two different learning centers). However, be sure to keep the centers focused on the same topic or concept so that you can help students build connections across the centers. Using centers that focus on a variety of topics will more likely result in a disconnected learning experience for students.

To ensure greater student success at the centers, review with your whole class any instructions you have provided at each center on cards. For students who have difficulty reading, provide audio-recorded directions at each center. If necessary, model or teach again any necessary skills. After students have had time to work in several centers, follow up with individual or class discussions to ensure that students are learning the essential ideas and connections that the centers are meant to elicit.

 ## Tiered Lessons

In a tiered lesson, you set the same learning goals for all students, but different pathways are provided to reach those learning goals, thereby creating the various tiers. First, you need to decide which category you wish to tier: content, process, or product. If you are new to preparing tiered lessons, tier only one category until you become more comfortable with the process. Once you decide which category to tier, determine the challenge of each of the defined tiers based on student readiness levels, interests, and learning profiles (Kingore, 2006; Murray & Jorgensen, 2007; Tomlinson, 1999). Murray and Jorgensen (2007) suggest starting by creating three tiers to make the process more manageable: a regular tier or lesson, an extension tier that provides extra challenge, and a scaffolding tier that provides more background or support. Once you have this framework, you can design as many tiers as needed to meet your students' needs. All tiered experiences should have the following characteristics (Sousa & Tomlinson, 2011):

- Address the same learning goals
- Require students to use reasoning
- Be equally interesting to students

We have already considered some ways to tier the content by using parallel tasks and open questions. However, varying the degree of challenge is not just about the *content*. You can also use any of the following four aspects to tier lessons (Kingore, 2006):

- *Degree of assistance.* If some students need additional support, you can partner students, provide examples, help them brainstorm ideas, or provide a cue sheet (Figure 4.3).
- *Structure of the task.* Some students, such as students with disabilities, benefit from highly structured tasks. However, gifted students often benefit from a more open-ended structure.
- *Complexity of the task(s).* Make tasks more concrete or more abstract, and include more difficult problems or applications.
- *Complexity of process.* As you think about your learners, ask yourself these questions: How quickly should I pace this lesson? How many instructions should I give at one time? How many higher-level thinking questions are included as part of the task(s)?

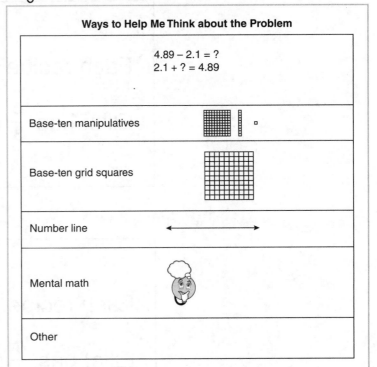

Figure 4.3 Problem-solving cue sheet.

Ways to Help Me Think about the Problem

$$4.89 - 2.1 = ?$$
$$2.1 + ? = 4.89$$

Base-ten manipulatives

Base-ten grid squares

Number line

Mental math

Other

Consider how the following original task is modified in the adapted task to change the level of the challenge. Assume that the students do not know the standard algorithm for dividing fractions.

ORIGINAL TASK (SIXTH GRADE):

Elliot is making cookies. Each recipe calls for $\frac{1}{2}$ cup of sugar. If he has $\frac{3}{4}$ cup of sugar, how many recipes can he make? Explain how you know. (Assume he can make part of a recipe.)

The teacher has distributed fraction bars to the students to model the problem, and paper and pencil to illustrate and record how they solved the problem. The teacher asks the students to model the problem and be ready to explain their solution.

ADAPTED TASK:

Elliott is making cookies. Each recipe calls for a certain amount of sugar. Elliot has some sugar. How many recipes can he make? Explain how you know. (Assume he can make part of a recipe.)

The teacher asks the students what is happening in this problem, how they might solve the problem, and what tools might help them solve the problem. Then the teacher distributes task cards that tell how much sugar is needed for each recipe and how much sugar Elliot has. The teacher has varied the difficulty of the tasks by considering how easy it is to relate the fractions to each other.

Card 1 (easier)

Each recipe uses $\frac{1}{3}$ cup of sugar.

Elliot has $\frac{4}{3}$ cups of sugar.

Card 2 (middle)

Each recipe uses $\frac{1}{2}$ cup of sugar.

Elliot has $\frac{4}{3}$ cups of sugar.

Card 3 (advanced)

Each recipe uses $\frac{5}{6}$ cup of sugar.

Elliot has $\frac{3}{4}$ cups of sugar.

In each case, the students must use words, pictures, models, or numbers to show how they figured out the solution. Various tools are provided (Cuisenaire rods, fraction bars, and grid paper) for the students' use.

Stop and Reflect

Which of the four aspects that change the challenge of tiered lessons was addressed in the adapted task? ■

You would preassess your students to determine the best ways to use these task cards. One option is to give students only one card, based on their current academic readiness (e.g., easy cards to those who struggle with division of fractions). A second option is to give out cards 1 and 2 based on readiness, then use card 2 as an extension for those who successfully complete card 1, and card 3 as an extension for those who successfully complete card 2. In each of these cases, you will need to record at the end of the lesson which students were able to model and explain the various levels of the problems so that the next lesson can be planned appropriately. Notice that this tiered lesson addresses both the complexity of the task (difficulty of different cards) and the process (instructions are broken down by starting with the no-numbers scenario).

The following example illustrates how to tier a lesson based on *structure*. Notice that the different tasks vary in how open-ended the work is, yet all tasks focus on the same learning goal of applying the Pythagorean theorem in a real-world problem.

LEARNING OBJECTIVE: Apply the Pythagorean Theorem (Grade 8)

Suppose students have been reading and discussing the World Series and so are familiar with the game of baseball. Give them a diagram of a baseball diamond with regulation dimensions (Figure 4.4). Students will be given different tasks to solve, based on their learning needs and prior success in applying the Pythagorean theorem.

- Group A: Identify and solve at least two situations that would require you to use the Pythagorean theorem to find distances on the baseball diamond. (open-ended)
- Group B: Suppose the second baseman is standing on second base with the ball and a runner is running toward home plate. How far will the second baseman need to throw the ball to throw the runner out at home plate? (slightly structured)

Figure 4.4 Application of the Pythagorean theorem.

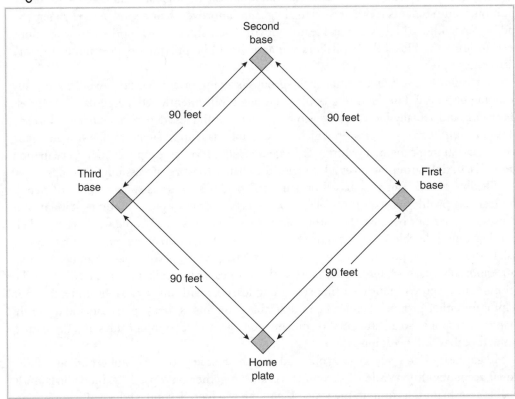

- Group C: Suppose the second baseman is standing on second base with the ball and a runner is running toward home plate. How far will the second baseman need to throw the ball to throw the runner out at home plate? Use the following suggestions and questions to work through the problem:
  1. On your diagram of the baseball diamond, draw a line between second base and third base, another line between third base and home plate, and another line between second base and home plate.
  2. What shape have you drawn? What do you know about the distance between bases? Which distance are you trying to find?
  3. Use the Pythagorean theorem ($a^2 + b^2 = c^2$) to help you find the unknown distance. (most structured)

The three tiers in this lesson reflect different degrees of difficulty in terms of task structure. However, all students are working on the same learning objective, and they all must engage in reasoning to use the Pythagorean theorem to find unknown distances.

In Chapter 6 you will read about response to intervention (RtI), a multi-tier student-support system that offers struggling students increasing levels of intervention. We want to distinguish between the tiers in RtI and tiered lessons used in differentiation. In RtI the tiers refer to the different degrees of intervention offered to students as needed—from the first tier that occurs in a general education setting and involves the core instruction for all students based on high-quality mathematics curriculum and instructional practices, to the upper tier that could involve one-on-one instruction with a special education teacher. Tiered lessons used in differentiation would be an avenue to offer high-quality core instruction for all students in the first tier or level of RtI.

◆ Flexible Grouping

Allowing students to collaborate on tasks supports and challenges their thinking and increases their opportunities to communicate about mathematics and build understanding. In addition, many students feel that working in groups improves their confidence, engagement, and understanding (Nebesniak & Heaton, 2010). Even students who prefer to work alone need to learn the life skill of collaboration and should be provided opportunities to work with others.

Determining how to place students in groups is an important decision. Avoid continually grouping by ability. This kind of grouping, although well-intentioned, perpetuates low levels of learning and actually increases the gap between more and less dependent students. Instead, consider using *flexible grouping*, in which the size and makeup of small groups vary in a purposeful and strategic manner (Murray & Jorgensen, 2007). When coupled with differentiation strategies, flexible grouping gives all students the chance to work successfully in groups.

Flexible groups can vary based on students' readiness, interests, language proficiency, and learning profiles, as well as the nature of the tasks. For example, sometimes students can work with a partner because the nature of the task best suits two people working together. At other times, flexible groups might be created with four students because their assigned task has enough components or roles to warrant a larger team. Note that it can be effective to periodically place struggling learners with more capable students who are likely to be helpful. However, constantly pairing struggling learners with more capable students is not helpful for either group. The idea behind flexible grouping is that groups can and do easily change in response to all students' readiness, interests, and learning profiles and the nature of the task they will be doing.

Regardless of how you group your students, the first key to successful grouping is individual accountability. While the group is working together on a product, individuals must be able to explain the content, the process, and the product. Second, and equally important, is building a sense of shared responsibility within a group. At the start of the year, it is important to engage students in team-building activities and to set expectations that all group members will participate in the assigned group task(s) and that all group members will be responsible for ensuring that the entire group understands the concept.

Reinforcing individual accountability and shared responsibility may create a shift in your role as the teacher. When a member of a small group asks you a question, pose the question to the whole group to find out what the other members think. Students will soon learn that they must use teammates as their first resource and seek teacher help only when the whole group needs help. Also, when you are observing groups, rather than asking a student what she is doing, ask another student in the group to explain what the first student is doing. Having all students participate in the oral report to the whole class also builds individual accountability. Letting students know that you may call on any member to explain what the group did is a good way to ensure that all group members understand what they did. In addition, having students individually write and record their strategies and solutions is important. Using these techniques will increase the effectiveness of grouping, which in turn will help students learn mathematical concepts more successfully.

Stop and Reflect

Why is teaching mathematics through problem solving (i.e., a problem-based approach) a good way to differentiate instruction and reach all students in a classroom? ■

5

Planning, Teaching, and Assessing Culturally and Linguistically Diverse Students

One of the aims of schools should be to produce citizens who treat one another with respect, who value the contributions of those with whom they interact irrespective of race, class, or gender, and who act with a sense of social justice.

Boaler (2006, p. 74)

Culturally and Linguistically Diverse Students

We are lucky to be in a country in which people from all over the world bring us rich diversity in cultural practices and languages. Students' native languages are not only an important part of their cultural heritage, but students also think, communicate, and learn in their native languages. Since 1980, the number of school-age children who speak a language other than English at home has risen from 4.7 million to 11.2 million (NCES, 2011).

Jo Boaler's quote captures the essence of the equity principle in *Principles and Standards for School Mathematics*: "Excellence in mathematics education requires equity—high expectations and strong support for all students" (NCTM, 2000, p. 12).

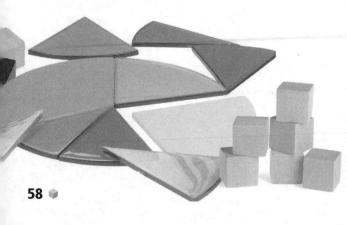

Teaching for equity is much more than providing students with an equal opportunity to learn mathematics. Attention to language and culture, two interrelated and critical considerations, is important in planning, teaching, and assessing students from diverse backgrounds. Students who are given instructional tasks that are well supported and thought-provoking— rather than low-level tasks with short-term gains—can reach higher levels of mathematical proficiency.

◆ Funds of Knowledge

Students from different countries, regions, or experiences, including those who speak different languages, are often viewed as challenges to a teacher or school. Rather, students' varied languages and backgrounds should be seen as a resource in teaching (Gutierrez, 2009). Valuing a person's cultural background is more than a belief statement; it is a set of intentional actions that communicate to the student, "I want to know about you, I want you to see mathematics as part of your life, and I expect that you can do high-level mathematics." In getting to know students, we access their funds of knowledge,—the essential knowledge or information that they use to survive and thrive (Gonzáles, Moll, & Amanti, 2005). Instead of teaching English language learners (ELLs) from a deficit model (lack of knowledge and experience), we can connect their experiences at home and with family to those of the mathematics classroom. The more we enhance learning for all students, regardless of their places of birth, the more enriched the opportunities for learning become.

◆ Mathematics as a Language

Mathematics is commonly referred to as a "universal language," but this is not entirely true. Conceptual knowledge (e.g., what division is) is universal. Procedures (e.g., how you divide or factor) and symbols are culturally determined and are not universal. For example, in the United States, the common algorithm for the division of fractions is to invert the second fraction and multiply, but in Mexico, the common algorithm is to cross-multiply (Perkins & Flores, 2002):

$$\frac{7}{8} \times \frac{1}{4} \times \frac{28}{8}$$

Figure 5.1 illustrates the process for factoring that is used in other countries, including Mexico.

Commas and periods are sometimes used in reverse; for example, 1, 4 means one and four tenths, and 1.400.000 means 1.4 million (Secada, 1983). In Mexico, textbooks may refer to angle B as $\hat{B}$ rather than as $\angle B$, or to angle ABC as $\widehat{ABC}$ rather than as $\angle ABC$, as is done in the United States. An ELL might not recognize the angle symbol and could confuse it with the "less than" symbol. What is called "billions" in the United States is called "thousand millions" in Mexico (Perkins & Flores, 2002). Treating mathematics as universally the same can lead to inequities in the classroom because students from other cultures may not understand the symbols and processes being used in their class and therefore not be able to participate and learn.

How we do mathematics is also influenced by culture. For example, mental mathematics is highly valued in other countries, whereas in the United States, recording every step is valued. Could you follow the factoring and common-multiple approach illustrated in Figure 5.1? It looks different from the factor trees or factor lists commonly taught in the United States. The critical equity question, though, is not just whether you can follow an alternative approach, but how you will you respond when you encounter a student using such an approach.

- Will you require the student to use trees or lists (disregarding the way he or she learned it)?
- Will you ask the student to elaborate on how he or she did it?
- Will you have the student show other students his or her way of thinking?

The latter two responses communicate to the student that you are interested in his or her way of knowing mathematics, and that there are many ways in which different people and different cultures approach mathematics. Supporting a range of strategies for algorithms is an important way to show that you value students as individuals and is a good way to gain insights into possible culturally influenced strategies.

Teaching Tip

Instead of requiring students to write all their steps, ask them to think aloud as they solve a problem, or ask how they did it in their head.

Figure 5.1 Steps and thought processes for finding factors and multiples in Mexico.

Step in the Algorithm			Explanation or Think Aloud for the Step
5.1a. Finding Prime Factors			
150			Start with the first prime number and see how many times it can be used as a factor. Record the remaining factor under the original number.
150 75	2		2 won't work a second time, so try the next prime number, 3.
150 75 25	2 3		3 won't work again, so try the next prime number, 5.
150 75 25 5 1	2 3 5 5		5 will work a second time, leaving 1 as the remaining factor, so the factoring is complete. The prime factors are the numbers in the right-hand column.
5.1b. Finding the Least Common Multiple			
24 12	18 9	2	As in 5.1a, the process begins with trying the first prime number, 2. 2 is a common factor.
24 12 6 3	18 9	2 2 2 3	2 will work again for 24, so factors for 24 are continued. The next prime to try is 3.
24 12 6 3 1	18 9 3 1	2 2 2 3 3	3 is a common factor. 3 works a second time for 18. This leaves factors of 1 for each column. The least common multiple is found by multiplying the values in the right-hand column: $2 \times 2 \times 2 \times 3 \times 3 = 72$.

Source: Adapted from Perkins & Flores (2002).

Culturally Responsive Instruction

Culture and language are interwoven and interrelated. Therefore, teaching strategies that support diverse learners often support both cultural diversity and language. For example, if you invite students to talk to a partner before sharing with the whole class, you not only provide ELLs with an additional speaking opportunity to support language development, but also distribute the sharing, listening, and teaching, so you are sharing power within the classroom community.

Culturally responsive mathematics instruction is not just for recent immigrants; it is for all students, including students from different ethnic groups, different socioeconomic levels, and so on. It includes consideration for content, relationships, cultural knowledge, flexibility in approaches, use of accessible learning contexts (i.e., contexts familiar or interesting to students), a responsive learning community, and working in cross-cultural partnerships (Averill, Anderson, Easton, Te Maro, Smith, & Hynds, 2009). As described in Chapter 4, differentiation can be accomplished by adapting the content, process, product, and the classroom environment (Tomlinson, 2003). Here are four strategies for differentiating that address the specific needs of linguistically and culturally diverse students. These ideas are also presented in an at-a-glance format in Table 5.1.

Table 5.1 At-a-Glance Focus on Culturally Responsive Mathematics Instruction

Aspect of Culturally Responsive Instruction	Reflection Questions to Guide Teaching and Assessing
Communicate high expectations.	Does the content include a balance of procedures and concepts? Are students expected to engage in problem solving and generate their own approaches to problems? Are connections made between mathematics topics?
Make content relevant.	In what ways is the content related to familiar aspects of students' lives? In what ways is prior knowledge elicited/reviewed so that all students can participate in the lesson? To what extent are students asked to make connections between school mathematics and mathematics in their own lives? How are student interests (events, issues, literature, or pop culture) used to build interest and mathematical meaning?
Communicate the value of students' identities.	In what ways are students invited to include their own experiences within a lesson? Are story problems generated from students and teachers? Do stories reflect the real experiences of students? Are individual student approaches presented and showcased so that each student sees his or her ideas as important to the teacher and peers? Are alternative algorithms shared as a point of excitement and pride (as appropriate)? Are the multiple modes used to demonstrate knowledge (e.g., visuals, explanations, models) valued?
Model shared power.	Are students (rather than just the teacher) justifying the correctness of solutions? Are students invited (expected) to engage in whole-class discussions in which they share ideas and respond to one another's ideas? In what ways are roles assigned so that every student feels that he or she is contributing to and learning from other members of the class? Are students given a choice in how they solve a problem? In how they demonstrate knowledge of the concept?

Focus on Important Mathematics

Too often, our first attempt to help ELLs is to simplify the mathematics and/or remove the language from the lesson. Simplifying or removing language can take away opportunities to learn. Culturally responsive instruction stays focused on the big ideas of mathematics (i.e., is based on standards such as the *Common Core State Standards*) and helps students engage in and stay focused on those big ideas. For example, a critical area in the sixth grade is division of fractions, including being able to "understand and explain why the procedures for dividing fractions make sense" (CCSSO, 2010, p. 44). Stories involving the division of fractions can be carefully selected for the use of contexts that are familiar to ELLs and for the use of visuals (e.g., rectangular plots of land or trays of brownies). Rather than every story having a new context, the stories can focus on the same theme (and connect to the English that students are learning in their English-as-a-second-language instruction, if possible). The teacher can incorporate opportunities for students to share their approaches to dividing fractions, for example, and illustrate (with visuals) how they thought about it. In this way, ELLs are able to learn the important content (connecting story situation to equation to meaning for division) and engage in classroom discourse.

Make Content Relevant

There are really two components to making content relevant. One is to think about the *mathematics*: Is the mathematics itself presented meaningfully, and is it connected to other content? The second is to contextualize the content so that it is grounded in familiarity.

Mathematical Connections.   Helping students see that mathematical ideas are interrelated will fill in or deepen their understanding of and connections to previously taught content. For example, consider the eighth-grade problem in Figure 5.2.

You may recognize that this task connects several representations, including graphs, symbols, and situations. It also connects meaning between fractions, ratios, and proportions. Just having students plot ratios on a graph to illustrate the relationship takes away

Figure 5.2

Sample problem for eighth-grade *Common Core State Standard* 8.EE.5: "Graph proportional relationships, interpreting the unit rate as the slope of the graph."

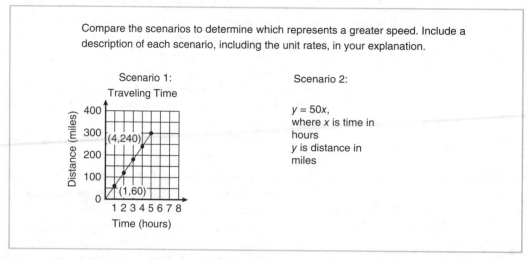

Source: Arizona Department of Education (2010). Reprinted with permission from Arizona Department of Education K–12 Mathematics Standards.

opportunities to emphasize the meaning among the representations and to connect what they already know about fractions to proportional reasoning and algebra. Instead, provide language support and other accommodations that help students make sense of the task and, in so doing, build strong mathematical connections and a strong understanding of addition and subtraction.

Context Connections.　Making content relevant is also about contexts. The problem in Figure 5.2 could be more explicitly connected to the speed of a car, and that context could be used for reasoning. For example, where are the two cars after one hour? After two hours? Using problems that connect students to developmentally appropriate social or peer connections is one way to contextualize learning. Another is to make connections to historical or cultural contexts. Seeing mathematics from various cultures provides opportunities for students to "put faces" on mathematical contributions. For example, students could analyze freedom quilts, which tell stories about the Underground Railroad (Neumann, 2005), or flags of various countries; this allows them to explore *Common Core State Standards* content by looking at the ratio of colors in an area (grade 6) or creating scale drawings of the design (grade 7). They could also look for or design their own quilts that include translations, rotations, reflections, and dilations (grade 8).

Incorporate Students' Identities

Incorporating students' identities in the mathematics they do overlaps with the previous category, but it merits its own discussion. Students should see themselves in mathematics and see that mathematics is a part of their culture. The classroom environment should incorporate students' cultural practices. For example, students from some countries may not feel comfortable challenging an approach used by another student in a classroom discussion.

Both researchers and teachers have found that telling stories about their own lives, or asking students to tell stories, makes mathematics relevant to students and can raise student achievement (Turner, Celedón-Pattichis, Marshall, & Tennison, 2009). Table 5.2 provides ideas for making mathematics relevant to a student's home and community.

> *Teaching Tip*
>
> Teachers can adapt the way students consider each other's ideas so that all members of the class feel comfortable participating in such a discussion. Try specific prompts such as, "Which strategy would you use if the numbers were more difficult? Why? Talk to your partner, and then we will share as a whole class."

Read the following teacher's story to see how she incorporated family history and culture into her class by reading *The Hundred Penny Box* (Mathis, 1986). In Mathis's story, a 100-year-old woman remembers an important event in every year of her life as she turns over each of her 100 pennies. Each penny is more than a coin; it is a "memory trigger" for her life.

> Taking a cue from the book, I asked all the students to collect one penny from each year they were alive, starting from the year of their birth and not missing a year. Students were encouraged to bring in additional pennies their classmates might need. Then, the students consulted with family members to create a penny time line of important events in their lives. Using information gathered at home, they started with the year they were born, listing their birthday and then recording first steps, accidents, vacations, pets, births of siblings, and so on.

> Students in grades 6–8 can prepare a "life line" of their key events, too, determining where between zero (i.e., the day they were born) and their current age a memorable event happened. The number line is an important model to use in teaching fractions, and in this context, students can build the meaning of fractions on the number line. Importantly, number line investigations should focus on the distance between two quantities (the intervals), and in this context, they can focus on the amount of time between events. For example, you

Table 5.2 Where to Find Mathematics in Students' Homes and Community

Where to Look	What You Might Ask Students to Record and Share (and Mathematics That Can Be Explored)
Grocery store or market	• Cost of an item of which they bought more than one (multiplication) • Cost of an item that came with a quantity (e.g., dozen eggs) (division) • Better buy of two items of different sizes (division) • Shapes of different containers (geometry) • Different types/brands of different foods they select, such as what kind of bread (data)
Photographs	• Of a person they admire (data) • Of a favorite scene (geometry, measurement) • Of 2-D and 3-D shapes in their home or neighborhood • Of a flower (multiplication with number of petals, algebraic thinking)
Artifact (game or measuring device) from their culture or that is a favorite	• The game likely naturally involves mathematics. • Measuring devices can be used to explore fractions and decimals.

can ask students what fraction of their life they have spent in school. Considering events that happened before their birth introduces integer values. They can ask parents, grandparents, and other relatives about key events that happened before they were born and add these to their life lines. Or, they can find coins dated before they were born and determine where they would go on their life lines.

Ensure Shared Power

When we think about creating a positive classroom environment, one in which all students feel as if they can participate and learn, we are addressing considerations related to power. The teacher plays a major role in establishing and distributing power, whether intentional or not. In many classrooms, the teacher has the power—telling students whether answers are right or wrong (rather than having students determine correctness through reasoning), dictating processes for how to solve problems (rather than giving choices for how students will engage in the problems), and determining who will solve which problems (rather than allowing flexibility and choice for students). The way that you assign groups, seat students, and call on students sends clear messages about who has power in the classroom.

 ## Teaching Culturally and Linguistically Diverse Students

Creating effective learning opportunities for ELLs involves integrating the principles of bilingual education with those of standards-based mathematics instruction. When learning about mathematics, students may be learning content in English for which they do not know the words in their native language. In middle school, these words are many. Examples include *transformation, proportional, transversal, polygon, system of equations, cylinder,* and *sphere.* In addition, there are many words in middle-school mathematics that are familiar to students but take on specialized meaning in mathematics, such as *mean, multiply, expression, reflection, translation, factor, acute,* and *similar.*

Stop and Reflect

In addition, story problems are difficult for ELLs not just because of the language but also because the sentences in story problems are often structured differently from sentences in conversational English (Janzen, 2008). Teachers of English to Speakers of Other Languages (TESOL), a professional organization focused on the needs of ELLs, argues that ELLs need to use both English and their native language to read, write, listen, and speak as they learn appropriate content—a position similarly addressed in NCTM standards documents and position statements. The strategies discussed in this section are

the ones that appear most frequently in the literature as critical to increasing the academic achievement of ELLs in mathematics classrooms (e.g., Celedón-Pattichis & Ramirez, 2012; Echevarria, Vogt, & Short, 2008). Table 5.3 offers an "at-a-glance" format of some reflective questions related to instructional planning and teaching in classes with ELLs.

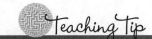
Teaching Tip

Any one of the categories in Table 5.3 could be the focus of a lesson study, discussions with colleagues, or the basis for individual reflection. The importance lies not in the specific suggestions, but in the concept of having an eye on language development *and* mathematics content.

Table 5.3 Reflective Questions for Planning and Teaching Mathematics Lessons for ELLs

Process	Mathematics Content Considerations	Language Considerations
Reflective Questions for Planning		
1. Determine the mathematics.	• What mathematical concepts (aligned to grade-level standards) am I teaching? • What student-friendly learning objectives will I post? • How does this mathematics concept connect to other concepts students have learned?	• What language objectives might I add (e.g., reading, writing, speaking, and listening)? • What visuals or words will I use to communicate the content and language objectives?
2. Consider student needs.	• How can I connect the content to be taught to content that students have learned? Or, how will I fill in gaps if students don't have prerequisite content needed for the lesson?	• What context or models might I select that are a good match to students' social and cultural backgrounds and previously learned vocabulary?
3. Select, design, or adapt a task.	• What task can I use that addresses the content identified in No. 1 and the needs of my students identified in No. 2? • How might I adapt a task so that it has multiple entry and exit points (i.e., is challenging and accessible to a range of students)?	• What context might I use that is meaningful to the students' cultures and backgrounds? • What language pitfalls does the task have? Which of these will I eliminate, and which of these need explicit attention? • Which words or phrases, even if familiar to students, take on new meaning in a mathematics context (e.g., homonyms, homophones, and words such as *mean, similar, find*)?

(continued)

Table 5.3 (Continued)

Process	Mathematics Content Considerations	Language Considerations
Reflective Questions for Teaching		
1. Introduce the task (the *Before* phase).	• How will I introduce the task in a way that elicits prior mathematics knowledge needed for the task? • Is a similar task needed to build background related to the content (or would such a preview take away from the purpose or challenge of the task)?	• How can I connect the task to students' experiences and to familiar contexts? • What key vocabulary do I want to introduce so that the words will be used throughout the lesson? (Post key vocabulary in a prominent location.) • What visuals and real objects can I use that bring meaning to the selected task? • How can I present the task in visual, written, and oral formats? • How will I be sure that students understand what they are to do in the *During* phase?
2. Work on the task (the *During* phase).	• What hints or assists might I give as students work that help them focus without taking away their thinking? • What extensions or challenges will I offer for students who successfully solve the task? • What questions will I pose to push the mathematics identified in the learning goals?	• Have I grouped students for both academic and language support? • Have I encouraged students to draw pictures, make diagrams, and/or use manipulatives? • Have I used strategies to reduce the linguistic demands (e.g., graphic organizers, sentence starters such as, "I solved the problem by . . .," recording tables, and concept maps) without hindering the problem solving?
3. Debrief and discuss the task and the mathematics (the *After* phase).	• How will students report their findings? • How will I format the discussion of the task? • What questions will I pose to push the mathematics identified in the learning goals?	• In what ways can I maximize language use in nonthreatening ways (e.g., think–pair–share)? • How can I encourage and reinforce different formats (multiple exit points) for demonstrating understanding of the lesson content? • How might I provide advance notice, language support, or rehearsal to English language learners so that they will be comfortable speaking to their peers? • Am I using appropriate "wait time"?
Formative Assessment		
Throughout lesson and unit	• What questions will I ask during the lesson, or what will I look for in the students' work as evidence of learning the objectives (*During* and *After* phases)? • What follow-up might I provide to students who are not demonstrating understanding of the mathematics?	• What words will I use in my questions to be sure the questions are understood? How might I use a translator to assist in assessing? • If a student is not succeeding, how might I diagnose whether the problem is with language, content, or both? • What accommodations can I provide to be sure I am accessing what the students know?

◈ Focus on Academic Vocabulary

ELLs enter the mathematics classroom from homes in which English is not the primary language of communication. Although a person may develop conversational English language skills in a few years, it takes as many as seven years to learn *academic language*, which is the language specific to a content area such as mathematics (Cummins, 1994). Academic language is harder to learn because it is not used in a student's everyday world. In addition, there are unique features of the language of mathematics that make it difficult for many students, in particular those who are learning English. Teaching the academic language of mathematics evolves over time and requires thoughtful and reflective instructional planning.

Honor Use of Native Language

Valuing a student's native language is one of the ways you value his or her cultural heritage. In a mathematics classroom, students can communicate in their native languages while continuing their English language development (Haas & Gort, 2009; Moschkovich, 2009; Setati, 2005). For example, a good strategy for students working individually or in small groups is having them think about and discuss the problem in their preferred language. If a student knows enough English, then the presentation in the *After* phase of the lesson can be shared in English. If the student knows little or no English and does not have access to a peer who shares his or her native language, then a translator, the use of a Web-based dictionary, or a self-made mathematics-focused dictionary can be a strong support. Students within the small group can also be coached to use visual aids and pictures to communicate. Bilingual students will often code-switch, moving between two languages. Research indicates that the practice of code-switching supports mathematical reasoning because students select the language in which they can best express their ideas (Moschkovich, 2009).

Certain native languages can support learning mathematical words. Because English, Spanish, French, Portuguese, and Italian all have their roots in Latin, many math words are similar across languages (Celedón-Pattichis, 2009; Gómez, 2010). For example, *aequus* (Latin), *equal* (English), and *igual* (Spanish) are cognates. See if you can figure out the English mathematical terms for the following Spanish words: *número, hexágano, ángulo, triángulo, álgebra, circunferencia, ángulo, triángulo, quadra,* and *cubo.* Students may not make this connection if you do not point it out, so it is important to explicitly teach students to look for cognates.

Use Content and Language Objectives

If students know the purpose of a lesson, they are better able to make sense of the details when they are challenged by some of the oral or written explanations. When language expectations are explicitly included, students will know that they will be responsible for reaching certain language goals alongside mathematical goals and will be more likely to attempt to learn those skills or words. Here are two examples of dual objectives:

1. Students will write and evaluate expressions with variables from story situations (mathematics).
2. Students will describe in writing and orally how the expression connects to the situation (language and mathematics).

Explicitly Teach Vocabulary

Intentional vocabulary instruction must be part of mathematics instruction for all students. This includes attention to terms within a lesson and additional opportunities to develop academic language. These additional opportunities can reinforce understanding as they help students learn the terminology. Examples include these:

- Self-made dictionaries that link concepts and terms with drawings or clip art pictures
- Foldables of key words for a topic
- Games focused on vocabulary development (e.g., "Pictionary" or "$10,000 Pyramid")
- Interactive word walls, including visuals and translations

In addition, many websites provide translations; students can create cards with terms and their translations, building personal math dictionaries (Kersaint, Thompson, & Petkova, 2009).

All students benefit from an increased focus on language; however, too much emphasis on vocabulary can diminish the focus on mathematics. Importantly, the language support should be *connected* to the mathematics and the selected task or activity.

Teaching Tip

Not all vocabulary should be "previewed" because the term (and its concept) can sometimes be better understood after some exploration has occurred.

As you analyze a lesson, you must identify terms related to the mathematics and to the context that may need explicit attention. Consider the following grade 8 short constructed response item (low level of difficulty), released from the 2007 National Assessment of Educational Progress (NCES, 2011).

Three tennis balls are to be stacked one on top of another in a cylindrical can. The radius of each tennis ball is 3 cm. To the nearest whole centimeter, what should be the minimum height of the can? Explain why you chose the height that you did. Your explanation should include a diagram.

In order for students to engage in this task, they need visuals or illustrations for the context words, such as *tennis balls* and *cylindrical can*. They also need support for the mathematical terminology they must learn and retain. The words *cylinder*, *radius*, and *height* are listed in the problem, but *sphere* and *diameter* are words that are also important to this task. Students need to know what is meant by *diagram* so that they can create one.

◆ Lesson Considerations

Support for academic language use is a significant part of lesson considerations. In addition, facilitating discourse that provides access to ELLs is critical. This includes (1) efforts to ensure that ELLs understand and have the background for engaging in the focus task(s), and (2) the need to put structures in place for student participation throughout the lesson.

Build Background

Similar to building on prior knowledge, building background also takes into consideration native language and culture as well as content (Echevarria, Vogt, & Short, 2008). If possible, use a context and appropriate visuals to help students understand the task you want them to solve. This is a nonthreatening and engaging way to help students make connections between what they have learned and what they need to learn. For example, if you are teaching operations with positive and negative numbers (integers), you can build background by using actual thermometers, which provide a visual and a context. You might display pictures of places covered in snow and position them near pictures of thermometers with low temperatures to build the meaning of the negative values (e.g., ⁻10 is colder and therefore less than ⁻3).

Some aspects of English and mathematics are particularly challenging to ELLs (Whiteford, 2009/2010). For example, teen numbers sound a lot like their decade number—if you say *sixteen* and *sixty* out loud, you can hear how similar they are. And, decimal fractions (e.g., 0.15) sound like whole numbers (e.g., 1500). Emphasizing the *n* in *teen* or the *ths* in decimal fractions helps ELLs hear the difference. Remember, too, that the U.S. measurement system may be unfamiliar to ELLs. When encountering content that may be unfamiliar or difficult for ELLs, devote additional time to building background so that students can engage in the mathematical tasks without also having to navigate language and background knowledge.

Use Comprehensible Input

Comprehensible input means that the message you are communicating is understandable to students. Modifications include simplifying sentence structures and limiting the use of nonessential or confusing vocabulary (Echevarria, Vogt, & Short, 2008). Note that these modifications do not lower expectations for the lesson. Sometimes, teachers put many unnecessary words and phrases into questions, making them less clear to nonnative speakers. Compare the following two sets of teachers' instructions:

NOT MODIFIED:

You have a worksheet in front of you that I just gave out. For every situation, I want you to determine the total surface area for the shapes. You will be working with your partner, but each of you needs to record your answers on your own paper and explain how you got your answer. If you get stuck on a problem, raise your hand.

MODIFIED:

Please look at your paper. (Holds paper and points to the first picture.) You will find the surface area. What does surface area mean? (Allows wait time.) How can you calculate surface area for the shapes? ("Calculate" is more like the Spanish word *calcular*, so it is more accessible to Spanish speakers.) Talk to your partner. (Points to mouth and then to a pair of students as she says this.) Write your answers. (Makes a writing motion over paper.) If you get stuck on a problem (shrugs shoulders and looks confused), raise your hand (holds hand up).

Notice that three things have been done: sentences have been shortened, confusing words have been removed, and related gestures and motions have been added to the oral directives. Also notice the "wait time" the teacher gives. It is very important to provide extra time after posing a question or giving instructions to allow ELLs time to translate, make sense of the request, and then participate.

Another way to provide comprehensible input is to use a variety of tools to help students visualize and understand what is verbalized. In the preceding example, the teacher models the instructions. Effective tools include manipulatives, real objects, pictures, visuals, multimedia, demonstrations, and literature (Echevarria, Vogt, & Short, 2008). When introducing a lesson, include pictures, real objects, and diagrams. For example, with surface area of rectangular solids, show different boxes that have been cut open into their nets. Ask students, "How many tiles will cover each of the faces of the box?" And, as you ask, physically move some tiles on top of the box to illustrate. Review terms for the box (net, side, length, width, height) and label a box for reference.

Engage Students in Discourse That Reflects Language Needs

Discourse, or the use of classroom discussion, is essential for *all* learning but is particularly important for ELLs, who need to engage in productive language (writing and speaking), not just receptive language (listening and reading), as noted in *Application of Common Core State Standards for English Learners* (CCSSO, 2011, p. 2):

> ELLs are capable of participating in mathematical discussions as they learn English. Mathematics instruction for ELL students should draw on multiple resources and modes available in classrooms—such as objects, drawings, inscriptions, and gestures—as well as home languages and mathematical experiences outside of school. Mathematical instruction should address mathematical discourse and academic language.

There are strategies you can use in classroom discourse that help ELLs understand and participate. As described in the quote above, the use of gestures and visuals is critical to learning English and mathematics. For example, revoicing is a research-based strategy that helps ELLs hear an idea more than once and hear it restated with the appropriate language applied to concepts. But, because ELLs cannot always explain their ideas fully, don't rush to call on someone else; instead patiently press for details. Pressing for details is not done just so the teacher can decide whether the idea makes sense; it allows other students to make sense of the idea, too (Maldonado, Turner, Dominguez, & Empson, 2009). Because practicing language is important for ELLs, having opportunities for students to practice phrases or words through pair–share or choral response also is effective. Finally, students from other countries often solve or record problems differently, so inviting ELLs to share how they solved a problem can enhance the richness of discussion around different approaches to problems.

Teaching Tip

Making the strategies of ELLs public and connecting their strategies to others is interesting, and it supports the learning of all students while building the confidence of the ELLs.

Plan Cooperative/Interdependent Groups to Support Language

The use of cooperative groups is a valuable way to differentiate instruction. For ELLs, groups provide the opportunity to use language, but only if the groups are carefully formed in a way that considers students' language skills. Placing an ELL with two English-speaking students may result in the ELL being left out. On the other hand, grouping all Spanish speakers together prevents these students from having the opportunity to hear and participate in mathematics in English. Consider placing a bilingual student in a group with a student who has limited English, or place students who have the same first language together with native speakers so that they can help one another understand and participate (Garrison, 1997; Khisty, 1997).

◆ Implementing Strategies for ELLs

The strategies just described are subtle moves in teaching. As you read the following vignette, look for strategies that the teacher applies to provide support for ELLs while keeping expectations high.

> Ms. Evers is teaching a seventh-grade lesson that involves determining whether a situation is proportional, and if so, what is the constant of proportionality. The lesson asks students to analyze a situation in which servings of trail mix are being made. Ms. Evers has four ELLs in her class, including a child from Korea who knows very little English and three children from Mexico who speak English at varying levels. All are recent arrivals in the United States. These students are not familiar with trail mix, or with the academic language of rates and proportions. Ms. Evers knows she needs to build background to ensure that they can participate in the lesson.
>
> The lesson begins with Ms. Evers placing cereal mix in two different bowls, one with twice the amount of mix as the other (neither bowl has enough for the whole class). She holds up the bowl with the smaller portion and asks what is in her mix. Students say Cheerios and chocolate chips (Ms. Evers emphasizes the word *mix* by saying she *mixed* Cheerios and chocolate chips in her *recipe*). As students say the terms, she shows the bags of each. She then shows the bowl with more in it and asks, "This has more, but is it the same *mix*?" She asks students to think (points at her head) yes or no, then share (points at her mouth) with a partner. After think–pair time, she gets some ideas from student pairs. Then, Ms. Evers says that the big idea today is to figure out if the mixes in the two bowls are in the same *ratio* of Cheerios to chocolate chips.

Ms. Evers then uses the context she started with—a mix of Cheerios and chocolate chips—and presents a table of how to make the mix. (The first two columns in the table represent the actual bowls.)

Mix	For 1 Person	For 2 People	For 3 People	For 4 People
Cups of Cheerios	2	4	6	8
Cups of chocolate chips	1	2	3	4

Ms. Evers asks, "Is this the same mix for all the different-sized recipes?" She gives students materials (grid paper, counters, cubes) and says, "Use these tools to show and tell me how you know if these are the same mix or not. Are the food items in the same *ratio*?"

This lesson is split into two parts. After students share their illustrations and explanations indicating that the ratios are the same, Ms. Evers asks students, "If we know how many chocolate chips, can we figure out how many Cheerios?" She asks students to work with their partners to answer the question and to see whether they can write an equation that fits all mixes. When the students share these responses, Ms. Evers teaches the new words—*proportional* and *constant of proportionality*, having students say the words, describe the words, and add the words to their personal math dictionaries.

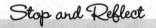

Stop and Reflect

What specific strategies to support ELLs can you identify? ■

There are a number of strategies that provided support for ELLs: recognizing the potential language support for *mix* and *ratio* initially, and later for *proportional* and *constant of proportionality*. Ms. Evers anticipated that the context (trail mix) might be unfamiliar, so she prepared two of the mixes to build background (and interest!). She employed a think–pair–share technique, concrete models (the cereal and chips), and scaffolded the lesson by separating it into part 1 (on ratios) and part 2 (on determining the constant). Most importantly, Ms. Evers did not diminish the challenge of the task with these strategies. If she had altered the task—for example, by having students find missing values in the table and telling them that they were related in the same way—she would have taken the reasoning out of the proportional reasoning lesson. Conversely, if she had simply asked students to decide whether the mixes were proportional and to find the constant of proportionality, she might have kept her expectations high but failed to provide the support that would enable all students to succeed.

◆ Assessment Considerations

Throughout the discussion of strategies for supporting ELLs are opportunities for assessment. Formative assessment, as described in Chapter 3, is embedded in instruction and informs instructional decisions. For example the use of visuals and gestures is important in helping ELLs to

- Understand the instructions and mathematical ideas (comprehensible *input*)
- Participate in the lesson (small groups or discussion)
- Communicate their own understanding (formative assessment)

The use of native language is also important for assessment. Research shows that ELLs perform better when a test is given in their native language (Robinson, 2010). If a teacher wants to understand what a student knows about mathematics, then the student should be able to communicate that understanding in a way that is best for the student, even if the teacher may need a translation.

Several strategies can assist teachers in using formative assessments with ELLs, including tasks with multiple entry and exit points, diagnostic interviews, tasks that limit the linguistic load, accommodations, and self-assessment.

Select Tasks with Multiple Entry and Exit Points

An aspect of teaching mathematics through problem solving that is important, particularly for ELLs, is to select tasks carefully. If a problem can be solved in multiple ways, an ELL is more likely to be able to design a strategy that makes sense and then illustrate that strategy. Inviting students to show and/or explain their strategy provides options for ELLs to use words and pictures to communicate their thinking.

Use Diagnostic Interviews

Chapter 3 provides a strong foundation on diagnostic interviews, which are critical for ELLs because of the insights they can provide related to language and mathematical understanding. When ELLs do not get a correct answer or cannot explain a response, teachers tend to think it is a lack of mathematical understanding rather than a language issue. This is particularly true with ELLs who have a pretty strong ability to communicate in everyday English (as opposed to academic English). Before drawing conclusions about what mathematics a student does and does not understand, it is important to observe whether it is content or language that is causing a problem. Consider the following task that could be part of a diagnostic interview focused on percent increase (grade 7) (Arizona Department of Education, 2010):

At a certain store, 48 television sets were sold in April. The manager at the store wants to encourage the sales team to sell more TVs and is going to give all the sales team members a bonus if the number of TVs sold increases by 30 percent in May. How many TVs must the sales team sell in May to receive the bonus? Justify your solution. (Reprinted with permission from Arizona Department of Education K–12 Mathematics Standards)

Stop and Reflect

If a student missed this problem, what do you think might be the reason? ◼

There are numerous reasons why students might struggle with this problem, including a lack of understanding mathematical concepts like percentage increase. Or, the difficulty could be due to context-related vocabulary, such as *sales*, *sell*, and *sold*. But, it could also be due to the sentence structure, in this case the "If . . . then" style common in math story problems. Diagnostic interviews have revealed that the word *if* can prevent students from comprehending what the sentence is asking (a challenge for native English speakers as well) (Fernandez, Anhalt, & Civil, 2009). The fact that there are many possible reasons why a student might not be able to solve a task, some related to language and some to mathematics, is a strong argument for using diagnostic interviews. If we misdiagnose the reason for a student's struggles, our interventions will be misguided.

Diagnostic interviews also can be used before instruction in order to assess the mathematical and language needs of students. Hearing an ELL's interpretation of a problem and seeing how he or she approaches the problem provide valuable insights that you can incorporate into your planning and teaching. For example, a student might say "three-hundredths from seven-tenths" rather than "seven-tenths minus three-hundredths," which indicates the way the student talks about subtraction at home. Using and connecting both ways of talking about subtraction strengthen everyone's understanding.

Limit Linguistic Load

If you are trying to assess student understanding, look for language that can interfere with students' understanding the situation (e.g., unneeded elaboration in a story, difficult or unfamiliar vocabulary). Removing pronouns such as *they, this, that, his,* and *her* and using actual names can assist ELLs in understanding some problems. For example, the television problem above could be rewritten as follows:

The sales team sold 48 televisions in April. The sales team wants to sell 30 percent more televisions in May so that they will earn a bonus. How many televisions must the sales team sell in May to receive the bonus? Justify your solution.

Notice that it is not only reducing the language, but also repeating the same terms (*sales team, television*) and adding specific referents that makes the meaning of the story more clear. Of course, this particular problem could be adapted further by using illustrations or manipulatives.

Another way to reduce the linguistic load is to pick a context and stay with it for an entire lesson or series of lessons. This allows students to focus their thinking on the mathematics without getting bogged down in the various contexts that might be on an assessment. For example, instead of using a different percentage increase situation (e.g., one about attendance at an event), stay with television sales but change the problem details (what is known, unknown). This reduces the linguistic load but keeps the mathematical challenge high.

Provide Accommodations

For assessing, *providing accommodations* refers to strategies for making sure that the assessment itself is accessible to children. This might mean allowing students to hear the question (students often can understand spoken English better than written English), shortening the assessment, or extending the time (Kersaint, Thompson, & Petkova, 2009). In addition, you can provide sentence starters so that the ELL knows what type of response you want. For example, "My equation fits the story because . . . ."

Incorporate Self-Assessment

It may take time to help students learn what it means to self-assess, but creating a list of content from a unit and asking students to rate how well they know it can be one way to gather information on what students know. Similarly, after a lesson or problem, students can rate or describe how hard they thought the lesson or problem was (and why). This is valuable not only for you in the formative assessment process, but also for students as they learn to self-monitor and look for ways to measure their own improvement.

Stop and Reflect

The goal of equity is to offer all students access to important mathematics. What might you have on the list of things to do (and things not to do) that provide culturally and linguistically diverse students with opportunities to learn mathematics? ■

6

Planning, Teaching, and Assessing Students with Exceptionalities

Most low achievers in mathematics are probably "instructionally disabled," not cognitively or "learning disabled."

Baroody (2011, p. 31)

Talented [mathematics] students need teachers who can move beyond the traditional "teacher role" of a dispenser of information to that of a role model who is passionate about learning, able to translate that passion into action, aggressively curious, and comfortable with this change of role.

Greenes, Teuscher, and Regis (2010, p. 80)*

Instructional Principles for Diverse Learners

The NCTM *Principles and Standards for School Mathematics* states, "All students, regardless of their personal characteristics, backgrounds, or physical challenges, must have

*Reprinted by permission from Greenes, C., Teuscher, D., & Regis, T., Preparing Teachers for Mathematically Talented Middle School Students, in M. Saul, S. Assouline, & L. J. Sheffield (Eds.), *The Peak in the Middle: Developing Mathematically Gifted Students in the Middle Grades* (pp. 77–91). Copyright 2010 by the National Council of Teachers of Mathematics. All rights reserved.

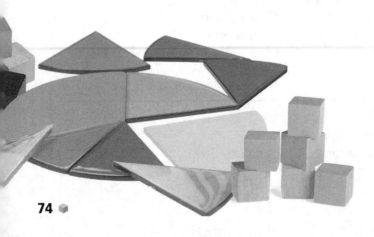

opportunities to study—and support to learn—mathematics" (NCTM, 2000, p. 12). Within the same document, and as previously noted in Chapter 5, the equity principle states, "Excellence in mathematics education requires equity—high expectations and strong support for all students" (NCTM, 2000, p. 12). We know that teaching for equity is much more than providing students with an equal opportunity to learn mathematics; instead, it attempts to attain equal outcomes for all students by being sensitive to individual differences.

Many *achievement* gaps are actually *instructional* gaps or *expectation* gaps. It is not helpful when teachers establish low expectations for students, such as when they say, "I just cannot put this class into groups to work; they are too unruly" or "My students with disabilities can't solve word problems—they don't have the reading skills." Operating under the belief that some students cannot "do mathematics" ensures that they don't have ample opportunities to prove otherwise. Instead, we suggest you consider Storeygard's (2010) mantra for teachers that proclaims, "My kids can!"

As can be gleaned from the opening quotations, there is a spectrum of learners who need to be considered if we intend to have equity in our instruction. Figuring out how you will maintain equal outcomes (high expectations) while providing for individual differences (strong support) can be challenging. Equipping yourself with an ever-growing collection of instructional strategies for a variety of students is critical. A strategy that works for one student may be completely ineffective with another, even a student who has the same exceptionality. Addressing the needs of *all* means providing access and opportunity for

- Students who are identified as struggling or having a disability
- Students who are mathematically gifted
- Students who are unmotivated or need to build resilience

You may think, "I do not need to read the section on mathematically gifted students because they will be pulled out for math enrichment." Students who are mathematically talented need to be challenged in the daily core instruction, not just when they are participating in a program for gifted students.

The goal of equity is to offer all students access to important mathematics during their regular classroom instruction. Yet inequities exist, even if unintentionally. For example, if teachers do not build in opportunities for student-to-student interaction in a lesson, they may not be addressing the needs of girls, who are often social learners, or English language learners, who need opportunities to speak, listen, and write in small-group situations. It takes more than just wanting to be fair or equitable; it takes knowing the strategies that accommodate each type of learner and making every effort to incorporate those strategies into your teaching. "Equity does not mean that every student should receive identical instruction; instead, it demands that reasonable and appropriate accommodations be made as needed to promote access and attainment for all students" (NCTM, 2000, p. 12).

Across the wonderful and myriad diversities of your students, all of them learn mathematics in essentially the same way (Fuson, 2003). The authors of *Adding It Up* (National Research Council, 2001) conclude that all students are best served when you give attention to the following three principles:

1. Learning with understanding is based on connecting and organizing knowledge around big conceptual ideas.

2. Learning builds on what students already know.

3. Instruction in school should take advantage of students' informal knowledge of mathematics.

These principles, also reflected in the tenets of constructivist theory, apply to all learners and therefore are essential in making decisions about how you can adapt instruction to meet individual learners' needs through accommodations and modifications. An accommodation is a response to the needs of the environment or the learner; it does not alter the task. For example, you might write down directions for a student instead of just presenting them orally. A modification changes the task, making it more accessible to the student. For example, if the student is asked to find the surface area of a complex shape, you might break the shape into all of its faces (as a net) and ask the student to find the area of each face and combine. Then the student will attempt the next shape without the modification. When modifications result in an easier or less demanding task, expectations are lowered. Modifications should be made in a way that leads back to the original task, providing scaffolding or support for learners who may need it. In the sections in this chapter, we share research-based strategies that reflect these principles while providing appropriate accommodations and modifications for the wide range of students in your classroom.

Figure 6.1

Multitiered systems of support—using effective strategies to support all students.

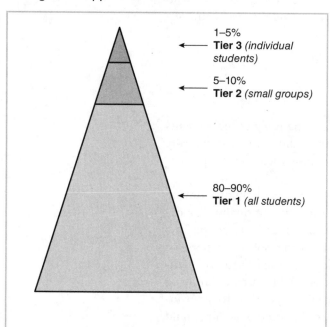

1–5%
Tier 3 *(individual students)*

5–10%
Tier 2 *(small groups)*

80–90%
Tier 1 *(all students)*

Common Features across Tiers

- **Research-Based Practices:** Prevention begins with practices based on students' best chances for success.
- **Data-Driven:** All decisions are based on clear objectives and formative data collection.
- **Instructional:** Prevention and intervention involve effective instruction, prompts, cues, practice, and environmental arrangements.
- **Context-Specific:** All strategies and measures are selected to fit individual schools, classrooms, or students.

Source: Based on Scott, T., and Lane, H. (2001). *Multi-Tiered Interventions in Academic and Social Contexts.* Unpublished manuscript, University of Florida, Gainesville.

◆ Multitiered Systems of Support

In many areas, a systematic process for achieving higher levels of performance for all students often includes a multitiered system of support sometimes called *response to intervention* (RtI). This approach commonly emphasizes ways for struggling students to get immediate assistance and support rather than waiting for them to fail before they receive help. This same multitiered support system can also be used to identify students who are far exceeding standards and need additional challenges. Multitiered models are basically centered on three interwoven elements: high-quality curriculum, instructional support (interventions), and formative assessments that capture students' strengths and weaknesses. These systems of support were initially designed to determine whether low achievement is due to a lack of high-quality mathematics (i.e., "teacher-disabled students") (Baroody, 2011; Ysseldyke, 2002) or to an actual learning disability. However, they can also help determine more intensive instructional options for students who need to catch up or who may need to have additional advanced mathematical challenges beyond what other students study.

Response to Intervention

RtI is a multitiered student support system that is frequently represented in a three-tier triangular format. As you move up the tiers, the number of students involved decreases, the teacher–student ratio decreases, and the level of intervention increases. As you might guess, there is a variety of RtI models in use as states and districts structure their unique approaches to meet local needs. Each tier in the triangle represents a level of intervention with corresponding monitoring of results and outcomes, as shown in Figure 6.1. The foundational and largest portion of the triangle, tier 1, represents the core instruction for all students based on a high-quality mathematics curriculum, instructional practices (i.e., manipulatives, conceptual emphasis), and progress-monitoring assessments. For example, if using a graphic organizer in tier 1 core instruction, the following high-quality practices would be expected in the three phases of the lesson—*Before*, *During*, and *After*.

- *Before:* States purpose, introduces new vocabulary, clarifies concepts from the prior knowledge in a visual organizer, and defines tasks of group members if groups are being used
- *During:* Displays directions in a chart, poster, or list; provides a set of guiding questions in a chart with blank spaces for responses
- *After:* Facilitates a discussion to highlight or make more explicit the significant concepts or skills and then presents a summary and list of important concepts as they relate to one another

Tier 2 represents students who did not reach the level of achievement expected during tier 1 instructional activities. Students in tier 2 should receive supplemental targeted instruction (interventions) outside the core mathematics lessons that uses more explicit strategies, with systematic teaching of critical skills and concepts, more intensive and frequent instructional opportunities, and more supportive and precise prompts (Torgesen, 2002). The National Council of Teachers of Mathematics *Position Statement on Interventions* (NCTM, 2011) states, "Although we do not specifically state the precise interventions, we endorse the use of increasingly intensive and effective instructional interventions for students who struggle with mathematics." Interventions are "reserved for disorders that prove resistant to lower levels of prevention and require more heroic action to preclude serious complications" (Fuchs & Fuchs, 2001, p. 86).

Identifying and using these supplemental interventions is a flexible process that can be adapted or tailored based on how students respond. If further assessments, such as diagnostic interviews, reveal favorable progress, the students are weaned from the extra intervention sessions. However, if difficulties and struggles remain, the interventions can be adjusted in intensity, and in rare cases, students are referred to the next tier of support. Tier 3 is for students who need more intensive periods of instruction, sometimes with one-on-one attention, which may include comprehensive mathematics instruction or a referral for special education evaluation or special education services. Instructional strategies for the three tiers are outlined in Table 6.1.

Progress Monitoring

A key to the multitiered system of support is monitoring students' progress. One way to collect evidence of students' knowledge of concepts is through the use of diagnostic interviews, examples of which are described throughout the book in a feature called "Formative Assessment Notes," marked with the following icon 📃. Another approach is to assess students' growth toward fluency in basic facts, an area that is a well-documented barrier for students with learning disabilities (Mazzocco, Devlin, & McKenney, 2008). Combining instruction with short daily assessments to monitor students' knowledge of number combinations that were already taught proved that the students with disabilities were better not only at remembering but also at generalizing to other facts (Woodward, 2006). The collection of information gathered from these assessments reveals whether students are making the progress expected or if more intensive instructional approaches need to be put into place.

◆ Planning, Teaching, and Assessing Students with Learning Disabilities

Each student has specific learning needs, and strategies that work for one student may not work for another. Yet, there are some general ideas that can help as you plan instruction

Table 6.1 Interventions for Teaching Mathematics in a Multitiered System of Support

Tie	Interventions
Tier 1	A highly qualified regular classroom teacher: • Incorporates a high-quality rigorous curriculum and has expectations for all students to be challenged • Builds in CCSS Standards for Mathematical Practice and NCTM Mathematical Process Standards • Commits to teaching the curriculum as defined • Supports student use of multiple representations such as manipulatives, visual models, and symbols • Monitors progress to identify struggling students and students who excel at high levels • Uses flexible student grouping • Fosters active student involvement • Communicates high expectations
Tier 2	A highly qualified regular classroom teacher, with possible collaboration from a highly qualified special education teacher: • Works with students (commonly in small groups) in supplemental sessions outside the core instruction • Conducts individual diagnostic interviews to target strengths and weaknesses • Collaborates with special education, gifted, or English language learner (ELL) teachers • Creates lessons that emphasize the big ideas (focal points) or themes • Incorporates CSA (concrete/semi-concrete/abstract) approach • Shares thinking in a think-aloud to show students how to make problem-solving decisions • Incorporates explicit systematic strategy instruction (summarizes key points and reviews key vocabulary or concepts before the lesson) • Models specific behaviors and strategies, such as how to handle measuring materials or geoboards • Uses mnemonics or steps written on cards or posters to help students follow problem-solving steps • Uses peer-assisted learning, in which another student can provide help to a student in need • Supplies families with additional support materials to use at home • Encourages student use of self-regulation and self-instructional strategies, such as revising notes, writing summaries, and identifying main ideas • Teaches test-taking strategies (allows students to use a highlighter on tests to emphasize important information) • Slices back (Fuchs & Fuchs, 2001) to material from a previous grade level to ramp back up
Tier 3	A highly qualified special education teacher: • Works one-on-one with students • Uses tailored instruction based on specific areas of weakness • Modifies instructional methods, motivates students, and adapts curricula further • Uses explicit contextualization of skills-based instruction

for students with learning disabilities. The following questions should guide your planning:

1. What organizational, behavioral, and cognitive skills are necessary for the students with disabilities to derive meaning from this activity?

2. Which students have known weaknesses in any of these skills or concepts?

3. How can I provide additional support in these areas of weakness so that students with learning disabilities can focus on the conceptual task in the activity? (Karp & Howell, 2004, p. 119)

Each phase of the lesson evokes specific planning considerations for students with disabilities. Some strategies apply throughout a lesson. The following discussion is not exhaustive, but it provides specific suggestions for offering support to students throughout the lesson while you maintain the challenge.

1. Structure the environment.

   • *Centralize attention.* Move the student close to the board or teacher. Face students when you speak to them, and use gestures. Where possible, remove competing stimuli.

   • *Avoid confusion.* Word directions carefully, and ask the student to repeat them. Give one direction at a time. Use the same language for consistency. For example, when teaching decimals, talk about base-ten materials as ones, tenths, and hundredths rather than interchanging with names such as "flats," "rods," and "cubes," which emphasize shape rather than value.

   • *Create smooth transitions.* Ensure that transitions between activities have clear directions and that there are limited chances to get "off task."

2. Identify and remove potential barriers.

   • *Find ways to help students remember.* Recognize that memory is often not a strong suit for students with disabilities, and therefore develop mnemonics (memory aids) for familiar steps or write directions that can be referred to throughout the lesson. For example, **STAR** is a mnemonic for problem solving: **S**earch the word problem for important information; **T**ranslate the words into models, pictures, or symbols; **A**nswer the problem; **R**eview your solution for reasonableness (Gagnon & Maccini, 2001).

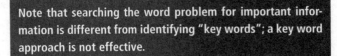

Teaching Tip

Note that searching the word problem for important information is different from identifying "key words"; a key word approach is not effective.

   • *Provide vocabulary and concept support.* Give explicit attention to vocabulary and symbols throughout the lesson. Preview essential terms and related prior knowledge/concepts, create a "math wall" of words and symbols to provide visual cues, and connect symbols to their precise meanings.

   • *Use "friendly" numbers.* Instead of using $6.13, use $6.00 to emphasize conceptual understanding rather than mixing computation and conceptual goals. Incorporate this technique when computation and operation skills are *not* the lesson objective.

   • *Vary the task size.* Students with learning disabilities can become frustrated by the enormity of the task. One way to address this problem is to assign students with disabilities fewer problems to solve.

   • *Adjust the visual display.* Design assessments and tasks so that there is not too much on a single page. The density of words, illustrations, and numbers on a page can be overwhelming for students with disabilities. Find ways to put only one problem on a page, increase the font size, or reduce the visual display. Be sure the visual displays support the meaning of the problem (rather than just unrelated clip art).

3. Provide clarity.

   • *Reiterate the time frame.* Give students additional reminders about the time left for exploring materials, completing tasks, or finishing assessments. This helps students with time management.

- *Ask students to share their thinking.* Use the think-aloud method or think–pair–share strategy.

- *Emphasize connections.* Provide concrete representations, pictorial representations, and numerical representations. Have students connect them through carefully phrased questions. Also, connect visuals, meanings, and words. For example, in teaching part–part and part–whole ratios, you can bring a group of eight students to the front of the class, placing part of the group (e.g., those wearing red) to the left and the other part (e.g., those not wearing red) to the right. Point out the part–part (red–not red) relationship and part–whole (red–total) relationship with gestures as you ask students to explain how the following symbols connect to the situation: 5:3, 3 to 8, $\frac{3}{5}$, 5:8, and $\frac{5}{8}$.

- *Adapt delivery modes.* Incorporate a variety of materials, images, examples, and models for visual learners. Some students may need to have the problem or assessment read to them or generated with voice creation software. Provide written instructions in addition to oral instructions.

- *Emphasize the relevant points.* Some students with disabilities may inappropriately focus on the color of a cube instead of the quantity of cubes.

- *Use methods for organizing written work.* Provide tools and templates so that students can focus on the mathematics rather than on the creation of a table or chart. Also use graphic organizers, picture-based models, and paper with columns or grids.

- *Provide examples and non-examples.* Give examples of dilations of triangles and triangles that are not dilations, or situations that are functions and situations that are not. Help students focus on the characteristics that differentiate the examples from the non-examples.

4. Consider alternative assessments.

- *Propose alternative products.* Provide options for how to demonstrate understanding (e.g., a verbal response that is written by someone else, voice-recorded, or modeled with a manipulative). Use voice recognition software or word prediction software that can generate a whole menu of word choices when students type a few letters.

- *Encourage self-monitoring and self-assessment.* Students with learning disabilities often are not good at self-reflection. Asking them to review an assignment or assessment to explain what was difficult and what they think they got right can help them be more independent and take greater responsibility for their learning.

- *Consider feedback charts.* Help students monitor their growth by charting progress over time.

5. Emphasize practice and summary.

- *Help students bring ideas together.* Initially, create study guides that summarize the key mathematics concepts and support students as they review key concepts. Then have students work toward independence by having them develop study guides by identifying, summarizing, and coordinating the big ideas.

- *Provide extra practice.* Use carefully selected problems (not a large number) and allow the use of familiar physical models.

Not all of these strategies will apply to every lesson and to every student with special needs, but as you are thinking about a particular lesson and certain students in your class, you will find that many of these will apply and will allow your students to engage in the task and accomplish the learning goals of the lesson.

◆ Implementing Interventions

NCTM (2007) has gathered a set of effective, research-based approaches for teaching students with difficulties in mathematics (e.g., students needing interventions in tier 2 or tier 3 of a support system such as RtI), highlighting the use of several key strategies that are also suggested by Gersten, Beckmann, Clarke, Foegen, Marsh, Star, and Witzel (2009). These strategies include systematic and explicit instruction, think-alouds, concrete and visual representations of problems, peer-assisted learning activities, and formative assessment data provided to students and teachers. These interventions, proven to be effective for students with disabilities, may represent principles quite different from those at tier 1. The strategies described here are interventions for use with the small subset of students for whom the initial core instruction has been ineffective.

Explicit Strategy Instruction

Explicit instruction is often characterized by highly structured, teacher-led instruction on a specific strategy. When engaging in this explicit instruction, you do not merely model the strategy and have students practice it; instead, you try to illuminate your decision making—a process that may be troublesome for these particular learners. In this instructional strategy, after you assess the students so that you know what to model, you use a tightly scripted sequence that goes from modeling to prompting students through the model to practice. Your instruction is highly organized in a step-by-step format and involves teacher-led explanations of concepts and strategies, including the critical connection building and meaning making that help learners relate new knowledge to concepts they know. Let's look at a classroom teacher who is using explicit instruction.

As you enter Mr. Logan's classroom, you see a small group of students who have struggled with understanding volume and being able to calculate volume with measurements of length, width, and height. They are seated at a table listening to the teacher's detailed explanation and watching his demonstration. The students are using manipulatives, as prescribed by Mr. Logan, and moving through carefully selected tasks. He tells the students to take out the open box (rectangular prism) and asks them how they could find a way to fill the box to see how much it holds. As he begins, Mr. Logan asks, "Is *volume* a word you know?" He suggests that they first think about the bottom of the box and how that might help. The students use the available cubes to cover the bottom of the box. Then, to make sure they don't allow for any gaps or overlaps in the pieces, he asks them to talk about their reasoning process with the question, "What are some things you need to keep in mind as you place the cubes?" Mr. Logan writes their responses to how many cubes cover the bottom of the box on the adjacent board as $5 \times 12 = 60$. He then shows a box with cubes covering the bottom layer, but with gaps between the cubes. He says, "I have only 50 cubes covering the bottom. Can that be correct, too?" Then, he asks them to estimate how many layers of cubes they might need to fill the box and records their responses. The students take turns answering these questions out loud. During the lesson, Mr. Logan frequently stops the group, interjects points of clarification, and directly highlights critical components of the task. For example, he asks, "Do you need to fill each layer with cubes to find the volume of the box? Is there another way to calculate the number of cubes that will be needed to fill the box?" Vocabulary words, such as *volume, base, height,* and *area,* are written and in some cases illustrated on the "math word wall" nearby, and the definitions of these terms are reviewed and reinforced throughout the lesson. Mr. Logan then turns the box so that a different side forms the base and asks, "What will the volume be now?"

He discusses with students what are now the base and height, helping students see that any two of the three dimensions can be used to form the base. At the completion of the lesson, students are given several similar pictures of rectangular solids (semi-concrete) and several examples with just the dimensions given (abstract) as independent practice.

A number of aspects of explicit instruction can be seen in Mr. Logan's approach to teaching concepts related to volume. He employs a teacher-directed teaching format, carefully describes the use of manipulatives, and incorporates a model–prompt–practice sequence. This sequence starts with verbal instructions and careful demonstrations with concrete models, followed by prompting, questioning, semi-concrete models, and more abstract thinking with formulas, then independent practice. Note that he also explicitly presents a non-example when he places the cubes in the bottom of the box in a haphazard way leaving gaps. The students are deriving mathematical knowledge from the teacher's oral, written, and visual clues.

As students with disabilities solve problems, explicit strategy instruction can help guide them in carrying out tasks. First ask the students to read and restate the problem, draw a picture, develop a plan by linking this problem to previous problems, write the problem in a mathematical sentence, break the problem into smaller pieces, carry out operations, and check answers with a calculator or other appropriate tools. These self-instructive prompts, or self-questions, structure the entire learning process from beginning to end. Unlike during more open-ended inquiry-based instruction, the teacher models these steps and explains the components with terminology that is easily understood by students with disabilities—students who did not discover these concepts independently through initial tier 1 or tier 2 activities. Yet, consistent with what we know about how all students learn, students are still developing an understanding of the meaning of volume and engaged in problem solving (not just in skill development).

Concrete models can support explicit strategy instruction for the students in your class with disabilities. For example, consider a lesson on multiplication of fractions using the example of $\frac{2}{3} \times \frac{1}{4}$. Create squares on two transparencies partitioned and shaded in the two different fractional amounts. You might say, "Watch me. Now find the square that shows two-thirds and the one that shows one-fourth." Then, the teacher will show the two squares aligned and layered (with one square turned in a 90-degree rotation) so that students are able to see what one-fourth of two-thirds looks like. In contrast, a teacher with a more inquiry-oriented approach might say, "Use a rectangle (on your grid paper) to show me a representation for one-fourth times two-thirds." Although initially more structured, the use of concrete models will provide access to the concept of multiplication of fractions, and will also lead to generalizing a procedure for finding the product.

There are a number of possible advantages to using explicit strategy instruction for students with disabilities. First, this approach helps you make more explicit for these students the covert thinking strategies that others use in mathematical problem solving. Second, although these students hear classmates' thinking strategies in the *After* component of each lesson, they frequently cannot keep up with the rapid pace of the sharing. Without extra time to reprocess the conversation, students with disabilities may not have access to these strategies. Finally, more explicit approaches are also less dependent on the students' ability to draw ideas from past experience or to operate in a self-directed manner.

Explicit strategy instruction can also have distinct disadvantages for students with disabilities. Some aspects of this approach rely on memorizing, which can be one of their weakest skills. Taking a known weakness and building a learning strategy around it is not productive. There is also the concern that highly teacher-controlled approaches promote long-term dependency on teacher assistance. This is of particular concern for students with disabilities because many are described as passive learners.

Students learn what they have the opportunity to practice. Students who are never given opportunities to engage in self-directed learning (based on the assumption that this is not an area of strength) will be deprived of the opportunity to develop skills in this area. In fact, the best explicit instruction is scaffolded, meaning it moves from a highly structured, single-strategy approach toward multiple models, including examples and nonexamples. It also includes immediate error correction followed by the fading of prompts to help students move to independence. Explicit instruction, to be effective, must include making mathematical relationships explicit (so that students make connections to other mathematical ideas rather than only learning that day's mathematics). Because making connections is a major component in how students learn, it must be central to instructional strategies for students with disabilities.

Concrete, Semi-Concrete, Abstract (CSA)

The CSA (concrete, semi-concrete, abstract) intervention has been used in mathematics education in a variety of forms for years (Heddens, 1964; Witzel, 2005). Based on the reasoning theory of Bruner (1966), this model reflects a sequence that begins with an instructional focus on concrete representations (manipulative materials) and tools, then moves to semi-concrete representations (drawings or pictures) and abstraction (using only numerals or mentally solving problems) over time. Built into this approach is the return to visual models and concrete representations as students need them or as they begin to explore new concepts or extensions of concepts learned previously. As students share reasoning that shows they are beginning to understand the mathematical concept, there can be a shift to semi-concrete representations. This is not to say that CSA is a rigid approach that moves to abstraction only after the other phases. Instead, it is essential that there be parallel modeling of number symbols throughout this approach to explicitly relate concrete models and visual representations to their corresponding values. Think back to the vignette in which Mr. Logan is teaching volume and uses cubes to fill a box, then semi-concrete drawings of rectangular prisms and formulas to link these ideas into a cohesive instructional sequence.

CSA also includes modeling the mental conversations that go on in your mind as you help students articulate their own thinking. Again, as you articulate your thought processes using an appropriate model for a student, your choice of a reasoning strategy and model should be based on evidence from the student's performance on targeted assessments. In the last component of CSA, students are capable of working with abstract aspects of the concepts without an emphasis on concrete or semi-concrete (drawings) images.

Peer-Assisted Learning

Students with special needs also benefit from other students' modeling and support (Fuchs, Fuchs, Yazdian, & Powell, 2002). The basic notion is that students learn best when they are placed in the role of an apprentice working with a more skilled peer or "expert." Although the peer-assisted learning approach shares some of the characteristics of the explicit strategy instruction model, it is different because knowledge is presented on an "as-needed" basis as opposed to a predetermined sequence. The students can be paired with older students or peers who have a more sophisticated understandings of a concept. At other times, tutors and tutees can reverse roles during the tasks. Having students with disabilities "teach" others is an important part of the learning process, so giving students with special needs a chance to explain concepts to another student is valuable.

Think-Alouds

When you use "think-aloud" as an instructional strategy, you demonstrate the steps to accomplish a task while verbalizing the thinking process and reasoning that accompany the steps. Remember, don't start with where your thinking is—assess and start where the student's thinking is. The student follows this instruction by imitating your process of "talking through" a solution on a different, but parallel, task. This is similar to the model in which "expert" learners share strategies with "novice" learners.

Consider a problem in which sixth-grade students are given the task of determining how much a hamburger costs given that 13 hamburgers cost $78.00. The think-aloud strategy would involve talking through the steps and identifying the reasons for each step as you progress through the task. As you write down the important information, you might state, "I need to find how much one hamburger would cost, the *rate*. How can I use what we have to find that amount? I know I have to use the total cost, but what other information do I need?" All of this dialogue occurs before an operation is finalized. What are other alternatives in carrying out the task? When you use this metacognitive strategy, try to talk about and model possible approaches in an effort to make your invisible thinking processes visible to students.

Although you can choose any of these strategies as needed, your goal is always to work toward a high level of student responsibility for learning. Movement to higher levels of understanding of content can be likened to the need to move to a higher level on a hill. For some, formal stair steps with support along the way are necessary (explicit strategy instruction); for others, ramps with encouragement at the top of the hill will work (peer-assisted learning). Other students can find a path up the hill on their own with some guidance from visual representations (CSA approach). All people can relate to the need to have different support during different times of their lives or under different circumstances, and it is no different for students with special needs (Table 6.2). Yet, they must eventually learn to create a path to new learning on their own, as that is what will be required in the real world after formal education ends. Leaving students knowing only how to climb steps with support and face hills with constant assistance and encouragement from others will not help them attain their life goals.

⬢ Adapting for Students with Moderate or Severe Disabilities

Students with moderate or severe disabilities often need extensive modifications and individualized support to learn mathematics. This population of students may include those with severe autism, sensory disorders, limitations affecting movement, cerebral palsy, processing disorders such as intellectual disabilities, and combinations of multiple disabilities.

Originally, the curriculum for students with severe disabilities was called "functional," in that it often focused on life-skills such as managing money, telling time, using a calculator, measuring, and matching numbers to complete such tasks as entering a telephone number or identifying a house number. Now, directives and assessments have broadened the curriculum to address the content strands that were specifically delineated by grade level in the *Common Core State Standards* (CCSSO, 2010).

At a basic level, students work on developing number sense, use measuring tools, compare graphs, explore place-value concepts (sometimes linked to money use), use the number line, and compare quantities. When possible, the content should be connected to life skills and features of jobs—shopping skills and activities in which food is prepared are both options for mathematical problem solving. At other times, you can just link mathematical learning objectives to everyday events in a practical way. For example, when the operation of division is studied, figuring how candy can be equally shared at Halloween or how game cards can be dealt would be appropriate. Students can also undertake a small project such as constructing a box to store different items as a way to explore shapes and measurements.

Do not believe that all basic facts must be mastered before students with moderate or severe disabilities can move forward in the curriculum; students can learn geometric or

Table 6.2 Common Stumbling Blocks for Students with Disabilities

Stumbling Block	What Will I Notice?	What Should I Do?
Student has trouble forming mental representations of mathematical concepts.	• Can't interpret a number line for fractions or for integers • Has difficulty going from a story about a garden plot (to set up a problem on finding area) to graph or dot paper	• Explicitly teach the representation—for example, exactly how to draw a diagram (e.g., partition the number line). • Use larger versions of the representation (e.g., number line) so that students can move to or interact with the model.
Student has difficulty accessing numeric meanings from symbols (issues with number sense).	• Has difficulty with the use of variables • Does not understand the meaning of the equal sign • Can't interpret whether an answer is reasonable	• Explicitly teach multiple ways of representing an unknown, showing the variations at exactly the same time (e.g., containers as models that hold an unknown quantity, algebra tiles). • Use multiple representations for a problem to show how the number would look with more concrete visuals.
Student is challenged to keep numbers and information in working memory.	• Gets confused when other students share multiple strategies during the *After* portion of the lesson • Forgets how to start the problem-solving process • Has difficulty keeping track of the meaning of the values in proportional situations (what varies with what)	• Record (in writing) ideas of other students during discussions. • Incorporate a chart that lists the main steps in problem solving as an independent guide, or make bookmarks with questions the student can ask himself or herself as self-prompts. • Use word labels with each numeric value.
Student lacks organizational skills and the ability to self-regulate.	• Loses track of steps in a process • Writes computations in a way that is random and hard to follow	• Use routines as often as possible, or provide self-monitoring checklists to prompt steps along the way. • Use graph paper to record problems or numbers. • Create "math word walls" for reference.
Student misapplies rules or overgeneralizes.	• Applies rules such as "always add a zero when you multiply by ten" too literally, resulting in errors such as $2.5 \times 10 = 2.50$ • Mechanically applies algorithms—for example, adds $\frac{7}{8} + \frac{12}{13} =$ and gives the answer $\frac{19}{21}$	• Always give examples as well as counterexamples to show how and when "rules" should be used and when they should not. • Tie all rules into conceptual understanding; don't emphasize memorizing rote procedures or practices.

measuring concepts without having mastered all basic facts. Geometry for students with moderate or severe disabilities is more than merely identifying shapes; it is critical for being oriented in the real world through interpreting maps of the local area. Students who learn to count bus stops and judge time can be helped to navigate their world successfully.

Table 6.3 offers ideas across the curriculum that are appropriate for teaching students with moderate or severe disabilities.

Planning for Students Who Are Mathematically Gifted

Students who are mathematically gifted include those who have a high level of ability or interest. Some may be gifted with an intuitive knowledge of mathematical concepts, whereas others have a passion for the subject even though they may have to work hard to learn it. Many students' giftedness becomes apparent to parents and teachers when they grasp and articulate mathematics concepts at an age earlier than expected. They are often found to make

Table 6.3 Activities for Students with Moderate or Severe Disabilities

Content Area	Activity
Number and operations	• Calculate the cost of field trips. • Create a list of supplies that need to be ordered for the classroom or a particular event and calculate cost. • Calculate the number of calories in a given meal.
Algebra	• Show an allowance or wage on a chart to demonstrate growth over time. • Write an equation to show how much the student will earn in a month or year. • Calculate the slope of a wheelchair ramp or driveway.
Geometry	• Use spatial relationships to identify a short path between two locations on a map. • Tessellate several figures to show how a variety of shapes fit together. Using tangrams to fill a space will also develop important workplace skills, such as packing boxes or organizing supplies on shelves.
Measurement	• Fill differently shaped items with water, sand, or rice to assess volume, ordering the vessels from least to most. • Take body temperature and use an enlarged thermometer to show comparison with outside temperatures. • Use area to calculate the amount of paint needed to cover the walls or ceiling of the classroom. • Use a map to estimate the amount of time it would take to travel to a known location.
Data analysis and probability	• Survey students on favorite games (electronic or other), and use the top five as choices for the class. Make a graph to represent and compare the results. • Examine the outside temperatures for the past week and discuss the probability that the temperatures the next day will be within a particular range.

connections between topics of study easily and frequently are unable to explain how they got an answer (Rotigel & Fellow, 2005). Many teachers have a keen ability to spot talent when they note students who have strong number sense or visual–spatial sense (Gavin & Sheffield, 2010). Note that these teachers are not pointing to students who are fast and speedy with their basic facts, but to those who have the ability to reason and make sense of mathematics.

Do not wait for students to demonstrate their mathematical talent; instead, develop it through a challenging set of tasks and inquiry-based instruction (VanTassel-Baska & Brown, 2007). Generally, as previously described in the RtI model, high-quality core instruction is able to respond to the varying needs of diverse learners, including the talented and gifted. Yet for some of your gifted students, the core instruction proves not to be enough of a challenge. The curriculum for these advanced learners should be adapted to consider level, complexity, breadth, depth, and pace (Assouline & Lupkowski-Shoplik, 2011; Renzulli, Gubbins, McMillen, Eckert, & Little, 2009; Saul, Assouline, & Sheffield, 2010).

There are four basic categories for adapting mathematics content for gifted mathematics students: *acceleration, enrichment* (depth), *sophistication* (complexity), and *novelty* (Gallagher & Gallagher, 1994; Ravenna, 2008). In each category, your students should apply rather than just acquire information. The emphasis on implementing and extending ideas must overshadow the mental collection of facts and concepts.

Acceleration

Acceleration recognizes that your students may already understand the mathematics content that you plan to teach. Some teachers use "curriculum compacting" (Reis & Renzulli, 2005) to give a short overview of the content and assess students' ability to respond to mathematics tasks that would demonstrate their proficiency. Another option is to reduce the amount of time these students spend on aspects of the topic or moving to more advanced content at the next grade level or beyond. Allowing students to increase the pace of their own learning can give them access to curriculum different from their grade level while demanding more independent study. However, moving students to higher mathematics (by moving them up a grade, for example) will not succeed in engaging them as learners if the instruction is still at a slow pace. Research reveals that when gifted students are accelerated through the curriculum, they become more likely to explore STEM (science, technology, engineering, and mathematics) fields (Sadler & Tai, 2007).

Enrichment

Enrichment activities go beyond the topic of study to content that is not specifically a part of your grade-level curriculum but is an extension of the original mathematical tasks. For example, while studying decimal place value concepts and powers of 10, mathematically gifted students can stretch their knowledge to study other bases, such as base five, base eight, and base twelve. This provides an extended view of how our base-ten numeration system fits within the broader system. Other times, the format of enrichment can involve studying the same topic as the rest of the class while differing on the means and outcomes of the work. Examples include group investigations, solving real problems in the community, writing letters to outside audiences, and identifying applications of the mathematics learned.

Sophistication

Another strategy is to increase the sophistication of a topic by raising the level of complexity or pursuing greater depth of content, possibly outside the regular curriculum or by connecting mathematics to other subject areas. Frequently, gifted students explore topics similar to those of their classmates but focus on higher-level thinking or on more complex or abstract ideas. This can mean exploring a larger set of ideas in which a mathematics topic exists. For example, while studying a unit on geometry, mathematically gifted students can deepen their knowledge to study fractals and how that topic links to geographic maps and fern fronds. In the algebra strand, when studying sequences or patterns of numbers, mathematically gifted students can learn about Fibonacci sequences and their appearances in the natural world in such things as shells and plant life.

Novelty

Novelty introduces completely different material from the regular curriculum and frequently occurs in after-school clubs, out-of-class projects, or collaborative school experiences. In collaborative experiences, students from a variety of grades and classes may volunteer for special mathematics projects, with a classroom teacher, principal, or resource teacher taking the lead. The novelty category includes having students explore topics that are within their developmental grasp but outside the curriculum. For example, students may look at mathematical "tricks," using binary numbers to guess classmates' birthdays or a logic matrix to solve reasoning problems. They may also explore topics such as topology through the creation of paper "knots" called flexagons (see www.flexagon.net) or conduct a large-scale investigation of the amount of food thrown away at lunchtime. A group might create tetrahedron kites or find mathematics in art, such as locating the golden rectangle in paintings. Another aspect of the novelty approach provides different options for students to culminate with performances of their understanding, such as demonstrating their knowledge through inventions, experiments, simulations, dramatizations, visual displays, and oral presentations.

Strategies to Avoid

There are a number of ineffective approaches for gifted students that find their way into classrooms. Five common ones are these:

1. *Assigning more of the same work.* This is the least appropriate way to respond to mathematically gifted students and the most likely to result in students hiding their ability. The approach is described by Persis Herold as "all scales and no music" (quoted in Tobias, 1995, p. 168).

2. *Giving free time to early finishers.* Although students find this rewarding, it does not maximize their intellectual growth and can lead to hurrying to finish a task.

3. *Assigning gifted students to help struggling learners.* Routinely assigning gifted students to teach students who are not meeting expectations that the gifted students have mastered does not stimulate their intellectual growth and can place them in a socially uncomfortable and/or undesirable situation. Consistently using this approach puts mathematically talented students in a constant position of tutoring rather than allowing them to create deeper and more complex levels of understanding.

4. *Providing additional opportunities.* Unfortunately, generalized gifted programs are often unrelated to the regular mathematics curriculum (Assouline & Lupkowski-Shoplik, 2011). While it can benefit students, add-on experiences are not enough. Gifted students need adaptations to the instruction in their mathematics classroom. Learners with a high level of ability shouldn't get one-stop shopping in a gifted program that focuses on all academic subjects; they need individual attention to develop depth and a more complex understanding of mathematics.

5. *Providing independent enrichment on the computer.* This practice often does not engage students with mathematics in a way that will enhance conceptual understanding and support their ability to justify their thinking to others. There are excellent enrichment opportunities on the Internet—such as the activities on NCTM's Illuminations website (http://illuminations.nctm.org)—but too often computer time becomes time to do games that simply practice skills.

Sheffield (1999, p. 46) writes that gifted students should be introduced to the "joys and frustrations of thinking deeply about a wide range of original, open-ended, or complex problems that encourage them to respond creatively in ways that are original, fluent, flexible, and elegant." Accommodations, modifications, and interventions for mathematically gifted students must strive for this goal.

Stop and Reflect

How is equity in the classroom different from teaching all students equitably? ■

7

Collaborating with Families, Community, and Principals

With students, parents and teachers all on the same page and working together for shared goals, we can ensure that students make progress each year and graduate from school prepared to succeed in college and in a modern workforce.

CCSSO (2010)

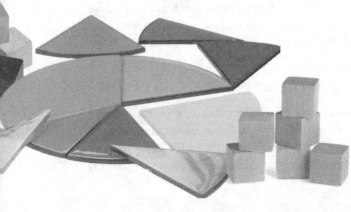

 Parental and Community Support for Mathematics

Teaching mathematics developmentally, addressing the increased content demands articulated in the *Common Core State Standards* initiative (CCSSO, 2010), and ensuring that students are mathematically proficient requires *everyone's* commitment. And, numerous studies have found a positive relationship between the level of parental involvement and their child's achievement in school (e.g., Aspiazu, Bauer, & Spillett, 1998; Henderson, Mapp, Jordan, Orozco, Averett, Donnelly, Buttram, Wood, Fowler, & Myers, 2002). We often hear educators make statements such as, "You must have the principal's support" and "You need to get parents on board," and we nod our heads in agreement. But knowing what this support looks like and recognizing how to get the support are less clear. In this chapter, we discuss ideas for developing a collaborative community that understands and is able to support high-quality mathematics teaching and learning for every student.

Parents know the importance of mathematics for their child's future. They participate in their child's learning by supporting homework, attending back-to-school nights or PTA meetings, and meeting with teachers, even if they may recall unpleasant experiences or difficulties with school mathematics from their own schooling. Understanding that memories of mathematics classes are not always pleasant for parents and appreciating parental support prepare us to suitably identify for parents the mathematics goals that students should be experiencing in the twenty-first century. Communication with parents is key to encouraging their support and involves using one-way, two-way, and three-way communication strategies (Figure 7.1).

Figure 7.1 Ways to communicate with families.

One-way communication strategies	Letters sharing the goals of a unit	Websites where resources and curriculum information are posted	Newsletters
Two-way communication strategies	Log of student work (signed or commented on by parent)	PTA meetings/open houses	One-on-one meetings, class or home visits
Three (or more)–way communication strategies	Family math nights	Conferences (with parent and child)	Log/journal of student learning with input from student, parent, and teacher

◆ Communicating Mathematics Goals

Every year, parents need opportunities to get information directly from the school leaders and teachers about their child's mathematics program, including the kind of instruction that might differ from what they experienced in their own schooling. For example, even if your school has been engaged in implementing a mathematics program for a decade that reflects the NCTM *Principles and Standards for School Mathematics* and now the *Common Core State Standards*, the program will still be new to the parents of your students.

Changes to the mathematics curriculum—new textbooks, new technologies, new philosophies—are all perfect reasons for communicating with parents. This interaction is one of the most important components of successfully implementing a standards-based mathematics curriculum (Bay, Reys, & Reys, 1999). Without such opportunities for communication, parents may draw their own conclusions about the effectiveness of the mathematics curriculum, develop frustrations and negative opinions about what is happening in their child's classroom or school, and communicate this apprehension to other parents. Table 7.1 highlights questions parents commonly ask about standards-based mathematics programs.

Providing a forum for parents around mathematics highlights the importance of the subject and gives parents confidence that your school is a great place for preparing their children for middle school and beyond. Be proactive! Don't wait for concerns or questions to percolate. Some early action strategies include engaging parents in family and community math nights, positive homework practices, and parent-coaching sessions, as well as sharing where to find mathematics-related resources for their children (e.g., websites and manipulatives). Let's discuss each.

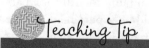 *Teaching Tip*

"Welcome Back" or "Family Math" nights are a great time to have parent–child teams experience working together on mathematics tasks.

Family and Community Math Nights

There are many ways to conduct a family or community mathematics event, such as including a math component in a back-to-school night, discussing it in a PTA meeting, or hosting a showcase for a new mathematics program. Critical

Table 7.1   Categories of Parent Questions Related to Standards-Based Mathematics

Category	Types of Questions
Pedagogy	• Why isn't the teacher teaching? (And what is the point of reinventing the wheel?) • Are students doing their own work when they are in groups? Is my child having to do the work of students who don't understand the work? • Why is there so much reading and writing in math class? • Why is my child struggling more than in previous years?
Content	• Is my child learning the basic skills? • Why is my child learning different ways (than I learned) for doing the operations? • Will my child be on track for Algebra I in eighth grade? ninth grade? • Where are the math topics I am used to seeing and why are there topics I never learned? • Is my child learning mathematics or just doing activities?
Evidence	• Is there any evidence that this approach or curriculum is effective? • Will my child do better on state/national standardized tests with this new approach? • Will this prepare my child for middle school, high school, college, and beyond?
Understanding	• Why is mathematics teaching changing? • How can I help my child [with their homework; to be successful]? • Where can I learn more about the *Common Core State Standards*?

Source: Adapted from Bay-Williams, J. M., & Meyer, M. R. (2003). What Parents Want to Know about Standards-Based Mathematics Curricula. *Principal Leadership, 3*(7), 54–60. Copyright 2003 National Association of Secondary School Principals. For more information on NASSP products and services to promote excellence in middle level and high school leadership, visit www.nassp.org.

to this plan is providing opportunities for parents to be learners of mathematics so that they can experience what it means to *do mathematics* (just like their children).

When choosing mathematical tasks to use with parents, be sure the tasks focus on content that really matters to them and relates to what they know is a part of the grades 6–8 curriculum, such as ratios and proportions or algebraic thinking. Tasks throughout this book are ideal for a math night. Figure 7.2 contrasts two sixth-grade problems for learning about ratio—one is straightforward and lends to a procedural approach (set up a proportion and find the missing value) and one that is designed for a teaching-through-problem-solving experience (explore and determine a way to compare ratios).

Stop and Reflect

What distinctions do you notice between the two tasks? What is valued as "doing mathematics" in both of the problems? ■

The contrasting ratio problems are ideal for discussing with parents what it means to do mathematics because they (1) offer a familiar context, (2) require minimal prior knowledge, (3) have multiple solution strategies, (4) can involve manipulatives (color tiles and/or grid paper), and (5) have the potential to connect the mathematical ideas of fractions, ratios, rates, and proportions, as well as algebra. The potential each of these problems has to support and challenge children in making sense of mathematics should be made explicit during a discussion with parents.

Figure 7.2 Problems to explore at a parent or community night.

Problem 1: For every point Angie scores, Erica scores 4. What is the ratio? If Erica scored 20 points, how many did Angie score?

Problem 2: You are painting your room and want a blue–green shade but are not sure which choice to make from the many colors offered. You want the one that will turn out the bluest of the following choices. Which one should you pick?

Ratio of blue to green is 9:4.   Ratio of blue to green is 3:2.

Ratio of blue to green is 15:6.   Ratio of blue to green is 12:5.

Ask parents to solve the first problem and share their strategies and answers. Repeat for the second problem. Be sure to ask for multiple approaches. Then, ask participants to consider the learning opportunities in the two contrasting tasks. Ask questions such as these:

- What skills are being developed in each problem?
- Which problem gives more opportunity to make connections between mathematics and the real world?
- Which task would your child be more motivated to solve? Why?

Help parents identify the depth of the mathematics in the teaching-through-problem-solving task. Remind parents that in grades 6 through 8, students are building important foundations for algebraic thinking—looking for patterns, reasoning, and generalizing. Help parents see these aspects in this ratio problem. Share the *Common Core State Standards* and/or the NCTM standards (in parent-friendly language), and focus on the goal of having students become mathematically proficient, as described in those standards. Ask parents, "Where do you see these proficiencies being supported in the two tasks we did?"

Revisit the first problem in Figure 7.2 and consider how it *could* be a problem in which reasoning is involved (e.g., using different approaches, creating visuals to illustrate the relationships among the values). Invite parents to see whether they can solve the following proportion in a way *other than* the cross-product method or if they can solve it in more than one way.

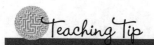 **Teaching Tip**

Provide copies of the appropriate *Common Core State Standards* Introduction and Overview pages (the first two pages for each grade), and allow parents time to think about each "Critical Area."

Alicia is reading a book. She read 40 pages in 1 hour. If she continues to read at that rate, how long will it take her to read the 200-page book?

Parents may recall their own confusion in how to set up a proportion—for example, not knowing where to put the *x* or not knowing if they should cross multiply. Reasoning through problems like this and hearing other ways to reason about the problems help students understand proportional situations, and then they are able to understand and use cross multiplication when needed, or reasoning strategies when such strategies are more meaningful.

Address any or all of the questions in Table 7.1 that apply to your setting. One way to do this is to have parents write their questions on note cards and collect them so you can identify common questions and decide the order in which to discuss each one. The sections that follow provide possible responses to questions that parents (or community members) commonly ask.

Pedagogy

When parents ask questions that point to their belief that mathematics is best learned through direct instruction—just as they learned it—remind them of the experience they had in *doing* mathematics with the ratio problems. Point to the difference between being *shown* how to do something (e.g., this is how you divide fractions, now practice this) and *developing* an understanding of something (e.g., what it means to divide fractions, and how you might solve this division problem). Point out that skills are (still) important, and that students benefit by generating their own procedures and connecting those procedures to a solid understanding. Explicitly promote the fact that a developmental approach to learning mathematics provides the means for students to (1) use prior knowledge, (2) make connections, (3) use alternative strategies and reasoning, (4) apply mathematical ideas to new situations, and (5) develop positive dispositions about being able to do mathematics.

Role of the Teacher

Similarly, address the role of the teacher as *organizer* (organizes a worthwhile mathematical task), *facilitator* (facilitates student interaction), and *questioner* (asks questions to help students make connections or to deepen their understanding). Remind parents that just because the teacher is not *telling* their child what to do does not mean that the teacher is not teaching. The teacher is orchestrating the class so that each student develops the ability to solve problems independently.

Cooperative Groups

Parents may also wonder about how frequently their child works in cooperative groups because this may differ from their own mathematics learning experiences. Help parents see the role of others in their learning as they solved the problems and as they heard solutions from those who were working at other tables. Connect that experience to the value of cooperative learning. You can do this in a variety of ways:

1. *Share the one-page parent overview from the NCTM Families Ask department titled "Cooperative Learning" (Coates & Mayfield, 2009).* "Families Ask," a feature posted on the NCTM website at www.nctm.org/resources/content.aspx?id=9292 and published in *Mathematics Teaching in the Middle School*, provides over 20 excellent, written-for-parents discussions on a range of topics relevant to middle school.

2. *Include a feature in your parent newsletter.* Early in the year, you can feature cooperative learning and address its importance across content areas. In mathematics, this can include the following benefits: hearing different strategies, building meaning, designing solution strategies, and justifying approaches—all of which are essential to building a strong understanding of mathematics and important life skills.

3. *Send home letters introducing math units of study.* If you are about to teach a unit on functions, a letter can help parents know the important aspects of the content. This is a great time to mention that students will work in groups so that they can see different ways to illustrate functions with tables, graphs, equations, and situations.

4. *Do a cooperative learning mathematics activity at a family math night or back-to-school event.* Use a task that lends itself to assigning roles to different members of the group and won't take long to solve. Have parents work with two to three others to solve the task.

Parents may initially worry that students working in groups are simply copying from other students and not learning. Share strategies you use to build in individual accountability and shared responsibility. For example, teachers

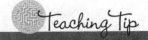

Being proactive about communicating the *benefits* of cooperative learning, as well as how you build in *individual accountability* and *shared responsibility,* will go a long way toward converting parent concerns into parent support.

may ask each student to record explanations in his or her notebook. At other times, you may assign specific roles to each member of the group.

Use of Technology

Parents may be avid users of technology yet still have concerns about their child's use of calculators and computers in middle school when they haven't yet mastered the basic facts or learned how to graph by hand. Even though research overwhelmingly finds that students using calculators achieve at least as much as those not using calculators, calculators are widely blamed for students' lack of reasoning and sense making. Reassure parents that students will learn to use calculators when it is appropriate. For example, students should notice that $x + 14 = 34$ can be solved by mentally thinking, "What number plus 14 is 34? 20," more quickly than it can be calculated on a calculator. Calculators support learning, and presenting examples to make this point is important. For example, consider sharing a measurement lesson (sixth grade) in which students are asked to measure the dimensions of boxes to the nearest centimeter to calculate surface area and volume. Without a calculator, such a lesson would get bogged down in calculations that take time and attention away from the goal of the lesson—measurement.

An important message to parents is that mastery of basic facts should *not* be a prerequisite to using a calculator. Instead, students (and teachers) should be making good decisions about whether a calculator supports or detracts from solving a particular problem (and learning the intended mathematics).

Practice and Problem Solving

Parents may also wonder why there are fewer skill/practice problems and more story problems in the curriculum. Effective mathematics learning environments are rich in language. Real mathematics involves more "word" problems and far fewer "naked number" skill problems. In contrast to when the parents went to school, skills are now less needed in the workplace because of available technology, but the importance of number sense, reasoning, and being able to solve real problems has increased. Because some students struggle with reading and/or writing, share strategies you use to help them understand and solve story problems (Figure 7.3).

Figure 7.3

Share with parents how you support reading and problem solving.

Reading Strategies for Mathematics Problems

- Read aloud (whole class)
- Read a math problem with a friend
- Find and write the question
- Draw a picture of the problem
- Act out the problem
- Use a graphic organizer (recording page with problem-solving prompts)
- Discuss math vocabulary
- Play math vocabulary games

Parents may worry when they see their child struggle with a single mathematics problem because they may believe that fast means successful. But faster isn't smarter. Cathy Seeley's book with this same title (2009) is a great read on this topic written for families, educators, and policy makers. Seeley offers 41 brief messages, many of which can address parent questions about mathematics (e.g., "A Math Message to Families: Helping Students Prepare for the Future," "Putting Calculators in their Place: The Role of Calculators and Computation in the Classroom," and "Do It in Your Head: The Power of Mental Math"). In terms of engaging students in productive struggle, explain that engaging students in productive struggle is one of the two most effective ways teachers can develop conceptual understanding in students (the other is making connections among mathematical ideas) (Bay-Williams, 2010; Hiebert & Grouws, 2007). Rather than presenting a series of simpler problems for students to practice, standards-based curricula characteristically focus on fewer tasks, each of which provides students with an opportunity for higher-level thinking, multiple strategy solutions, and more time focused on math learning.

Share the first Standard for Mathematical Practice (Figure 7.4), and ask the parents what they notice. Focus on the importance of *perseverance*. This is true in mathematics and in life. Reassure parents that some tasks take longer because of

Figure 7.4 Standard 1 from the Standards for Mathematical Practice.

> **1. Make sense of problems and persevere in solving them.**
> Mathematically proficient students start by explaining to themselves the meaning of a problem and looking for entry points to its solution. They analyze givens, constraints, relationships, and goals. They make conjectures about the form and meaning of the solution and plan a solution pathway rather than simply jumping into a solution attempt. They consider analogous problems, and try special cases and simpler forms of the original problem in order to gain insight into its solution. They monitor and evaluate their progress and change course if necessary. Older students might, depending on the context of the problem, transform algebraic expressions or change the viewing window on their graphing calculator to get the information they need. Mathematically proficient students can explain correspondences between equations, verbal descriptions, tables, and graphs or draw diagrams of important features and relationships, graph data, and search for regularity or trends. Younger students might rely on using concrete objects or pictures to help conceptualize and solve a problem. Mathematically proficient students check their answers to problems using a different method, and they continually ask themselves, "Does this make sense?" They can understand the approaches of others to solving complex problems and identify correspondences between different approaches.

Source: Page 6 of CCSSO (Council of Chief State School Officers), *Common Core State Standards.* Retrieved from http://corestandards.org. Copyright © 2010. National Governors Association Center for Best Practices and Council of Chief State School Officers. All rights reserved.

the nature of the tasks, not because their child lacks understanding. Mathematics is not nearly as much about speed and memorization as it is about being able to grapple with a novel problem, try various approaches from a variety of options, and finally reach an accurate answer.

Mathematics Content

A common concern of parents is that their children are not learning standard algorithms or the procedures they remember using when they were in middle school. You must address (at least) two points related to this critical issue. First, the skills that parents are looking for (e.g., invert and multiply for dividing fractions) are still in the curriculum—they just may look different because they are presented in a way based on understanding, not just memorization. Standard algorithms are still taught but they are taught *along with* alternative (or invented) strategies that build on students' number sense and reasoning. Let parents experience that both invented and standard algorithms are important in being mathematically proficient by inviting them to solve the following problems:

$$1399 + 547 = \underline{\hspace{1cm}} \qquad 5009 - 998 = \underline{\hspace{1cm}}$$

$$487 + 345 = \underline{\hspace{1cm}} + 355$$

Ask for volunteers to share the ways that they thought about the problems. For the subtraction problem, for example, the following might be shared:

5000 take away 1000 is 4000, then add the 9 and 2 back on to get 4011.

998 up to 1000 is 2, up to 5000 is 4002, and up 9 more is 4011.

5009 to 5000 is 9, then down to 1000 is 4000 more (4009), and then down to 998 is 2 more (4011).

These invented strategies, over numerous problems, reinforce place-value concepts and the relationship between addition and subtraction. Noticing that these values are both near

1000 helps to select a strategy. The standard algorithm for this problem is very messy, and one that frequently results in computational errors. The best choice for solving this problem is one of the ways described above. The key to procedural fluency is to first assess the values in the problem and then decide how to solve it. This bird's-eye view of the problem is important in doing mathematics—rather than always doing the same thing no matter what the numbers. This is very evident in the third example, which can be solved with no computation if the relationships among the numbers are first noticed.

Second, what is "basic" in the twenty-first century is much more than computation. Many topics in middle school were not a part of the curriculum a generation ago (e.g., functions). Looking together through the essential concepts in the *Common Core State Standards* or the NCTM *Curriculum Focal Points* helps parents see that the curriculum is not just an idea generated at their child's school but the national consensus on what middle-school students need to learn.

Student Achievement

At the heart of parents' interest in school mathematics is wanting their child to be successful, not only in the current classroom but also at the next level of school and later on in the high-stakes assessments like the ACT or SAT for college entrance. If your state has implemented the *Common Core State Standards*, you can share that the standards are for K–12 and designed to prepare students for college and future careers. The *Common Core State Standards* website has an increasing number of resources for parents (http://corestandards.org) to help them ensure that their child is college and career ready.

Another approach to inform parents about student achievement is to share research on the *ineffectiveness* of the traditional U.S. approach to teaching mathematics. The Trends in International Mathematics and Science Study (TIMSS), an international study conducted regularly that includes many countries, continues to find that U.S. students achieve at an average level in fourth grade, then score lower in mathematics than international students do in eighth grade and high school. Discuss the implications of unpreparedness for students who want to seek higher-paying jobs on what is now an international playing field.

Parents may be more interested in how your specific school is doing in preparing students for the future. Share evidence from your school of mathematics success, including stories about an individual student (no name given) or the success of a particular classroom, like the following one received by a middle-school principal:

> I was worried at the start of the year because my son has never liked math and was coming home with pretty complicated problems to solve. I wondered why the teacher hadn't shown him *how* to add and subtract integers, for example. But, now I can really see his number sense—he uses various ways to add, including that he can do it in his head and use a number line! He is also doing very well with problem solving and writing his own story problems! As an aside, I am also learning a lot—I didn't learn this way, but I am finding the homework problems are really interesting. Best of all, his confidence has skyrocketed. Is this something that will be continued next year and when he takes algebra?

Such communications help parents see that there is a transition period and that, in the end, a standards-based approach helps engage students and build their understanding over time.

 ## Homework Practices and Parent Coaching

The way in which parents are involved in homework can make a difference in student attitudes and learning (Cooper, 2007; Else-Quest, Hyde, & Hejmadi, 2008; Patall, Cooper, & Robinson, 2008). For example, students perform better when parents provide a quiet environment and establish rules about homework completion. Also, a parent's emotions are connected to the student's emotions, and these positive emotions are connected to better performance (Else-Quest et al., 2008). Therefore, parents who exhibit positive interest, humor, and pride in their child's homework support the child's mathematics learning.

You may have heard parents say, "I am not good at math" or "I don't like solving math problems." Parents may feel this way, and given the research just described, it is particularly important to redirect parents to portray mathematics in a positive light. For example, "Even though math can be hard, stick with it and you will figure it out." Teaching parents how to help their children has also been found to make a difference in supporting student achievement (Cooper, 2007).

How do you effectively encourage students and their families to support mathematics learning at home? Here, we break down the many possible ways into four categories: (1) parent participation, (2) homework support, (3) resources for parents, and (4) beyond-homework experiences.

Parents' Participation

Some parents who may have been very engaged in their child's elementary education are not as involved in middle school. They may feel their involvement is not as critical in middle school as it was in elementary school, or that their child may not want to see them at school. In any case, an invitation to come to a mathematics lesson or a math event gives parents the chance to witness firsthand such things as how you ask questions, how problems can be solved in many ways, and how calculators can be used to support reasoning. They may notice that you encourage students to select their own strategy and explain how they know it works. Parents will also pick up on the language that you are using and will be able to reinforce that language at home. You can even provide a note-taking template that includes categories such as the following: What is the big idea of the lesson? What illustrations or tools are being used to help students understand? What are some questions the teacher is asking that I could also ask? What does the teacher do when a student is stuck?

Homework Support

Homework can be a positive experience for students, families, and the teacher. Take the following recommendations into consideration when thinking about the homework that you will assign to your students.

1. *Mimic the three-phase lesson model.* Complete a brief version of the *Before* phase of a lesson to be sure the homework is understood before students go home. At home, students complete the *During* phase. When they return with the work completed, apply the sharing techniques of the *After* phase of the homework. Students can even practice the *After* phase with their family if you encourage this through parent or guardian communications. Some form of written work must be required so that students are held responsible for the task and are prepared for the class discussion.

2. *Use a distributed-content approach.* Homework can address content that has been taught earlier in the year as practice, that day's content as reinforcement, or upcoming content as groundwork. Interestingly, research has found that distributed homework (homework that combines all three components) is more effective in supporting student learning (Cooper, 2007). The exception is students with learning disabilities, who perform better when homework focuses on reinforcement of skills and current class lessons.

3. *Promote an "ask-before-tell" approach with parents.* Parents may not know how best to support their child when he or she is stuck or has gotten a wrong answer. One

$\mathcal{Figure}$ 7.5 Questions for families to help their children with homework.

These guiding questions are designed to help your child think through his or her math homework problems. When your child gets stuck, ask the following:

* What do you need to figure out? What is the problem about?
* What words are confusing? What words are familiar?
* Did you solve problems like this one in class today?
* What have you tried so far? What else can you try?
* Can you make a drawing, table, or diagram to help you think about the problem?
* Does your answer make sense?
* Is there more than one answer?
* What math words or steps do you use in class?

important thing you can do is to ask parents to implement an "ask-before-tell" approach (Kliman, 1999). This means that before parents explain something, they should ask their child to explain how he or she did it. The child may self-correct (a life skill), and if not, at least the parents can use what they heard from their child to provide targeted assistance.

4. *Provide good questioning prompts for parents.* Providing guiding questions for parents or guardians supports a problem-based approach to instruction as they help their children. Figure 7.5 provides guiding questions that can be included in the students' notebooks and shared with families. Translating questions for parents who are not native speakers of English is important. Often, a student can help you with this task.

Homework of this nature communicates to families the problem-based or sense-making nature of your classroom and might help them see the value in this approach. A final note: A little bit goes a long way—if students are to spend time solving meaningful problems, then just a few engaging problems a night can accomplish more than a long set of practice problems.

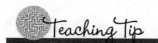 *Teaching Tip*

Providing specific guidance to families makes a big difference in what to do (and *not* do) to help their children learn mathematics and be confident in doing mathematics.

Resources for Families

Parents will be better able to help to their child if they know where to find resources. The Internet can either provide a wealth of information or be an overwhelming distraction. Help parents locate the good places to find math support. First, check whether your textbook provides websites with online resources for homework, including tutorials, video tutoring, videos, connections to careers and real-world applications, multilingual glossaries, audio podcasts, and more. Second, post websites that are good general resources. Here are some examples:

* *Figure This! Math Challenges for Families* (www.figurethis.org/index.html). This website has a teacher corner and a family corner. It offers outstanding resources to help parents understand standards-based mathematics, help with homework, and engage in *doing* mathematics with their children. It is also available in Spanish.

* *National Council of Teachers of Mathematics (NCTM)* (www.nctm.org/resources/families .aspx). This frequently updated site connects families to help on homework, current trends in mathematics, and resources.

* *Math Forum* (http://mathforum.org/parents.citizens.html). This site includes many features for teachers and families. For example, "Ask Dr. Math" is a great homework resource because students can write in their questions and get answers fairly quickly.

Parents may also want to read or participate in math discussion groups, read about key issues for the mathematics community, or download some of the very interesting problems posted here.

- *National Library of Virtual Manipulatives* (http://nlvm .usu.edu/en/nav/vlibrary.html) This site has numerous applets and virtual tools for learning about many mathematics topics.

There are also great websites for specific content. For example, Conceptua Math (www .conceptuamath.com) has excellent applets for exploring fraction operations.

Beyond Homework: Seeing Mathematics in the Home

In the same way that families support literacy by reading and talking about books with their children, families can and should support numeracy. Because this has not been the practice in many homes, it means you, as the teacher, have the responsibility to help parents see the connection between numeracy and everyday life. In her article "Beyond Helping with Homework: Parents and Children Doing Mathematics at Home," Kliman (1999) offers some excellent suggestions, which include asking parents to share anecdotes, find mathematics in the books they read, and create opportunities during household chores. Figure 7.6 provides a sample letter home that suggests these ideas to parents.

Adults constantly use estimation and computation while doing everyday tasks. If you get parents to talk about these instances with their children, imagine how much it can help students learn about mathematics and its importance as a life skill.

Involving ALL Families

Some families are at all school events and conferences; others rarely participate. However, all families want their children to be successful in school. Parents who do not come to school events may have anxiety related to their own school experiences, or they may feel completely confident that the school and its teachers are doing well by their child and that they do not need to participate. In some cultures, questioning a teacher may be perceived as disrespectful. Rodríguez-Brown (2010, p. 352), a researcher on Hispanic families, writes, "It is not that Latino parents do not want to support their children's learning. . . . [They] believe that it is disrespectful to usurp the teacher's role."

Try to find ways to build a strong rapport with all families. Some strategies to consider include the following:

1. *Honor different strategies for doing mathematics.* Although this is a recommendation in standards documents, it is particularly important for students from other countries because they may have learned different ways to do the operations (Civil & Planas, 2010).

2. *Communicate with positive notes and phone calls.* Be sure to find a way to compliment each student's mathematical thinking (not just a good score on quiz) at some point early in the school year.

3. *Host informal gatherings to discuss mathematics teaching and learning.* Having regular opportunities to meet with the parents allows the development of rapport and trust. Consider hosting events in out-of-school facilities. Schools in communities with a high level of poverty have found that having parent events at a community center or religious institution brings in families that are reluctant to come into a school.

Figure 7.6
Sample letter to parents regarding ways to infuse mathematics into their interactions with their child.

Making Math Moments Matter (M^4)

Dear Families:

As a seventh grader, your child is increasingly interested in what is happening in the community and the world. In that world is a lot of math! In our class this year we are working on four critical areas: **proportional reasoning, operations with all rational numbers (including algebraic equations), geometry,** and **statistics.** It will really help your child to <u>understand</u> and <u>see the importance</u> of math if you find ways to talk about "math moments" (on any math topic, but especially the four mentioned here). We call it Making Math Moments Matter (M^4 for short). Here are some ways to have fun with M^4 at home.

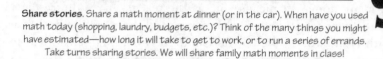

Share stories. Share a math moment at dinner (or in the car). When have you used math today (shopping, laundry, budgets, etc.)? Think of the many things you might have estimated—how long it will take to get to work, or to run a series of errands. Take turns sharing stories. We will share family math moments in class!

Connecting to art. Art is a great connect to seventh-grade geometry, as we will be looking at scale drawings and finding surface area and volume of different three-dimensional shapes. If your child has an interest in cartoons, encourage him or her to create scale drawings.

Chores. Yes, chores! If it takes $\frac{3}{4}$ of an hour to do a load of laundry, how long will it take to do 3 loads? If you walk the dog for 0.25 hour twice each day, how many hours do you walk the dog in a week? A month? If you earn $5 an hour walking dogs, what might you earn in a week?

Newspaper data. The paper is full of numeric information. Asking your child how the number 1.6 million is written out, or how it compares to 1.6 billion, is a good way to support his or her number sense. Also, you can review sports statistics, asking about what they mean and how they will be affected by more [hits, yards, goals].

4. *Incorporate homework that involves the family.* When a student brings in homework that tells about his or her family and you provide positive feedback or a personal comment, then you are establishing a two-way communication with the family via homework.

5. *Translate letters that are sent home.* If you are doing a class newsletter (for families) or a letter describing the next mathematics unit, make an effort to translate the letter into the native language of the families represented in your class. If you cannot do this, consider having the first class session include a component in which students write to their families about what they are about to do. Ask them to write in their parents' first language and to include visuals to support their writing. Ask parents to respond (in their language of choice). This is a great practice for helping students know what they need to learn, and it communicates to families that they are an important part of that learning.

6. *Post homework on your webpage.* For parents who are not native speakers of English, posting problems on your site makes it easier to take advantage of online translations. Although these translations may not be perfectly accurate, they can help parents and students understand the language in the problems.

For more suggestions on ensuring that your mathematics tasks and homework are meeting the needs of culturally and linguistically diverse students, see Chapter 5 and read "NCTM Research Brief: Involving Latino and Latina Parents in Their Children's Mathematics Education" (Civil & Menéndez, 2010). For suggestions on students with special needs, see Chapter 6.

 # Principal Engagement and Support

Teachers cite a supportive principal as one of the most essential components in successfully implementing a standards-based curriculum (Bay, Reys, & Reys, 1999). Therefore, a principal plays a pivotal role in establishing a shared vision for a problem-based mathematics program. Principals, who have many competing priorities, often cannot take the time to attend the professional development workshops that are designed for teachers who will be teaching the mathematics program. And what they need to know is qualitatively different from what a classroom teacher needs to know.

Since the launch of the *Common Core State Standards*, school administrators, parents, and community members are more aware than ever about mathematics standards. If your state has not adopted the *Common Core State Standards*, there are still state-level standards that are the focus of mathematics goals and assessments. So, while it may seem that the need to communicate with administrators is something to simply check off your list—STOP—it must be a top priority.

Even though principals are hearing more about mathematics standards, higher standards, and the need to ensure that all students are successful, it does not mean they understand what standards-based mathematics curriculum *is* in terms of the content or the related CCSS Standards for Mathematical Practice or NCTM Process Standards. The principal is likely to get bombarded with broad or specific questions from parents: "Is 'New Math' back?" "Why isn't the teacher teaching the procedures for multiplying and dividing?" "What are the Standards for Mathematical Practice?" When a principal is asked these questions, he or she needs to give a convincing response that is accurate and that also addresses the heart of the parents' concerns (that their child is going to get a good, sound math experience that will prepare him or her for college and career).

Meyer and Arbaugh (2008) suggest professional development specifically for principals. Although their focus is on the adoption of standards-based textbooks, the plan they outline applies to all principals who are seeking to be knowledgeable and effective advocates for implementing new standards or mathematics curricula. The following ideas are adapted from their suggested professional development to focus on one-on-one conversations.

1. *Contrast old and new curriculum.* As a first step, it is important to know what is new and different in the mathematics program. One way to start is to provide a set of materials that represent typical *Common Core State Standards*–aligned tasks alongside the previous curriculum. Point out the noticeable similarities and differences or the key features of the curriculum. (Note: It is important to focus on *both* similarities *and* differences—not *everything* is being replaced, and this is an important message.)

2. *Discuss how parents and students will respond.* Anticipate what will be noticed by parents (or their children): Which changes might be welcomed? Which changes might be worrisome? How will the welcome aspects be promoted and the worrisome aspects be explained?

3. *Experience the curriculum.* Invite the principal to visit your classroom or other classrooms where the Standards for Mathematical Practice or the NCTM Process

Standards are being infused. Ask the principal to join a group of students and listen to their discussion of how they are solving a problem. Or organize a lesson when, in the *After* phase, the students actually present their solutions to the principal. For example, in the sixth grade, have students use visuals and explanations to show their different ways of dividing fractions. If possible, ask the principal to solve one of the problems the students are doing and share his or her strategy with the class. This firsthand experience can provide the principal with a wonderful story to share with parents and insights that won't be gained from reviewing standards documents.

4. *Discuss emerging issues.* Plan a regular time to meet with the principal to discuss what he or she has heard from families about the mathematics program. Discuss what you might do to respond to questions (some of the anticipated issues may already have been described in the preceding section on parents' concerns). If there is a question about a problem-based approach, Chapter 2 should be a great read for a principal, and contains talking points to share with others.

Finally, keep your principal apprised of successes and breakthroughs. These stories provide the principal with stories and evidence to share when pressed by parents or community members. Principals are very often your strongest advocates and are in a position to serve as buffers between school mathematics and the community.

 # Communicating with Stakeholders

A final and critical point is to be careful in how we communicate with stakeholders (e.g., parents, district administrators, other teachers, community partners). Without knowing, we sometimes say things that, although well intentioned, increase the concerns of stakeholders rather than helping to ease stakeholder anxiety. Table 7.2 provides three such examples.

Table 7.2 Statements and Possible (Unintended) Interpretations of the Statements

Original Statement	What a Parent/ Administrator Might Think	A Stronger, Carefully Composed Statement
"The [mathematics program] still addresses skills, but it also includes concepts."	"Why are they bringing skills up? They must be taking those away. My child/U.S. kids have to know basics. How can I put a stop to this?"	"The skills in the [mathematics program] are expanding from what we once learned and now include . . ."
"It is important for students to learn from one another, so I will be more in the role of facilitator."	"The teacher is not teaching? My child does better when things are explained clearly. When I come to see you teach, what am I looking for if you are just letting the kids learn on their own?"	"In our classroom, we learn from one another. I give carefully selected tasks for students to discuss, and then we talk about them together so that everyone has a chance to learn the mathematics we are doing, and that approach gives me the chance to work one-on-one as needed."
"This year, we are doing a whole new mathematics program that the state has adopted."	"My worst nightmare—an experiment of something new during the years my child is in middle school. This will cause problems for the rest of his life."	"We are doing some new things in order to make sure your child is well prepared for . . . [or that our program is the best available]. You might have noticed that last year we [added writing as a component to our math program]. This year, here are the big things we hope to accomplish. . . ."

Stop and Reflect

Consider a statement you have heard or used with families. Ask yourself, "How might a parent respond if he or she heard this statement?" "What might the parent misinterpret?" "How might my principal respond?" Then, read the responses in the table to see whether they represent stakeholders like those in your setting. As a rule, it is a good idea to filter your statements through these questions. ■

Initially the statements may not seem harmful, but they can set off alarms from the lens of a stakeholder. Consider these reactions, and then review the shifted language in the third column, which communicates a stronger (and less potentially disconcerting) message. Along these lines, it is very important to convey to parents an excitement for and pride in your mathematics program. Being tentative, reserved, vague, or silent on the mathematics program can only raise concerns in the community. Help parents and administrators to understand that the mathematics program students are experiencing aligns with best practices in education, represents what they need to know in today's world, and prepares them for mathematics at the next level as well as the mathematics they need for life.

Stop and Reflect

What do you think the parents of your students would most value about "teaching mathematics *through* problem solving," and how will you use your response to this question to build strong family support and engagement? (Repeat the question for other stakeholders, such as your principal.) ■

8

Fraction Concepts and Computation

BigIDEAS

1 For students to really understand fractions, they must experience fractions across many constructs, including part of a whole, ratios, and division.

2 Three types of models exist for fractions: area (e.g., $\frac{1}{3}$ of a garden), length (e.g., $\frac{3}{4}$ of an inch), and set (e.g., $\frac{1}{2}$ of the class).

3 Partitioning and iterating are ways for students to understand the meaning of fractions.

4 The meanings of each operation with fractions are the same as the meanings of the operation with whole numbers. Operations with fractions should begin with an application of these same meanings to fractional parts.

5 Repeated addition and area models support the development of concepts and algorithms for the multiplication of fractions.

6 Partition and measurement models lead to two different thought processes for the division of fractions.

7 Estimation should be an integral part of computation development to keep students' attention on the meanings of the operations and the expected sizes of the results.

 ## Why Students Struggle with Fractions

If you think about the way in which students learn to add whole numbers and the way in which they learn to add fractions, you will see some stark differences that provide insights into why students struggle with fraction concepts and operations. Adding with whole numbers begins with counting, then counting on, then mental strategies, and as the numbers get bigger, students learn algorithms. All the while, they are using concrete objects, which include counters, ten-frames, hundreds charts, and number lines. In addition, story situations (concrete examples) are provided on a regular basis. Equations are written to model

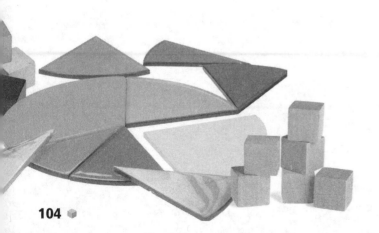

what has been illustrated with the manipulatives or the story. Yet, as students learn about fraction operations, far fewer manipulatives or visuals are used, mental strategies are rare, and story situations tend to be used only as an application problem after the algorithms have been learned. It is no surprise that students poorly understand the meaning behind fraction computation, and that leads to the many errors they make in performing fraction computations. Finally, the time devoted to learning whole-number addition is significant, whereas instruction in fraction computation is often limited to several days.

In addition to the instructional approach to operations with fractions, other reasons why fractions are difficult for students include these:

- There are many meanings of fractions (see later section "Fraction Constructs").
- Fractions are written in a unique way.
- Students overgeneralize their whole-number knowledge (McNamara & Shaughnessy, 2010).

This last point is very important in middle school as students focus on operations. An explanation of common misapplications of whole-number knowledge to fractions follows, along with ways you can help. Misconceptions are presented here, as well as at the conclusion of each operation section in this chapter.

> **Teaching Tip**
>
> Anticipating student misconceptions is a critical part of planning—it can greatly influence task selection and how the lesson is structured.

Misconception 1.   Students think that the numerator and denominator are separate values and have difficulty seeing them as a single value (Cramer & Whitney, 2010). It is hard for them to see that $\frac{3}{4}$ is one number.

How to Help.   Find fraction values on a number line. This can be a fun warm-up activity each day, with students placing particular values on a classroom number line or a number line on their warm-up page. Measure with inches to various levels of precision (e.g., to the nearest fourth, eighth, or sixteenth). Avoid the phrase "three out of four" (unless you are talking about ratios or probability) or "three over four"; instead, say "three-fourths" (Siebert & Gaskin, 2006).

Misconception 2.   Students do not understand that $\frac{2}{3}$ means two equal-size parts (although not necessarily equal-shape objects). For example, students may think that the accompanying shape shows $\frac{3}{4}$ light gray rather than $\frac{1}{2}$ light gray.

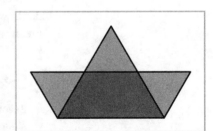

How to Help.   Students need to create their own representations of fractions across various types of models. In addition, provide problems like the one illustrated here, in which all the partitions are not already drawn.

Misconception 3.   Students think that a fraction such as $\frac{1}{5}$ is smaller than a fraction such as $\frac{1}{10}$ because 5 is less than 10. Conversely, students may be told that fractions are the reverse—the bigger the denominator, the smaller the fraction. Teaching such rules, without providing the reason, may lead students to overgeneralize that $\frac{1}{5}$ is more than $\frac{7}{10}$.

How to Help.   Many visuals and contexts that show parts of the whole are essential in helping students understand. For example, ask students whether they would rather go outside for $\frac{1}{2}$ of an hour, $\frac{1}{4}$ of an hour, or $\frac{1}{10}$ of an hour and to explain why. Ask students to provide their own example to justify which fraction is larger.

Misconception 4.   Students mistakenly use the operation "rules" for whole numbers to compute with fractions—for example, $\frac{1}{2} + \frac{1}{2} = \frac{2}{4}$.

How to Help. As before, ask students to connect to a meaningful visual or example. Include estimation in teaching operations with fractions.

Students who make these errors do not understand fractions. Until they understand fractions meaningfully, they will continue to make errors by overapplying whole-number concepts (Cramer & Whitney, 2010; Siegler, Carpenter, Fennell, Geary, Lewis, Okamoto, & Wray, 2010). Although the focus of this chapter is primarily on operations, we begin with important ideas of how to develop a conceptual understanding of fractions.

 Fraction Concepts

Fraction concepts are emphasized in the *Common Core State Standards* beginning in grade 3 and continuing through grade 7, with a focus on topics such as equivalence, the operations, and proportional reasoning. This emphasis over years is an indication of both the complexity and the importance of fraction concepts.

The National Assessment of Education Progress, commonly called the "Nation's Report Card," continues to show that middle-school students have a weak understanding of fraction concepts and operations (Sowder & Wearne, 2006; Wearne & Kouba, 2000). A lack of understanding of fractions is considered one of the major reasons students are not successful in algebra (Brown & Quinn, 2007; National Mathematics Advisory Panel, 2008). This means that even if students should have learned foundational concepts before middle school, if they have not, then you must infuse such meaning-making as you work on developing an understanding of the operations. The following sections identify some of these critical foundations.

◆ **Fraction Constructs**

Part–whole (for example, shading part of a whole rectangle) is the most common way that fractions are represented. But part–whole is not the only meaning of fractions. In fact, part–whole is so often the way fractions are represented, it may be difficult for you to think about what else fractions might represent. Many who research fraction understanding believe students would understand fractions better if there were more emphasis across the different meanings of fractions (Clarke, Roche, & Mitchell, 2008; Siebert & Gaskin, 2006).

Stop and Reflect

Beyond shading a region of a shape, how else are fractions used? How are these other ways alike and different from a part of a region or an area? ■

The different meanings associated with fractions, referred to as fraction "constructs" to differentiate from the different types of visuals that can be used, are the focus of this section.

Part–Whole

Using the part–whole construct is an effective starting point for building the meaning of fractions (Cramer & Whitney, 2010). Part–whole goes well beyond shading a region. For example, it could be part of a group of people ($\frac{3}{5}$ of the class went on the field trip), or it could be part of a length (we walked $3\frac{1}{2}$ miles).

[Handwritten notes at top of page: How many 1/6th are between 0 and 1? How many 12th are equivalent to 1 whole - show with manipulatives. How to find 1/6. Then translate it into number line.]

Measure

Measurement involves identifying a length and then using that length as a measuring unit to determine the length of an object. For example, in the fraction $\frac{5}{8}$, you can use the unit fraction $\frac{1}{8}$ as the selected length, then count or measure to show that it takes five of those to reach $\frac{5}{8}$. Notice that, conceptually, this is different because part–whole focuses on how many parts, while measure focuses on how much or how long (Behr, Lesh, Post, & Silver, 1983; Martinie, 2007).

Division

Consider the idea of sharing $10 with 4 people. This is not a part–whole scenario, but it still means that each person will receive one-fourth ($\frac{1}{4}$) of the money, or $2\frac{1}{2}$ dollars. Division is often not connected to fractions, which is unfortunate. Students should understand and feel comfortable with this example written as $\frac{10}{4}$, $4\overline{)10}$, $10 \div 4$, $2\frac{2}{4}$, and $2\frac{1}{2}$ (Flores, Samson, & Yanik, 2006). Division of fractions is addressed in detail later in this chapter.

Operator

Fractions can be used to indicate an operation, as in $\frac{4}{5}$ of 20 square feet, or $\frac{2}{3}$ of the audience was holding banners. These situations indicate a fraction of a whole number, and students may be able to use mental math to determine the answer. This construct is not emphasized enough in school curricula (Usiskin, 2007). And even when students have learned to multiply by fractions, they may not recognize the operation in applications, for example in solving an area problem with fractional side lengths (Johanning, 2008).

Ratio

Ratios are part–whole and part–part fraction constructs. For example, the ratio $\frac{3}{4}$ could be the ratio of those wearing jackets (part) to those not wearing jackets (part), or it could be part–whole, meaning the ratio of those wearing jackets (part) to those in the class (whole). When working with ratios, students have to use the context to make sense of the part–part and part–whole relationships.

◆ Fraction Models

There is substantial evidence to suggest that the effective use of models in fraction tasks can help students understand fractions (Cramer & Henry, 2002; Siebert & Gaskin, 2006). Unfortunately, textbooks rarely use models, and when they do, they tend to use only area models (Hodges, Cady, & Collins, 2008). This means that students often do not explore fractions in a variety of situations or have sufficient time to develop a conceptual understanding. Yet, critical to learning fractions is the use of physical models, which leads to mental models and then an understanding of fractions (Cramer & Whitney, 2010; Petit, Laird, & Marsden, 2010). Table 8.1 illustrates three categories of fraction models: area, length, and set.

Standards for
Mathematical Practice

1 Make sense of problems and persevere in solving them

An increasing number of Web resources are available to help students model fractions. One excellent source is Conceptua Fractions, developed by Conceptua Math (www.conceptuamath.com). This site offers tools that help students explore various fraction concepts with area, set, and length models (including the number line).

Table 8.1 Models for Fraction Concepts and How They Compare

Model	What Defines the Whole	What Defines the Parts	What the Fraction Means
Area	The area of the defined region	Equal area	The part of the area covered, as it relates to the whole unit
Length or number line	The unit of distance or length	Equal distance or length	The location of a point in relation to zero and other values on the number line
Set	Whatever value is determined as one set	Equal number of objects	The count of objects in the subject, as it relates to the defined whole

Source: Adapted from Petit, M. M., Laird, R. E., & Marsden, E. L. (2010). *A Focus on Fractions: Bringing Research to the Classroom (Studies in Mathematical Thinking and Learning series)*. New York, NY: Taylor & Francis.

Area Models

Circular fraction piece models are the most commonly used area model. The circle emphasizes the part–whole concept of fractions and the meaning of the relative size of a part to the whole (Cramer, Wyberg, & Leavitt, 2008). But circles can be overdone and are difficult to partition into same-size sections. There are many area model manipulatives, including pattern blocks, geoboards, color tiles, and fraction pieces. Regions can also be drawn on blank or grid paper. Drawing rectangles is especially flexible and allows you to see if students partition correctly.

Length Models

With length models, lengths or measurements are compared instead of areas. Music, for example, can be a length example if you imagine partitioning a measure into halves, fourths, eighths, and sixteenths (Goral & Wiest, 2007). Length models include Cuisenaire rods, paper strips (e.g., adding machine tape), fraction strips, and the number line.

Teaching Tip

> Linear models are closely connected to the real-world contexts in which fractions are commonly used for measuring. Ask students to think of examples of when they have seen or used fractions—most of these will be length situations.

Cuisenaire rods or strips provide flexibility because any length can represent the whole. The number line is a significantly more sophisticated measurement model (Bright, Behr, Post, & Wachsmuth, 1988). Reviews of research on fractions (Petit et al., 2010; Siegler et al., 2010) report that the number line helps students to understand a fraction as a number (rather than as one number over another number). The Institute of Educational Sciences report on the effective teaching of fractions argues that number lines should be a "central representational tool" (Siegler et al., 2010, p. 1).

The *Common Core State Standards* emphasize the importance of the number line across the grades, beginning with whole-number operations in the early grades and continuing through algebra in high school. Specific to fractions and middle school, sixth-grade standard 6.NS6 states, "Understand a rational number as a point on the number line" (CCSSO, 2010, p. 43), and in eighth grade, this is expanded to finding rational number estimations of irrational numbers on a number line. The following activity is a fun way to use a familiar context to engage students in thinking about fractions through a linear model.

◢ *Activity 8.1* **WHO IS WINNING?**

The friends below are playing the game red light–green light. Who is winning? The fractions tell how much of the distance they have already moved. Can you place these friends on a line to show where they are between the start and finish?

Mary: $\frac{3}{4}$ Harry: $\frac{1}{2}$ Larry: $\frac{5}{6}$ Han: $\frac{5}{8}$ Miguel: $\frac{5}{9}$ Angela: $\frac{2}{3}$

The game red light–green light may not be familiar to English language learners (ELLs). Role playing the game with people in the class and using estimation are good ways to build background and support students with disabilities.

Source: Adapted from Bay-Williams, J. M., & Martinie, S. L. (2003). Thinking rationally about number in the middle school. *Mathematics Teaching in the Middle School, 8*(6), 282–287.

Set Models

The whole in a set model is a set of objects, and subsets of the whole make up fractional parts. For example, 3 red counters are one-fourth of a set of 12 counters. Set models include counters, people, or any discrete objects. The idea of referring to a collection of counters as a single entity makes set models difficult for some students. To help students make the distinction, put a piece of yarn in a loop around the items in the set to help them "see" the whole. Students will frequently focus on the size of the set rather than the number of equal sets in the whole. For example, if 12 counters make a whole, then a set of 4 counters is one-third, not one-fourth, because 3 equal sets make the whole. However, the set model helps establish important connections with many real-world uses of fractions and with ratio concepts. The activity below can be done as an energizer or as a quick activity when you find you have five minutes.

Activity 8.2 CLASS FRACTIONS

Use a group of students as the whole—for example, use six students if you want to work on halves, thirds, and sixths. Ask students, "What fraction of our group [are wearing tennis shoes, have brown hair, etc.]?" Change the number of people over time.

When you are determining what students already know about fractions, it is important to assess across each of these model types. For example, give students a piece of paper, fold it into thirds, and at the top of each section write *area*, *length*, and *set*. Have them show you a picture and write a sentence describing a context or example for a selected fraction (e.g., $\frac{3}{4}$) for all three models. This can be done exactly for commonly used fractions or can be an estimation activity with fractions like $\frac{31}{58}$. Each of these models will be important in fraction operations, as well as operations with other rational numbers, so it is important to determine students' strengths and needs and plan experiences accordingly.

Iterating and Partitioning

These two terms may not be common in middle school, but they are two foundational (and underemphasized) ideas for fractions that can greatly support student understanding of fraction operations, especially multiplication and division of fractions, which involve both processes. Each term is briefly discussed here.

Partitioning

When you ask students to show eighths on a rectangle, or on a number line, they are not *dividing* (a commonly used term that can lead to confusion with the operation division) the

Figure 8.1

Students learning about fractional parts should be able to tell which of these figures are correctly partitioned in fourths. They should also be able to explain why the other figures are not showing fourths.

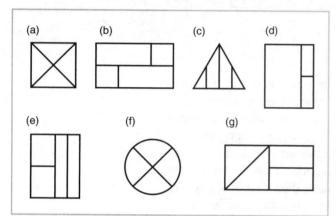

shape or line, they are *partitioning* it. This term emphasizes the concept of part–whole (part-ition) and avoids the confusion with division. Students should partition regions or shapes, lengths, and sets. Using examples and non-examples helps students strengthen their understanding of fractions.

Activity 8.3 CORRECT SHARES

Draw regions like the ones in Figure 8.1, showing examples and non-examples (which are very important to use for students with disabilities) of fractional parts. Have students identify the wholes that are correctly partitioned into the requested fractional parts and those that are not. For each response, have students explain their reasoning.

The regions in this activity fall into each of the following categories:

1. Same shape, same size: (a) and (f) [equivalent]
2. Different shape, same size: (e) and (g) [equivalent]
3. Different shape, different size: (b) and (c) [not equivalent]
4. Same shape, different size: (d) [not equivalent].

Activity 8.4 involves partitioning with a length context.

Activity 8.4 HOW FAR DID SHE GO?

Give students number lines partitioned such that only some of the partitions are showing. Use a context such as walking to school. For each number line, ask, "How far has [Nicole] gone? How do you know?"

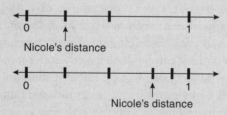

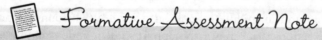

Students can justify their reasoning by measuring the size of the sections that have been partitioned.

Formative Assessment Note

Activities 8.3 and 8.4 are good diagnostic assessments to see whether students understand that it is the size that matters, not the shape. If, for Activity 8.3, students identify all the wholes that are correctly partitioned into fourths except (e) and (g), they do not understand this concept, and you need to plan future tasks that focus on equivalence—for example, asking students to take a square and partition it in at least four different ways.

Partitioning is a strategy commonly used in Singapore as a way to solve story problems. Consider the following story problem (Englard, 2010):

A nurse has 54 bandages. Of those, $\frac{2}{9}$ have designs and the rest are just tan. How many of the bandages have designs?

Students who have learned the Singapore bar diagram model solve the problem by partitioning a strip into nine parts and figuring out how many bandages go into each part, and then how many are in two of the nine parts, as shown.

Set models can also be used to see if students understand fractional parts. Consider the following problem:

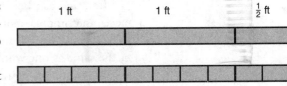

Eloise has 6 trading cards, André has 4 trading cards, and Lu has 2 trading cards. What fraction of the trading cards does Lu have?

A student who answers "one-third" is not thinking about equal shares but about the number of people with trading cards.

Understanding that parts of a whole must be partitioned into equal-size pieces across different models is an important step in conceptualizing fractions and provides a foundation for exploring sharing and equivalence tasks, which are prerequisite to performing fraction operations (Cramer & Whitney, 2010).

Iterating

The term *iterating* means repeating a process, and in fractions that translates into counting by fifths or tenths or whatever fractional parts you are using. In whole-number learning, counting precedes addition and subtraction and helps students add and subtract. This is also true with fractions. Counting fractional parts to see how multiple parts compare with the whole helps students understand the relationship between the parts (the numerator) and the whole (the denominator). Understanding that $\frac{3}{4}$ can be thought of as a count or unit of three parts called *fourths* is an important idea for students to develop (Post, Wachsmuth, Lesh, & Behr, 1985; Siebert & Gaskin, 2006; Tzur, 1999).

Iterating makes sense with length models because iteration is like measuring. Consider that you have $2\frac{1}{2}$ feet of ribbon and are trying to figure out how many fourths you have. You can draw a strip and start counting (iterating) the fourths, as shown.

Using a ribbon that is $\frac{1}{4}$ foot long as a measuring tool, a student counts off 10 fourths, as shown.

Students can participate in many tasks that involve iterating lengths, progressing in increasing difficulty, as in Activity 8.5.

Activity 8.5 HOW LONG IS THIS PART?

Give students a rectangular strip of paper—for example, by cutting strips from blank paper—as shown.

Explain that this paper measures $\frac{3}{4}$ of the whole. Ask students to find $\frac{1}{2}$ of the whole, $1\frac{1}{2}$ of the whole, $2\frac{1}{4}$ of the whole, 3 of the whole, and so on. To find these lengths, students should partition the original paper strip into three parts to find $\frac{1}{4}$ of the whole, then iterate the $\frac{1}{4}$ to find the various fractions listed. For each quantity students are asked to find (e.g., $\frac{1}{2}$ of the whole), ask students to justify how they determined the length. Have students compare their lengths, and if there are different results, engage students in determining which one must be correct.

Standards for
Mathematical Practice

3 Construct
viable arguments
and critique the
reasoning of others

Figure 8.2

Given the whole and the fraction, find the part.

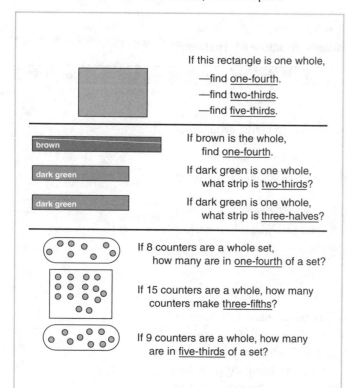

If this rectangle is one whole,
—find one-fourth.
—find two-thirds.
—find five-thirds.

If brown is the whole,
find one-fourth.

If dark green is one whole,
what strip is two-thirds?

If dark green is one whole,
what strip is three-halves?

If 8 counters are a whole set,
how many are in one-fourth of a set?

If 15 counters are a whole, how many
counters make three-fifths?

If 9 counters are a whole, how many
are in five-thirds of a set?

Figure 8.3

Given the part and the fraction, find the whole.

If this rectangle is one-third, what
could the whole look like?

If this rectangle is three-fourths,
draw a shape that could be the
whole.

If this rectangle is four-thirds, what
rectangle could be the whole?

If purple is one-third, what strip is
the whole?

If dark green is two-thirds, what
strip is the whole?

If yellow is five-fourths, what strip
is one whole?

If 4 counters are one-half of a
set, how big is the set?

If 12 counters are three-fourths of
a set, how many counters are in
the full set?

If 10 counters are five-halves of a
set, how many counters are in
one set?

Iterating can be done with a variety of models. For example, you can display fraction pieces and simply count them together: "one-fourth, two-fourths, three-fourths, four-fourths, five-fourths." Ask, "If we have five-fourths, is that more than one whole, less than one whole, or the same as one whole?" Figures 8.2, 8.3, and 8.4 provide rich examples across models of engaging students in iterating and partitioning in order to strengthen their understanding of fractions.

Stop and Reflect

Explore the problems in these three figures. If you do not have access to rods or counters, just draw illustrations on paper or solve mentally. Which problems and which models do you find easier to solve? Which ones do you think your students will find easier? Harder? ■

Questions involving unit fractions are generally easier for students, and questions involving fractions greater than one are harder. For example, "If 15 chips are five-thirds of one whole set, how many chips are in a whole?" will generally be more difficult for students. However, in these kinds of questions, the unit fraction plays a significant role (found through partitioning). If you have $\frac{2}{3}$ and want the whole, you first need to find $\frac{1}{3}$.

Calculators are an excellent tool for iteration activities that can provide the beginning concepts for the division of fractions.

Activity 8.6 **CALCULATOR FRACTION COUNTING**

Calculators that permit fraction entries and displays are now quite common in schools. Many, like the TI-15, now display fractions in correct fraction format and offer a choice of showing results as mixed numbers or simple fractions. Counting by fourths with the TI-15 is done by first storing $\frac{1}{4}$ in one of the two operation keys: $\boxed{\text{Op1}}$ $\boxed{+}$ 1 $\boxed{\text{n}}$ 4 $\boxed{\text{d}}$ $\boxed{\text{Op1}}$. To count, press 0 $\boxed{\text{Op1}}$ $\boxed{\text{Op1}}$ $\boxed{\text{Op1}}$, repeating to get the number of fourths wanted. The display will show the counts by fourths and also the number of times that the $\boxed{\text{Op1}}$ key has been pressed. Ask students questions such as the following: "How many $\frac{1}{4}$s to get to 3?" "How many $\frac{1}{5}$s to get to 5?" These can become increasingly more challenging: "How many $\frac{1}{4}$s to get to $4\frac{1}{2}$?" "How many $\frac{2}{3}$s to get to 6? Estimate, and then count by $\frac{2}{3}$s on the calculator." Students, particularly students with disabilities, should coordinate their counts with fraction models, adding a new fourths piece to the pile with each count. At any time, the display can be shifted from mixed form to simple fractions with a press of a key. The TI-15 can be set so that it will not simplify fractions automatically, which is the appropriate setting before the introduction of equivalent fractions.

Figure 8.4
Given the whole and the part, find the fraction.

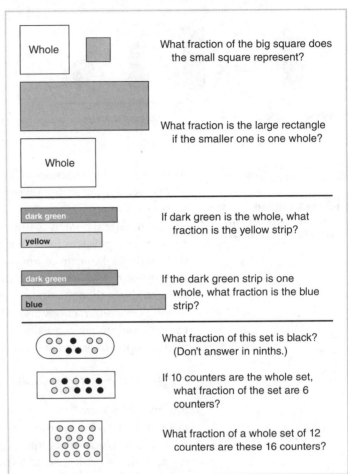

Fraction calculators provide a powerful way to help students develop fraction meaning. A variation on Activity 8.6 is to show students a mixed number such as $3\frac{1}{8}$ and ask how many counts of $\frac{1}{8}$ on the calculator it will take to count that high. The students should try to stop at the correct number ($\frac{25}{8}$) before pressing the mixed-number key.

🔺 Foundations for Fraction Operations

Fraction operations involve a significant amount of working with fraction equivalences. If students know only rules for finding an equivalent fraction, they will struggle with all operations. Instead, equivalences must be well understood. Although this content is addressed in elementary school, any of the ideas in this section can be used as readiness lessons or warm-up activities, or they can be integrated with instruction on the operations. The key is for your language and discussion to focus on the meaning, as we describe below.

 Teaching Tip

🔷 Fractions Greater Than One

Fractions less than and greater than one should be mixed together in fraction instruction. Too often, students aren't exposed to numbers greater than one (e.g., $\frac{5}{2}$ and $4\frac{1}{4}$), and then when they are added into the mix (no pun intended!), they find them confusing.

The term *improper fraction* for fractions greater than one can be a source of confusion because it implies "not acceptable." In algebra, fractions are often preferred to mixed numbers. Replace this phrase with *fraction* or *fraction greater than one,* which is consistent with *Common Core State Standards* and National Council of Teachers of Mathematics (NCTM) terminology.

Figure 8.5

Stacking cubes illustrate the equivalence of $\frac{12}{5}$ and $2\frac{2}{5}$.

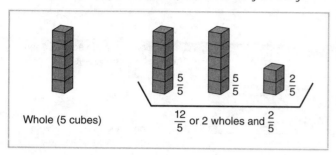

Whole (5 cubes)

$\frac{5}{5}$ $\frac{5}{5}$ $\frac{2}{5}$

$\frac{12}{5}$ or 2 wholes and $\frac{2}{5}$

Standards for Mathematical Practice

8 **Look for and express regularity in repeated reasoning** ▶

If students have had opportunities to iterate fractional parts beyond one whole, as in the previous section, they already know how to write $\frac{13}{6}$ or $\frac{13}{5}$. Ask students to select a manipulative or create a drawing to illustrate these values and find equivalent representations by using wholes and fractions (mixed numbers). Multilink (connecting) cubes are a very effective way to help students see both forms for recording fractions greater than one (Figure 8.5).

Students identify one cube as the unit fraction ($\frac{1}{5}$) for the problem ($\frac{12}{5}$). They count out 12 fifths and build wholes. Conversely, they can start with the mixed number, build it, and find out how many total cubes (or fifths) were used. Repeated experiences in building and solving these tasks will lead students to see a pattern of multiplication and division that closely resembles the algorithm for moving between these two forms.

By middle school, it is important that students use mental images. Challenge students to visualize equivalent forms without using actual tools. A good explanation for $3\frac{1}{4}$ might be that there are 4 fourths in one whole, so there are 8 fourths in two wholes and 12 fourths in three wholes. The extra fourth makes 13 fourths in all, or $\frac{13}{4}$. (Note the iteration within this process.) Even though middle-school students may already know the standard algorithm for moving between fractions and mixed numbers, it is important for them to be able to explain the relationship conceptually. This conceptual basis is critical for the reasoning needed in fraction operations and in algebra.

⬡ Estimating Fraction Size

Students must know "about" how big a particular fraction is if they are going to be able to estimate sums, differences, products, and quotients. As with whole numbers, students are less confident and less capable of estimating than they are at computing exact answers. Here, we share a few activities to reinforce (and formatively assess) student understanding of the size of a fraction. First, see if students can identify approximate fractional amounts from visuals, as in Activity 8.7.

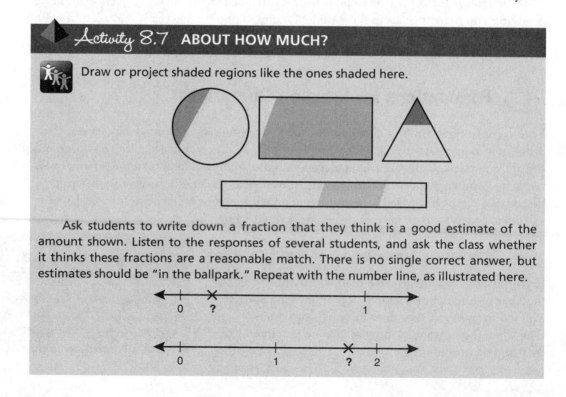

Activity 8.7 ABOUT HOW MUCH?

Draw or project shaded regions like the ones shaded here.

Ask students to write down a fraction that they think is a good estimate of the amount shown. Listen to the responses of several students, and ask the class whether it thinks these fractions are a reasonable match. There is no single correct answer, but estimates should be "in the ballpark." Repeat with the number line, as illustrated here.

If students have difficulty coming up with an estimate, ask whether they think the amount is closer to 0, $\frac{1}{2}$, or 1. You may want to give students with disabilities a set of cards with possible options for estimates. Then, they can match a card to one of the pictures.

The number line is a good model for helping students develop a better understanding of the relative size of a fraction (Petit, Laird, & Marsden, 2010). Remember also to estimate with values greater than greater than one—for example, $3\frac{3}{7}$ or $\frac{19}{5}$ to the nearest benchmark, $3, 3\frac{1}{2}$, or 4.

Comparing Fractions

Being able to reason about the size of fractions is helpful when comparing fractions. Too often, middle-school students use an algorithm (cross-products) for comparing two fractions, which they do not understand. Comparison activities (Which fraction is more? Which is less?) can play a significant role in helping students develop concepts of relative fraction sizes. Mathematically proficient students can compare fractions with a variety of strategies. Try reasoning strategies on the problems in Activity 8.8.

 Activity 8.8 **WHICH FRACTION IS GREATER?**

Ask students to use a reasoning strategy to determine which fraction is greater. For each problem, ask students to explain how they determined their answer. Encourage students to use different strategies across the problems. Encourage the use of benchmarks, and explain that they cannot use common denominators or cross multiplication.

Which fraction in each pair is greater?
Give one or more reasons. Try not to use drawings or models. <u>Do</u> <u>not</u> use common denominators or cross-multiplication. Rely on concepts.

A. $\frac{4}{5}$ or $\frac{4}{9}$ G. $\frac{7}{12}$ or $\frac{5}{12}$

B. $\frac{4}{7}$ or $\frac{5}{7}$ H. $\frac{3}{5}$ or $\frac{3}{7}$

C. $\frac{3}{8}$ or $\frac{4}{10}$ I. $\frac{5}{8}$ or $\frac{6}{10}$

D. $\frac{5}{3}$ or $\frac{5}{8}$ J. $\frac{9}{8}$ or $\frac{4}{3}$

E. $\frac{3}{4}$ or $\frac{9}{10}$ K. $\frac{4}{6}$ or $\frac{7}{12}$

F. $\frac{3}{8}$ or $\frac{4}{7}$ L. $\frac{8}{9}$ or $\frac{7}{8}$

The strategy used for comparing should vary with the size of the fractions. Here we share four different ways, which are more efficient than either common denominators or cross products, to determine the greater fraction. The first two comparison schemes listed here rely on the meanings of the top and bottom numbers in fractions and on the relative sizes of unit fractional parts. The third and fourth ideas use the additional ideas of 0, $\frac{1}{2}$, and 1 as convenient anchors or benchmarks for thinking about the size of fractions. Comparing two fractions can develop and strengthen a general sense of fractions.

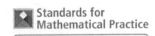
Standards for Mathematical Practice

7 Look for and make use of structure

More of the Same-Size Parts

To compare $\frac{3}{8}$ and $\frac{5}{8}$, it is easy to think about having 3 parts of something compared to 5 parts of the same thing.

Same Number of Parts but Parts of Different Sizes

Consider the case of $\frac{3}{4}$ and $\frac{3}{7}$. If a whole is partitioned into 7 parts, the parts will certainly be smaller than if the same-sized whole is partitioned into only 4 parts. Many students will select $\frac{3}{7}$ as larger because 7 is more than 4 and the top numbers are the same.

More and Less Than One-Half or One Whole

The fraction pairs $\frac{3}{7}$ versus $\frac{5}{8}$ and $\frac{5}{4}$ versus $\frac{7}{8}$ do not lend themselves to either of the previous thought processes. In the first pair, $\frac{3}{7}$ is less than half of the number of sevenths needed to make a whole, so $\frac{3}{7}$ is less than a half. Similarly, $\frac{5}{8}$ is more than a half. Therefore, $\frac{5}{8}$ is the larger fraction. The second pair is determined by noting that one fraction is less than one and the other is greater than one.

Distance from One-Half or One Whole

Standards for
Mathematical Practice

2 Reason abstractly
and quantitatively

▶

Why is $\frac{9}{10}$ greater than $\frac{3}{4}$? Not because the 9 and 10 are big numbers, although that may be a student's explanation. Each is one fractional part away from one whole, and tenths are smaller than fourths (i.e., $\frac{9}{10}$ is only one-tenth less than 1). Similarly, notice that $\frac{5}{8}$ is smaller than $\frac{4}{6}$ because $\frac{5}{8}$ is only one-eighth more than a half, while $\frac{4}{6}$ is one-sixth more than a half. Can you use this basic idea to compare $\frac{3}{5}$ and $\frac{5}{9}$? (Hint: Each is half of a fractional part more than $\frac{1}{2}$.)

Stop and Reflect

If students do not have all of these reasoning strategies, what strategies might you use to showcase the ones that are not as familiar? ■

◆ *Activity 8.9* **CHOOSE, JUSTIFY, PROVE**

Standards for
Mathematical Practice

3 Construct
viable arguments
and critique the
reasoning of others

▶

Present two or three pairs of fractions to students. The students' task is to decide which fraction is greater (choose), explain why they think this is so (justify), and then prove by using their choice of a manipulative or picture. Ask other students if they are convinced by the explanation and illustration provided. Include fractions that are equivalent.

An adaptation of this activity is to ask students to place the fractions on the number line and justify the relative size of each fraction. See also Activity 8.1 for a fun context for comparing and ordering fractions.

Smith (2002, p. 9 [emphasis added]) suggests that comparison questions ask, "Which of the following two (or more) fractions is greater, *or are they equal?*" This question leaves open the possibility that two fractions that may look different can, in fact, be equal.

◆ Equivalent Fractions

Equivalence is a critical but often poorly understood concept, whether for whole-number equations or for finding equivalent fractions.

How do you know that $\frac{4}{6} = \frac{2}{3}$? Explain in two different ways.

Here are some possible student responses:

- They are the same because you can simplify $\frac{4}{6}$ and get $\frac{2}{3}$.
- If you have a set of 6 items, 4 of them would be $\frac{4}{6}$. But you can think of the 6 as 3 groups with two in each group, and the 4 would be 2 groups with two in each group. So, $\frac{2}{3}$ groups is equivalent to $\frac{4}{6}$ items.
- If you start with $\frac{2}{3}$, you can multiply the top and the bottom numbers by 2, and that will give you $\frac{4}{6}$, so they are equal.
- If you had a square, partitioned it into 3 parts, and shaded 2 parts, that would be $\frac{2}{3}$ shaded. If you partitioned all 3 of these parts in half, that would be 6 parts in all, with 4 parts shaded. That's $\frac{4}{6}$, and it would be the same amount.

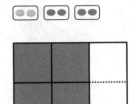

Response 2 illustrates what is happening in response 1, and response 4 illustrates what is happening in response 3. You can reinforce a conceptual understanding of fraction equivalence by using language that focuses on the concept (responses 2 and 4). Consider how different the conceptual and procedural explanations are.

- *Concept:* Two fractions are equivalent if they are representations for the same amount or quantity—if they are the same number.
- *Procedure:* To get an equivalent fraction, multiply (or divide) the top and bottom numbers by the same nonzero number.

Equivalence across Fraction Models

Note that the two examples above were area and set models. The following discussion and Activities 8.10, 8.11, and 8.12 similarly include attention to area and set models, along with length models.

Activity 8.10 **DIFFERENT FILLERS**

Using an area model for fractions that is familiar to your students (Figure 8.6), prepare a recording sheet with shapes that are outlined to show a part of a whole. For example, if the model consists of circular fraction pieces, you might draw an outline for $\frac{2}{3}$, $\frac{1}{2}$, and $\frac{3}{4}$. The students' task is to use their own fraction pieces to find as many equivalent fractions for the area as possible.

Activity 8.11 **DOT-PAPER EQUIVALENCES**

Use Blackline Master 6 or create your own with isometric or square dot grid paper (Blackline Masters 2–4). On the grid, draw the outline of an area and designate it as one whole. Draw a part of the area within the whole. Use different-sized parts of the whole to find names for the shaded part. See Figure 8.6, which includes an example drawn on an isometric grid. Students should draw a picture of the unit fractional part that they use for each fraction name. The larger the size of the whole, the more names the activity will generate.

The "Dot-Paper Equivalences" activity helps students do what Lamon (2002) calls "unitizing"—that is, given a quantity, finding different ways to chunk the quantity into parts in order to name it. She points out that this is a key ability related not only to equivalent fractions but also to proportional reasoning, especially in the comparison of ratios.

Figure 8.6 Area models for equivalent fractions.

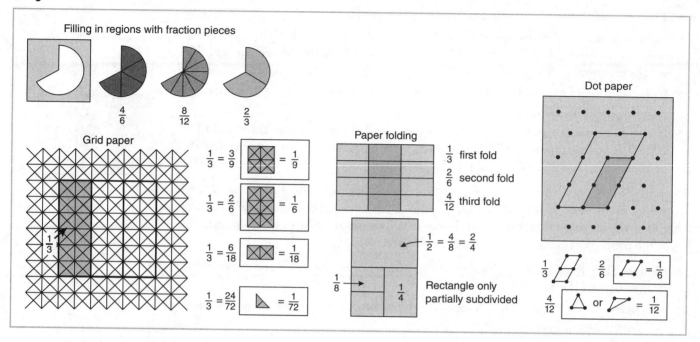

Figure 8.7 Length models for equivalent fractions.

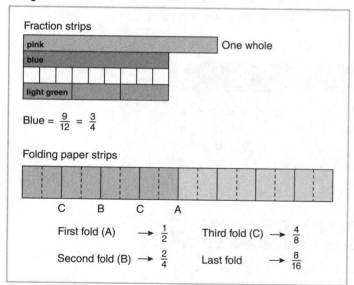

Length models should be used in activities similar to the "Different Fillers" activity. Asking students to locate $\frac{2}{5}$ and $\frac{4}{10}$ on a number line, for example, can help them see that the two fractions are equivalent (Siegler et al., 2010). Measuring in inches is an excellent context for working on fraction equivalences with halves, fourths, eighths, and sixteenths. Using Cuisenaire rods, students find smaller rods to find fraction names for the given part (see the first example in Figure 8.7). To have larger wholes and thus more possible parts, use a train of two or three rods for the whole and the part. Folding paper strips is another method of creating fraction names. In the second example in Figure 8.7, one-half is partitioned by successive folding in half. Other folds would produce other equivalent fraction names.

One excellent way to make a direct connection to algebra is to have students think of fractions as slope and find their locations on a coordinate axis (Cheng, 2010). For example, the fraction $\frac{3}{4}$ can represent the rise and run for slope (rise is the y-value, and run is the x-value). So, $\frac{3}{4}$ is plotted at (4,3). Similarly, the fraction $\frac{6}{8}$ is plotted at (8,6).

 *Formative Assessment Note*

Consider using a diagnostic interview to see if students are making the connection between equivalence and slope. Ask students to find other values that lie on this line. Ask what they know about the fraction they selected. Students should be able to explain that they are equivalent fractions and that they are fractions that represent the same slope. Conversely, you can give students fractions and ask, "Is this fraction equivalent to $\frac{3}{4}$?" and "Will this fraction be on the same line with $\frac{3}{4}$?"

Set models can also be used to develop the concept of equivalence. The following activity is also a unitizing activity in which students look for different units or chunks of the whole in order to name a part of the whole in different ways.

Activity 8.12 APPLES AND BANANAS

Have students set out a specific number of counters in two colors—for example, 24 counters, 16 of them red (apples) and 8 yellow (bananas). The 24 counters make up the whole. The task is to group the counters into different fractional parts of the whole and use the parts to create fraction names for the fractions that are apples and the fractions that are bananas. In Figure 8.8, 24 counters (pieces of fruit) are arranged in different groups and arrays. ELLs may not know what is meant by the term *group* because this is often used in classrooms to arrange students. Spend time before the activity modeling what it means to group objects.

Ask questions such as, "If we make groups of four, what part of the set is red?" With these prompts, you can suggest fraction names that students are unlikely to suggest.

Across the models, two instructional practices are critical in reinforcing the concept of equivalence:

- Notice that the phrase *reducing fractions* was not used. This terminology implies making the amount smaller and should be avoided. Fractions are simplified, *not* reduced.

- Do not tell students their answer is incorrect if not in the simplest or lowest terms. This also misinforms students about the equivalence of fractions. If you want the answer in a simplified form, provide feedback to the student that the answer is correct but must be simplified.

Figure 8.8 Set models for equivalent fractions.

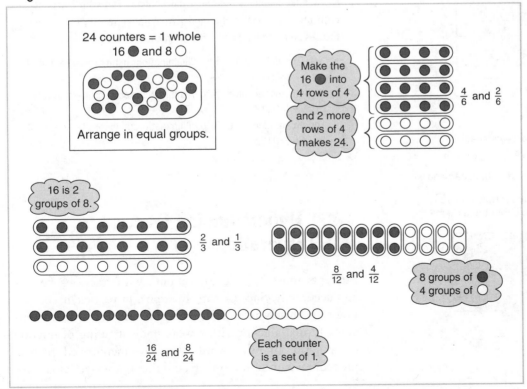

Equivalent-Fraction Algorithm

Middle-school students need to be able to use and understand the equivalent-fraction algorithm. Activity 8.13 is designed to build this connection. Adding a context can help struggling learners understand why the fractions are equivalent.

◢ *Activity 8.13* **GARDEN PLOTS**

Have students draw a square "garden" on blank paper, or hand students a square of paper (like origami paper). Begin by explaining that the garden is divided into rows of various vegetables. In the first example, you might illustrate four columns (fourths) and designate $\frac{3}{4}$ rows as corn. Then, explain that the garden is going to be shared with family and friends in such a way that each person has an equal share. Show how the garden can be partitioned horizontally to represent sharing with two people (Figure 8.9a). Ask, "What fraction of our newly partitioned garden is corn?" $\frac{6}{8}$. Next, tell students to come up with other ways to share the garden with friends. (They can choose how many, or you can structure it.) For each newly partitioned garden, ask students to record an equation showing the equivalent fractions.

Figure 8.9

Conceptual illustration of equivalent fraction algorithm. (a) Partition to show equivalence. (b) Cover part of the square and ask, "How can you count the fraction parts if you cannot see them?"

(a) Partition to show equivalence

Start with each square showing $\frac{3}{4}$.

$$\frac{4}{4} = \boxed{\frac{3 \times 3}{3 \times 4}} = \frac{9}{12} \qquad \frac{3}{4} = \boxed{\frac{4 \times 3}{4 \times 4}} = \frac{12}{16}$$

$$\frac{3}{4} = \boxed{\frac{2 \times 3}{2 \times 4}} = \frac{6}{8} \qquad \frac{3}{4} = \boxed{\frac{5 \times 3}{5 \times 4}} = \frac{15}{20}$$

What <u>product</u> tells how many parts are shaded?

What <u>product</u> tells how many parts in the whole?

Notice that the same factor is used for both part and whole.

(b) Cover part of square and ask, "How can you count the fraction parts if you cannot see them?"

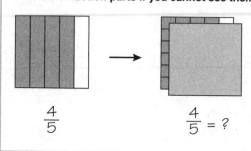

$$\frac{4}{5} \qquad\qquad \frac{4}{5} = ?$$

After students have prepared their own examples, provide time for them to look at their fractions and gardens and notice patterns about the fractions and the diagrams. To help students see the connection of the garden plot to the algorithm, cover a part of the plot so that they cannot see all the sections (Figure 8.9b).

t·e·c·h·n·o·l·o·g·y ⏻
note

NCTM's Illuminations has three units called "Fun with Fractions." Each unit uses one of the model types (area, length, or set) and focuses on comparing and ordering fractions and equivalence.

- Set model unit: http://illuminations.nctm.org/LessonDetail.aspx?id=U112
- Region model unit: http://illuminations.nctm.org/LessonDetail.aspx?id=U113
- Length model unit: http://illuminations.nctm.org/LessonDetail.aspx?id=U152.

◢ Understanding Fraction Operations

Students must be able to compute with fractions flexibly and accurately. Success with fractions, in particular computation, is closely related to success in Algebra I. If students enter formal algebra with a weak understanding of fraction computation (in other words, they have memorized the four procedures but do not understand them), they are at risk for struggling, which in turn can limit college and career opportunities. Deeper understanding and flexibility take time! This is recognized by research and the *Common Core State Standards*, which suggest the following developmental process:

Grade 4: Add and subtract fractions with like denominators, and multiply fractions by whole numbers (p. 27).

Grade 5: Develop fluency with addition and subtraction of fractions, and develop understanding of the multiplication of fractions and the division of fractions in limited cases (unit fractions divided by whole numbers and whole numbers divided by unit fractions) (p. 33).

Grade 6: Apply and extend previous understandings of multiplication and division to divide fractions by fractions (p. 41).

Similarly, the NCTM *Curriculum Focal Points* (NCTM, 2006) place addition and subtraction of fractions (and decimals) as a focal point in grade 5, and multiplication and division of fractions as a focal point in grade 6. Collectively, these guides recognize that the development of understanding and procedural proficiency for fraction operations requires significant time.

Some teachers may argue that they can't or don't need to devote so much time to fraction operations—that sharing one algorithm for each operation is quicker and leads to less confusion for students. This approach does not work. First, none of the algorithms helps students think conceptually about the operations and what they mean. When students follow a procedure they do not understand, they have no means of knowing when to use it, and no way of assessing whether their answers make sense. Second, mastery of poorly understood algorithms in the short term is quickly lost, particularly by students who struggle in mathematics. When combined with the differing procedures for each operation, the algorithms all soon become a meaningless jumble. Students ask, "Do I need a common denominator, or do I just add or multiply the bottom numbers?" "Which one do you invert, the first or the second number?" Third, students can't adapt to slight changes in the fractions. For example, if a mixed number appears, students don't know how to apply the algorithm.

◆ Effective Teaching Process

In a report that summarizes what works for teaching fraction operations, four steps are suggested: (1) use contexts, (2) use a variety of models, (3) include estimation and informal methods, and (4) address misconceptions (Siegler et al., 2010). Each is briefly described here and then addressed within the discussion of each operation.

1. *Use contextual tasks.* Contexts are concrete and provide the chance for students to see what is happening with each operation. Problem contexts need not be elaborate. What you want is a context that fits both the meaning of the operation and the fractions involved.

2. *Explore each operation with a variety of models.* Use area, length, and set models, and be sure students connect the models to the symbolic operations. The tools will help students learn to reason, contribute to mental methods, and provide a useful background for developing the standard algorithms.

3. *Let estimation and informal methods play a big role in the development of strategies.* "Should $2\frac{1}{2} \times \frac{1}{4}$ be more or less than 1? More or less than 2?" Estimation keeps the focus on the meanings of the numbers and the operations, encourages reflective thinking, and helps build informal number sense with fractions. Can you reason to get an exact answer without using the standard algorithm? One way is to apply the distributive property, splitting the mixed number and multiplying both parts by $\frac{1}{4}$: $(2 \times \frac{1}{4}) + (\frac{1}{2} \times \frac{1}{4})$. Two $\frac{1}{4}$s are $\frac{2}{4}$ or $\frac{1}{2}$, and a half of a fourth is $\frac{1}{8}$. So, add an eighth to a half and you have $\frac{5}{8}$.

4. *Address common misconceptions regarding the operations.* Students naturally apply their prior knowledge—in this case, whole-number knowledge—to new knowledge. Using whole-number knowledge can support fraction understanding. For example, ask, "What does 2×3 mean?" Follow this with, "What might $2 \times 3\frac{1}{2}$ mean?" But because the procedures are different, whole-number knowledge also leads to errors in computing with fractions (e.g., adding denominators when fractions are being added). Teachers should present common misconceptions and discuss why some approaches lead to right answers and why others do not (Siegler et al., 2010). For example, show students an incorrectly solved problem (e.g., $\frac{2}{3} + \frac{1}{2} = \frac{3}{5}$) and ask students to describe how they would help this student understand addition of fractions.

◈ Computational Estimation

Estimation is one of the most effective ways to build understanding and procedural fluency with fractions. A frequently quoted result from the Second National Assessment (Post, 1981) concerns the following item:

Estimate the answer to $\frac{12}{13} + \frac{7}{8} =$ ___
You will not have time to solve the problem with paper and pencil.

Here is how 13-year-olds answered:

Response	Percentage of 13-Year-Olds
1	7
2	24
19	28
21	27
Don't know	14

There are different ways to estimate for fraction computation (Siegler et al., 2010):

- *Benchmarks.* Decide whether the fractions are closest to 0, $\frac{1}{2}$, or 1 (or to 3, $3\frac{1}{2}$, or 4—the closest whole numbers and the half in between them for mixed numbers). After making the determination for each fraction, mentally add or subtract.

Addition example: $\frac{7}{8} + \frac{1}{10}$. Think "$\frac{7}{8}$ is close to 1, and $\frac{1}{10}$ is close to 0, so the sum is about $1 + 0$, or close to 1."

Division example: $5\frac{1}{3} \div \frac{3}{5}$. Think "$5\frac{1}{3}$ is close to 5, and $\frac{3}{5}$ is close to $\frac{1}{2}$. How many halves in 5? 10."

- *Relative size of unit fractions.* Decide how big the fraction is based on its unit (denominator), and apply this information to the computation.

Addition example: $\frac{7}{8} + \frac{1}{10}$. Think "$\frac{7}{8}$ is just $\frac{1}{8}$ away from a whole (1), and $\frac{1}{8}$ is a close to (but bigger than) $\frac{1}{10}$, so the sum will be close to, but less than, 1."

Multiplication example: $\frac{1}{3} \times 3\frac{4}{5}$. Think "I need a third of this value. A third of 3 is 1, and $\frac{1}{3}$ of $\frac{4}{5}$ is going to be just over $\frac{1}{5}$ (since there are four parts), so about $1\frac{1}{5}$."

The following activity can be done regularly as a short full-class warm-up or can be a focus activity for a full lesson.

Activity 8.14 OVER OR UNDER ONE

 Tell students that they are going to estimate the answers to fraction operation problems. They are to decide only whether the exact answer is more than one or less than one. Project a problem for no more than 10 seconds, then hide or remove it. Ask students to write down on paper or on a mini whiteboard their choice of "over" or "under" one. You can also ask students to show you "thumbs up" or "thumbs down" to indicate over or under one. Or use clickers to quickly gather data (see www.iclicker.com). Do several problems. Then return to each problem and discuss how students decided on their estimates. Students, in particular students with disabilities, may benefit from having a number line as a tool to think about the problems. Students also benefit when they are asked to connect their estimate to a real-life situation, a number line, or a picture.

In the discussions following these estimation exercises, ask students if they think that the exact answer is more or less than the estimate that they gave. What is their reasoning? Over time, Activity 8.14 can include tasks that are more challenging, or it can be differentiated with different groups of students working on different "over" and "under" values. Consider the following variations:

- Use a target answer that is different from one. For example, estimate more or less than $\frac{1}{2}$, $1\frac{1}{2}$, 2, or 3.
- Choose fraction pairs in which the fractions are both less than one or both greater than one.
- Ask students to create equations that are slightly less than or slightly more than one (or other values). They can trade equations with other students, who in turn need to decide whether the sum, difference, product, or dividend is over one or under one (or other value).

A more challenging estimation activity is shared in Activity 8.15, which can provide good insights into what students know about the relationship between numerator and denominator.

 Activity 8.15 CAN YOU MAKE IT TRUE?

Share equations with two missing values (in the numerators, or denominators, or one of each). Explain that students cannot use the digits already in the problem. Encourage students to use fraction benchmarks (0, $\frac{1}{2}$, 1) to support their thinking. A few examples are shared here (one of them is impossible—can you find it?):

$$\frac{\square}{6} + \frac{\square}{8} = 1 \qquad \frac{\square}{5} - \frac{\square}{3} = 1 \qquad \frac{9}{\square} + \frac{\square}{8} = 3$$

$$\frac{6}{n} + \frac{5}{n} = \frac{1}{2} \qquad \frac{1}{n} - \frac{5}{n} = 2 \qquad \frac{n}{7} - \frac{5}{n} = \frac{1}{2}$$

Source: Adapted from Fung, M. G., & Latulippe, C. L. (2010). Computational estimation. *Teaching Children Mathematics, 17*(3), 170—176, and from Hynes, M. C. (Ed.). (1996). *Ideas: NCTM standards-based instruction, grades 5—8.* Reston, VA: NCTM.

All of these equations require reasoning and thinking about the relative sizes of fractions, which builds a critical foundation for success in developing and understanding fraction operations.

Addition and Subtraction

Addition and subtraction of fractions are taught in grade 5, but middle-school teachers may find that students need additional experience. Here, we briefly discuss the four steps previously introduced.

Figure 8.10 Using models to add fractions.

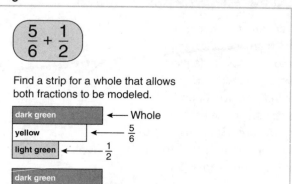

$\frac{5}{6} + \frac{1}{2}$

Find a strip for a whole that allows both fractions to be modeled.

The sum is 1 whole and a red strip more than a whole. A red strip is 1/3 of a dark green strip.

So $\frac{5}{6} + \frac{1}{2} = 1\frac{1}{3}$.

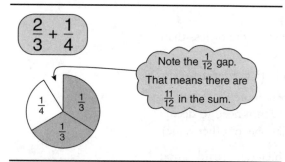

$\frac{2}{3} + \frac{1}{4}$

Note the $\frac{1}{12}$ gap. That means there are $\frac{11}{12}$ in the sum.

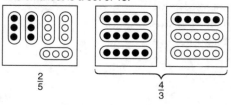

$\frac{2}{5} + \frac{4}{3}$

What set size can be used for the whole? The smallest is a set of 15.

$\frac{2}{5}$ $\frac{4}{3}$

Combine (add) the fractions.
$\frac{2}{5}$ is 6 counters, and $\frac{4}{3}$ is 20 counters.
In sets of 15, that is $\frac{26}{15}$, or $1\frac{11}{15}$.

1     $\frac{11}{15}$

Contextual Examples and Invented Strategies

Consider the example of measuring something in inches (e.g., sewing, cutting molding for a doorway, hanging a picture). These measures are typically in halves, fourths, eighths, and/or sixteenths—fractions that can be added mentally by considering the relationship between the sizes of the parts (e.g., $\frac{1}{2} = \frac{2}{4} = \frac{4}{8} = \frac{8}{16}$). If you can easily find the equivalent fraction, then you can count parts—no algorithm is needed, although informally you did find a common denominator and added.

Pose problems in a familiar context, as in the four problems posed here.

- Megan gathered 4 pounds of walnuts, and Aimee gathered another $2\frac{7}{8}$ pounds. How many pounds did they gather?
- On Saturday, Lisa walked $1\frac{1}{2}$ miles, and on Sunday she walked $2\frac{1}{8}$ miles. How far did she walk over the weekend?
- Jacob ordered $4\frac{1}{4}$ pizzas. Before his guests arrived, he ate $\frac{7}{8}$ of one pizza. How much was left for the party?
- In measuring the wood needed for a picture frame, Elise figured that she needed two pieces that were $5\frac{1}{4}$ inches and two pieces that were $7\frac{3}{4}$ inches. What length of wood board does she need to buy to build her picture frame?

Notice that these problems (1) use a mix of area and linear models; (2) use a mix of whole numbers, mixed numbers, and fractions; (3) use a variety of different contexts; and (4) include both addition and subtraction situations. Did you notice that the last problem involves adding four fractions, not just two fractions? Adding a series is important with fractions, just as it is with whole numbers.

◆ Models

Figure 8.10 illustrates addition across all three models. Area and length models are very effective in illustrating the meaning of adding fractions. Set models can also be used, but they can be more confusing for students.

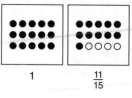

Teaching Tip

The key to which manipulative to use lies in the context—if a context is round, fraction circles are a good match. If the context is distance, then a number line is a better match.

Area Models

Cramer et al. (2008) suggest that circles are the best model for adding and subtracting fractions because circles allow students to develop mental images of the sizes of different pieces (fractions) of the circle. Consider this problem, in which the context is circular:

Jack and Jill ordered two medium pizzas, one cheese and one pepperoni. Jack ate $\frac{5}{6}$ of a pizza and Jill ate $\frac{1}{2}$ of a pizza. How much pizza did they eat together?

There are many other area models that can be used. Pattern blocks, for example, have pieces such that the hexagon can be one whole, the blue parallelogram $\frac{1}{3}$, the green triangle $\frac{1}{6}$, and the red trapezoid $\frac{1}{2}$. Like circles, rectangles can be drawn for any fractional value, depending on how they are partitioned. In addition, the partitioning can be easier and more accurate in a rectangle.

Al, Bill, Carrie, Danielle, Enrique, and Fabio are each given a portion of the school garden for spring planting. Here are the portions:

$$\text{Al} = \frac{1}{4} \quad \text{Bill} = \frac{1}{8} \quad \text{Carrie} = \frac{3}{16} \quad \text{Danielle} = \frac{1}{16} \quad \text{Enrique} = \frac{1}{4} \quad \text{Fabio} = \frac{1}{8}$$

They decide to pair up to share the work. What fraction of the garden will each of the following pairs or groups have if they combine their portions of the garden? Show your work.

- Bill and Danielle
- Al and Carrie
- Fabio and Enrique
- Carrie, Fabio, and Al

Linear Models

An important model for adding or subtracting fractions is the number line (Siegler et al., 2010). One advantage of the number line is that it can be connected to the ruler, which is the most common real context for adding or subtracting fractions. The number line is also a more challenging model than the circle model because it requires that the student understand $\frac{3}{4}$ as 3 parts of 4, and also as a value between 0 and 1 (Izsák, Tillema, & Tunc-Pekkam, 2008). Using the number line in addition to area representations can strengthen students' understanding of fractions (Clarke et al., 2008; Cramer et al., 2008; Petit et al., 2010).

Activity 8.16 JUMPS ON THE RULER

Tell students to model the given examples on the ruler. A linear context can be added (length of grass in the yard, hair growing or being cut), but if students have been doing many contextual tasks, it is important to see whether they can also add and subtract without a context. Use the ruler as a visual, and find the results of these three problems without applying the common denominator algorithm. ELLs may not be as familiar with inches because most countries measure in metric units. In this case, be sure to spend time before the activity discussing how the inch is partitioned, and/or add labels for fourths as a reminder that the inch is different from metric system units.

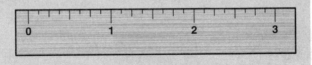

$\frac{3}{4} + \frac{1}{2}$ $\qquad$ $2\frac{1}{2} - 1\frac{1}{4}$ $\qquad$ $1\frac{1}{8} + 1\frac{1}{2}$

These jumps encourage students to invent strategies without having to find a common denominator (Taber, 2009). In the first problem, students might use 1 as a benchmark. They use $\frac{1}{4}$ from the $\frac{1}{2}$ to get to a whole, then have $\frac{1}{4}$ more to add on—so, $1\frac{1}{4}$. Similarly, they could take the $\frac{1}{2}$ from the $\frac{3}{4}$ to make a whole with the $\frac{1}{2}$, then add on the $\frac{1}{4}$. The more students illustrate problems on the number line, the more flexible they will become in adding or subtracting fractions.

Figure 8.11

Rewriting addition and subtraction problems involving fractions.

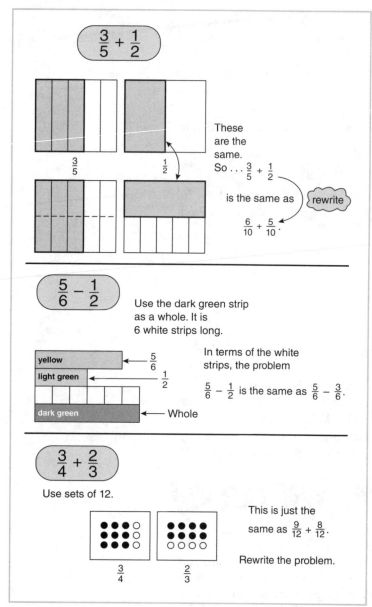

◆ Developing the Algorithms

Students can build on their invented strategies and knowledge of equivalence to develop the common-denominator approach for adding and subtracting fractions. The idea that the top number counts and the bottom number tells what is counted makes addition and subtraction of like fractions very similar to adding and subtracting whole numbers. When students are working on adding with like denominators, it is important to be sure that they are focusing on the key idea—the units are the same, so they can be combined (Mack, 2004).

When working with unlike denominators, students may have memorized an algorithm that did not make sense. Reminders such as "you can't add apples and oranges" work against students' understanding why, and the statement is essentially false. A correct statement might be, "Remember that we must add equal-size parts. The algorithm is designed to find common denominators because that means the parts that are being added or subtracted are the same size."

If students are making errors, they likely do not understand adding and subtracting fractions with unlike denominators and need experiences with visuals. Have students use models or drawings. Ask students to explain why they are finding the same denominator (so that equal-size parts can be combined). These ideas are illustrated in Figure 8.11.

◆ Fractions Greater Than One

Include mixed numbers in all of your activities with addition and subtraction, and let students solve these problems in ways that make sense to them. Students will tend naturally to add or subtract the whole numbers and then the fractions. Sometimes, this is all that needs to be done, but in other cases, regrouping across the whole number and fraction is needed.

Several strategies can be used. Consider this problem: $2\frac{1}{8} - \frac{5}{8}$. Some will take $\frac{5}{8}$ from the whole part, 2, leaving $1\frac{3}{8}$, and then add $\frac{1}{8}$ more to get $1\frac{4}{8}$. Others may take away the $\frac{1}{8}$ that is there and then $\frac{4}{8}$ from the remaining 2. A third but unlikely method is to trade one of the wholes for $\frac{8}{8}$, add it to the $\frac{1}{8}$, and then take $\frac{5}{8}$ from the resulting $\frac{9}{8}$. This last method is the same as the standard algorithm, and parallels the regrouping process in whole number addition and subtraction.

One underemphasized technique that is a great strategy is to change the mixed numbers to single fractions. Let's revisit $2\frac{1}{8} - \frac{5}{8}$. This can be rewritten as $\frac{17}{8} - \frac{5}{8}$. Because $17 - 5$ is 12,

To reinforce equivalences, ask students, "What equivalent fractions might you use so that you have equal-size parts?" rather than "What is the common denominator?"

the solution is $\frac{12}{8}$, or $1\frac{1}{2}$. This is certainly efficient and will always work. The message here is to provide options to students that make sense to them.

Addressing Misconceptions

By the time students are in the middle school, they will have had experiences with adding fractions. It is important assess students' understanding and keep an eye on common misconceptions that will need to be addressed. Here are the most common misconceptions related to the addition and subtraction of fractions.

Adding Both Numerators and Denominators

The most common error in adding fractions is to add both the numerators and the denominators. Consider the following task:

Ms. Rodriguez baked a pan of brownies for the bake sale and cut the brownies into 8 equal-size parts. In the morning, three of the brownies were sold; in the afternoon, two more were sold. What fractional part of the brownies had been sold? What fractional part was still for sale?

Students solving this task are able to effectively draw a rectangle partitioned into eighths and are able to shade $\frac{3}{8}$ and $\frac{2}{8}$, as shown here. However, about half of students will write $\frac{3}{8} + \frac{2}{8} = \frac{5}{16}$, even after drawing the model correctly. And they won't seem to be bothered that the two answers ($\frac{5}{8}$ and $\frac{5}{16}$) are different (Bamberger, Oberdorf, & Schultz-Ferrell, 2010). In such a case, ask students to decide whether both answers can be right. Ask them to defend which is right and why the other answer is not right. You cannot just tell students which is right—the key is for them to be able to overcome their misconceptions (influenced by their knowledge of how to add whole numbers) and for them to connect the model to the symbols.

Even after students have more experience with adding and subtracting, they can forget about the meaning of the denominator, so it is important to challenge potential misconceptions. For example, one teacher asked her fifth graders if the following was correct: $\frac{3}{8} + \frac{2}{8} = \frac{5}{16}$. A student correctly replied, "No, because they are eighths (holds up one-eighth of a fraction circle). If you put them together, you still have eighths (shows this with the fraction circles). See, you didn't make them into sixteenths when you put them together. They're still eighths" (Mack, 2004, p. 229).

Failing to Find Common Denominators

Less common, but still prevalent, is the tendency to just ignore the denominator and add the numerators (Siegler et al., 2010). For example, $\frac{4}{5} + \frac{4}{10} = \frac{8}{10}$. This is an indication that students do not understand that the different denominators indicate different-size pieces. Using a number line or fraction strip, where students must pay attention to the relative sizes of the fractions, can help develop a stronger understanding of the role of the denominator in adding.

Difficulty Finding Common Multiples

Many students have trouble finding common denominators because they are not able to come up with common multiples of the denominators quickly. This skill requires having a good command of multiplication facts. Activity 8.17 is aimed at the skill of finding least common multiples or common denominators. Students benefit from knowing that *any* common denominator will work. Least common denominators are preferred because the computation is more manageable with smaller numbers, and there is less simplifying to do after adding or subtracting. Do not require least common multiples—support all common denominators, and through discussion students will see that finding the smallest multiple is more efficient.

Figure 8.12

Least common multiple (LCM) flash cards.

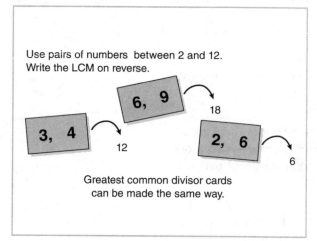

Use pairs of numbers between 2 and 12. Write the LCM on reverse.

3, 4 → 12

6, 9 → 18

2, 6 → 6

Greatest common divisor cards can be made the same way.

Activity 8.17 COMMON MULTIPLE FLASH CARDS

Make flash cards with pairs of numbers that are potential denominators. Most should be less than 12 (Figure 8.12). Place students with partners and give them a deck of cards. At a student's turn, he or she turns over a card and states a common multiple (e.g., for 6 and 8, a student might suggest 48). The partner gets a chance to suggest a smaller common multiple (e.g., 24). The student suggesting the least common multiple gets to keep the card. Be sure to include pairs that are prime, such as 9 and 5; pairs in which one is a multiple of the other, such as 2 and 8; and pairs that have a common divisor, such as 8 and 12. Start students with disabilities with the card on which one member of the pair is a multiple of the other.

Difficulty with Mixed Numbers

Too often, instruction with mixed numbers is not well integrated into fraction instruction, and therefore students find these values particularly troubling. Here are three misconceptions described in the research (Petit et al., 2010; Siegler, et al., 2010).

- When given a problem like $3\frac{1}{4} - 1\frac{3}{8}$, students subtract the smaller fraction from the larger ($\frac{3}{8} - \frac{1}{4}$). Although this occurs with whole-number subtraction, it is more prevalent with mixed numbers.

- When given a problem like $4 - \frac{7}{8}$, students don't know what to do with the fact that one number is not a fraction. They will tend to place an 8 under the 4 ($\frac{4}{8} - \frac{7}{8}$) in order to find a solution.

- When given a problem like $14\frac{1}{2} - 3\frac{1}{8}$, students focus only on the whole-number aspect of the problem and don't know what to do with the fractional part.

There are ways to avoid and address these misconceptions. Include more mixed numbers and whole numbers with fractions less than one. Use models and contexts. And, importantly, take on these misconceptions by making them part of class discussions about whether they are correct and why.

 ## Multiplication

Can you think of a situation that requires using multiplication of fractions? Do you use this algorithm outside teaching? Often, the answer to these questions is no. It is not that there are no situations involving fraction multiplication, but the connection between the concept and the procedure is not well understood, so the algorithm is never used. Here, we will share contexts and models that can be used to develop the algorithm meaningfully.

◆ Contextual Examples and Models

When working with whole numbers, we would say that 3×5 means "3 sets of 5" (equal sets) or "3 rows of 5" (area or array), or "5 three times" (number line). Different visuals must be used and aligned with contexts so that students get a comprehensive understanding of multiplication of fractions. The story problems that you use to pose multiplication tasks to students need not be elaborate, but it is important to think about the numbers and contexts that you use in the problems.

Multiplication of fractions is really about scaling. If you scale something by a factor of 2, you multiply it by 2. When you scale by 1 (1 times the size), the amount is unchanged (identity property of multiplication). Similarly, multiplying by $\frac{1}{2}$ means taking half of the original size, while multiplying by $1\frac{1}{2}$ means the original size plus half the original size. This scaling concept can enhance students' ability to decide whether their answers are reasonable. A possible progression of problem difficulty is developed in the sections that follow.

Fractions of Whole Numbers

Students' first experiences with fraction multiplication should involve finding fractions of whole numbers. Figure 8.2 includes problems that can serve as a starting point for finding fractions of a whole, and Figure 8.13 shows how to use manipulatives to illustrate the operation. Contexts are critical in making sense of finding a fraction of a whole. Activity 8.18 also provides some great starting tasks.

Figure 8.13

Modeling multiplication problems in which the unit pieces do not require further subdivision.

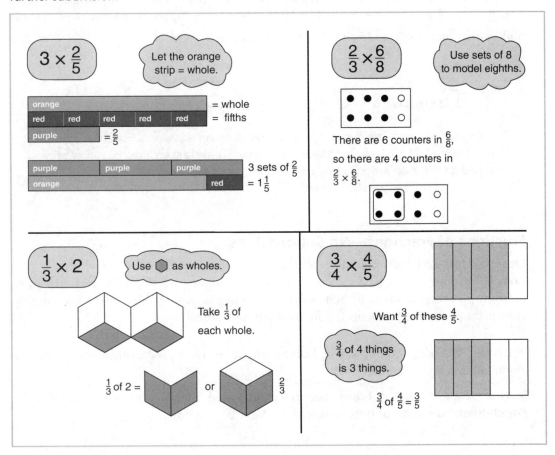

Activity 8.18 WATER, WALKING, AND WHEELS

Ask students to use any manipulative or drawing to figure out the answers to the next three tasks. As you will notice, they represent area, linear, and set models in different contexts.

1. The walk from school to the public library takes 15 minutes. When Anna asked her mom how far they had gone, her mom said that they had gone $\frac{2}{3}$ of the way. How many minutes had they walked? (Assume a constant walking rate.)

2. There are 15 cars in Michael's matchbox car collection. Two-thirds of the cars are red. How many red cars does Michael have?

3. Wilma filled 15 glasses with $\frac{2}{3}$ cup of milk in each. How much milk did Wilma use?

Rather than having to deal with three different contexts, ELLs will benefit from three stories in the same context (vocabulary). They should still involve three different models. For example, all three could be about cars but include parking lot (area), line of cars (linear), and collection (set).

How might students think through each problem? For the first two, students might partition 15 into three groups (or partition a line into three parts), then see how many are in two parts. Recording this in symbols ($\frac{2}{3}$ of 15) gives the following result: $15 \div 3 \times 2$.

Notice that Wilma's situation is "15 groups of $\frac{2}{3}$," not "$\frac{2}{3}$ of a group of 15." Although the commutative property means that these numbers can be switched, it is important that students understand each type as a representation with a different meaning. The problem may be solved in a counting-up strategy. It may be solved by repeated addition: $\frac{2}{3} + \frac{2}{3} + \frac{2}{3} + \ldots + \frac{2}{3} = 30/3 = 10$. Students may notice that what they did was multiply the numerator by 15 and then they divided by 3, so $15 \times \frac{2}{3} = \frac{(15 \times 2)}{3} = \frac{30}{3} = 10$.

Formative Assessment Note

These "fraction-of-a-whole" problems can be used as a performance assessment. From their written solutions and from what you observe as students work, record your insights on a checklist about which of these models (area, linear, and set) are easy or challenging for different learners.

Fractions of Fractions—No Subdivisions

Once students have had experiences with fractions of a whole ($\frac{2}{3}$ of 15) or wholes of fractions (15 groups of $\frac{2}{3}$), a next step is to introduce finding a fraction of a fraction, but to carefully pick tasks in which no additional partitioning is required. See if you can mentally answer the next three problems (again, by using each model type):

You have $\frac{3}{4}$ of a pizza left. If you give $\frac{1}{3}$ of the leftover pizza to your brother, how much of a whole pizza will your brother get?

Someone ate $\frac{1}{10}$ of a loaf of bread, leaving $\frac{9}{10}$. If you use $\frac{2}{3}$ of what is left of the loaf to make French toast, how much of the whole loaf will have been used?

Gloria used $2\frac{1}{2}$ tubes of blue paint to paint the sky in her picture. Each tube holds $\frac{4}{5}$ ounce of paint. How many ounces of blue paint did Gloria use?

Figure 8.13 shows how to use different manipulatives to illustrate multiplication. However, there is more than one way to partition. In $\frac{1}{3} \times \frac{3}{4}$, for example, you can find one-third of the three-fourths (as in Figure 8.13), or you can find one-third of each fourth and then combine the pieces (Izsák, 2008).

Fractions of Fractions—Subdividing the Unit Parts

When the pieces must be subdivided into smaller unit parts, the problems become more challenging.

Zack had $\frac{2}{3}$ of the field left to cut. After lunch, he cut $\frac{3}{4}$ of the field that was left to cut. How much of the whole field did Zack cut after lunch?

The zookeeper had a huge bottle of the animals' favorite liquid treat, Zoo Cola. The monkey drank $\frac{1}{5}$ of the bottle. The zebra drank $\frac{2}{3}$ of what was left. How much of the bottle of Zoo Cola did the zebra drink?

In Zack's lawn problem, it is necessary to find fourths of two things, the 2 thirds of the grass left to cut. In the Zoo Cola problem, you need thirds of four things, the 4 fifths of the Zoo Cola that remain. Again, the concepts of the top number counting and the bottom number naming what is counted play an important role. Figure 8.14 shows a possible solution for Zack's lawn problem. Using a paper strip and partitioning is an effective way to solve multiplication problems, especially when they require additional partitioning (Siebert & Gaskin, 2006). A similar approach can be used for the Zoo Cola problem.

The area model is also an effective visual for fraction problems in which subdividing is required. It provides a powerful visual to show that a result of a fraction times a fraction can be quite a bit smaller than either of the fractions, or that if the fractions are both close to 1, then the result is also close to 1. And it is a good model for connecting to the standard algorithm for multiplying fractions.

Provide students with a square, and ask them to partition and shade to illustrate the fraction that is the initial value. For example, in $\frac{3}{5} \times \frac{3}{4}$, you are finding $\frac{3}{5}$ of $\frac{3}{4}$, so you start with $\frac{3}{4}$ (Figure 8.15a). To find fifths of the $\frac{3}{4}$, draw five horizontal lines through the $\frac{3}{4}$ (Figure 8.15b) or all the way across the square so that the whole is in same-size partitions, and shade three of the five (Figure 8.15c). The overlap of the shading illustrates what is $\frac{3}{5}$ of $\frac{3}{4}$ of the original whole.

Using a context and building on whole-number knowledge can support student reasoning about a fraction of a fraction. Quilting is a good context because quilts are rectangles and the individual rectangles (or squares) within the quilt are fractions of the whole quilt. Activity 8.19 is a two-step activity with quilts.

Figure 8.14

Solutions to a multiplication problem when the parts must be subdivided.

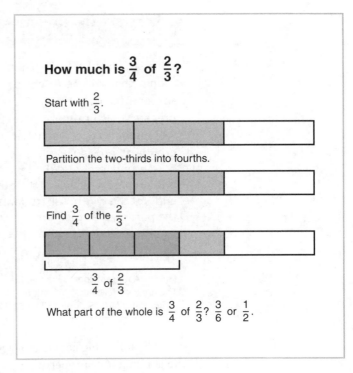

How much is $\frac{3}{4}$ of $\frac{2}{3}$?

Start with $\frac{2}{3}$.

Partition the two-thirds into fourths.

Find $\frac{3}{4}$ of the $\frac{2}{3}$.

$\frac{3}{4}$ of $\frac{2}{3}$

What part of the whole is $\frac{3}{4}$ of $\frac{2}{3}$? $\frac{3}{6}$ or $\frac{1}{2}$.

Figure 8.15 Modeling multiplication with squares (area model).

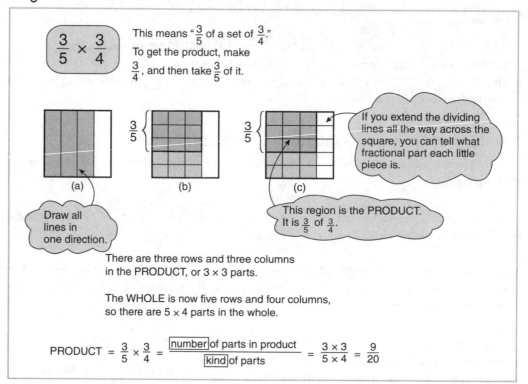

$$\text{PRODUCT} = \frac{3}{5} \times \frac{3}{4} = \frac{\boxed{\text{number}} \text{ of parts in product}}{\boxed{\text{kind}} \text{ of parts}} = \frac{3 \times 3}{5 \times 4} = \frac{9}{20}$$

Activity 8.19 QUILTING PIECES

Have students use grid paper to sketch a drawing of a quilt that will be 8 feet by 6 feet (or create a full-size one for your class!). Explain that each group will prepare a picture that is 3 feet by 2 feet for the quilt. Ask students to tell you what fraction of the quilt each group will provide.

Second, rephrase the task. Explain that each group is to prepare a section of the quilt that is $\frac{1}{4}$ of the length and $\frac{1}{2}$ of the width. Ask students to sketch the quilt and the portion that their group will prepare.

Help students make the connection that $\frac{1}{4}$ the length $\times \frac{1}{2}$ the width $= \frac{1}{8}$ the area ($\frac{1}{4} \times \frac{1}{2} = \frac{1}{8}$).

Source: Adapted from Tsankova, J. K., & Pjanic, K. (2009/2010). The area model of multiplication of fractions. *Mathematics Teaching in the Middle School, 15*(5), 281–285.

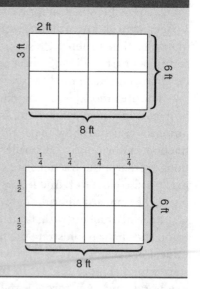

The following activity engages students in exploring the multiplication of fractions and the commutative property.

Activity 8.20 PLAYGROUND PROBLEM

Show students the following problem. Ask students to predict which community will have the bigger playground. Record the predictions. Place students with partners and ask one to solve the problem for community A and the other to solve for community B. Once they have completed their illustration and solution, ask students to compare their responses and to be ready to report to the class what they decided.

Two communities, A and B, are building playgrounds in grassy lots that are 50 yards by 100 yards. Community A has decided to convert $\frac{3}{4}$ of its lot to a playground and to cover $\frac{2}{5}$ of the playground with blacktop. Community B is building its playground on $\frac{2}{5}$ of the lot and covering $\frac{3}{4}$ of the playground with blacktop. In which park is the grassy playground bigger? In which lot is the blacktop bigger? Illustrate and explain.

Source: Adapted from Imm, K. L., Stylianou, D. A., & Chae, N. (2008). Student representations at the center: Promoting classroom equity. *Mathematics Teaching in the Middle School, 13*(8), 458–463.

technology note

The National Library of Virtual Manipulatives (http://nlvm.usu.edu) offers many explorations for fractions. The Fractions Rectangle Multiplication applet allows you to explore the multiplication of any two fractions up to 2 × 2. Another wonderful interactive site where the area model can be explored is at www.sci.sdsu.edu /CRMSE/IMAP/applets/IE_Win/FracFracStory33_IE_WIN_jar/FracFracClass.html.

◆ Developing the Algorithms

Students are introduced to multiplication algorithms before middle school, but if they lack an understanding of why they work, it will be important to connect visuals with the operations, as illustrated above. Ask students to solve three examples such as the following, and to illustrate the solution by partitioning a square that represents the whole:

$$\frac{5}{6} \times \frac{1}{2} \qquad \frac{3}{4} \times \frac{1}{5} \qquad \frac{1}{3} \times \frac{9}{10}$$

Ask questions that press the students to tell how the computation connects to the illustration: "How did you figure out how what the unit of the fraction [the denominator] was for the answer?" Or, more specifically, "How did you figure out that the denominator would be twelfths?" It is important to emphasize the meaning of what they are doing. Ask students to estimate how big they think the answer will be and why. In the first example here, a student might note that the answer will be slightly less than $\frac{1}{2}$ since $\frac{5}{6}$ is close to, but less than, 1.

◆ Factors Greater Than One

Multiplying fractions in which at least one factor is greater than one—for example, $\frac{3}{4} \times 2\frac{1}{2}$— should be integrated into multiplication with fractions less than one. When these problem types are mixed, students can see the impact of multiplying by a number less than one and a number more than one. Activity 8.21 is a way to focus on this reasoning (Thompson, 1995).

▶ Activity 8.21 CAN YOU SEE IT?

Post a partially shaded illustration like the one shown here.

Ask students the following questions and have them explain what they see and how they see it.

Can you see $\frac{3}{5}$ of something?   Can you see $\frac{5}{3}$ of $\frac{3}{5}$?

Can you see $\frac{5}{3}$ of something?   Can you see $\frac{2}{3}$ of $\frac{3}{5}$?

Figure 8.16

Multiplication of fractions with factors greater than one.

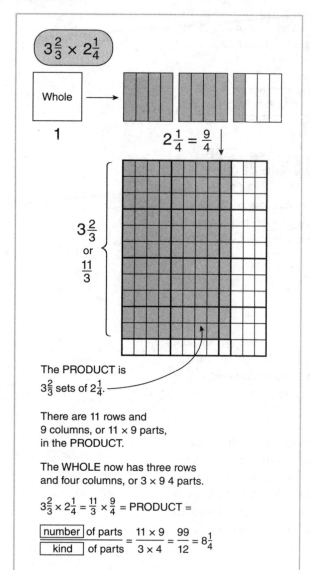

The PRODUCT is $3\frac{2}{3}$ sets of $2\frac{1}{4}$.

There are 11 rows and 9 columns, or 11 × 9 parts, in the PRODUCT.

The WHOLE now has three rows and four columns, or 3 × 9 4 parts.

$$3\frac{2}{3} \times 2\frac{1}{4} = \frac{11}{3} \times \frac{9}{4} = \text{PRODUCT} =$$

$$\frac{\boxed{\text{number}} \text{ of parts}}{\boxed{\text{kind}} \text{ of parts}} = \frac{11 \times 9}{3 \times 4} = \frac{99}{12} = 8\frac{1}{4}$$

Figure 8.17

Partial-product approach to multiplying fractions.

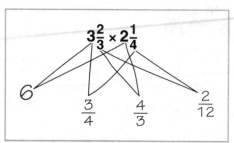

The area model is a good way to illustrate the product of fractions greater than one (Figure 8.16). But they can be left as mixed numbers, as illustrated in Figure 8.17. Notice that the same four partial products in Figure 8.17 can be found in the rectangle in Figure 8.16. The partial-products process is conceptual and lends itself to estimation. Just as with whole numbers, various strategies for multiplying fractions should be encouraged.

♦ Addressing Misconceptions

Students' concepts of whole-number multiplication and fraction addition and subtraction can lead to confusion with fraction multiplication. This is exaggerated when students have not developed a conceptual understanding of multiplication of fractions and have only memorized an algorithm, such as "multiply both the bottom numbers and the top numbers." The result of memorizing rules that don't make sense is an inability to solve multiplication problems. This becomes a significant barrier for solving proportions and algebraic expressions. Here are some common misconceptions and suggestions for helping students.

Treating the Denominator the Same as in Addition and Subtraction Problems

Why is it that the denominators stay the same when fractions are added but are multiplied when fractions are multiplied? (What is a conceptual explanation for this?) Compare the two operations with various visuals, such as a rectangle, circle, and number line to see how these are conceptually different.

Inability to Estimate the Approximate Size of the Answer

Students often think multiplication makes bigger. So, they have much difficulty in deciding if their answers make sense. On the one hand, they may never even think about whether their answer makes sense, so any answer looks good to them (e.g., $\frac{1}{2} \times 6\frac{1}{4} = 12\frac{1}{8}$). On the other hand, they may actually notice the answer ($\frac{1}{2} \times 6\frac{1}{4} = 3\frac{1}{8}$) but become concerned that it can't be right because the answer should be bigger. Estimation and the use of contexts and visuals help students think about whether their answers are reasonable.

Matching Multiplication Situations with Multiplication (and Not Division)

Multiplication and division are closely related, and our language is sometimes not as precise as it needs to be. In the question, "What is $\frac{1}{3}$ of 24?" students may think divide by 3 or multiply by $\frac{1}{3}$. But they may also divide by $\frac{1}{3}$, confusing the idea that they are finding a fraction of the whole. This becomes more evident when the numbers are more complex or the story is more involved. Estimation can help students. This is particularly true for ELLs, who become confused by language such as "divide it in half" and "divide it by half" (Carr, Carroll, Cremer, Gale, Lagunoff, & Sexton, 2009). One way to help is to ask, "Should the result be larger or smaller than the original amount?" Also, having students rewrite a phrase to state the problem more clearly can help them determine whether the appropriate operation is multiplication or division.

Division

According to the *Common Core State Standards*, division of fractions begins in fifth grade but is a major focus of sixth grade. Division of fractions is one of the least understood topics in the K–8 curriculum. Can you think of a real-life example of dividing by a fraction? Many people cannot, even though we conceptually use division by fractions in many real-life situations. Division of fractions remains one of the most mysterious algorithms in mathematics. We want to avoid this mystery at all costs and help students really understand when and how to divide fractions.

◆ Contextual Examples and Models

As with the other operations, connect to students' prior knowledge of division with whole numbers. Recall that there are two meanings of division: measurement and partition (Gregg & Gregg, 2007; Kribs-Zaleta, 2008; Tirosh, 2000). We will review each separately here and look at story problems in each problem type. In the classroom, the types of problems should eventually be mixed.

Measurement Interpretation of Division

The measurement interpretation is also called *repeated subtraction* or *equal groups*. In these situations, an equal group is repeatedly taken away from the total. For example, if you have 13 quarts of lemonade, how many canteens, each holding 3 quarts, can you fill? Notice that this is not a sharing situation but rather an equal subtraction situation.

The measurement model is a good model for beginning fraction division because students can draw illustrations to show the measures (Cramer, Monson, Whitney, Leavitt, & Wyberg, 2010). And the measurement model is a connection to iteration and a good way to develop an algorithm for dividing fractions, so it is important for students to explore this idea in contextual situations.

Figure 8.18 includes a set of tasks focused on servings (measurement) to build meaning for division of fractions (Gregg & Gregg, 2007). As the figure shows, moving gradually to more complex examples will enable students to use

Figure 8.18

Tasks that use the measurement interpretation of "how many servings?" to develop the concept of division.

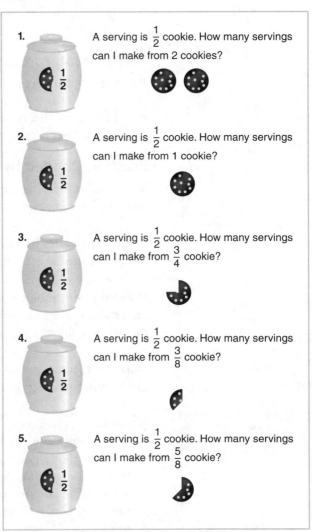

their whole-number concepts to build an understanding of division with fractions. Over time, students will be able to take on problems that are more complex both in the context and in the numbers involved, as in the following examples.

You are going to a birthday party. From Mitch and Bob's Ice Cream Factory, you order 6 pints of ice cream. If you serve $\frac{3}{4}$ of a pint of ice cream to each guest, how many guests can be served? (Schifter, Bastable, & Russell, 1999)

Farmer Brown found that he had $2\frac{1}{4}$ gallons of liquid fertilizer concentrate. It takes $\frac{3}{4}$ gallon to make a tank of mixed fertilizer. How many tankfuls can he mix?

Stop and Reflect

Try solving these problems yourself. Ask yourself how many servings/tanks of three-fourths you can get from the total available. ■

Partitive Interpretation of Division

Partitive problems are ones that involve sharing (partitioning) the whole. Partition problems include classic sharing problems (24 apples shared with 4 friends) and rate problems (If you walk 12 miles in 3 hours, how many miles do you walk per hour?). The focus of these situations is on what is one portion: "How many for one friend?" "How many miles walked in one hour?"

Fraction Divided by a Whole Number

This is not really a big leap from whole-number division. Notice that each situation focuses on one of these questions: "How much is the whole?" or "How much for one?"

Cassie has $6\frac{2}{3}$ yards of ribbon to make four bows for birthday packages. How much ribbon should she use for each bow if she wants to use the same length of ribbon for each?

When the $6\frac{2}{3}$ is thought of as fractional parts, there are 20 thirds to share, or 5 thirds for each ribbon. The unit parts (thirds) require no further partitioning in share equally. In the following problem, the parts must be split into smaller parts.

Mark has $1\frac{1}{4}$ hours to finish his three chores. If he divides his time evenly, how many hours can he give to each chore?

Note that the question is, "How many hours for one chore?" The 5 fourths of an hour that Mark has do not split neatly into three parts. So, some or all of the parts must be partitioned. Figure 8.19 shows how to model these with each type of model (area, linear, and set). In each case, all of the fourths are subdivided into three equal parts, producing twelfths. There are a total of 15 twelfths, or $\frac{5}{12}$ hour for each chore. (Test this answer against the solution in minutes: $1\frac{1}{4}$ hours is 75 minutes, which divided between 3 chores is 25 minutes per chore. $\frac{25}{60} = \frac{5}{12}$.)

Fraction Divided by a Smaller Fraction

The sharing concept is more difficult to conceptualize when the divisor is a fraction. Keep in mind that for partition and rate problems, the fundamental question is, "How much is one (portion/share)?" Activities on finding the whole given a part (see Figure 8.3) build a foundation for finding a fraction of a fraction. For example, if 18 counters represent $2\frac{1}{4}$ sets,

Figure 8.19 Three models of partition division with a whole-number divisor.

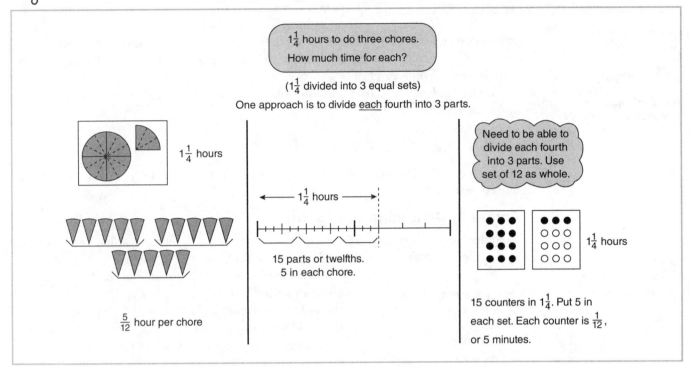

how much is one whole set of counters? Think about how many fourths are in the total, then how much in one-fourth as a way to figure out how much in one. Activity 8.22 focuses on this reasoning process.

◢ *Activity 8.22* **HOW MUCH FOR ONE?**

Pose contextual problems, like the ones here, in which the focus question is, "How much for one ___?"

1. Dan paid $3.00 for a $\frac{3}{4}$-pound box of cereal. How much is that per pound?
2. Andrea found that if she walks quickly during her morning exercise, she can cover $2\frac{1}{2}$ miles in $\frac{3}{4}$ hour. She wonders how fast she is walking in miles per hour. Draw pictures or use models to illustrate your answer.

Answers That Are Not Whole Numbers

Most problems are not going to come out evenly. If Cassie has 5 yards of ribbon to make bows and each bow needs $1\frac{1}{6}$ yards, she can make only four bows because a part of a bow does not make sense. But if Farmer Brown begins with 4 gallons of concentrate, after making five tanks of mix, he will have used $\frac{15}{4}$, or $3\frac{3}{4}$, gallons of the concentrate. With the $\frac{1}{4}$ gallon remaining, he can make a partial tank of mix. He can make $\frac{1}{3}$ tank of mix because it takes 3 fourths to make a whole, and he has 1 fourth of a gallon (he has one of the three parts he needs for a tank).

Here is another problem to try:

John is building a patio. Each patio section requires $\frac{1}{3}$ of a cubic yard of concrete. The concrete truck holds $2\frac{1}{2}$ cubic yards of concrete. If there is not enough for a full section at the end, John can put in a divider and make a partial section. How many patio sections can John make with the concrete in the truck?

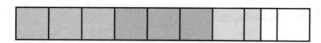

One way to do this is counting how many thirds in $2\frac{1}{2}$? Here you can see that you get 3 patio sections from the dark whole, 3 more from the light whole, and then you get 1 more full section and $\frac{1}{2}$ of what you need for another patio section. The answer is $7\frac{1}{2}$. Students will want to write the "remainder" as $\frac{1}{3}$ because they were measuring in thirds, but the question is how many sections can be made—$7\frac{1}{2}$.

▶ Invite students to debate what the remainder should be, justifying with the context and visuals.

◆ Developing the Algorithms

There are two different algorithms for division of fractions. Both algorithms are discussed here.

Common-Denominator Algorithm

Common denominators are a great strategy for dividing, although not widely known or used in the United States. Let's revisit $2\frac{1}{2} \div \frac{1}{3}$. The problem would become $2\frac{3}{6} \div \frac{2}{6}$, or $\frac{15}{6} \div \frac{2}{6}$. The question becomes, "How many sets of 2 sixths are in a set of 15 sixths?" Or, "How many 2s in 15?" $7\frac{1}{2}$. Figure 8.20 shows how to illustrate this idea with an area model using the problem $\frac{5}{3} \div \frac{1}{2}$. Notice that once a common denominator is found, the thought process is the same as in the whole-number problem $10 \div 3$. The resulting algorithm, therefore, is as follows: To divide fractions, first get the common denominators, then divide the numerators. For example, $\frac{5}{3} \div \frac{1}{4} = \frac{20}{12} \div \frac{3}{12} = 20 \div 3 = \frac{20}{3} = 6\frac{2}{3}$.

Figure 8.20

Common-denominator method for fraction division.

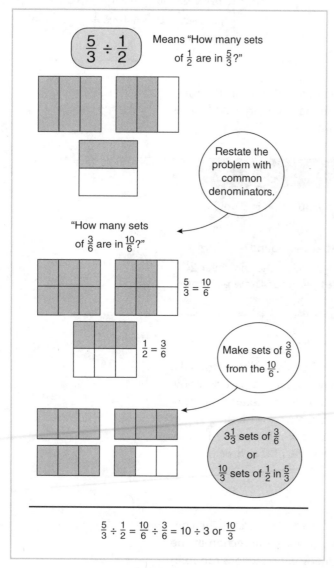

$$\frac{5}{3} \div \frac{1}{2} = \frac{10}{6} \div \frac{3}{6} = 10 \div 3 \text{ or } \frac{10}{3}$$

Invert-and-Multiply Algorithm

Providing a series of tasks and having students look for patterns in how they are finding the answers can help them discover this poorly understood and commonly taught algorithm. For example, consider this first set, in which the divisor is a unit fraction. Pose the question that goes with each equation.

$3 \div \frac{1}{2} =$ (How many servings of $\frac{1}{2}$ in 3 containers?)

$5 \div \frac{1}{4} =$ (How many servings of $\frac{1}{4}$ in 5 containers?)

$8 \div \frac{1}{5} =$ (How many servings of $\frac{1}{5}$ in 8 containers?)

$3\frac{3}{4} \div \frac{1}{8} =$ (How many servings of $\frac{1}{8}$ in $3\frac{3}{4}$ containers?)

Ask students to look across these problems (and others) for a pattern. They will notice that they are multiplying by the denominator of the second fraction. For example, in the third example, a student might say, "You get five for every whole container, so 5×8 is 40." You can also consider these expressions as partitive situations, which answers the question "How much in one?" For example, Mary paid \$3 for half a pound of coffee. How much did she pay for one pound? The computation is $3 \div \frac{1}{2}$. To find a whole pound, you would double what you have to get to one pound for \$6.

Then move to similar problems, but with a second fraction that is not a unit fraction:

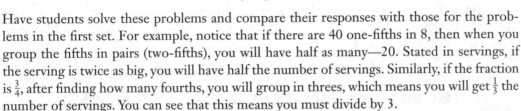

$$5 \div \tfrac{3}{4} =$$
$$8 \div \tfrac{2}{5} =$$
$$3\tfrac{3}{4} \div \tfrac{3}{8} =$$

8 Look for and
express regularity in
repeated reasoning

Have students solve these problems and compare their responses with those for the problems in the first set. For example, notice that if there are 40 one-fifths in 8, then when you group the fifths in pairs (two-fifths), you will have half as many—20. Stated in servings, if the serving is twice as big, you will have half the number of servings. Similarly, if the fraction is $\tfrac{3}{4}$, after finding how many fourths, you will group in threes, which means you will get $\tfrac{1}{3}$ the number of servings. You can see that this means you must divide by 3.

The examples given were measurements because the size of the group (serving) was known, but not the number of groups. Using partitioning, or sharing, examples nicely illustrates the standard algorithm. Consider this example:

You have $1\tfrac{1}{2}$ oranges, which is $\tfrac{3}{5}$ of an adult serving. How many oranges (and parts of oranges) make up 1 adult serving?

Source: Kribs-Zaleta, C. (2008). Oranges, posters, ribbons, and lemonade: Concrete computational strategies for dividing fractions. *Mathematics Teaching in the Middle School, 13*(8), 453–457.

You may be thinking that you first need to find what one-fifth would be—which would be one-third of the oranges you have—or $\tfrac{1}{2}$ of an orange (notice you are dividing by the numerator). Then, to get the whole serving, you multiply $\tfrac{1}{2}$ by 5 (the denominator) to get $2\tfrac{1}{2}$ oranges in 1 adult serving.

In either the measurement or the partitive interpretation, the denominator leads you to find out how many fourths, fifths, or eighths you have (multiply by this value to determine total parts), and the numerator tells you the size of the serving (divide by this value as you group). At some point, someone thought, "Well, if they just flipped the fraction, then it would be more straightforward—multiplying by the top and dividing by the bottom"—and that is why we have learned to "invert and multiply."

◆ Addressing Misconceptions

The biggest misunderstanding for division of fractions is just not knowing what the algorithm means. Once students realize the meaning of division, they are able to begin thinking of different ways to approach problems and decide whether their answers make sense. Within division, there are other common misconceptions that need to be addressed.

Thinking the Answer Should Be Smaller

Based on their experiences with whole-number division, students think that when they divide by a fraction, the answer should be smaller. This is true if the divisor is a fraction greater than one (e.g., $\tfrac{5}{3}$), but it is not true if the fraction is less than one. Include estimating when you teach division of fractions.

Connecting the Illustration with the Answer

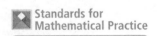

Students may understand that $1\tfrac{5}{3} \div \tfrac{1}{4}$ means, "How many fourths are in $1\tfrac{1}{2}$?" So, they may set out to count how many fourths—6. But in recording their answer, they can get confused as to what the 6 refers to and think it should be a fraction, and they record $\tfrac{6}{4}$ when actually it is 6 groups of one-fourths, not 6 fourths (Cramer et al., 2010).

Writing Remainders

As noted above, knowing what the unit is (the divisor) is critical and must be understood in giving the remainder (Coughlin, 2010/2011; Lamon, 1999). In the problem $3\frac{3}{8} \div \frac{1}{4}$, students are likely to count 4 fourths for each whole (12 fourths) and one more for $\frac{2}{8}$, but then not know what to do with the extra eighth. It is important to be sure they understand the measurement concept of division. Ask, "How much of the next piece do you have?" Context can also help. In this case, if the problem was about pizza servings, there would be 13 full servings and $\frac{1}{2}$ of the next serving.

 ## Teaching Considerations for Teaching Fractions

One reason why fractions are not well understood is that there is a lot to know about them—from part–whole relationships to division. In addition, building understanding means representing across area, length, and set models—and including contexts that fit these models. Estimation activities can support student understanding of fractions and are an important skill in and of themselves. Equivalence, including comparisons, is a central idea for which students must have sound understanding and skill. Connecting visuals with the procedure and not rushing the algorithm too soon are important aspects of the process. We close this chapter with a summary of recommendations on effective fraction instruction (Clarke et al., 2008; Cramer & Whitney, 2010):

1. Give a greater emphasis to number sense and the meaning of fractions, rather than to rote procedures for manipulating them.
2. Provide a variety of models and contexts to represent fractions.
3. Emphasize that fractions are numbers, making extensive use of number lines in representing fractions.
4. Spend whatever time is needed for students to understand equivalences (concretely and symbolically), including flexible naming of fractions.
5. Link fractions to key benchmarks, and encourage estimation.

Expanded Lesson

Division-of-Fractions Stories

Content and Task Decisions

Grade Level: 5–6

Mathematics Goals

- To develop the partitive meaning of division with fractions through investigating various contexts.

Grade Level Guide

NCTM Curriculum Focal Points	Common Core State Standards
Understanding of division of fractions is one of the three focal points in grade 5. "Number and Operations: Developing an understanding of and fluency with multiplication and division of fractions and decimals" (NCTM, 2006, p. 18).	In fifth grade, students begin their understanding of division of fractions, in particular of unit fractions (continuing work in sixth grade). In grade 5, students will "Apply and extend previous understandings of division to divide unit fractions by whole numbers and whole numbers by unit fractions" (CCSSO, 2010, p. 36). In grade 6, students will "Interpret and compute quotients of fractions, and solve word problems involving division of fractions by fractions, e.g., by using visual fraction models and equations to represent the problem" (CCSSO, 2010, p. 42).

Consider Your Students' Needs

Students have solved both partition and measurement problems with whole numbers. They understand the symbolic notation of fractions (i.e., they know what the numerator in the fraction means—the number of parts—and what the denominator in the fraction means—the kind of parts we are counting). The students can add fractions and find equivalent fractions.

For English Language Learners

- Use visuals for the opening story problem (real gum or counters to represent gum) and model the problem with people in the class.

- Provide an opportunity for students to work with a partner who will be able to help with vocabulary.
- Encourage students to use both their native language and English as they work in groups.

For Students with Special Needs

- After debriefing the problem with the gum, use a think-aloud to highlight some of the thinking strategies that come into the decision making as you solve the problem. Jot down some of these ideas so that students can use them as a reference.
- Try suggesting that students who are struggling while using a single representation, such as a bar diagram, possibly use cash register tape.

Materials

- The teacher will want to have a way to project the stories and the solutions.

Lesson

Before

Begin with a simpler version of the task:

- Ask students how they would solve the following story problem if they did not know their multiplication facts: "Marie bought 24 pieces of bubble gum to share between her 3 friends and herself. How many pieces of gum will each person get?"
- Have them draw a picture or think about how they would act out the story to determine the answer. Listen to the students' ideas. Capitalize on ideas that emphasize the sharing action in the problem.

Present the focus task to the class:

- Students are to solve the following problems:

Cassie has $5\frac{1}{4}$ yards of ribbon to make three bows for birthday packages. How much ribbon should she use for each bow if she wants to use the same length of ribbon for each?

Mark has $1\frac{1}{4}$ hours to finish his three household chores. If he divides his time evenly, how much time can he spend on each chore?

- Students should draw pictures and have a written explanation for their solutions. They should also be prepared to explain their thinking. Before you come together as a class, have students explain their ideas to a partner.

Provide clear expectations:

- Have students work independently and then share their work with a partner.

During

Initially:

- Be sure that students are drawing pictures to help them think about how to do the problems and explain their thinking.

Ongoing:

- Look for students who use different representations to think about the problems. Highlight those different ways in the *After* section of the lesson.

- To differentiate for advanced learners, pose another problem to them in which the parts must be split into smaller parts (as in the second problem in the task). For example, "Ryan has $6\frac{2}{3}$ yards of rope to hang 4 bird feeders. How much rope will he use for each feeder if he wants to use the same length of rope for each?"

- Monitor partner discussions as students explain their thinking in order to address any misconceptions or difficulties during the whole-class discussion.

After

Bring the class together to share and discuss the task:

- For each problem, first get answers from the class. If more than one answer is offered, simply record them and offer no evaluation.

- Have students come to the board to explain their strategies for thinking about the problem. You may need to ask questions about drawings or explanations to make sure everyone in the class follows the rationale. Encourage the class to comment or ask questions about each student's representation or thinking. Ask if others used a different representation or solved the problem in a

different way. If so, have the students come forward to share their solutions. If there are different answers, the class should evaluate the solution strategies and decide which answer is correct and why.

- Discuss the different representations students use (e.g., some students use circles or rectangles, whereas others may use a number line) and how the action in the story is one of sharing.

- For problems that require the parts to be split into smaller parts, students will likely use different approaches. For example, for the second problem in the given task, some students will first divide the hour into thirds and then the quarter hour into twelfths, whereas other students will divide the hour into twelfths and share the twelfths between the three chores. It is important to have students compare and contrast the different approaches. Some solutions that at first appear to be different are actually equivalent in many ways. Through questioning, help students make these connections.

- Help students notice that while they are answering these questions they are also asking, "How much is in the whole?" or "How much for one?" This mode of thinking will help students when the divisor is a fraction.

Assessment

Observe

- Are students using their understanding of the meaning of fractions to help them draw a representation or solve the problem in another way? Using the meaning of the fraction is imperative when the problem requires splitting the part into smaller parts.

- Look for students who struggle with identifying the whole. These students need more experience working with part–whole tasks.

Ask

- What is the problem asking you to partition?
- How many parts/groups will you have?
- What is the size of each part?

9

Decimal Concepts and Computation

Big IDEAS

1 Decimals (also called *decimal fractions*) are a way of writing fractions within the base-ten system (tenths, hundredths, etc.).

2 The base-ten place-value system extends infinitely in two directions—to tiny values as well as to large values. Between any two place values, the 10-to-1 ratio remains the same.

3 Percents are hundredths and are a third way of writing both fractions and decimals.

4 Operations with decimals are based on the fundamental concepts of the operations. Connecting to whole-number and fraction operations can help build meaning for operations involving decimals.

We use decimals for such varied needs as reading metric measures, calculating distances, and understanding sports statistics. Decimals are important in many occupations, ranging from nursing and pharmacy to airplane construction, in which the level of precision affects the safety of the general public. In the *Common Core State Standards for Mathematics*, students are introduced to decimals in the fourth grade, where they develop an understanding of decimal notation (to hundredths), and in the fifth grade, where one of the critical areas in the CCSS includes operations with decimals (to hundredths). In the sixth grade, students extend this work with tenths and hundredths to all decimals, developing standard algorithms. In the seventh grade, they develop a "unified understanding of number" (CCSSO, 2010, p. 46) so as to be able to move fluently between decimals, fractions, and percents.

Extending the Place-Value System

Decimals, like whole numbers, are written in a base-ten format, so connection to whole-number place value can help students understand place value of very small numbers. Here, we share three important ideas that apply to decimal fractions.

The 10-to-1 Relationship

One of the most basic of these ideas is the 10-to-1 multiplicative relationship between the values of any two adjacent positions. In terms of a base-ten model such as paper strips

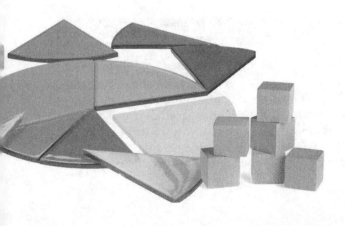

Figure 9.1 The 10-to-1 place-value relationship extends infinitely in both directions.

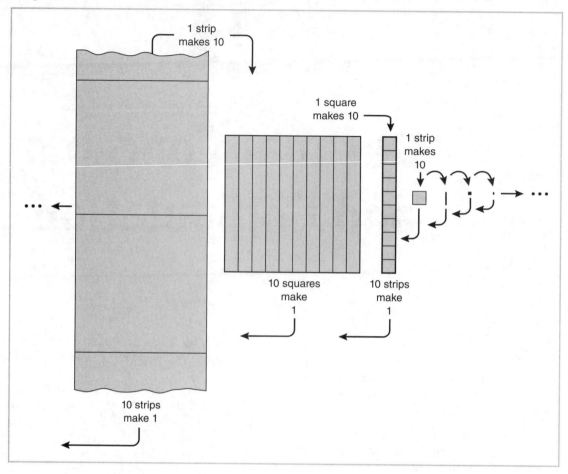

and squares, 10 of any one piece will make 1 of the next larger (to the immediate left) piece; for example, 10 tens makes 1 hundred, and 10 millions makes 1 ten-million. This is also true for decimal fractions; for example, 10 ten-thousandths makes 1 thousandth, and 10 thousandths makes 1 hundredth. And movement of a piece to the immediate right involves division by 10 (1 divided by 10 is one-tenth). The ratio can be stated as 1 to 10 as the place values move to the right: 1 hundred is 10 tens, 1 million is 10 hundred-thousands, and 1 thousandth is 10 ten-thousandths. These values continue *infinitely in two directions*, as illustrated in Figure 9.1. The 10-to-1 relationship can be explored meaningfully with the calculator.

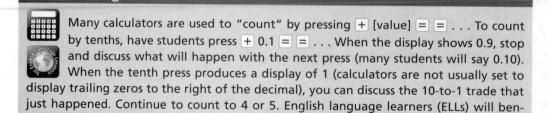

Activity 9.1 CALCULATOR DECIMAL COUNTING

Many calculators are used to "count" by pressing ⊞ [value] ⊟ ⊟ . . . To count by tenths, have students press ⊞ 0.1 ⊟ ⊟ . . . When the display shows 0.9, stop and discuss what will happen with the next press (many students will say 0.10). When the tenth press produces a display of 1 (calculators are not usually set to display trailing zeros to the right of the decimal), you can discuss the 10-to-1 trade that just happened. Continue to count to 4 or 5. English language learners (ELLs) will benefit from counting aloud. Ask, "How many presses to get to the next whole number?"

For students with disabilities or who are struggling with the decimal notation, pair the calculator counting with adding in base-ten strips for tenths. Ten presses equates to 10 strips (10 tenths). Repeat for other small values, like 0.001 and 0.0001. Ask, "How many [ten-thousandths] to make one-thousandth? How many to make one-hundredth? One-tenth? One?" Allow students to explore and respond to these questions.

Regrouping

Even middle-school students need to be reminded that regrouping really means that it takes 10 of a group to make one of the place value to the immediate left. Students can benefit from flexible regrouping—for example, regrouping 2451 into 24 hundreds, 5 tens, and 1 unit, or 245 tens and 1 unit or 2,451 units. This work with whole numbers prepares students to think about 0.6 as 6 tenths as well as 60 hundredths.

Measurement and Monetary Units

Decimal values often determine a measurement or an amount, and the unit must be stated in order to understand the number. For example, the metric system has seven place values with names (Figure 9.2). The decimal can be used to designate any of these places as the unit without changing the actual measure.

Our monetary system is also a decimal system. The amount $1,727,000.00 has ones as the unit. But this can also be written as $1.727 million, with the unit shifted to millions. And $5.72 can also be written as 572 cents, with hundredths designated as the unit.

Precision and Equivalence

Common Core State Standards Mathematical Practice 6 states, "Mathematically proficient students ... express numerical answers with a degree of precision appropriate for the problem context" (p. 7).

Consider the two values 0.06 and 0.060. They are equivalent in terms of numeric value. But the latter is more *precise*. It makes clear that the item was measured to the nearest thousandth and that there were 60 thousandths. In the first case, the measurement was completed only to the nearest hundredth, so the measure might have been 0.058 or 0.063,

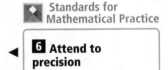

Standards for Mathematical Practice

◀ **6 Attend to precision**

Figure 9.2

In the metric measurement system, each place-value position has a name. The decimal point follows the unit length. Any of the metric positions can be the unit length, as illustrated here.

kilometer	hectometer	dekameter	meter	decimeter	centimeter	millimeter	
		4	3	8	5		

4 dekameters, 3 meters, 8 decimeters, and 5 centimeters =

43.85	meters
43850	millimeters
0.04385	kilometers
4385	centimeters

Unit names

but not necessarily precisely at 0.060. Various sports measure to different levels of precision. For example, in basketball, a player's free throws are often measured in hundredths (and stated as a percent): *Reagan is an 87 percent free throw shooter.* In baseball, batting averages are measured in thousandths: *Willie has a batting average of .345 for the season.* Precision becomes important when very small items are measured. So, although 0.04500 may be equivalent to 0.045, it may be relevant to record the entire value to communicate the level of precision.

 ## Connecting Fractions and Decimals

Did you know that students have greater difficulty understanding decimals than understanding fractions? This may be a surprise, given the computation for decimals may seem easier than the computation for fractions. Conceptual understanding of decimals and their connections to fractions must be carefully developed (Martinie, 2007). Decimals are sometimes referred to as decimal fractions, in particular in the research and in the *Common Core State Standards.* This is because, conceptually, a decimal is a fraction. It is a special case of a fraction in which the denominator is part of the base-ten number system, so it can be written in this way as a convention. For example, 0.03 is "three-hundredths," which can be written as $\frac{3}{100}$ or as 0.03. When the curriculum treats decimals and fractions separately, students are less likely to see this connection and realize that they are simply different ways to write the same value. The focus of this chapter is on how to ensure that middle-school students have a sound understanding of the different ways to represent rational numbers.

The symbols 3.75 and $3\frac{3}{4}$ represent the same quantity, yet on the surface the two appear quite different. For students, the world of fractions and the world of decimals are very distinct. Developing an understanding that 0.75 is the same as $\frac{3}{4}$ is difficult because the denominator (of 100) is hidden when decimals are written. By the end of middle school, students must see that both systems represent the same concepts and can be interchanged based on the demands of the problem. Here we share some ways to ensure that the connection between fractions and decimals is understood.

Say Decimal Fractions Correctly

You must make sure you are reading and saying decimals in ways that support students' understanding. *Always* say "five and two-tenths" instead of "five point two." Using the "point" terminology results in a disconnect to the fractional part that exists in every decimal. This is not unlike the ill-advised reading of fractions as "two over ten" instead of the correct "two-tenths." This level of precision in language will provide your students with the opportunity to *hear* the connections between decimals and fractions, so that when they hear "two-tenths," they will think of both 0.2 and $\frac{2}{10}$.

**Teaching Tip**

Tell students that you want to hear the "ths" as they talk about decimals. Exaggerate "ths" in your own speaking. This is important for everyone, but especially for ELLs and students with disabilities, who may not notice the difference if it is not emphasized.

Use Fraction Models

Fractions with denominators of 10, 100, 1000, and so on will be referred to as *decimal fractions.* Fractions such as $\frac{7}{10}$ and $\frac{63}{100}$ can also be written as 0.7 and 0.63, so they are called *decimal fractions.* Recall that fractions can be represented in areas, lengths, and sets. When you are trying to make the connection to decimal fractions, the goal is to find a model for which tenths and hundredths (at least) are possible. Area models for this include circles partitioned into hundredths, base-ten materials (see Blackline Master 9), 10 × 10 geoboards (see Blackline Master 11), and grid

BLM

Figure 9.3

The rational number wheel can show decimal fraction quantities. Turn the wheel to show 0.25, which is also $\frac{25}{100}$ or $\frac{1}{4}$ of the circle (Blackline Master 10).

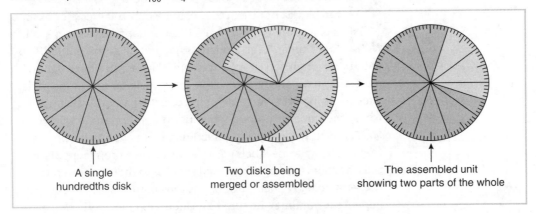

A single
hundredths disk

Two disks being
merged or assembled

The assembled unit
showing two parts of the whole

paper (see Blackline Master 7 or 8). Length models (a great connection to measurement) include Cuisenaire rods (at least for tenths), meter sticks, and the number line. Sets can be created in any number, so sets of 10, 100, and 1000 can be made, but typically these are best counted when in arrays with rows of 10, which then can be connected to an area model.

Area Models

As with fractions, area models are a good beginning. Figure 9.3 shows how two disks (each of a different color), cut along a radius and slipped together, can be used to model fractions or decimal fractions less than 1 (Blackline Master 10).

The most common area model for decimal fractions is a 10×10 square (Figure 9.4 and Blackline Master 11). Base-ten blocks are often used for this, with the 10-cm square that was used as the "hundreds" now representing the whole, or 1. Each rod (strip) is then 1 tenth, and each small cube ("tiny") is 1 hundredth. With base-ten blocks, the thousands block can be the whole, and consequently the flats (squares) are then tenths, the rods hundredths, and small cubes thousandths.

Figure 9.4

These 10×10 squares show decimal fractions (Blackline Master 9).

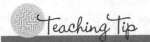**Teaching Tip**

Blackline Master 8 provides a large square that is subdivided into 10,000 tiny squares. Students can identify how many squares are needed for 0.1, 0.01, 0.001, and 0.0001, using appropriate names for the values. Notice that any one of the pieces can be assigned the value of 1, and that affects the values of the other pieces (Figure 9.5).

Because students may be accustomed to a particular piece being used as the unit (e.g., the little square or cube being 1), they can benefit from activities in which the unit changes, such as Activity 9.2.

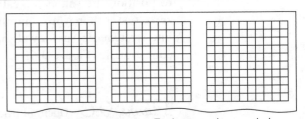

10×10 squares on paper. Each square is one whole. Students shade fractional parts.

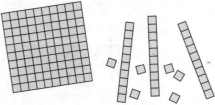

A 10×10 square, strips (representing tenths), and individual squares (representing hundredths) can be used to illustrate decimal fraction values, such as 1.36.

Figure 9.5

The decimal point indicates that the rods or strips are each one unit, so the 10 × 10 square is ten, and the little squares are tenths.

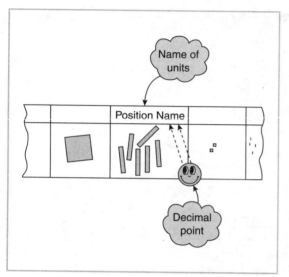

Activity 9.2 SHIFTING UNITS

Give students a collection of paper base-ten pieces or base-ten blocks. Ask them to pull out a particular mix; for example, a student might have three squares, seven strips, and four "tinies." Tell students that you have the unit behind your back; when you show it to them, they are to figure out how much they have and to record the value. Hold up one of the units, like the strip. Observe students record their value. Ask students to say their quantity aloud while using appropriate terminology. For ELLs and students with disabilities, it is particularly important that you write these labels with the visuals in a prominent place in the classroom (and in student notebooks) so that they can refer to the terminology and illustrations as they participate in the activity. Repeat several times. Be sure to include examples in which a piece is not represented so that students will understand decimal values like 3.07. Continue playing in partners. One student selects a mix of base-ten pieces. The student's partner then tells him or her which one is the unit, and the student writes and says the number.

Length Models

As discussed in Chapter 8, length models are very important and often underutilized. In fact, linear models are particularly helpful in making the connection between fractions and decimals because students can see that values such as $\frac{3}{4}$ and 0.75 are the same length from zero. One of the best length models is a meter stick. Each decimeter is one-tenth of the whole stick, each centimeter is one-hundredth, and each millimeter is one-thousandth. Any number line model broken into 100 subparts is likewise a useful model for hundredths. Empty number lines like those used with whole-number computation are also very useful in helping students compare decimals and think about scale and place value (Martinie & Bay Williams, 2003). Given two or more decimals, students can use the empty number line to position the values, revealing what they know about the size of these decimals by using zero, one, other whole numbers, or other decimal values as benchmarks. A large number line stretched across a wall or on the floor can be an excellent tool for exploring decimals conceptually (Figure 9.6).

Figure 9.6 Decimal fraction number line.

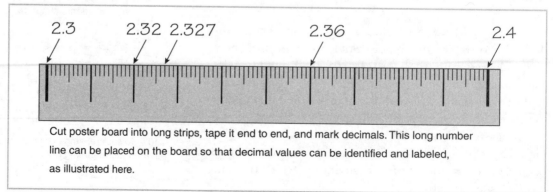

Cut poster board into long strips, tape it end to end, and mark decimals. This long number line can be placed on the board so that decimal values can be identified and labeled, as illustrated here.

Set Models

Money is a model for decimals, which has the advantage of being a familiar context. The disadvantage of money as a model is that it is always written to the hundredths place. Numbers like 3.2 and 12.1389 do not relate to money and can cause confusion (Martinie, 2007). The important thing is to use multiple representations, which will broaden students' understanding and their skill at decimal operations.

◆ From Fractions to Decimals

Before learning about decimals, students should have developed a conceptual familiarity with fractions, such as halves, thirds, fourths, fifths, and eighths, across models. This familiarity must be extended to decimals. Students need to make concept-based translations—that is, translations based on understanding rather than on a rule or algorithm.

To understand decimals in terms of place value, a number must be understood in terms of its expanded form, in which the place values are written as individual parts (e.g., 0.45 as 4 tenths and 5 hundredths) and as one number (e.g., 45 hundredths). Base-ten pieces can help students see the expanded form, which is the focus of Activity 9.3.

 Activity 9.3 **BUILD IT, NAME IT**

For this activity, have students use their base-ten strips and squares (Blackline Master 9). Assign the large square to be one unit. Ask students to use their pieces to show the fraction you are about to display. Display a mixed number like $2\frac{35}{100}$ and wait until students have collected the matching pieces. Ask students to tell you how many units, how many tenths, and how many hundredths they used. Ask students to write and say their amount as a decimal while using the terms *tenths, hundredths,* and *thousandths* (not *point*!). Repeat the activity by starting with the decimal (e.g., 4.6 or 3.712) and ask students determine the fraction.

Calculators that permit entry of fractions have a fraction–decimal conversion key. Some calculators will convert a decimal such as 0.25 to the fraction $\frac{25}{100}$ and allow either manual or automatic simplification. Graphing calculators can be set so that the conversion is either with or without automatic simplification. The ability of fraction calculators to go back and forth between fractions and decimals makes them valuable tools as students begin to connect fraction and decimal symbolism.

In Activity 9.3, the fraction is already written in base-ten format, but typically, the fractions we are converting to decimals are familiar fractions, such as $\frac{3}{4}$ and $\frac{2}{5}$. The following two activities are designed to focus on decimal equivalences for familiar fractions in a conceptual manner.

Activity 9.4 **FAMILIAR FRACTIONS TO DECIMALS**

Students are given a familiar fraction (e.g., $\frac{3}{5}$) to convert to a decimal. Ask students to shade a 10 × 10 grid to illustrate that value (or build it with base-ten blocks). Referring to their visual or blocks, ask students to write the decimal equivalent. A good sequence is to start with halves and fifths, then fourths, and possibly eighths. Thirds are best done as a separate activity, since the decimal form is a repeating decimal.

Figure 9.7

A 10 × 10 square can be used to convert familiar fractions to decimals.

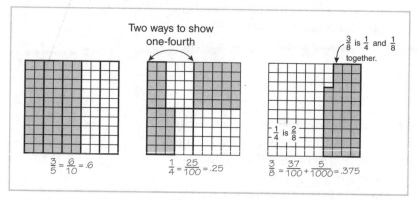

$$\frac{3}{5} = \frac{6}{10} = .6 \qquad \frac{1}{4} = \frac{25}{100} = .25 \qquad \frac{3}{8} = \frac{37}{100} + \frac{5}{1000} = .375$$

Figure 9.7 shows three examples of how fractions might be illustrated on a 10 × 10 grid. Notice that for fourths, two ways are shown. The question becomes how to translate this to decimals. In either case, students may see the 25 pieces representing 25 hundredths, but only one of the representations shows tenths and hundredths. Both ways are appropriate, but be sure that students see the connection between tenths and hundredths. The fraction $\frac{3}{8}$ represents a wonderful challenge. A hint might be to find $\frac{1}{4}$ first, and then notice that $\frac{1}{8}$ is half of a fourth. Remember that the next-smaller pieces are tenths of the tinies. Therefore, half of a tiny is $\frac{5}{1000}$.

The circle is also effective in making the fraction-to-decimal connections because it can be partitioned into any fractional amount.

Figure 9.8

The rational number wheel can be cut apart to illustrate tenths and hundredths.

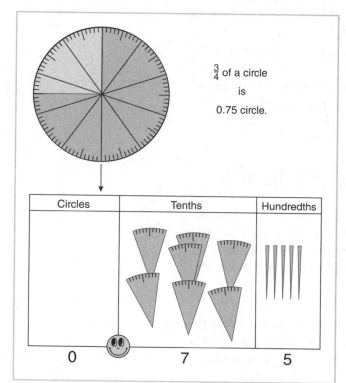

$\frac{3}{4}$ of a circle

is

0.75 circle.

Circles	Tenths	Hundredths
0	7	5

Activity 9.5 RATIONAL NUMBER WHEEL: ESTIMATE AND VERIFY

Use the rational number wheel (Blackline Master 10 and Figure 9.3). With the blank side of the wheel facing them, have students adjust the wheel to show a particular fraction—for example, $\frac{3}{4}$. Next, ask students to estimate how many hundredths they think are equivalent. Then, ask students to turn the wheel over and check their answer (note that the color reverses when the wheel is turned over). Ask students to justify how they decided what the decimal equivalent was. Repeat with other common fractions. For students with disabilities, you may need to use pieces from the rational number wheel (on the hundredths side) that are cut into tenths; then, the students can use those pieces as comparison tools (Figure 9.8). The estimation component of the last activity adds the visual "feeling" for decimals.

The exploration of modeling $\frac{1}{3}$ as a decimal is a good introduction to the concept of an infinitely repeating decimal, which is a standard for seventh grade (CCSSO, 2010). Try to partition the whole 10 × 10 square into 3 parts by using strips and little squares. Each part receives 3 strips, with 1 strip left over. To divide the leftover strip, each part gets 3 little squares, with 1 left over. To divide the tiny, each part gets 3 tiny strips, with 1 left over. (Recall that with base-ten pieces, each smaller piece must be $\frac{1}{10}$ of the preceding-size piece.) It becomes apparent that this process is never-ending. As a result, $\frac{1}{3}$ is the same as 0.333333 . . ., or $0.\overline{3}$. For practical purposes, $\frac{1}{3}$ is about 0.333. Similarly, $\frac{2}{3}$ is a repeating string of sixes, or about 0.667. Later, students will discover that many fractions cannot be represented by a finite decimal.

Students must also understand decimals on a number line, a more difficult representation than area or money based on data from the National Assessment of Educational Progress (NAEP). Over the years, NAEP results showed that most students could not find a decimal equivalent for a mixed number (Kouba, Brown, Carpenter, Lindquist, Silver, & Swafford, 1988) and struggled with finding decimals on a number line where the subdivisions on the number line were written as fractions (Kouba, Zawojewski, & Strutchens, 1997).

Even when partitions were written as decimals (increments were multiples of 0.2), only 56 percent of eighth graders correctly placed decimal numbers on a number line (Wearne & Kouba, 2000). This is a strong reminder that just telling students to convert to decimals by using division contributes nothing to their understanding of decimal equivalence. Note that this method has not been and will not be suggested in this chapter. The following activity continues the development of fraction–decimal equivalences with a focus on the number line.

Teaching Tip

Length models need more emphasis in the teaching of decimals. Use paper strips, Cuisenaire rods, and number lines—all of which can show tenths and hundredths, and the relationship between them.

Activity 9.6 **DECIMALS LINEUP**

Give students decimal numbers that have familiar fraction equivalents. At first, keep the numbers between two consecutive whole numbers. For example, use 3.5, 3.125, 3.4, 3.75, and 3.66. Show a number line encompassing the same whole numbers. You can use an empty number line (no partitions), or you can have the line partitioned by halves or fourths as benchmarks. The students' task is to locate each of the decimal numbers on the number line and to provide the fraction equivalent for each.

 Formative Assessment Note

A simple yet powerful *performance assessment* to evaluate decimal understanding has students represent two related decimal numbers, such as 0.6 and 0.06, by using each of three or four different representations: a number line (not provided but student-drawn), a 10 × 10 grid, money, and base-ten materials (Martinie & Bay-Williams, 2003). Ask students to describe their representations. If students have significantly more difficulty with one model than with others, this may mean that they have learned how to use certain models but have not necessarily developed deep conceptual understanding of decimal fractions. Placement of decimals on an empty number line is perhaps the most interesting task—and provides the more revealing information (Figure 9.9). The insights from this assessment can inform which models you need to emphasize.

Figure 9.9

Three different sixth-grade students attempt to draw a number line and show the numbers 0.6 and 0.06.

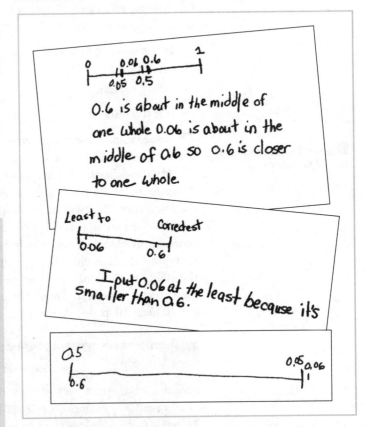

Source: Reprinted with permission from Martinie, S. L., & Bay-Williams, J. (2003). Investigating students' conceptual understanding of decimal fractions using multiple representations. *Mathematics Teaching in the Middle School, 8*(5), p. 246. Copyright © 2003 by the National Council of Teachers of Mathematics. All rights reserved.

Solving interesting problems that involve both decimals and fractions can strengthen student understanding of both fractions and decimals. The following are interesting investigations to be explored with a calculator:

- Which fractions have decimal equivalents that terminate? Can you discover a pattern? Is the answer based on the numerator, the denominator, or both?

- For a given fraction, how can you tell the maximum length of the repeating part of the decimal? Try dividing by denominators of 7 and 11 and 13 and then make a conjecture.

- Explore all of the ninths—$\frac{1}{9}, \frac{2}{9}, \frac{3}{9}, \cdots \frac{8}{9}$. Remember that $\frac{1}{3}$ is $\frac{3}{9}$ and that $\frac{2}{3}$ is $\frac{6}{9}$. Use only the pattern you discover to predict what $\frac{9}{9}$ should be. But doesn't $\frac{9}{9} = 1$?

- How can you find what fraction produces this repeating decimal: 3.454545 . . . ?

The last question can be generalized for any repeating decimal, illustrating that every repeating decimal is a rational number.

◆ Decimals to Fractions

In the real world, decimal numbers are rarely those with exact equivalents to familiar fractions. What fraction would you say approximates the decimal 0.52? Eighth-grade NAEP found that only 51 percent of eighth graders selected $\frac{1}{2}$. The other choices were $\frac{1}{50}$ (29 percent), $\frac{1}{5}$ (11 percent), $\frac{1}{4}$ (6 percent), and $\frac{1}{3}$ (4 percent) (Kouba et al., 1997). This mediocre performance on such a basic problem is an indication that too many students are learning rules rather than developing an understanding of decimals. Through warm-up problems or full lessons, you can ask students to tell you what they know about 0.65 by using fraction statements (or vice versa). They may write or say such things as these:

- It is greater than $\frac{1}{2}$ but less than $\frac{3}{4}$.
- It is about $\frac{2}{3}$.
- It is the fraction $\frac{65}{100}$.
- It is the same as $\frac{6}{10} + \frac{5}{100}$ *or* $0.6 + 0.05$ ("6 tenths and 5 hundredths").

Standards for Mathematical Practice

7 Look for and make use of structure ▶

The last example is very important to understanding decimal notation and building the connection back to what they know about whole numbers and fractions.

Middle-school students should have this conceptual foundation, but if they do not, doing approximation activities through warm-ups or learning centers can help them develop the foundation they will need for learning the operations. The first benchmarks that should be developed are 0, $\frac{1}{2}$, and 1. For example, is 7.3962 closer to 7 or to 8? Why? Expand these types of problems to other familiar fractions (thirds, fourths, fifths, and eighths). In this example, 7.3962 is close to 7.4, which is $7\frac{2}{5}$. A good number sense with decimals includes the ability to think of a familiar fraction that is a close equivalent to a decimal. This is what the *Common Core State Standards* mean by developing a "unified understanding of number" (CCSSO, 2010, p. 46). Activity 9.7 focuses on approximating the relative size of decimals.

▶ *Activity 9.7* **CLOSE TO A FAMILIAR FRACTION**

Make a list of about five decimals that are close to but not exactly equal to a familiar fraction equivalent. For example, use 24.8025, 6.59, 0.9003, 124.356, and 7.7. Ask students to find a familiar fraction that is close to each of these decimals. You may want to discuss strategies, such as thinking first of decimals that are close to the same value. For example, 6.59 is close to 6.6, which is $6\frac{3}{5}$. Ask students to write (or say) an explanation for their choices. If different students select different equivalent fractions, discuss the reasonableness of the different choices.

For a fun alternative or extension of this activity, students can be given a familiar fraction to start and be asked to create a decimal value that is close. They can then trade and quiz their peers to see if the peers can determine which fraction they originally had.

 ## Emphasizing Equivalence between Fractions and Decimals

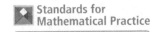 Standards for
Mathematical Practice

1 Make sense of problems and persevere in solving them

The last two sections have shared conceptual ideas for converting fractions to decimals and then decimals to fractions, but the goal is *not* that students can convert, but that they can recognize equivalent representations and easily switch representations to the form that fits the situation. It is important in middle school to continue to reinforce this flexible approach to rational number, accepting responses in either form and asking students questions such as, "Who solved it using decimals? Fractions? What are the advantages or disadvantages of the two ways?" Activities like Activity 9.8 can be used for centers or even homework to continue to reinforce equivalence representations.

Activity 9.8 BEST MATCH

Create a deck of cards with familiar fractions on half of the cards and the decimals that are close to the fractions, but not exact, on the other half. Using concentration or another matching game, have students find the best fraction match for the decimal values. The difficulty is determined by how close the various fractions are to one another, so this game can be differentiated by providing different sets of cards to different students. Students with disabilities may benefit from prompts such as, "Is the decimal close to 0, close to $\frac{1}{2}$, or close to 1?" Or have a list of all the possible compatible fractions as a reference.

 ## *Formative Assessment Note*

You can find out if your students have a unified understanding of fractions and decimals with a *diagnostic interview*. Here are a few examples:

- Write the fraction $\frac{5}{8}$ as a decimal. Use a drawing or a physical model (meter stick or 10×10 grid), and explain why your decimal equivalent is correct.
- What fraction is also represented by the decimal 0.004? Use words, physical model, pictures, and numbers to explain your answer.
- Use both a fraction and a decimal to tell the name of this marked point on the number line. Explain your reasoning.

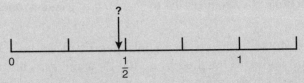

In the last example, it is especially interesting to see which representation students select first—fraction or decimal. Furthermore, do they then translate this number to the other representation or make a second independent estimate?

Comparing and Ordering Decimal Fractions

Comparing decimal fractions and putting them in order from least to greatest involves understanding the relative size of a number. But comparing decimal fractions has some important distinctions from comparing whole numbers, and because of that, students can make errors.

Stop and Reflect

What errors do you think students might make in ordering the following list from smallest to largest: 0.36, 0.058, 0.375, 0.97, 0, 2.0, and 0.4? ■

◆ **Common Misconceptions**

There are six common errors and misconceptions that students exhibit when comparing and ordering decimals (Desmet, Gregoire, & Mussolin, 2010; Steinle & Stacey, 2004a, 2004b).

1. *Longer is larger.* This is the most common initial error, in which students select the number with more digits as the largest. This is an incorrect application of whole-number ideas as students just look at the number beyond the decimal point and judge it as they would a whole number. So, under this misconception, they would say that 0.375 is greater than 0.97.

2. *Shorter is larger.* Here, the students think that because the digits far to the right represent very small numbers, longer numbers are smaller. For example, they would choose 0.4 as larger than 0.97 because "a tenth is larger than a hundredth." This error is very persistent.

3. *Internal zero.* In this case, students are confused by a zero in the tenths position, as in 0.058. Here, they would see 0.58 as less than 0.078, thinking that "zero has no impact" when written to the left, as is the case with a whole number. This has also been shown to be an issue when decimals are placed on the number line.

4. *Less than zero.* This misconception with zero is that when some students compare 0.36 with 0, they choose 0 as larger. This is due to the thinking that zero is a whole number positioned in the ones column (to the left of the decimal point) and so is greater than a decimal fraction (to the right of the decimal point). They are unsure if a decimal fraction is greater than zero.

5. *Reciprocal thinking.* This error usually takes teachers by surprise. If students are asked to compare 0.4 and 0.6, they incorrectly select 0.4 as larger. Using their knowledge that decimals are like fractions, they connect 0.4 to $\frac{1}{4}$ and 0.6 to $\frac{1}{6}$ and erroneously decide 0.4 is greater.

6. *Equality.* Another surprise is that students don't integrate the idea of regrouping decimals and that 4 tenths is equal to 40 hundredths or 400 thousandths. This misconception has them thinking that the 0.4 in the group above is not close to 0.375 and/or that 0.3 is smaller than 0.30.

All of these common errors reflect a lack of conceptual understanding of how decimal fractions are constructed.

Relative Size of Decimals

Because misconceptions stem from not understanding the size of values in the tenths, hundredths, and thousandths places and beyond, it is important to have students find values on the number line or other model. The following activity can help promote discussion about the relative sizes of decimal numbers.

▶ *Activity* 9.9 LINE 'EM UP

Prepare a list of four or five decimal numbers that students might have difficulty putting in order. Use a context such as the height of plants. The numbers should all be between the same two consecutive whole numbers. Have students first predict the order of the numbers, from least to greatest. Require students to use a model (e.g., a line if the context is plant height). As students wrestle with using the numbers to represent which plant (value) is taller, they will develop a deeper understanding of which digits contribute the most to the size of a decimal.

Determining how close a particular decimal is to different place values can strengthen students' understanding of the place values. For example, for 3.0917, ask, "Is this number closer to 3 or to 4?" Then, go to the tenths: "Is it closer to 3.0 or to 3.1?" Repeat with hundredths and thousandths. Students may revert to thinking that tenths are comparable to tenths and that there are no hundredths between. When asked which decimal is closer to 0.19—0.2 or 0.21—students select 0.21 (ignoring the decimal point). They also are not sure that 0.513 is near 0.51 but just a little larger. They may also think that 0.3 is near 0.4 but far away from 0.31784. These examples are evidence that students are in need of additional experiences focused on the relative size of decimals.

Density of Rational Numbers

An important concept for middle-school students is that there is *always* another number between any two numbers. When students see only decimals rounded to two places, this may reinforce the notion that there are no numbers between 2.37 and 2.38 (Steinle & Stacey, 2004b). Finding the decimal located between any two decimals requires that students understand the density of decimals. Using a linear model helps to show that there is always another decimal to be found between any two decimals—an important concept that is emphasized in the following activity.

▶ *Activity* 9.10 CLOSE DECIMALS

Have your students name a decimal between 0 and 1.0. Next, have them name another decimal that is even closer to 1.0 than the first. Continue for several more decimals in the same manner, each one closer to 1.0 than the previous decimal. Similarly, try close to 0 or close to 0.5. If students struggle, encourage them to use a number line to help them with their decision making.

Adding and Subtracting Decimal Fractions

There is much more to adding and subtracting decimals than knowing to "line up the decimal points." The *Common Core State Standards* (CCSSO, 2010, p. 33) say that fifth graders should "apply their understandings of models for decimals, decimal notation, and properties of operations to add and subtract decimals to hundredths. They develop fluency in these computations, and make reasonable estimates of their results."

Estimating Decimal Sums and Differences

Estimation is important. Often, an estimate is all that is needed. Even if an exact answer is required, estimating a reasonable answer helps students know if their answer makes sense. As with fractions, until students have a sound understanding of place value, equivalence, and relative size of decimals, they are not ready to develop understanding of the operations (Cramer & Whitney, 2010). An emphasis on estimation is very important, especially for students in the seventh and eighth grades who have learned the rules for decimal computation and may not be considering whether their answer is reasonable. Many students who rely on rules for decimals make mistakes without being aware of them because they are not using number sense.

---

1. 45.907 + 123.01 + 56.1234
2. 459.8 − 12.345
3. 0.607 + 0.18
4. 89.1 − 0.998

Stop and Reflect

What strategies can be applied to these problems (front end, rounding, compatibles)? What strategies might students use? ■

Your estimates might be similar to the following:

1. Between 210 and 240
2. A little less than 450
3. Close to 0.8
4. About 88

In these examples, an understanding of decimal numeration and whole-number estimation skills (e.g., front end, rounding, and compatibles) can produce reasonable estimates. When encouraging students to estimate, do not use rigid rules for rounding; instead, encourage a range of strategies.

Developing Algorithms

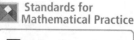
Standards for Mathematical Practice

1 Make sense of problems and persevere in solving them

Invented strategies receive significant attention with whole-number computation, but less with fraction and decimal computation. Yet, invented strategies are grounded in place value, are efficient, and are often times more conceptual for students than standard algorithms. This is certainly true for adding and subtracting decimal fractions. Even after the standard ▶ algorithm is learned and understood, middle-grade students should be encouraged to pick the best method given the situation. This is what mathematically proficient students do. Consider this problem:

Sumiko and Tiana each timed their own quarter-mile run with a stopwatch. Jessica says that she ran the quarter mile in 74.5 seconds. Tiana was more accurate in her timing, reporting that she ran the quarter mile in 81.34 seconds. Who ran it the fastest and how much faster was she?

Students who understand decimal numeration should be able to tell approximately what the difference is—close to 7 seconds. Then, students can figure out the exact difference by using various methods. First, students might note that 74.5 and 7 more is 81.5, then figure out how much extra that is (0.16) and subtract the extra to get a total difference of 6.34. Second, students might use a counting-up strategy (e.g., on a number line), adding 0.5 to 74.5 to get 75, then 6 more seconds to 81, then add the remaining 0.34 to 6.5 for a total difference of 6.84. Third, students might change 74.5 to 74.50 and subtract with regrouping. Similar story problems for addition and subtraction, some involving different numbers of decimal places, will help develop students' understanding.

In addition to using many contexts, students should illustrate addition and subtraction with different tools. The number line is an important tool. Using an empty number line allows students to estimate different-size jumps for tenths, hundredths, and so on. The number line is a good connection to length contexts, like the race story above. Since many uses of decimals are measurements, the number line should receive significant emphasis.

The base-ten pieces discussed earlier in this chapter are also an excellent tool for modeling addition and subtraction of decimals, in particular because students have often used them for modeling whole-number computation. This tool is a good match to the standard algorithm for adding and subtracting decimals, which the *Common Core State Standards* place in grade 6. As students solve various problems with base-ten pieces, they will notice the regrouping process and be able to generalize that place values must be added to (or subtracted from) the same place values (hundredths with hundredths and tenths with tenths, for example). This then leads them to the reason why the decimal points are lined up for adding and subtracting decimals.

5 Use appropriate tools strategically

8 Look for and express regularity in repeated reasoning

technology note

The National Library of Virtual Manipulatives (NLVM) site (http://nlvm.usu.edu/en/nav/category_g_3_t_1.html) offers a virtual activity, "Base Blocks—Decimals," that allows students to place base-ten blocks on a place-value chart to illustrate and solve addition and subtraction problems with decimals. The problems can be created or generated randomly. And the number of decimal places can be selected, so that any of the four blocks can be designated as the unit.

In middle school, students will have had experience adding and subtracting decimals. One way to assess how well they understand adding and subtracting decimals is to see if they can illustrate and come up with a context for a given problem, as in the next activity.

Activity 9.11 REPRESENT AND REVIEW

Give students a piece of paper. Ask them to fold it in half and in half again, creating four sections (as in the translation task discussed in Chapter 3). In the first section, ask students to record a decimal fraction expression—for example, 6.2 + 0.58. Next to it, ask them to write a situation that fits that problem. In the bottom two quadrants, students are to illustrate the operation by using (a) a number line and (b) base-ten pieces. Once they have finished, they can trade with someone else and review to see if their peer's representations accurately represent the problem.

 *Formative Assessment Note*

As students complete Activity 9.11, use a *checklist* to record whether they are showing evidence of having an understanding of decimal concepts by determining a context, illustrating on the number line, and illustrating with base-ten pieces. Look to see whether students can do these representations with problems of varying difficulty.

As students become more proficient in adding and subtracting with the standard algorithm, continue to provide opportunities for them to estimate, illustrate by using one of the two models discussed here, use invented strategies, and explain a context to fit the situation. For example, the NLVM game "Circle 3" is a great reasoning experience that challenges students to use logic as they combine decimals to add to 3. (It is not as easy as it sounds!) These types of continued experiences will ensure that students develop procedural proficiency for decimal addition and subtraction.

 Multiplication

Multiplication of decimals tends to be poorly understood. Students (and adults) blindly count over how many decimal places they have to decide where the decimal goes in the answer. No attempt is made to assess if the answer is reasonable. Yet, being mathematically proficient means having a much deeper understanding of multiplication of decimals. Students need to be able to use concrete models or drawings, strategies based on place value (invented strategies), and properties of operations, and must be able to explain the reasoning used (CCSSO, 2010). Estimation is essential in building that understanding.

 Estimating Products

Estimate the problems listed below. Which ones were easy to estimate? Difficult?

1. 5.91×6.1
2. 145.33×0.109
3. 0.58×9.67023

A student's reasoning might be similar to the following:

1. This is about 6 times 6, so the answer is about 36.
2. This is like 145 dimes, so divide by 10 and it is about 14.50. *Or,* this is about a tenth of 145, so 14.5.
3. The first value is about one-half, so half of about 10 is about 5.

When problems involve two very small decimals, estimation is difficult, but it is still possible to look at the answer to see if it is relatively smaller than what the initial factor was (taking a small part of a small part results in an even smaller part).

 *Teaching Tip*

As with any new operation, it is important to begin with the concrete. Situations (story problems) and visuals (manipulatives) provide that concrete foundation.

 Developing Algorithms

Begin exploring multiplication of decimals by using problems in a context and by using physical models.

Using decimal values that include small whole-number values can help students estimate and begin to see the impact of multiplying decimals.

The farmer fills each jug with 3.7 liters of cider. If you buy 4 jugs, how many liters of cider is that?

Ask students, "Is it more than 12 liters? What is the most it could be?" Second, let students use their own methods for determining an exact answer (based on place value and properties). One strategy is repeated addition: 3.7 + 3.7 + 3.7 + 3.7. Another is to multiply 3 × 4, then count up 0.7 four times. Or, students may double 3.7 (getting 7.4) and double it again. Eventually, students will agree on the exact result of 14.8 liters. Connect these strategies to the number line, showing how jumps on the decimal number line match the invented strategies. Explore other problems involving whole-number multipliers. Multipliers, such as 3.5 and 8.25, that involve common fractional parts—here, one-half and one-fourth—are a good next step.

Figure 9.10

A student's use of grids to reason about 1.5 × 0.6.

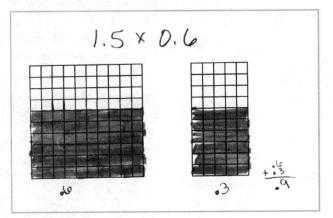

The area model is particularly useful in illustrating decimal multiplication because students know this model from whole-number multiplication (Rathouz, 2011). The rectangle model is especially useful for developing the standard algorithm for decimal multiplication, so creating stories that fit with a rectangle visual is a good idea.

A gardener can plant flowers in 1.5 m² of her garden. She decides to plant bluebells on an area that is 0.6 of the garden. On how many square meters can she plant bluebells?

In this problem, we are looking for 0.6 of 1.5 m², or 0.6 × 1.5. Begin with an estimate. An estimation might be 0.8 m², reasoning that it will be a little more than half of the available part of the garden. Figure 9.10 shows a student's solution on a grid diagram. Each large square represents 1 m², with each row of 10 small squares as 0.1 m² and each small square as 0.01 m². The shaded section shows 0.6 m² + 0.3 m² = 0.9 m². Notice that this is a proportional model, allowing students to "see" the values of the factors.

Use problems that can be illustrated with base-ten pieces or on the number line, such as these:

1. Four-tenths of an 8.5-acre farm is used for growing corn. How many acres of corn does the farm have?
2. A frog hops 4.2 inches at every hop. How far away is she from her starting point after 5 hops?

Figure 9.11 provides illustrations of each of these multiplication situations, a grid to illustrate the farm example (9.11a), and a line to illustrate frog leaps (9.11b). These illustrations of decimal multiplication should remind students of the strategies they used to learn whole-number multiplication, and this connection can be used in developing meaning for the standard algorithm for decimal multiplication.

Figure 9.11

Visuals (tools) used to illustrate multiplication of decimals.

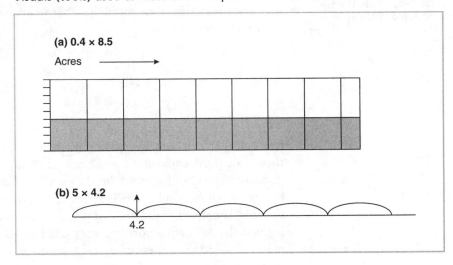

Ask students to compare a decimal product with one involving the same digits but no decimal. For example, how are 23.4×6.5 and 234×65 alike? Interestingly, both products have exactly the same digits: 15210. (The zero may be missing from the decimal product.) Have students use a calculator to explore other products that are alike except for the location of the decimals involved. The digits in the answer are always the same. After seeing how the digits remain the same for these related products, do the following activity.

Activity 9.12 WHERE DOES THE DECIMAL GO? MULTIPLICATION

Have students compute the following product: 24×63. Using only the result of this whole number computation (1512) and estimation, have them give the exact answer to each of the following:

$$0.24 \times 6.3 \qquad 24 \times 0.63 \qquad 2.4 \times 63 \qquad 0.24 \times 0.63$$

For each computation, have students write a rationale for how they placed the decimal point. For example, on the first one a student might explain that 0.24 is close to one-fourth and one-fourth of 6 is less than two, so the answer must be 1.512. They can check their results with a calculator. ELLs may apply a different mental strategy that is common in their country of origin. Even if they have trouble articulating their reasoning, it is important to consider alternative ways to reason through the problem. It is also important to have a class discussion about errors and how to avoid them.

Stop and Reflect

What is the value in having students explain how they placed the decimal, rather than just having students count over the number of places? ∎

Another way to support full understanding of the algorithm is to rewrite the decimals in their fraction equivalents. So, if you are multiplying 3.4×1.7, that is the same as $\frac{34}{10} \times \frac{17}{10}$. With multiplication, you would get $\frac{578}{100}$. When this is rewritten as a decimal fraction, it is 5.78, which corresponds to moving the decimal two places to the left (Rathouz, 2011).

The method of placing the decimal point in a product by way of estimation is more difficult as the product gets smaller. For example, knowing that 37×83 is 3071 does not make it easy to place the decimal in the product of 0.037×0.83. But the standard algorithm can be developed from this problem, all the while helping students understand properties of number.

Here is the process:

$$0.037 \times 0.83 = (37 \times \tfrac{1}{1000}) \times (83 \times \tfrac{1}{100})$$
$$(37 \times \tfrac{1}{1000}) \times (83 \times \tfrac{1}{100}) = 37 \times 83 \times \tfrac{1}{1000} \times \tfrac{1}{100}$$
$$37 \times 83 \times \tfrac{1}{1000} \times \tfrac{1}{100} = (37 \times 83) \times (\tfrac{1}{1000} \times \tfrac{1}{100})$$
$$(37 \times 83) \times (\tfrac{1}{1000} \times \tfrac{1}{100}) = 3071 \times \tfrac{1}{100,000} = 0.03071$$

This may look too complicated, but if you just look at what is happening with the decimal fractions, you can see why you count the number of values to the right of each factor, and then place the decimal in the product so that it has the same number of decimal places. The standard algorithm for multiplication is the following: Do the computation as if all numbers were whole numbers. When finished, place the decimal by reasoning or estimation if possible. If not, count the decimal places, as illustrated above. Even if students have already learned the standard algorithm, they need to know the conceptual rationale centered on place value and the powers of ten for "counting" and shifting the decimal places. By focusing on rote applications of rules, students lose out on opportunities to understand the meaning

---

◆ **Standards for Mathematical Practice**

2 Reason abstractly and quantitatively

and effects of operations and are more prone to misapply procedures (Martinie & Bay-Williams, 2003).

Questions such as the following keep the focus on number sense and provide useful information about your students' understanding.

---

1. Consider these two problems: $3\frac{1}{2} \times 2\frac{1}{4}$ and 2.276×3.18. Without doing the calculations, which product do you think is larger? Provide a reason for your answer that can be understood by someone else in this class.
2. How much larger is 0.76×5 than 0.75×5? How can you tell without doing the computation? (Kulm, 1994)

Student discussions and explanations as they work on these or similar questions can provide insights into their decimal and fraction number sense and the connections between the two representations.

 ## Division

Like multiplication of decimals, division of decimals is often poorly understood, and estimation and concrete experiences are needed to build a strong understanding. Returning to the whole-number understanding of division can help build meaning for the division of decimals.

Estimating with Decimal Division

Division can be approached in a manner exactly parallel to that for multiplication. In fact, the best approach to a division estimate generally comes from thinking about multiplication rather than division. Consider the following problem:

The trip to Washington was 280 miles. It took exactly 4.5 hours to drive. What was the average rate in miles per hour?

To make an estimate of this quotient, think about what times 4 or 5 is close to 280. You might think $60 \times 4.5 = 240 + 30 = 270$, so maybe about 61 or 62 miles per hour.

Here is a second example without context.

Make an estimate of $45.7 \div 1.83$. Think only of what times $1\frac{8}{10}$ is close to 46.

Because 1.83 is close to 2, the estimate is near 23. And since 1.83 is less than 2, the answer must be greater than 23—say 25 or 26. (The actual answer is 24.972677.)

Developing the Algorithm

Estimation can produce a reasonable result, but you may still require an exact answer. Figure 9.12 shows division by a whole number and how that can be carried out to as many places as you wish. (The explicit-trade method for whole numbers developed by John Van de Walle is shown on the right.)

Figure 9.12

Extending the whole-number division algorithm to decimal values.

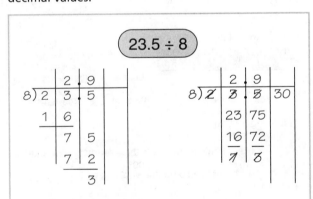

Trade 2 tens for 20 ones, making 23 ones.
Put 2 ones in each group, or 16 in all.
That leaves 7 ones.

Trade 7 ones for 70 tenths, making 75 tenths.
Put 9 tenths in each group, or 72 in all.

Trade the 3 tenths for 30 hundredths.

(Continue trading for smaller pieces as long as you wish.)

Activity **9.13**   **WHERE DOES THE DECIMAL GO? DIVISION**

Provide a quotient such as 146 ÷ 7 = 20,857 correct to five digits but without the decimal point. The task is to use only this information and estimation to give a fairly precise answer to each of the following:

$$146 ÷ 0.7 \quad 1.46 ÷ 7 \quad 14.6 ÷ 0.7 \quad 1460 ÷ 70$$

For each computation, students should write a rationale for their answer and then check their results with a calculator. As noted in the section on multiplication on page 160, ELLs may apply a different mental strategy, and it is important to value alternative approaches. Again, engage students in explicit discussions of common errors or misconceptions and how to fix them.

An algorithm for division is parallel to that for multiplication: Ignore the decimal points, and do the computation as if all numbers were whole numbers. When finished, place the decimal by estimation. This is reasonable for divisors greater than 1 or close to a familiar value (e.g., 0.1, 0.5, 0.01). If students have a method for dividing by 45, they can divide by 0.45 and 4.5 thinking they will get ten times as many (since 4.5 is one-tenth of 45), so multiply the answer by ten.

Percents

The term *percent* is simply another name for *hundredths* and as such is a standardized ratio with a denominator of 100. If students can express fractions and decimals as hundredths, the term *percent* can be substituted for the term *hundredth*. Consider the fraction $\frac{3}{4}$. As a fraction expressed in hundredths, it is $\frac{75}{100}$. As a decimal, it is 0.75. Both $\frac{75}{100}$ and 0.75 are read in exactly the same way: "seventy-five hundredths." When used as an operator, $\frac{3}{4}$ of something is the same as 0.75 or 75 percent of that same thing. Thus, percent is merely a new notation and terminology, not a new concept.

Chapter 8 explored fractions in which one part was unknown (see Figures 8.2 through 8.4). Figure 9.13 illustrates how these can be modified to focus on percents. Emphasize equivalence, but seek the equivalence for *hundredths*. Connect hundredths to percent, and replace fraction language with percent language.

Models and Terminology

Physical models provide the main link between fractions, decimals, and percents (Figure 9.14 and Blackline Masters 10 and 11). Students should develop an understanding of the percent equivalence of familiar fractions (halves, thirds, fourths, fifths, and eighths). Three-fifths, for example, is 60 percent as well as 0.6. Base-ten models, like the rational number wheel (see Figure 9.3), are suitable for fractions, decimals, and percents. The same is true of a 10×10 grid where each little square inside is 1 percent of the grid. Each row or strip of 10 squares is not only a tenth but also 10 percent of the grid. Zambo (2008) recommends linking fractions to percents

Figure **9.13**

Part–whole fraction problems can be adapted to percent challenges.

(From Figure 8.2)

                                    100%
If this strip is ~~one whole~~,
                                    66⅔%
what strip is ~~two-thirds~~?
                                    150%
What strip is ~~three-halves~~?

(From Figure 8.3)

                            75%
If this rectangle is ~~three-fourths~~, draw a shape
                            100%
that could be ~~the whole~~.

(From Figure 8.4)

                        percent
What ~~fraction~~ of this set is black?

with a 10×10 grid. By marking one of every four squares on the grid, students can discover the link between $\frac{1}{4}$ and $\frac{25}{100}$ or 25 percent. He goes on to suggest that even more complex representations, such as $\frac{1}{8}$, can lead to interesting discussions about the remaining squares left at the end, resulting in $12\frac{1}{2}$ of 100 squares or $12\frac{1}{2}$ percent.

Figure 9.14

Visuals illustrate three different representations.

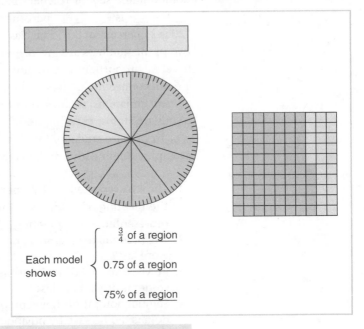

Each model shows $\begin{cases} \frac{3}{4} \text{ of a region} \\ 0.75 \text{ of a region} \\ 75\% \text{ of a region} \end{cases}$

Activity 9.14 PERCENT MEMORY MATCH

Create a deck of cards of circle graphs with a percentage shaded in and cards that have the matching percents (like a circle with $\frac{1}{2}$ shaded and 50 percent). (A spreadsheet program like Excel can generate these graphs when you enter the percent of each part.) Students are to pair each circle graph with the percent that best matches it in a memory game in which they must flip over matching cards to make a pair. For students with disabilities, provide a rational number wheel (see Figure 9.3) as a movable representation to help support their matching. For a virtual game that has the same goal, see the NCTM Illuminations virtual "Concentration" (http://illuminations.nctm.org/ActivityDetail.aspx?ID=73), which uses representations of percents and fractions and a regional model. It is designed for one or two players.

Length representations are also important. A number line can be created that has 0 and 100 percent as end points, or 0 to 1, and percents can be posted on the number line in their appropriate places. In fact, an advantage of the number line is that it lends to showing percentages greater than 100 percent.

Another length representation is the percent necklace. Using fishing line or sturdy string, link 100 same sized beads and knot them in a tight, circular necklace. Have students count the number of beads between any two lines that represent a wedge of the circle. For example, they might find that 24 beads are in the section of the circle graph that shows how many students' favorite music is country. That is an estimate that approximately 24 percent of the students favor country music. Counting the beads in a given category gives students an informal approach to estimating percent while investigating a meaningful physical model for thinking about the concept of per 100.

Teaching Tip

Use a classroom-long number line, and have students place fractions, decimals, and percents. Equivalent representations are placed on top of one another. This can be a lesson or a daily routine for five minutes at the start of class.

technology note

The NCTM Illuminations activity "Fraction Models" (http://illuminations.nctm.org/activitydetail.aspx?ID =11) explores equivalence of fractions, mixed numbers, decimals, and percents. You select the fraction and pick the type of model (length, area [rectangle or circle], or set), and it shows the corresponding visual and all the equivalences.

◆ Percent Problems in Context

Some middle-school teachers may talk about "the three percent problems." The sentence "_____ is _____ percent of _____" has three spaces for numbers—for example, "20 is 25 percent of 80." The classic three percent problems come from this sterile expression; two of the numbers are given, and the students are asked to produce the third. Students tend to set up proportions but are not quite sure which numbers to put where. In other words, they are not connecting understanding with the procedure. Furthermore, commonly encountered percent situations, such as sales figures, taxes, food composition (percent fat), and economic trends are almost never in the "_____ is _____ percent of _____" format.

To prepare students for these short statements, provide more elaborate and authentic examples. Begin with problems that involve familiar fractions and compatible numbers.

1. The PTA reported that 75 percent of the total number of families were represented at the meeting. If students from 320 families go to the school, how many families were represented at the meeting?
2. The baseball team won 80 percent of the 25 games it played this year. How many games were lost?
3. In Ms. Glasser's class, 20 students, or $66\frac{2}{3}$ percent, were on the honor roll. How many students are in her class?
4. Samuel bought his new computer at a $12\frac{1}{2}$ percent discount. He paid $700. How many dollars did he save by buying it at a discount?
5. If Nicholas has read 60 of the 180 pages in his library book, what percent of the book has he read so far?
6. The hardware store bought widgets at 80 cents each and sold them for $1 each. What percent did the store mark up the price of each widget?

Figure 9.15

Students use bar diagrams to solve percent problems.

Stop and Reflect

Which types of problems might be more challenging to students? What visuals or physical models might be used to support their thinking? ■

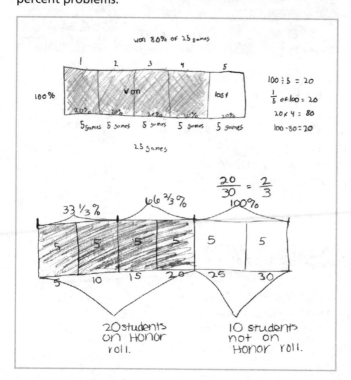

Examples of students' reasoning with bar diagrams are illustrated in Figure 9.15.

The results of the 2005 NAEP exam revealed that only 37 percent of eighth graders could determine an amount following a given percent of increase. Many selected the answer obtained by adding the percent itself to the original amount. That is, for a 10 percent increase, they would select an answer that was 10 more than the original amount. In another question, only 30 percent could accurately calculate the percent of the tip when given the cost of the meal and the amount of the tip left by the diners. A reason for this weak performance is a failure to develop percent concepts meaningfully (a recurring theme related to rational numbers).

◆ Estimation

Many percent problems do not have simple (familiar) numbers. Frequently, in real life an approximation or estimate in percent situations is enough to help one think

Formative Assessment Note

These context-based percent problems are an effective *performance assessment* to evaluate students' understanding. Assign one or two, and have students explain why they think their answers make sense. You might take a realistic percent problem and substitute a fraction for a percent (e.g., use $\frac{1}{8}$ instead of $12\frac{1}{2}$ percent) to compare how students handle the problems with fractions and with percents. If your focus is on reasoning and justification rather than number of problems correct, you will be able to collect all the assessment information you need.

through the situation. Even if a calculator will be used to get an exact answer, an estimate based on an understanding of the relationship confirms that a correct operation has been performed or that the decimal point is positioned correctly.

To help students with estimation in percent situations, two ideas that have already been discussed can be applied. First, when the percent is not a simple one, substitute a close percent that is easy to work with. Second, select numbers that are compatible with the percent involved to make the calculation easy to do mentally. In essence, convert the complex percent problem into one that is more familiar. Here are some examples.

1. The 83,000-seat stadium was 73 percent full. How many people were at the game?
2. The treasurer reported that 68.3 percent of the dues had been collected, for a total of $385. How much more money can the club expect to collect if all dues are paid?
3. Max McStrike had 217 hits in 842 at-bats. About what percent of the time is he getting a hit?

 Possible Estimates

1. Use $\frac{3}{4}$ and 80,000 → about 60,000
2. Use $\frac{2}{3}$ and $380; will collect $\frac{1}{3}$ more, which is half of $\frac{2}{3}$ → about $190
3. 217 is about $\frac{1}{4}$ of 842; $\frac{1}{4}$ is the same as 25 percent → about 25%

Here are three percent problems with two sets of numbers. The first number in the set is a compatible number that allows the problem to be worked out mentally by using fraction equivalents. The second number requires a substitution with an approximation or estimation, as in the last activity.

1. The school enrolls {480, 547} students. Yesterday {10 percent, 12 percent} of the students were absent. How many came to school?
2. Mr. Carver sold his lawn mower for {$45, $89}. This was {60 percent, 62 percent} of the price he paid for it when it was new. What did the mower cost when it was new?
3. When the box fell off the shelf, {90, 63} of the {360, 250} widgets broke. What percentage was lost in the breakage?

The first problem asks for a part (whole and fraction given), the second asks for a whole (part and fraction given), and the third asks for a fraction (part and whole given).

It is also convenient at times to use simple base-ten equivalents: 1 percent and 10 percent and multiples of these (including halves). For example, we often use 10 percent plus half of that much to compute a 15 percent tip at a restaurant. To find 0.5 percent, we can think of half of 1 percent.

There are several common uses for estimating percentages in real-world situations. As students gain full conceptual understanding and flexibility, there are ways to think about percents that are useful as you are shopping or in situations that bring thinking about percents to the forefront.

1. *Tips.* As mentioned previously, to figure a tip, you can find 10 percent of the amount and then half of that again to make 15 percent.

2. *Taxes.* The same approach is used for adding on sales tax. Depending on the amount, you can find 10 percent, take half of that, and then find 1 percent and add or subtract that amount as needed. But encourage other approaches as well. Students should realize that finding percents is a process of multiplication; therefore, finding 8 percent (tax) of $50 will generate the same result as finding 50 percent (half) of 8, or $4.

3. *Discounts.* A 30 percent decrease is the same as 70 percent of the original amount, and sometimes, depending on the original amount, one of those percents is easier to use in mental calculations than the other. If a $48 outfit is discounted 30 percent, for example, you are paying 70 percent. Round $48 to $50. And you have .70 × 50 (think 7 × 5), so your cost is about $35.

Again, these are not rules to be taught; they are reasoning activities to be developed that require a full understanding of percent concepts and the commutative property.

◆ Teaching Percents

In summary, here are suggestions for effective instruction with percents:

- Emphasize percents of familiar fractions (halves, thirds, fourths, fifths, eighths, and tenths), and use numbers compatible with these fractions. The focus of these exercises is on the relationships involved, not complex computation.

- Do not rush to develop rules or procedures for different types of problems—encourage students to notice patterns.

- Use the terms *part*, *whole*, and *percent* (or *fraction*). *Fraction* and *percent* are interchangeable. Help students see these percent exercises as the same types of exercises they did with fractions.

- Require students to use manipulatives, drawings, and contexts to explain their solutions. It is wiser to assign three problems requiring a drawing and an explanation than to give 15 problems requiring only computation and answers. Remember that the purpose is the exploration of relationships, not computational skill.

- Encourage mental computation and estimation.

E x p a n d e d L e s s o n

Zoom: Finding Rational Numbers on the Number Line

Content and Task Decisions

Grade Level: 6–7

Mathematics Goals

- To understand a rational number as a point on the number line
- To use both fraction and decimal representations of a quantity flexibly
- To develop the concept of density of rational numbers (another fraction/decimal fraction can always be found between any two given fractions/decimal fractions).

Grade Level Guide

NCTM *Curriculum Focal Points*	Common *Core State Standards*
Connecting fractions to decimals and comparing decimals (and fractions) are part of a focal point in grade 4: "Number and Operations: Developing an understanding of decimals, including the connections between fractions and decimals" (NCTM, 2006, p. 16).	In sixth grade, students study rational numbers in more depth: "Apply and extend previous understandings of numbers to the system of rational numbers" (CCSSO, 2010, p. 43). Specifically, "Understand a rational number as a point on the number line" (p. 43). A critical area in seventh grade is that "students develop a unified understanding of number, recognizing fractions, decimals (that have a finite or a repeating decimal representation), and percents as different representations of rational numbers" (p. 46).

Consider Your Students' Needs

Students are skilled at finding equivalent fractions and at converting fractions to decimals.

For English Language Learners

- The word *between* needs attention in the *Before* phase. In particular, *between* doesn't mean that the value has to be exactly in the middle. This can be modeled with people in front of the room, and the word can be written and described on the board.

- Students from other countries often do more mental math, and this should be valued. If you are not clear on how someone found an "in-between" fraction or decimal, ask the student to explain or write how he or she thought about it. Having the student share a clever mental strategy is also a good idea.

For Students with Disabilities

- You may need to scaffold this task for students who are struggling by selecting the first two fractions for them to work on rather than using what the class suggests. In that way, you can select fractions with denominators that are easily compared, such as thirds and twelfths. Once students explore an approach to finding fractions between those limits, then they can move on to more challenging combinations.

Materials

- Number line (in front of class)
- Adding machine paper or paper strips (one per group)

Lesson

Before

Begin with a simpler version of the task:

- Stretch a number line (e.g., clothes line) across the front of the room. Ask students to mark where 0.75 and 1 are on the line. Tell students you are going to "zoom in" and find more values between those two values. Then, ask students to write down three possible numbers that go between those two numbers. Have students share a few ideas of fractions and decimals that go between 0.75 and 1. Ask students to share their thinking strategies for how they found the number.

- Present the focus task to the class: You are going to select a card with two values on it. You are going to create a number line that "zooms in" on that part of the number line. You are going to find five numbers that are between the two values. (Note: Differentiate by using tiers—provide different starting decimals or fractions that vary in difficulty for different groups of students.)

Provide clear expectations:

- Students can use any method they wish to find their "in-between" values, but they have to be able to explain their methods in the *After* phase.

- Explain that their list of five values must include both fractions and decimals, but each answer must be distinct (e.g., .9 and $\frac{9}{10}$ are the same answer and count only once).

- Students are to write the values on a "zoomed-in" number line on their paper strip.

During

Ongoing:

- Look for students who are using various strategies to identify decimals and fractions. Possible strategies include these:

  - Folding/partitioning the line in half and in half again in order to find values in between, and noting the related fractional or decimal value

  - Extending out one decimal place, then using consecutive values

  - Getting a large common denominator, then using consecutive numerators.

- Observe the extent to which students are reasoning with the numbers (fractions and/or decimals) and to what extent they are using the number line to support their reasoning.

- Have students post their number lines with their starting values and five "in-between" values.

After

Bring the class together to share and discuss the task:

- Have groups of students bring their number line to front of room. Ask each student in the group to explain how he or she located one of the decimals or fractions.

- If students convert the fractions to decimals, see if they can convert one or more of the decimal numbers to fractions. Use this strategy to highlight that these are different symbolic notations for the same quantities. If you suspect that students are not convinced that the fraction and decimal number represent the same quantity, give them a copy of the 10 × 10 grids and ask them to represent the fraction quantity on one grid and the decimal quantity on another grid and compare the amounts.

- After students have shared the number lines, ask, "Do you think you could find five more decimals between your values? Five more fractions?" Ask how many decimals they think exist between their two values. Provide small-group time for them to discuss this question before having groups share their thinking.

- At the conclusion of this lesson, explain that what the students have been exploring is the concept of the *density of rational numbers*. Students may be able to come up with their own definition of what it means to say that rational numbers are *dense*.

Assessment

Observe

- Do students have a systematic way to determine decimals or fractions on the number line between the given values, or are they haphazardly identifying possibilities?

- Are students using benchmarks or other strategies in deciding where to place the values on the number line?

- Are they overly reliant on either fractions or decimals, or can they reason in both domains?

Ask

- How can you find a decimal whose value is between those of any two other decimals?

- How are finding numbers between decimals and finding numbers between fractions similar? Different?

- How many values can we find between the two numbers we used? (This is what it means to say that rational numbers are "dense.")

10

The Number System

BigIDEAS

1 Our number system includes whole numbers, fractions, decimals, and integers, all of which are rational numbers. Every rational number can be expressed as a fraction.

2 *Integers* are the negative and positive counting numbers and zero. Positive and negative numbers describe quantities having both magnitude and direction (e.g., temperature above or below zero).

3 *Exponential notation* is a way to express repeated products of the same number. Specifically, powers of ten express very large and very small numbers in an economical manner.

4 Many numbers are not rational; the irrationals can be expressed only symbolically or approximately by using a close rational number. Examples include $\sqrt{2} \sim 1.41421$ and $\pi \sim 3.14159\dots$.

Before middle school, students have explored whole numbers and positive fractions and decimals, but in middle school, they begin to focus on more complicated number sets. First, students learn additional ways to represent numbers by using scientific and exponential notation. Second, they learn that the number system expands to the left of zero, exploring integers and negative fractions and decimals. Finally, students explore irrational numbers, where they begin to appreciate the completeness of the real-number system.

The ideas presented in this chapter build on ideas that have been developed throughout the book. Exponents are used in algebraic expressions and add to the operations. Scientific notation employs place-value concepts and expands options for how large and small numbers are represented. Integers move beyond the set of positive counting numbers to numbers less than zero and therefore extend the number line (as well as operations) to include negative values. This is a critical area of study in sixth grade: "Students extend their previous understandings of number and the ordering of numbers to the full system of rational numbers, which includes negative rational numbers, and in particular negative integers" (CCSSO, 2010, p. 39). And it continues as a critical area in seventh grade: "Students develop a unified understanding of number, recognizing fractions, decimals (that have a finite or a repeating decimal representation), and percents as different representations of rational numbers" (CCSSO, 2010, p. 46).

Exponents

As numbers in our increasingly technological world get very small or very large, expressing them in standard form can become cumbersome. Exponential notation is more efficient for conveying numeric or quantitative information. In the *Common Core State Standards*, exponents are first introduced in fifth grade related to powers of ten and place value. In sixth grade, students learn to write and evaluate numeric expressions involving whole-number exponents. And in eighth grade, students work with radicals and integer exponents. Similarly, the NCTM *Curriculum Focal Points* (NCTM, 2006, p. 20) state that in eighth grade, "students use exponents and scientific notation to describe very large and very small numbers. They use square roots when they apply the Pythagorean Theorem."

◆ Exponents in Expressions and Equations

Standards for Mathematical Practice

8 Look for and express regularity in repeated reasoning

▶

The "rules" of exponents may be confusing for students. For example, with only a rule-based background, they may not remember whether you add or multiply the exponents when you raise a number to a given power. This is an indication that students lack a conceptual understanding of the operations and the notation. Students need to explore exponents with whole numbers before they use exponents with variables. By looking at whole-number exponents, they are able to notice patterns in solving problems and are able to generate (and understand) the "rules" of exponents themselves. A whole-number exponent is simply shorthand for repeated multiplication of a number times itself—for example, $3^4 = 3 \times 3 \times 3 \times 3$.

Exponential notation is unfamiliar and difficult to understand, and therefore requires explicit attention. First, an exponent applies to its immediate base. For example, in the expression $2 + 5^3$, the exponent 3 applies only to the 5, so the expression is equal to $2 + (5 \times 5 \times 5)$. However, in the expression $(2 + 5)^3$, the 3 is an exponent of the quantity $2 + 5$ and is evaluated as $(2 + 5) \times (2 + 5) \times (2 + 5)$, or $7 \times 7 \times 7$. Notice that the process follows the order of operations. As with any topic, start with what is familiar and concrete. With exponents, this means beginning by exploring powers of 2 and 3—operations that can be represented geometrically.

Minia knows that square animal pens are the most economical for the amount of area they provide (assuming straight sides). Can you provide a table for Minia that shows the areas of square pens that have between 4 m and 10 m of fence on each side?

Figure 10.1

A student records possibilities for making a square pen.

Side length	pen picture	equation	area
4 meters	4 ☐	$4 \times 4 = 4^2$	$16 m^2$
5 meters	5 ☐ 5	$5 \times 5 = 5^2$	$25 m^2$
6 meters	6 ☐ 6	$6 \times 6 = 6^2$	$36 m^2$
7 meters	7 ☐ 7	$7 \times 7 = 7^2$	$49 m^2$
8 meters	8 ☐	$8 \times 8 = 8^2$	$64 m^2$
9 meters	9 ☐ 9	$9 \times 9 = 9^2$	$81 m^2$
10 meters	10 ☐ 10	$10 \times 10 = 10^2$	$100 m^2$

Students may set up a table similar to the one in Figure 10.1, showing possible areas for square pens with different side lengths.

Another way to explore exponents is to explore algebraic growing patterns, such as the classic "Painted Cube" problem. This appears in *Connected Mathematics Project 2*, as seen in Figure 10.2. (See also http://connectedmath.msu.edu/CD/Grade8/Painted/PaintedCubes.html.)

As the painted cube grows, so does the size of each square face (excluding the edges), as well as the number of cubes hidden inside the large painted cube. In a $2 \times 2 \times 2$ painted cube, the faces are 2×2; in a $3 \times 3 \times 3$ painted cube, the faces are 3×3. Note that although each face is 3×3, the outer cubes are corners, so that more sides are painted, whereas the inner 2×2

$\mathcal{F}igure$ 10.2   The "Painted Cube" problem provides a context for exploring squares and cubes.

Organize your data in a table like the one below.

Edge Length of Large Cube	Number of Centimeter Cubes	Number of Centimeter Cubes Painted On			
		3 faces	2 faces	1 face	0 faces
2					
3					
4					
5					
6					

Study the patterns in the table.

1. Describe the relationship between the edge length of the large cube and the total number of centimeter cubes.

2. Describe the relationship between the edge length of the large cube and the number of centimeter cubes painted on.

  a. 3 faces   **b.** 2 faces   **c.** 1 face   **d.** 0 faces

Source: Adapted from *Connected Mathematics: Frogs, Fleas and Painted Cubes: Quadratic Relationships* by Glenda Lappan, James T. Fey, William M. Fitzgerald, Susan N. Friel, and Elizabeth Difanis Phillips. Copyright 2006 by Michigan State University, Glenda Lappan, James T. Fey, William M. Fitzgerald, Susan N. Friel, and Elizabeth Difanis Phillips. Used by permission of Pearson Education, Inc. All rights reserved.

square on each face is a centimeter cube with one side painted. Consider what is happening with the cubes in the middle of the painted cube. In a $2 \times 2 \times 2$ cube, there are no inside cubes; in a $3 \times 3 \times 3$ cube, there is a $1 \times 1 \times 1$ (1) "hidden" centimeter cube inside that will not be painted on any face. In a $4 \times 4 \times 4$ cube, there will be $2 \times 2 \times 2$ (8) hidden cubes. As you can see, the number of cubes with one side painted grows at a quadratic rate, and the number of "hidden" cubes grows at a cubic rate. In exploring the pattern, students get experience with algebraic rules that are linear, squared, and cubed.

Exponential growth is very interesting to explore in real-world contexts. The website "Otherwise" offers an applet that can engage students in experiments with population (exponential) growth (www.otherwise .com/population/exponent.html). Another powerful exploration of exponential growth is to look at powers of ten. The website "Molecular Expressions" (http://micro.magnet.fsu.edu/primer/java/scienceopticsu /powersof10) illustrates this by comparing the size of the Milky Way with the size of a plant cell.

◆ Order of Operations

Working with exponents extends the *order of operations*. An exponent indicates the number of times the base is used as a factor, so it indicates repeated multiplication and therefore precedes other multiplication and division, as well as addition and subtraction. In the expression $5 \times 4^2 - 6$, the 4^2 is acted upon first because in expanded form this would be $5 \times 4 \times 4 - 6$. Multiplying 5 times 4 and then squaring changes the result because the 5 is not meant to be squared.

You can see why multiplying before computing the exponent changes the meaning of the problem (and the answer), while doing exponents first results in the same quantity. When we want to communicate that operations are to be computed in a different order, we have to use grouping symbols, such as parentheses.

Teaching Tip

Order of operations is not just a convention; it is based on the meaning of the operations! Pose a problem like the one here, and ask students to explain why exponents are computed before multiplication.

Although part of the order of operations is due to convention (e.g., working from left to right, using parentheses), the order of the computations is due to the meanings of these operations. A context can make this point clearer, which is the focus of Activity 10.1.

Activity 10.1 STACKS OF COINS

Select a story situation that includes such things as stacks of coins, bricks, or notebooks. If you have the book *Two of Everything,* by Lily Hong, you can show that the Haktaks have stacks of coins from their magic pot and use that as the context. Tell stories and ask students to (1) write an expression and (2) tell you how many. For example: "Mrs. Haktak had one stack with seven coins and four stacks with ten coins. How many coins did she have? (Students should write $7 + 4 \times 10$ or $4 \times 10 + 7$ for the expression.) Ask, "Could we write it either way? Why or why not?" and "Could we add the seven to the four and then multiply by 10? Why or why not?" Then, write expressions with addition and multiplication and ask students to tell their own stories as they solve the problem.

Another way to illustrate why the order of operations is true is to write an expression, such as $4^2 - 3 + 2 \times 5$, as all addition: $4^2 + 3 + 2 \times 5 = 4 + 4 + 4 + 4 + 3 + 5 + 5$. How would you combine if you wanted to be efficient? Add all the fours $(4 \times 4 = 4^2)$, then add $5 + 5$ (2×5), then add 3.

The phrase "**P**lease **E**xcuse **M**y **D**ear **A**unt **S**ally," or more simply PEMDAS, is sometimes used to help students remember the order of operations. Although this mnemonic may be helpful, it often leads students to think that addition is done before subtraction and that multiplication comes before division. An improved version involves writing the order in hierarchical levels:

Teaching Tip

Mnemonics should not replace an understanding of why the order of operations is what it is.

P = parenthesis
E = exponents
MD = multiplication and division (whichever is first from left to right)
AS = addition and subtraction (whichever is first from left to right)

The order of operations is not as rigid as the list might imply. For example, consider the expression $10 \times 4 - 5 \times 2$. It doesn't matter which product is figured first.

An applet, "Rags to Riches" (www.quia.com/rr/116044.html), provides practice for doing the order of operations in a game format, similar to "Who Wants to Be a Millionaire." You can also strengthen students' understanding of order of operations by having them use appropriate symbols to record expressions, as in the activity here.

Activity 10.2 GUESS MY NUMBER

In this activity, you will give hints about a number, and students will think backward to find it (by using logical reasoning). For ELLs and students with disabilities, provide the statements in writing and verbally. Students create equations, using parentheses appropriately to reflect the clues you give, as in the following three examples:

Standards for Mathematical Practice

4 Model with mathematics

- I am thinking of a number; I add 5, double it, and I get 22. $[(n + 5) \times 2 = 22]$
- I am thinking of a number; I subtract 2, square it, and I get 36. $[(n - 2)^2 = 36]$
- I am thinking of a number; I double it, add 2, cube it, and I get 1000. $[(2n + 2)^3 = 1000]$

For students with disabilities, you may want to start with a known number rather than an unknown number—for example, start with 5, square it, add 11, and divide by 6. They should write $(5^2 + 11) \div 6 = n$.

Formative Assessment Note

Give students an expression that includes all the operations and the use of parentheses—for example, $(4 + 2)^2 \times 2 \div 4$—and ask them to write a matching story, using a context of their choice, to fit the expression. Having students write these stories in *journals* provides an excellent assessment of their understanding of the order of operations.

As you review students' stories, see if the stories show students' understanding that multiplication and division (and addition and subtraction) are equal in the hierarchy of order and should therefore be solved from left to right.

Another way to engage students or assess their understanding of exponents and order of operations is to have them determine if given equations are true or false. This is the focus of Activity 10.3.

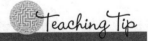
Teaching Tip

Students can be overzealous in using parentheses when writing expressions. Regularly ask students, "Are the parentheses required or optional in this equation?"

Activity 10.3 TRUE OR FALSE EQUATIONS

Write an equation that addresses one or more aspects of the order of operations. For example: $24 \div (4 \times 2) = 24 \div 4 \times 2$. If students think that multiplication comes before division, they will write "true." Or, if they are not aware of the left-to-right prioritizing, they may also write "true." Other examples include these:

Standards for Mathematical Practice

3 Construct viable arguments and critique the reasoning of others

$$15 + 2^3 = 15 + 2 \times 3 \qquad 3.2 - 1.2 + 0.04 = (3.2 - 1.2) + 0.04$$
$$2 + 5^3 = 7^3 \qquad (3.6 + 0.4)^2 = 4^2$$
$$3.2^2 + 3.2^2 = 3.2^4 \qquad 6 \bullet 2^4 = 12^4$$

There are several ways to incorporate true/false equations into instruction. First, one or two of these equations can be part of a daily warm-up routine. Second, equations can be written on cards, and partners can work together. Both partners think of the answer. One student says "true" or "false," and the partner agrees or disagrees. If the partners disagree, they try to convince each other of the correct responses. They create a stack of their true equations and a stack of their false equations. When you check each group's progress, you can formatively assess by seeing if the cards in the true and false piles are correct.

Stop and Reflect

The true/false statements can address commonly misunderstood aspects of the order of operations. How does the strategy of true/false statements support the learning of students with disabilities and students who struggle? What aspects of the order of operations do you think are commonly misinterpreted by students? ■

Exponent Notation on the Calculator

Most simple four-function calculators do not use algebraic logic, so operations are processed as they are entered. On calculators without algebraic logic, the following two keying sequences produce the same results:

Key: →	3 ⊞ 2 ⊠ 7 🟰
Display → 3	2 ⌒ 5 7 35

Key: →	3 ⊞ 2 🟰 ⊠ 7 🟰
Display → 3	2 5 7 35

Whenever an operation sign is pressed, the effect is the same as pressing = and then the operation. Of course, neither result is correct for the expression $3 + 2 \times 7$, which should be evaluated as $3 + 14$, or 17.

Calculators designed for middle grades often use algebraic logic (follow the order of operations) and include parenthesis keys, so that both $3 + 2 \times 7$ and $(3 + 2) \times 7$ can be keyed in the order in which the symbols appear. See the difference in the following displays:

Key: →	3 ⊞ 2 ⊠ 7 🟰
Display → 3	2 7 17

Notice that the following display does not change when × is pressed and a right parenthesis is not displayed. Instead, the expression that the right parenthesis encloses is calculated and that result displayed.

Key: →	⦗ 3 ⊞ 2 ⦘ ⊠ 7 🟰
Display → [3	2 5 7 35

Some calculators show the expression $3 + 2 \times (6^2 - 4)$. Nothing is evaluated until you press Enter or EXE. Then, the result appears on the next line to the right of the screen:

$$3 + 2 * (6^2 - 4) \qquad 67$$

The last expression entered can be recalled and edited so that students can see how different expressions are evaluated.

$3 + 2 * (6^2 - 4)$	67
$(3 + 2) * (6^2 - 4)$	160
$(3 + 2) * 6^2 - 4$	176
$3 + 2 * 6^2 - 4$	71

Calculators remain a powerful tool for exploring the impact of operations. For example, to evaluate 3^8, press 3 $\boxed{\times}$ $\boxed{=}$ $\boxed{=}$ $\boxed{=}$ $\boxed{=}$ $\boxed{=}$ $\boxed{=}$ $\boxed{=}$. (The first press of $\boxed{=}$ will result in 9, or 3 $\boxed{\times}$ 3.) Students will be fascinated by how quickly numbers grow. Enter any number, press $\boxed{\times}$, and then repeatedly press $\boxed{=}$. Try two-digit numbers. Try 0.1.

Give students many opportunities to explore expressions involving exponents and the order of operations.

Activity 10.4 ENTERING EXPRESSIONS

Provide students with numeric expressions to evaluate with simple four-function calculators. Ask, "How will you have to enter these to apply the order of operations correctly?" Rewrite the expression the way it needs to be entered. Here are some examples of expressions to try:

$3 + 4 \times 8$ $4 \times 8 + 3$	$3^6 + 2^6$ $(3 + 2)^6$	$3^4 \times 7 - 5^2$ $(3 \times 7)^4 - 5 \times 2$	$3^4 \times 5^2$ $(3 \times 5)^6$

$\dfrac{5^3 \times 5^2}{5^6}$ $4 \times 3 - 2^3 \times 5 + 23 \times 9$ $\dfrac{4 \times 3^5}{2}$ $4 + \dfrac{3^5}{2}$

A common misconception with exponents is to think of the two values as factors, so 5^3 is thought of as 5×3 rather than as the correct equivalent expression of $5 \times 5 \times 5$. This becomes still more problematic when students hear such things as, "It is five three times." Avoid confusing language and spend significant time having students state and write the equivalent expressions. Students should write equivalent expressions without exponents or include parentheses to indicate explicit groupings. For example:

$$\begin{aligned}(7 \times 2^3 - 5)^3 &= [7 \times (2 \times 2 \times 2) - 5] \times [7 \times (2 \times 2 \times 2) - 5] \times [7 \times (2 \times 2 \times 2) - 5] \\ &= [(7 \times 8) - 5] \times [(7 \times 8) - 5] \times [(7 \times 8) - 5] \\ &= (56 - 5) \times (56 - 5) \times (56 - 5) \\ &= 51 \times 51 \times 51\end{aligned}$$

For many expressions, there is more than one way to proceed, and sharing different ways is important. Activity 10.3, "True or False Equations," can be adapted to focus on the equivalence of simplified and expanded forms of a variety of equations.

Even though calculators with algebraic logic will automatically produce correct results (i.e., follow the order of operations), students must know the order of operations, including when they have to do one operation before another and when it doesn't matter which goes first. This flexibility and awareness become the foundation for symbolic manipulation in algebra.

◆ Negative Exponents

Standards for Mathematical Practice

7 Look for and make use of structure ▶

What does 2^{-4} mean? This is a good question to ask students who have been working with positive exponents. The following two related options can help students explore the possibilities of negative exponents. The powers of ten are good to explore because they directly relate to place value. Ask students to continue the pattern of 10^n as follows:

$$
\begin{aligned}
10^4 &= 10{,}000 \\
10^3 &= 1000 \\
10^2 &= 100 \\
10^1 &= 10 \\
10^0 &= ? \\
10^{-1} &= ?
\end{aligned}
$$

To continue the pattern, 10^0 would be 1, which it is! (This is the definition of 10^0, in fact, any number to the zero power is 1). The next value would be one-tenth of 1. And, each successive number is one-tenth of the one that comes before it:

$$10^{-1} = 0.1 = \tfrac{1}{10}$$

$$10^{-2} = 0.01 = \tfrac{1}{100} = \tfrac{1}{10^2}$$

$$10^{-3} = 0.001 = \tfrac{1}{1000} = \tfrac{1}{10^3}$$

Students may notice that the negative exponent is the reciprocal of the value it would be without the negative sign.

Figure 10.3

Graphing calculators evaluate expressions as decimals. However, they also convert decimals to fractions. This figure shows the screen of a TI-73 calculator. The F←→D key converts fractions to decimals (and decimals to fractions), as shown here.

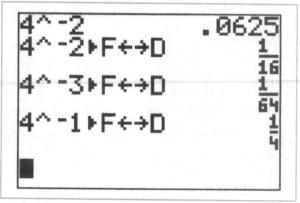

technology note

Students can explore negative exponents on a calculator. For example, ask students to figure out what 4^{-3} or 2^{-5} equals. If the calculator has the decimal-to-fraction conversion function, suggest that students use that feature to help develop the meaning of negative exponents. Figure 10.3 gives an example of how this might look on a graphing calculator. Ask students to notice patterns that they think can be generalized and to test their conjectures.

Students often confuse exponent rules. Identifying a mistake in someone else's work is another effective way to help students think about the correct (and incorrect) order in a problem, as illustrated in Activity 10.5.

Activity 10.5 FIND THE ERROR

Create a set of problems that are solved incorrectly, and ask students to explain what was done wrong and how to do it correctly. A few examples are provided here:

Zach: $3(4)^2 = 24$ Yoli: $(5^3)^2 = 5^5$ Wilma: $\frac{20x^8}{5x^2} = 4x^4$

Examples can be increasingly more challenging and can be mixed with correct solutions. For activity sheets with more examples, see Johnson and Thompson (2009).

Standards for Mathematical Practice

◀ **3 Construct viable arguments and critique the reasoning of others**

Scientific Notation

The more common it becomes to find very large or very small numbers in our daily lives, the more important it is to have convenient ways to represent them. Numbers can be written in common form, but when this becomes cumbersome, a better option is scientific notation. In the *Common Core State Standards*, scientific notation is an eighth-grade expectation within the domain of Expressions and Equations (CCSSO, 2010). In scientific notation, a number is changed to a number greater than or equal to 1 and less than 10 multiplied by a power of ten. For example, 3,414,000,000 can also be written as 3.414×10^9.

Stop and Reflect

What strategies can you use to bring real-life contexts into exploring scientific notation so that students understand the relative sizes of the numbers, as well as how to write them symbolically? ■

Different notations have different purposes and values. For example, the population of the world on July 7, 2012, was estimated to be 7,024,764,005 (U.S. Census Bureau, n.d.). This can be expressed in various ways:

7024 million

7.0×10^9

About 7 billion

Each way of stating the number has value and purpose in different contexts. Rather than spend time with exercises converting numbers from standard form to scientific notation, consider large numbers found in newspapers, magazines, and atlases. How are they written? How are they said aloud? When are they rounded and why? What forms of the numbers seem best for the purposes? What level of precision is appropriate for the situation? And, how do these numbers relate to other numbers? How does the population of the world relate to the population in your state or your continent?

Standards for Mathematical Practice

◀ **6 Attend to precision**

Websites like that of the U.S. Census Bureau (www.census.gov) make population data readily available. The NCTM Illuminations lesson "The Next Billion" (http://illuminations.nctm.org/LessonDetail.aspx?id=L715) is a high-quality lesson for exploring when the world population will reach 8 billion. Students discuss their predictions, past trends in population growth, and social factors—a good interdisciplinary opportunity.

Contexts for Very Large Numbers

The real world is full of very large quantities and measures. We see references to huge numbers in the media all the time. Unfortunately, most of us have not developed an appreciation for extremely large numbers, such as those in the following examples:

- A state lottery with 44 numbers from which to pick 6 has over 7 million possible combinations. There are $44 \times 43 \times 42 \times 41 \times 40 \times 39$ possible ways in which the balls can come out of the hopper (5,082,517,440). But generally, the order in which they are picked is not important. Because there are $6 \times 5 \times 4 \times 3 \times 2 \times 1 = 720$ different arrangements of six numbers, each collection appears 720 times. Therefore, there are *only* $5,082,517,440 \div 720$ possible lottery numbers, or 1 in 7,059,052 chances to win.

- The estimated size of the universe is 40 billion light-years. One light-year is the number of miles light travels in *1 year*. The speed of light is 186,281.7 miles per *second*, or 16,094,738,880 miles in a single day.

- The human body has about 100 billion cells.

- The distance to the sun is about 150 million kilometers.

Connect large numbers to meaningful points of reference to help students get an idea of their true magnitude. For example, suppose students determine that the population in their city or town is about 500,000 people. They can then figure that it would take approximately 13,300 cities of the same population size to generate the population of the world. Or, suppose students determine that it is about 4600 km between San Francisco, California, and Washington, D.C. This means that it would take more than 32,000 trips back and forth between these two cities to equal the distance between the earth and the sun.

The following activity uses real data to develop an understanding of scientific notation and the relative size of numbers.

◆ *Activity* 10.6 **HOW FAR AWAY FROM THE SUN?**

 Explain to students that they are going to research planetary distances from the sun (in kilometers), record the data in scientific notation, and create a scaled illustration of the distances. If gathering data is not practical, provide the following figures:

Mercury	57,909,000	Jupiter	778,400,000
Venus	108,200,000	Saturn	1,423,600,000
Earth	149,600,000	Uranus	2,867,000,000
Mars	227,940,000	Neptune	4,488,400,000

Encourage students to develop strategies to figure out the relative distances between two planets. You can give a long strip of cash register tape to each group and have the students mark the sun on one end and Neptune on the other. For ELLs, reinforce the names of thousands, millions, and billions. (Note that billion can mean 1 million millions in some countries, not 1000 millions, as it does in the United States.)

Contexts for Very Small Numbers

It is also important to use real examples of very small numbers. As with large numbers, connecting very small numbers to points of reference can help students conceptualize how tiny these numbers really are, as shown by the following real-world examples:

- The length of a DNA strand in a cell is about 10^{-7} m. This is also measured as 1000 *angstroms*. (Based on this information, how long is an angstrom?) For perspective, the diameter of a human hair is about 2.54×10^{-5} m.

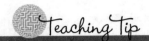

- Human hair grows at the rate of 10^{-8} miles per hour. Garden snails have been clocked at about 3×10^{-2} mile per hour (see more below).
- The mass of one atom of hydrogen is 0.000 000 000 000 000 000 000 001 675 g; for comparison, the mass of one paper clip is about 1 g.
- Sound takes $0.28 (2.8 \times 10^{-1})$ seconds to travel the length of a football field. In contrast, a TV signal travels a full mile in about $0.000005368 (5.3 \times 10^{-6})$ second. So a TV viewer at home hears the football being kicked before the receiver on the field does.

Teaching Tip

> Finding real data that are very, very small or very, very large can build the meaning of small and large numbers *and* insights into various aspects of the world.

Activity 10.7 AT A SNAIL'S PACE

The speed of garden snails has been clocked at about 3×10^{-2} mile per hour. Ask students to estimate how long it will take a snail to travel 1 mile. To explore, have them record the decimal equivalent of 3×10^{-2} (0.03). They can use the calculator's counting function (enter .03 + .03 =). On most calculators, when you hit = repeatedly, the calculator counts by the last value entered (.03). Each press of the = represents 1 hour. Ask students figure it out mathematically or by counting. Share strategies. When students have shared their results, ask what it would mean if the rate had been 3×10^{-3}. They can explore this problem, too, and should conclude that it would take 10 times longer.

Scientific Notation on the Calculator

Students may learn how to multiply by 10, by 100, and by 1000 simply by moving the decimal point. Help students expand this idea by examining powers of ten on a calculator that permits entry of exponents.

Activity 10.8 EXPLORING POWERS OF TEN

Have students use any calculator that permits entering exponents to explore some of the following:

- Explore 10^n for various values of n. What patterns do you notice? What does 1E15 mean? (1E15 is the typical calculator form of 1×10^{15}.) What does 1E−09 mean?
- What does 4.5E10 mean? 4.5E−10?
- What does 5.689E6 mean? Can you enter this another way?
- Try sums like $(4.5 \times 10^n) + (27 \times 10^k)$ for different values of n and k. What can you find out? Does it hold true when n and k are negative integers?
- What happens with products of numbers like those in the previous item?

Students need to become familiar with the power-of-ten expressions in written forms and the calculator form. For example, on a calculator, the product of $45,000,000 \times 8,000,000$ is displayed as 3.6E14, meaning 3.6×10^{14}, or 360,000,000,000,000 (360 trillion).

One misconception students can develop is that the exponent tells the number of zeros to add onto the number. Address this explicitly in class discussions. For example, ask students,

"Why are there 13 zeros and not 14? Is there a relationship between the exponent and the number of zeros?" (No, it depends on how many nonzero digits are in the number.)

Scientific notation has advantages in terms of operating on large or small numbers, especially for multiplication.

Compute $(4.5 \times 10^7) \times (8 \times 10^6)$, or 4.5E7 $\times$ 8.0E6, mentally.

Notice that the significant digits can be multiplied mentally ($4.5 \times 8 = 36$) and the exponents added to produce 36×10^{13} or 3.6×10^{14}.

Integers

Every day, students experience phenomena that involve negative numbers, as shown in the following list:

- Temperature
- Altitude (above and below sea level)
- Golf (above and below par)
- Money
- Time lines, including Before Common Era (BCE)
- Football yardage (gains/losses)

Generally, negative numbers are introduced with integers—the whole numbers and their negatives or opposites—instead of with fractions or decimals. However, it is a mistake to stop with integer values because students must understand where numbers like ⁻4.5 and ⁻1¼ are positioned on the number line in relation to integer values. In fact, because noninteger negative numbers are not addressed adequately in middle school, many students have misconceptions about where noninteger negative numbers are located on the number line. For example, students will place ⁻1¼ between ⁻1 and 0 instead of between ⁻2 and ⁻1. In the *Common Core State Standards*, integers are introduced and developed in sixth grade, and in seventh grade, students "solve multi-step real-life and mathematical problems posed with positive and negative rational numbers in any form (whole numbers, fractions, and decimals), using tools strategically" (CCSSO, 2000, p. 49).

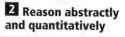
Standards for Mathematical Practice

2 Reason abstractly and quantitatively

◆ Contexts for Exploring Integers

▶ As with any new topic or type of number, it is important to start with familiar contexts so that students can use prior knowledge to build meaning. With integers, students often get confused about which number is bigger or in which direction they are moving when they compute, so having a context is particularly important.

For many students, in particular ELLs, it is important to include visuals with the contexts, to support language development (Swanson, 2010). As students learn to compare and compute, they can use the contexts to ground their thinking and justify their answers. The importance of using contexts is emphasized in the *Common Core State Standards* in sixth grade: "[Students must] understand that positive and negative numbers are used together to describe quantities having opposite directions or values (e.g., temperature above/below zero, elevation above/below sea level, credits/debits, positive/negative electric charge); use positive and negative numbers to represent quantities in real-world contexts, explaining the meaning of 0 in each situation" (CCSSO, 2010, p. 43). These contexts and others are described in the next sections.

◆ Quantity Contexts

Golf Scores

In golf, scores are often written in relationship to a number considered par for the course. So, if par for the course is 70, a golfer who ends the day at 67 has a score of $^-3$, or 3 strokes under par. Consider a player in a four-day tournament with day-end scores of $^+5$, $^-2$, $^-3$, $^+1$. What would be his or her final score for the tournament? How did you think about it? You could match up the positive and the negatives (in this case, $^+5$ with $^-2$ and $^-3$ to get a net result of 0), then see what is left (in this case, $^+1$). The notion that opposites (5 and $^-5$) equal zero is an important concept in teaching integers. You can post a mixed-up set of golf scores and ask students to order the players from first through tenth place. Emphasize that first place is the *lowest* score—and therefore the *smallest* number.

Money: Payments and Deposits

Suppose that you have a bank account. At any time, your records show how many dollars are in your account. The difference between the payments and deposit totals tells the amount of money in the account. If there is more money deposited than paid out, the account has a positive balance, or is "in the black." If there are more payments than deposits, the account is in debt, showing a negative cash value, or is "in the red." This is a good context for exploring addition and subtraction of integers, as in Figure 10.4. Net worth is a similar way to look at integers (assets and debts). Considering the net worth of famous people can engage students in making sense of integers (Stephan, 2009), and students can successfully draw on their experiences with assets, debts, and net worth values to create meaning for integer addition and subtraction (Stephan & Akyuz, 2012).

Figure 10.4

A checkbook used as a context for adding and subtracting integers.

Item	Payments or Deposits	Balance
Mowing lawn	+12.00	$34.00
Phone bill	−55.00	−21.00
iTunes downloads	−9.00	−30.00
Paycheck	+120.00	90.00

▲ *Activity* 10.9 **WHAT IS HER NET WORTH?**

On the Internet, look up the net worth of someone interesting to your students (e.g., a singer, athlete, or actor). Make up two to three assets and two to three debts, and ask your students to figure out her net worth. Then, with the students, look up the net worth of other people of their choice. Have them suggest possible assets and debts for that person. One clever way to do this is to have a net worth page filled out with two to three assets and two to three debts, but a smudge on the paper so that all students can see is the net worth (Stephan, 2009). This visual is particularly important for students with disabilities because they can see the missing value in a real situation.

Eventually, debts can be represented as negative values, and a connection is made to integer addition and subtraction.

◆ Linear Contexts

Many of the real contexts for negative numbers are linear. In addition, the number line provides a good tool for learning the operations that relate well to what the students have done with whole-number and fraction operations. The *Common Core State Standards* emphasize the need for sixth graders to be able to represent integers on a number line as well as on a coordinate axis (CCSSO, 2010). See www.mathgoodies.com/lessons/vol5/intro_integers .html for a good introduction to integers on a number line.

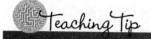

Teaching Tip

Temperature as a context for negative numbers has the advantage that you can also use fraction and decimal values.

Temperature

The "number line" measuring temperature is vertical. This context demonstrating negative integers may be the most familiar to students because they either have experienced temperatures below zero or know about temperatures at the North or South Pole. A good starting activity for students is finding where various temperatures belong on a thermometer. For example, Figure 10.5 displays a thermometer marked in increments of five degrees, and students are asked to place on the number line the following temperatures from a week in North Dakota: 8°, ⁻2°, ⁻12°, 4°, ⁻8°, 0°, ⁻3°. Ask students to order the temperatures from the coldest to the warmest (least to greatest).

Figure 10.5

Thermometers are excellent tools for exploring positive and negative numbers.

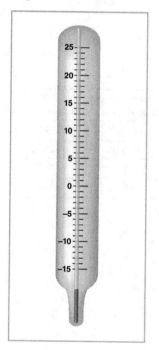

Altitude

Another vertical number-line model, altitude, is also a good context for integers. The altitudes of sites below sea level are negative, such as that of the town of Dead Sea, Israel (with an altitude of ⁻1371 feet) and Badwater, California, in Death Valley (which has an altitude of ⁻282 feet). Positive values for altitude include Mount McKinley (the tallest mountain in North America), at 20,322 feet. Students can order the altitudes of various places around the world (data easily found on the Internet) or find the difference between the altitudes of two different places—a good context for subtraction of integers.

Time Lines

Asking students to place historical events on a time line is an excellent interdisciplinary opportunity. The time line is useful for examples with larger values (e.g., 1950) as well as negative values (e.g., ⁻3000, or 3000 BCE). Or, students can explore their own personal time line (Weidemann, Mikovch, & Hunt, 2001), in which students find out key events that happened before they were born (e.g., the birth of an older sibling) and have happened since they were born (e.g., the move to a new house). Students place these events on a number line, with zero representing the day they were born. By partitioning a year into months, students can gain experience with rational numbers (halves, fourths, or twelfths) on the number line. Continue to reinforce the connection to the size of numbers, asking students, "Which number (year) is the smallest (earliest)?"

Football

A statistic reported on every play in a football game is yards gained and yards lost, which provides a good context for exploring integers, especially when it comes to comparing and adding integers. Students can be asked questions like these: "If the Steelers started their drive on the 20-yard line and the first three plays were recorded as ⁻4,⁺9,⁺3, did they get a first down?" "On the Ravens' first play, the yardage is ⁻4. Where are they in relation to the line of scrimmage?" (Use negatives if they are behind the line of scrimmage, in this case ⁻4.) "Where are they in relation to the first down marker?" (⁻14).

Activity 10.10 (AMERICAN) FOOTBALL STATISTICS

 Look up the average yards gained for some of the best running backs in the NFL or from college teams popular with your students. Ask students to use average yards gained per down to create a possible list of yardage gains and losses for each player. For example, if a player had an average of 4 yards per carry in a game, the following could have been his data:

$$10, \ ^-3, \ ^-2, 21, \ ^-5, 3, \ ^-1, 5, \ ^-1, 13$$

You may want to do one like this together, then have students create their own. The football context provides an excellent way to *use* integers meaningfully, integrated with the important concept of averages. ELLs may not be familiar with American football because football in most countries is what is called *soccer* in the United States. Role playing the game with students is a fun way to be sure the game is understood by all. Also, a yard is a U.S. measurement that may not be familiar and could be confused with the other meaning of *yard*. Comparing a yard to a meter can provide a point of reference that will help build meaning for this activity.

◆ Meaning of Negative Numbers

Negative numbers are defined in relation to their positive counterparts. For example, the definition of negative 3 is the solution to the equation $3 \ + \ ? \ = \ 0$. In general, the *opposite of n* is the solution to $n \ + \ ? \ = \ 0$. If *n* is a positive number, the *opposite of n* is a negative number. The set of integers, therefore, consists of the positive whole numbers, the opposites of the whole numbers (or negative integers), and zero, which is neither positive nor negative. Like many aspects of mathematics, abstract or symbolic definitions are best understood when conceptual connections link to the formal mathematics.

Absolute Value

Absolute value is introduced in sixth grade in the *Common Core State Standards*. The *absolute value of a number* is defined as the distance between that number and zero. Knowing the distance between two points, either on a number line or on a plane, is often needed in applications of mathematics. For example, we need to be able to determine how far a helicopter is from a hospital, regardless of its direction. Opposites, such as $^-12$ and 12, are the same distance from zero and therefore have the same absolute value.

  When students' absolute value experiences are limited to simplifying expressions like $|^-8|$ or $|6 - 10|$, they do not connect the procedure with the meaning of absolute value or see any real purpose for doing this. Add in a context to make it meaningful. For example, $|6 - 10|$ can be the distance between the 10-mile marker and the 6-mile marker. In this example, you can see that both $10 - 6$ and $6 - 10$ can lead to the answer and that distance is positive (absolute value), so the answer is 4.

Stop and Reflect

What other contexts can be used to build meaning for absolute value? ■

Notations

Because students have seen the negative sign only when doing subtraction, the symbolic notation for integers may be confusing. It may also be confusing that sometimes the negative sign appears at different heights (e.g., –7 and ⁻7). Also, sometimes parentheses are placed around the number so that it is separate from the operation—for example, 8 − (⁻5). Students have not seen parentheses used in this way and may think they should multiply. It is important to connect to their prior knowledge and explicitly build meaning for the new symbols. In this case, you might ask students, "When do we use parentheses in mathematics?" Students may say they are used for grouping a series of computations to show what to do first and that they can also mean multiplication. Point out that parentheses are also used to make a number sentence more readable—separating the negative number from the operation.

⬙ Tools for Teaching Integers

Two models, one denoted by quantity and the other by linear operations, are popular for helping students understand comparisons and the four operations (+ , − , × , and ÷) with integers.

Counters

Any counters with a different color on either side or counters in two colors (e.g., tiles of two different colors) can work to represent integers. But, two-color counters are a great fit for showing positive and negative because one side (color) can represent positive counts and the other side (color) can represent negative counts. One counter of each type results in zero (⁺1 + ⁻1 = 0), illustrating that they are opposites. Consider money: If yellow counters are credits and red counters are debits, having 5 yellows and 7 reds is the same as having 2 reds or 2 debits and is represented as ⁻2 (Figure 10.6). It is important for students to understand that it is always possible to add to or remove from a collection of any number of pairs consisting of one positive and one negative counter without changing the value (i.e., it is like adding equal quantities of debits and credits).

Figure **10.6**

Each collection is a model of negative 2.

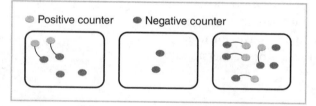

Number Lines

The number line is the second (and important) tool for computing with negative numbers. A number line has several advantages. Importantly, it is familiar to students from their computations with whole numbers, fractions, and decimals (see Chapters 8 and 9). Second, it is an excellent tool for representing the operations conceptually in terms of increasing or decreasing amounts. To add a context, consider using small cutouts of grasshoppers that jump up and down the line (Swanson, 2010). Or, use your school's mascot! Students can see that as the animal moves to the left, it goes to smaller numbers, and as it moves to the right, it goes to larger numbers. Third, the number line shows the distance from zero (or the absolute value of the number). Fourth, the number line allows students to explore noninteger negative and positives values (e.g., $⁻4\frac{1}{4} + 3\frac{3}{3}$ or ⁻9.2 − 4.5), which is difficult to do with counters. Finally, the number line is an important connection to the coordinate axis, which involves two perpendicular number lines.

Figure **10.7**

Number-line model for integers.

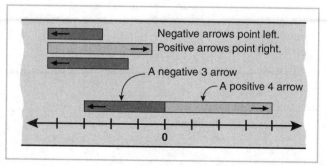

Arrows can be used in integer computation to show distance and direction. For example, 4 can be modeled with an arrow four units long starting at any location on the number line and pointing to the right, and ⁻3 can be modeled with an arrow three units long starting at any location on the number line and pointing to the left (Figure 10.7). The arrows help students think of integer quantities as directed distances. A positive arrow never points left, and a negative arrow never points right. Furthermore, each arrow is a quantity with both length (magnitude or absolute value) and direction (sign). These properties are constant for each arrow regardless of its position on the number line.

Which Model to Use

Although the two models of counters and the number line appear quite different, they are alike mathematically. Integers involve two concepts—magnitude and direction. Quantity is modeled by the number of counters or the length of the arrows. Opposites are represented by different colors or different directions.

Seeing how integers are represented across these two models while making connections between the models can help students extract the intended concepts. The context should also decide the representation because if students are exploring a context that is a length context, the number-line visual is a fit, and if they are exploring a quantity model, such as money, then the counters are a better match.

 # Operations with Integers

Once your students understand how integers are represented by each of the models, you can present the operations for the integers in the form of story problems.

◆ Addition and Subtraction

Introduce negative values in one of the contexts discussed earlier, such as golf scores. Personalize the story by telling students that each weekend, you golf a round on Saturday and on Sunday. The first weekend, your results were $^+3$ and $^+5$, the next weekend you scored $^+3$ and $^-5$, and on the last weekend you scored $^-6$ and $^+2$. How successful was your game each weekend? Overall? Because this is a quantity model, counters are a good choice for illustrating (although number lines can also be used). A linear context could be used with football yards gained and lost on two plays. See Figure 10.8 for illustrations of how to use both models for addition.

Conversely, ask students to create their own stories for integer operations. One way to scaffold this is to ask students the following three prompts: Where did you start? How far did you go? Where are you now? (Swanson, 2010). So, for example, a student might write, "I was 3 feet under water, then dove down 5 feet. Where am I now?"

Contexts are an important place to begin, but students also need to be able to reason about the numbers themselves. It is important to focus on the meaning of opposites. Activity 10.11 provides an excellent way to explore integers quantitatively, with a focus on having students use opposites as they think about integer addition (Friedmann, 2008).

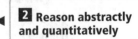
Standards for Mathematical Practice

◀ **2 Reason abstractly and quantitatively**

▶ *Activity* 10.11 **FIND THE ZERO**

Before beginning the activity, ask students to tell you the sums of several opposites, such as 4 + $^-$4. Then, ask students to look at a sum of integers that are not opposites, such as 7 + $^-$4, and see if they can "find a zero" by decomposing one of the numbers—for example, (3 + 4) + $^-$4—and solve. Students, particularly students with disabilities, may benefit from creating a "zero box" below each problem as they solve it, as illustrated. (For details, see Expanded Lesson.)

$$12 + {}^-5 =$$

Zero box: $\boxed{5 + {}^-5}$

$$(7 + 5) + {}^-5 = 7 + (5 + {}^-5) = 7 + 0 = 7$$

Figure 10.8

Integer addition with counters and number lines. The first example in both cases illustrates with whole numbers as a way to build background for integer addition.

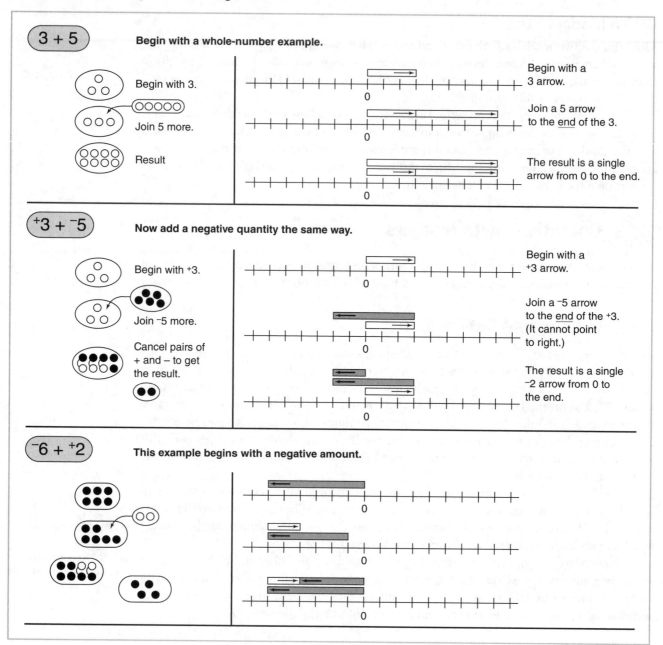

Students must continue to illustrate what is happening when they are adding and subtracting negative numbers. If they do not, they will get lost in the symbols and will not know in which direction to head on the number line. Figure 10.8 provides examples of addition problems that are illustrated by using different approaches with the two models: with positive and negative counters and with the number line and arrows.

To add with the number line, each added arrow begins at the head of the previous arrow. Subtraction can be used for separate (take-away) situations (e.g., start with 7 and take away 10) or for comparison situations (e.g., what is the difference or distance between 7 and ⁻3?). An advantage to the number-line model is that it can be used for both separate and comparison situations.

Consider the problem ⁻5 − ⁺2, the second example modeled in Figure 10.9. If a quantity model is used, the context could be money, such as, "I start with a debit of $5 and then

Figure 10.9

Integer subtraction with both counters and number lines (shown first with a whole-number example to build background).

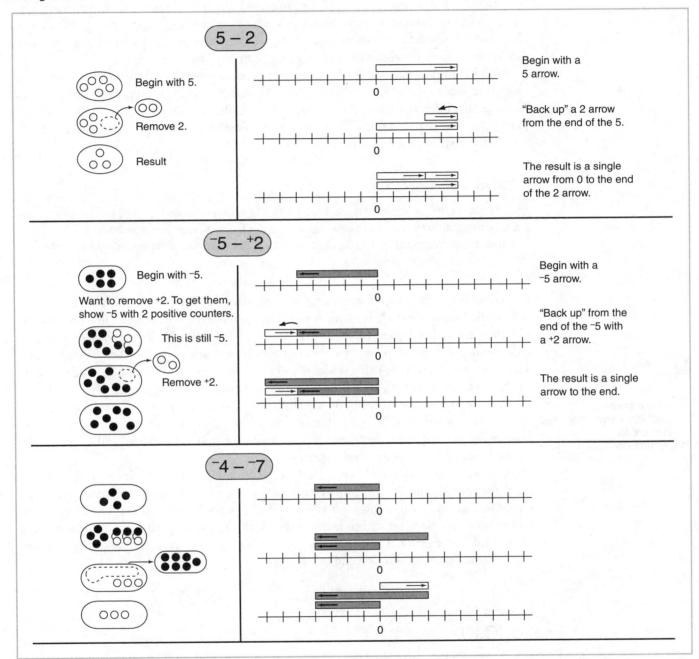

withdraw (take out) $2 more from my account. What balance will my bank account show (if no fees have been charged yet for my overdrawn account)?"

To show this problem, you start with the five red counters. To remove two positive counters from a set that has none, a different representation of ⁻5 must first be made. Because any number of neutral pairs (one positive, one negative) can be added without changing the value of the set, two pairs are added so that two positive counters can be removed. The net effect is to have more negative counters.

With the number line, subtraction can be illustrated by using arrows for separate and comparison situations. Consider a separate (take-away) situation as a way to think about the second example in Figure 10.9. Using temperature as a context, the explanation could be,

"The day begins at 5° below zero. Then the temperature drops $^+2$, which means it just got colder and is now $^-7$°." The difficulty in the take-away thinking comes when you try to provide an authentic explanation of subtracting a negative value.

Consider, for example, $^-4 - ^-7$ (see the third example in Figure 10.9). You start with taking away, but because it is negative temperature (or coldness) that is being taken away, you are in fact doing the opposite—warming up by 7°. With the number line, you start at $^-4$, then reverse the arrow going left to one going right for 7 moves.

Number lines can also be used for comparison situations. For subtraction, this can make a lot more sense to students (Tillema, 2012). In this example, the comparison question is, "What is the difference from $^-7$ to $^-4$?" In other words, how do you get from $^-7$ to $^-4$? You count up 3. Notice that if this were written in reverse ($^-4 - ^-7$), it would be the difference from $^-4$ to $^-7$, still 3, but the direction is to the left, so $^-3$.

Stop and Reflect

Try to explain the problems in Figures 10.8 and 10.9 by using both a quantity and a linear context. For subtraction, explain each in a separate situation and a comparison situation. What kinds of stories or contexts might fit with these different ways to think about addition and subtraction? ■

◆ Standards for
Mathematical Practice

1 Make sense
of problems and
persevere in
solving them

A significant challenge for students is to connect visual representations to their symbolic work. One way to help students is to ask them to notate basic number line illustrations with their equations. Figure 10.10 illustrates how a student might draw arrows to represent addition and subtraction exercises. You can also have students write story situations as a third representation. This helps students to build a stronger understanding, while helping you better identify any misconceptions or error patterns.

It is important for students to see that $^+3 + ^-5$ is the same as $^+3 - ^+5$, and that $^+2 - ^-6$ is the same as $^+2 + ^+6$. Illustrating addition and subtraction problems on the number line and explicitly discussing how the two expressions are related will help students see the connections between these expressions.

In seventh grade, students must learn to "solve multi-step real-life and mathematical problems posed with positive and negative rational numbers in any form (whole numbers, fractions, and decimals), using tools strategically" (CCSSO, 2010, p. 49). The examples in this section have been limited to integers, but with the use of a ruler or any number line partitioned into fractional amounts, the same arrow illustrations can help students reason about rational number addition and subtraction.

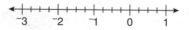

Figure 10.10

Students can use simple arrow sketches to represent addition and subtraction with negative numbers.

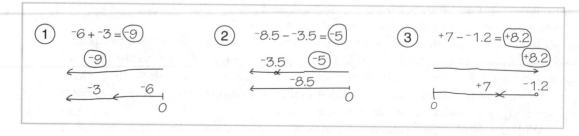

◆ Multiplication

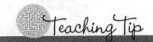

Multiplication of integers is an extension of multiplication of whole numbers, fractions, and decimals. One way to think of whole-number multiplication is equal groups, or repeated addition. The first factor tells how many sets there are or how many are added in all, beginning with zero. This translates to integer multiplication quite readily when the first factor is positive, regardless of the sign of the second factor. The first example in Figure 10.11 illustrates a positive first factor and a negative second factor ($3 \times {}^-4$), which translates into the question, "If I have three groups of $^-4$, how much do I have?" With a context, this could be any of the following: I lost four dollars three days in a row; how much have I lost? Three days in a row Hans scored $^-4$ in his golf tournament; what is his score? Three times today the temperature dropped four degrees; how much has the temperature changed?

What could the meaning be when the first factor is negative, as in $^-2 \times {}^-3$? If a positive first factor means repeated addition (how many times added to zero), a negative first factor should mean repeated subtraction (how many times subtracted from zero). The second example in Figure 10.11 illustrates how multiplication with the first factor negative can be represented.

◆ Division

Connect division of negative numbers with what students know about positive numbers. Recall that $8 \div 4$ with whole numbers has two possible meanings corresponding to two missing-factor expressions. The equation $4 \times ? = 24$ asks, "Four sets of what make twenty-four?" (group size unknown), whereas the equation $? \times 6 = 24$ asks, "How many

Figure 10.11

Multiplication by a positive first factor is repeated addition. Multiplication by a negative first factor is repeated subtraction.

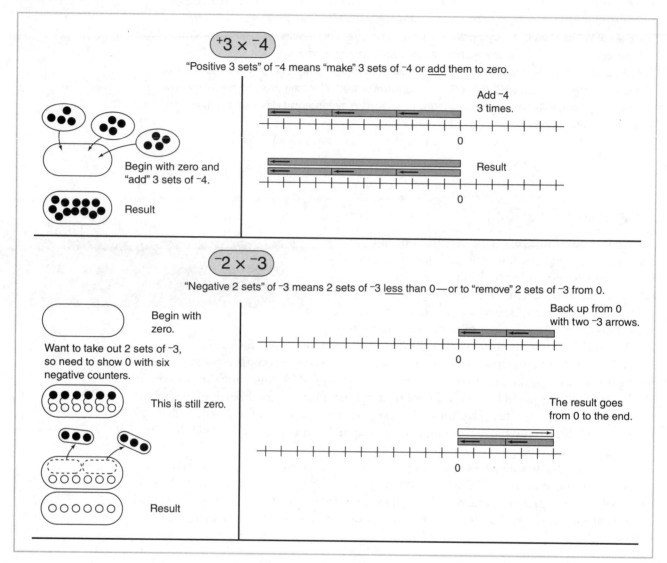

fours make twenty four?" (number of groups unknown). The latter question (? × 4 = 24) is the one that fits well with thinking about negative values because it lends to skip counting to 24. The first example in Figure 10.12 illustrates how the two visual models (two-color counters and number line) work for whole numbers. Following that is an example in which the divisor is positive but the dividend is negative.

Stop and Reflect

Try talking through examples and drawing pictures for ⁻8 ÷ 2. Check your understanding with the examples in Figure 10.12. Now try 9 ÷ ⁻3 and ⁻12 ÷ ⁻4. What contexts can fit these equations? ■

Figure 10.12   Division of integers following a measurement approach.

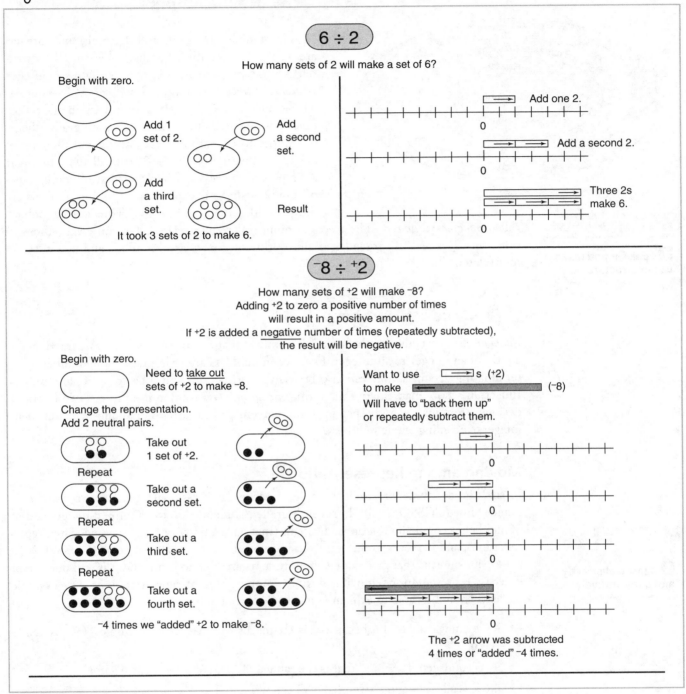

Understanding integer division rests on a good conceptual understanding of multiplication problems in which the first factor is negative (e.g., ⁻3 × 5) and knowledge of the relationship between multiplication and division. Encourage students to think first about how to visualize the whole-number situation and then connect that understanding to negative numbers. Extend these explorations to decimal and fraction values, and continue to have students draw illustrations to accompany their equations.

Figure 10.13 An illustration of the real numbers.

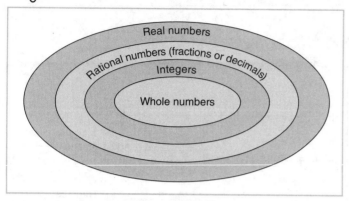

Real Numbers

Whole numbers, fractions and decimals, and integers are all rational numbers because they can all be written as a fraction with an integer over a nonzero integer. *Irrational numbers* are numbers such as $\sqrt{2}$—numbers whose value cannot be written as a fraction and whose exact value can only be estimated. Eighth graders begin to explore irrational numbers and to find their rational approximation (CCSSO, 2010). All these numbers are a part of the *real numbers*, which are the only types of numbers students explore until high school, where they consider the square roots of negative numbers, called *imaginary numbers*. These sets of numbers are interrelated, and some are subsets of other sets. Figure 10.13 provides an illustration of the types of numbers and how they are interrelated.

◆ Rational Numbers

Rational numbers comprise the set of all numbers that can be represented as a fraction—or a ratio of an integer to an integer. Even when numbers are written as whole numbers or as terminating decimals, they can also be written as fractions and thus are rational numbers. In fact, in school mathematics the term *rational numbers* is often used to refer to fractions, decimals (terminating and repeating), and percents. These are rational numbers, but so are integers, including whole numbers.

Moving among Representations

In sixth grade, students should be able to recognize a rational number as a point on a number line (CCSSO, 2010). In seventh grade, "students develop a unified understanding of number, recognizing fractions, decimals (that have a finite or a repeating decimal representation), and percents as different representations of rational numbers" (CCSSO, 2010, p. 46). This means that given any value, students are able to think about it and operate on it across representations, moving flexibly among different representations. For example, students should be able to explain equivalence, as noted here:

- $4\frac{3}{5}$ is equivalent to 4.6 because $\frac{3}{5}$ is six-tenths of a whole, so 4 wholes and six-tenths is 4.6.

- $4\frac{3}{5}$ is equivalent to $\frac{23}{5}$, and that is the same as $23 \div 5$, or 4.6 if I use decimals.

- 4.6 is read "four and six-tenths," so I can write that as $4\frac{6}{10} = 4\frac{3}{5}$.

  Similarly, compare these three expressions:

$$\tfrac{1}{4} \text{ of } 24 \qquad \tfrac{24}{4} \qquad 24 \div 4$$

This discussion can lead to a general development of the idea that a fraction can be thought of as division of the numerator by the denominator, or that $\frac{a}{b}$ is the same as $a \div b$.

When a fraction is converted to a decimal, the decimal either terminates (e.g., 3.415) or repeats (e.g., 2.5141414 . . .). Is there a way to tell in advance whether a given fraction is a terminating decimal or a repeating decimal? The following activity can be used to discover whether that prediction is possible.

Activity 10.12 **REPEATER OR TERMINATOR?**

Have students generate a table listing in one column the first 20 unit fractions ($\frac{1}{2}, \frac{1}{3}, \frac{1}{4}, \cdots, \frac{1}{21}$). The second column is for listing the prime factorization of the denominators, and the third column is for listing the decimal equivalents of the fractions (use calculators to get the precise decimal form).

After they have completed the table, ask students if they can determine a rule that will tell in advance whether the decimal will repeat or terminate. They can test the rule with fractions that have denominators beyond 21. Challenge students to confirm that their rule applies even if the numerator changes.

◀ ◆ **Standards for Mathematical Practice**

8 Look for and express regularity in repeated reasoning

As students work on this task, they will notice various patterns, as can be seen in the student work provided in Figure 10.14. As this student has discovered, the only fractions with terminating decimals have denominators that factor only with combinations of twos and fives. Why is this so?

Middle-school students must understand that any rational number, positive or negative, whole or not whole, can be written as a fraction and as a decimal. So, ⁻8 can be written as the fraction $\frac{-8}{1}$ or $\frac{-16}{2}$ or $\frac{-800}{100}$, or as the decimal ⁻8 or ⁻8.0. In fact, there are infinite ways to write equivalences for ⁻8. Fluency with equivalent representations is critical and requires much more than teaching an algorithm for moving from one representation to another.

◆ Irrational Numbers

Students encounter *irrational numbers* in seventh grade when they learn about π. Additional exploration of irrational numbers occurs in eighth grade (CCSSO, 2010). As noted earlier, *irrational* numbers are not rational, meaning they cannot be written in fraction form. The irrational numbers together with the rational numbers make up the *real numbers*. The real numbers fill in all the holes on the number line, even when the holes are infinitesimally small.

Figure 10.14

A student notes patterns while exploring the "Repeater or Terminator" activity.

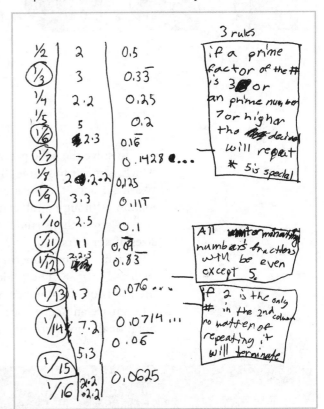

A very old but great middle-school video, "The Weird Number," has recently been posted (www.youtube .com/watch?v=SbjtIRp9C6A). This is a scary (funny) story of a village of whole numbers in the mountains that "hear" there are other numbers beyond the hills. See also a Discovery Education video about rational, irrational, and real numbers at www.youtube.com/watch?v=oORCAz-V_Bg.

◆ **Standards for Mathematical Practice**

1 Make sense of problems and persevere in solving them ◀

Students' first experiences with irrational numbers typically occur when they explore square roots of whole numbers. The following activity provides a good introduction to square roots and cube roots.

Figure 10.15

A geometric interpretation of square roots and cube roots.

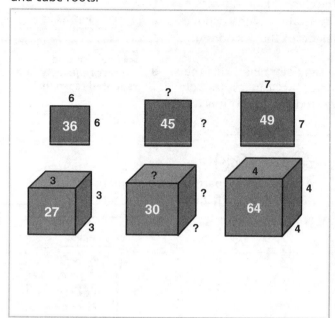

Show students pictures of three squares (or three cubes), as in Figure 10.15. The sides (squares) and edges (cubes) of the first and last figure are consecutive whole numbers. The areas or volumes of all three figures are provided. Ask students to use a calculator to find the length of the sides (squares) or edges (cubes) of the figure in the center. Explain to students that they are not to use the square root or cube root key, but to estimate what they think the length of the side would be and test it by squaring or cubing it. Ask students to continue to estimate until they have found a value to the hundredths place that gets as close to 45 as possible (or 30 in the case of the cube). Solutions will satisfy these equations:

$$\square \times \square = 45, \quad \text{or} \quad \square^2 = 45$$

and

$$\square \times \square \times \square = 30, \quad \text{or} \quad \square^3 = 30$$

To solve the cube problem, students might start with 3.5 and find that 3.5^3 is 42.875, which is much too large. Through trial and error, they will find that the solution is between 3.1 and 3.2. Continued use of strategic trial and error will lead to a close approximation. Although a calculator can find these square or cube roots quickly, the estimation activity strengthens students' understanding of squares and square roots and the relative sizes of numbers.

From this introduction, students can be challenged to find solutions to equations such as $\square^2 = 8$. The students are now prepared to understand the general definition of the *n*th root of a number, *x*, as the number that when raised to the *n*th power equals *x*. The square and cube roots are simply other names for the second and third roots. The notational convention of the radical sign comes last.

In middle school, students encounter irrational numbers primarily when working with the Pythagorean theorem ($a^2 + b^2 = c^2$), which is used to find the distance between two points (the distance being the diagonal, or *c*). If $a = 3$ and $b = 4$, then $c = 5$. All sides are rational numbers. But this result is only in special cases. More often, sides will be something like 4 and 7 units, in which case $c = \sqrt{16 + 49} = \sqrt{69}$. Although there is sometimes a perfect square that can be simplified, in this case there isn't one, and the distance is $\sqrt{69}$, an irrational number.

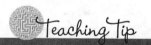

Teaching Tip

Point out that $\sqrt{6}$ is a number, *not* a computation. (This is a significant point of confusion for students because the symbol looks like a division problem.) $\sqrt[3]{8}$ is equivalent to 2. Both are numbers.

An engaging middle-school project applying the Pythagorean theorem and irrational numbers is a Wheel of Theodorus, described in Activity 10.14. Theodorus was one of the early believers in the existence of irrational numbers. (This was quite a contentious issue for the Pythagoreans, who were against the idea of irrationals!)

Activity 10.14   WHEEL OF THEODORUS

Ask students to construct a right triangle that measures 1 cm on each side adjacent to the right angle and then draw the hypotenuse and record its measure. They then use the hypotenuse as side *a* of a new right triangle, drawing side *b* 1 cm long. Connect the end points of side *a* and side *b*. Draw and record the new hypotenuse ($\sqrt{3}$). Create the next triangle, which will have sides of $\sqrt{3}$ and 1 and a hypotenuse of $\sqrt{4}$ or 2, and so on. Doing this about 30 times will form a wheel. (See Bay-Williams & Martinie, 2009, for a complete lesson, or search online for instructions and diagrams of a Wheel of Theodorus.)

Visit "The Evolution of the Real Numbers" at www.themathpage.com/areal/real-numbers.htm. This is an interesting description of many topics related to the real-number system. Although mostly text, the pages are filled with interactive questions.

Expanded Lesson

Find the Zero

Content and Task Decisions

Grade Level: 6–7

Mathematics Goals

- To find sums of integers
- To describe and illustrate integer addition and connect equations to other representations

Grade Level Guide

NCTM *Curriculum Focal Points*	Common *Core State Standards*
As a focal point in seventh grade, students extend their understanding of the operations to "all rational numbers, including negative integers" (NCTM, 2006, p. 19).	In sixth grade, students "recognize opposite signs of numbers as indicating locations on opposite sides of 0 on the number line; recognize that the opposite of the opposite of a number is the number itself, e.g., $-(^-3) = 3$, and that 0 is its own opposite" (CCSSO, 2010, p. 43). In seventh grade, students "describe situations in which opposite quantities combine to make 0" and "show that a number and its opposite have a sum of 0 (are additive inverses)" (CCSSO, 2010, p. 48).

Consider Your Students' Needs

For English Language Learners

- Provide language support for the story writing. This might include sentence frames. For example, "The temperature began as _____ , then _____ by _____ and _____ , and now the temperature is _____ . Providing a one-sentence frame can support students in writing their own sentences.
- Build meaning for the words *opposite* and *inverse*. In Spanish, the word for "inverse" is *inverso,* but as in English, this word is not commonly used and so may be unfamiliar.

For Students with Disabilities

- Use whichever model makes the most sense to the student (two-color counters or a number line). If you are using counters, tape two together with one of each color showing to make a sample of "zero" to help students see the connected counters as a single grouping. If you are using the number line, place it on the floor with painter's tape so that students can walk out the equations, or explore the difference between two numbers by having two students stand on those locations (with another student walking the difference).
- Students with disabilities may benefit from creating a "zero box" below each problem as they solve it, as illustrated below.

  $12 + ^-5 =$

  Zero box: $\boxed{5 + ^-5}$

  $(7 + 5) + ^-5 = 7 + (5 + ^-5) = 7 + 0 = 7$

Materials

- Two-color counters
- Number line (drawn on board or created with a rope)

Lesson

Before

Present the task to the class:

- Ask students to tell you the sums of several opposites (e.g., $4 + ^-4$). Have a volunteer come up to a number line and illustrate the moves (e.g., up four and back four).
- Ask students to create a story that fits the situation. For example, a student might say, "I walked four blocks and then returned four blocks, so I am back where I started" (at zero).
- Repeat with the counters, illustrating what $4 + ^-4$ looks like. A story that fits the counters might be, "I earned four dollars and then spent four dollars, and now I have zero change in my pocket."
- Ask students what they notice about the problems in which opposites are added together. Discuss whether

this will always be true. Then ask, "How can this be helpful in solving problems that are *not* opposites (e.g., 7 + ⁻4)?". Can they "find a zero" by decomposing one of the numbers (e.g., (3 + 4) + ⁻4) to solve it?

Set clear expectations:

- Explain that students will be creating a trifold to illustrate integer addition. Take a piece of paper and fold it in thirds in both directions so that the paper has nine sections. Each column includes a different representation: *expression* (rewritten with opposites), *illustration* (either a number line or counters), and *story*.

- Give students three problems to record in the left-hand column. They are to fill out each column as illustrated here:

Expression: ⁻3 + 8 = Equivalent expression: ⁻3 + (3 + 5)	Illustration:	Story: The temperature was 3° below, then it went up 8° degrees, which means it got back to 0 and then went up 5° more.

Alternatively, or as an extension, do this same activity, but for each example, give students a *different* representation (fill in a different column) and have them find the other two.

During

Initially:

- Observe whether students are clear on what to record in each box on their folded paper.

Ongoing:

- As students are working, observe whether they are struggling. If students are struggling with their own example or story, use the following three prompts: Where did you start? How far did you go? Where are you now? So, for example, a student might write, "I was

3 feet under water, then I dove down 5 feet. Where am I now?" As students are working, ask them to show you the connections between the three representations (columns).

- Ask questions that encourage students to explain how the information in each column is connected.

After

Bring the class together to share and discuss the task:

- Ask a volunteer to share what the first problem looks like with counters and another student volunteer to illustrate what the problem looks like on the number line.

- Discuss the number line visual. Ask students to raise their hands if they chose this model, and invite them to tell the stories they wrote for this illustration.

- Repeat for counters, asking who selected counters as their visual and what stories they used to match the counters.

- Ask how opposites are shown in the two visual models.

- Close by asking students to explain in writing how they can use opposites as a strategy for adding negative and positive numbers.

Assessment

Observe

- Are students using the same story contexts or varying their stories?

- Are students using all number-line illustrations or all counters, or do they have a blend?

- Do the stories align with the models they selected?

- Is the illustration or the story challenging for students?

- Are students recording the equivalent equations in a way that shows one number decomposed such that two of the addends are opposites?

Ask

- How are you deciding to rewrite your expressions?

- What do your pictures have in common?

- Can you solve any integer addition problem by using the "Finding the Zero" strategy? When will it be helpful? When is it not helpful?

11

Proportional Reasoning

BigIDEAS

1 A *ratio* is a multiplicative comparison of two quantities or measures. A key developmental milestone is the ability of a student to begin to think of a ratio as a distinct entity, different from the two measures that make it up.

2 Ratios and proportions involve multiplicative rather than additive comparisons. This means that equal ratios result from multiplication or division, not from addition or subtraction.

3 *Rate* is a way to represent a ratio and in fact represents an infinite number of equivalent ratios.

4 *Proportional thinking* is developed through activities and experiences involving comparing and determining the equivalence of ratios. This means solving proportions in a wide variety of problem-based contexts and situations through reasoning, not the rigid use of formulas.

Proportional reasoning goes well beyond the notion of setting up a proportion to solve a problem—it is a way of reasoning about multiplicative situations. Proportional reasoning, like equivalence, is considered a unifying theme in mathematics. It is estimated that among the population of adults, more than half are not proportional thinkers (Lamon, 2006). This is a direct result of mathematics experiences that exclusively focused on solving missing-value proportions. Such rote practice is particularly troubling in the area of proportional reasoning because proportional reasoning is at the core of so many important concepts, including "similarity, relative growth and size, dilations, scaling, pi, constant rate of change, slope, speed, rates, percent, trigonometric ratios, probability, relative frequency, density, and direct and inverse variations" (Heinz & Sterba-Boatwright, 2008, p. 528). Wow!

 Ratios

A *ratio* is a number that relates two quantities or measures within a given situation in a multiplicative relationship (in contrast to a difference or additive relationship). Reasoning with ratios involves paying attention to two quantities that covary. Ratios and rates are described as one of the four critical areas in grade 6 (CCSSO, 2010). These concepts grow out of students' prior understanding of multiplicative reasoning, in particular multiplicative comparisons.

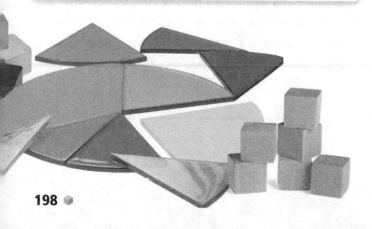

◆ Types of Ratios

Part-to-Part Ratios

A ratio can relate one part of a whole (9 girls) to another part of the same whole (7 boys). This can be represented as $\frac{9}{7}$, meaning "a ratio of nine to seven," not "nine-sevenths" (the fraction). In other words, a part-to-part ratio is not a fraction, although it can be written with the fraction bar; the context is what tells you it is a part-to-part ratio.

Part-to-part ratios occur across the curriculum. In geometry, corresponding parts of similar geometric figures are part-to-part ratios. The ratio of the diagonal of a square to its side is $\sqrt{2}$. In algebra, the slope of a line is a ratio of rise for each unit of horizontal distance (called the run). The probability of an event is a part-to-whole ratio, but the odds of an event occurring are a part-to-part ratio.

Part-to-Whole Ratios

Ratios can express comparisons of a part to a whole—for example, the ratio of the number of girls in a class (9) to the number of students in the class (16). This can be written as the ratio $\frac{9}{16}$ or can be thought of as nine-sixteenths of the class (a fraction). Percentages and probabilities are examples of part–whole ratios.

Ratios as Quotients

Ratios can be thought of as quotients. For example, if you can buy 4 kiwis for $1.00, the ratio of money for kiwis is $1.00 to 4 kiwis. The cost per kiwi ($0.25) is the unit rate.

Ratios as Rates

Miles per gallon, square yards of wall coverage per gallon of paint, passengers per busload, and roses per bouquet are all rates. Rates involve two different units and how they relate to each other. Relationships between two units of measure are also rates—for example, inches per foot, milliliters per liter, and centimeters per inch. A rate represents an infinite set of equivalent ratios (Lobato, Ellis, Charles, & Zbiek, 2010).

Ratios Compared with Fractions

Ratios are closely related to fractions, but ratios and fractions should be thought of as overlapping concepts with important distinctions (Lobato et al., 2010). Because they are both represented symbolically with a fraction bar, it is important to help students see that fractions and ratios are related. Here are three examples to make this point:

1. The ratio of cats to dogs at the pet store is $\frac{3}{5}$.
   This ratio is not a fraction because fractions are not part-to-part ratios.
2. The ratio of cats to pets at the pet store is $\frac{3}{8}$.
   This can be adapted to say that three-eighths of the pets are cats. Since this is a part-to-whole ratio, it is both a ratio and a fraction.
3. Mario walked three-eighths of a mile ($\frac{3}{8}$ mile).
   This is a fraction of a length and is not a ratio because there is not a multiplicative comparison.

Unfortunately, ratios are often addressed in a superficial manner, with students recording the symbols (3:5) to tell the ratio of girls to boys. Instead, ratios should be taught as relations that involve multiplicative reasoning.

Stop and Reflect

The distinctions between ratios and fractions are subtle. How might you help students notice and be able to articulate these distinctions? ■

◆ Two Ways to Think about Ratio

Lobato et al. (2010, p. 22) point out that "forming a ratio is a cognitive task—not a writing task." What they mean is that ratio is a relationship, and that the relationship can be thought of in different ways, regardless of whether its notation is $\frac{2}{5}$ or 2:5 or 2 ÷ 5. It is important to understand two ways to think about ratios: as multiplicative comparisons and as composed units.

Multiplicative Comparison

A ratio represents a multiplicative comparison, and that comparison can go either way. Consider the following relationship: Wand A is 8 inches long, and wand B is 10 inches long.

The ratio of the two wands is 8 to 10. But this statement does not necessarily communicate the *relationship* between the measures. There are two ways to compare the relationship multiplicatively:

The short wand is eight-tenths as long as the long wand (or four-fifths the length).

The long wand is ten-eighths as long as the short wand (or five-fourths or $1\frac{1}{4}$ the length).

This multiplicative relationship is the ratio. It involves asking the question, "How many times greater is one thing than another?" or "What fractional part is one thing of another?" (Lobato et al., 2010, p. 18). The *Common Core State Standards* emphasize the importance of comparisons in elementary school, explicitly describing the importance of using comparison situations across the operations. This trajectory should better prepare students to reason about ratios and rates in middle school.

Composed Unit

The term *composed unit* refers to thinking of the ratio as one unit. For example, if kiwis are 4 for $1.00, you can think of this as a unit and then think about other multiples that would also be true, like 8 for $2.00, 16 for $4.00, and so on. (Each of these would be a unit composed of the original ratio.) This is iterating (also discussed in Chapter 8). There can also be other partitioning of the composed unit: 2 for $0.50 and 1 for $0.25. Any number of kiwis can be priced by using these composed units.

It is important that students be able to apply both types of ratios. Activity 11.1 provides a context for thinking of a composed unit and then a multiplicative comparison.

 Activity 11.1 **BIRTHDAY CUPCAKES**

 Explain to students that they are going to be icing cupcakes and selling them at school. In a recipe for icing, the instructions say that to ice 1 batch of cupcakes with aqua icing, you will need 2 green drops of food coloring and 5 blue drops of food coloring. Ask students to figure out how many drops of food coloring will be needed for 1 batch of cupcakes, 2 batches, 5 batches, and so on (composed-unit thinking). Students may want to record their data in a table.

Next, ask students to figure out how many blue drops for 1 drop of green, and how much green for 1 drop of blue (multiplicative comparison). Ask students to think about how this information helps them in determining the number of drops of each color for the various numbers of batches. Students—particularly students with disabilities—may benefit from visualizing this comparison, which can be done by lining up green and blue tiles or counters (or by using drawings).

Proportional Reasoning

Ratios are extended to understanding and applying proportional reasoning—for example, investigating contexts such as interest, taxes, and tips as well as connecting to work with similar figures, graphing, and slope. Developing an understanding of and applying proportional relationships are a focus in grade 7 (CCSSO, 2010; NCTM, 2006). But reasoning proportionally doesn't begin in middle school; one-to-one correspondence, place value, fraction concepts, and multiplicative reasoning are all elementary topics that are the beginnings of proportional reasoning (Seeley & Schielack, 2007).

Proportional reasoning is difficult to define in a simple sentence or two. It is not something that you either can or cannot do. According to Lamon (1999), proportional thinkers do the following:

- Understand a *ratio as a distinct entity* representing a relationship different from the quantities it compares (See earlier discussion about the composed units.)
- Recognize proportional relationships as distinct from nonproportional relationships in real-world contexts
- Have a sense of *covariation* (They understand relationships in which two quantities vary together and are able to see how the variation in one coincides with the variation in the other.)
- *Develop a wide variety of strategies* for solving proportions or comparing ratios, most of which are based on informal strategies rather than prescribed algorithms

These last three areas are addressed in the sections that follow.

Proportional and Nonproportional Situations

Students should be able to compare situations and discuss whether the comparison is due to an *additive*, *multiplicative*, or *constant* relationship (Van Dooren, De Bock, Vleugels, & Verschaffel, 2010). Importantly, a ratio is a number that expresses a multiplicative relationship (part-to-part or part-to-whole) that can be applied to a second situation in which the relative quantities or measures are the same as in the first situation. For example, in the kiwi problem, the first situation was 4 kiwis for $1.00, and this relative quantity (4 for $1.00 or 1 for $0.25) is true regardless of how many kiwis you buy (the second situation).

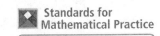
◀ Standards for Mathematical Practice

2 Reason abstractly and quantitatively

---

1. Janet and Jeanette are walking to school, each at the same rate. Jeanette started first. When Jeanette has walked 6 blocks, Janet has walked 2 blocks. How far will Janet have walked when Jeanette is at 12 blocks?
2. Lisa and Linda are planting corn on the same farm. Linda plants 4 rows, and Lisa plants 6 rows. If Linda's corn is ready to pick in 8 weeks, how many weeks will it take for Lisa's corn to be ready?
3. Kendra and Kevin are using the same recipe to bake cookies. Kendra will make 6 dozen cookies, and Kevin will make 3 dozen cookies. If Kevin uses 6 ounces of chocolate chips, how many ounces will Kendra need?

Stop and Reflect

Can you figure out which of the three problems above is an *additive, multiplicative,* or *constant* relationship? What are the differences in the wording of these situations that make each one an *additive, multiplicative,* or *constant* relationship? How can you help students distinguish between these types? ■

The first situation is additive. Janet will still be 4 blocks behind, so 8 blocks. If the problem is incorrectly solved through multiplicative reasoning, however, you will get 4 blocks. The second situation is constant. It will take 8 weeks for the corn to grow, regardless of how many rows are planted. If the problem is solved through multiplicative reasoning, the incorrect answer is 12 weeks. The final situation is multiplicative, and the answer is 12 ounces. How did you do?

The way to get students to distinguish between these types of reasoning is to provide opportunities for them to discuss and compare the distinctions between these problem types. Consider the following sample problem, suggested by Cai and Sun (2002, p. 196) in their discussion of how teachers in Chinese classrooms introduce the concept of ratio:

Mr. Miller's 25 students are asked if they are basketball fans (yes or no). Of these students, 20 say yes and 5 say no. Describe as many relationships as you can about those who are basketball fans and those who are not.

Students might describe several different relationships:

- There are 15 more fans than nonfans.
- There are 4 times as many fans as nonfans.
- For every 4 students who like basketball, there is 1 student who does not.

Of these, the first is an additive relationship—focusing on the difference between the two numbers. The other two are variations of the multiplicative relationship, each expressing the 4-to-1 ratio of fans to nonfans in a slightly different way.

The following problem, adapted from the book *Adding It Up* (National Research Council, 2001), involves a comparison.

Two weeks ago, two flowers were measured at 8 inches and 12 inches. Today they are 11 inches and 15 inches tall. Did the 8-inch or the 12-inch flower grow more?

Additive reasoning would lead to the response that they both grew the same amount— 3 inches. Reasoning multiplicatively leads to a different conclusion: The first flower grew $\frac{3}{8}$ of its height, while the second grew $\frac{3}{12}$ of its height. So the first flower grew more. This is a proportional view of the change situation. Here, both additive reasoning and multiplicative reasoning produce valid, albeit different, answers. As students critique these different approaches, they are better able to understand the difference between additive and multiplicative comparisons.

The following activities provide more opportunities for students to make the distinction between additive reasoning and multiplicative reasoning.

Standards for
Mathematical Practice

**3 Construct
viable arguments
and critique the
reasoning of others**

▶

 Activity 11.2 **WHICH HAS MORE?**

Provide students with situations similar to those in Figure 11.1. Ask students to decide which has more and share a rationale for their thinking. As students share their reasoning, help them see the difference between looking at the difference (additive reasoning) and looking at the ratio (multiplicative reasoning). For English language learners (ELLs), take time to build meaning for what these terms mean—connect *additive* with the word *add,* and *multiplicative* with *multiple* and *multiply.* Reasoning can be modeled through illustrations or explanations. If no one suggests one of the options, introduce it. For example, say, "Amy says it is the second group. Can you explain why she made that choice?" or "Which class team has a larger proportion of girls?"

Activity 11.3 WEIGHT LOSS

Show students the data in the following chart:

Week	Max	Moe	Minnie
0	210	158	113
2	202	154	107
4	200	150	104

Max, Moe, and Minnie are all on a diet and have recorded their weights at the start of their diet and at two-week intervals. After four weeks, which person is the most successful dieter?

Ask students to make three different arguments—each favoring a different dieter. (The argument for Moe is that he is the steadiest in his loss.)

Figure 11.1

Two pictorial situations that can be interpreted with either additive or multiplicative comparisons.

(a) Which team has more girls?

The Stars   The Comets

(b) Which set has more circles?

A   B

Additive and Multiplicative Comparisons in Story Problems

When comparisons are embedded in a story situation, they may be additive *or* multiplicative. Using additive reasoning in a situation that calls for multiplicative reasoning, or vice versa, leads to incorrect answers.

Stop and Reflect

Solve the five-item assessment shown in Figure 11.2, devised to examine students' appropriate use of additive or multiplicative reasoning (Bright, Joyner, & Wallis, 2003). Which ones are multiplicative situations? Additive? What is the difference between items 2 and 4? ■

Notice that the items involving rectangular representations (1, 2, and 5) cannot be answered correctly by using additive reasoning. Students are often challenged to determine which type of reasoning to use. When 132 eighth- and ninth-grade students were asked these questions, scores on items 1 through 4 ranged from 45 percent to 67 percent correct. Item 5 proved very difficult (37 percent correct for most square, 28 percent correct for least square).

Figure 11.2   Five items that can be used to assess proportional reasoning.

For each problem, circle the correct answer.

1. Mrs. Allen took a 3- by 5-inch photo of the Cape Hatteras Lighthouse and made an enlargement on a photocopier. She used the 200 percent option. Which is "more square," the original photo or the enlargement?
   a. The original photo is "more square."
   b. The enlargement is "more square."
   c. The photo and the enlargement are equally square.
   d. There is not enough information to determine which is "more square."

2. The Science Club has four separate rectangular plots for experiments with plants:

   1 foot by 4 feet   7 by 10 feet
   17 by 20 feet   27 by 30 feet

   Which rectangular plot is most square?
   a. 1 foot by 4 feet
   b. 7 by 10 feet
   c. 17 by 20 feet
   d. 27 by 30 feet

3. Sue and Julie were running equally fast around a track. Sue started first. When Sue had run 9 laps, Julie had run 3 laps. When Julie completed 15 laps, how many laps had Sue run?
   a. 45 laps
   b. 24 laps
   c. 21 laps
   d. 6 laps

4. At the midway point of the basketball season, you must recommend the best free-throw shooter for the all-star game. Here are the statistics for four players:

   Novak: 8 of 11 shots   Peterson: 22 of 29 shots
   Williams: 15 of 19 shots   Reynolds: 33 of 41 shots

   Which player is the best free-throw shooter?
   a. Novak
   b. Peterson
   c. Williams
   d. Reynolds

5. Write your answer to this problem:
   A farmer has three fields. One is 185 feet by 245 feet, one is 75 feet by 114 feet, and one is 455 feet by 508 feet. If you were flying over these fields, which one would seem most square? Which one would seem least square? Explain your answers.

Source: Reprinted with permission from Bright, G. W., Joyner, J. J., & Wallis, C. (2003). Assessing Proportional Thinking. *Mathematics Teaching in the Middle School, 9*(3), p. 167. Copyright 2003 by the National Council of Teachers of Mathematics. All rights reserved.

 Formative Assessment Note

All five of these items could be used as *performance assessments,* or a few of them (at least one additive) could be used as a *diagnostic interview.* For example, item 5 was given to an eighth grader, who first solved it incorrectly by using an additive strategy (subtracting the sides). When asked if a very large rectangle, 1,000,000 feet by 1,000,050 feet, would look less square, he replied, "No—*oh,* this is a proportional situation." He then solved it with a novel strategy (Figure 11.3).

Return for a moment to item 3 in Figure 11.2. This item has been used in other studies showing that students try to solve this as a proportion problem, although it is an additive situation. (The two runners will end up six laps apart, which is how they began.) Watson and Shaughnessy (2004) note that the way in which we word problems is a clue that a proportion is involved. Students begin to recognize that the wording is related to proportions and automatically arrange four quantities (three known and one unknown) into a proportion, without paying attention to whether the numbers have a multiplicative relationship. They are focused on the structure of the proportion, not the concept of the proportion (Heinz & Sterba-Boatwright, 2008).

Activity 11.4 can help students move from additive to multiplicative reasoning.

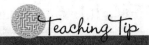

Teaching Tip

Acting out a proportional situation can help students make sense of it. For example, have students act out item 3 after they have attempted it.

Activity 11.4 PENCIL TO PENCIL

Hold up a cutout of a very large pencil (e.g., 30 inches in length). Explain to students that this is the exact size of a pencil used by a giant.

Ask, "If this is her pencil, what else can you tell me about her?" For students (particularly those with disabilities) who need more structure or guidance, ask specific questions: "How tall is the giant? How long would her hand be?" After students have found out things about the giant, have them list their findings on posters and have them illustrate or explain how they found the measures. ELLs are likely to be more familiar with centimeters, so have students choose what measurement system they use, or have all students use centimeters. As an alternative, begin with a tiny pencil (figurine size) and consider the size of the tiny person.

Source: Adapted from Che, S. M. (2009). Giant pencils: Developing proportional reasoning. *Mathematics Teaching in the Middle School, 14*(7), 404–408.

Figure 11.3

Jacob noticed that each length was divisible by 5; therefore, he simplified each ratio to have a side of 5 and then compared the widths.

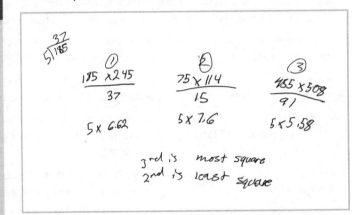

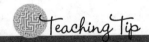

Teaching Tip

There are many great books and poems about very large or very small people, and literature is an excellent way to bring meaning and relevance to mathematics! See Table 11.1.

When students first engage in this activity, they may focus on the (additive) difference of the pencil they are shown and a real pencil they have. If they reason about this difference, then they will find that the giant is only 24 inches taller than they are. Thinking about this should raise some doubt about this line of reasoning because there are real people who are 2 feet taller, and a 30-inch pencil would still be too big for them to manage. They might then start thinking of how many of their pencils would equal the extra large pencil. By counting (iterating), they might notice it takes about 5 lengths of their pencils. In debriefing this activity with students, it is important to discuss the thought processes and why the situation is a multiplicative comparison, not an additive comparison.

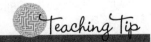

Teaching Tip

Ask students to write examples of additive differences and multiplicative differences. This can help them distinguish between these ideas, which they must be able to do to reason with ratios (which is multiplicative).

Table 11.1 Great Middle-School Books for Ratio and Proportions

Literature with Proportional Situations
Many books include multiplicative comparisons and therefore can be used for proportional reasoning. Here are two that are favorites in middle school.

If You Hopped Like a Frog Schwartz, 1999	David Schwartz compares features of various creatures with those of humans. For example, in the title comparison, Schwartz deduces that if a person had a frog's jumping ability, he or she could jump from home plate to first base in one hop. This short picture book contains 12 more fascinating comparisons. Schwartz also provides the factual data on which the proportions are based. Students can figure out how strong or tall they would be if they were one of the featured animals.
Holes Sachar, 2000	A popular book and movie, this novel tells the story of boys in a "camp" who are digging holes every day, which provides an opportunity to look at daily rates of dirt removal. Pugalee, Arbaugh, Bay-Williams, Farrell, Mathews, and Royster (2008) describe an excellent activity with this book that involves not only proportional reasoning but also measurement and algebra.

Literature with Large and/or Small People
There is a plethora of literature involving very little or very big people (or animals). With any of these books, lengths of arms, legs, or noses can be compared as a way to explore within and between ratios. Several favorites are shared below.

Alice's Adventures in Wonderland Carroll, 1865/1982	In this classic, Alice becomes very small and very tall, opening doors to many ratio and proportion investigations. See Taber (2005) for ideas on using this book to teach proportions.
The Borrowers Norton, 1953	A classic tale of little folk living in the walls of a house. Furnishings are created from odds and ends of the full-size human world.
Gulliver's Travels Swift, 1726; amended 1735/1999	Yet another classic story. In this case, Gulliver first visits Lilliput, where he is 12 times the size of the inhabitants, and then goes to Brobdingnag, where he is one-tenth the size of the inhabitants.
Harry Potter and the Sorcerer's Stone Rowling, 1997	In the book, Hagrid is described as twice as tall and nearly five times as wide as the usual man. Students can measure their own shoulder width and height and create a scatter plot. Placing Hagrid's measurements on the graph illustrates that he is not made in proportion to the usual person. In the movie, he is more proportional to the other characters, although still nearly twice their height. Students can explore the size of his house, furniture, and motorcycle based on an estimated scale of how much bigger he is than the usual person.
Jim and the Beanstalk Briggs, 1970	What happened to the giant after Jack? Jim comes along. Jim wants to help the poor, pessimistic giant. This heartwarming story is great for multiplicative or proportional reasoning.
Kate and the Beanstalk Osborne, 2000	This version of the traditional *Jack and the Beanstalk* tale includes a giantess. The giantess falls to earth, and Kate finds out that the castle belongs to her family.
The Lord of the Rings Tolkien, 1965	Hobbits are described as approximately 3 feet tall (which can be estimated at 100 cm). This height can be used to set up a ratio with the height of the typical sixth grader and the ratio then used to determine the size of various objects. To connect to the movie, ask students to be in the role of producer and figure out the size of objects used in the movie. See Beckman, Thompson, and Austin (2004) for elaboration on this activity.
"One Inch Tall" in *Where the Sidewalk Ends* Silverstein, 1973	Shel Silverstein is a hit with all ages. This poem asks what it would be like if you were one inch tall.
Swamp Angel Isaacs, 1999	A swamp angel named Angelica grows into a giant. Students can compare birth height with current height or compare Angelica's measurements with their own.

Contrasting two very similar problems can also support students' emerging skills at reasoning proportionally (Lim, 2009). Consider these two tasks and how they are the same and how they are different:

1. A red car and a silver car are traveling at the same constant rate. When the red car has traveled 20 miles, the silver car has traveled 12 miles. How far will the red car be when the silver car has traveled 32 miles?
2. A red car and a silver car are traveling at different but constant rates. They pass Exit 95 at the same time. When the red car has traveled 20 miles past Exit 95, the silver car has traveled 16 miles. How far will the red car have traveled when the silver car has traveled 32 miles?

Standards for Mathematical Practice

4 Model with mathematics

Use equations to consider the situation. In the first case, the relationship is red = silver + 8 because the red car is 8 miles in front of the silver car. In the latter case, the relationships is red = $\frac{5}{4}$ silver because for every 5 miles the red car travels, the silver car travels 4 miles (Lim, 2009).

Teaching Tip

Asking students to use variables to write the relationships can help them see the difference between additive and multiplicative situations.

◆ Covariation

Covariation can sound like a high school or college concept, but it simply means that two different quantities vary together. For example, 5 mangos cost $2.00 (two quantities in a multiplicative relationship); as the number of mangos varies (for example, to 10 mangos), so does the cost. And, as the cost changes, so does the number of mangos you will get. Once you know either a new price or a new number of mangos, you can determine the missing variable.

Within Ratios and Between Ratios

A ratio of two measures in the same setting is a *within* ratio. For example, in the case of the mangos, the ratio of mangos to money is a within ratio—that is, it is "within" the context of that example.

A *between* ratio is a ratio of two corresponding measures in different situations. In the case of the

Figure 11.4

Given a proportional situation, the two between ratios will be equivalent, as will the two within ratios.

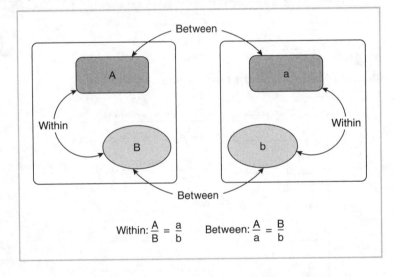

Within: $\frac{A}{B} = \frac{a}{b}$ Between: $\frac{A}{a} = \frac{B}{b}$

mangos, the ratio of the original number of mangos (5) to the number of mangos in a second situation (10) is a between ratio—that is, it is "between" the two situations. The drawing in Figure 11.4 is an effective way of looking at two ratios and determining whether a ratio is between or within.

Standards for Mathematical Practice

5 Use appropriate tools strategically

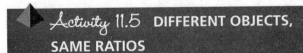

Activity 11.5 **DIFFERENT OBJECTS, SAME RATIOS**

Prepare cards with different numbers of two distinctly different objects, as shown in Figure 11.5. Given the set of cards, students are to select the cards on which the ratio of

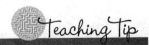

Teaching Tip

Have students create a drawing similar to the one in Figure 11.4. This representation will be very helpful in setting up and understanding proportions, especially for students who struggle with the abstract.

Figure 11.5 Ratio cards for exploring ratios and rates.

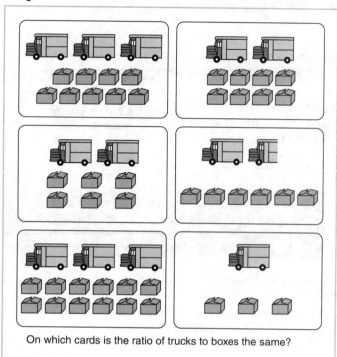

On which cards is the ratio of trucks to boxes the same?

Figure 11.6

Blackline Masters 12 and 13 for use with Activity 11.6.

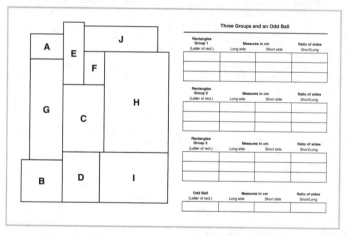

the two types of objects is the same. This task moves students toward a numeric approach rather than a visual one and introduces the notion of ratios as rates. In this context, it makes the most sense to find the boxes per truck as the rate (rather than trucks per box). Finding the rate (amount for one unit) for pairs of quantities facilitates comparisons (just as the unit prices provided in grocery stores allow you to compare different brands).

Covariation in Geometry and Measurement

Within and between ratios are particularly relevant in exploring similarity with geometric shapes (topic in grade 8 in the *Common Core State Standards*). Students often struggle to determine which features to compare. The following activity can help students begin to analyze which features to compare.

Activity 11.6 LOOK-ALIKE RECTANGLES

BLM

Provide students with copies of Blackline Masters 12 and 13 (Figure 11.6) and have them cut out the 10 rectangles. Three of the rectangles (A, I, and D) have sides in the ratio of 3 to 4. Rectangles C, F, and H have sides in the ratio of 5 to 8. Rectangles J, E, and G have sides in the ratio of 1 to 3. Rectangle B is a square, so its sides are in the ratio of 1 to 1.

Ask students to group the rectangles into three sets that "look alike." If your students know the word *similar* from geometry, use that term. To explain what "look alike" means, draw three rectangles on the board with two that are similar and one that is clearly dissimilar, as in the following example. Have students use their language to explain why rectangles 1 and 3 are alike.

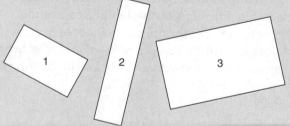

When students have decided on their groupings, stop and discuss the reasons why they classified the rectangles as they did. Be prepared for some students to try to match sides or look for rectangles that have the same amount of difference between the sides. Encourage students to critique the explanations given. Next, have the students measure and record the sides of each rectangle to the nearest half centimeter with Blackline Master 13. Discuss the results and ask students to offer explanations of how the ratios and groupings are related. If the groups are formed of proportional (similar) rectangles, the ratios within each group will be equivalent. Students with disabilities may need to have examples of one rectangle from each grouping as a starting point.

Standards for Mathematical Practice

3 Construct viable arguments and critique the reasoning of others

The connection between proportional reasoning and the geometric concept of similarity is very important. Similar figures provide a visual representation of proportions, and proportional thinking enhances the understanding of similarity. Discussion of the similar figures should focus on the ratios between and within the figures.

technology note

Dynamic geometry software such as *GeoGebra* (a free download from www.geogebra.org/cms) or *The Geometer's Sketchpad* (Key Curriculum Press) offers a very effective method of exploring the idea of ratio. In Figure 11.7, two lengths are drawn on a grid with the software's "snap-to-grid" option. The lengths are measured, and two ratios are computed. As the length of either line is changed, the measures and ratios are updated instantly. A screen similar to Figure 11.7 can be used to discuss ratios of lengths as well as inverse ratios with your full class. In this example, notice that the difference between the first pair and second pair of lines is the same, but the ratios are not the same.

You can also use dynamic geometry software to explore similar figures and corresponding measures. The "Dilate" feature in *The Geometer's Sketchpad* can be used to draw a figure and then dilate it (reduce or enlarge it proportionally) according to any scale factor. The ratios of beginning and ending measures (lengths and areas) can then be compared with the scale factor.

Figure 11.7

Dynamic geometry software can be used to discuss the ratios of two lengths.

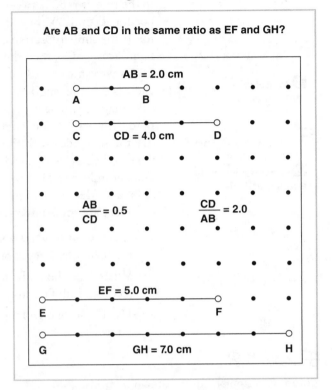

Source: The Geometer's Sketchpad, Key Curriculum Press, 1150 65th Street, Emeryville, CA 94608, 1-800-995-MATH, www.keycurriculum.com. Reprinted by permission.

Creating scale drawings is an application of similarity. Multiplication *is* scaling (e.g., making something three times bigger or one-half the size). Scale drawings, then, are an important way for students to see the connection between multiplicative reasoning and proportional reasoning. Students are asked to resize a sketch that is similar to one they are given. The next activity is about scaling.

Activity 11.7 SCALE DRAWINGS

On grid or dot paper (see Blackline Masters 1–5), have students use straight lines with vertices on the dots to draw a simple shape. After one shape is complete, have them draw a "scaled" drawing—a larger or smaller shape that looks similar to the first. With ELLs, be sure the term *scale* is understood, so that they don't confuse this use of the word with a machine that weighs things or what fish have. This can be done on a grid of the same size or a different size, as shown in Figure 11.8. First, compare ratios within (see the first problem in Figure 11.8). Then compare ratios between the figures (see the second problem in Figure 11.8).

Corresponding sides from one figure to the next should all be in the same ratio. The ratio of two sides within one figure should be the same as the ratio of the corresponding two sides in another figure.

The third problem in Figure 11.8 involves the measure of area as well as length. Comparisons of corresponding lengths, areas, and volumes in proportional figures lead to some interesting patterns. If we know the length of the side of a figure, we can create the ratio of 1 to k, for example, to represent the relationship to a proportional figure. (The variable k is often used with proportions, whereas m is used with equations to describe slope—both refer to the rate or ratio between two values, which is called the *scale factor*.) If two figures are proportional (similar), then any corresponding linear dimensions will have the same scale factor. If the similar figure has sides that are three times the length of the sides of the original figure (scale of 3), then the ratio of the sides of the original to the sides of the new figure is 1:3, or we can write it symbolically as $y = 3x$, where x is the side length of the original figure and y is the side length of the new figure.

Imagine you have a square that is 3 by 3 and you create a new square that is 6 by 6. The ratio between the side lengths is 1:2. What is the ratio between the two areas? Why is it 1:4? Try the same idea with the volume of a cube—what is the relationship of the original volume to the new volume when you double the length of the edges? Why? Returning to the sailboat in Figure 11.8, what would you conjecture is the ratio between the areas of the two sailboats? Measure and test your hypothesis.

Here are some interesting situations to consider for scale drawings:

- If you want to make a scale model of the solar system and use a Ping-Pong ball for the earth, how far away should the sun be? How large a ball do you need to represent the sun?

- What scale should be used to draw a scale map of your city (or some region of interest) so that it will fit onto a standard piece of poster board?

- Use the scale on a map to estimate the distance and travel time between two points of interest.

- Roll a toy car down a ramp, timing the trip with a stopwatch. How fast was the car traveling in miles per hour? If the speed is proportional to the size of the car, how fast would this have been for a real car?

- Your little sister wants a table and chair for her doll. Her doll is 14 inches tall. How tall should you make the table? The chair?

Standards for Mathematical Practice

4 Model with mathematics

Standards for Mathematical Practice

2 Reason abstractly and quantitatively

Figure 11.8

Comparing similar figures drawn on grids.

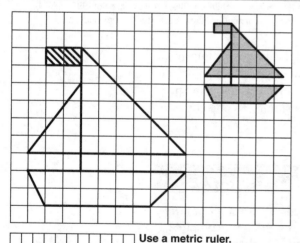

Use a metric ruler.
- Choose two lengths on one boat and form a ratio (use a calculator). Compare to the ratio of the same parts of the other boats.
- Choose two boats. Measure the same part of each boat, and form a ratio. Compare with the ratios of another part.
- Compare the areas of the big sails with the lengths of the bottom sides.

technology note

Google Earth (www.google.com/earth) is a great resource for doing authentic scaling activities (Roberge & Cooper, 2010). If you get a Google Earth diagram that includes something for which the measure is known, students can figure out other measures. For example, you know that a standard football field is 100 yards from end zone to end zone (120 yards if you include the end zones), so zoom in on your school football field. By zooming to different levels, students can build an understanding of scale factor in an interesting context. Or, you can do some interdisciplinary teaching by exploring regions that align with what is being studied in social studies! "Scale City" (www.ket.org/scalecity) is an online mathematics resource for middle-grade students that features fun and engaging videos and interactive simulations to teach the mathematics of scale and scaling with connections to the *Common Core State Standards*.

Covariation in Algebra

Let's extend the "Look-Alike Rectangles" activity (Activity 11.6) to introduce the concept of covariation. Stack like rectangles so that that they are aligned at one corner, as in Figure 11.9. Place a straightedge across the diagonals, and you will see that opposite corners also line up. If the rectangles are placed on a coordinate axis with the common corner at the origin, the slope of the line joining the corners is the ratio of the sides. A great connection to algebra!

Proportional situations are linear situations. Ratios are a special case of linear situations that will always go through the origin because they are multiplicative relationships. The ratio or rate is the slope of the graph. In the *Common Core State Standards*, eighth graders explore and understand the connection between proportional situations and linear situations (CCSSO, 2010).

Figure 11.9

The slope of a line through a stack of proportional rectangles is equal to the ratio of the two sides.

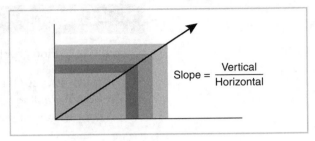

$$\text{Slope} = \frac{\text{Vertical}}{\text{Horizontal}}$$

Standards for Mathematical Practice

◀ **4 Model with mathematics**

◀ **Activity 11.8 RECTANGLE RATIOS—REVISITED GRAPHICALLY**

BLM

Have students graph the data from a collection of equal ratios that they have scaled or discussed (see Blackline Master 1, 3, or 42). For example, the graph in Figure 11.10 is based on the ratios of two sides of similar rectangles. If only a few ratios have actually been plotted, the graph can be drawn carefully and then used to determine other equivalent ratios. In the rectangle example, students can draw rectangles with sides determined by the graphs. Then they can compare them with the original rectangles. A unit ratio can be found by locating the point on the line at $x = 1$ or at $y = 1$. Ask students to find the rate each way. Also see if students can find a rectangle that has a non-integer side length (e.g., $4\frac{1}{2}$ units). Then ask students how, if they know the short side, they can find the long side (and vice versa).

Figure 11.10 Graphs show the ratios of sides in similar rectangles.

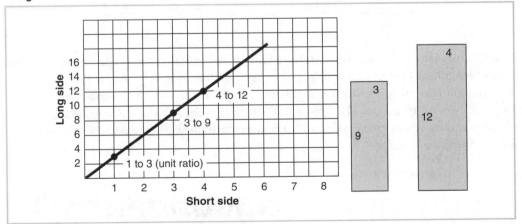

Graphs provide another way of thinking about proportions, and they connect proportional thought to algebraic interpretations. All graphs of equivalent ratios fall along straight lines that pass through the origin. If the equation of one of these lines is written in the form $y = mx$, the slope m is always one of the equivalent ratios.

The following is a relevant context that applies algebraic thinking to develop proportional reasoning.

Activity 11.9 **DRIPPING FAUCET**

Pose the following problem to students:

If you brush your teeth twice a day and leave the water running when you brush, how many gallons of water will you waste in one day? In two days? In a week? A month? Any number of days?

Have students actually gather real data, if possible. Then compute the mean. Ask students to figure out the answers to the questions posed and justify their answers.

Source: Adapted from Williams, M., Forrest, K., & Schnabel, D. (2006). Water wonders (math by the month). *Teaching Children Mathematics, 12*(5), 248–249.

This environmental investigation involves real measurement and authentic data. Stemn (2008) implemented this investigation with students and found that it aided their understanding of the difference between multiplicative and additive situations. Students in her class were challenged to figure out how many of the paper cups that they used for measuring would fill a gallon. The class figured out that 2 paper cups were equal to one-quarter gallon. Each student reasoned how many gallons he or she wasted in a day. For example, a student who wasted 5 paper cups of water reasoned that this would be two-fourths, plus a half of another fourth (or one-eighth). So, in total, five-eighths of a gallon of water is wasted per day. The class recorded what they knew in a table:

Paper cups of water wasted	1	2	3	4	5
Gallons of water wasted	$\frac{1}{8}$	$\frac{1}{4}$	$\frac{3}{8}$	$\frac{2}{4}$	$\frac{5}{8}$

The teacher encouraged students to rewrite the table with common denominators. Students recognized that the ratio of paper cups to gallons was $1:\frac{1}{8}$. Notice the connection to algebraic reasoning and to measurement. The formula $y = \frac{1}{8}x$ describes the number of paper cups (x) to gallons (y). This investigation also showed the students how to reason through measurement conversions with a nonstandard measure (the paper cup), which is a very challenging concept.

technology note

For a good selection of challenging ratio and proportion problems that involve work and everyday life tasks, see NCTM's "Figure This! Math Index: Ratio and Proportions" (www.figurethis.org/challenges/math _index.htm).

Develop a Wide Variety of Strategies

Proportional reasoning includes comparing two ratios as well as identifying equivalent ratios. Posing problems that have multiple solution strategies can help students (Berk, Taber, Gorowara, & Poetzl, 2009; Ercole, Frantz, & Ashline, 2011). Strategies for solving missing value proportions include the following:

- Rate
- Scaling up or down
- Scale factors (within or between measures)
- Ratio tables
- Double-line comparison
- Graphs
- Cross products

It is worth repeating that all of these strategies are useful in particular situations, and all should be understood. The first three are the most intuitive; therefore, they are the ones students might invent, and a good place to begin.

Reasoning Strategies

Unit rate and scale factor can be used to solve many proportional situations mentally. The key is to know both strategies and pick the one that best fits the particular numbers in the problem, as the next examples illustrate.

Tammy bought 3 widgets for $2.40. At the same price, how much would 10 widgets cost?

Tammy bought 4 widgets for $3.75. How much would a dozen widgets cost?

Stop and Reflect

Consider how students might use an approach other than the cross-product algorithm to solve these two problems. If they know the cross product, how might you encourage them to use a mental strategy? ■

In the first situation, it is perhaps easiest to determine the cost of one widget—the *unit rate* or unit price. This can be found by dividing the price of 3 widgets by 3. Multiplying this unit rate of $0.80 per widget by 10 will produce the answer. This approach is referred to as a *unit-rate* method. Notice that the unit rate is a within ratio. This approach applies the ratio as a multiplicative comparison.

In the second problem, a unit-rate approach could be used, but the division does not appear to be easy. Because 12 is a multiple of 4, it is easier to notice that the cost of a dozen is 3 times the cost of 4, or that the scale factor between the ratios is 4. This is called a *buildup strategy*. (This strategy could have been used for the first problem but would have been more difficult because the scale factor between 3 and 10 is $3\frac{1}{3}$.) Notice that the buildup approach

Teaching Tip

Give students problems in which the numbers lend themselves to both the unit-rate approach and the buildup approach (but let them choose their approach). This way, they learn not only that two different approaches are possible, but also that sometimes one approach works better than another.

applies the ratio as a composed unit. Although scale factors (the buildup strategy) are a useful way to think about proportions, they are most frequently used when the numbers are compatible (i.e., the scale factor is a whole number).

At the office superstore, you can buy 4 pencils for $0.59, or you can buy the same pencils in a large box of 5 dozen for $7.79. How much will you save per pencil if you buy the large box?

The price of a box of 2 dozen gumballs is $4.80. Bridget wants to buy 5 gumballs. What will she have to pay?

To solve the pencil problem, you might notice that the between ratio of pencils to pencils is 4 to 60 (5 dozen), or 1 to 15. If you multiply the $0.59 by 15, the factor of change, you will get the price of the box of 60 if the pencils are sold at the same price. In the gumball problem, the within ratio of 24 to $4.80 lends to finding the unit rate of $0.20 per gumball, which can then be multiplied by 5 to find the cost of 5 gumballs.

It is important to follow these tasks with problems that have more difficult numbers, asking students to apply the same strategies to reason to an answer. For example, try to apply both strategies to the next problem.

Brian can run 5 km in 11.4 minutes. If he keeps running at the same speed, how far can he run in 23 minutes?

Figure 11.11

A comparing-ratios problem: In which pitcher will the lemonade have the stronger lemon flavor, or will the flavor be the same in both pitchers?

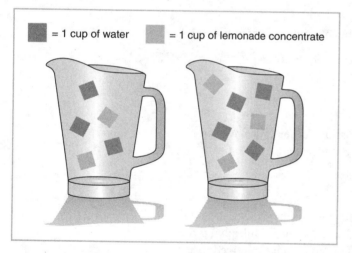

= 1 cup of water   = 1 cup of lemonade concentrate

Selecting problems that can be solved many ways is important. The following activity has been used in various studies and curricula because it can be approached in so many ways.

Activity 11.10 LEMONADE RECIPES

Show students a picture of two pitchers of lemonade, as in Figure 11.11. The little squares indicate the amounts of water and lemonade concentrate used in each pitcher. A light grey square is a cup of lemonade concentrate, and the dark grey is a cup of water. Ask whether the lemonade in one of the pitchers will have a stronger lemon flavor or whether the lemonade in the two pitchers will taste the same. Ask students to justify their answers.

Standards for Mathematical Practice

1 Make sense of problems and persevere in solving them

▶

3 Construct viable arguments and critique the reasoning of others

▶

Stop and Reflect

There are many ways to solve the lemonade problem through reasoning (see if you can think of three). How might you have students share their ways so that other students can understand and critique their approach? How will you help students see connections between the strategies? ◼

The task in "Lemonade Recipes" is interesting because of the number of ways in which the comparison can be made. A common method is to figure out how much water goes with each cup of concentrate. As we will see later, this approach uses a unit rate: cups of water per cup of lemonade concentrate ($1\frac{1}{2}$ vs. $1\frac{1}{3}$). Other approaches use fractions instead of unit rates and attempt to compare the fractions: concentrate compared with water ($\frac{2}{3}$ vs. $\frac{3}{4}$) or the reverse, and also lemonade concentrate as a fraction of the total ($\frac{2}{5}$ vs. $\frac{3}{7}$). This can also be done with water as a fraction of the total. Some students may also use percentages instead of fractions, creating the same arguments. Another way for them to justify their answers is to use multiples of one or both of the pitchers until either the amounts of water or the amounts of lemonade concentrate are equal.

One interesting argument is that the lemonade in the two pitchers will taste the same: If the concentrate and water are matched up in each pitcher, then there will be one extra cup of water in each recipe. Although this argument is incorrect (can you tell why?), your class will likely have a spirited discussion of these ideas.

The lemonade task can be adjusted for difficulty. As given, there are no simple relationships between the two pitchers. If the solutions are 3 to 6 and 4 to 8 (equal flavors), the task is much simpler. For a 2-to-5 recipe versus a 4-to-9 recipe, it is easy to double the first and compare it with the second. When a 3-to-6 recipe is compared with a 2-to-5 recipe, the unit rates are perhaps more obvious (1 to 2 vs. 1 to $2\frac{1}{2}$).

The following problem provides another context for comparing ratios with a variety of approaches.

Two camps of Scouts are having pizza parties. The leader of the Bear Camp ordered enough so that every 3 campers will have 2 pizzas. The leader of the Raccoon Camp ordered enough so that there will be 3 pizzas for every 5 campers. Did the Bear campers or the Raccoon campers have more pizza?

Figure 11.12 shows two different reasoning strategies. When the pizzas are sliced into fractional parts, as in Figure 11.12a, the approach is to look for a unit rate—pizzas per camper. A partitioning approach has been used for each ratio (as in division). But, notice that this problem does not say that the Bear Camp and the Raccoon Camp have only 3 and 5 campers, respectively. Any multiples of 2 to 3 and 3 to 5 can be used to make the appropriate comparison, the same as in making multiple pitchers of lemonade. The iterative approach is illustrated in Figure 11.12b. Three "clones" of the 2-to-3 ratio and two clones of the 3-to-5 ratio are made so that the number of campers getting a like number of pizzas can be compared. From the vantage of fractions, this is like getting common numerators. Because there are more campers in the Raccoon Camp ratio (larger denominator), there is less pizza for each camper. These strategies, and the strategies in the lemonade activity, emerge as students reason multiplicatively about the situations.

Perhaps you have noticed that some of the problems shared in this section include all the values and ask students to compare, whereas others ask for a missing value. Some lend themselves to a unit-rate method, some to a buildup strategy, and some to other strategies. The more experiences students have in comparing and solving situations that are proportional in nature, the better they will be able to reason proportionally.

Figure 11.12
Two reasoning methods for comparing two ratios.

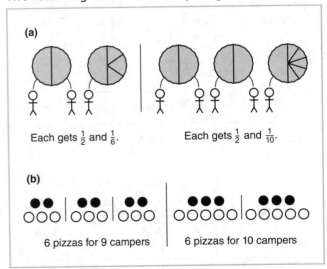

(a)

Each gets $\frac{1}{2}$ and $\frac{1}{6}$.   Each gets $\frac{1}{2}$ and $\frac{1}{10}$.

(b)

6 pizzas for 9 campers   6 pizzas for 10 campers

◆ Ratio Tables

Ratio tables, or charts that show how two variable quantities are related, are good ways to organize information. They serve as tools for applying buildup strategy but can also be used to determine unit rate. Consider the following table:

Acres	5	10	15	20	25
Pine trees	75	150	225		

If the task is to find the number of trees for 65 acres of land, or the number of acres needed for 750 trees, students can proceed by using addition—that is, they can add 5 along the top row until they reach 65. This is a recursive pattern, or repeated-addition strategy. The pattern that connects acres to pine trees (× 15) is the generative pattern and the multiplicative relationship between the values. This is the rate (15 pine trees per acre). The equation for this situation is $y = 15x$, where x is number of acres and y is the number of pine trees. Once this is discovered, students can figure out that 15×65 acres $= 975$ pine trees. But, the nice thing about the ratio table is that neither variables nor equations are needed, so it is less abstract than using proportions.

Ratio tables can be used to find a specific equivalent ratio. Then the ratio table can be used as a strategy for solving a proportion. The following activity provides examples, and Figure 11.13 gives illustrations of this use of a ratio table.

Figure 11.13

Something weighing 160 pounds on Earth weighs 416 pounds on Jupiter. If something weighs 120 pounds on Earth, how many pounds will it weigh on Jupiter? Three solutions obtained with ratio tables.

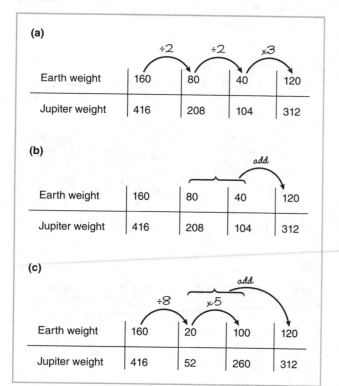

Activity 11.11 USING RATIO TABLES

Build a ratio table and use it to answer missing value questions. Be sure the context is relevant to ELLs and other students in the classroom. If the examples below are not relevant to your students, select something of interest from their culture or experiences.

- Plants come in boxes of 35 plants. How many plants would be in 16 boxes?
- If 5 tire rotations on a bike take you 8 yards, how many tire rotations are needed to take you 50 yards?
- A person who weighs 160 pounds on Earth will weigh 416 pounds on Jupiter. How much will a person weigh on Jupiter who weighs 120 pounds on Earth?
- At the local college, 5 of every 8 seniors live in apartments. How many of the 300 seniors are likely to live in apartments?
- The tax on a purchase of $20 is $1.12. How much tax will there be on a purchase of $45.50?

Source: Based on Dole, S. (2008). Ratio tables to promote proportional reasonings in the primary classroom. *Australian Primary Mathematics Classroom, 13*(2), 18–22, and Lamon, S. J. (1999). *More: In-depth discussion of the reasoning activities in "Teaching fractions and ratios for understanding."* Mahwah, NJ: Lawrence Erlbaum Associates.

You likely recognize these tasks as typical "solve-the-proportion" tasks. One ratio and part of a second are given, with the task being to find the fourth number. Figure 11.13 shows three different ways to use ratio tables to solve the Jupiter weight task. As this example illustrates, the ratio table has several advantages over the missing-value proportion. Students label each row, are more successful at placing the values appropriately, and therefore are able to compare. And working within the ratio table is more directly connected to the concept of seeking an equivalent ratio than to the concept of solving a missing-value proportion. For all these reasons, the ratio table should be introduced before missing-value proportions and then used as a bridge to understanding them.

 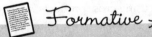 *Formative Assessment Note*

Because there are many ways to reason about proportional situations, it is important to capture *how* students are reasoning. *Writing* is an effective way to do this. Ask students to tell how they solved a problem or to explain how they used the ratio table. You can provide more structure by using specific writing prompts or sentence starters, such as, "In the ratio table, I used the values _____ to . . . ." or by asking students to describe two different ways they can use the ratio table to arrive at the solution.

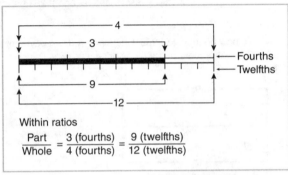

Figure 11.14
Double-line (strip) comparison.

◆ Double-Line (Strip) Comparison

In Figure 11.14, a line segment is partitioned in two different ways: in fourths on one side and in twelfths on the other. In previous examples in this chapter, proportions were established based on two categories of students, two flowers, and two different Scout camps. Here, only one thing is measured—the part of a whole—but it is measured or partitioned two ways: in fourths and in twelfths.

A simple line segment drawing similar to the one in Figure 11.14 can be drawn to set up a proportion to solve any equivalent-fraction problem, even one that does not result in a whole-number numerator or denominator.

Standards for Mathematical Practice

◀ **5** Use appropriate tools strategically

For a nice virtual model that compares a double-line strip, go to "Math Playground" (www.mathplayground .com/thinkingblocks.html) and scroll down to "Ratio Models." This site has instructions and practice that connects the two strips to different types of proportional situations.

◆ Percents

All percent problems can be set up as equivalent fractions. They involve a part and a whole measured in some unit and the same part and whole measured in hundredths—that is, in percents. A simple line segment drawing can be used for each of the three types of percent problems. Let the measures on one side of the line correspond to the numbers or measures in the problem. On the opposite side of the line, indicate the corresponding values in terms of percents. Examples are shown in Figure 11.15.

Notice how flexible this double-line strip is for different types of percent problems. It allows modeling of not only part–whole scenarios but also increase–decrease situations, and those in which there is a comparison between two distinct quantities. Another advantage of the double-line strip is that it does not restrict students from thinking about percents greater than 100 since the line can represent more than 100 percent, which is not true for a circle model (Parker, 2004).

Figure 11.15

Percentage problems can be solved by setting up a proportion with a line segment model.

In 1960, U.S. railroads carried 327 million passengers. Over the next 20 years, there was a 14 percent decrease in passengers. How many passengers rode the railroads in 1980?

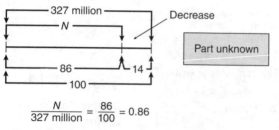

$$\frac{N}{327 \text{ million}} = \frac{86}{100} = 0.86$$

$$N = 0.86 \times 327 \text{ million} \rightarrow \text{about } 281 \text{ million}$$

Sylvia's new boat cost $8950. She made a down payment of $2000. What percent of the sales price was Sylvia's down payment?

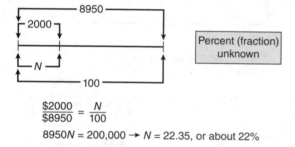

$$\frac{\$2000}{\$8950} = \frac{N}{100}$$

$$8950N = 200,000 \rightarrow N = 22.35, \text{ or about } 22\%$$

The average dressed weight of a beef steer is 62.5 percent of its weight before it has been slaughtered. If a dressed steer weighs 592 pounds, how much did it weigh "on the hoof"?

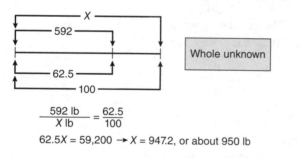

$$\frac{592 \text{ lb}}{X \text{ lb}} = \frac{62.5}{100}$$

$$62.5X = 59,200 \rightarrow X = 947.2, \text{ or about } 950 \text{ lb}$$

◆ Cross Products

Traditional textbooks show students how to set up an equation of two ratios involving an unknown, "cross multiply," and solve for the unknown. "The central challenge of developing students' capacity to think with ratios (to reason proportionally) is to teach ideas and restrain the quick path to computation" (Smith, 2002, p. 15). Even when using cross products, students should be encouraged to reason in order to find the missing value, rather than just to apply the cross-product algorithm.

Sixth- and seventh-grade students rarely use cross multiplication to solve proportion problems, even when that method has been taught (Smith, 2002). A possible reason is that, although the method is relatively efficient, it does not look like the earlier conceptual approaches.

Create a Visual

Rather than telling students to cross multiply, build understanding through visuals. Figure 11.16 shows the double-line strip model connected to the cross product, and Figure 11.17 illustrates how a picture of the context can support setting up a proportion. The two equations (proportions) in the Figure 11.17 come from setting up within and between ratios. Different students will find different strategies more logical, so encourage students to select a strategy that makes sense to them.

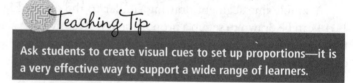

Teaching Tip

Ask students to create visual cues to set up proportions—it is a very effective way to support a wide range of learners.

Figure 11.18 shows a different visual that integrates the double number line. Different students will find different strategies more logical—encourage students to select a strategy that makes sense to them.

Solve the Proportion

Look at the situations in Figures 11.16, 11.17, and 11.18. As students (and adults) often do naturally, you can determine the *unit rate* to solve these problems. For example, you can find the price for 1 pound of apples by dividing the $0.80 by 4 and then multiplying this result by 6 to determine the price of 6 pounds. The equation is ($0.80 ÷ 4) × 6 = $1.20. Or you can examine the *scale factor* from 4 to 6 pounds (within ratio), which is 1.5. Multiply $0.80 by the same scale factor to get $1.20. The equation is (6 ÷ 4) × $0.80 = $1.20. One equation uses $0.80 in multiplication, and the other equation uses $0.80 in division. These are exactly the two devices we employed in the other two approaches: (1) *scale factor* and (2) *unit rate*. If you cross multiply the between ratios, you get exactly the same result. Furthermore, you get the same result as if you had written the two ratios inverted—that is, with the reciprocals of each fraction. Try it!

The cross product is not the only way to solve proportions, but if it is used, it should be understood. This strategy, when understood, is useful when numbers are more challenging and the unit rate or scale factor is not as easy to calculate.

Figure 11.16

The number line is an effective tool for building and understanding proportions and cross products.

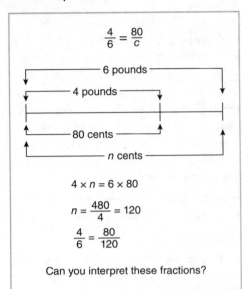

$$\frac{4}{6} = \frac{80}{c}$$

6 pounds

4 pounds

80 cents

n cents

$$4 \times n = 6 \times 80$$

$$n = \frac{480}{4} = 120$$

$$\frac{4}{6} = \frac{80}{120}$$

Can you interpret these fractions?

Figure 11.17

A simple drawing helps establish correct proportion equations.

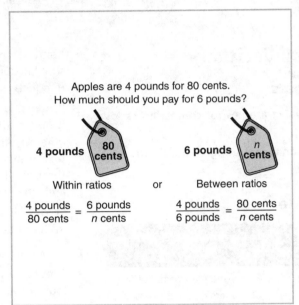

Apples are 4 pounds for 80 cents. How much should you pay for 6 pounds?

4 pounds — 80 cents   6 pounds — n cents

Within ratios   or   Between ratios

$$\frac{4 \text{ pounds}}{80 \text{ cents}} = \frac{6 \text{ pounds}}{n \text{ cents}}$$ $$\frac{4 \text{ pounds}}{6 \text{ pounds}} = \frac{80 \text{ cents}}{n \text{ cents}}$$

Teaching Proportional Reasoning

Considerable research has been conducted to determine how students reason in various proportionality tasks and to determine whether developmental or instructional factors are related to proportional reasoning (e.g., see Bright et al., 2003; Lamon, 1999, 2007; Lobato et al., 2010; Siegler, Carpenter, Fennell, Geary, Lewis, Okamoto, & Wray, 2010). The findings are shared here as a way to summarize the chapter.

1. Use composed-unit and multiplicative-comparison ideas in building understanding of ratio. Learning more about multiplicative comparisons should lead to an understanding of rate, which is a strategy to be applied to proportions.

2. Help students distinguish between proportional and nonproportional comparisons by providing examples of each and discussing the differences.

3. Provide ratio and proportion tasks in a wide range of contexts, including situations involving measurements, prices, geometric and other visual contexts, and rates of all sorts.

4. Engage students in a variety of strategies for solving proportions. In particular, use ratio tables, visuals, and equations to solve problems—always expecting students to apply reasoning strategies.

5. Recognize that symbolic or mechanical methods, such as the cross-product algorithm, for solving proportions do not develop proportional reasoning and should not be introduced until students have had many experiences with intuitive and conceptual methods.

Figure 11.18

Line segments can be used to model both time and distance.

Jack can run an 8-km race in 37 minutes. If he runs at the same rate, how long should it take him to run a 5-km race?

| 8 km | 5 km |
| 37 min. | x min. |

Within ratios

$$\frac{8 \text{ km}}{37 \text{ min.}} = \frac{5 \text{ km}}{x \text{ min.}}$$

Between ratios

$$\frac{8 \text{ km}}{5 \text{ km}} = \frac{37 \text{ min.}}{x \text{ min.}}$$

Expanded Lesson

Comparing Ratios

Content and Task Decisions

Mathematics Goals

- To develop conceptual strategies for comparing ratios in various contexts
- To develop proportional reasoning (multiplicative as opposed to additive)

Grade Level Guide

NCTM Curriculum Focal Points	Common Core State Standards
Ratios appear as part of a focal point in grade 6: "Number and Operations: Connecting ratio and rate to multiplication and division" (NCTM, 2006, p. 18) and are embedded in the algebraic thinking in grade 6 as well. Applying ratio understanding to proportions is a focal point in grade 7: "Number and Operations and Algebra and Geometry: Developing an understanding of and applying proportionality, including similarity" (NCTM, 2006, p. 19).	Ratios and rates comprise one of four critical areas in grade 6: "connecting ratio and rate to whole number multiplication and division and using concepts of ratio and rate to solve problems" (CCSSO, 2010, p. 39). Specifically, sixth graders "expand the scope of problems for which they can use multiplication and division to solve problems, and they connect ratios and fractions. Students solve a wide variety of problems involving ratios and rates" (CCSSO, 2010, p. 39).

Consider Your Students' Needs

Students understand equivalent fractions. They are also familiar with the term *unit fraction* (e.g., $\frac{1}{3}, \frac{1}{4}, \frac{1}{9}$). Students have had experiences with ratios, but some may still not be able to distinguish between additive and multiplicative relationships. Some students may also have used symbolic or mechanical methods for solving proportions, but these methods are not well understood.

For English Language Learners

- For the warm-up, show an illustration of a running track (e.g., the one at your school or one from the Internet).

- Reinforce the terms *ratio* and *rate* throughout the lesson. Encourage all students to use the appropriate language in their small groups and in their presentations.
- When solving tasks 2 through 4, be sure the context is understood through the use of visuals or realia (real objects). Alternatively, problem 3 can be the one context used and three examples given (that mirror tasks 2 through 4). This is a way to engage in the content but limit the linguistic demands.
- Students should be encouraged to discuss the problem in their native language, as well as in English.

For Students with Disabilities

- Support students by explicitly sharing that they should look for a strategy to find how much time it takes for Terry to run one lap. Describe this as a unit rate. Have students find the unit rate for other problems.
- You may want to consider modifying problem 2 to having Jill walk 3 steps every 12 seconds. This will give students who struggle a bit more practice in finding the unit rate with more compatible numbers. Then you can change the original problem with Jill walking 3 steps every 10 seconds.

Materials

Each student will need:

- "It's a Matter of Rates" worksheet (Blackline Master 14)
- Ratio tables (optional)

The teacher will need:

- A copy of "It's a Matter of Rates" (Blackline Master 14) to display

Lesson

Before

Present the focus task to the students:

Note: This is a longer *Before* phase that includes solving one problem before doing the others—it could be that the *Before* takes up a full lesson and the next two phases are the focus of day 2.

- Read the first problem on the "It's a Matter of Rates" worksheet to students. Ask them to guess which runner is faster. Get a show of hands for Terry and then for Susan.

- Next, have students think for a moment about how they determine which runner is actually faster. Students should share their ideas with a partner.

- Listen to student ideas without evaluating them. If a ratio table has not been introduced, share it as one tool you have used for thinking about this type of problem. Ask students to work with a partner on one of the strategies they have been shown.

- Ask students to prepare illustrations and explanations of their solution to Terry's and Susan's rates. Discuss the different approaches, and ask questions that help students see how one solution connects to another solution.

- Focus discussion on generalizing the strategies that worked—for example, that people found something the same about the two (either the laps or the time) so that they could compare.

- Assign the other three problems for students to solve. Notice that problem 2 has a context similar to that of problem 1, but the others are quite different examples of ratio or rate.

During

Ongoing:

- For students who are having difficulty, look at one ratio in a problem and ask what the unit rate is. For example, "How fast can Terry run in 1 minute? How often does Jack take a step up the hill?" In the first three problems, one or both of the ratios can be converted to a unit rate.

- For students who are ready for a challenge, differentiate by changing the numbers so that neither rate is easily simplified to a unit rate.

- Do not give students an algorithm. Instead, encourage them to make sense of the numbers in the given context.

After

Bring the class together to share and discuss the task:

- For each problem, ask students to share their strategies. Do not evaluate students' approaches, but allow the class to discuss and question the different strategies

and make connections between them. Through questioning, help the students compare and contrast the different approaches.

- If students use unit rates in their strategies, help the class relate unit rates to the concept of unit fractions.

- Change the numbers in one or more problems so that the unit rates are not easy to use. For example, suppose that Terry runs 5 laps in 12 minutes and Susan runs 2 laps in 5 minutes. How students respond to this problem will give you insight into choosing problems for the next lesson.

- As an extension, have students create their own problems while using proportional reasoning with two ratios that are not easily compared or easily simplified to unit rates.

Assessment

Observe

- Look for students who are still focusing on additive relationships. These students are not seeing the multiplicative relationship of proportionality.

- Which students are using a unit-rate approach? Which are not? Are students using different forms of the ratios to create two fractions with the same numerators? With the same denominators?

- Watch for students who are using a mechanical method (such as the cross-product algorithm). These methods do not develop proportional reasoning and should not be encouraged (or introduced) until students have had many experiences with intuitive and conceptual methods. If students are using such methods, ask them to explain why it works, or ask if they can find the solution another way.

Ask

- What strategies are you using for comparing ratios?

- How are unit ratios like or different from unit fractions?

- How does a ratio table help with comparing two ratios?

- Can you have a common numerator to compare two ratios?

12

Exploring Algebraic Thinking, Expressions, and Equations

Big IDEAS

1 *Algebra* is a useful tool for generalizing arithmetic and representing patterns in our world. Explaining the regularities and consistencies across many problems gives students the chance to generalize.

2 *Symbols*, especially those involving equality and variables, must be well understood conceptually for students to be successful in mathematics, particularly algebra.

3 The methods we use to compute and the structures in our number system can and should be generalized. For example, the generalization that $a + b = b + a$ tells us that $83 + 27 = 27 + 83$ without the need to compute the sums on each side of the equal sign.

4 *Patterns,* both repeating and growing, can be recognized, extended, and generalized.

5 *Functions* are a special type of relationship that uniquely associates members of one set with members of another set.

6 The understanding of functions is strengthened when they are explored across representations because each one provides a different view of the same relationship.

Algebra is an established content strand in grades K–12. Although the level of sophistication changes across grade levels, one thing is clear: The algebra envisioned for middle school—and for high school as well—is not the algebra that you most likely experienced. That traditional algebra course of the eighth or ninth grade consisted primarily of symbol manipulation procedures and artificial applications with little connection to the real world. The focus now is on the type of thinking and reasoning that prepares students to use algebra to make sense of all areas of mathematics and real-world situations.

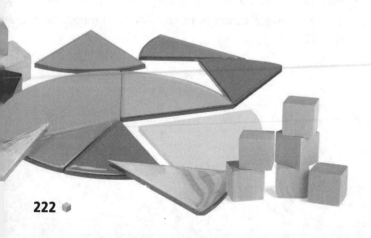

In the *Common Core State Standards* (CCSSO, 2010), the close connections between arithmetic and algebra are noted in every grade from kindergarten through fifth grade, where number and algebra are combined in the discussions of clusters and standards under the domain of Operations and Algebraic Thinking. In middle school (grades 6–8), students begin to study algebra in more abstract and symbolic ways, focusing on understanding and using variables, expressions, and equations. In addition, in eighth grade, students begin to explore functions and use functions to model relationships between quantities.

 # Algebraic Thinking

Algebraic thinking or algebraic reasoning involves forming generalizations from experiences with number and computation, formalizing these ideas with the use of a meaningful symbol system, and exploring the concepts of pattern and functions. Far from being a topic with little real-world use, algebraic thinking pervades all of mathematics and is essential for making mathematics useful in daily life.

Researchers suggest three strands of algebraic reasoning, all infusing the central notions of generalization and symbolization (Kaput, 2008; Blanton, 2008):

1. The study of structures in the number system, including those arising in arithmetic (algebra as generalized arithmetic)

2. The study of patterns, relations, and functions

3. The process of mathematical modeling, including the meaningful use of symbols

Thus, algebraic thinking is composed of different forms of thought and an understanding of symbols. Algebra is a separate strand of the mathematics curriculum but is also embedded in all areas of mathematics. These three big strands are presented in this chapter, with the third strand addressed in two separate sections—the meaningful use of symbols (a priority in sixth grade with the introduction of variables) and mathematical modeling (a priority in eighth grade with the introduction of functions).

 # Structures in the Number System

 ## Generalization through Number

Even the most basic arithmetic situation can be extended to look at generalizations about numbers. Consider the example below, which is an early elementary task (Neagoy, 2012):

Seven birds have landed in your backyard on your favorite bush and in your favorite tree. How many birds might be up high in the tree, and how many might be down low on the bush?

Stop and Reflect

Can you list all the ways in which this can occur? If there were only 5 birds, how many possible ways would there be for them to be in the tree and on the bush? What if there were 10 birds? Is there a rule that can be generalized to determine how many ways in which the 10 birds can be sitting in the tree and on the bush? ■

A significant algebra question is how to decide when all of the solutions have been found. As early as second grade, children can generalize this pattern, but it is also a good opening task in sixth grade to see to what extent students notice patterns and can develop generalized rules by using symbols. In this pattern, there are 8 ways in which to put 7 birds in the tree and on the bush, 6 ways for 5 birds, and 11 ways for 10 birds. Middle-school students should be able to explain why this is the case: For any number of birds (n), there are $n + 1$ ways because there can be 0, 1, 2, . . . n birds sitting on the bush. This is a *generalization* for how to determine the number of solutions without listing them. In the *Common Core State Standards* for sixth grade, students are asked to solve real-world and mathematical problems by writing and solving equations of the form $x + p = q$. Using a problem that is concrete and that begins with listing numeric possibilities is a way to help students learn to generalize and use variables. To extend the discussion, ask students questions such as these: "What if there were 340 birds? Would the rule still hold? How do you know? What if you knew there were 20 different ways in which the birds could be on the bush and in the tree? Could you figure out how many birds were there? Is there a rule for that?"

Generalizations can be described with symbols, something that elementary students can do (as seen in this vignette) and that middle-school students must do. For example, in the problem of the birds on the bush and in the tree, the teacher might ask, "If I have some birds in the tree, let's use a t for the number of birds in the tree. How might you describe how many birds are in the bush?" Students might answer, "Seven minus t." If the students answer "b," then the teacher can ask how t and b are related in an equation. Middle-school students doing a similar problem with 8 mice in blue and green cages, for example, discovered three equations to describe the situation: $b + g = 8$, $8 - g = b$, and $8 - b = g$ (Stephens, 2005).

Standards for Mathematical Practice

8 Look for and express regularity in repeated reasoning

▶ Slight shifts in how arithmetic problems are presented can open up opportunities for generalizations (Blanton, 2008). For example, instead of a series of unrelated computation problems, consider a list that can lead to a discussion of a generalization:

$$\tfrac{1}{2} \times 12 = \qquad \tfrac{1}{4} \times 12 = \qquad \tfrac{1}{8} \times 12 = \qquad \tfrac{3}{4} \times 12 = \qquad \tfrac{3}{8} \times 12 =$$

Once students have solved these problems, you can focus attention on the factors and the products, asking questions like these: "What do you notice? Will this always be true? Why is this true?" In their own words, students will explain the relationship between the numerator and the denominator and what that means in multiplication situations with a fraction and a whole number. Similarly, you can pose tasks that connect to the properties for addition or for multiplication:

$$\tfrac{1}{6} \times 12 = \qquad 12 \times \tfrac{1}{6} = \qquad \tfrac{2}{3} \times 12 = \qquad 12 \times \tfrac{2}{3} =$$

Standards for Mathematical Practice

7 Look for and make use of structure

▶ Although students may already understand the commutative property of multiplication when using whole numbers, they may not recognize that the property can be generalized to fractions. Ask students to prove that this is true and to connect to story situations that illustrate why it is true.

If students are to be successful in algebra, which is more abstract and symbolic, such discussions must be a part of the daily middle-school mathematics experience (Mark, Cuoco, Goldenberg, & Sword, 2010). Algebraic thinking is central to mathematical proficiency. Note that two Standards for Mathematical Practice margin notes have been presented above, but others could have been listed, too (which is true throughout this chapter). The explicit focus on seeking generalizations and looking for structure is also important in supporting the range of learners in the classroom, from those who struggle to those who excel (Schifter, Russell, & Bastable, 2009). Doing so requires planning in advance—deciding what questions you can ask to help students think about generalized characteristics within the problem they are working on across the mathematical strands (not just when they are in an "algebra" unit).

Meaningful Use of Symbols

Perhaps one reason that students are unsuccessful in algebra is that they do not have a strong understanding of the symbols they are using. For many adults, the word *algebra* elicits memories of simplifying long strings of variable-filled equations with the goal of finding *x*. These experiences of manipulating symbols were often devoid of meaning and resulted in such a strong dislike for mathematics that algebra has become a favorite target of cartoonists and Hollywood writers. In reality, symbols represent real events and should be seen as useful tools for solving important problems that aid in decision making (e.g., calculating how many boxes of cookies we need to sell to make *x* dollars, or the rate at which a given number of employees need to work to finish a project on time).

Looking at equivalent expressions that describe a context is an effective way to bring meaning to numbers and symbols. The classic task in Activity 12.1 involves such reasoning.

Figure 12.1

How many different ways can you find to count the border tiles of an 8 × 8 pool without counting them one at a time?

Activity 12.1 BORDER TILES

Ask students to build an 8 × 8 square array representing a swimming pool with colored tiles such that tiles of a different color are used around the border (Figure 12.1). Challenge students to find at least two ways to determine the number of border tiles used without counting them one by one. Students should use their tiles, words, and number sentences to show how they counted the squares. Ask students to illustrate their solution on centimeter grid paper. For English language learners (ELLs), the drawing will be a useful support, but be sure the instructions are clear and that they understand that they are counting the outside tiles and need to find more than one way. There are at least five different methods of counting the border tiles around a square other than counting them one at a time.

A great tool to help students explore the border tiles problem is the site "Plan Your Room" (www.planyourroom.com). Input your dimensions (e.g., 8 feet 0 inches × 8 feet 0 inches) and click "Start with a Room."

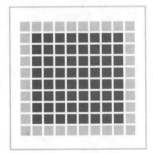

Stop and Reflect

See whether you can find four or five different counting schemes for the border tiles problem. Can you see how the different expressions are equivalent? What questions might you pose to students in order to help them focus on these equivalent expressions? ■

A very common solution to the border tiles problem is to notice that there are 10 squares across the top and also across the bottom, leaving 8 squares on either side. This might be written as follows:

$$10 + 10 + 8 + 8 = 36 \qquad \text{or} \qquad (2 \times 10) + (2 \times 8) = 36$$

Each of the following expressions can likewise be traced to looking at the squares in various groupings:

$$4 \times 9 \qquad 4 \times 8 + 4 \qquad 4 \times 10 - 4 \qquad 100 - 64$$

More equivalent expressions are possible because students may use addition instead of multiplication. In any case, once the generalizations are created, ask students to justify how the elements in the expression map to the physical representation. Ask students to compare

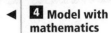

Standards for Mathematical Practice

◄ **4 Model with mathematics**

the different ways and discuss whether they are all correct (and therefore equivalent) expressions for describing the general rule.

Notice that the task just completed involved numeric expressions—a good place to start making meaning for symbols. These expressions did not involve the two types of symbols that are perhaps the most important to understand—and, unfortunately, not well understood by many middle-school students. The equal sign ($=$) and inequality signs ($<, \leq, >, \geq$) are the first type. Variables are the second type. The sections that follow provide strategies for helping students understand these symbols.

Equal Sign and Inequality Signs

The equal sign is one of the most important symbols in elementary arithmetic, in algebra, and in all mathematics using numbers and operations. At the same time, research dating from 1975 to the present indicates clearly that the equal sign ($=$) is a very poorly understood symbol (Kieran, 2007; RAND Mathematics Study Panel, 2003) and rarely represented in U.S. textbooks in a way that encourages students to understand the equivalence relationship—an understanding that is critical to understanding algebra (McNeil, Grandau, Knuth, Alibali, Stephens, Hattikudur, & Krill, 2006). The *Common Core State Standards* explicitly address developing an understanding of the equal sign as early as the first grade. These authors recognized the critical importance of the equal sign in general, and particularly in preparation for the algebraic manipulation that begins in middle school and continues throughout high school and college mathematics.

Stop and Reflect

In the following expression, what number do you think belongs in the box?

$$8 + 4 = \Box + 5$$

How do you think students in middle school typically answer this question? ◼

In a classic study, not one sixth grader among 145 put a 7 in the box (Falkner, Levi, & Carpenter, 1999). Try it with your students!

Where do such misconceptions come from? Most, if not all, equations that students encounter in elementary school look like this: $5 + 7 =$ _____, or $8 \times 45 =$ _____. This unfortunate situation continues in the middle-school curriculum, where problem numbers change but are still written in the same format: $5.6 \times 12.06 =$ _____, or $\frac{3}{4} \times 4\frac{1}{2} =$ _____. Naturally, students come to see $=$ as a symbol signifying "and the answer is" rather than as a symbol indicating the relationship of equivalence (Carpenter, Franke, & Levi, 2003; McNeil & Alibali, 2005; Molina & Ambrose, 2006). Subtle shifts in the way you approach teaching computation can alleviate this major misconception. For example, rather than ask students to *solve* a problem (e.g., $4.5 + 0.61$ or 0.25×26), ask them to *find an equivalent (simplified) expression*, then write the equivalent expressions as an equation (Blanton, 2008). So, for $4.5 + 0.61$, students might write $4.5 + 0.61 = 4 + 0.6 + 0.5 + 0.01$, illustrating what place values they will add.

For a multiplication problem, students might write $0.25 \times 26 = \frac{1}{2}(\frac{1}{2} \times 26)$. If students record their mental math or invented strategies numerically as an equivalence statement such as this one, their understanding of the equal sign will be much stronger, *and* they will be more aware of the relationships among numbers and forms of numbers (e.g., $\frac{1}{2} \times \frac{1}{2} = \frac{1}{4}$, so $0.5 \times 0.5 = 0.25$) and therefore more flexible with their approaches to problems.

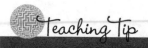

Teaching Tip

Rather than have them solve an expression, just ask students to rewrite it in an equivalent way—this takes the focus *off* answers and puts the focus *on* equivalence.

Why is it so important that students correctly understand the equal sign? First, it is important for them to understand and symbolize relationships in our number system. The equal sign is a principal method of representing these relationships. For example,

$0.6 \times 11 = 0.6 \times 10 + 0.6 \times 1$ shows a mental strategy for computation based on the distributive property. When these ideas, initially and informally developed through arithmetic, are generalized and expressed symbolically, powerful relationships are available for working with numbers in new situations. In this case, for any number n, $n \times a = n \times (a - 1) + n \times a$.

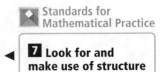

Standards for Mathematical Practice

7 **Look for and make use of structure**

A second reason is that when students fail to understand the equal sign, they typically have difficulty with algebraic expressions (Knuth, Stephens, McNeil, & Alibali, 2006). Consider the equation $5x - 24 = 81$. It requires students to see the expressions on the two sides of the equal sign as equivalent. It is not possible to "do" the left-hand side. However, if both sides are understood as being equivalent, students will see that $5x$ must be 24 more than 81, or $5x = 81 + 24$.

Inequalities are also poorly understood and have not received the attention that the equal sign has received, likely because inequalities are not as prevalent in the curriculum or in real life. Still, understanding and using inequalities is important and will require significant time and experiences to develop. A context such as money can provide a good way to make sense of inequalities, as in the example below.

You have $100 for purchasing gift cards for your 5 friends. You want to spend the same on each, and you will also need to spend $10 to buy a package of card holders for the gift cards. Describe this situation with symbols.

Stop and Reflect

How would you write this inequality? How might students write it? What difficulties do you anticipate? And, importantly, what questions will you pose to help students build meaning for the inequality symbols? ■

Students might record the situation in any of the following ways (using a for the amount of money for the gift):

$$5a + 10 \leq 100 \qquad 10 + 5a \leq 100 \qquad 100 \geq 10 + 5a \qquad 100 \geq 5a + 10$$

Another set of four possibilities are these four inequalities without the equal signs. Discuss with students what it means to say "less than" or "less than or equal to." Allow them to debate which makes more sense given the situation. In particular, bring attention to the ways in which to write the inequality with a less-than sign and with a greater-than sign. The dilemma of which way to place the sign is what makes understanding inequalities even more challenging than understanding equations. Invite students to say exactly what each of these statements means. For example, the first statement directly translates to 5 gift cards and $10 for a package of holders must be less than or equal to $100. The final example directly translates to I have $100, which must be more than or the same as the cost of 5 cards and the holders. Ask questions that help students analyze the situation quantitatively, such as, "Which has to be more, the amount you have or the amount you spend?"

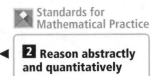

Standards for Mathematical Practice

2 **Reason abstractly and quantitatively**

Conceptualizing the Equal and Inequality Signs with a Balance

Students' understanding of the idea of equivalence can be developed concretely, as in Activity 12.2.

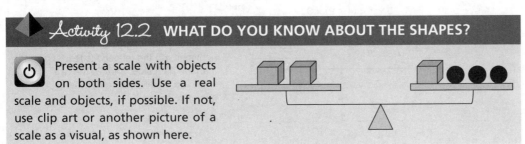

Activity 12.2   WHAT DO YOU KNOW ABOUT THE SHAPES?

Present a scale with objects on both sides. Use a real scale and objects, if possible. If not, use clip art or another picture of a scale as a visual, as shown here.

Ask students what they know about the shapes. "The cubes weigh the same. The spheres weigh the same. What do you know about how the weights of the cubes and the spheres compare?" For more explorations like this, see "Pan Balance—Shapes" on the NCTM Illuminations website at http://illuminations.nctm.org/ActivityDetail.aspx?id=33.

After students have experiences with these shapes, they can then explore numbers and focus on equal and not-equal situations. Figure 12.2 offers examples that connect the balance to the related equation. This model of the two-pan balance also illustrates that the expressions on each side represent a number.

Activity 12.3 TILT OR BALANCE

Draw or project a simple two-pan balance. In each pan, write a numeric expression and ask whether one pan will go down or whether the two pans will balance (see Figure 12.2a). Challenge students to write number sentences. Note that when the scale "tilts," either a "greater-than" or "less-than" symbol ($>$ or $<$) is used, and if it is balanced, an equal sign ($=$) is used. Include examples (like the third and fourth balances in the figure) for which students can make the determination by analyzing the relationships on the two sides rather than by doing the computation. For students with disabilities, instead of having them write expressions for each side of the scale, share a small collection of cards with expressions and have them identify the ones that will make the scale balance.

As an alternative or extension, use missing-value expressions. Ask students to find a number that will result in one side tilting downward, a number that will result in the other side tilting downward, and one that will result in the two sides being balanced (see Figure 12.2b).

Figure 12.2

Using expressions and variables in equations and inequalities. The two-pan balance helps develop the meaning of $=$, $<$, and $>$.

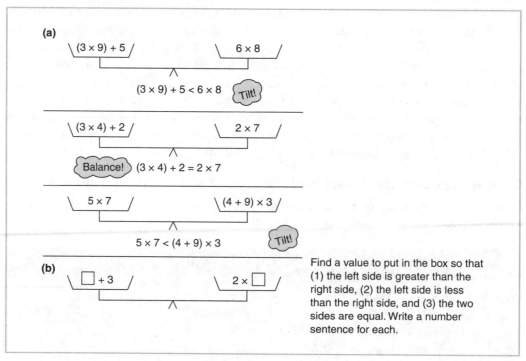

(a)

$(3 \times 9) + 5$ 6×8

$(3 \times 9) + 5 < 6 \times 8$ Tilt!

$(3 \times 4) + 2$ 2×7

Balance! $(3 \times 4) + 2 = 2 \times 7$

5×7 $(4 + 9) \times 3$

$5 \times 7 < (4 + 9) \times 3$ Tilt!

(b)

$\square + 3$ $2 \times \square$

Find a value to put in the box so that (1) the left side is greater than the right side, (2) the left side is less than the right side, and (3) the two sides are equal. Write a number sentence for each.

The balance is a concrete tool that can help students understand that if you add or subtract a value from one side, you must add or subtract a like value from the other side to keep the equations balanced. Another NCTM Illuminations applet, "Pan Balance—Expressions" (http://illuminations.nctm.org/ActivityDetail.aspx?id=10), provides a virtual balance where students can enter what they believe to be equivalent expressions (with numbers or symbols), each in a separate pan, to see whether the expressions do in fact balance.

Figure 12.3 shows solutions for two equations, one in a balance and the other without. Even after you have stopped using the balance, it is a good idea to refer to the two-pan balance concept of equality and the idea of keeping the sides balanced. This use of concrete (an actual balance) or semi-concrete (drawings of a balance) representations helps students develop a strong understanding of the abstract concept of equality.

The notion of preserving balance also applies to inequalities—but what is preserved is imbalance. In other words, if one side is 5 more than the other side, then subtracting 5 from both sides results in the same side being 5 more.

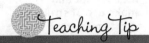
Teaching Tip

Use real scales to show that adding or subtracting the same object (quantity) from both sides preserves the inequality.

True/False and Open Sentences

Carpenter and colleagues (2003) suggest that a good starting point for helping students with the equal sign is to explore equations as either true or false. Clarifying the meaning of the equal sign is just one of the outcomes of this type of exploration, as seen in the following activity.

 Activity 12.4 **TRUE OR FALSE**

Introduce true/false sentences or equations with simple examples to explain what is meant by a true equation and a false equation. Then put several simple equations on the board, some true and some false. Keep the computations simple so that the focus is on equivalence. Ask students to decide which of the equations are true and which are not. For each response, the students must explain their reasoning. The following are appropriate for middle grades:

$$120 = 60 \times 2 \qquad 1 = \frac{3}{4} + \frac{2}{1} \qquad 318 = 318$$

$$\frac{1}{2} = \frac{1}{4} + \frac{1}{4} \qquad 345 + 71 = 70 + 344$$

$$1210 - 35 = 1310 - 45 \qquad 0.4 \times 15 = 0.2 \times 30$$

Listen to the types of reasons that students use to justify their answers, and plan additional equations accordingly. ELLs and students with disabilities will benefit from first explaining (or showing) their thinking to a partner (a low-risk speaking opportunity) and then sharing with the whole group. For false statements, ask students to rewrite the statement with > or < to make the statement true. "Pan Balance—Numbers" on the NCTM Illuminations website (http://illuminations.nctm.org/ActivityDetail.aspx?id=26) can be used to model and/or verify equivalence.

Figure 12.3

Using a balance scale to think about solving equations.

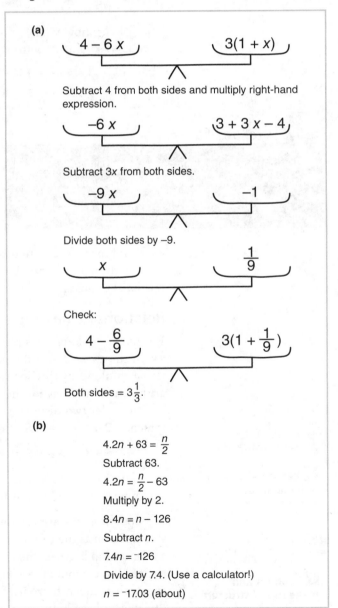

(a)

$4 - 6x$ | $3(1 + x)$

Subtract 4 from both sides and multiply right-hand expression.

$-6x$ | $3 + 3x - 4$

Subtract 3x from both sides.

$-9x$ | -1

Divide both sides by −9.

x | $\frac{1}{9}$

Check:

$4 - \frac{6}{9}$ | $3\left(1 + \frac{1}{9}\right)$

Both sides = $3\frac{1}{3}$.

(b)

$$4.2n + 63 = \frac{n}{2}$$

Subtract 63.

$$4.2n = \frac{n}{2} - 63$$

Multiply by 2.

$$8.4n = n - 126$$

Subtract n.

$$7.4n = {}^-126$$

Divide by 7.4. (Use a calculator!)

$$n = {}^-17.03 \text{ (about)}$$

An equation with no operation ($318 = 318$) can raise questions for students who have not seen the equal sign without an operation on one side. Reinforce that the equal sign means "is the same as" by using that language when you read the symbol. In other words, expressions can be related in one of three ways: an expression is less than, the same as, or greater than another expression.

After students have experienced true/false sentences, introduce an open sentence—one with a box to be filled in or a letter to be replaced. To develop an understanding of open sentences, encourage students to look at a number sentence holistically and discuss in words what the equation represents.

◆ **Standards for Mathematical Practice**

▸ **7 Look for and make use of structure**

◆ Activity 12.5 OPEN SENTENCES

Pose several open sentences. Here is a sampling for operations with decimals:

$$0.5 + \square = 5 \qquad 0.4 + \square = 0.6 \qquad 4.5 + 5.5 = \square - 1$$

$$0.3 \times 7 = 7 \times \square \qquad \square \times 4 = 4.8 \qquad \square = 2.3 - 0.5 \qquad 2.4 \div \square = 4.8 \div 6$$

Discuss how students solved the problems. After using open boxes, begin to mix in variables so that students can see the variable as representing a missing value:

$$3.6 - n = 3.7 - 4 \qquad n + 0.5 = 0.5 + 4.8 \qquad 1.5 + 2.7 = n + 2.8$$

$$6 \times n = 3 \times 8 \qquad 15 \times 27 = n \times 27 + 5 \times 27 \qquad 1 = 0.5 \div n$$

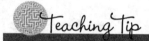
Teaching Tip

Notice that each open sentence is simultaneously addressing important number relationships and number sense, so they are excellent choices for warm-up problems or learning centers.

Open sentences are an excellent opportunity to explore inequalities. Consider replacing the equal sign in any of the equations in Activity 12.5 with a $>$ or $<$. What is now possible for the missing value or the variable? Not just one answer, but many (in fact, infinitely many). Since students are more used to equations, they are likely to find the value that makes it equal and then struggle to decide how to adjust the answer to create the inequality. They may begin with trial and error, but students eventually should be able to use reasoning, also called relational thinking.

Relational Thinking

Relational thinking takes place when a student observes and uses numeric relationships between the two sides of the equal sign rather than actually computing the amounts. Relational thinking of this sort is a first step toward generalizing the relationships found in arithmetic to the relationships used when variables are involved.

Consider two distinctly different explanations for placing a 3 in the box for this open sentence: $2.4 \div \square = 4.8 \div 6$.

◆ **Standards for Mathematical Practice**

▸ **2 Reason abstractly and quantitatively**

"Since $4.8 \div 6$ is 0.8, then $2.4 \div$ something is also 0.8, so that must be 3."

"I noticed that 2.4 is half of 4.8, so I need to divide by a number half the size of 6 in order to maintain equivalence, so the answer is 3."

◆ **Standards for Mathematical Practice**

▸ **7 Look for and make use of structure**

Both students are reasoning abstractly. The first student computes the result on one side and adjusts the result on the other to make the sentence true. The second student uses a relationship between the expressions on the two sides of the equal sign. This student does not need to compute the values on each side. When the numbers are large, the relationship approach is much more useful. Having students share their thinking promotes relational thinking and can help other students improve in analyzing relationships in a problem.

Formative Assessment Note

As students work on these types of tasks, you can conduct a *diagnostic interview* (although you may not get to everyone, so you may want to start with students you think are having difficulty). Listen for whether they are using relational thinking. If they are not, ask, "Can you find the answer without actually doing any computation?" This questioning nudges students toward relational thinking and helps you decide what instructional steps are next.

In order to nurture relational thinking and the meaning of the equal and inequality signs, continue to explore an increasingly complex series of true/false and open sentences with your class. Select numbers and operations that lend to relational thinking, like the examples above. Use numbers that make actual computation difficult (not impossible) as a means to encourage relational thinking. Here are some examples:

True/False

$$6.74 - 3.89 = 6.64 - 3.79 \qquad 42 = 0.5 \times 84$$
$$\tfrac{2}{5} = \tfrac{1}{2} + \tfrac{1}{3} \qquad 64 \div 14 = 32 \div 28$$

Open Sentences

$$7.03 + 0.056 = 7.01 + \square \qquad 0.126 - 0.37 > \square - 0.4$$
$$20 \times 4.8 = n \times 2.4 \qquad \tfrac{2}{5} + \tfrac{1}{5} < \tfrac{3}{10} + \tfrac{1}{10} + n$$

Stop and Reflect

Two of the true/false statements are false. Can you use relational thinking to explain why? Non-examples help students learn about properties of numbers. How can you use these false statements to help students address misconceptions or to deepen their understanding of number relationships? ■

Standards for
Mathematical Practice

7 **Look for and make use of structure**

Asking students to explain why something is false or asking if it can be changed to make it true (i.e., by changing to an inequality or by adapting the numbers) can help students focus on the important details within an equation that they may not have noticed initially. Molina and Ambrose (2006) found that asking students to write their own open sentences was particularly effective in helping them solidify their understanding of the equal sign.

Activity 12.6 **WRITING TRUE/FALSE SENTENCES**

After students have had ample time to discuss true/false and open sentences, ask them to make up their own true/false sentences that they can use to challenge their classmates. Each student should write a collection of three or four sentences with at least one true and at least one false sentence. Encourage them to include one "tricky" one. Their equations can either be traded with a partner or used in full-class discussions.

> Repeat for open-sentence problems. For students needing additional structure, in particular students with disabilities, consider providing frames such as these:
>
> _____ + _____ = _____ + _____   _____ + _____ > _____ + _____
>
> _____ − _____ = _____ − _____   _____ − _____ < _____ − _____
>
> _____ + _____ = _____ − _____   _____ + _____ < _____ − _____

When students write their own true/false sentences, they often are intrigued with the idea of using large numbers or lots of numbers in their sentences. This encourages them to create sentences involving relational thinking.

The Meaning of Variables

Expressions or equations with variables are a means for expressing patterns and generalizations. In the *Common Core State Standards*, variables are first introduced, and are part of a critical area, in sixth grade: "Students understand the use of variables in mathematical expressions" (CCSSO, 2010, p. 39). The series of standards in this domain address the importance of understanding the multiple uses of variables in mathematics.

Variables can be used as unique unknown values or as quantities that vary. Unfortunately, students often think of the former (the variable as a placeholder for one exact number), and not the latter (that a variable can represent multiple, even infinite, values).

Variables are difficult for students to understand. Students also struggle with the meaning of variables in expressions such as $3a + 2b$, where they commonly think of the variables as labels such as 3 apples and 2 bananas (Gray, Loud, & Sokolowski, 2005). Experiences in elementary and middle school should focus on building meaning for variables, as well as addressing common misconceptions, as delineated in the next two sections.

Teaching Tip

Write variables as lowercase letters in italics. This will help distinguish the multiplication symbol × from the variable *x*.

Variables Used as Unknown Values

In open-sentence explorations, the □ is the precursor of a variable used as an unknown or missing value, and it is used throughout elementary school. In grades 4 and 5, students are to begin using variables to represent missing values, so students should have some initial experiences with variables.

One-Variable Situations. Initial work with finding the value of the variable that makes the sentence true should rely on relational thinking (reasoning). Starting in sixth grade, students will begin developing specific techniques for solving equations when relational thinking or reasoning is insufficient.

Context can also help students develop meaning for variables. Many story problems involve a situation in which the variable is a specific unknown, as in the following basic example:

Gary ate 14 strawberries, and Jeremy ate some, too. The container of 25 strawberries was gone! How many did Jeremy eat?

Although students can solve this problem mentally without using algebra, they can begin to learn about variables by expressing it in symbols: $14 + n = 25$, where the n represents the number of strawberries that Jeremy ate. These problems can grow in difficulty over time.

Activity 12.7 TELEPHONE: TRANSFORMING WORDS TO EQUATIONS/INEQUALITIES

 This activity is based on the classic game of "telephone," in which a statement is whispered to a person and passed from that person to another. The goal is for the phrase to stay the same all the way around the group (see Bay & Ragan, 2000, for details). Place students in small groups. Prepare simple situations (one for each group) like the one in the example above with a missing value. Label each one with a number (story 1). In round 1, students write an equation that communicates exactly what the story states. They label their equation (e.g., story 1). At your direction, they pass that equation to the next group (keeping the original story), which will re-create a story that exactly matches the equation (preserving the missing value). The group labels the story as story 1 (or whatever number they received). The group passes the story to the next group (keeping the equation the group had received for story 1). This continues until the stories make it back to the original groups. Each group has all the notes it received (all labeled by story number). Give all the story 1 cards to group 1, story 2 cards to group 2, and so on. Each group is to see if its story made it around correctly, and if not, where it got mixed up (and why). Each group shares what happened with its story as it passed through the groups. The process is the same whether the stories involve equations or inequalities. If you have ELLs or students with disabilities, rather than have students write stories about any context, have them write stories about a given situation (like shopping for particular items at the store with a particular budget).

This activity helps students go both ways with variables and words, deepening the connection between the two. In addition, it helps students find errors and misconceptions. Finally, it helps students to recognize equivalent expressions versus not-equivalent expressions because groups may have written an equation that is correct but written it slightly differently.

Two-or-More-Variables Situations. Systems of equations (or inequalities) are examples of two or more variables serving as placeholders for missing values or unknowns. With a context, students can explore and solve such situations by using relational understanding, as in Activity 12.8.

Activity 12.8 BALLS, BALLS, BALLS

In this activity, students will figure out the weight of three balls, given the following three facts:

1.　◖◗　+　🏈　= 1.25 pounds

2.　◖◗　+　⚽　= 1.35 pounds

3.　⚽　+　🏈　= 1.9 pounds

Ask students to look at each fact and make observations that help them generate other facts. For example, they might notice that the soccer ball weighs 0.1 pound more than the football. Write this in the same fashion as the other statements. Continue until these discoveries lead to finding the weight of each ball. Encourage students to use tools or pictures to represent and explore the problem.

One possible approach: Add equations 1 and 2.

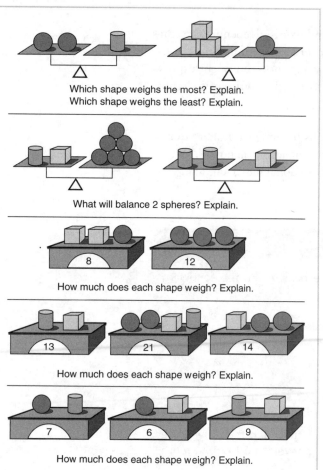

Then take away the football and soccer ball, reducing the weight by 1.9 pounds (based on the information in equation 3), and you have two baseballs that together weigh 0.7 pound. Divide by 2, so one baseball is 0.35 pound.

Source: Adapted from Maida, P. (2004). Using algebra without realizing it. *Mathematics Teaching in the Middle School, 9*(9), 484–488.

This activity is an appropriate sixth- or seventh-grade task to be solved by reasoning, or a great introduction for eighth graders as they begin work with systems of equations.

Another concrete way to work on systems of equations is through balancing. Notice that the work done in building the concept of the equal sign is now applied to understanding and solving for two or more variables. In Figure 12.4, a series of examples shows problems in which each shape on the scales represents a different value. Two or more scales representing a single problem provide different information about the shapes or variables.

When no numbers are involved, as in the top two examples of Figure 12.4, students can find combinations of numbers for the shapes that make all of the examples balance. If an arbitrary value is given to one of the shapes, then values for the other shapes can be found accordingly. In the second example, if the sphere equals 2, then the cylinder must be 4 and the cube equals 8. If a different value is given to the sphere, the other shapes will change accordingly.

Figure 12.4

Examples of problems with multiple variables and multiple scales.

Which shape weighs the most? Explain.
Which shape weighs the least? Explain.

What will balance 2 spheres? Explain.

How much does each shape weigh? Explain.

How much does each shape weigh? Explain.

How much does each shape weigh? Explain.

Stop and Reflect

How would you solve the last problem in Figure 12.4? Can you solve it in two ways? How can you help students bridge the connection from these informal investigations with variables to a more formal understanding of systems of equations? ■

Ask algebra students what the purpose is of solving a system of equations, and at best they might examples they are solving for *x* and for *y*. Students should be able to explain what *x* and *y* tell you (as it connects to a situation and in general) and why this might be important. Eighth graders must "understand that solutions to a system of two linear equations in two variables correspond to points of intersection of their graphs, because points of intersection satisfy both equations simultaneously" (CCSSO, 2010, p. 55).

Simplifying Expressions and Solving Equations

Simplifying equations and solving for x have often been meaningless tasks, and students are unsure of why they need to know what x is or what steps to do and in what order. This must be taught in a more meaningful way! Knowing how to simplify and recognizing equivalent expressions are essential skills for working algebraically. Students are often confused about what the instruction "simplify" means. (Imagine an ELL wondering why the teacher is asking students to change the original problem to an easier one.) The border tiles problem in Activity 12.1 provides a good context for thinking about simplifying and equivalence. Recall that there are at least 5 possibilities for finding the number of border tiles. If the pool had dimensions other than 8×8, those equations would be structurally the same, but with different values. If the square had a side of length p, the total number of tiles could be found in similar ways:

10 + 10 + 8 + 8	$(2 \times 10) + (2 \times 8)$	4×9	$100 - 64$
$(p + 2) + (p + 2) + p + p$	$2 \times (p + 2) + (2 \times p)$	$4 \times (p + 1)$	$(p + 2)^2 \; p^2$

Invite students to enter these expressions into the TABLE function on their graphing calculator and graph them to see whether they are equivalent (Brown & Mehilos, 2010). Looking at these options, the connection can be made for which one is stated the most simply (briefest or easiest to understand).

Students need an understanding of how to apply mathematical properties and how to preserve equivalence as they simplify. (This is one of the *Common Core State Standards* in grade 7.) In addition to the ideas that have been offered (open sentences, true/false sentences, etc.), one way to do this is to have students look at simplifications that have errors and explain how to fix the errors (Hawes, 2007). Figure 12.5 shows how three students have corrected the simplification of $(2x + 1) - (x + 6)$.

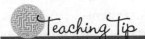

Teaching Tip

Create your own examples of simplified expressions that have an error in them—select an error that is commonly made in your classroom so that the class can discuss why the expression is not correct.

Activity 12.9 provides an engaging way for students to explore properties and equivalent expressions.

Activity 12.9   NUMBER TRICKS

Begin by having students do the following sequence of operations:

Write down any number.
Add to it the number that comes after it.
Add 9.
Divide by 2.
Subtract the number you began with.

Now you can "magically" read their minds. Everyone ended up with 5! Ask students, "How does this

Figure 12.5

Three students provide different explanations for fixing the flawed simplification given.

Explain how to fix this simplification. Give reasons.
$(2x + 1) - (x + 6) = 2x + 1 - x + 6$

Gabrielle's solution

If $x = 3$ then the order of operations would take place, so the problem would look like $(2 \cdot 3 + 1) - (3 + 6) = 2 \cdot 3 + 1 - 3 + 6$ you would have to do $1 - 3$ instead of $1 + 6$. But its actually $3 + 6$. So that's the mistake.

Prabdheep's solution

The problem will look like this in its correct form $(2x + 1) - (x + 6) = 2x + {}^-1x + {}^-6$ because there is a minus sign right outside of the () on the left side it means its -1. So if you times -1 by x its $-1x$ not $1-x$. When you times -1 by 6 its 6 not 6.

Briannon's solution

Explain how to fix this problem. Give Reasons
$(2x + 1) - (x + 6) = 2x + 1 - x + 6$
you are subtracting x and 6 not subtracting x and adding 6
Correctly simplified the problem is
$(2x + 1) + (-(x + 6))$ - distribute negative
$2x + 1 + {}^-x + {}^-6$
$\boxed{x + {}^-5}$

Figure 12.6

Cubes can illustrate the steps in "Number Tricks."

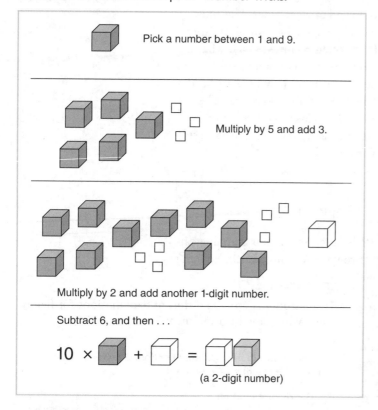

Pick a number between 1 and 9.

Multiply by 5 and add 3.

Multiply by 2 and add another 1-digit number.

Subtract 6, and then . . .

$10 \times$ ▢ $+$ ▢ $=$ ▢▢

(a 2-digit number)

trick work? Start with n. Add the next number: $n + (n + 1) = 2n + 1$. Adding 9 gives $2n + 10$. Dividing by 2 leaves $n + 5$. Now, subtract the number you began with, leaving 5. As a follow-up or for enrichment, students can generate their own number tricks. For students with disabilities or students who struggle with variables, suggest that instead of using an actual number they use an object, such as a cube, and physically build the steps of the problem, as illustrated in Figure 12.6.

Solving systems of equations has also been presented in a way that includes a series of procedures with little attention to meaning (e.g., by graphing, by substitution, and simultaneously). Mathematically proficient students should have access to multiple approaches, including these three. However, rather than learn one way by rote each day or be tested on whether they can use each approach, they should encounter a system and be guided by the question when you ask, "How can we determine the point of intersection of this system?"

Graphing calculators make the choice of using a graph to determine the point of intersection an efficient option, whereas graphing by hand used to be one of the most tedious methods. And among the strategies that students must try is observation. Too often, students leap into solving a system algebraically without stopping to observe the values in the two equations. Look at the systems of equations here, and see which ones might be solved for x or y without using algebra.

Teaching Tip

Just as they did with the operations, students should *choose* a method for solving a system of equations that fits the situation, using appropriate tools.

Standards for Mathematical Practice

5 Use appropriate tools strategically ▶

$$x + y = 25 \text{ and } x + 2y = 25 \qquad 3x + y = 20 \text{ and } x + 2y = 10$$

$$8x + 6y = 82 \text{ and } 4x + 3y = 41 \qquad \tfrac{y}{3} = 5 \text{ and } y + 5x = 60$$

Variables Used as Quantities That Vary

Variables that vary are most commonly used to describe functions (e.g., $y = 3x - 5$). This shift from the variable as an unknown in equations/inequalities to a variable that represents a functional relationship is a critical distinction that must be made; it is also one of the things that is a particular struggle for students in algebra (Kieran, 2007). The difficulty can be alleviated if students have experiences with variables that vary throughout middle school—certainly in sixth grade as they focus on the meaning and use of variables and as they explore patterns. The opening problem about the bush and the tree is an excellent way to introduce variables that vary in two ways: first, in representing the way birds can be on the bush and in the tree as $t + b = 7$, and second, as the general case of number of birds (b) to number of ways they can be in the tree (w) ($w = b + 1$).

Teaching Tip

When working with variables that can represent more than one number, ask students, "What are possible values for the variable?" and "What values are *not* possible for the variable?" Highlight the fact that when a variable is used in an equation, it always represents the same value.

Help students recognize that when there is more than one variable in a single equation, each variable can represent many, even infinitely many, numbers (or at times the same number). And, at the same time, each variable may represent numerous but limited values. In the example just given, there are only eight things that t can be. In the second equation, b can be infinitely many numbers, but they must be whole numbers. This discussion builds important ideas of range and domain of functions in a concrete manner.

Build on students' understanding of rational numbers, and contrast variables-as-unknowns equations with variables-that-vary equations. Compare the two problems below.

$$\tfrac{1}{4} + n = 1 \qquad m + n = 1$$

Ask students to find one answer for n for each problem. Then ask if they think they can find a different answer. In the first case, they may be able to find equivalent forms for n, but n is still the same number (e.g., 0.75, $\tfrac{3}{4}$, $\tfrac{6}{8}$). But, in the second example, there are literally infinitely many values that n can be. Students can be challenged to create at least 10 expressions with decimals, integers, and fractions—enhancing their understanding of rational numbers while expanding their understanding of what a variable can mean in an expression.

Another difficulty with variables that vary is determining how to represent situations to show the relationship between the two variables correctly.

Stop and Reflect

We know there are 3 feet in a yard. Using f for number of feet and y for number of yards, which of these equations correctly expresses the relationship: $3f = y$ or $f = 3y$? Make your choice before reading on. ■

Teaching Tip

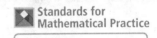

Rather than saying, "Use x for feet and y for yards," say the precise statement, "Use x for the number of feet and y for the number of yards." This helps students to remember that the variable is the "number of" units.

Many students will (incorrectly) pick $3f = y$ because there are 3 feet in a yard. But, try putting some numbers in $3f = y$. For example, if f is 5, then y will be 15, but 5 feet is not equal to 15 yards. Recall that students confuse variables with labels, a particular challenge when using a measurement context. One instructional strategy is to choose variables of x and y to remove the confusion with measurement errors. Another strategy is to analyze the situation by testing for specific examples (as was done here by trying 5 feet).

Standards for
Mathematical Practice

◀ **6** **Attend to precision**

Slightly altering number tasks can help students figure out how to relate two variables. Instead of "Marta has \$6 and Nathan has \$3 more than Marta; how much more money does Nathan have?" use "If Marta has some money in her bank and Nathan has \$3 more than Marta, how much more money does Nathan have?" (Blanton, 2008, p. 18). Symbolically, this is Marta + 3 = Nathan, or $m + 3 = n$. Picture this on the number line. It can start anywhere (m), jump 3 to the right, and land on anything (n):

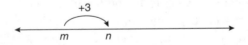

Comparing number lines with numbers and those with variables can help students understand expressions with variables (Darley, 2009) (Figure 12.7). When students are looking at the number line, ask questions like these: "What is the value of x? Can it be any number? If we don't know what x is, how can we place $\tfrac{1}{3}x$ on the number line? Think of a value that x cannot be." Notice that in the two examples, x really can be any positive value. However, if you place $x + 2$ on the number line somewhere close to x, the space between these is 2, and you can use this distance as a "measure" to approximate the size of x. Because students

Figure 12.7

Number lines for arithmetic and algebra.

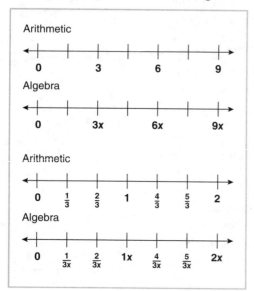

use the number line extensively with whole numbers, it is a good way to bridge to algebra. An open number line posted in your room, where you can post values, and then trade out for new values, can provide many opportunities to think about the relative value of variables.

The following example is appropriate for middle-school students as a context for exploring variables that vary:

If you have $10 to spend on $2 granola bars and $1 fruit bars, how many ways can you spend all your money without receiving change?

To begin exploring this problem, students record data in a table and look for patterns. They notice that when the number of granola bars changes by 1, the number of fruit bars changes by 2. Symbolically, this representation is $2g + f = \$10$, where g is the number of granola bars and f is the number of fruit bars.

Include decimal and fraction values in the exploration of variables. As any algebra teacher will confirm, students struggle most with these numbers—likely a result of limited concrete and visual experiences in mixing fractions and decimals. The following example includes a context to support student reasoning.

You bought $1.75 pencils and $1.25 erasers from the school store, and you spent exactly $35.00. What might you have purchased? What equation represents this situation?

For students with disabilities or students who might be unfamiliar with using a table, it is helpful to adapt the table to include both how many and how much, as shown in Figure 12.8 (Hyde, George, Mynard, Hull, Watson, & Watson, 2006). Reinforce the two elements with each entry (how many? how much?). In addition, calculators can facilitate the exploration of possible solutions. To increase the challenge for advanced or gifted students, ask students to graph the values or to consider more complex situations (see Blackline Master 42).

Once students have the expression in symbols (in this case, $1.75x + 1.25y = 35.00$), ask them to tie each number and variable back to the context. In this way, students can make sense of what is often poorly understood and develop a strong foundation for algebraic situations with no context.

 ## Making Structure in the Number System Explicit

Before middle school, students apply properties of addition and multiplication as they learn basic facts and invented and standard algorithms for the four operations. For example, understanding the commutative property for both addition and multiplication reduces substantially the number of facts to be memorized. In middle school, students examine these properties explicitly and express them in general terms without reference to specific numbers. For example, a student solving $394 + 176 = n + 394$ may say that n must be 176 because $394 + 176$ is the same as $176 + 394$. This is a specific instance of the commutative property. To articulate this (and other structural properties of our number system) in a general way, either in words or in symbols (e.g., $a + b = b + a$), noting that it is true for all numbers, is what making structure explicit means. When made explicit and understood, these structures not only add to students' tools for computation but also enrich their understanding of the number system, providing a base for even higher levels of abstraction (Carpenter et al., 2003).

◆ Making Sense of Properties

Properties of the number system can be built into students' explorations with true/false and open-number sentences. For example, elementary students will generally agree that the true/false sentence $41 \times 3 = 3 \times 41$ is true. The pivotal question for middle school is, "Is this true for any two numbers?" Some students will argue that although it seems to be true all of the time, there may be two numbers that haven't been tried yet for which it does not work.

The following problem and discussion are focused on investigating the distributive and associative properties, not on whether the equation is true or false:

Ms. J: [*Pointing at* $(2 \times 8) + (2 \times 8) = 16 + 16$ *on the board*] Is it true or false?

LeJuan: True, because two 8s is 16 and two 8s is 16.

Lizett: $(2 \times 8) + (2 \times 8)$ is 32 and $16 + 16$ is 32.

Carlos: 8 plus 8 is 16, so 2 times 8 is 16, and 8 plus 8 is 16, and 2 times 8 is 16.

Ms. J: [*Writing* $4 \times 8 = (2 \times 8) + (2 \times 8)$ *on the board*] True or false?

Students: True.

Ms. J: What does the 2 stand for?

Reggie: Two boxes of eight.

Ms. J: So, how many boxes are there?

Students: Four.

Ms. J: [*Writing* $32 + 16 = (4 \times 8) + (a \times 8)$ *on the board*] What is a?

Michael: Two, because 4 times 8 is 32, and 2 times 8 is 16.

Ms. J: [*Writing* $(4 \times 8) + (2 \times 8) = (b \times 8)$ *on the board*] What is b?

Students: Six.

Source: Baek, J. M. (2008). Developing algebraic thinking through exploration in multiplication. In Greenes, C. E., & Rubenstein, R. (Eds.), *Algebra and algebraic thinking in school mathematics: 70th NCTM yearbook* (pp. 151–152). Reston, VA: NCTM.

Notice how the teacher is developing the aspects of these properties in a conceptual manner—focusing on exemplars to guide students to generalize, rather than asking students to memorize the properties as they appear in Table 12.1 as their first experience, which can be a meaningless, rote activity.

The structure of numbers can sometimes be illustrated geometrically. For example, 43×8 can be illustrated as a rectangular array. That rectangle can be partitioned into two rectangles [e.g., $(40 \times 8) + (3 \times 8)$], preserving the quantity:

Figure 12.8

A table adapted to include how many and how much for each row.

	Total $35.00		
$1.75 item		**$1.25 item**	
	$35.00		$0
20		0	
	$0		$35
0		28	

Source: Hyde, A., George, K., Mynard, S., Hull, C., Watson, S., & Watson, P. (2006). Creating Multiple Representations in Algebra: All Chocolate, No Change, *Mathematics Teaching in the Middle School, 11*(6), 262–268. Reprinted with permission. Copyright © 2006 by the National Council of Teachers of Mathematics. All rights reserved.

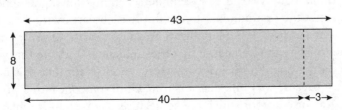

Table 12.1 Properties of the Number System

Name of Property	Symbolic Representation	How Children Might Describe the Pattern or Structure
Addition		
Commutative	$a + b = b + a$	"When you add two numbers in any order, you'll get the same answer."
Associative	$(a + b) + c = a + (b + c)$	"When you add three numbers, you can add the first two and then add the third or add the last two numbers and then add the first number. Either way, you will get the same answer."
Additive Identity	$a + 0 = 0 + a = a$	"When you add zero to any number, you get the same number you started with."
	$a - 0 = a$	"When you subtract zero from any number, you get the number you started with."
Additive Inverse	$a + (^-a) = 0$	"When you subtract a number from itself, you get zero."
Inverse Relationship of Addition and Subtraction	If $a + b = c$ then $c - b = a$ and $c - a = b$	"When you have a subtraction problem you can 'think addition' by using the inverse."
Multiplication		
Commutative	$a \times b = b \times a$	"When you multiply two numbers in any order, you will get the same answer."
Associative	$(a \times b) \times c = a \times (b \times c)$	"When you multiply three numbers, you can multiply the first two and then multiply the answer by the third or multiply the last two numbers and then multiply that answer by the first number. Either way, you will get the same answer."
Multiplicative Identity	$a \times 1 = 1 \times a = a$	"When you multiply one by any number, you get the same number you started with."
Multiplicative Inverse	$a \times \frac{1}{a} = \frac{1}{a} \times a = 1$	"When you multiply a number by its reciprocal, you will get one."
Inverse Relationship of Multiplication and Division	If $a \times b = c$ then $c \div b = a$ and $c \div a = b$	"When you have a division problem, you can 'think multiplication' by using the inverse."
Distributive (Multiplication over Addition)	$a \times (b + c) = a \times b + a \times c$	"When you multiply two numbers, you can split one number into two parts (5 can be 2 + 3), multiply each part by the other number, and then add them together."

Standards for Mathematical Practice

2 Reason abstractly and quantitatively ▶

Challenge students to think about this idea *in general*. This may be described in words (at first) and then as symbols: $a \times b = (c \times b) + (d \times b)$, where $c + d = a$. Be sure students can connect the examples to general ideas and the general ideas back to examples. This is the distributive property, and it is perhaps the most important central idea in arithmetic (Goldenberg, Mark, & Cuoco, 2010).

Making Conjectures Based on Properties of Addition and Multiplication

Most of the properties are ones students have experienced in their work with number. A great way to make these properties explicit is to pursue students' ideas on what they notice always to be true. A good way to start is to ask students to try to state in words an idea of something they think is always true. For example, when multiplying a number by a second number, you can split the first number and multiply each part by the second number, and you will get the same answer. If a generalization is not clear or entirely correct, have students discuss the wording until all agree that they understand. Write this verbal statement of the property on the board. Call it a conjecture, and explain that it is not necessarily a true statement just because we think that it is true. Until someone either proves it or finds a counterexample—an instance for which the conjecture is not true—it remains a conjecture.

Standards for Mathematical Practice

3 Construct viable arguments and critique the reasoning of others ▶

Activity 12.10 CONJECTURE CREATION

Because this is a creative and challenging activity, begin with a problem like the one described previously, or post the following on the board: $2 \times 5 + 5 = 3 \times 5$. Ask students, "Could I trade 5 for another number and still have a true statement? What other numbers will work?" Allow time for students to explore, and then have them share their ideas. They will share that it works for any number (even fractions, decimals, and negative numbers). Propose to students that they are suggesting a conjecture that $2 \times n + n = 3 \times n$. Encourage conjectures in words as well as symbols. The full class should discuss the various conjectures, asking for clarity or challenging conjectures with counterexamples. Conjectures can be added to a class list written in words and in symbols. All students, but particularly ELLs, may struggle with correct and precise terms. You can "revoice" their ideas with appropriate phrases to help them learn to communicate mathematically, but be careful to not make this the focus—the focus should be on the ideas presented. Importantly, students with disabilities are helped by the presentation and discussion of counterexamples. They cement their thinking by focusing on the critical elements.

Table 12.1 lists basic properties of the number system for which students may make conjectures.

Attempting to justify or prove that a conjecture is true is a significant form of algebraic reasoning and is at the heart of what it means to do mathematics (Ball & Bass, 2003; Carpenter et al., 2003; Schifter, 1999; Schifter, Monk, Russell, & Bastable, 2007). Researchers and recent standards (NCTM *Curriculum Focal Points* and *Common Core State Standards*) argue that making conjectures and justifying that they are always true are central to reasoning and sense making. Therefore, when conjectures are made in class, rather than respond by telling students whether that conjecture is true or false, ask, "Do you think that is always true? How can we find out?" Students need to reason through ideas based on their own thinking and not simply rely on the word of others.

The most common form of justification is the use of examples. Students will try lots of specific numbers in a conjecture. "It works for any number you try." They may try very large numbers as substitutes for "any" number, and they may try fractions or decimal values. It is hoped that proof by example will lead to someone asking, "How do we know there aren't some numbers that it doesn't work for?"

Second, students may reason with physical materials or illustrations to show the reasoning behind the conjecture (like the rectangular arrays demonstrating the distributive property). What moves this beyond "proof by example" is an explanation such as, "It would work this way no matter what the numbers are." Activity 12.11 explores properties of odd and even numbers with the calculator and can lead into a proof with physical materials or variables.

Activity 12.11 BROKEN CALCULATOR: CAN YOU FIX IT?

Explore these two challenges; afterward, ask students for conjectures they might make about odds and evens.

1. If you cannot use any of the even keys (0, 2, 4, 6, 8), can you create an even number in the calculator display? If so, how?
2. If you cannot use any of the odd keys (1, 3, 5, 7, 9), can you create an odd number in the calculator display? If so, how?

Patterns and Functions

Patterns are found in all areas of mathematics. Learning to look for patterns and how to describe, translate, and extend them is part of thinking algebraically. Two of the eight Standards for Mathematical Practice begin with the phrase "look for," implying that students who are mathematically proficient pay attention to patterns as they do mathematics. In middle school, the study of patterns and functions is addressed as follows in the *Common Core State Standards*:

- Represent and analyze quantitative relationships between dependent and independent variables (grade 6)

- Solve real-life and mathematical problems using numerical and algebraic expressions and equations (grade 7)

- Understand the connections between proportional relationships, lines, and linear equations (grade 8)

- Define, evaluate, and compare functions (grade 8)

- Use functions to model relationships between quantities (grade 8)

This list is an indication of the importance of focusing on patterns and functions within the algebra curriculum.

Looking for and Analyzing Patterns

Students are surrounded by patterns in the world around them. Keep a look out for patterns that can be analyzed and used to make predictions. Encourage students to do the same. This can be as simple as asking students to look for numeric patterns and, when they spot one, bring it back to class to share. Or, they can be assigned to look for patterns in the newspaper or activities in which they participate. One context is the Olympics. The Summer Olympics will be held in 2016, 2020, and every four years after that. The Winter Olympics will be held in 2014, 2018, and so on. Ask students to create a way to determine if *x* year will be an Olympic year (in general), a Summer Olympic year, and/or a Winter Olympic year (Bay-Williams & Martinie, 2004).

Hurricanes also are named in a repeating manner and can be analyzed and generalized. For each letter of the alphabet, there are six names that are used cyclically (except that a name is retired when a major hurricane, like Katrina, occurs) (Fernandez & Schoen, 2008). The six names beginning with *A*, for example, will be used as follows: Andrea in 2013, Arthur in 2014, Ana in 2015, Alex in 2016, Arlene in 2017, and Alberto in 2018. (Did you notice the pattern regarding gender?) Assuming the names are not retired, students can answer questions such as these:

- In what year in the 2020s will the first hurricane of the year be named Alex?

- What will be the name of the first hurricane in the year 2020? In 2050?

- Can you describe in words or symbols how to figure out the name of a hurricane, given the year?

Functions

Functions are situations that covary. Yet functions and function notation are very abstract and difficult for students. Experiences with function situations must begin with meaning-making experiences. Geometric growing patterns provide a concrete and engaging way to introduce functions. Second, contexts build meaning for functions and for the relevance of algebra in general. Third, thinking of functions in an input–output manner helps students develop the meaning of what a function is. Let's revisit the border tiles problem (see Figure 12.1), which both provides a context and illustrates a geometric growing pattern. Once students have explored and solved this pattern numerically, they can explore pools (squares) of other dimensions (3×3, 4×4, 10×10, etc.). Ask students to use their counting strategy for these different-size pools to see if they can come up with a general rule for finding the number of tiles needed to create a border for a square pool of any length.

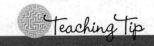

Teaching Tip

Two important questions help students analyze specific examples in order to determine the general relationship: What is changing? What is staying the same? What is changing is what becomes the variable.

Analyzing numerous examples can lead to a generalized statement. For example, see how these examples help generalize a relationship:

$$(2 \times 6) + (2 \times 4)$$

$$(2 \times 7) + (2 \times 5)$$

$$(2 \times 10) + (2 \times 8)$$

$t = 2 \times (s + 2) + 2s$, where s is the length of the side and t is the total number of tiles

This growing pattern is a function; the number of tiles required is a function of the length of the sides. Students can struggle with recognizing the difference between equations and functions (Kieran, 2007). An equation with one variable is a situation in which the goal is to determine what the variable is (variable as an unknown). A function is a situation with two variables, in which the goal is to represent the relationship between the two variables.

To build on the border tiles problem, students can explore other perimeter-related growing patterns, such as a triangle made of dots with 3, 4, or 5 dots on each side. Students should reason that this is the same type of pattern, except that it has three sides, and be able to use their previous generalization (Steele, 2005).

Geometric Growing Patterns

The problems just described are geometric growing patterns. They provide a good introduction to functions because students can extend the pattern, examine the examples, and then look for a generalization for the nth term. Figure 12.9a is a growing pattern in which design 1 requires three triangles, design 2 requires six triangles, and so on. The questions in Activity 12.12, mapped to the pattern in Figure 12.9a, are good ones to help students begin to think about the functional relationship.

Activity 12.12 **PREDICT HOW MANY**

Have students work in pairs or small groups to explore a pattern and respond to these questions:

- Complete a table that shows the number of triangles for each step.

Step Number (Term)	1	2	3	4	5...	10	20
Number of Triangles (Element)							

If the list of fractions above continues in the same pattern, which term will be equal to 0.95?

- How many triangles are needed for step 10? How many for step 20? How many for step 100? Explain your reasoning.
- Write a rule (in words and/or symbols) that gives the total number of pieces to build any step number (*n*).

Keep in mind that ELLs need clarification on the specialized meanings of *step* and *table* because these words mean something else outside mathematics.

Figure 12.9

Demonstrating geometric growing patterns with manipulatives.

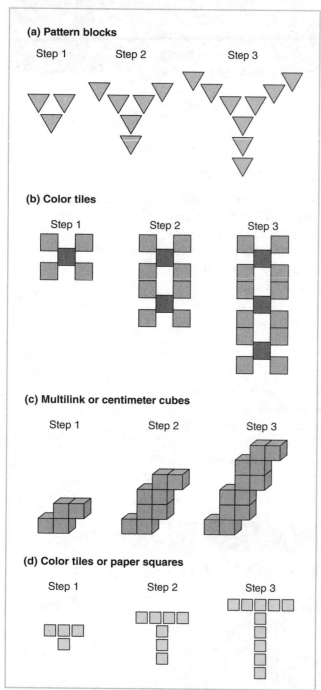

(a) Pattern blocks

Step 1   Step 2   Step 3

(b) Color tiles

Step 1   Step 2   Step 3

(c) Multilink or centimeter cubes

Step 1   Step 2   Step 3

(d) Color tiles or paper squares

Step 1   Step 2   Step 3

Notice that the number of triangles needed is a function of the design number. In this case, the number of triangles needed is three times the design number, or $t = 3d$.

Teaching Tip

Where did the multiplication sign go? Writing equations to describe patterns is often the first time students see multiplication written in different ways ($3 \times d$, $3 \cdot d$, $3d$). Reinforce that all of these are appropriate and can be used interchangeably, although the common form is to drop any multiplication symbol when variables are used ($3d$).

We also say that d is the independent variable and t is the dependent variable (the number of triangles needed *depends on* the design number).

Additional geometric growing patterns with different manipulatives are shown in Figure 12.9b–d, although the possibilities are endless. An analysis of growing patterns should include the developmental progression of reasoning by looking at the visuals, then reasoning about the numeric relationships, and then extending to a larger (or *n*th) case (Friel & Markworth, 2009). Students' experiences with growing patterns should start with fairly straightforward patterns (such as those in Figure 12.9) and continue with patterns that are somewhat more complicated, such as the dot pattern in Figure 12.10.

Contexts with Growing Patterns

In addition to geometric growing patterns, the use of contexts builds the meaning of functions.

Activity 12.13 TWO OF EVERYTHING

Two of Everything: A Chinese Folktale (Hong, 1993) is a story about a poor old couple. One day, the husband and wife discover a pot that doubles whatever goes into it, including the wife! Begin by exploring the doubling pattern in the story. Use tables of data to help students generalize and write an equation to describe the function. Ask students questions like these: "What if 200 pencils were dropped in the pot? If 60 tennis balls were pulled out, how many were dropped in the pot?" Second (the next day), explain that the magic pot has been acting up! It is not just doubling; each day, it is using some different rule. Give students a list of partially completed tables that represent different functions (e.g., 3 rows completed for the rule "+ 5," "4x," "½x," and so on. For each, ask students to add examples to the table, explaining the rule in words and as an equation. This lesson is good for ELLs because it introduces them to another culture through the book and has a concrete situation that is easily acted out or illustrated. Additionally, completing the tables for the different rules does not entail an overwhelming use of language, and there is a lot of student interaction (speaking and listening) within the lesson.

Notice what a great connect this story is to the input–output concept of functions. Something goes into (the) pot, and then something comes out (of the) pot (in-pot, out-pot). You can invite students to create a mystery magic pot rule, generate the beginning of a table, give a hint about the rule the pot is using, trade it with another student, and try to figure out the rule.

The choices for function contexts are endless because functions are everywhere in our world. The price of most things is a functional relationship (and a good way to connect functions to rate, as discussed later).

Input–Output Functions

After students have explored many contexts and visual growing patterns that are related in functional ways, they are ready to explore functions in more abstract ways. As noted above, the "Two of Everything"activity is an introduction to this idea. The input–output idea can be explored without a context, but with a physical "function machine" into which some value goes and another number comes out. Students figure out the function machine rule. This can become a fun daily routine, trading out whoever is the function operator (Figure 12.11).

Encourage students to record the examples they try in a table, so that they can see how the numeric values are related as they consider what the rule might be. For easier examples, this may not seem necessary, but in learning this process, students will be better able to analyze examples in a table to determine the explicit pattern when the problems are more difficult.

Figure 12.10

Two different ways to analyze relationships in the dot pattern.

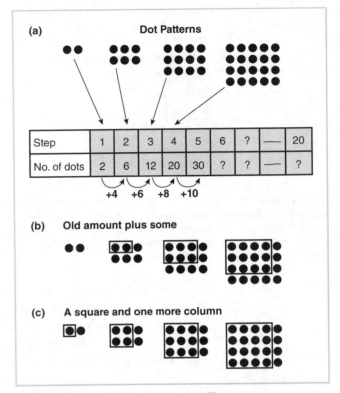

With a large empty box, you can have a student inside a function machine generating the output.

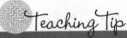

Numerous websites offer "function machine" investigations. Here are four:

- National Library of Virtual Manipulatives (http://nlvm.usu.edu/en/nav/frames_asid_191_g_3_t_1.html)
- "Math Playground" (www.mathplayground.com/functionmachine.html)
- Shodor "Interactivate" (www.shodor.org/interactivate/activities/LinearFunctMachine)
- CyberChase "Stop That Creature!" (http://pbskids.org/cyberchase/games/functions/functions.html)

Figure 12.11

A function machine illustrates the relationship between the independent and the dependent variable in a concrete manner.

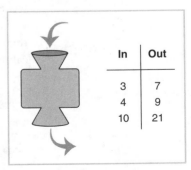

Include fractions and decimals in working with growing patterns. In 2003, the National Assessment of Educational Progress (NAEP) tested 13-year-olds on the item in Figure 12.12. Only 27 percent of students answered the problem correctly (Lambdin & Lynch, 2005).

When looking for relationships, some students will focus on the table, and others will focus on the physical pattern. It is important for students to see both forms.

Figure 12.12 NAEP item for 13-year-olds.

Term	1	2	3	4
Fraction	$\frac{1}{2}$	$\frac{2}{3}$	$\frac{3}{4}$	$\frac{4}{5}$

If the list of fractions above continues in the same pattern, which term will be equal to 0.95?

Ⓐ The 100th
Ⓑ The 95th
Ⓒ The 20th
Ⓓ The 19th
Ⓔ The 15th

Source: Lambdin, D. V., & Lynch, K. (2005). Examining Mathematics Tasks from the National Assessment of Educational Progress. *Mathematics Teaching in the Middle School, 10*(6), 314–318. Reprinted with permission. Copyright 2005 by the National Council of Teachers of Mathematics. All rights reserved.

So, if a relationship is found in a table, challenge students to see how that plays out in the physical version and vice versa.

Recursive Patterns and Formulas

For most students, it is easier to see the patterns from one step to the next. In Figure 12.10a, the number in each step can be determined from the previous step by adding successive even numbers. A pattern that changes from step to step in a way that can be described is known as a *recursive* pattern (Bezuszka & Kenney, 2008; Blanton, 2008).

The recursive pattern can also be observed in the physical pattern and in the table. In Figure 12.10b, notice that in each step, the previous step has been outlined. That lets you examine the amount added and see how it creates the pattern of adding on even numbers.

Explicit Formulas

To find the table entry for the hundredth step, the only way a recursive formula can help is to find all of the prior 99 entries in the table. If a formula (or rule) can be discovered that connects the number of the step to the number of objects at that step, any table entry can be determined without building or calculating all of the previous entries. A rule that determines the number of elements in a step from the step number is called an *explicit formula*. It allows you to determine the output, given an input (or vice versa).

Stop and Reflect

Can you determine an explicit formula for the pattern in Figure 12.10? How did you find the formula? ■

Students are likely to discover the explicit formula for a given situation in different ways. Some will analyze the table and notice that if they multiply the step number by the next step number, they will get the number of circles for that step. This leads to the explicit formula: $d = n(n + 1)$, where d is the number of dots and n is the step number. Some will examine the physical pattern to see what is changing. In Figure 12.10c, a square array is outlined for each step. Each successive square is one unit larger on a side. In this example, the side of each square is the same as the step number. The column to the right of each square is also the step number. At this point, writing a numeric expression for each step number can help students write the explicit formula. For example, the first four steps in Figure 12.10 are $1^2 + 1$, $2^2 + 2$, $3^2 + 3$, and $4^2 + 4$. The explicit formula is therefore $d = n^2 + n$.

Students will likely be able to describe the explicit formula in words before they can write it in symbols. If the goal of your lesson is to find "the rule," then stopping with the verbal formula is appropriate. If your instructional goal is to write formulas with symbols, then ask students first to write the formula, or rule, in words and then think about how they can translate that statement into numbers and symbols.

◆ Linear Functions

Linear functions are a subset of all functions, but because linearity is a major focus of middle-school mathematics, it appears here in its own section. The NCTM *Curriculum Focal*

Points and the *Common Core State Standards* emphasize the importance of linear functions across the middle grades, with a strong focus on linearity in the seventh and eighth grades (CCSSO, 2010; NCTM, 2006).

Stop and Reflect

Think back to example tasks shared in this chapter—birds, border tiles, the magic pot, and the dot pattern. Which are linear functions? Which are not linear, but are still functions? ■

The examples that involved linear functions include the birds (how many ways they could be on the bush and in the tree), the border tiles problem, $m + n = 1$, the geometric growing patterns, and the "Two of Everything" activity, which can be nonlinear if the rule of the magic pot is something nonlinear (like "square the number"). The dot pattern (Figure 12.10) is nonlinear (it is quadratic).

In middle school, students are to notice if situations are linear or not. Consider the example below.

You are asked to build a rectangular pen with 24 yards of fence. (1) Write an equation with variables to describe the relationship between the length and the area. (2) Write an equation with variables to describe the relationship between the length and width (Figure 12.13).

An explicit formula for determining the width is $w = 12 - l$ (l is the length), which decreases at a constant rate and is linear. The explicit formula for the area of the pen is $a = l(12 - l)$, which is not linear.

Figure 12.13

The width and area graphs as functions of the length of a rectangle with a fixed perimeter of 24 units.

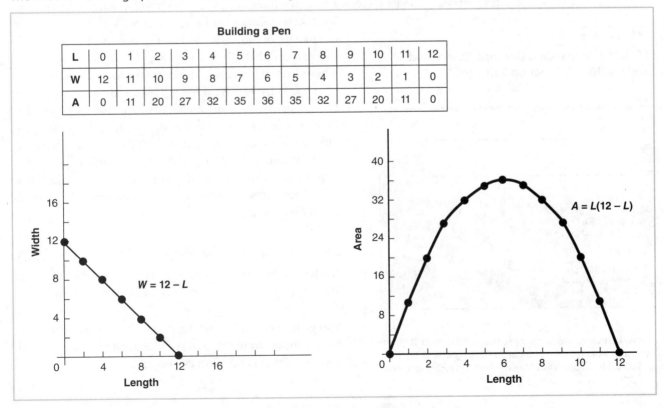

L	0	1	2	3	4	5	6	7	8	9	10	11	12
W	12	11	10	9	8	7	6	5	4	3	2	1	0
A	0	11	20	27	32	35	36	35	32	27	20	11	0

Linear (and nonlinear) situations should be analyzed across representations. In a situation, students should be able to describe a constant rate of change related to the situation. In a graph, this can be established by seeing that the plotted points lie on one line. In a table, the change will be constant (e.g., a recursive pattern is + 4 each time). In the equation, linearity can be determined by looking at the part of the expression that changes and seeing if it represents constant change or not.

Rate of Change and Slope

Rate, whether constant or varying, is a type of change often associated with how fast something is traveling. Rate is an excellent context for exploring linearity because constant rates can be seen in a wide range of contexts, such as the geometric model of the pattern block perimeters or the rate of growth of a plant. Other rate contexts in numeric situations include hourly wages, gas mileage, profit, and even the cost of an item, such as a bus ticket.

For an interactive tool that connects linear equations in the form $y = mx + b$ to graphs, try "Interactive Linear Equation" at Math Warehouse (www.mathwarehouse.com/algebra/linear_equation/linear-equation-interactive-activity.php). In addition, try the NCTM e-Examples (www.nctm.org/standards/content.aspx?id=24600) that target rate, connecting linear functions to a real-world context and graphs. In Applet 5.2, students can adjust the speed, direction, and starting position of two runners. As the runners are set in motion, a time–distance graph is generated (Figure 12.14). In Applet 6.2, phone call rates are explored.

These explorations of rate develop the concept of *slope*, which is the numeric value that describes the rate of change for a linear function. Conceptually, then, slope signifies how much *y* increases when *x* increases by 1. If a line contains the points (2,4) and (3,¯5), you can see that as *x* increases by 1, *y* decreases by 9. So the rate of change, or slope, is –9. For the points (4,3) and (7,9), you can see that when *x* increases by 3, *y* increases by 6. Therefore, an increase of 1 in *x* results in a change of 2 in *y* (dividing 6 by 3). The slope is 2. After further exploration and experiences, your students will begin to generalize that you can find the rate of change or slope by finding the difference in the *y* values and dividing by the difference in the *x* values. Exploring this first through reasoning is important for students if they are to be able to make sense of and remember the formula for calculating slope when given two points.

Figure 12.14

Applet 5.2: "Understanding Distance, Speed, and Time Relationships Using Simulation Software."

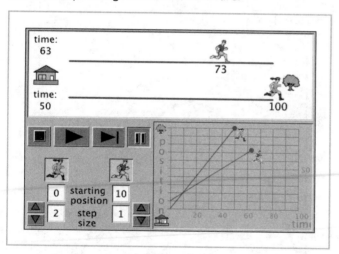

Zero Slope and No Slope

Understanding these two easily confused slopes requires contexts, such as walking rates. Consider this story:

You walk for 10 minutes at a rate of 1 mile per hour, stop for 3 minutes to watch a nest of baby birds, then walk for 5 more minutes at 2 miles per hour.

What will the graph look like for the 3 minutes when you stop? What is your rate when you stop? In fact, your rate is zero, and because you are at the same distance for 3 minutes, the graph at that timeframe will be a horizontal line.

Let's say that you see a graph of a walking story that includes a vertical line—a line with no slope. What would this mean? It means that there is no change in the x variable—you traveled a distance with no time passing! Now, even if you were a world record sprinter, this would be impossible. Remember that rate is based on a change of 1 in the x value.

Proportional and Nonproportional Situations

Linear functions can be proportional or nonproportional. The rate example just described is *proportional*. The distance you walk is proportional to how much time you have walked. As another example, your pay for babysitting is proportional to the hours you work. All proportional situations, then, are equations in the form $y = mx$. Notice that the graphs of all proportional situations are straight lines that pass through the origin. Students will find that the slope of these lines is also the rate of change between the two variables. (See Chapter 11 for many interesting problems that focus on rates and proportions.)

Look back at the geometric growing patterns in Figure 12.9. Figure 12.9d demonstrates a nonproportional situation—it is increasing at a constant rate of $+ 3$ (and is therefore linear), but the variables are not related in a proportional way (i.e., $y \neq 3x$). Proportional representations are shown in Figure 12.9a–c. However, if you slightly altered the patterns, they could become nonproportional. For example, in the pattern in Figure 12.9a, if the triangles were added to two of the prongs, like an upside-down V, then you could no longer find the nth term simply by multiplying the step number by a factor.

In nonproportional situations, one value is constant. The "Pattern Block Perimeter" problem provides an excellent exploration of linear, but nonproportional, functions (Figure 12.15). (Note: This is a good pattern to explore in the same manner as the border tiles problem, beginning with a string of seven or eight blocks and finding equivalent ways to determine the perimeter without counting.)

Figure 12.15

For each string of pattern blocks, can you determine the perimeter for *n* pattern blocks?

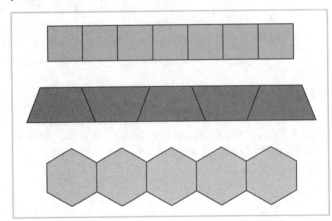

Stop and Reflect

Can you answer the following questions: What is the perimeter for any string of triangles? Any string of squares? Hexagons? What is the same across each of these growing patterns? And the proportional question: Is the number of pieces needed proportional to the string length? ∎

The equation representing the triangles is $y = x + 2$, for the squares is $y = 2x + 2$, and for the hexagons is $y = 4x + 2$. No matter which step number you are on, or which shape you are using, there are 2 units of perimeter on each end. The perimeter of the hexagon pattern blocks is not proportional to the number of blocks used. Said another way, you cannot get from the input (number of blocks) to the perimeter by multiplying by a factor, as you can in proportional situations.

If you are walking but have a head start of 50 meters, or if you are selling something and have an initial expense, those values are constants in the linear function that make it nonproportional.

The constant value, or initial value, can be found across representations beyond the contexts described here. In the table, it is the value when $x = 0$, which means it is the point where the graph crosses the y axis. All situations that have this initial or constant value are nonproportional.

Nonproportional situations are more challenging for students to generalize. Students want to use the recursive value (e.g., $+ 4$) as the factor ($\times 4$). Students often make the common error of using the table to find the tenth step and doubling it to find the twentieth step, which works in proportional situations but does not work in nonproportional situations. Mathematics education researchers have found that having students analyze errors such as these supports their learning of mathematics concepts (Lannin, Arbaugh, Barker, & Townsend, 2006).

Parallel, Same, and Perpendicular Lines

Students in eighth grade should be comparing different linear situations that result in parallel, same, or perpendicular lines (CCSSO, 2010). Using a context is necessary to build understanding. Consider the situation of Larry and Mary, each earning $30 a week for the summer months. Mary starts the summer $50 dollars in debt, and Larry already has $20. When will Mary and Larry have the same amount of money? In week 3, how much more money does Larry have? How much more does he have in week 7? In any week, what is the difference in their wealth? The rates for Larry's and Mary's earnings are the same—and the graphs therefore go up at the same rate—that is, the slopes are the same. We can tell that the graphs of $y = 30x + 20$ (Larry's money) and $y = 30x - 50$ (Mary's money) are parallel without even making the graphs because the rates (or slopes) are the same.

Can you think of what change in Larry's and Mary's situations might result in the same line? Remember the equivalent expressions discussed earlier? As illustrated on the calculator, they will have the same line. Slopes can also tell us when two lines are perpendicular, but it is less obvious. A little bit of analysis with similar triangles will show that for perpendicular lines, the slope of one is the negative reciprocal of the other.

Graphs

So far, patterns and functions have been represented by (1) physical materials or drawings, (2) tables, (3) words, and (4) symbols. A graph adds a fifth representation (see Blackline Master 42 for a coordinate axis). Figure 12.16 provides a graph of the "Pattern Blocks Perimeter" problem (presented in Figure 12.15), and Figure 12.17 shows a graph for the border tiles problem (Figure 12.1) and the "Dot Pattern" problem (Figure 12.10).

BLM

Figure 12.16

Graphs of the perimeters of three different strings of pattern blocks. The lines are not drawn because, for this context, there are no solutions between the points.

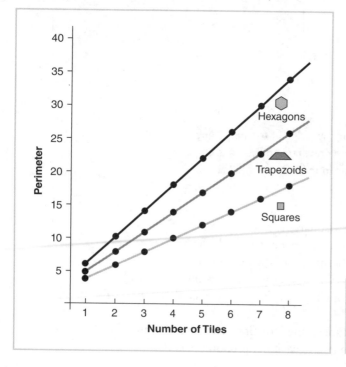

Notice that the first graph in Figure 12.17 is a straight-line (linear) relationship, and the other is a curved line that would make half of a parabola if the points were joined. The horizontal axis is always used for the step numbers, the independent variable. Having graphs of three related growing patterns offers the opportunity to compare and connect the graphs to the patterns and to the tables (see Figure 12.16). For example, ask students to discuss how to get from one to the next (over 1, up 6), and then ask how that information can be found in the table. Second, identify a particular point on the graph, and ask what it tells about the pattern. You can also pose questions such as these (referring to Figure 12.16) to help students understand the graphic representation of the function:

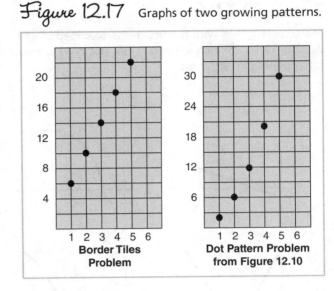

Figure 12.17 Graphs of two growing patterns.

- How does each graph represent each of the string patterns?
- Why is there no line connecting the dots?
- Why is one line steeper than the others?
- What does this particular point on the graph match up to in the model and in the table?

 Formative Assessment Note

Being able to make connections across representations is important for understanding functions, and the only way to know if a student is seeing the connections is to ask. In a *diagnostic interview*, ask questions like the ones just listed, and look to see whether students are able to link the graph to the context, to the table, and to the formula.

In addition to a graphing calculator, there are some excellent websites for generating graphs of functions. For example, GraphSketch.com (http://graphsketch.com) is an effective tool for making graphs of equations.

Graphs and Contexts

It is important for students to be able to interpret and construct graphs related to real situations; they should be able to sketch the shape of a graph without using any specific data, equations, or numbers, and they should be able to look at the shape of a graph and tell a possible story about the data. The advantage of activities such as these is the focus on how a graph can express the relationships involved.

Activity 12.14 **SKETCH A GRAPH**

 Sketch a graph for each of these situations. No numbers or formulas are to be used.

1. The temperature of a frozen dinner from 30 minutes before it is removed from the freezer until it is removed from the microwave and placed on the table (with the moment the dinner is removed from the freezer considered to be time 0)

Figure 12.18

Match each graph with the situations described in Activity 12.14, "Sketch a Graph." Talk about what change is happening in each case.

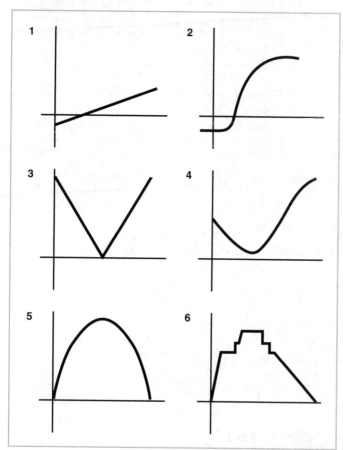

2. The value of a 1970 Volkswagen Beetle from the time it was purchased to the present (assuming it was kept in perfect condition)
3. The level of water in the bathtub from when you start filling it to when it is empty after a bath
4. Profit in terms of number of items sold
5. The height of a thrown baseball from when it is released to when it hits the ground
6. The speed of the same baseball

Be sure that the contexts you pick are familiar to ELLs (and other students). If they are not, change the context or illustrate what it is. For students with disabilities, you may want to have them match graphs (Figure 12.18) before drawing them.

Stop and Reflect

Can you sketch a graph for each situation in the last activity? ■

Graphs and Rate of Change

Analysis of the graphs should focus on how the function is changing—whether it is increasing or decreasing rapidly or gradually. A graph is a picture of the rate of change of one variable in terms of the other. Essentially, graphs can have only one of the seven characteristics shown in Figure 12.19 or some combination of these. These types of change will be seen in the following activity.

Figure 12.19

Seven ways in which graphs can change. A graph often has combinations of these characteristics.

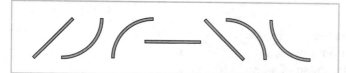

Activity 12.15 BOTTLES AND VOLUME GRAPHS

Figure 12.20 shows six vases and six graphs. Assume the bottles are filled at a constant rate. Because of bottle shape, the height of the liquid will increase either more slowly or more quickly as the bottle gets wider or narrower. Match the graphs with the bottles. Find some containers that have different shapes. Give each group one vase to use. Fill a small medicine cup with water and empty it into the container, recording in a table the number of little cups used and the height of the water. After each group gathers the data, they graph their findings. Graphs are collected and matched with the container.

◆ Connecting Representations

Students must understand the connections between context, tables, graphs, equations, and verbal descriptions; it is not enough just to teach each one separately (Hackbarth & Wilsman, 2008). So, pose tasks and questions that will help your students make these connections (Earnest & Balti, 2008). Each representation supports understanding of the function as a whole, as we illustrate with the following task.

Brian is trying to make money by selling hot dogs from a cart at the stadium during music performances and ball games. He pays $35 per night for the use of the cart. He sells hot dogs for $1.25 each. His costs for the hot dogs, condiments, napkins, and other paper products are on average $0.60 per hot dog. The profit from a single hot dog is, therefore, $0.65.

Context

This function begins with a context: selling hot dogs and the resulting profit. The context helps students make sense of what changes (number of hot dogs sold) and what stays the same ($35 rental), which can help them figure out the explicit formula. The context supports students' conceptual understanding of the other, more abstract representations.

Table

Brian might sit down and calculate some possible profits based on anticipated hot dog sales. The table provides a concise way to look at the recursive pattern and the explicit pattern. The recursive pattern can lead to seeing what changes, whether it changes at a constant rate, and how that information can help find the explicit formula.

Verbal Description

Brian's profit depends on the number of hot dogs that are sold. In functional language, "Profit is a function of the number of hot dogs sold." The verbal description of the explicit formula for the hot dog stand might be stated by students as, "You multiply each hot dog sold by $0.65; then subtract $35 for the cart." The verbal explanation of the explicit formula provides a connection from the context to the symbolic representation (Lannin, Townsend, Armer, Green, & Schneider, 2008).

Symbols

Brian's profit is represented by the equation $p = (0.65 \times h) - 35$, where p stands for profit. This equation defines a function between two variables, profit and hot dogs. By expressing a function as an equation, it is possible to find the profit for any number of hot dogs.

Figure 12.20

Assuming the bottles are filled at a constant rate, match the graphs with the vases.

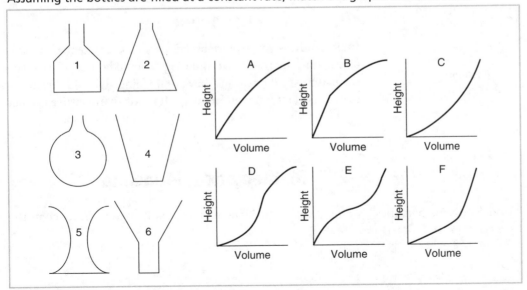

Figure 12.21

A graph showing profit as a function of hot dogs sold.

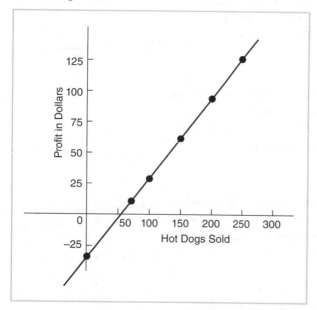

Graphs

Figure 12.21 shows the graph of the hot dog problem. As we have already established, the profit increases as the sales increase. There is, in this situation, a linear pattern, meaning that the profit is increasing at a constant rate—namely, at $0.65 per hot dog.

The graph allows one to observe "at a glance" that the relationship between sales and profits is linear and increasing. The context gives meaning to the graph, and the graph adds understanding to the context.

Graphs are easily created with technology. For example, GraphSketch (http://graphsketch.com) works very much like a graphing calculator and can graph functions of any type.

Figure 12.22 illustrates the five representations of functions for the hot dog context. Such a diagram could be used with any function, with one of the representations given and students asked to create the others.

Figure 12.22

Five different representations of a function. For any given function, students should see that all the representations are connected and illustrate the same relationship.

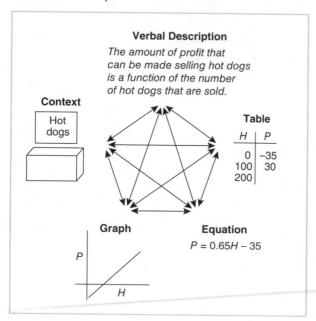

Formative Assessment Note

The hot dog problem is a good *performance assessment*. A good question (which can be adapted to any task) is, "Can you show me where in the table, the graph, and the equation you can find the profit for selling 225 hot dogs?"

⬡ Function Language

Importantly, as you explore functions across representations, students, using appropriate terminology, should be able to articulate the patterns and functions they are noticing. Table 12.2 summarizes important function language. It is not an exhaustive list, but it adds to what has already been discussed in this chapter.

 Mathematical Modeling

"Model with mathematics" is one of the eight Standards for Mathematical Practice in the *Common Core State Standards*.

Table 12.2 Function Language

Concepts	Description	Example
Independent and dependent variables	The *independent variable* is the input, or whatever value is being used to find another value. For example, in the case of the strings of pattern blocks, the independent variable is the number of blocks in the string. The *dependent variable* is the number of objects needed, the output, or whatever value you get from using the independent variable.	In the "Pattern Blocks Perimeter" problem, the dependent variable is the perimeter. You can say that the perimeter of the block structure depends on the number of blocks used.
Discrete and continuous functions	When isolated or selected values are the only ones appropriate for a context, the function is *discrete*. If all values along a line or curve are solutions to the function, then the function is *continuous*.	Discrete: "Pattern Blocks Perimeter" problem (Figure 12.15). Only whole-number values make sense. Continuous: "How Many Gallons Left?" (Activity 12.16). There can be any value for miles and gallons (within the appropriate domain).
Domain and range	The *domain* of a function comprises the possible values for the independent variable. The *range* is the corresponding possible values for the dependent variable.	In the "Pattern Blocks Perimeter" problem, the domain and range are all positive whole numbers. In the "Building a Pen" problem (Figure 12.13), the domain and range are all real numbers between 0 and 12.

Modeling links classroom mathematics and statistics to everyday life, work, and decision making. Modeling is the process of choosing and using appropriate mathematics and statistics to analyze empirical situations, to understand them better, and to improve decisions (CCSSO, 2010, p. 72).

We have already seen many examples of mathematical models (e.g., the model or equation for describing the number of border tiles required for different-size pools). How is modeling used to make decisions? Take the example of selling widgets marked up at some percentage over wholesale. Once a formula is derived for a given price and markup, it can be used to determine the profit at different sales levels. The model (equation) can be adjusted in the price and markup percentage, in order to adjust the profit.

You can create a mathematical model to describe the depreciation of a car at 20 percent each year. If the car loses 20 percent of its value in 1 year, then it must be worth 80 percent of its value after a year. So, after 1 year, the $15,000 car is worth $15,000 × 0.8. In the second year, it loses 20 percent of that value, so it will be worth only 80 percent of its value at the end of year 1, which was $15,000 × 0.8. The value at the end of year 2 would be ($15,000 × 0.8) × 0.8, and so on. At the end of y years, the value of the car can be expressed in this equation: value = $\$15,000 \times 0.8^y$. Figure 12.23 shows the graph and the table of values on a graphing calculator.

The next activity provides another context appropriate for developing a mathematical model.

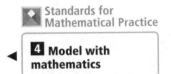

Standards for Mathematical Practice

◄ **4** Model with mathematics

Teaching Tip

Mathematical models are not to be confused with tools (such as manipulatives or visuals for building a pattern). And, as the *Common Core State Standards* indicate, modeling with mathematics is something students do across the curriculum as they think numerically and symbolically about the mathematics they are doing.

Figure 12.23

The graph and table for $V = 15,000 \times 0.8^y$. Year, the independent variable, is shown under X, and value of the car, the dependent variable, is shown under $Y1$.

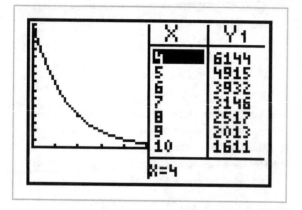

Activity 12.16 HOW MANY GALLONS LEFT?

A car gets 23 miles per gallon of gas. It has a gas tank that holds 20 gallons. Suppose that you were on a trip and had filled the tank at the outset. Determine a mathematical model that describes the gallons left for given miles traveled. ELLs may be more familiar with kilometers per liter, which means you can adapt the problem to those units or connect the meaning of the two.

Notice that the word *rule* could replace "mathematical model." In this case, one possible equation is $g = 20 - \frac{m}{23}$. Use the model, or equation, to make predictions. For example, "How can you tell from the model how much gas will be left after driving 300 miles? How many miles can you drive before the gas tank has only 3 gallons left?" Two more engaging contexts are provided in Figure 12.24.

Sometimes, a model is provided, and the important task is for students to understand and use the formula. Consider the following water pumping problem and related equation from the Michigan Algebra Project (Herbel-Eisenmann & Phillips, 2005):

Suppose you turn a pump on and let it run to empty the water out of a pool. The amount of water in the pool (W, measured in gallons) at any time (T, measured in hours) is given by the following equation: $W = {}^-350\,(T - 4)$.

Stop and Reflect

What questions might you pose to middle-school students to help them make sense of this equation? Try to think of three. ∎

In the Michigan Algebra Project, students were asked to solve several problems and explain how the equation was used to find the answer. Those questions and one student's responses are provided in Figure 12.25.

Figure 12.24 Mathematical modeling problems for further exploration.

1. Pleasant's Hardware buys widgets for \$4.17 each, marks them up 35 percent over wholesale, and sells them at that price. Create a mathematical model to relate widgets sold (w) to profit (p). The manager asks you to determine the formula if she were to put the widgets on sale for 25 percent off. What is your formula or mathematical model for the sale, relating widgets sold (s) to profit (p)?

2. In Arches National Park in Moab, Utah, there are sandstone cliffs. A green coating, caused by cyanobacteria, covers some of the sandstone. Bacteria grow by splitting in two (or doubling) in a certain time period. If the sandstone started with 50 bacteria, create a mathematical model for describing the growth of cyanobacteria on the sandstone. (Buerman, 2007)

Figure 12.25

One student's explanations of questions regarding what a mathematical model means.

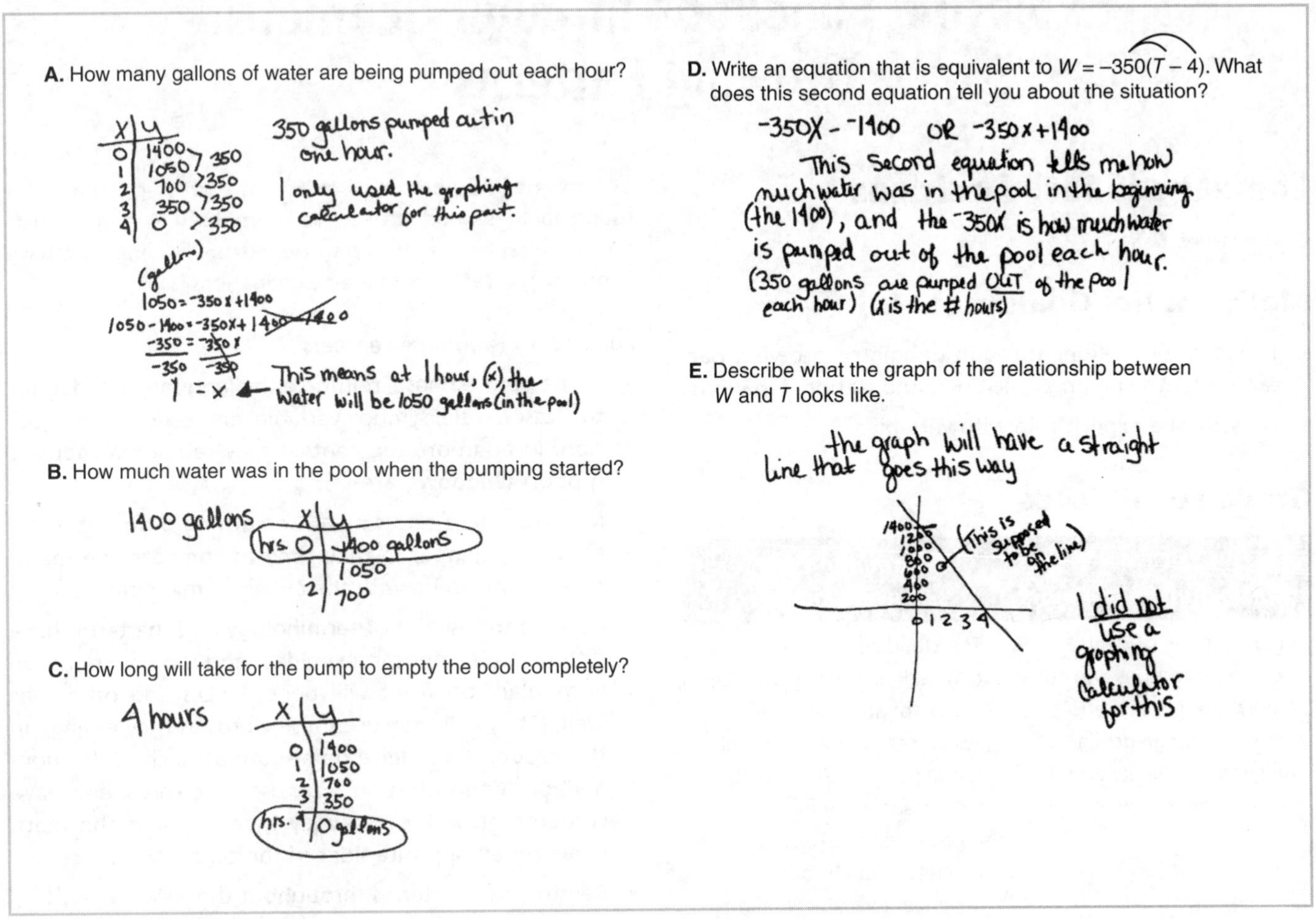

A. How many gallons of water are being pumped out each hour?

350 gallons pumped out in one hour.

I only used the graphing calculator for this part.

(handwritten table and work)

x | y
0 | 1400 ⌉ 350
1 | 1050 ⌉ 350
2 | 700 ⌉ 350
3 | 350 ⌉ 350
4 | 0 ⌉ 350
(gallons)

$1050 = -350x + 1400$
$1050 - 1400 = -350x + 1400 - 1400$
$-350 = -350x$
$-350 / -350 = x$
$1 = x$ ← This means at 1 hour, (x), the water will be 1050 gallons (in the pool)

B. How much water was in the pool when the pumping started?

1400 gallons

x | y
hrs 0 | 1400 gallons
1 | 1050
2 | 700

C. How long will take for the pump to empty the pool completely?

4 hours

x | y
0 | 1400
1 | 1050
2 | 700
3 | 350
hrs. 4 | 0 gallons

D. Write an equation that is equivalent to $W = -350(T - 4)$. What does this second equation tell you about the situation?

$-350X - 1400$ or $-350X + 1400$

This second equation tells me how much water was in the pool in the beginning (the 1400), and the -350X is how much water is pumped out of the pool each hour. (350 gallons are pumped OUT of the pool each hour) (x is the # hours)

E. Describe what the graph of the relationship between W and T looks like.

the graph will have a straight line that goes this way

(handwritten graph)
1400, 1200, 1000, 800, 600, 400, 200
0 1 2 3 4
(This is supposed to be the line)

I did not use a graphing calculator for this

Expanded Lesson

Exploring Functions through Geometric Growing Patterns

Content and Task Decisions

Grade Level: 6–8

Mathematics Goals

- To explore functions through geometric growing patterns, identifying an explicit rule and stating it in words
- To write the explicit rule with variables

Grade Level Guide

NCTM Curriculum Focal Points	Common Core State Standards
In sixth grade, students explore expressions and equations related to sequences, and in eighth grade, linear functions and linear equations are a focal point.	The Standards for Mathematical Practice, in particular, "Look for and make use of structure," are central to this lesson (CCSSO, 2010, p. 8). In sixth grade, students "write an equation to express one quantity, thought of as the dependent variable, in terms of the other quantity, thought of as the independent variable. Analyze the relationship between the dependent and independent variables using graphs and tables, and relate these to the equation" (CCSSO, 2010, p. 43). In eighth grade, students explore functions, a critical area, with numerous important standards.

Consider Your Students' Needs

Students have had some experience with growing patterns. They have extended growing patterns with appropriate materials and explained why their extensions followed a rule. Students have created tables to record the numeric component of patterns (the number of objects at each step). They have found and described recursive relationships (i.e., how the pattern changes from one step to the next). They may not have begun to use variables in their explanations.

For English Language Learners

- In the *Before* phase, reinforce the language needed for the lesson: rule, symbol, variable, expression, and equation. In addition, the context may require vocabulary support (windows, arrays).
- Many of these terms mean something different in everyday language, so take time to compare the mathematical meaning with the everyday meaning.
- Because this is a lot of terminology and the terms have different meanings in everyday language, working on vocabulary up front will benefit ELLs and others, as well. (They will then use these words as they engage in the lesson.) Consider a game format, such as "Pictionary" or "Concentration." Or, use note cards, and have students draw the everyday meaning and the math meaning on opposite sides of the card.
- Reinforce these terms throughout the lesson.

For Student with Disabilities

- Consider having toothpicks or rods available for modeling the steps in the window problem. Then move to two-color counters to create the arrays in the dot-array pattern.

Materials

Each student will need:

- "Predict How Many" ("Windows") worksheet (Blackline Master 18)
- "Predict How Many" ("Dot Arrays") worksheet (Blackline Master 19)

The teacher will need:

- Transparencies or copies of "Predict How Many" worksheets (Blackline Masters 18 and 19) for projection

Lesson

Before

Present the focus task to the class:

- Distribute the "Windows" pattern worksheet and display it on the overhead. Explain that the table shows how many sticks are needed to make all of the windows for that step. Have students look at the next two steps and fill in the next two entries of the table.

- Ask, "Can you predict how many sticks you will need to build the 20th step?" Explain that they are going to explore this pattern, recording their data in a table. The goal is to be able to tell a way to find how many sticks are needed for any step number.

Provide clear expectations:

- Students may work with partners to share ideas, but each student needs to complete the recording sheet.

- Tell students that the goal is for them to be able to tell the rule in words and in symbols, and to be able to connect both the words and symbols to the pattern.

During

Initially:

- Observe whether students are recording data in the table.

Ongoing:

- Use questions to encourage students to connect the windows pattern with the table data.

- If students are having difficulty finding a relationship, suggest that they look for ways to count the dots without having to count each one. If they use the same method of counting for each step, they should begin to see how their counting method relates to the step numbers. Have them write a numeric expression for each step that matches their counting procedure. For example, step 2 is 2 × 3, step 4 is 3 × 4, and so on.

- Once students think they have identified a relationship, make sure they test their conjecture with other parts of the table and picture.

After

Bring the class together to share and discuss the task:

- Ask what entry students found for step 20.

- Ask students what general rule they found for finding the number of sticks needed. Ask students to explain their thinking to the class. Here are some possible ideas that students may suggest:

  1. "There is a square of four sticks, then each new step adds three more. That is, four plus three times one less than the step number."
  2. "One stick at the start, then there are as many sets of three as the step number." [$1 + (3 \cdot \text{step})$]
  3. "The tops and bottoms of the windows have the same number of sticks as the step number. There is one more vertical stick than the step number." [step (top) + step (bottom) + (step + 1) (vertical sides)]

- After students have described their pattern in words, ask them to write the explicit rule as an equation. You can use x and y, or you can use s for step number and n for number of sticks needed. The equations that align with the explanations above are these:

$$n = [4 + 3(s - 1)]$$
$$n = 1 + 3s$$
$$n = (s + s) + (s + 1) \text{ or } 2s + s + 1$$

- Point to various parts of each equation, and ask students what that means in the context of the windows.

- Ask students, "Can each of these equations be correct?" Allow them to discuss and prove that these expressions are equivalent.

- To see if students understand their formulas, ask questions such as, "Which step number would have 40 sticks? 70 sticks? Will there be a step number with 100 sticks?"

- As a follow-up experience, allow students time to explore "Dot Arrays," writing words and equations to describe the explicit rule.

Assessment

Observe

- Are students able to see the connections between the pictorial representation, the table, and the equation?

- Are students using variables accurately in writing their expressions and equations?

Ask

- What do you notice is changing with each new window (pattern)?

- Where do you see that change in the pattern? In the table?

- How can you use the pattern in the drawing or table to write a rule for the situation (in words)?

- How do the words in your rule fit with your equation?

13

Developing Geometry Concepts

BigIDEAS

1 What makes shapes alike and different can be determined by geometric properties. For example, shapes have sides that are parallel, perpendicular, or neither; they have line symmetry, rotational symmetry, or neither; they are similar, congruent, or neither.

2 Shapes can be moved in a plane or in space to make congruent or similar shapes. These transformations include translations, reflections, rotations, and dilations.

3 Shapes can be described in terms of their location in a plane or in space. Coordinate systems can be used to describe these locations precisely. Coordinates can be used to measure distance, an important application of the Pythagorean theorem.

4 The ability to perceive shapes from different viewpoints helps us understand relationships between two- and three-dimensional figures and mentally change the position and size of shapes.

Geometry is a "network of concepts, ways of reasoning and representation systems" used to explore and analyze shape and space (Battista, 2007, p. 843). This critical area of mathematics appears in everything from global positioning systems to computer animation. Unique to the *Common Core State Standards for Mathematics*, geometry appears as a domain across all grades, K–12: "The notion of building understanding in geometry across the grades, from informal to more formal thinking, is consistent with the thinking of theorists and researchers" (CCSSO, 2010, p. 41). In middle school, the primary focus of geometry is on the following concepts:

- Exploring shapes on the coordinate plane (drawing them in grade 6 and performing transformations on

them in grade 8); finding lengths of line segments on the coordinate plane (vertical and horizontal lines in grade 6 and all lines in grade 8 with the Pythagorean theorem)

- Constructing triangles with given conditions, with and without technology, and exploring properties of triangles (grade 7)
- Exploring relationships between two-dimensional and three-dimensional shapes—for example, by slicing three-dimensional figures (grade 7)
- Exploring congruence and similarity with physical models, visuals, and technology, focusing on scale drawings (grade 7) and transformations (grade 8)
- Analyzing the relationship of angles related to triangles and parallel lines (grade 8)

For too long, the geometry curriculum in the United States has emphasized learning terminology and labeling in low-level tasks, such as "this is an obtuse or a right triangle." Geometry is much more than this. First, it involves developing and applying *spatial sense*. Spatial sense is an intuition about shapes and the relationships among shapes, and it includes the ability to visualize objects and spatial relationships mentally—to turn things around in one's mind. It includes a comfort with geometric descriptions of objects and position. People with well-developed spatial sense appreciate geometric forms in art, nature, and architecture, and they use geometric ideas to describe and analyze their world.

Second, geometry involves significantly more content than shapes, as indicated by the four major geometry strands:

- *Shapes and properties:* the properties of shapes, as well as the relationships built on properties
- *Transformations:* translations, reflections, rotations, and dilations
- *Location:* coordinate geometry and other ways of specifying how objects are located in a plane or in space
- *Visualization:* the recognition of shapes in the environment, the development of relationships between two- and three-dimensional objects, and the ability to construct and draw figures from different viewpoints

All four of these are significant in the middle-school curriculum. Therefore, the content in this chapter is divided according to these four categories, with the discussion of each category beginning with foundational experiences and moving through more challenging experiences.

Developing Geometric Thinking

All students can develop the ability to think and reason in geometric contexts, but this ability requires ongoing and significant experiences across a developmental progression. The research of two famous Dutch educators, Pierre van Hiele and Dina van Hiele-Geldof (husband and wife), provides insights into the differences in geometric thinking through the description of different levels of thought. The van Hiele levels of geometric thought have been a major influence in the mathematics curriculum worldwide.

Van Hiele Levels of Geometric Thought

Figure 13.1 illustrates the five levels of geometric thought. Each level describes how we think and what types of geometric ideas we think about (called *objects of thought*) and what students can do (called *products of thought*). The levels are developmental in nature—students (regardless of age) begin at level 0 and through experiences progress to the next level. The work in middle school is targeted primarily at level 2, but you may need to pull in level 0 and level 1 experiences for students who are not ready to reason at level 2. Characteristics of the van Hiele levels of geometric thought are provided in Figure 13.2.

Figure 13.1   The van Hiele levels of geometric thought.

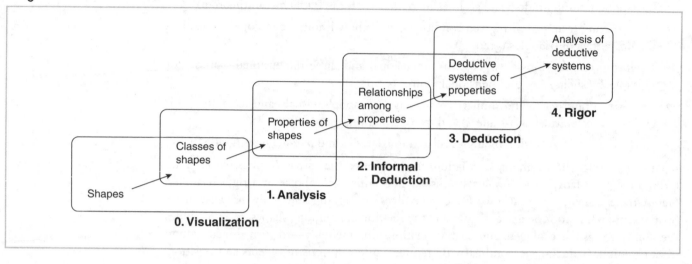

Figure 13.2   Characteristics of the van Hiele levels.

Characteristic	Implication
1. Developmental	To arrive at any level, students must move through all prior levels. (For students to be ready for high school geometry, middle school must focus on developing level 2 geometric thought.) When instruction or language is at a level higher than that of the students, students cannot understand the concept being developed. A student can, for example, memorize a fact (e.g., all squares are rectangles) but not mentally construct the actual relationship of how the properties of a square and rectangle are related.
2. Age-independent	Although a seventh grader should be working at level 2, he or she may be at level 0 or 1. Some adults remain forever at level 0, and a significant number of adults never reach level 2.
3. Experience-dependent	Advancement through the levels requires geometric experiences. (The eighth grader operating at level 0 needs numerous and carefully selected activities to help him or her move to level 1, and then additional carefully selected experiences to move to level 2.)

Level 0: Visualization

The objects of thought at level 0 are shapes and what they "look like."

Students at level 0 recognize and name figures based on the global visual characteristics of the figure. For example, a square is defined by a level 0 student as a square "because it looks like a square." Appearance is dominant at level 0 and can therefore overpower the properties of a shape. A level 0 thinker, for example, may see a square with sides that are not horizontal or vertical (it appears tilted) and believe it is a diamond and no longer a square.

The products of thought at level 0 are classes or groupings of shapes that seem to be "alike."

The emphasis at level 0 is on shapes that students can observe, feel, build, take apart, or work with in some manner. How are shapes alike and different? Some of these classes of shapes have names—rectangles, triangles, rhombi, and so on. Properties of shapes (e.g., parallel sides, right angles) are included at this level, but only in an informal manner.

Level 1: Analysis

The objects of thought at level 1 are classes of shapes rather than individual shapes.

You will know your students are at the analysis level if they are able to consider all shapes within a class rather than just the single shape on their desk. Instead of talking about *this* particular rectangle, they can talk about *all* rectangles. Students focus on what makes a rectangle a rectangle (four sides, four right angles, etc.). The irrelevant features (e.g., size or orientation) fade into the background. If a shape belongs to a particular class, it has the corresponding properties of that class. "All cubes have six congruent faces, and each of those faces is a square." Students operating at level 1 may be able to list all the properties of squares, rectangles, and parallelograms but may not see that each of these classes is a subclass of the next (e.g., that all squares are rectangles, and all rectangles are parallelograms). In defining a shape, level 1 thinkers are likely to list as many properties of a shape as they know.

The products of thought at level 1 are the properties of shapes.

Level 1 students continue to use manipulatives and drawings of shapes, but they also see these individual shapes as representatives of classes of shapes. Their understanding of the properties of shapes—such as symmetry, perpendicular and parallel lines, and so on—continues to be refined. This identification of geometric properties is an important cognitive activity (Yu, Barrett, & Presmeg, 2009).

The following activity is targeted at developing level 1 thinkers because the goal is to explore and conjecture about the properties of quadrilaterals.

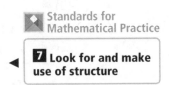

Standards for Mathematical Practice

◄ **7 Look for and make use of structure**

Activity 13.1 PROPERTY LISTS FOR QUADRILATERALS

Prepare handouts for parallelograms, rhombi, rectangles, and squares (see Blackline Masters 20–23 and Figure 13.3). Assign groups of three or four students to work with one type of quadrilateral (for English language learners [ELLs] and students with disabilities, post labeled shapes as a reference). Their task is to list as many properties as they can that apply to all of the example shapes on their sheet. They will need tools such as index cards (to check right angles, compare side lengths, and draw straight lines); mirrors (to check line symmetry); and tracing paper (for angle congruence). Encourage students to use the words *at least, only, at most, always* to describe how many of something. For example, "rectangles have at least two lines of symmetry"—because squares, included in the category of rectangles, have four.

Figure 13.3

Shapes for "Property Lists for Quadrilaterals" activity.

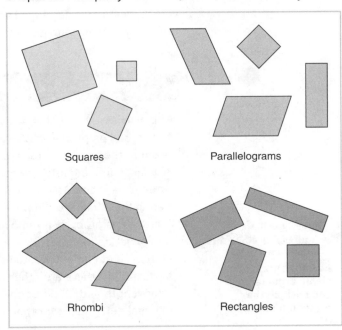

Squares   Parallelograms

Rhombi   Rectangles

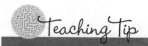

Have students prepare their property lists under these headings: Sides, Angles, Diagonals, and Symmetries. Groups then share their lists with the class, and eventually, a class list for each category of shape will be developed.

For ELLs, emphasizing these words, having students say the words aloud, and having students point to each word as you say it are ways to reinforce meaning and support their participation and comprehension during the sharing time. For students with disabilities, provide a structured recording sheet with a table listing the headings. This will help organize their thinking around the many diverse possibilities.

Notice that students must assess whether the properties apply to all shapes in the category. If they are working on squares, for example, their observations must apply to a square mile as well as a square centimeter.

Level 2: Informal Deduction

The objects of thought at level 2 are the properties of shapes.

After students are able to think about the properties of geometric objects, they are ready to develop relationships between and among these properties. "If all four angles are right angles, the shape must be a rectangle. If it is a square, all angles are right angles. If it is a square, it must be a rectangle." Once students have greater ability to engage in "if–then" reasoning, they can classify shapes with a minimal set of defining characteristics. For example, four congruent sides and at least one right angle are sufficient to define a square. Observations extend beyond properties themselves and begin to focus on logical arguments *about* the properties. When your students are at level 2, they will be able to follow and appreciate informal deductive arguments about shapes and their properties.

The products of thought at level 2 are relationships among properties of geometric objects.

The hallmark of level 2 activities is the inclusion of informal logical reasoning. Since your students have developed an understanding of the various properties of shapes, it is now time for you to encourage conjecture and to ask "why?" or "what if?"

◀ *Activity* 13.2 **MINIMAL DEFINING LISTS**

This activity is a sequel to Activity 13.1, "Property Lists for Quadrilaterals." Once the class has agreed on property lists for the parallelogram, rhombus, rectangle, and square (and possibly the kite and trapezoid), post the lists. Have students work in groups to find "minimal defining lists" for each shape. This product will be a subset of all the properties listed for a shape. The term *defining* here means that any shape that has all the properties on the minimal defining list must be the defined shape. The term *minimal* means that if any single property is removed from the list, the list is no longer defining. For example, a minimal defining list for a square is a quadrilateral with (1) four congruent sides and (2) four right angles (two items on the list). If a shape has these two properties, it must be a square. But there are other minimal defining lists for a square, such as (1) all sides the same length and (2) perpendicular diagonals. Challenge students to find more than one minimal defining list for their shape.

◆ Standards for
Mathematical Practice

3 Construct
viable arguments
and critique the
reasoning of others ▶

A proposed list can be challenged as being either not minimal or not defining. A list is not defining if a counterexample—a shape other than one being described—can be produced by using only the properties on the list.

The hallmark of this and other level 2 thinking activities is the emphasis on logical reasoning. "*If* a quadrilateral has these properties, *then* it must be a square." Logic is also involved in proving that a list is faulty—either not minimal or not defining. Here, students begin to learn the nature of a definition and the value of counterexamples. The other aspect of this activity that clearly involves level 2 thinking is that students focus on analyzing the relationships between properties (e.g., if a quadrilateral has four right angles, it also has diagonals of the same length).

> **Teaching Tip**
>
> Use "if–then" sentence frames to help students analyze the relationships between properties. Or create a matching game of "if" statements and "then" statements.

Level 3: Deduction

The objects of thought at level 3 are relationships among properties of geometric objects.

At level 3, students analyze informal arguments; the structure of a system complete with axioms, definitions, theorems, corollaries, and postulates begins to develop; and they begin to appreciate the necessary means of establishing geometric truth. The student at this level is usually in high school and is able to work with abstract statements about geometric properties and make conclusions based on logic.

The products of thought at level 3 are deductive axiomatic systems for geometry.

Level 4: Rigor

The objects of thought at level 4 are deductive axiomatic systems for geometry.

At the highest level of the van Hiele hierarchy, the objects of attention are axiomatic systems themselves, not just the deductions within a system. This is generally the level of a college mathematics major who is studying geometry as a branch of mathematical science.

The products of thought at level 4 are comparisons and contrasts among different axiomatic systems of geometry.

 Formative Assessment Note

How do you discover the van Hiele level of each student? Once you know, how will you select the right activities to match your students' levels? As you conduct an activity, listen to the types of observations that students make and record them on a checklist. Can your students talk about shapes as classes? Do they refer, for example, to "rectangles," or do they base their discussion around a particular rectangle? Do they generalize that certain properties are attributable to a type of shape, or simply to the shape at hand? Do they understand that shapes do not change when the orientation changes? With simple observations such as these, you will soon be able to distinguish between levels 0, 1, and 2. If students are not able to follow logical arguments or make conjectures about the properties of shapes, they are likely at level 1 or below and will need interventions to prepare them for level 2.

◆ Implications for Instruction

As described in Figure 13.2, carefully selected and implemented tasks are the way to move students up through the levels of geometric thought. The geometry taught in high school is primarily at level 3, so a priority in middle school is to provide instruction to students so that they are at least strong level 2 thinkers, ready for success in high school and beyond. Many activities can be implemented to span two levels of thinking, helping students move from one level to the next.

Moving from Level 0 to Level 1

If middle-school students are still at level 0, they need targeted interventions that will move them to level 1. Memorization or drill is not the answer. Students need experiences that start at level 0 thinking and include introductory level 1 thinking. Instructional activities that support students' movement are as follows:

- *Challenge students to test ideas about shapes by using a variety of examples from a particular category.* Say, "Let's see if that is true for other rectangles," or "Can you draw a triangle that does *not* have a right angle?" In general, question students to see if the observations they make about a particular shape apply to other shapes of a similar kind.

- *Focus on the properties of figures rather than on simple identification.* As new geometric concepts are learned, students should be challenged to use these features to classify shapes.

- *Provide ample opportunities to draw, build, make, put together (compose), and take apart (decompose) shapes in both two and three dimensions.* These activities should be built around the understanding and use of specific characteristics or properties.

- *Apply ideas to entire classes of figures* (e.g., *all* rectangles, *all* prisms) *rather than to individual shapes in a set.* For example, find ways to sort all possible triangles into groups. From these groups, define types of triangles.

Dynamic geometry software, such as *The Geometer's Sketchpad* (from Key Curriculum Press) or the free public domain software from GeoGebra, is especially useful for exploring many examples of a class of shapes and is appropriate for middle-school students.

Moving from Level 1 to Level 2

Level 2 thinking should begin about grade 5, when students begin to classify two-dimensional figures based on their properties in large categories and subcategories. Middle-school students who are still at level 1 need to transition to level 2. The following strategies are effective interventions for moving from level 1 to level 2:

- *Challenge students to explore or test examples.* Ask questions such as these: "If the sides of a four-sided shape are all congruent, will you always have a square? Can you find a counterexample?"

- *Encourage the making and testing of hypotheses or conjectures.* "Do you think that will work all the time? Is that true for all triangles, or just equilateral triangles?"

- *Examine the properties of shapes to determine the necessary and sufficient conditions for a shape to be a particular shape.* "What properties must diagonals have to guarantee that a quadrilateral with these diagonals will be a square?"

- *Encourage students to attempt informal proofs.* As an alternative, require them to make sense of informal proofs that you or other students have suggested.

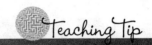

> Ask questions that use the language of informal deduction: *all, some, none, if–then, what if?* Place these prompts prominently on your walls (on posters) to encourage students to ask these questions as they work.

In each of the sections in this chapter ("Shapes and Properties," "Location," "Transformations," and "Visualization"), many activities are shared, and they follow the van Hiele levels of geometric thought. If one activity is beyond the reach of a student or a class, drop back to an earlier one. These four sections are quite fluid—that is, the content areas overlap and build on one another. Activities in one section may help develop geometric thinking in another area.

 Shapes and Properties

This is the content area most often associated with geometry in pre-K–grade 8 classrooms, when young students begin to "perceive, say, describe/discuss and construct objects in 2-D space" (National Research Council, 2009, p. 177).

Middle-school students need experience with a wide variety of two- and three-dimensional shapes. Polygons should not always be regular (all sides the same), and they should not always be shown with a base horizontal to the line on the paper in which it appears. (If you have students say a triangle is upside down, it is because they have rarely seen triangles illustrated differently.) Shapes should have curved sides, straight sides, and combinations of these. Along the way, as students describe the shape or property, the terminology can be introduced.

 Describing and Classifying Shapes

Even before children enter school, they begin sorting experiences. As they get older, they begin to classify the categories they have sorted. In the *Common Core State Standards*, classifying two-dimensional shapes into categories based on their properties (a level 1 thinking task) is a fifth-grade concept (with some sorting by properties in grades 3 and 4). In middle school, the categories of two-dimensional shapes are analyzed by determining the relationship between the sides and angles of a given shape, particularly triangles and quadrilaterals. The categories of two-dimensional shapes are provided in Table 13.1.

Activity 13.3 is a describing-and-classifying activity that can be at level 0 or level 1, depending on the shapes you place in the folder. It is therefore a good task for students who need more experiences in moving toward level 2 thinking.

 Activity **13.3** WHAT'S MY SHAPE?

Make a double set of two-dimensional shapes on card stock (two sets per group). You can use the shapes from Blackline Masters 24–30 (Figure 13.4) or other shapes. See, for example the NCTM Illuminations lesson "Shape Up" (http://illuminations.nctm.org/LessonDetail.aspx?id=L813), which includes a shapes template and a virtual sorting applet.

Cut out one set of shapes, and glue each shape inside a folded sheet of construction paper (or a file folder) to make a "secret-shape" folder. Cut out the other set and place it in an envelope or container.

Table 13.1   Categories of Two-Dimensional Shapes

Shape	Description
Simple Closed Curves	
Concave, convex	An intuitive definition of *concave* might be "having a dent in it." If a simple closed curve is not concave, it is convex. A more precise definition of *concave* may be interesting to explore with older students.
Symmetric, nonsymmetric	Shapes may have one or more lines of symmetry and may or may not have rotational symmetry. These concepts will require more detailed investigation.

Polygons
    Concave, convex
    Symmetric,
    nonsymmetric
    Regular
	Simple closed curves with all straight sides.
	
	All sides and all angles are congruent.

Triangles	
Triangles	Polygons with exactly three sides.

Classified by sides
    Equilateral
    Isosceles
    Scalene
	
	All sides are congruent.
	At least two sides are congruent.
	No two sides are congruent.

Classified by angles
    Right
    Acute
    Obtuse
	
	One angle is a right angle.
	All angles are smaller than a right angle.
	One angle is larger than a right angle.

Convex Quadrilaterals	

Convex quadrilaterals
    Kite
    Trapezoid
        Isosceles trapezoid
    Parallelogram
        Rectangle
        Rhombus
        Square
	Convex polygons with exactly four sides.
	Two opposing pairs of congruent adjacent sides.
	At least one pair of parallel sides.
	A pair of opposite sides is congruent.
	Two pairs of parallel sides.
	Parallelogram with a right angle.
	Parallelogram with all sides congruent.
	Parallelogram with a right angle and all sides congruent.

Figure 13.4

An assortment of shapes for sorting.

In a group or pair, one student is designated the leader and given a secret-shape folder. The other student(s) ask yes-or-no questions to figure out what the shape is. Students cannot point to a piece and ask, "Is it this one?" Instead, they ask questions such as these: "Does it have all straight sides? Is it concave?" The group looks at the shapes in the full set and eliminates shapes as they ask questions to narrow the possibilities. The final piece is checked against the one in the leader's folder. Students with disabilities or students who are not yet at level 1 thinking may need a list of possible properties and characteristics (e.g., number of sides) for support as they ask questions.

You can adapt Activity 13.3 to focus on types of triangles, types of quadrilaterals, or types of three-dimensional shapes (place three-dimensional shapes in an opaque bag). For three-dimensional shapes, use a collection of solids with a lot of variation (curved surfaces, etc.). Power Solids and other collections of three-dimensional shapes are available through various catalogs, or use real objects such as cans, containers, and balls. For the categories of two-dimensional shapes, see Figure 13.5.

 ## Formative Assessment Note

Activity 13.3 can be adapted to be a *diagnostic interview*. You hold the hidden shape and see what questions the students ask. The ways students describe two-dimensional shapes are good evidence of their level of geometric thinking. Level 0 thinkers may ask, "Is it a parallelogram?" (because it looks like a rectangle), while level 1 thinkers may ask the same question but see the shape as a group of shapes. When you respond yes, look to see if the students include squares and rectangles. If they do not, point at a rectangle and ask, "Is this a parallelogram?" With level 1 thinkers, you may also hear these questions: "Is it convex? Is it obtuse? Does it have line symmetry? Rotational symmetry?" These questions focus on the properties of shapes and indicate that the students are at level 1 thinking.

Seventh graders learn to draw geometric shapes with given conditions (CCSSO, 2010). Geoboards are excellent tools for building shapes with various properties or conditions and provide a way to scaffold to being able to draw shapes freehand. Rather than draw and erase sketches with a geoboard, you simply move the rubber band.

 ### Teaching Tip

To avoid rubber band "incidents," require that students place a thumb over the peg where they first place the rubber band. This way, if the rubber band comes off as they stretch it, it will stay on their thumb.

Activity 13.4 CAN YOU MAKE IT?

Create a collection of challenges. Each challenge describes one or more properties of a shape, and the student challenge is to create a shape with these properties on the geoboard. The list of properties of shapes that follows is only a sample. Try combining two or more properties to create new challenges. Also, have students create challenges that can be posted for others to try.

- A shape with just one square corner and four sides
- A shape with two square corners (or three, four, five, or six square corners)
- A shape with one line of symmetry (or two lines of symmetry)
- A shape with two pairs of parallel lines
- A shape with two pairs of parallel lines and no right angles

If the class keeps track of solutions to the challenges in the last activity, there is an added possibility of creating classes of shapes with certain properties, resulting in definitions of new classes of shapes. The list (like the one above) can also include impossible tasks—for example, a four-sided shape with exactly three right angles. Finally, a connection to measurement can be added. Tasks can include the requirement of having a particular area or a particular perimeter, or both. Measurement tasks can be easily joined with geometric tasks.

Figure **13.5** Categories of two-dimensional shapes.

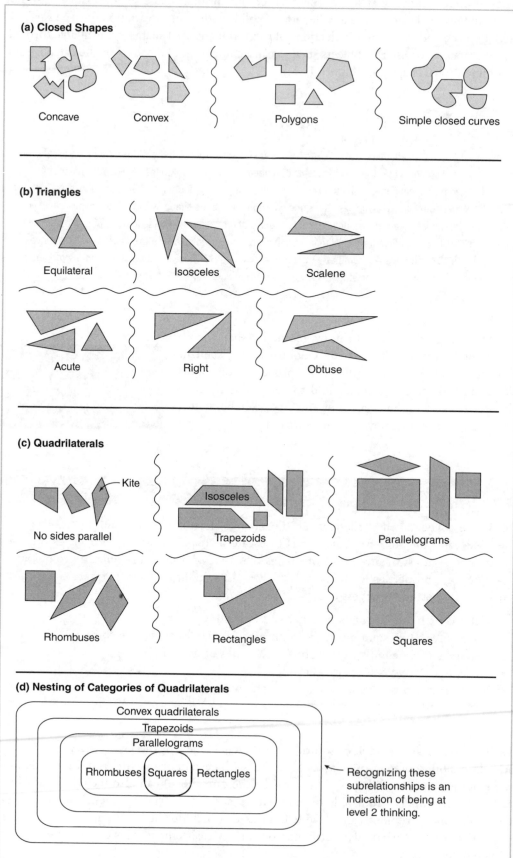

(a) Closed Shapes

Concave   Convex   Polygons   Simple closed curves

(b) Triangles

Equilateral   Isosceles   Scalene

Acute   Right   Obtuse

(c) Quadrilaterals

Kite

No sides parallel   Isosceles   Trapezoids   Parallelograms

Rhombuses   Rectangles   Squares

(d) Nesting of Categories of Quadrilaterals

Convex quadrilaterals
Trapezoids
Parallelograms
Rhombuses | Squares | Rectangles

Recognizing these subrelationships is an indication of being at level 2 thinking.

Classifying Triangles

Determining types of triangles is introduced in grade 4 with the concept of right triangles. It is then emphasized in seventh grade, where the focus is on properties based on the measures of the sides and angles (CCSSO, 2010). Figure 13.5b illustrates the categories of triangles. Activity 13.5 explores all the ways to classify triangles.

Activity 13.5   TRIANGLE SORT

Make copies of the "Assorted Triangles" sheet (Blackline Master 31). Note the examples of right, acute, and obtuse triangles; examples of equilateral, isosceles, and scalene triangles; and triangles that represent every possible combination of these categories. Have students cut them out. Ask students to sort the entire collection into three groups so that no triangle belongs to two groups. When this is done and descriptions of the groups have been written, students should find a second criterion for creating three different groups. Students with disabilities may need a hint to look only at angle sizes or only at the issue of congruent sides, but delay giving these hints if you can.

Once the groups have been determined, provide appropriate terminology. For ELLs and other students who may struggle with the vocabulary, it is important to focus on the specialized meanings of the terms (e.g., contrasting *acute pain* and *acute angle*) as well as on root words (*equi-* meaning "equal" and *-lateral* meaning "side"). As a follow-up activity, challenge students to sketch a triangle in each of the nine cells of the chart.

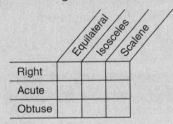

	Equilateral	Isosceles	Scalene
Right			
Acute			
Obtuse			

Stop and Reflect

Of the nine cells in the chart, two of them are impossible to fill. Can you tell which ones and why? ∎

Activity 13.5 can also be explored with a piece of string. Ask students to create a triangle with specific conditions, like two congruent sides and one obtuse angle.

An important aspect of looking at types of triangles in seventh grade is to consider when given conditions result in a unique triangle, more than one triangle, or no triangle. For example, an equilateral triangle with sides of 4 cm is unique, a triangle with two sides the same and one angle the same can be made in many ways, and a triangle with two obtuse angles is impossible to make.

Activity 13.4, "Can You Make It?" can also be adapted to explore the conditions of triangles. Adapt the list of properties to read, "A triangle with," and then add the question, "How many ways?"

Can you make a triangle with one 90-degree angle and two sides of 5 cm and 8 cm? How many ways?

Can you make a triangle with two angles of 45 degrees? How many ways?

Can you make a triangle with sides of 4 cm, 8 cm, and 13 cm? How many ways?

Notice that these examples address both sides and angles (or a combination). You can also identify a single problem for investigation, pressing students to prove (informally, through the use of tools) whether the conditions make the triangle unique or not, as in these next two examples.

ARE THESE TRIANGLES UNIQUE?

A right triangle with legs of 3 units and 4 units

An isosceles triangle with an 80-degree angle and a side of 5 units

 *Teaching Tip*

Once right triangles are introduced, the term *legs* is used for the two sides adjacent to the right angle, and the term *hypotenuse* is used to name the third side. Encourage students to use this language when discussing right triangles.

Students need many experiences with such activities (with triangles and other polygons). Thinking about how the conditions of a triangle define it is the foundation for high school geometry, in which, for example, students prove why angle-side-angle (ASA) makes a triangle unique. In doing transformations and scale drawings in middle school, students are better able to recognize what is true about congruent and similar shapes.

Middle-school students should explore the relationship of angles within a triangle (adding to 180 degrees). They should also use facts about supplementary, complementary, vertical, and adjacent angles to solve for an unknown angle in a figure (CCSSO, 2010). Activity 13.6 explores interior angles.

◄ *Activity* **13.6** **ANGLE SUMS IN A TRIANGLE**

Ask students to cut out three congruent triangles. (Stack three sheets of paper, and cut three shapes at one time.) Label each triangle with angles a, b, and c, making sure the corresponding angles are labeled with the same letter. Place one triangle on a line and the second directly next to it in the same orientation. Place the third triangle in the space between the triangles, as shown in Figure 13.6a. Ask, "Will this relationship be true for

Figure **13.6** Interior and exterior angles of triangles can be explored with various tools.

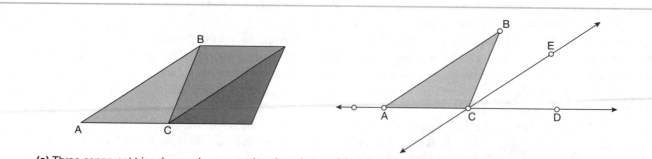

(a) Three congruent triangles can be arranged to show that the sum of the interior angles will always be a straight angle or 180 degrees.

(b) Draw CE parallel to AB. Why is angle BAC congruent to angle ECD? Why is angle ABC congruent to angle BCE?

any kind of triangle?" Have them make two more triangles (in triplicate) that are different from each other to answer the question. Based on this experience, what conjecture can you make about the sum of the angles in a triangle?

Technology can be an important tool in exploring these relationships. In a dynamic geometry program, the three triangles in Figure 13.6a can be drawn by starting with one triangle, translating it to the right the length of AC, and then rotating the same triangle about the midpoint of side BC. When the vertices of the original triangle are dragged, the other triangles will change accordingly and remain congruent. Although this exploration demonstrates to students that the angle sum is always a straight angle, it does not show them why. This requires examining exterior angles, as illustrated in Figure 13.6b. Students can look at relationships among the interior and exterior angles, making and testing conjectures, which builds important foundations for the proofs they will do in high school.

Activity 13.7 is another example of a way to informally investigate important properties of triangles. (Also see the Expanded Lesson at the end of this chapter.)

▶ *Activity* **13.7 TRIANGLE MIDSEGMENTS**

Using a dynamic geometry program, draw a triangle, and label the vertices A, B, and C. Draw the segment joining the midpoints of AB and AC, and label this segment DE (Figure 13.7). Measure the lengths of DE and BC. Also measure angles ADE and ABC. Drag points A, B, and C. What conjectures can you make about the relationships between segment DE (the midsegment of triangle ABC) and segment BC (the base of triangle ABC)?

Figure 13.7
The midsegment of a triangle is always parallel to the base and half as long.

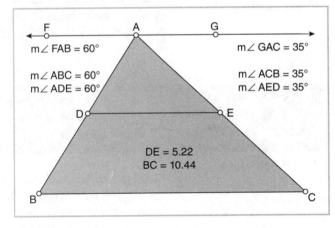

The midsegment is half the length of the base and parallel to it. Students can explore why this is so by drawing a line through point A parallel to BC. List all pairs of angles that they know are congruent. Why are they congruent? Note that triangle ABC is similar to triangle ADE. Why is it similar? Encourage students to make logical arguments for why the things they observe to be true are in fact true for any triangle.

Classifying Quadrilaterals

Like triangles, quadrilaterals have subcategories with names (see Figure 13.5c). The activities described previously can be used to explore quadrilaterals as well as triangles. An important and difficult concept within quadrilaterals is how they relate to one another—for example, which is a subcategory of which? (See Figure 13.5d.) This concept is a focus of fifth grade in the *Common Core State Standards* expectations but continues to be important in seventh grade, as students explore the conditions that make a shape unique, possible, or impossible. The minimal defining list in Activity 13.2 begins to address these relationships. The next activity uses examples and non-examples to explore the subcategories.

Figure **13.8** Solve the mystery. What do these shapes have in common?

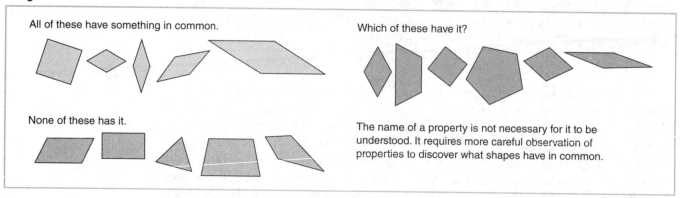

Through activities like "Mystery Definition" with two- and three-dimensional shapes, students develop informal definitions based on their own analysis of relevant properties. Developing such definitions should be a meaning-making experience, not a memorizing task.

Figure 13.5a–c illustrates various categories of two-dimensional shapes, any of which can be used for "Mystery Definition." After students' definitions have been discussed and compared, you can compare their ideas with the common definition for each shape and determine whether their definitions captured all of the necessary aspects of the shape and stated them precisely.

Quadrilaterals are an especially rich source of investigations. In addition to Activity 13.8, "Mystery Definition," Activities 13.1 and 13.2, "Property Lists for Quadrilaterals" and "Minimal Defining Lists," focus on having students generate definitions and compare them with the common definition for each shape. In defining shapes, it is important for students to explore which of these shapes are subcategories of other shapes (e.g., squares are a subset of rectangles). This is a fifth-grade expectation in the *Common Core State Standards* but is particularly difficult for students (and adults) and likely will need to be revisited through middle school. Figure 13.5d illustrates the nesting of categories of quadrilaterals.

Three-dimensional figures also have subcategories (Figures 13.9 and 13.10). Important and interesting relationships exist in three dimensions, and these relationships are important in measurements such as surface area and volume. Table 13.2 describes the categories of solids (Zwillinger, 2011).

As new relationships come up in student presentations and related discussions of defining properties, you can introduce proper terminology.

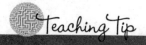

► **3 Construct viable arguments and critique the reasoning of others**

Activity **13.8** **MYSTERY DEFINITION**

Use a projection device to conduct the "Mystery Definition" activities, such as the examples in Figure 13.8. With your first collection, be certain that you have allowed for all possible variables. In Figure 13.8, for example, a square is included in the set of rhombi. Similarly, choose non-examples to be as close to the positive examples as is necessary to help with an accurate definition. The third, or mixed, set should include shapes with which students are most likely to be confused. For each shape in the third set, students should justify their choices in a class discussion. This activity can also be used with three-dimensional figures. Note that the use of non-examples is particularly important for students with disabilities.

Teaching Tip

The word *definition* is not used in the CCSS for grades 6–8, but informal definitions lay the foundation for learning precise definitions in high school geometry.

► **6 Attend to precision**

Figure 13.9 Defining and categorizing cylinders and prisms (Zwillinger, 2011).

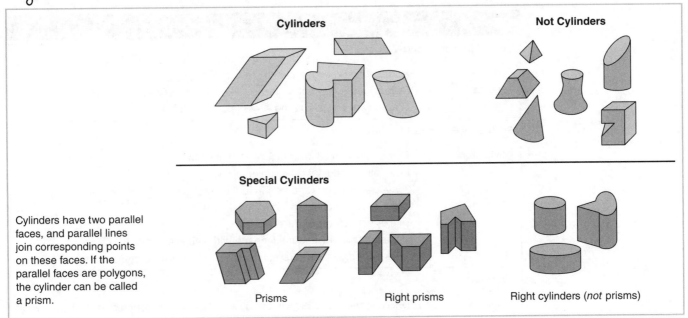

Cylinders have two parallel faces, and parallel lines join corresponding points on these faces. If the parallel faces are polygons, the cylinder can be called a prism.

Figure 13.10 Cones and pyramids.

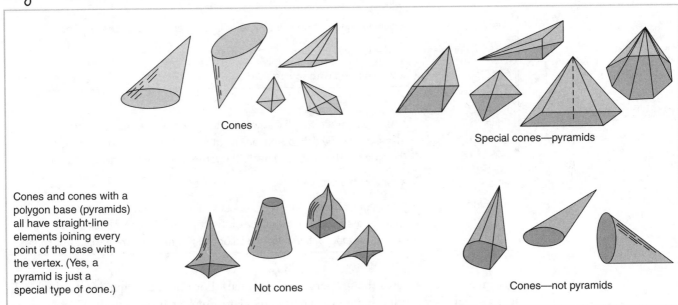

Cones and cones with a polygon base (pyramids) all have straight-line elements joining every point of the base with the vertex. (Yes, a pyramid is just a special type of cone.)

For example, if two diagonals intersect such that they form 90-degree angles, then they are *perpendicular*. Other terms, such as *parallel, congruent, bisect,* and *midpoint,* can be clarified as you help students write their descriptions. This is also a good time to introduce symbols, such as ≈ for *congruent* and || for *parallel*.

Recall that at van Hiele level 2, the focus of thought shifts to properties for categories of shapes. At this level, it is essential to encourage conjecture and explore informal deductive arguments. Middle-school students should begin to understand and use simple proofs. Let's revisit Activity 13.2, "Minimal Defining Lists," which is a level 2 activity. The parallelogram, rhombus, rectangle, and square all have at least four minimal defining lists. One of the less obvious but

Teaching Tip

Vocabulary support can also occur in the *After* phase of the lesson, not just in the *Before* phase. This allows vocabulary to grow out of students' meaningful experiences.

𝒯𝒶𝒷𝓁ℯ **13.2** Categories of Three-Dimensional Shapes

Shape	Description
Sorted by Edges and Vertices	
Sphere and "egglike" shapes	Shapes with no *edges* and no *vertices* (corners). Shapes with *edges* but no *vertices* (e.g., a flying saucer). Shapes with *vertices* but no *edges* (e.g., a football).
Sorted by Faces and Surfaces	
Polyhedron	Shapes made of all faces (a *face* is a flat surface of a solid). If all surfaces are faces, all the edges will be straight lines. Some combination of faces and rounded surfaces (cylinders are examples, but this is not a definition of a cylinder). Shapes with curved surfaces. Shapes with and without edges and with and without vertices. Faces can be parallel. Parallel faces lie in places that never intersect.
Cylinders	
Cylinder	Two congruent, parallel faces called *bases*. Lines joining corresponding points on the two bases are always parallel. These parallel lines are called *elements* of the cylinder.
Right cylinder	A cylinder with elements perpendicular to the bases. A cylinder that is not a right cylinder is an *oblique cylinder.*
Prism	A cylinder with polygons for bases. All prisms are special cases of cylinders.
Rectangular prism	A cylinder with rectangles for bases.
Cube	A square prism with square sides.
Cones	
Cone	A solid with exactly one face and a vertex that is not on the face. Straight lines (elements) can be drawn from any point on the edge of the base to the vertex. The base may be any shape at all. The vertex need not be directly over the base.
Circular cone	A cone with a circular base.
Pyramid	A cone with a polygon for a base. All faces joining the vertex are triangles. Pyramids are named by the shape of the base: *triangular* pyramid, *square* pyramid, *octagonal* pyramid, and so on. All pyramids are special cases of cones.

very interesting lists uses the properties of diagonals. For example, a quadrilateral with diagonals that bisect each other and are perpendicular (intersect at right angles) is a rhombus. Activity 13.9 explores the properties of diagonals in two-dimensional shapes.

◀▲ 𝒜𝒸𝓉𝒾𝓋𝒾𝓉𝓎 **13.9** **DIAGONAL DESIGNATIONS**

For this activity, students need three strips of card stock about 2 cm wide. Two strips should be of the same length (about 30 cm), and the third should be shorter (about 20 cm). Punch nine holes equally spaced along the strip. (Punch a hole near each end. Divide the distance between the holes by 8. This will be the distance between the remaining holes.) Use a brass fastener to join two strips. A quadrilateral is formed by joining the four holes (Figure 13.11). Provide students with the following list of possible

Figure 13.11

Handmade strips can be used to explore diagonals (and other properties) of shapes.

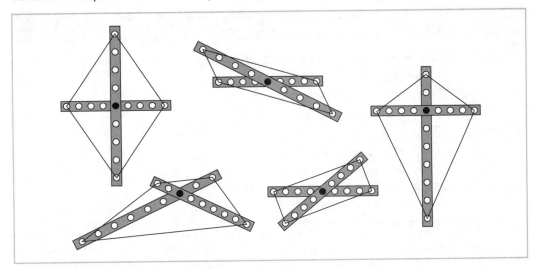

relationships to investigate for quadrilaterals. For ELLs, provide a list of the quadrilaterals with pictures next to the names of the various shapes (or refer them to a word wall or journal entry with each option). Ask, "What quadrilaterals can these diagonals form?"

- Diagonals that are the same length
- Diagonals that are perpendicular
- Diagonals that bisect each other
- Diagonals that are perpendicular and of the same length

Students use the strips to build shapes that fit these conditions. They may want to make shapes on geoboards or dot paper, or they can use dynamic geometry software to explore the tasks and test hypotheses. With dynamic software (e.g., *The Geometer's Sketchpad* or *GeoGebra*), objects can be moved and manipulated easily. Lines can be drawn and designated as perpendicular, or a point can be placed as the midpoint of a segment. The most significant idea is that when a geometric object is created with a particular relationship to another, that relationship is maintained no matter how either object is moved or changed. This is a very powerful way to see how diagonals relate to the type of quadrilateral formed. Some students will work with the diagonal relationships to see what shapes can be made. Others will begin with examples of the shapes and observe the diagonal relationships.

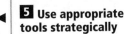

Standards for
Mathematical Practice

◀ **5** Use appropriate tools strategically

Notice that the "Minimal Defining List" and "Diagonal Designations" activities focus on the relationships among properties within a shape. Students are engaged in the general process of deciding the following question: "If we specify only this list of properties, will that guarantee this particular shape?" These tasks provide a rich opportunity to discuss what constitutes a definition and to develop foundations for informal proofs.

Stop and Reflect

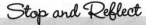

Use the property list for squares and rectangles to prove that all squares are rectangles. Notice that you must use logical reasoning to understand this statement. It does little good simply to force definitions on students who are not ready to develop the relationship. ■

The next activity is also a good follow-up to "Minimal Defining Lists" and requires level 2 thinking about shapes and properties.

Activity 13.10 TRUE OR FALSE?

Prepare statements such as the following: "If it is a _____, then it is also a _____. All are _____. Some are _____." A few examples are suggested here, but numerous possibilities exist.

- If it is a square, then it is a rhombus.
- All squares are rectangles.
- Some parallelograms are rectangles.
- All parallelograms have congruent diagonals.
- If it has exactly two lines of symmetry, it must be a quadrilateral.
- If it is a cylinder, then it is a prism.
- All pyramids have square bases.

Select several of these for investigation. Students determine whether the statements are true or false and in the *After* phase of the lesson present an argument to support their decision. Once this format is understood, let students challenge their classmates by making their own statement(s). Extend to three-dimensional shapes. Each list should have a mix of true and false statements. Students' lists can be used in subsequent lessons, with a focus on informal ways to prove whether a statement is true or false.

◆ Standards for Mathematical Practice

3 Construct viable arguments and critique the reasoning of others

 *Teaching Tip*

In number and algebra, students make conjectures about properties of operations (see Chapter 12, p. 240); in geometry, students make conjectures about properties of shapes. When a student makes an observation or a statement about a geometric concept, write it the board. Ask, "Is it always true? How can we prove it?"

Polygons

Although more attention is given to triangles and quadrilaterals, middle-school students should also explore various polygons, examining their properties and the conditions that make such shapes unique or possible. In addition, investigating polygons is a good connection to generalizations and algebraic thinking (see Chapter 12 for examples of geometric growing patterns). The next task engages students in exploring patterns and developing informal proof. It is excellent for eighth graders because it connects to both function and geometry expectations.

◆ Standards for Mathematical Practice

3 Construct viable arguments and critique the reasoning of others

Draw a line through a polygon to form two new polygons. Is there a relationship between the number of sides of the original polygon and the number of sides of the two new polygons? For example, the accompanying pentagon has been partitioned into a quadrilateral and a pentagon.

The number of sides of the original shape was five, and the number of sides of the two new shapes (combined) is nine. Will a pentagon always form two shapes with a sum of nine sides? Is there a relationship between the starting number of sides and the ending number of sides? Does the pattern for pentagons extend to other shapes? Make a conjecture, and prepare a justification for why you think it is true.

Source: Adapted from Sconyers, J. M. (1995). Proof and the middle school mathematics student. *Mathematics Teaching in the Middle School, 1*(7), 516–518.

The number of resulting sides depends on where the slice is made (from a vertex or from a side). With the exception of triangles, there are three possibilities. For each case, a pattern emerges across polygons.

◆ Composing and Decomposing Shapes

Students must see shapes as composed of other shapes. This work begins as early as first grade and is an important component in middle school, where students are ex-pected to decompose shapes in order to measure sur-face area and volume (addressed in Chapter 14). In addition, in grade 7, students compose (draw) shapes in order to study the properties of the shape: "Draw (freehand, with ruler and protractor, and with tech-nology) geometric shapes with given conditions. Focus on constructing triangles from three measures of angles or sides, noticing when the conditions deter-mine a unique triangle, more than one triangle, or no triangle" (CCSSO, 2010, p. 50).

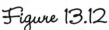

Provide free exploration time with these manipulatives before starting a task—it helps students notice how the shapes are related and minimizes off-task behaviors with the pieces dur-ing the lesson.

Students need to explore freely how shapes fit together to form larger shapes (com-pose) and how larger shapes can be taken apart into smaller shapes (decompose). Pattern blocks and tangrams (see Blackline Master 32) are good tools for composing and decomposing shapes. Less known, but very interesting, is the mosaic puzzle (van Hiele, 1999), which contains five different angles (lend-ing to discussions of types of angle measures). Figure 13.12 illustrates the different tools and provides an ex-ample of a template that you can make.

BLM

Figure 13.12

Tools for exploring composing and decomposing shapes.

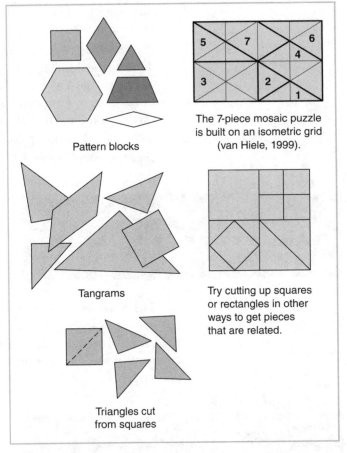

Pattern blocks

The 7-piece mosaic puzzle is built on an isometric grid (van Hiele, 1999).

Tangrams

Try cutting up squares or rectangles in other ways to get pieces that are related.

Triangles cut from squares

technology note

Tangram geometry activities and puzzles are readily available on the Internet. For example, "Logicville" (www.logicville.com /tangram.htm) posts lessons for geometry and fractions, as well as dozens of tangram puzzles that can be composed with an applet. The National Library of Virtual Manipulatives (http://nlvm .usu.edu) also offers a tangram applet with a set of 14 puzzle figures. Sharing these websites with families through newsletters can encourage students to solve such puzzles at home.

The geoboard is one of the best devices for com-posing and decomposing two-dimensional shapes, and middle-school students find it highly engaging. The geoboard, for example, would be an excellent tool for ex-ploring the splitting-a-polygon task described previously. There are many possible activities to develop facility with composing and decomposing shapes. Activity 13.4, "Can You Make It?" is a good example. Geoboard activities can also be done on dot or grid paper. Allow students to choose the tool (geoboard, grid paper, dot paper, or blank paper) that best supports their thinking for the given problem.

Commercial materials, such as Geoshapes and Polydron, permit the creative construc-tion of geometric solids. They include plastic polygons that can be snapped together to

Standards for Mathematical Practice

◄ **3** Use appropriate tools strategically

technology note

There are excellent electronic versions of the geoboard. One of them, found at the National Library of Virtual Manipulatives (http://nlvm.usu.edu), includes an option to calculate perimeter and area of a shape. The University of Illinois Office for Mathematics, Science, and Technology Education (http://mste.illinois.edu/users/pavel/java/geoboard) has a virtual geoboard with a clickable option that shows the lengths of the sides of the figure.

make three-dimensional models. With the Zome System, sticks and connectors are used to form three-dimensional skeletal shapes. Students are able to "see" slices of a shape by holding a card at various angles, which demonstrates what two-dimensional shape would be formed if the card fit exactly inside the three-dimensional shape in the designated position. Homemade constructions can be highly engaging for middle-school students. Here are three excellent options for skeletal models:

- *Plastic coffee stirrers with pipe cleaners.* Plastic stirrers can be easily cut to different lengths. To connect the corners, cut the pipe cleaners into 2-inch lengths. These are inserted into the ends of the stirrers.

- *Plastic bendable drinking straws.* With scissors, cut the straws lengthwise from the top down to the flexible joint. The slit ends can then be inserted into the uncut bottom ends of other straws, making a strong but flexible joint. Three or more straws are joined in this fashion to form two-dimensional polygons. To make three-dimensional shapes, use wire twist ties to join polygons side to side.

- *Rolled newspaper rods.* Fantastic large three-dimensional shapes can be built with newspaper and masking tape. Roll three large sheets of newspaper on the diagonal to form a rod. The more tightly the paper is rolled, the less likely the rod is to bend. Secure the roll at the center with a piece of tape. The ends of the rod are thin and flexible for about 6 inches, where there is less paper. Connect rods by bunching and taping (use a lot of tape!) the thin parts together. Additional rods can be joined after two or three are already taped (Figure 13.13).

Teaching Tip

Asking students to create such homemade three-dimensional shapes can be an excellent homework assignment, especially if they have a model created in class to use as a reminder of how to build it.

The newspaper rod method is exciting because the structures quickly become large. Let students work in groups of four or five. They will soon discover what makes a structure rigid and will acquire ideas of balance and form. (They can also create poster-size two-dimensional slices to insert inside these shapes, as discussed in the "Visualization" section of this chapter.)

Teaching Tip

One way to acknowledge the importance of the Pythagorean theorem is through learning about Pythagorus. Try *Mathematical Scandals* by Theoni Pappas, or find interesting facts online.

◆ Pythagorean Theorem

The *Pythagorean theorem*, explored in eighth grade, is one of the most important mathematical relationships and warrants in-depth conceptual investigation. In geometric terms, this relationship states that if a square is constructed on each side of a right triangle, the areas of the two smaller squares will together equal the area of the square on the longest side, the hypotenuse.

Figure 13.13

Large, skeletal, three-dimensional shapes can be made from newspapers and used to look at the shapes of slices through them.

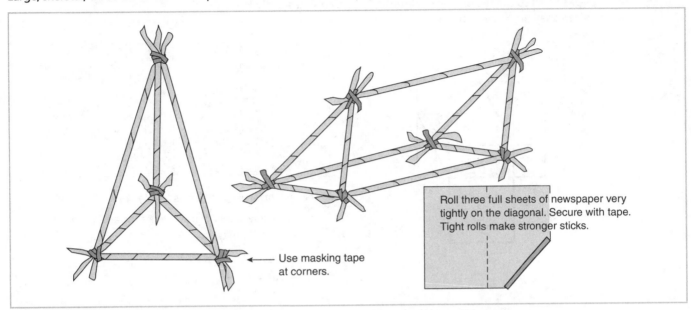

Use masking tape at corners.

Roll three full sheets of newspaper very tightly on the diagonal. Secure with tape. Tight rolls make stronger sticks.

Activity 13.11 THE PYTHAGOREAN RELATIONSHIP

BLM

Have students draw a right triangle on half-centimeter grid paper (see Blackline Master 5). Assign each student a different triangle by specifying the lengths of the two legs. Students are to draw a square on each leg and on the hypotenuse and find the areas of all three squares. (For the square on the hypotenuse, the exact area can be found by making each of the sides the diagonal of a rectangle.) See Figure 13.14. Make a table of the area data (square on leg a, square on leg b, square on hypotenuse c), and ask students to look for a relationship between the squares.

Standards for Mathematical Practice

◄ **4 Model with mathematics**

The two large, congruent squares in Figure 13.15 together show a proof of the Pythagorean theorem (Nelson, 2001). Note that both squares contain four triangles that are the same but arranged differently. If the areas of the squares and the triangles are added and set equal, the Pythagorean relationship can be found by subtracting out the common areas in both squares. An algebraic recording of the thinking process is shown below the drawings. Instead of using a, b, and c, students can explore the relationship with examples. Pythagorean triples work well for this (e.g., 3-4-5, 6-8-10, or 5-12-13).

Standards for Mathematical Practice

◄ **2 Reason abstractly and quantitatively**

technology note

For an NCTM Illuminations applet, "Proof without Words: Pythagorean Theorem," see http://illuminations .nctm.org/ActivityDetail.aspx?ID=30.

Eighth graders should be familiar with Pythagorean triples. Any set of three whole numbers that satisfy the Pythagorean theorem is called a *Pythagorean triple*. Pythagorean triples occur often in geometry tasks and are often "disguised" as multiples of commonly recognized triples.

Figure 13.14

The Pythagorean relationship. The areas of all squares can be calculated when they are drawn on a grid.

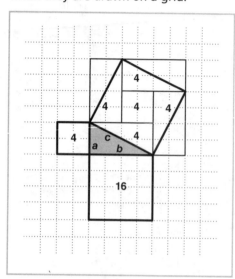

Figure 13.15

The two squares together form a "proof without words." Can you supply the words?

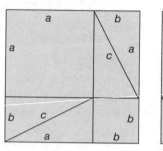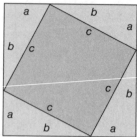

The area of the large square is $(a + b)^2 = a^2 + 2ab + b^2$.

The same area is also c^2 plus 4 times the area of one triangle.

$$= c^2 + 4\left(\tfrac{1}{2}ab\right) = c^2 + 2ab$$

So $c^2 + 2ab = a^2 + 2ab + b^2$.

$$c^2 = a^2 + b^2.$$

◆ Standards for
Mathematical Practice

4 Look for and
make use of structure

▶

◆ Standards for
Mathematical Practice

8 Look for and
express regularity in
repeated reasoning

▶

Activity 13.12   FINDING PYTHAGOREAN TRIPLES: 3-4-5 IN DISGUISE

Begin with the most common Pythagorean triple, 3-4-5. Ask, "Will triangles that are similar to the 3-4-5 triangle also be Pythagorean triples?" Give students a ruler, grid paper, and a calculator (or have them explore the options with dynamic geometric software). Ask students to find at least three triples that form triangles similar to the 3-4-5 triangle. (Note: There are infinitely many, so once students notice a pattern, stop the exploration and discuss strategies for how to recognize the 3-4-5 in disguise.)

Recognizing Pythagorean triples saves the step of having to use the Pythagorean theorem to find the length of a missing side.

---

1. Banners are being hung around the classroom to celebrate the upcoming championship game. Each banner is a meter wide. How many banners need to be purchased to go end to end around the perimeter of the room?

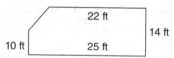

2. Find the perimeter of the trapezoid.

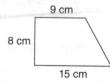

These two tasks both have a Pythagorean triple relationship that leads to finding the missing side. But these types of tasks should be mixed with tasks that use numbers that are not Pythagorean triples.

Transformations

Transformations are changes in the position or size of a shape and are a major focus of eighth grade in the *Common Core State Standards*. Movements that do not change the size or shape of the object moved are called *rigid motions*. *Translations, reflections,* and *rotations* are rigid transformations that result in congruent shapes (Figure 13.16). *Dilations* preserve shape, but not size, and therefore result in similar shapes. Students need to know how to recognize and construct each transformation, and particular information (set in italics) is required for each transformation if it is to be performed.

Translation

A translation requires a *direction* and a *distance*. In a translation, every point on the preimage moves in the same direction for the same distance to form the image. In middle school, this may be a move of "up 2 and over 3" on the coordinate axis.

Reflection

A reflection requires a *line of reflection*. A reflection is a transformation in which an object is flipped across a line of reflection. The line of symmetry can be the *x*-axis or the *y*-axis, or any other line. If a shape is reflected over the *y*-axis, for example, the *x*-values of the preimage are the opposite of the *x*-values of the image, and the *y*-values in both images are the same.

Rotation

A rotation requires a *center of rotation (point)* and a *degree of rotation*. The point can be any point on the coordinate axis, although in middle school, rotation around the origin is most common. A figure can be rotated up to 360 degrees.

Beginning work with transformations can involve sketches on paper, without the use of a coordinate axis, as in Activity 13.13.

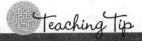

Teaching Tip

Build meaning for the words *translation*, *reflection*, and *rotation* by connecting each one to ideas associated with the word in everyday language. For example, the earth *rotates* around the sun.

Figure 13.16 Translation, reflection, and rotation.

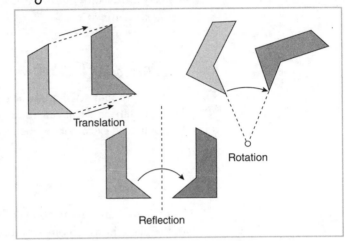

Figure 13.17

Motion Man can be used to begin an exploration of transformations.

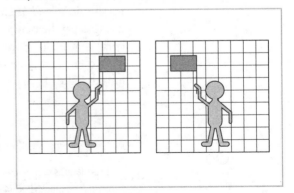

Activity 13.13 MOTION MAN

 Using Blackline Masters 33 and 34, make copies of the first Motion Man, and then copy the mirror image on the backs of these copies (Figure 13.17). You want the back image to match the front image when the paper is held to the light. Give all students a two-sided Motion Man.

Give students the required criteria for each type of transformation, and ask them to trace it on paper. For example, for the translation, students need to know distance and direction. Write or say, "Translate Motion Man 4 inches right and 2 inches down." A reflection requires a line. Write or say, "Draw a vertical or horizontal line and reflect Motion Man over that line."

A rotation requires a center and a degree measure. Write or say, "The center of Motion Man is the center of rotation; rotate him 90 degrees (clockwise)." For all students, ELLs in particular, it is important that these demonstrations include explicit practice with the terms and that visuals are posted for reference. Practice by having everyone start with his or her Motion Man in the same orientation. As you announce one of the moves, students translate, reflect, or rotate Motion Man accordingly.

As a follow-up, display two Motion Men side by side in any orientation. The task is to decide what motion or combination of motions will get the man on the left to match the man on the right. Students use their own man to work out a solution. Test the solutions that students offer.

Stop and Reflect

In the previous activity, instructions were given for one way to do each transformation. What slight shifts in the directions can adapt this task to provide more and different experiences for students to explore translations, reflections, and rotations in meaningful ways? ■

⬡ Tessellations

Tessellations are a motivating and artistic application of transformations. A *tessellation* is a tiling of the plane in which one or more shapes appear in a repeating pattern with no gaps or overlaps (Figure 13.18a). Tessellations are based on the circle—if the angle measures add up to 360 degrees, the shapes will fit together at a vertex with no overlaps or gaps. A *regular tessellation* is made of a single polygon. Therefore, only certain polygons can be used for regular tessellations.

Stop and Reflect

Which regular polygons can be used to form regular tessellations? Which combinations of polygons can be used to form semi-regular tessellations? ■

A regular triangle (equilateral) has angles of 60 degrees, so six triangles can form a tessellation. Likewise, four squares can form a tessellation, and so can three regular hexagons.

A *semi-regular tessellation* is made of two or more different regular polygons. These tessellations are defined by the series of shapes meeting at a vertex. An excellent activity for middle-school students is to explore which polygons can form a semi-regular tessellation and design their own illustration of that tessellation (Figure 13.18b).

The Dutch artist M. C. Escher is well-known for his tessellations, in which the tiles are very intricate and often shaped like birds, horses, or lizards. Escher took a simple shape such as a triangle, parallelogram, or hexagon and performed transformations on the sides. For example, a curve drawn along one side might be *translated* (slid) to the opposite side (Figure 13.18c). If the altered line is rotated to an adjacent side, the shape will also be tessellated, and the objects will look as if they have turned. Once a tile has been designed, it can be traced over and over again.

Tessellations can be created by hand or with technology. See, for example, "Semi-regular Tessellations" at http://nrich.maths.org/4832 or "Tessellate!" at www.shodor.org/interactivate/activities/Tessellate.

Figure 13.18 Regular and semi-regular tessellations with polygons.

(a) Regular Tessellations

  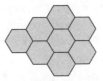

(b) Semi-Regular Tessellations

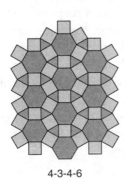  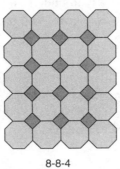 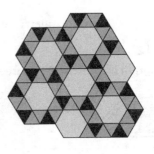

4-3-4-6   3-4-3-3-4   8-8-4   3-3-3-3-6

(c) Altering a Parallelogram to Create an Escher-Like Design

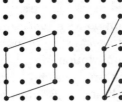 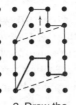  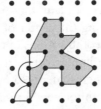

1. Start with a simple shape.

2. Draw the same curve on two opposite sides. This tile will stack up in columns.

3. Rotate a curve on the midpoint of one side.

4. Rotate a curve on the midpoint of the other side. Use this tile for tessellation (below).

A column of this tile will now match a like column that is rotated one complete turn. Find these rotated columns in the tessellation below.

◆ Symmetry

Symmetry is established through transformations. If a shape can be folded on a line so that the two halves match exactly, then it is said to have *line symmetry* (or *mirror symmetry*). Notice that the fold line is actually a *line of reflection*—the portion of the shape on one side of the line is reflected onto the other side.

A shape has *rotational symmetry* (also referred to as *point symmetry*) if it can be *rotated* about a point and land in a position exactly matching the one in which it began. A square has rotational symmetry, as does an equilateral triangle.

A good way to understand rotational symmetry is to take a shape with rotational symmetry, such as a square, and trace around it on a piece of paper. Call this tracing the shape's "footprint." The order of rotational symmetry will be the number of ways in which the shape can fit into its footprint without being flipped over. The parallelogram in Figure 13.19 has *180-degree rotational symmetry*. The degrees refer to the smallest angle of rotation required before the shape matches itself or fits into its footprint. A square has *90-degree rotational symmetry*.

Figure 13.19

A parallelogram is rotated 180 degrees.

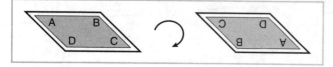

◆ Composition of Transformations

There are many ways in which Motion Man can be used for a single transformation (e.g., changing the center of rotation or line of reflection). Motion Man can also be used to explore combinations of translations (called *compositions of translations*)—for example, reflected over a line and then translated 3 inches. You can position Motion Man in two places and challenge students to figure out how he got there. At first, students may be confused when they cannot get Motion Man into the new position with one transformation. Encourage them to work together with several Motion Men to see how they might move Motion Man to his new position. Oftentimes, there are numerous ways to get him to the new position.

Have students experiment with compositions of transformations by using a simple shape on a rectangular dot grid, as a step toward using coordinates on the coordinate axis. For example, have students draw an L shape on a dot grid and label it L_1 (Figure 13.20). Reflect it through a line, and then rotate the image $\frac{1}{4}$ turn clockwise about a point not on the shape. Call this image L_2. L_2 is the image of a composition of a reflection followed by a rotation. Notice that if L_1 is rotated $\frac{1}{4}$ turn clockwise about the same point used before (the result of which we will call L_3), there is a relationship between L_2 and L_3. Continue to explore different combinations of transformations.

◆ Standards for
Mathematical Practice

7 **Look for and
make use of structure** ▶

Figure 13.20

Transformations on dot paper.

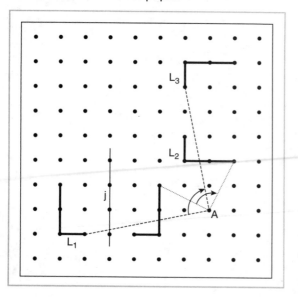

◆ **t e c h n o l o g y** ⏻
note

NCTM's e-Example "Understanding Congruence, Similarity, and Symmetry Using Transformations and Interactive Figures" (Applet 6.4, at www.nctm .org/standards/content.aspx?id=26885) is one of the best applets to support students' understanding of all three rigid motions. In the last two parts of the applet, students explore compositions of reflections and then other compositions of up to three transformations.

◆ Congruence

Congruent shapes are defined in terms of transformations. Two shapes are considered congruent if you can apply rigid transformations from one shape to the other. The *Common Core State Standards* for eighth grade state that students should "understand that a two-dimensional figure is congruent to another if the second can be obtained from the first by a sequence of rotations, reflections, and translations; given two congruent figures, describe a sequence that exhibits the congruence between them" (CCSSO, 2010, p. 55).

Having explored foundational experiences like Motion Man and transformations on dot paper, students are ready to explore transformations and compositions of transformations on the coordinate axis. A focus on congruence helps connect these two related ideas, as in Activity 13.14.

◆ *Activity* 13.14   ARE THEY CONGRUENT?

BLM

Place various triangles on the coordinate axis, some of which are congruent and some not (see Blackline Master 42). Ask students to find a match of two congruent triangles and prove they are congruent by stating the transformations that they applied in order to get one shape to cover exactly the one they selected as a match.

The coordinate axis is addressed in detail in a later section, "Location," in which transformations will continue to be explored.

◆ Similarity

Two figures are *similar* if all of their corresponding angles are congruent and the corresponding sides are proportional. As noted in Chapter 11, proportional reasoning activities are good connections to geometry, such as Activity 11.6, "Look-Alike Rectangles," and Activity 11.7, "Scale Drawings."

A *dilation* is a nonrigid (can change size) transformation that produces similar two-dimensional figures. Figure 13.21 shows how a given figure can be dilated to make larger or smaller figures. In order to dilate a preimage, you must know the *scale factor*. A dilation can make the image smaller or larger, depending on whether the scale factor is less than or greater than 1.

If different groups of students use the same scale factor to dilate the same figure, they will find that the resulting figures are all congruent, even with each group using different dilation points. Dynamic geometry software makes the results of this exercise quite dramatic. The software allows the scale factors to be set at any value. Once a dilation is performed, the dilation point can be dragged around the screen, and the size and shape of the image clearly stay unchanged.

▲ Location

Location activities begin early in school, when young children describe objects as *under, near, far, between, left,* and *right.* The coordinate plane is introduced in grade 5 with a focus on quadrant I and

Figure 13.21

Begin with figure *ABCDE* and place point *P* anywhere. Draw lines from *P* through each vertex. Place point *A'* twice as far from *P* as *A* is from *P* (scale factor of 2). Repeat for the other points.

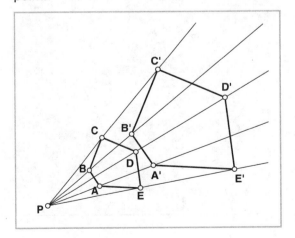

is extended to all four quadrants in grade 6, when students connect and apply their understanding of rational numbers and draw polygons on the coordinate axis (CCSSO, 2010). This knowledge is needed for scale drawings and constructions in grade 7 (described previously) and is used extensively in grade 8 for graphing lines on the coordinate axis and performing transformations. Finally, the coordinate plane is used to explore the distance (length) of vertical and horizontal lines in grade 6 and of any lines (by using the Pythagorean theorem) in grade 8. It is clear that understanding and being able to use the coordinate plane is critical in middle-school mathematics.

These next three quick activities are designed simply to get students familiar with plotting points on the coordinate plane (see Blackline Master 42). Any or all of these can be used in sixth grade for full-class instruction, or as intervention or review for students who will need to be accurate in graphing on the coordinate plane.

Dot to Dot

Ask students to create a dot-to-dot picture with fewer than 10 coordinates. They prepare two products—one is the labeled graph, and the second is the list of coordinates. Collect the second item (lists of coordinates), mix them up, and redistribute the lists to other students. Students create the graph of the new dot-to-dot picture. As a final step, they get the labeled graph from the original group to see if they completed the diagram accurately. Differences are studied to see where an error occurred.

Four in a Row

Adapt this classic game by requiring students to name the coordinates of the position they wish to mark with their color. If they name the coordinates backward or forget the negative value, then mark the point they named, not the point they meant to name. This can be done with the whole class (to start) or with partners.

Simon Says

Give students starting coordinates—for example, begin at (⁻3, 4). Give a series of instructions, such as "Simon says move 3 units to the right. Simon says move 2 units up. Move 5 units down. Where are you?" Have students compare their final locations and figure out what might have caused different results. (Remember, if Simon does not say it—don't move!)

◈ Transformations on the Coordinate Plane

Transformations were the focus of the previous section, in which the experiences prepared students to explore transformation on the coordinate plane. Experiences on the coordinate plane can begin with a single transformation, as in Activity 13.15, in which the focus is on translations.

$\mathcal{F}igure$ 13.22

Example translations on a coordinate axis.

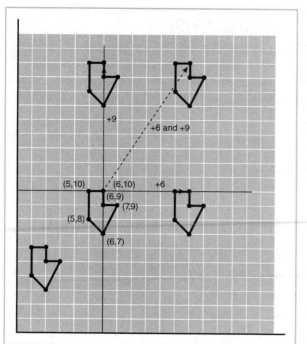

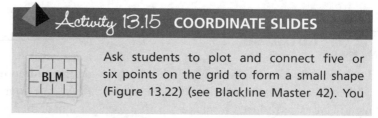

Activity 13.15 **COORDINATE SLIDES**

Ask students to plot and connect five or six points on the grid to form a small shape (Figure 13.22) (see Blackline Master 42). You may want to begin with all coordinates in quadrant I, with *x* values and *y* values less than 12, so there is room on the graph to draw the translated shapes. Next, ask students to add 6 to each of the *x*-values of their shape, leaving the *y*-values the same. This new figure should be congruent to the original and translated to the right. Third, ask students to create another figure by adding 9 to each *y*-value of the original coordinates.

Ask students to conjecture and test what could be done to the coordinates to move the figure along a diagonal line up and to the right. Figure 13.22 shows a slide created by adding 6 to the *x*-values and 9 to the *y*-values.

After this first experience with positive values, explore shapes that are positioned in the other quadrants. Explore moves that go down and to the left, as well. Also include fractional values.

Reflections and rotations can also be explored on a coordinate grid. For reflections, begin with using the *x*- or *y*-axis as the line of reflection, as in the following activity.

Activity 13.16 COORDINATE REFLECTIONS

◆ Standards for Mathematical Practice

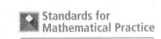

5 Use appropriate tools strategically

BLM

Ask students to draw a five-sided shape in the first quadrant on coordinate grid paper (see Blackline Master 42 or use dynamic geometry software).

Label the figure ABCDE and call it Figure 1 (Figure 13.23). Use the *y*-axis as a line of symmetry, and draw the reflection of the shape in quadrant II. Label the reflected points A'B'C'D'E' and call this figure Figure 2. Now, use the *x*-axis as the line of reflection and create Figure 3 (in quadrant III) and Figure 4 (in quadrant IV). Write in the coordinates for each vertex of all four shapes. Explore the following:

- How is Figure 3 related to Figure 4? How else could you have gotten Figure 3? How else could you have found Figure 4?
- How are the coordinates of Figure 1 related to its image in the *y*-axis, Figure 2? What can you say about the coordinates of Figure 4?
- Make a conjecture about the coordinates of a shape reflected over the *y*-axis and a different conjecture about the coordinates of a shape reflected over the *x*-axis.
- Draw lines from the vertices of Figure 1 to the corresponding vertices of Figure 2. What can you say about these lines? How is the *y*-axis related to each of these lines?

Figure 13.23

Figure 1 (*ABCDE* in quadrant I) is reflected across the *y*-axis. Then both figures are reflected across the *x*-axis.

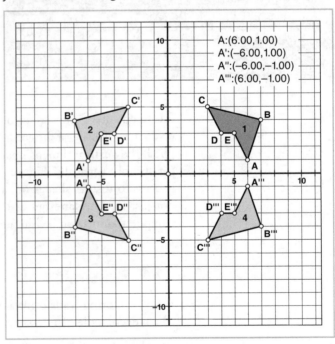

The following activity illustrates how multiplying a constant times the coordinates is a transformation that is not a rigid motion.

Figure 13.24

Dilation of a trapezoid (original is dark gray) when the scale factors are 0.5 and 2.0.

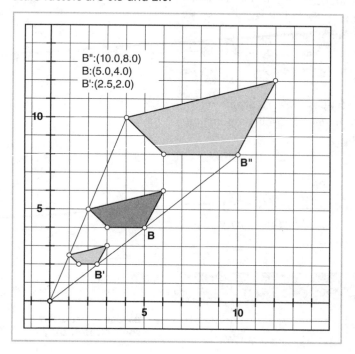

B":(10.0,8.0)
B:(5.0,4.0)
B':(2.5,2.0)

Activity 13.17 COORDINATE DILATIONS

BLM

Students begin with a four-sided shape in the first quadrant (see Blackline Master 42). They then make a list of the coordinates and make a new set of coordinates by multiplying each of the original coordinates by 2. They plot the resulting shape. What is the result? Now, have students multiply each of the original coordinates by $\frac{1}{2}$ and plot that shape. Next, ask students to draw a line from the origin to a vertex of the largest shape. Repeat for one or two additional vertices, and ask for observations. (An example is shown in Figure 13.24.)

Stop and Reflect

How do the lengths of sides and the areas of the shapes compare when the coordinates are multiplied by 2? What if they are multiplied by 3 or by $\frac{1}{2}$? ◼

Teaching Tip

Invite students to bring a picture of a favorite TV, book, video, or comic strip character. They can use coordinate points to create a modified version of the picture and dilate it to form a larger or smaller character.

Your students may enjoy exploring dilations a bit further, including the connection to scale drawings. Any diagram (e.g., a sailboat) can undergo a dilation, resulting in a larger or smaller diagram of the same shape.

Distortions can also be engaging, and they communicate the impact of the scale of a coordinate on the outcome of the transformation. If students start with a drawing of a simple face, boat, or some other shape drawn with straight lines connecting vertices, they will create an interesting effect by multiplying just the first coordinates, just the second coordinates, or using a different factor for each. When only the second coordinate is multiplied, the vertical dimensions alone are dilated, so the figure is proportionately stretched (or shrunk) vertically. Figure 13.25 illustrates such a distortion. Students can explore this process to distort shapes in various ways. Imagine being able to control transformations, not just in the plane but also for three-dimensional figures. The process is identical to computer animation techniques.

◆ Reasoning about Transformations

While exploring transformations, challenge students with questions such as the following, which deepen their understanding of transformations:

- How should the coordinates be changed to cause a reflection if the line of reflection is not the *y*-axis but is parallel to it?

- Can you discover a single rule for coordinates that would cause a reflection across one of the axes followed by a rotation of a quarter turn? Is that rule the same for the reverse order—a quarter turn followed by a reflection?

Figure 13.25

A distortion that is dilated differently for *x*- and *y*-values. This distortion was (*x* + 10, 3*y*).

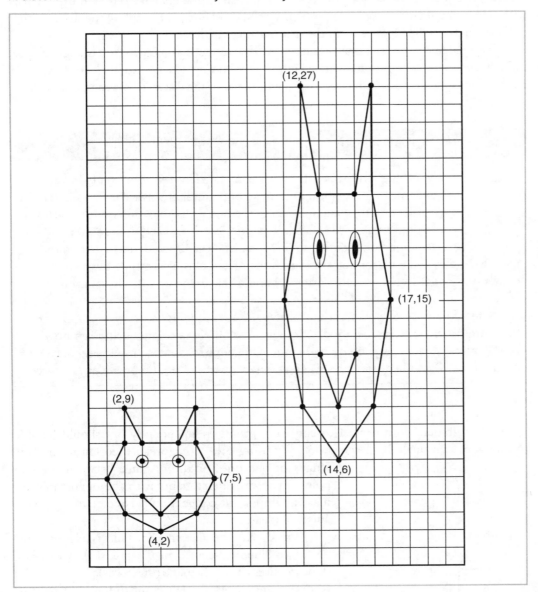

- If two successive translations are made with coordinates and you know what numbers were added or subtracted, what number should be added or subtracted to get the figure there in only one move?

- What do you think will happen if different factors are used for different coordinates in a dilation?

◆ Measuring Distance on the Coordinate Plane

Measuring in the coordinate plane begins with measuring vertical and horizontal lines.

How far apart are these points?

(⁻3,5) and (4,5)   (10,⁻5) and (10,25)

(⁻25,⁻10) and (⁻25,⁻35)   (⁻4$\frac{3}{4}$,⁻3) and (1$\frac{1}{4}$,⁻3)

Students can explore a variety of vertical lines by drawing them and conjecturing on how to find the distance without drawing it and counting units. Then they can see whether these conjectures also hold for horizontal lines. If sixth graders have repeated experiences with such tasks, including real-life problems, they will be ready to explore the distance formula in grade 8, when it appears in the mathematics curriculum.

If you can find a vertical distance and a horizontal distance, you can make a triangle and use the Pythagorean theorem to find any length. The following activity uses the coordinate grid and the Pythagorean relationship to develop a formula for the distance between two points.

◆ *Activity 13.18* DEVELOPING THE DISTANCE FORMULA

BLM

Begin by asking students to draw a line between two points in the first quadrant that are not on the same horizontal or vertical line. Ask students to draw a right triangle by using the line as the hypotenuse (the vertex at the right angle will share one coordinate with each end point). Students then apply the Pythagorean theorem to find the distance. Ask students to do two to four more examples and look for patterns across their examples. This can be done with coordinate grid paper (see Blackline Master 42) and a calculator, or with dynamic geometry software.

After they have explored various examples, ask students to analyze the examples for patterns. Next, have them look through all of their calculations and see how the coordinates of the two end points were used. Challenge students to use the same type of calculations to get the distance between two new points without drawing any pictures.

Figure 13.26

The slope of a line.

Eighth graders do not need to construct proofs independently but should be able to follow the rationale if shown proofs. By using the Pythagorean theorem to find the length of one line (or the distance between the end points), you provide students with the opportunity to make an important connection between two big mathematical ideas.

Notice that the distance formula is closely connected to slope (discussed in Chapter 12). Measuring slope requires a reference line (the *x*-axis). The *rise* is the vertical change from the left point to the right point—positive if up, negative if down. The *run* is the horizontal distance from the left point to the right point. Slope is then defined as the ratio of rise to run, or the ratio of the vertical change to the horizontal change. Figure 13.26 illustrates slope and the close connection to the distance formula.

▲ Visualization

Visualization might be called "geometry done with the mind's eye." It involves being able to create images of shapes and then turn them around mentally, thinking about how they look from different viewpoints—predicting the results of various transformations. It includes the mental coordination of two and three dimensions—in sixth grade, for example, by determining the net for a three-dimensional shape. Any activity that requires students to think about, manipulate, or transform a shape mentally or to represent a shape as it is seen visually will contribute to the development of their visualization skills.

Nets

A flat shape that can be folded up to make a solid figure is called the *net* of that solid. The following activity suggests several challenges involving nets. Sixth graders construct nets and describe the faces of three-dimensional shapes made up of rectangles and triangles, and they use the nets to calculate the surface area.

 Activity 13.19 **NET CHALLENGES**

The following tasks can be done as a series of activities, or any one of them can be selected to explore nets.

- Examine a set of pentominoes and determine which ones are "box makers." Test conjectures by cutting out the pentominoes and trying to use them to make a box. For each that is a box maker, see in how many different places a sixth square can be attached to create a top for the box (a net for a cube). Are there other nets for a cube that do not begin with a pentomino?

- Begin with a solid, such as a rectangular prism or square pyramid. Sketch as many nets as possible for this shape. Add to the collection some arrangements of the sides of the solid that are not nets. Challenge a friend to decide which are nets of the shape and which are not.

- Use a Polydron or a three-dimensional Geoshape to create a flat figure that you think will fold up into a solid. Test the result. If the number and/or type of flat shapes is specified, the task can be made more or less difficult. Can you make the net of a solid with 12 regular pentagons or 8 equilateral triangles? (These can be made into a *dodecahedron* and an *octahedron,* respectively, two of the five completely regular polyhedra, also known as the five *Platonic solids.*)

Standards for Mathematical Practice

1 **Make sense of problems and persevere in solving them**

Students can use "Dynamic Paper" from NCTM Illuminations (http://illuminations.nctm.org/ActivityDetail .aspx?ID=205) to create nets of three-dimensional figures with specified dimensions. This multipurpose tool creates custom graph paper, number grids, nets, number lines, shapes, spinners, and tessellations that can be exported in .jpeg and .pdf formats.

Perspective Drawings

One of the main goals of visualization in the geometry strand of the *Common Core State Standards* is to be able to identify and draw two-dimensional images of three-dimensional figures and to build three-dimensional figures from two-dimensional images. Activities aimed at this goal often involve drawings of small "buildings" made of 1-inch cubes.

Figure 13.27

"Building Views" tasks. Students are given one representation and build another.

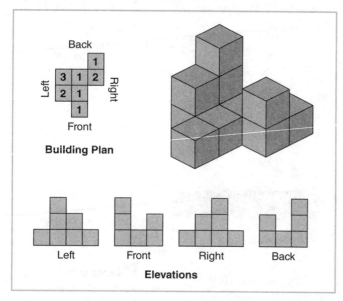

Building Plan

Elevations

Left   Front   Right   Back

Activity 13.20 BUILDING VIEWS

For this activity, students will need paper for drawing a building plan and 1-inch blocks for constructing a building.

Version 1: Students begin with a building made of the blocks and draw the left, right, front, and back views (these are called *elevations*). In Figure 13.27, the building plan shows a top view of the building and the number of blocks in each position. After students build a building from a plan like this, they draw the elevations (views) of the front, right, left, and back, as shown in the figure.

Version 2: Students are given right and front elevations. Ask students to build the corresponding building. To record their solution, they draw a building plan (top elevation with numbers).

Notice that the front and back elevations are symmetric, as are the left and right elevations. That is why only one of each is given in the second part of the activity. To expand "Building Views" into a more challenging activity, students can prepare three-dimensional drawings (isometric) of the block buildings or match three-dimensional drawings with buildings. Isometric grids (Blackline Master 2) are a form of *axonometric* drawing in which the scale is preserved in all dimensions (height, depth, width). The next activity provides a glimpse of this form of visualization activity.

Figure 13.28

Develop visual perception with elevations and building plan views.

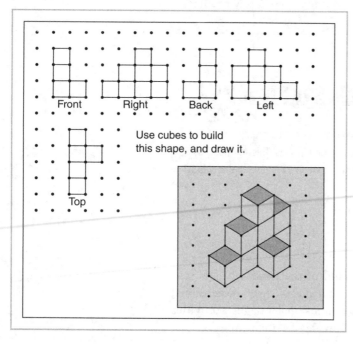

Front   Right   Back   Left

Use cubes to build this shape, and draw it.

Top

Activity 13.21 THREE-DIMENSIONAL DRAWINGS

Version 1: Students begin with an isometric three-dimensional drawing of a building. The assumption is that there are no hidden blocks. From the drawing, the students build the actual building with their blocks. To record the result, they draw a building plan (top view) indicating the number of blocks in each position.

Version 2: Students are given the four elevation views and a building plan (top view) (Figure 13.28). They build the building accordingly and draw two or more of the elevation views. There are four possible views: the front left and right and the back left and right. For students who struggle, have them build the building on a sheet of paper with the words *front, back, left,* and *right* written on the edges to keep them from confusing the different views.

◆ Two-Dimensional Slices of Three-Dimensional Shapes

Another connection between two- and three-dimensional shapes is found by slicing solids in different ways. This is a standard for grade 7 (CCSSO, 2010). When a solid is sliced into two parts, a two-dimensional figure is formed on the slice faces. Slices of solids made of clay sliced with a potter's wire can be explored. Figure 13.29 shows a cube sliced off at the corner, leaving a triangular face. Another engaging method is to fill a plastic solid (such as one of the Power Solids) partially with water. The surface of the water simulates a slice and models the face of the solid as if it had been cut at that location. By cutting the shape in different ways, every possible "slice" can be observed. Ask students to see if they can find a particular plane shape by slicing the three-dimensional shape they have. For example, ask, "Can you slice the rectangular solid to have a trapezoid face? A triangle face? A square face?"

These explorations of two- and three-dimensional shapes illustrate not only real-life connections (between two-dimensional representations and our three-dimensional world), but also the importance of exploration, conjecture, and proof in learning about shapes.

Figure 13.29 Predict the shape of the slice, then cut with a potter's wire.

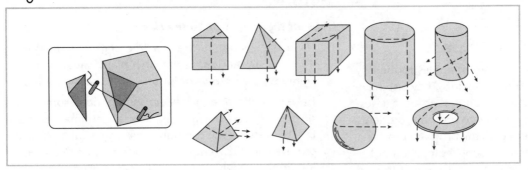

Expanded Lesson

Triangle Midsegments

Content and Task Decisions

Grade Level: 7–8

Mathematics Goals

- To investigate the relationship between a triangle's midsegment and its base
- To develop the rationale for why particular relationships exist in a triangle
- To develop logical reasoning in a geometric context

Grade Level Guide

NCTM Curriculum Focal Points	Common Core State Standards
Students in seventh grade explore proportionality by investigating similar objects. By using scale factors, they compare lengths in two figures. In eighth grade, students prove that certain configurations of lines result in similar triangles (NCTM, 2006).	In the seventh grade, students should be able to draw and describe geometric figures, including the relationships between the figures. Students in the eighth grade explore angle measures of triangles, including the measures of angles that are created when parallel lines are cut by a transversal.

Consider Your Students' Needs

Students are aware of the properties of angles formed by cutting parallel lines with a transverse line. They also have experience working with similar triangles. To do the lesson with a dynamic geometry software program, students should be relatively competent with the program tools and be able to draw different geometric objects (e.g., triangles, lines, line segments), label vertices, find midpoints, and measure lengths and angles while working independently.

For English Language Learners

- Before the lesson begins, use student-friendly words and visuals to communicate the goal of the lesson—to see whether the midsegment is somehow related to the base.
- Discuss with students what *conjecture* means and what *justification* means.

- Encourage students to use both words and pictures in the development of their conjectures.

For Students with Disabilities

- During the phase of the lesson in which conjectures are made and supported with reasoning, you may want to support students with disabilities by creating a table. Here, you can ask them first to measure and record the angles ADE, ABC, AED, and ACB. Also, have them measure the line segments AD, AE, AB, and AC (they already have BD and DE). They can then use this organized information to support ideas about relationships.

Materials

This lesson can be done either with computers or on paper. As described, the lesson assumes only a demonstration computer with a display screen. Although desirable, a computer is not required. The computer used in this lesson requires a dynamic geometry program, such as *The Geometer's Sketchpad* or *Wingeom* (free software).

Each student will need:

- Ruler that measures in centimeters

Lesson

Before

Present the focus task to the class:

- Have each student draw a line segment measuring 16 cm near the long edge of a blank sheet of paper. Demonstrate on the computer. Label the segment BC.
- Have students randomly select another point somewhere on their papers but at least several centimeters above BC. Illustrate on the computer that you want all students to have very different points. Some may be in the upper left, in the upper right, near the center, and so on. Have them label this point A and then draw segments AB and AC to create triangle ABC. Do the same on the computer.

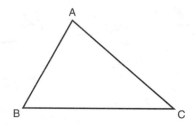

- Ask students to find the midpoints D and E of AB and AC, respectively, and draw the midsegment DE. Do the same on the computer. Introduce the term *midsegment* as the line joining the midpoints of two sides of a triangle.

- Have students measure their midsegments and report what they find. Amazingly, all students should report a measure of 8 cm. On the computer, measure BC and DE. Drag point A all over the screen. The two measures will stay the same, with the length of DE half that of BC. Even if B or C is moved, the ratio of BC to DE will remain 2:1.

- Ask students for any conjectures they may have about why this relationship exists.

- On the computer, draw a line through A parallel to BC. Have students draw a similar line on their papers. Label points F and G on the line, as shown here.

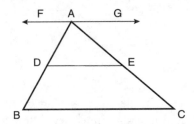

- Ask students what else they know about the figure now that line FG has been added. List all ideas on the board.

- Ask the students what conjecture can be made about the midsegment of any triangle. What reason can be given for why the conjecture might be true?

- Students are to write a conjecture about the midsegment of a triangle. In pairs, students are to continue to explore their sketches, looking for reasons why this particular relationship between the midsegment of a triangle and its base exists. They should record all of their ideas and justifications and be ready to share them with the class. If they wish to explore an idea on the computer sketch, they should be allowed to do so.

Provide clear expectations:

- Students can work alone or in pairs. Each student should record his or her own reasoning concerning the conjectures.

During

- Notice what students focus on in forming conjectures (and use for *After* phase sharing).

- For students having difficulty, suggest that they focus on angles ADE and ABC, as well as angles AED and ACB. (These pairs of angles are congruent.)

- Suggest that they list all pairs of angles that they know are congruent. Why are they congruent?

- If necessary, ask students to compare triangle ABC with triangle ADE. What do they notice? They should note that the triangles are similar. Why are they similar?

After

Bring the class together to share and discuss the task:

- Have students discuss their initial arguments for why the midsegment relationship holds. They can use the demonstration computer to share their ideas.

Assessment
Observe

- Look for students who struggle seeing the connections or relationships between properties. These students may not be functioning at level 2 of the van Hiele levels of geometric thought.

- Do students see the difference between simply observing a relationship and considering the reasons why the relationship exists?

Ask

- Can you convince me that your conjecture about the midsegment of a triangle is true?

- Why doesn't the size of your triangle affect the ratio of the midsegment to the base?

- Would the conjecture hold true if you used a different side of the triangle for the base? Why?

- Why are triangles ABC and ADE similar?

14

Exploring Measurement Concepts

BigIDEAS

1 Measurement involves a comparison of an attribute of an item or situation with a unit that has the same attribute. Lengths are compared with units of length, areas with units of area, time with units of time, and so on.

2 The estimation of measures and the development of benchmarks for frequently used units of measure help students increase their familiarity with units, preventing errors and aiding in the meaningful use of measurement.

3 Area and volume formulas provide a method of measuring these attributes with only measures of length.

4 Area, perimeter, surface area, and volume are related. For example, as the shapes of regions or of three-dimensional objects change while their areas or volumes are maintained, their perimeters and surface areas are affected.

From gigabytes that measure amounts of information, to font size on computers, to miles per gallon, to recipes for a meal, people are surrounded daily with measurement concepts that apply to a variety of real-world contexts and applications. Measurement is not an easy topic for students to understand. Data from international studies consistently indicate that U.S. students are weaker in the area of measurement than in any other topic in the mathematics curriculum (Thompson & Preston, 2004).

The focus of measurement in middle school is on area, surface area, and volume. Sixth graders investigate formulas for the area of triangles and quadrilaterals, use nets to explore the surface area of three-dimensional shapes, and find the volume of right rectangular prisms. In grade 7, the focus of measurement is on circles (circumference and area) and angles, and in grade 8, students continue to learn about the volume of three-dimensional shapes, with a focus on cylinders, cones, and spheres.

 Foundations of Measuring

Suppose that you asked your students to measure an empty bucket, as in Figure 14.1. The first thing they would need to know is *what* about the bucket is to be measured. They might measure the height (depth), diameter (distance across), or circumference (distance around). All of these are length measures. The surface area of the side could be determined. A bucket also has volume (or capacity) and weight. Each aspect that can be measured is an *attribute* of the bucket.

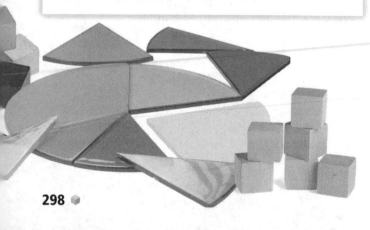

Once students determine the attribute to be measured, they then choose *how* they will measure it. This involves determining an appropriate unit that has the same attribute being measured. Length is measured with units that have length, volume with units that have volume, and so on.

🔹 Meaning of Measuring

Technically, a *measurement* is a number that indicates a comparison between an attribute of the object (or situation or event) being measured and the same attribute of a given unit of measure. We commonly use small units of measure to determine a numeric relationship (the measurement) between what is measured and the unit. For example, to measure a length, the comparison can be done by lining up copies of the unit directly against the length being measured. For most of the attributes measured in schools, we can say that *measuring* means that the attribute being measured is being "filled" or "covered" or "matched" with a unit of measure that has the same attribute.

🔹 Process of Measuring

In brief, to measure something, one must perform three steps:

1. Decide on the attribute to be measured.

2. Select a unit that has that attribute.

3. Compare the units—by filling, covering, matching, or using some other method—with the attribute of the object being measured. The number of units required to match the object is the measure.

The skill of measuring with a unit must be explicitly linked to the concept of measuring as a process of using measuring units and measuring instruments to compare attributes, as outlined in Table 14.1. This may seem simple, but middle-school students struggle to match appropriate units with length, area, and volume measures.

Making Comparisons

Sometimes, with a measure such as length, a direct comparison can be made in which one object is lined up and matched with another. But often, an indirect method in which a third object (e.g., a ruler) is used is necessary. For example, if students compare the volume of one box with the volume of another, they must devise an indirect way to compare the sizes of the two boxes (i.e., using a measuring instrument).

Figure 14.1

Measuring different attributes of a bucket.

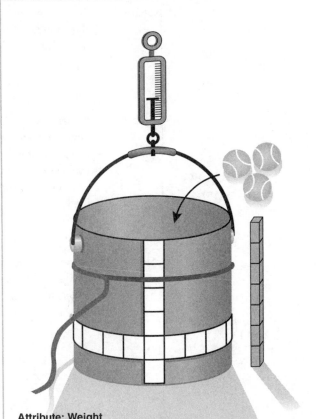

Attribute: Weight
Units: objects that <u>stretch</u> the spring in the scale
How many units will pull the spring as far as the bucket will?

Attribute: Volume/Capacity
Units: cubes, balls, cups of water
How many units will <u>fill</u> the bucket?

Attribute: Length
Units: rods, toothpicks, straws, string
How many units are <u>as tall as</u> the bucket?
How much string is needed to <u>go around</u> the bucket?

Attribute: Area
Units: index cards, squares of paper, tiles
How many cards will <u>cover</u> the surface of the bucket?

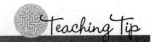
Teaching Tip

Use precise language when helping students make comparisons. Avoid using *bigger than,* and instead use language such as *longer than* or *holds more than.*

Table **14.1** Plan for Measurement Instruction

	Goal	Type of Activity	Notes
Step 1	Students will understand the attribute to be measured.	Make comparisons based on the attribute—for example, longer or shorter, heavier or lighter. Use direct comparisons whenever possible.	When it is clear that the attribute is understood, there is no further need for comparison activities.
Step 2	Students will understand how filling, covering, matching, or making other comparisons of an attribute with measuring units produces a number called a *measure*.	Use physical models of measuring units to fill, cover, match, or make the desired comparison of the attribute with the unit.	In most instances, it is appropriate to begin with informal units. Progress to the direct use of standard units when appropriate, and certainly before using formulas or measuring tools.
Step 3	Students will use common measuring tools with understanding and flexibility.	Make measuring instruments, and use them in comparison with the actual unit models to see how the measurement tool is performing the same function as the individual units. Be certain to make direct comparisons between the student-made tools and the standard tools.	Student-made tools are usually best made with informal units. Without a careful comparison with the standard tools, much of the value in making the tools can be lost.

Using Physical Units to Measure

All measurement is actually a comparison. The object being measured is being compared with the unit. A 15-inch book is measured by placing a unit of 1 inch down and counting how many units will match the length of the book. This process, called *iteration*, was also discussed with fractions—for example, how many fourths are in $3\frac{1}{2}$? Although iteration is learned early in elementary school, it is worth revisiting in middle school because this understanding will support students' thinking as they develop formulas for measuring the area of triangles and quadrilaterals.

Figure **14.2**

How long is this crayon?

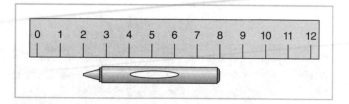

Using Measuring Instruments

In the 2003 National Assessment of Educational Progress (NAEP) examination, only 56 percent of eighth graders could give the correct measure of an object not aligned with the end of a ruler, as in Figure 14.2 (Kloosterman, Rutledge, & Kenney, 2009). These results point to the need to teach explicitly how to use measuring devices. Students also experienced difficulty when the increments on a measuring device were not one unit.

If students use unit models with which they are familiar to construct simple measuring instruments, it is more likely that they will understand how an instrument measures. A ruler is a good example. If students line up individual physical units along a strip of card stock and mark them off, they can see that it is the *spaces* on rulers, not the hash marks or numbers, that are important. It is essential that students discuss how measurement with the iteration of individual units compares with measurement with an instrument. Without this comparison and discussion, students may not understand that these two methods are essentially the same.

 Formative Assessment Note

Use *observation* to see whether students are using measuring tools accurately and meaningfully. Rulers and protractors are often poorly understood. Or, in a *diagnostic interview*, ask students to measure using a unit that they iterate and measure using a measuring tool. Second, ask them react to the technique used by another student. ("Monique measured the width of her locker. She lined up the 10-cm mark on one side. The measure of the other side of the locker ended up between the 42- and 43-cm marks. Monique is confused about how wide her locker is. Without measuring the locker again, how would you help Monique?")

◀ **3** Construct viable arguments and critique the reasoning of others

Choosing Appropriate Units

Should the room be measured in square feet or square inches? Should the concrete blocks be weighed in grams or kilograms? The answers to questions such as these involve more than simply knowing how big units are, although that is certainly required. Another consideration involves the need for precision. If you were measuring your wall in order to cut a piece of molding to fit, you would need to measure it very precisely. The smallest unit would be an inch or a centimeter, and you would also use fractional parts. But, if you were determining how many 8-foot molding strips to buy, the nearest foot would probably be sufficient.

◀ **6** Attend to precision

 Activity 14.1 **GUESS THE UNIT**

 Find examples of measurements of all types in newspapers, on signs, or in other everyday situations. Present the context and measures, but without units. For example, a recent story in a national newspaper described Abe Lincoln's Manchester, Vermont, home as 8000-square-foot (almost 750 square meters). Show students text that reads "Abe Lincoln had a built a home in Vermont that was 750 [smudge]." Ask students to predict what units of measure were used. Then share the actual article. Have students discuss their choices. For students with disabilities, you may want to provide the possible units so they can sort the real-world measures into groups.

⬡ Important Standard Measures and Units

In the United States, both metric and customary units of measure are important. Results of the 2004 NAEP revealed that only 37 percent of eighth graders knew how many milliliters were in a liter (Perie, Moran, & Lutkus, 2005). Interestingly, U.S. students do better with metric units than with customary units (Preston & Thompson, 2004). Familiarity with the units in both systems helps students consider reasonableness of their measurements. A doorway is a bit more than 2 m high, and a doorknob is about 1 m from the floor. A bag of flour is a good reference for 5 pounds. A paper clip weighs about a gram and is about 1 cm wide. A gallon of milk weighs a little less than 4 kg.

As students grasp the structure of decimal notation, develop the metric system with all seven places: three prefixes for smaller units (*deci-*, *centi-*, *milli-*), one for the unit itself (e.g., meters), and three for larger units (*deka-*, *hecto-*, *kilo-*). Avoid mechanical rules, such as this one: "To change centimeters to meters, move the decimal point two places to the left." Instead, use measurement conversions as an application of the proportional reasoning that is central to middle school.

◆ Estimation and Approximation

Measurement estimation is the process of using mental and visual information to measure or make comparisons without measuring instruments. It is a practical skill used almost every day. Do I have enough sugar to make cookies? Can you throw the ball 15 m? Is this suitcase over the weight limit? Here are several reasons for including estimation in measurement activities:

- Estimation helps students focus on the attribute being measured and the measuring process. Think about how you would estimate the area of the cover of this book in square centimeters. To do so, you would have to think about what area is and how the units might be placed on the book cover.

- Estimation provides an intrinsic motivation for measurement activities. It is interesting to see how close to the actual measurement you can come in your estimate.

- When standard units are used, estimation helps develop familiarity with the units. If you estimate the height of the door in meters before measuring, you must think about the size of a meter.

- The use of a benchmark to make an estimate promotes multiplicative reasoning. The width of the building is about one-fourth of the length of a football field—perhaps 25 yards.

Approximation is different from estimation—it does not have to do with predicting the result, it has to do with the actual result. All measurements are approximations. If you measure to the nearest inch, the object is only approximately 6 inches. If you decide to measure to the nearest eighth of an inch, you may measure the same object at $6\frac{3}{8}$ inches. Still, it could be measured to the nearest sixteenth of an inch, or even to a higher level of precision. Emphasize that all measures are approximate, and that smaller units lead to a greater degree of *precision*. A length measure can never be more than one-half unit in error. Because there is mathematically no "smallest unit," there is always some measurement error.

Standards for
Mathematical Practice

6 **Attend to precision** ▶

◆ Strategies for Estimating Measures

Begin measurement activities with estimates. Students need explicit guidance on effective measurement estimation. Here are four instructional strategies to support student competency with estimation:

Standards for
Mathematical Practice

7 **Look for and make use of structure** ▶

1. *Develop and use benchmarks or referents for important units.* Students who have acquired mental benchmarks for measurements *and* have practiced using them in class activities are much better estimators than students who have not learned to use benchmarks (Joram, 2003). Students must pay attention to the size of the unit to estimate well (Towers & Hunter, 2010). Referents should be things that are easily envisioned by the student.

2. *Use "chunks" of objects.* It may be easier to estimate short chunks along a wall than to estimate the whole length of the wall. The weight of a stack of books is easier to estimate if some estimate is given for the weight of an "average" book.

3. *Partition objects.* This is a similar strategy to chunking, with the estimator imposing chunks on the object. For example, if the wall length to be estimated has no useful chunks, it can be mentally divided in half and then in fourths or even eighths by halving it repeatedly until a more manageable length is found. Length, volume, and area measurements all lend themselves to this technique.

4. *Iterate a unit mentally or physically.* For length, area, and volume, it is sometimes easy to mark off single units visually. You might use your hands or make marks or folds to keep track as you go. If you know, for example, that your stride is about $\frac{3}{4}$ meters long, you can walk off a length and then multiply to get an estimate.

Tips for Teaching Measurement Estimation

Each of the previous strategies should be explicitly taught and discussed with students; then students should have more opportunities for selecting from among the strategies a method that works best in a particular situation. Consider these additional teaching tips:

1. *Create lists of visible benchmarks for students to use.* Record and post on a class chart.

2. *Discuss how different students made their estimates.* This will confirm that there is no single right way to estimate while reminding students of other useful approaches.

3. *Accept a range of estimates.* Think in relative terms about what is a good estimate. Within 10 percent for length is quite good. Even 30 percent off may be reasonable for weights or volumes.

4. *Encourage children to give a range of estimates (e.g., the door is between 7 and 8 feet tall) that they believe includes the actual measure.* Rather than just give a single value, stating a range helps students focus on reasonable minimum and maximum values.

Teaching Tip

Do not promote a "winning" estimate. It discourages estimation and promotes only seeking the exact answer.

5. *Make measurement estimation an ongoing activity.* Post a weekly measurement to be estimated. Students can record their estimates and discuss them for five minutes at the end of the week. Invite students to select measurements to estimate, with a student or team of students assigned this task each week.

6. *Be precise with your language, and do not use the word "measure" interchangeably with the word "estimate"* (Towers & Hunter, 2010). Randomly substituting one word for the other will cause uncertainty and possibly confuse students.

Measurement Estimation Activities

Estimation activities need not be elaborate. Any measurement activity can have an "estimate-first" component but also include tasks in which estimates are all that are needed. Here are some measurement estimation activities that can be done briefly and repeatedly.

◀ *Activity* 14.2 **ESTIMATION QUICKIE**

Select a single object, such as a box, a pumpkin, a painting on the wall of the school, a jar, or even the principal! Each day, select a different attribute or dimension to estimate. For the pumpkin or watermelon, for example, students can estimate its height, circumference, weight, volume, and surface area.

Activity 14.3 **ESTIMATION SCAVENGER HUNT**

 Conduct estimation scavenger hunts. Give teams a list of measurements, and have them find things that are close to having those measurements. Do not use measuring instruments. A list might include the following items:

- Something with a length of 3.5 m
- Something that is as long as your math book
- Something that weighs more than 1 kg but less than 2 kg
- A container that holds about 200 ml
- An angle of 45 degrees or 135 degrees

Let students suggest how to judge results in terms of accuracy.

 Activity 14.4 **E–M–E SEQUENCES**

Use estimate–measure–estimate (E–M–E) sequences to help students practice with benchmarks. Select pairs of objects to estimate that are somehow related or close in measure but not the same. Have students estimate the measure of the first and check by measuring. Then have them estimate the second. Here are some examples of pairs:

- Width of a window, width of a wall
- Volume of a coffee mug, volume of a pitcher
- Distance between the eyes, width of the head
- Weight of a handful of marbles, weight of a bag of marbles

 Formative Assessment Note

Estimation tasks are a good way to assess students' understanding of both measurement and units. Use a *checklist* while students estimate measures of real objects and distances inside and outside the classroom. Prompt students to explain how they arrived at their estimates to get a more complete picture of their measurement knowledge. Asking only for a numeric estimate can mask a lack of understanding and will not give you the information you need to provide appropriate remediation.

Angles

"Understand concepts [or attributes] of angle and measure angles" is one of the *Common Core State Standards for Mathematics* beginning in grade 4 (CCSSO, 2010, p. 28). This is developed in middle school as seventh graders use "facts about supplementary, complementary, vertical, and adjacent angles in a multi-step problem to write and solve simple equations for an unknown angle in a figure" (CCSSO, 2010, p. 50). Working with angle measures continues to be emphasized in grade 8 and is critical to high school geometry.

Angle measurement can be a challenge for two reasons: The attribute of angle size is often misunderstood, and protractors are often used without students understanding how they work. Angle units are based on an angle formed by rays extending from the center of a circle. An angle of 1 degree is one whose arc is $\frac{1}{360}$ of a circle (see Blackline Master 35). In this section, and the others in this chapter, we follow an instructional sequence that starts with comparison, then considers informal units, and finishes with the use of measurement tools.

 BLM

◆ Comparison Activities

The attribute of angle size might be called the "spread of the angle's rays." Angles are composed of two infinitely long rays with a common vertex. They differ in size only by how widely or narrowly the two rays are spread apart. To help students conceptualize the attribute of the spread of the rays, two angles can be directly compared by tracing one and placing it over the other (Figure 14.3). Be sure to have students compare angles with sides of different lengths. A wide angle with short sides may seem smaller than a narrow angle with long sides. This is a common misconception among students (Munier, Devichi, & Merle, 2008).

◆ Tools for Angular Measure

A unit for measuring an angle must be an angle. Nothing else has the same attribute of spread that we want to measure.

Activity 14.5 A UNIT ANGLE

Give each student an index card. Have students draw a narrow angle on the card with a straight-edge and then cut it out (or use wedges made from Blackline Master 35). The resulting wedge can then be used as a unit of angular measure by counting the number of wedges that will fit in a given angle (Figure 14.4). Distribute copies of a previously prepared page with assorted angles on it, and have students use their angle unit to measure the angles. Because the students made different unit angles, the results will differ and can be discussed and compared in terms of unit size.

Activity 14.5 illustrates that measuring an angle is like measuring length or area; unit angles are used to fill or cover the spread of an angle, just as unit lengths fill or cover a length.

Middle-school students need an approximate mental image of angle size for common benchmark angle measures, such as 30, 45, 60, 90, 180, 270, and 360 degrees. The activity below develops a tool that can be used to help students develop a familiarity with these angle measures.

Activity 14.6 WAX PAPER PROTRACTOR PROJECTS

The first part of this activity involves making the tool, incorporating concepts of circles and angles.

Make the protractor: Give each student a piece of wax paper that has been cut into a circle. Ask, "How many degrees in a full circle?" Ask students to fold the wax paper carefully in half and in half again, forming fourths. Ask, "How many degrees in the angles

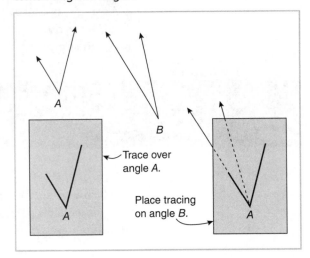

Figure 14.3
Which angle is larger?

Trace over angle A.

Place tracing on angle B.

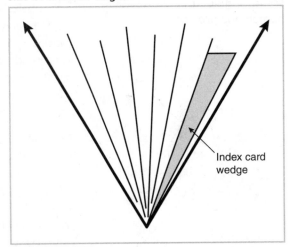

Figure 14.4
When a small wedge is cut from an index card and used as a unit angle, this angle measures about $7\frac{1}{2}$ wedges. The accuracy of measurement with nonstandard angles is less important than the idea of how an angle is used to measure the size of another angle.

Index card wedge

in the center?"[90 degrees] Next, ask students to refold the circle in fourths, and then to fold that fourth into thirds, crease, and open. Ask, "How many pieces?" [12 pieces] What is the angle measure of each twelfth (sector)?"[30 degrees]

Use the protractor: Point to or hold up various objects with vertices, and ask students to use their protractor to estimate the angle measure of those objects. Discuss the reasonableness of their estimates. Then have students use their wax paper protractor to measure. For example, challenge students to find five objects, each of which has a different angle measure and at least two of which have an angle measure greater than 90 degrees.

Teaching Tip

Be sure to include measurements of 180 degrees and greater so that students realize there are measures beyond 180 degrees.

The importance of angle measures is that they can provide important information about polygons, which is particularly relevant in grades 7 and 8 as students study special triangles and quadrilaterals (CCSSO, 2010). The next activity is targeted at building this connection.

Standards for Mathematical Practice

8 Look for and express regularity in repeated reasoning ▶

Figure 14.5

Measuring quadrilaterals with a homemade protractor.

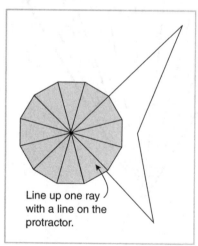

Line up one ray with a line on the protractor.

BLM

Activity 14.7 ANGLE SUMS OF POLYGONS

Ask students what they think the sum of the angles in a quadrilateral (or triangle or other polygon) might be. Collect their conjectures. Explain that students are going to investigate this question and report back what they learn. To do this, they must measure as many different kinds of quadrilaterals as they can. (Students may choose to draw the quadrilaterals, to build them on a geoboard or to create them by using short pieces of uncooked spaghetti as sides and taping them down.) Discuss with students the types of shapes they might include, including concave and convex shapes (Figure 14.5). For students with special needs, you may prepare a page of quadrilaterals with different shapes, rather than having them generate the shapes. Students use their wax paper protractor (or angle ruler) to measure the angles.

Such investigations build familiarity with angle units in general and important angle benchmarks, and they build the foundation for noticing properties of polygons.

Another tool similar to the wax paper protractor is the rational number wheel adapted to measure angles instead of hundredths (see Blackline Master 10 and Figure 9.3 on p. 147). It is an excellent reasoning task for students to create labels for the benchmark angle measures on the "Degree Wheel," which is now based on 360 degrees rather than one whole or 100 percent. For example, students might recognize that 30 degrees is one-third of 90 degrees (one-fourth of 360 degrees), so one-third of one-fourth, or one-twelfth. Or they might think that 30 degrees is one-third of 90 degrees, which is the same as one-third of 25 percent, so approximately 8 percent.

◆ Using Protractors and Angle Rulers

The two tools commonly used for measuring angles are the protractor and the angle ruler (Figure 14.6). The protractor is one of the most poorly understood measuring instruments. Part of the difficulty arises because the units (degrees) are so small. In addition, the numbers on most protractors run clockwise and counterclockwise along the edge, making the scale hard to interpret without a strong conceptual foundation. Angle rulers are a good choice for measuring angles, but they also require experience in order to understand how to set the tool on the angle to be measured and how to read the scale.

When introducing these tools, have students check their measures with one of their home-made tools, engage students in making an estimate, or do both. The best way to reduce errors in reading the protractor or angle ruler is to have students monitor their measuring, asking themselves, "Is this angle measure reasonable?" When students ask this question, they will not record 200 degrees when the angle is less than 180 degrees and will recognize that the value they should be reading on the protractor is 160 degrees.

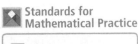

◆ Using Angle Measures to Determine Angle Measures

In middle school, students explore how other measures can be used to determine what a missing angle measure is. This includes knowing that the sum of the angles in a triangle is 180 degrees, that the sum of the angles in a quadrilateral is 360 degrees, that the sum of two adjacent angles that form a right angle must be 90 degrees (*complementary angles*), and that the sum of two adjacent angles that form a line must be 180 degrees (*supplementary angles*).

To explore the sum of angles within a triangle, see Activity 13.6, "Angle Sums in a Triangle," or adapt Activity 14.5, "A Unit Angle." To explore the other relationships, invite students to discover the relationship, employing their algebraic reasoning skills. The process emerges like this:

- Give a set of tasks in which students are looking for a missing angle that can be found because it is [a complementary angle, supplementary angle, etc.].

- Have students use one of their measuring tools to find the missing measures for the set of tasks.

- Discuss what relationships they notice across the set of tasks.

- Explore if this is always true and why.

The examples here can be used to explore supplemental angles and angles in a triangle.

What is the measure of angle *a*?

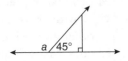

What is the measure of angle *b*?

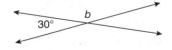

Figure 14.6

Tools used to measure angles.

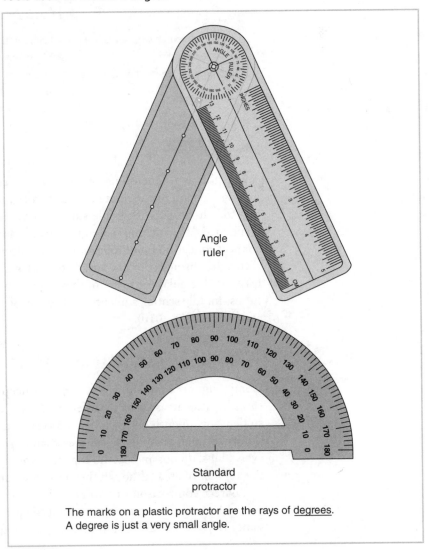

Angle ruler

Standard protractor

The marks on a plastic protractor are the rays of <u>degrees</u>. A degree is just a very small angle.

What is the measure of angle *c*?

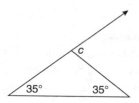

 Formative Assessment Note

Journal entries are a good way to evaluate what relationships students notice between angles. Give students a diagram with some angles labeled with measures and some angles not labeled.

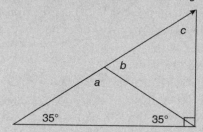

In their journals, have them explain the properties or relationships they used to figure out each missing angle measure ("I knew angle *a* was 110 degrees because . . ."). Writing an explanation such as this one reinforces the concept as well as the vocabulary.

 ## Area

Area is the two-dimensional space inside a region. As with other attributes, students must first understand the attribute of area before measuring. Data from the 2003 NAEP suggest that fourth- and eighth-grade students have an incomplete understanding of area (Blume, Galindo, & Walcott, 2007). Estimating area and measuring area begin in third grade, as they connect to learning multiplication, and continue in grades 4 and 5 with finding the area of rectangles through tiling. In grade 6, students explore area of a wide range of polygons and learn the formulas for many of these polygons. In grade 7, students explore area of circles. Across middle school, students apply concepts of area to surface area and to real-world situations (CCSSO, 2010).

◆ Comparison Activities

Comparing area measures is a bigger conceptual challenge than comparing length measures because areas come in different shapes. Comparison activities with areas should help students distinguish between size (or area) and shape, length, and other dimensions. A long, skinny rectangle may have less area than a triangle with shorter sides. Many students, and even adults, do not understand that rearranging an area into different shapes does not affect the amount of area (although the perimeter can change).

Direct comparison of two areas is frequently impossible except when the shapes involved have some common dimension or property. For example, two rectangles with the same width can be compared directly, as can any two circles. Comparison of these special shapes, however, fails to deal with the attribute of area. Instead, activities in which one area is rearranged (conservation of area) are suggested.

Tangrams can be used for this purpose (for a template, see Blackline Master 32 or http://nlvm.usu.edu/en/nav/frames_asid_289_g_2_t_3.html?open=activities&from= category_g_2_t_3.html). The two small triangles can be used to make the parallelogram, the square, and the medium triangle. This permits a similar discussion about pieces having the same size (area) but different shapes (and is great foundation for sixth-grade investigation of area formulas of triangles and quadrilaterals).

Activity 14.8 TANGRAM AREAS

 Give students outlines of several shapes made with tangram pieces that have the same area but different shapes. (You do not need to use a full set; it is good to start with three or four pieces.) See http://nlvm.usu.edu/en/nav/frames_asid_289_g_2_t_3.html? open=activities&from=category_g_2_t_3.html for an applet that allows students to cover various pictures with a full set of tangrams. Ask groups to estimate which one they think is the largest (or smallest). Let students use tangrams to decide which shapes have the same area, which are larger, and which are smaller. Students can also explore tangram shapes in a full set to see whether they are congruent.

This activity can (and should) be repeated with different shapes that *do vary in size*—that is, use more or fewer of the tangram pieces (Figure 14.7). Let students explain how they came to their conclusions.

◆ Tools for Area Measure

Before learning formulas, students should have significant "cover-the-surface" experiences with area. Tools for covering include manipulatives, which tend to be squares (but don't have to be) and grid paper. Both are discussed here.

Tiles

Square tiles are the most commonly used tools for exploring area, although any object that has area as its main attribute can be used. Square tiles can be easily cut from card stock or construction paper, so that each student will have a set that he or she can keep and use at home. Square manipulatives also come in other forms, for example, the 1-inch or 6-inch tiles found at a home improvement store or 5-foot square table cloths. The unit does not have to be a square. Surfaces can be covered with rectangles such as sticky notes, sheets of notebook paper, or sheets of newspaper.

In activities that involve covering surfaces, there are typically units that only partially fit in, or spaces that are too small for another full unit to fit in. Students should estimate about how many units will fill those gaps (Figure 14.8). Beginning in fifth grade, students begin using fractional units of measure, so covering a surface with partial pieces is a good way to start thinking about parts of units. The following activity is a good starting point to see what ideas your students have about units of area.

Teaching Tip

Two good literature links for tangrams are the popular *Grandfather Tang's Story* (Tompert, 1997) and the middle-school-friendly *The Legend of the Tangram Prince* (Foster, 2007). The illustrations in the first book use one full set, and those in the second book use two full sets, so the areas of the various figures within each book are congruent.

Figure 14.7

Compare shapes made of tangram pieces.

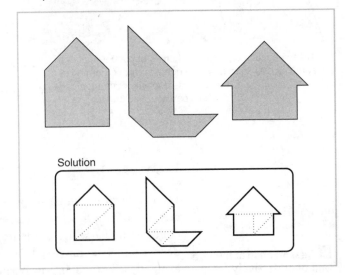

Activity 14.9 COVER AND COMPARE

Draw three shapes of different sizes on a sheet of paper: two rectangles and one irregularly curved shape. Make sure it is not obvious which shape is largest or smallest. Ask students to predict which shape has the smallest and which has the largest area. Next, ask students to find the approximate area of each shape by using a comparing technique that they design. Ask the groups to brainstorm strategies for comparing before they get started.

There are several approaches to this problem. One is to measure each shape with tiles and compare the approximate areas. Or students can select one shape as the basis for comparison and cut out the others, laying them over the first. Or students can cut out each shape and place it over grid paper. Students should explain their strategy and justify their choice of the shape with the largest and smallest area.

Figure 14.8

Measuring the area of a large shape drawn with tape on the floor. Units are card stock squares of the same size.

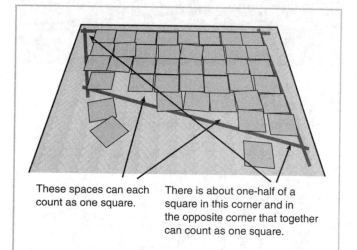

These spaces can each count as one square.

There is about one-half of a square in this corner and in the opposite corner that together can count as one square.

Your initial objective is to develop the idea that area is measured by covering or tiling, and that shape and size are two related but different attributes.

Grids

Grids of various types can be thought of as "area rulers." A grid of squares does for area what a ruler does for length. It lays out the units for you. Square grids on transparencies can be made from Blackline Masters 1, 3, and 5. Have students place the clear grid over a region to be measured and count the units inside. An alternative method is to trace a region onto a piece of grid paper.

Standards for Mathematical Practice

2 Reason abstractly and quantitatively

◆ Perimeter and Area

Using tiles or outlining shapes on grid paper allows the simultaneous exploration of perimeter and area. These concepts have been taught in elementary school, but they continue to confuse middle-school students. The next activities are designed to help students develop a deeper understanding of the relationship between perimeter and area; after exploring each, explicitly ask students how perimeter and area are related.

Activity 14.10 FIXED PERIMETERS

Explain to students that they are building a pen for a rabbit and that you have 24 feet of wire fence. Ask, "Will it matter what shape rectangle I use to make my pen?" Give students a piece of nonstretching string that is 24 cm long and a sheet of 1-cm grid paper. Ask students to explore how many different-size rectangles can be made with a perimeter of 24 cm, recording the perimeter and area for each new sketch of the pen. As a way to incorporate non-whole rational numbers, change the total number of feet to 30, and encourage students to measure sides to the nearest one-half inch.

Activity 14.11 **FIXED AREAS**

Using the same context, explain to students that when you bought your rabbit, you were told that the best space for outdoor exercise is 36 square feet. You need to buy the wire fence and are wondering how much to buy, but you haven't yet decided on a shape for the rectangle. Provide students with 1-cm grid paper. Ask them to design several options for you and for each one tell you the area and the perimeter (fence) needed.

Stop and Reflect

Let's think about the two preceding activities. For "Fixed Areas," will all of the perimeters be the same? If not, what can you say about the shapes with longer or shorter perimeters? For "Fixed Perimeters," will the areas remain the same? Why or why not? ■

◀  Standards for Mathematical Practice

7 **Look for and make use of structure**

When students complete Activity 14.10 or 14.11, have them cut out all the figures. Label either two charts or two locations on the board "Perimeter" and "Area," and have teams come up and place their figures (left to right) from smallest perimeter (or area) to largest perimeter (or area) on the appropriate chart. Ask students to state what they observe, make conjectures, and see whether any conclusions can be drawn. Students may be surprised to find out that rectangles with the same areas do not necessarily have the same perimeters, and vice versa. And, of course, this fact is not restricted to rectangles.

Students will notice interesting relationships between perimeter and area. When the area is fixed, the shape with the smallest perimeter is "squarelike," as is the rectangle with the largest area. If you allow any shape whatsoever, the shape with the smallest perimeter for a fixed area is a circle. Also, students will notice that the "fatter" a shape, the smaller its perimeter; the "skinnier" a shape, the larger its perimeter. (This is true in three dimensions—replace perimeter with surface area and area with volume.)

note

A virtual exploration of area and perimeter with Amy and Ben is available at "Math Playground" (www.mathplayground.com/area_perimeter.html). After the exploration, you can measure the lengths and widths of a variety of rectangles and calculate the area and perimeter of each.

 ## Developing Formulas for Area

Ask students, "What is area?" and the response you may hear is, "Area is length times width." This is not a definition of area—it is the formula for the area of (some) shapes. First and foremost, students must understand what area is, explore informal ways to find area, and then connect those to the formulas. When students *develop* formulas, they gain conceptual understanding of the ideas and relationships involved, and they engage in "doing mathematics." Also, there is less chance that students will confuse formulas or forget them altogether. And, if they are forgotten, with a conceptual understanding of how the formulas are related, students can regenerate the formulas.

It is important for students to understand how shapes are related and how formulas for finding their areas are also related. In the *Common Core State Standards* for sixth grade,

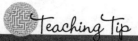

◆ **Standards for Mathematical Practice**

8 Look for and express regularity in repeated reasoning

students are to "find the area of right triangles, other triangles, special quadrilaterals, and polygons by composing into rectangles or decomposing into triangles and other shapes" (CCSSO, 2010, p. 44). The formula for the area of a rectangle is one of the first that is developed and is usually written as $A = L \times W$, or stated as "area equals length times width." Thinking ahead to other area formulas, an equivalent but more unifying idea might be $A = b \times h$, or "area equals base times height."

The formula *base × height* can be generalized to all parallelograms (not just rectangles) and is useful in developing the area formulas for triangles and trapezoids.

Furthermore, the same approach can be extended to three dimensions—volumes of cylinders are given in terms of the *area of the base* times the height.

◆ Student Misconceptions

Students have various challenges with area formulas. The common error of confusing the formulas for area and perimeter has already been discussed. Second, students can know a formula, but not understand that area is the measure of the surface. Therefore, when a shape does not fit into one of the formulas that they know, they cannot solve the task. The tasks in Figure 14.9 cannot be solved with simple formulas; an understanding of concepts and how formulas work is required.

Another common error when students use formulas comes from a failure to conceptualize the meaning of *height* and *base* in geometric figures. For each of the shapes in Figure 14.10, a slanted side and a height are given. Students tend to confuse these two.

Any side of a figure can be called a *base*. For each base that a figure has, there is a corresponding height. If the figure were to slide into a room on a selected base, the *height* would be the height of the shortest door it could pass through without tipping—that is, the perpendicular distance to the base.

Figure 14.9
Understanding the attribute of area.

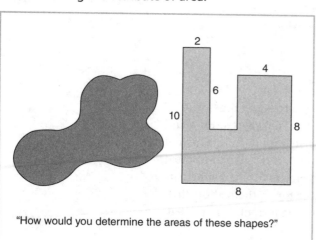

"How would you determine the areas of these shapes?"

Figure 14.10
Heights of figures are not always measured along an edge or a surface.

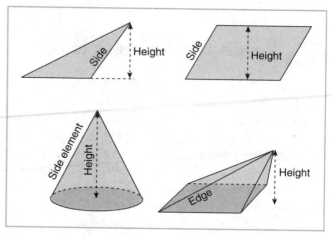

◆ Rectangles

Research suggests that it is a significant leap for students to move from counting squares inside a rectangle to acquiring a conceptual development of a formula. Students often try to fill in empty rectangles with drawings of squares and then count the result one square at a time (Battista, 2003). Although area of rectangles (and the formula) have been taught in elementary school, it is important to assess whether middle-grade students have a strong understanding of the formula because it will be used to develop the other area formulas.

Do students connect area to multiplication (of whole numbers or fractions), in which rectangles were used as a visual representation? When we multiply a length times a width, we are not multiplying "squares times squares." Rather, the *length* of one side indicates how many squares will fit on that side. If this set of squares is taken as a unit, then the *length* of the other side (not a number of squares) will determine how many of these *rows of squares* can fit in the rectangle. Then the amount of square units covering the rectangle is the product of the length of a row and the number of rows (column × row = area).

Do students connect length to the idea of base? Explain to students that you like the idea of measuring one side to tell how many squares will fit in a row along that side. You would like them to call or think of this side as the *base* of the rectangle, even though some people call it the *length* or the *width*. Then the other side can be called the *height*. Which side is the base? It can be either side—and students should realize that they can always rotate a shape in order to use more convenient numbers and use any side as the base. ◄

Standards for Mathematical Practice

1 Make sense of problems and persevere in solving them

◆ From Rectangles to Other Parallelograms

Once students understand the base-times-height formula for rectangles, the next challenge is to determine the areas of parallelograms. Rather than providing a formula, use the following activity, which asks students to devise their own formula, building on what they know about rectangles.

 Activity 14.12 **AREA OF A PARALLELOGRAM**

Give students two or three parallelograms, drawn either on grid paper or, for a slightly greater challenge, on plain paper labeled with all dimensions—the lengths of all four sides and the height. Ask students to use what they have learned about the area of rectangles to determine the areas of these parallelograms. Students should find a method that will work for any parallelogram, even if it is not drawn on a grid.

If students are stuck, ask them to examine ways in which the parallelogram is like a rectangle or how it can be changed into a rectangle. As shown in Figure 14.11, a parallelogram can always be transformed into a rectangle with the same base, the same height, and the same area. Thus, the formula for the area of a parallelogram is exactly the same as that for a rectangle: base times height.

Figure 14.11
Area of a parallelogram.

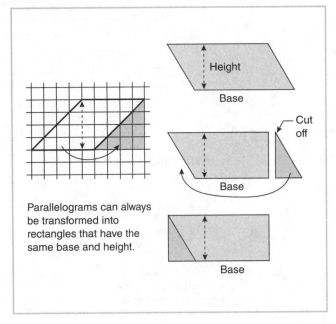

Parallelograms can always be transformed into rectangles that have the same base and height.

◆ From Parallelograms to Triangles

With that background, the area of a triangle can logically follow. Again, use a problem-based approach, as in the next activity.

 Activity 14.13 **AREA OF A TRIANGLE**

Provide students with at least two triangles drawn on grid paper. Avoid right triangles because they are an easier special case. Challenge the students to use what they have learned about the area of parallelograms to find the area of each of the triangles and to develop a method that will work for any triangle. They should be sure that their method works for all the triangles given to them, as well as at least one more that they draw. For students with disabilities or those that need more structure, ask, "Can you find a parallelogram that is related to your triangle?" Then suggest that they fold a piece of paper in half, draw a triangle on the folded paper, and cut it out, making two identical copies. Use the copies to fit the triangles together into a parallelogram. This provides a nice visual of how a triangle is related to a parallelogram.

As shown in Figure 14.12, two congruent triangles can always be arranged to form a parallelogram with the same base and same height as those of the triangle. The area of the triangle will, therefore, be one-half that of the parallelogram.

Stop and Reflect

There are three possible parallelograms, one for each triangle side that serves as a base. Will the computed areas always be the same? How might you engage students in exploring the three different parallelograms? ∎

◆ From Parallelograms to Trapezoids

After developing formulas for parallelograms and triangles, students are ready to develop the formula for area of a trapezoid. There are at least 10 different methods of arriving at a formula for trapezoids, each related to the area of parallelograms or triangles. One method uses the same general approach that was used for triangles. Suggest that students work with two trapezoids that are identical, just as they did with triangles. Figure 14.13 shows how this method results in the formula. Not only are all of these formulas connected, but similar methods were used to develop them, as well.

Figure 14.12

Two triangles always make a parallelogram.

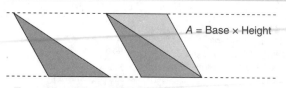

$A = \text{Base} \times \text{Height}$

Two copies of any triangle will always form a parallelogram with the same base and height; therefore, the triangle has an area of half of the parallelogram, $A = \frac{1}{2}(\text{Base} \times \text{Height})$.

Figure 14.13

Two trapezoids always form a parallelogram.

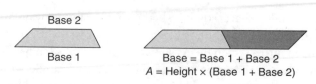

Base 2

Base 1

Base = Base 1 + Base 2
$A = \text{Height} \times (\text{Base 1} + \text{Base 2})$

Two trapezoids always make a parallelogram with the same height and a base equal to the sum of the bases in the trapezoid. Therefore, $A = \frac{1}{2} \times \text{Height} \times (\text{Base 1} + \text{Base 2})$.

Here are a few suggestions, each leading to a different approach to finding the area of a trapezoid:

• Make a parallelogram inside the given trapezoid by using three of the sides.
• Make a parallelogram by using three sides that surround the trapezoid.
• Draw a diagonal, forming two triangles.
• Draw a line through the midpoints of the nonparallel sides. The length of that line is the average of the lengths of the two parallel sides.
• Draw a rectangle inside the trapezoid, leaving two triangles, and then put those two triangles together.

Or give students an example of a trapezoid with the measurements labeled and ask them to try the following:

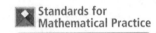

Find the area of the trapezoid by using only the formulas for area of rectangles, area of parallelograms, and area of triangles.

After they have worked through several related problems, ask students what they notice across the situations that they might generalize to all trapezoids.

 Stop and Reflect

Do you think that students should learn special formulas for the area of a square? Why or why not? Do you think students need formulas for the perimeters of squares and rectangles? ■

◀ ◆ **Standards for Mathematical Practice**

8 Look for and express regularity in repeated reasoning.

t e c h n o l o g y ⏻
note

The relationship between the areas of rectangles, parallelograms, and triangles can be dramatically illustrated with a dynamic geometry program such as *The Geometer's Sketchpad* (from Key Curriculum Press) or *GeoGebra* (free public domain software). Draw two congruent segments on two parallel lines (Figure 14.14). Then connect the end points of the segments to form a parallelogram and two triangles. The height is indicated by a segment perpendicular to the parallel lines. Either of the two line segments can be dragged left or right to slant the parallelogram and triangle without changing the base or height.

Figure 14.14
Dynamic geometry software shows that figures with the same base and height have the same area.

🔺 Surface Area

After learning how to find area of two-dimensional shapes, students are ready to explore surface area of three-dimensional shapes composed of two-dimensional faces. According to the *Common Core State Standards*, sixth graders are expected to find the surface area of shapes composed of faces of rectangles and triangles. In seventh grade, this requirement is extended to shapes composed of faces of triangles, quadrilaterals, and polygons, and to structures composed of cubes and right prisms (CCSSO, 2010). Nets are an effective strategy for introducing surface area. A great way to illustrate nets is to create several rectangular or triangular prisms made of card stock, including cubes

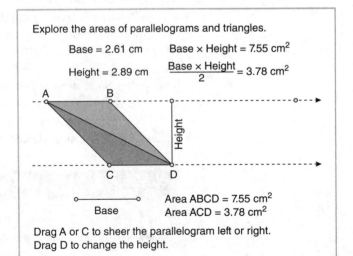

Explore the areas of parallelograms and triangles.

Base = 2.61 cm   Base × Height = 7.55 cm²

Height = 2.89 cm $\frac{\text{Base} \times \text{Height}}{2}$ = 3.78 cm²

Area ABCD = 7.55 cm²
Area ACD = 3.78 cm²

Drag A or C to sheer the parallelogram left or right.
Drag D to change the height.

with sides held together by small pieces of Velcro. In this way, students can think about the net of the figure as they break the figure into faces and calculate the surface area.

Activity 14.14 MAKING "TO-GO" BOXES

 This activity engages students in a context that involves nets. Begin by sharing the situation with the students: Joan's Dine & Dessert Shop orders to-go boxes in three sizes (dinner, pie, and cake), but the boxes are getting very expensive. Joan wants an estimate of how much cardboard is used for each size so that she can decide whether she should make her own boxes. Please share with her how much cardboard is used for these boxes (assume no overlap of cardboard—it is taped at the edges).

- Dinner box: 7 in. × 7 in. × 3 in.
- Pie box: 5 in. × 4 in. × 3 in.
- Cake box: 8 in. × 8 in. × 5 in.

Have grid and blank paper available to students for creating their net for each box. Have students compare their diagrams and surface areas. They may have picked different bases, and the illustrations may look different. This provides a great opportunity to talk about why these different nets are equivalent. For English language learners (ELLs), the word *net* may be confusing because it may connect to the Internet or to nets used for fishing or basketball. Also, getting food in a "to-go" box may not be a practice in a student's country of origin.

technology ⏻
note

See "Surface Area and Volume" at www.shodor.org/interactivate/activities/SurfaceAreaAndVolume to explore how changing the dimensions of a polyhedron changes its surface area (and volume), or see "Interactives: Geometry 3D Shapes" at www.learner.org/interactives/geometry/index.html for explorations of surface area through animations ("Surface Area & Volume" tab).

🔺 Circles

⬢ Circumference

The relationship between the *circumference* of a circle (the distance around, or the perimeter) and the *diameter* (a line passing through the center and joining two points on the circle) is one of the most interesting that students can discover and is a *Common Core State Standards* topic for seventh grade (CCSSO, 2010). The circumference of every circle is about 3.14 times as long as the diameter. The exact ratio is an irrational number close to 3.14, represented by the Greek letter pi (π). So, $\pi = \frac{C}{D}$, the circumference divided by the diameter. In a slightly different form, $C = \pi D$. Half the diameter is the radius (r), so the same equation can be written $C = 2\pi r$.

There are many ways to explore the ratio of circumference and diameter of a circle. Activity 14.15 engages students in measuring to analyze the relationship.

Activity 14.15 WHAT IS THE RATIO OF DIAMETER TO CIRCUMFERENCE?

 Place circular items such as jar lids, cans, wastebaskets, and even hula hoops at various stations around the room. Explain to students that they will be going to each station and carefully measuring the diameter and circumference of the shapes and recording their data in a table. Give each group of students a string and a ruler. Model how to measure each attribute: To measure the diameter, stretch the string across the circle, through the center. Since the diameter is the widest segment through a circle, students should look for where the string can be the longest as it is pulled across the circle; to measure the circumference wrap the string once around the object, and then measure the length of string needed to go around exactly once.

After students have been to every station, have them add a column to their table in which they record the ratio of circumference to diameter for each circle.

With graphing calculators, you can have each group enter its measures for diameter (*x*) and circumference (*y*) into the TABLE function of a graphing calculator, view the graph, and find the line of best fit.

(Recall from Chapter 11 that graphs of equivalent ratios are always straight lines through the origin.) If measured carefully, the ratio of circumference to diameter will be close to 3.14.

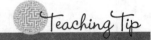
Teaching Tip

Outliers (data that do not result in a ratio close to 3.14) can be examined to see if there was measurement error, focusing student thinking on data (outliers) and measurement (precision)!

Another way to investigate the relationship is to cut a set of strings in a particular length (e.g., 8 cm). Use one string as a diameter, and use a compass to draw a circle around it. Then see how many of the remaining strings are needed to go around the circle. Repeat for different-size circles. Students are likely to be surprised that regardless of the size of a circle, they need only a little more than three strings to go around it.

What is most important in this activity is that students develop a clear understanding of π as the ratio of circumference to diameter (whole-to-part ratio) in any circle, regardless of size. If you know one measure, you can find the other. The quantity π is not some mystical number that appears in mathematics formulas; it is a naturally occurring and universal ratio.

◆ Area

As with polygons, students should investigate the area formula for circles, rather than just be given the formula. One way is to cover a circle with square units and see how many cover a circle. Use square tiles (e.g., color tiles), or cut out squares that can be placed on the circle and glued. The advantage of cutouts is that students can cut some that are only partially inside the circle and place the extra pieces somewhere else in the circle. The key to this approach is that the students need to get a measure of the radius from the sides of the tiles. One group, for example, might have a circle that has a radius of 3 tiles, while another group explores a circle that has a radius of 5 tiles.

Another, similar way to see the relationship is to set the radius as the unit. Use the radius unit to make squares—we will call them *radius squares*. Form a grid that is 2 × 2 radius squares, and draw a circle inside. By observation, you can see that the circle inscribed in this grid has an area of less than 4 radius squares (because so much of the grid is outside the circle). Students need two identical copies of this picture. They use one set to cut out the radius squares to see how many it takes to cover the circle in the other picture exactly. Students can reach an estimate that the number of radius squares needed is about 3.1 or 3.2. This is not as accurate a technique, but it does reinforce the geometric idea that r^2 is a square with a side of r.

A third approach is something close to the method that Archimedes actually used to approximate π. In this approach, students draw a circle on grid paper with a given radius (or the circle can be drawn beforehand on a handout). They draw a square inside the circle

Figure 14.15

Using inscribed and superscribed squares to estimate the area of a circle.

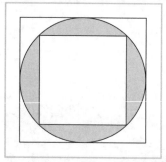

and outside the circle (Figure 14.15). Find the areas of the two squares, and average them to find the area of the circle. Archimedes began this way and then started using polygons that got closer to the shape of the circle. See www.pbs.org/wgbh/nova/teachers/activities/3010_archimed.html or http://illuminations.nctm.org/LessonDetail.aspx?ID=L574 for full lessons in which this approach is used.

A final and very effective approach is to cut a circle apart into sectors and rearrange them to look more like a parallelogram. For example, students can cut from 3 to 12 sectors from a circle and build them into what looks like parallelogram. Recall that in the angle investigation, students made a wax paper circle. This same circle can be remade and cut to form the pieces to explore area of a circle. You may need to help them notice that the smaller the size of the sectors used, the closer the arrangement gets to a rectangle. Figure 14.16 presents a common development of the area formula $A = \pi r^2$. See Flores and Regis (2003) for three different ways to illustrate the formula for the area of a circle.

technology note

See the NCTM Illuminations applet "Circle Tool" (http://illuminations.nctm.org/ActivityDetail.aspx?ID=116), which allows students to investigate the relationship between radius, diameter, circumference, and area of circles in a dynamic way.

Figure 14.16 Development of the formula for area of a circle.

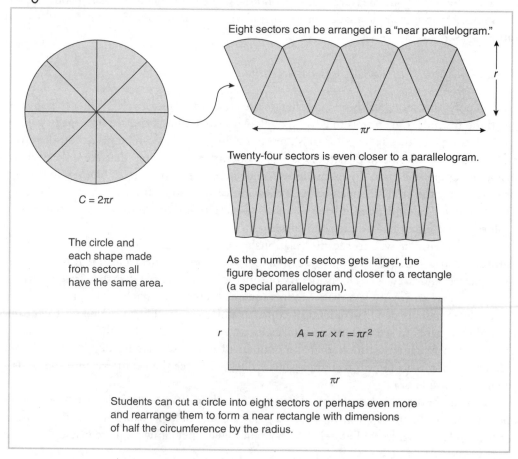

Volume and Capacity

Volume and *capacity* are two terms for the measure of the "size" of a three-dimensional region. This topic begins in fifth grade. It continues to be emphasized throughout middle school as students solve real problems involving volume and develop the formula for volume of right rectangular prisms in grade 6 and for cylinders, cones, and spheres in grade 8 (CCSSO, 2010).

The term *capacity* is generally used to refer to the amount that a container will hold. Standard units of capacity include quarts, gallons, liters, and milliliters. The term *volume* can be used to refer to the capacity of a container but is also used for the size of solid objects. Standard units of volume are expressed in terms of length units, such as cubic inches or cubic centimeters.

Comparison Activities

One method of comparing capacities is to fill one container with something and then pour this amount into the comparison container. Students and adults can have difficulty accurately predicting which of two containers will hold more. The apparent volumes of solid objects are sometimes misleading, and a method of comparison is also difficult. To compare the volumes of solids, such as a ball and an apple, a displacement method must be used. You can have students predict which object has the smaller or greater volume and then place the object in a measuring cup or beaker filled with water to see how much the water rises.

Surface Area and Volume

Just as students should understand the relationship between perimeter and area (see Activities 14.10 and 14.11), they should understand the relationship between volume and surface area, as in Activity 14.16.

Activity 14.16 FIXED VOLUME: COMPARING PRISMS

 Give each pair of students a supply of centimeter cubes or wooden cubes. If you have ELLs, provide a visual of a rectangular solid, labeling all the key words they will need for the lesson (*length, width, height, surface area, cube, volume, side*). Ask students to use 64 cubes (or 36, if you prefer) to build different rectangular prisms and record in a table the surface area for each prism formed. Then ask students to describe any patterns that they notice. In particular, what happens to the surface area as the prism becomes less like a tall, skinny box and more like a cube? (See Expanded Lesson for details.)

Another highly engaging way to compare surface area and volume is through the demonstration described in Activity 14.17.

Activity 14.17 WHICH SILO HOLDS MORE?

 Take two sheets of construction paper. Make a tube shape (cylinder) from one sheet by taping the two long edges together. Make a shorter, fatter cylinder from the other sheet by taping the short edges together. Ask, "If these were two silos, would they hold the same amount, or would one hold more than the other?" Survey students first to see how many select each option. To test the conjectures, use a filler, such as beans. Place the skinny cylinder inside the fat one. Fill the inside tube and then lift it up, allowing the filler to empty into the fat cylinder. Surprising to many, the volumes are different, even though the sizes of the papers holding the filler are the same. Ask students to investigate why this is true.

The goal of these activities is for students to realize that volume does not dictate surface area, but that there is a relationship between surface area and volume, just as there is between perimeter and area—namely, that cubelike prisms have less surface area than long, narrow prisms with the same volume.

Once students have developed formulas for computing area and volume, they can continue to explore the relationships between surface area and volume without actually building the prisms.

Tools for Volume and Capacity Measures

Two types of units can be used to measure volume and capacity: solid units and containers. Solid units are objects like wooden cubes or old tennis balls that can be used to fill the container being measured. The other type of unit model is a small container that can be filled; the filler is then poured repeatedly into the container being measured. The following are a few examples of units that you might want to collect:

- Liquid medicine cups
- Plastic jars and containers of almost any size
- Wooden cubic blocks or blocks of any shape (as long as you have a lot of the same size)
- Styrofoam packing peanuts (which still produce conceptual measures of volume despite not packing perfectly)

◤ *Activity* 14.18 BOX COMPARISON—CUBIC UNITS

Provide students with a pair of small boxes that you have folded up from poster board (Figure 14.17). For units, use dimensions that match the cube blocks that you have. Students are given two boxes, one block, and an appropriate ruler. (If you use 2-cm cubes, make a ruler with the unit equal to 2 cm.) Ask students to decide which box has the greater volume or if the volumes of the two boxes are the same. Here are some suggested box dimensions ($L \times W \times H$):

$$6 \times 3 \times 4 \quad 5 \times 4 \times 4 \quad 3 \times 9 \times 3 \quad 6 \times 6 \times 2 \quad 5 \times 5 \times 3$$

Students should use words, drawings, and numbers to explain their conclusions.

Figure 14.17

Make small boxes by starting with a rectangle and drawing a square on each corner as shown. Cut on the solid lines and fold the box up, wrapping the corner squares to the outside and taping them to the sides as shown.

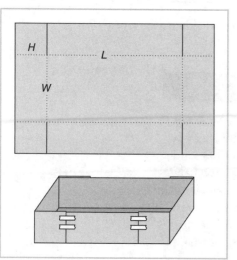

A useful hint in the last activity is to first figure out how many cubes will fit on the bottom of the box. Some students will discover a multiplicative rule for the volume. The boxes can be filled with cubes to confirm conjectures.

Instruments for measuring capacity are generally used for small amounts of liquids or pourable materials, such as rice or water. These tools are commonly found in kitchens and laboratories. Students should use measuring cups to explore recipes for foods, papier-mâché, or Oobleck for science experiments (google "making Oobleck" for recipes).

Developing Formulas for Volumes of Common Solid Shapes

The relationships in the formulas for volume are completely analogous to those for area. A common error that is repeated from two- to three-dimensional shapes occurs when students confuse the meaning of *height* and *base* in their use of formulas (see Figure 14.10). The base of the figure can be any flat surface of a figure.

As you read, notice the similarities between rectangles and prisms, between parallelograms and slanted (oblique) prisms, and between triangles and pyramids. Not only are the formulas related, but the processes for developing the formulas are similar.

Teaching Tip

A way to help students think about height (versus side length) is to picture an upright stick entering through a doorway: The *height* would be the height of the shortest door the stick could pass through without bending.

Volumes of Cylinders

A *cylinder* is a solid with two congruent, parallel bases and sides with parallel elements that join corresponding points on the bases. There are several special classes of cylinders, including *prisms* (with polygons for bases), *right prisms, rectangular prisms,* and *cubes* (see Chapter 13) (Zwillinger, 2011). Interestingly, all of these solids have the same volume formula, and that one formula is analogous to the area formulas for rectangles and other parallelograms.

Review Activity 14.18, "Box Comparison—Cubic Units." The development of the volume formula from this box exploration is parallel to the development of the formula for the area of a rectangle (Figure 14.18). The *area* of the base (instead of *length* of the base for rectangles) determines how many *cubes* can be placed on the base to form a single unit—a layer of cubes. The *height* of the box then determines how many of these *layers* will fit in the box, just as the height of the rectangle determined how many *rows* of squares will fill the rectangle.

Recall that a parallelogram can be thought of as a slanted rectangle, as was illustrated with dynamic geometry software (see Figure 14.14). Show students a stack of three or four decks of playing cards (or a stack of books). When stacked straight, they form a rectangular solid. The volume, as just discussed, is $V = A \times H$, with A equal to the area of one playing card. If the stack is now slanted to one side (Figure 14.19), what will the volume of this new figure be? Students should be able to argue that this figure has the same volume (and same volume formula) as the original stack.

What if the cards in this activity were some other shape? If they were circular, the volume would still be the area of the base times the height; if they were triangular, still the same. The conclusion is that the volume of *any* cylinder is equal to (*area of the base*) × *height*.

Volumes of Cones and Pyramids

Recall that when a parallelogram and a triangle have the same base and height, the areas are in a 2-to-1 relationship. Interestingly, the relationship between the volumes of a cylinder and a cone with the same base and height is 3 to 1. That is, *area* is to *two-dimensional* figures what *volume* is to *three-dimensional* figures. Furthermore, triangles are to parallelograms as cones are to cylinders.

To investigate the relationship, use plastic models of these related shapes (e.g., translucent Power Solids). Have students estimate the number of times the pyramid will fit into the prism. Then have them test their predictions by filling the pyramid with water or rice and emptying the filler into the prism. They will discover that exactly three pyramids will fill a prism with the same base and height (Figure 14.20).

Figure 14.18

Volume of a right prism: area of the base × height.

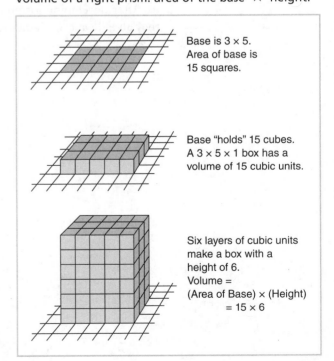

Base is 3 × 5.
Area of base is 15 squares.

Base "holds" 15 cubes.
A 3 × 5 × 1 box has a volume of 15 cubic units.

Six layers of cubic units make a box with a height of 6.
Volume =
(Area of Base) × (Height)
= 15 × 6

Figure 14.19

Two prisms with the same base and same height have the same volume.

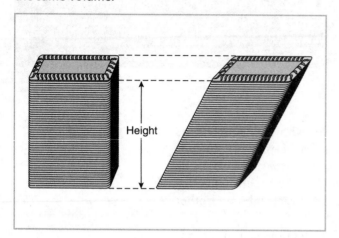

Height

Figure 14.20

Comparing the volume of a prism with the volume of a pyramid, and the volume of a cylinder with the volume of a cone.

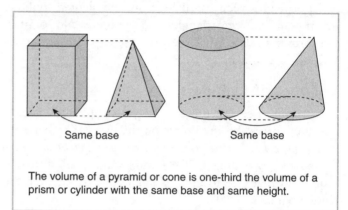

Same base   Same base

The volume of a pyramid or cone is one-third the volume of a prism or cylinder with the same base and same height.

The volume of a cone or pyramid is exactly one-third the volume of the corresponding cylinder with the same base and height.

Using the same idea of base times height, it is possible to explore the surface area of a sphere (4 times the area of a circle with the same radius) and the volume of a sphere ($\frac{1}{3}$ the surface area times the radius). That is, the surface area of a sphere is $4\pi r^2$, and the volume is $\frac{1}{3}(4\pi r^2)r$, or $\frac{4}{3}\pi r^3$.

◆ Connections between Formulas

The connectedness of mathematical ideas can hardly be better illustrated than with the connections of all of these formulas to the single concept of *base times height*.

A conceptual approach to the development of formulas helps students understand that they are meaningful and efficient ways to measure different attributes of the objects around us. After developing formulas in conceptual ways, students can derive formulas from what they already know. Mathematics does make sense!

Expanded Lesson

Fixed Volume

Content and Task Decisions

Grade Level: 6–7

Mathematics Goals

- To contrast the concepts of surface area and volume
- To develop an understanding of the relationship between surface area and volume of different shapes when the volume is fixed

Grade Level Guide

NCTM Curriculum Focal Points	Common Core State Standards
One of the three focal points in grade 7 is that students understand and be able to apply the concepts of volume and surface area.	An emphasis in grade 6 is on surface area (with nets) and developing the formula for rectangular prisms. In grade 7, students continue to "solve real-life and mathematical problems involving angle measure, area, surface area, and volume" (CCSSO, 2010, p. 47).

Consider Your Students' Needs

Students have worked with nets composed of rectangles and triangles and with volume of rectangular prisms.

For English Language Learners

- Build background for the terms *base, height, nets, volume, faces,* and *surface area.* Ask students whether they have heard these words, and use their ideas to talk about their mathematical meaning. You can create a chart on the wall comparing the everyday meaning and the mathematical meaning of these words.
- Use visuals (tiles, cubes, and a cardboard box that can be opened and closed) as you model the mathematical terms.

For Students with Disabilities

- Students who struggle may need to use either a computer-based program to model different surface areas or a geoboard. They may need to break a net into its component pieces and connect (even tape) each of the two-dimensional pieces to a face of the rectangular prism.
- Sometimes, the addition of a third dimension can be difficult. Focus first on the idea of (*area of*) *base* × *height.* Have students select a possible height (must be a factor of 60) and then think, "What are options for the base if the volume is 60 cubes?" For example, if they think of the height as 6 units, then they know the base must be 10 square units and can determine the length and width of the base. Have a collection of concrete materials available to model these dimensions.

Materials

Each student will need:

- Sixty cubes, such as wooden cubes or sugar cubes (multilink cubes can also be used, but the notches can create difficulties for students, slowing the constructions and challenging the visualizations)
- Two or three sheets of grid paper per person (for drawing nets)
- "Fixed-Volume Recording Sheet" (Blackline Master 37)
- Calculators

The teacher will need:

- Copy of "Fixed-Volume Recording Sheet" (Blackline Master 37) to project (with a document camera or overhead projector)

Lesson

Before

Begin with a simpler task exploring volume and nets:

- Give each student 12 cubes, and ask each one to build a rectangular prism. Ask, "Is there more than one way to build it?" (The only other way is 1 × 1 × 12.) Some students may have a base of 2 × 2 units and a height of 3 units, while others have a base of 2 × 3 units and a height of 2 units. Help them see that if they rotate the prism, it is the same (congruent).
- Ask, "If we were going to outline paper wrapping to cover this prism, what would the outline on my paper look like?"

- Ask students to draw a sketch on their grid paper (scaled down) of the net that would wrap the prism.

- As students share their nets and the area of the components of their nets, reinforce the meaning of surface area.

- Ask, "What do we mean by volume? How do we measure volume? What unit do we use to measure volume? How is surface area different from volume?" Make explicit that the units used to measure area are two-dimensional and therefore cover a region.

Present the focus task to the class:

- Ask, "If you had more cubes, like 1000 cubes, would there be more than one way to build a rectangular prism?" Invite students to list some ways, such as 10 × 10 × 10, 10 × 25 × 4, and 5 × 20 × 10. (They may be able to find ways mentally, or they may want to use a calculator.) Ask, "Would the volumes be different? Why?"

- Ask the focus question, "Will a rectangular prism of a fixed volume have the same surface area?"

- Record their predictions. Explain that you are going to explore this problem by building rectangular prisms with a volume of 60 cubic units.

Provide clear expectations:

Write the following directions on the board:

1. Use all 60 cubes to build a rectangular prism.

2. Sketch a net for the prism on the grid paper. (You may want to illustrate how they can trace the base, but only if you have grid paper with exactly the same scale as the cubes. Then roll the prism to trace the next side.)

3. Find the surface area of the net. Record the dimensions, volume, and surface area of the prism on the recording chart.

4. Repeat steps 1 through 3.

Place students in groups, but require that each student be responsible for drawing his or her own sketches and use his or her own recording sheet.

During

- Question students to be sure they understand the task and the meaning of *volume* and *surface area*. Look for students who are confusing these terms or units.

- Be sure students are drawing nets that would actually fold up to make the prism. You may want students to cut out and test their nets to confirm that they fit the prism they built.

- Watch for students who are building prisms that are actually congruent to prisms they have already built but

rotated to have a different base. Discuss with students that the dimensions are the same, and therefore the students should consider the prism congruent to the ones they have already built.

- Observe and ask the assessment questions, posing one or two to a student and moving to another student (see the "Assessment" section of this lesson).

- Ask students how they can be sure they have all of the possible rectangular solids. If they have not found one, suggest a base they might try. How can they logically come up with all possible dimensions?

After

Bring the class together to share and discuss the task:

- Ask students what they have found out about the surface areas (nets) and volumes of the different prisms. Ask, "Did the volume change when you changed the dimensions? Why or why not? Did the surface area (area of the net) change when you changed the dimensions? Why or why not?"

- Ask students to make observations about the connection between volume and surface area. They might notice, for example, that the more cubelike the prism, the smaller the surface area. How does this link to area and perimeter?

Assessment
Observe

- Are students using appropriate terminology?

- As students form new prisms, are they aware that the volume is not changing because they are building the new prisms with the same number of cubes each time?

- What strategies are students using to determine the dimensions for the cube? The nets for the cube?

- Are students stating important concepts or patterns to their partners? Are they making logical connections between surface area and volume?

Ask

- What is the area of the base of the prism you just made? What is the volume?

- How many rectangles will be in your net? Will this always be true?

- How do you know whether the net will actually fit the prism?

- How is area different from volume? What role does area play in finding the volume of a solid figure?

- How do you measure area? Surface area? Volume? How are the units different?

15

Working with Data and Doing Statistics

Big IDEAS

1 Statistics is its own field, different from mathematics; one key difference is the focus on the variability of data in statistical reasoning.

2 Doing statistics involves a four-step process: formulating questions, collecting data, analyzing data, and interpreting results.

3 Data are gathered and organized in order to answer questions about the populations from which the data came. With data from only a sample of the population, inferences are made about the population.

4 Various types of graphs and other data representations provide different information about the data and, hence, the population from which the data were taken.

5 Measures that describe data with numbers are called *statistics*. The use of a particular statistic can provide different information about the population.

6 Both graphs and statistics can provide a sense of the shape of the data, including how spread out or how clustered they are. To acquire a sense of the shape of data, the data must be recognized as a whole rather than as a collection of numbers.

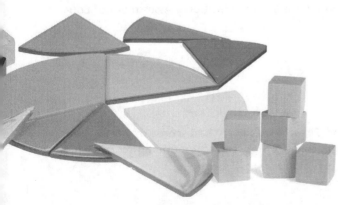

Graphs and statistics bombard the public in areas such as advertising, opinion polls, population trends, health risks, and the progress of students in schools. We hear that the average amount of rainfall this summer is more than it was last summer, or that the average American family consists of 3.19 people. We read on the U.S. Census website (www.census.gov) that the median home price in 2000 was $119,600. In October 2011, the median price of a home in the United States was $212,300, and the mean price was $242,300. These statistics prompt an array of questions: How were these data gathered? What was the purpose? What does it mean to have an average of 3.19 people? Why are the median and the mean for home sales so different, and which one is more helpful to me?

Statistical literacy is critical to understanding the world around us, essential for effective citizenship, and vital for developing the ability to question information presented in the media (Shaughnessy, 2007). Misuse of statistics occurs even in trustworthy sources like newspapers, where graphs are often designed to exaggerate a finding. In elementary school, students learn how data can be categorized and displayed in various graphical forms (grades K–1). They collect and organize sets of data, using frequency tables, bar graphs (horizontal and vertical), line plots (including fractional units), and pictographs to display and analyze data (grades 2–5) (CCSSO, 2010). But, based on recommendations in the *Common Core State Standards*, the study of statistics becomes a priority in and of itself in middle school. In grade 6, students explore data, looking at statistical variability and the distribution of data. In grade 7, students build on their understanding of single data distributions to compare two data distributions, and they are introduced to random sampling as a means of learning about a population. In grade 8, statistics blends with algebra as students explore bivariate data through examining lines, scatter plots, and tables.

 ## What Does It Mean to Do Statistics?

Doing statistics is, in fact, a different process from doing mathematics (Burrill & Elliott, 2006; Franklin, Kader, Mewborn, Moreno, Peck, Perry, & Scheaffer, 2005; Shaughnessy, 2003). As Richard Scheaffer (2006, p. 310–311), past president of the American Statistics Association, notes,

> Mathematics is about numbers and their operations, generalizations and abstractions; it is about spatial configurations and their measurement, transformations, and abstractions. . . . Statistics is also about numbers—but numbers in context: these are called data. Statistics is about variables and cases, distribution and variation, purposeful design or studies, and the role of randomness in the design of studies, and the interpretation of results.

Statistical literacy is a life skill as necessary as being able to read. We interpret data every day and base important life decisions on that data. This section describes some of the big ideas and essential knowledge regarding statistics and explains a general process for doing statistics.

 ### Is It Statistics or Is It Mathematics?

Statistics and mathematics are two different fields; however, assessment questions are often considered "statistics" when what is really being tested is more focused on a computational skill, as shown by the following examples (Scheaffer, 2006).

Read the questions below, and label each as "doing mathematics" or "doing statistics."

1. The average weight of 50 prize-winning tomatoes is 2.36 pounds. What is the combined weight, in pounds, of these 50 tomatoes? (This is an NAEP [National Assessment of Educational Progress] sample question.)
   a. 0.0472
   b. 11.8
   c. 52.36
   d. 59
   e. 118

2. Joe had three test scores of 78, 76, and 74, whereas Mary had scores of 72, 82, and 74. How did Joe's average (mean) compare with Mary's average (mean) score? (This

is a TIMSS [Trends in International Mathematics and Science Study] eighth-grade re-leased item.)

   a. Joe's was 1 point higher.

   b. Joe's was 1 point lower.

   c. The two averages were the same.

   d. Joe's was 2 points higher.

   e. Joe's was 2 points lower.

3. The following table gives the times each of three girls has recorded for seven trials of the 100-m dash this year. Only one girl may compete in the upcoming track meet. Which girl would you select for the meet and why?

Runner	Race 1	2	3	4	5	6
Suzie	15.2	14.8	15.0	14.7	14.3	14.
Tanisha	15.8	15.7	15.4	15.0	14.8	14.
Dara	15.6	15.5	14.8	15.1	14.5	14.

Stop and Reflect

Which of these involves statistical reasoning? What do you consider to be th[e] [...] of a task that make it a statistics-focused task versus a mathematics-focused task? ■

Questions 1 and 2 test mathematical knowledge. The first requires knowing the formula for averages, but the reasoning involves working backward through a formula—which is mathematical thinking, not statistical thinking. Similarly, in the second problem, one must know the formula for the mean, but the question is about a simple comparison of the results found with the formula. In both of these, you might notice that the *context is irrelevant* to the problem. The final question is statistical in nature because the situation requires analysis—graphs or averages might be used to determine a solution. The mathematics here is basic; the focus is on statistics. Notice that the *context is central* to responding to the question, which is an indication that statistical reasoning is involved.

In statistics, the context is essential to analyzing and interpreting the data (Franklin & Garfield, 2006; Franklin et al., 2005; Langrall, Nisbet, Mooney, & Jansem, 2011; Scheaffer, 2006). The spread, or shape, of the data and the meaning of unusual data points (outliers) are determined based on the context.

> ### Teaching Tip
> A good way to decide whether the task you are selecting is statistical in nature (as opposed to mathematical) is to ask yourself, "Does the context matter in answering the question posed in this task?"

◆ The Shape of Data

A big idea in the analysis of data and interpretation of the results is the *shape of the data*: a sense of how the data are spread out or grouped, what characteristics of the data set as a whole can be described, and what the data tell us in a global way about the population from which they were taken. In sixth grade, students must understand that the "set of data collected to answer a statistical question has a distribution which can be described by its center, spread, and overall shape" (CCSSO, 2010, p. 45).

In middle school, measures of center include the median and the mean; measures of spread (variability) include range, interquartile range, and absolute deviation. In particular, students must be able to describe the overall shape, noting the variability based on the context of the data that were gathered. This focus on describing the data based on the context is the key to teaching statistics effectively. This is a very different approach from the one offered in many textbooks, in which students work primarily on skills (e.g., "find the mean" and "make a scatter plot") for the sake of the skills. Instead, these skills must be embedded in collection and analysis of meaningful data with the purpose of having students be able to describe something about the population from which the data came.

Figure 15.1

The process of doing statistics.

I. Formulate Questions
   - Clarify the problem at hand.
   - Formulate one (or more) questions that can be answered with data.

II. Collect Data
   - Design a plan to collect appropriate data.
   - Employ the plan to collect the data.

III. Analyze Data
   - Select appropriate graphical and numerical methods.
   - Use these methods to analyze the data.

IV. Interpret Results
   - Interpret the analysis.
   - Relate the interpretation to the original question.

Source: Franklin, C., Kader, G., Mewborn, D., Moreno, J., Peck, R., Perry, M., & Scheaffer, R. (2005, August). *Guidelines for Assessment and Instruction in Statistics Education (GAISE) Report: A Pre-K–12 Curriculum Framework,* p. 11. Reprinted with permission. Copyright by the American Statistical Association. All rights reserved.

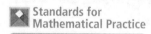
Standards for
Mathematical Practice

1 **Make sense of problems and persevere in solving them**

The Process of Doing Statistics

As the discussion of the shape of data suggests, if students are to be engaged *meaningfully* in learning and doing statistics, they should be involved in the full process, from asking and defining questions to interpreting results. This broad approach provides a framework and purpose in which students learn how to create graphs, compute the mean, and analyze data in other ways. This chapter is organized around this four-step process, which is presented in Figure 15.1.

Formulating Questions

Statistics begins with asking and answering questions about our world. Data collection should be for a purpose—to answer a question of interest to ourselves and others! We may want to learn about some aspect of our world, just like the political pollsters, advertising agencies, market researchers, census takers, wildlife managers, medical researchers, and hosts of others who gather data to answer questions and make informed decisions.

Students should be given opportunities to generate their own questions, decide on appropriate data to help answer these questions, and determine methods of collecting the data. When students formulate the questions, the data they gather become more meaningful. The methods for organizing the data and the techniques for analyzing them have a purpose.

Often, the need to gather data will come from the class naturally in the course of discussion, or from questions arising in other content areas. Science, of course, is full of measurements and thus abounds in possibilities for data analysis. The subject of social studies is also full of opportunities to pose questions requiring data collection. The next two sections suggest some additional ideas.

Classroom Questions

Students want to learn about themselves and each other's families. What does the "typical" student look like? What are students' interests, their likes and dislikes? What measures, such as arm span or time to get to school, apply to them? The easiest questions to begin with are those that can be answered by having each class member contribute one piece of data. Here are a few ideas:

- *Favorites.* TV shows, games, movies, ice cream, video games, sports teams, music
- *Numbers.* Number of pets or siblings, hours spent watching TV or sleeping, bedtime, time spent on the computer
- *Measures.* Height, arm span, area of foot, long-jump distance, shadow length, seconds to run around the track, minutes spent traveling to school

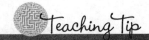

When a "favorite" is likely to have lots of possibilities, restrict the number of choices and have students select from a list.

Beyond One Classroom

The questions in the previous section are designed for students to contribute data about themselves. The results can be expanded by asking comparison questions: "How would this result compare with that of another class or of a nonstudent group?" Comparison questions are a good way to help students focus on the data they have collected and the variability within those data (Russell, 2006). In seventh grade, students begin to compare two populations and observe differences between them (CCSSO, 2010). Students might examine questions in which they compare the responses of boys versus girls, adults or teachers versus students, or categories of full-time workers versus college students. These situations involve issues of sampling and making generalizations and comparisons. In addition, students can ask questions about things beyond school. Discussions about communities provide a good way to integrate social studies and mathematics.

Activity 15.1 WHO'S IN OUR VILLAGE?

The picture book *If the World Were a Village: A Book about the World's People* (Smith, 2011) provides an excellent opportunity to compare class data or school data with data from the wider population in the world. The book explores global wealth, culture, language, and other influences, providing statistics in the adapted case of the world being a village of 100 people. Read the book to the class (or at least several of the comparisons). Ask students if they think the data in the book for particular topics represents their class (or school). Gather data and compare. Then ask students what else they think might be interesting data about our world that could be added to the pages of this book. (See Riskowski, Olbricht, and Wilson, 2010, for details on a project exploring concepts of statistics with 100 students.)

Newspapers suggest all sorts of data-related questions. For example, how many full-page ads occur on different days of the week? What types of stories are on the front page? Which comics are really for kids, and which are not?

Science is about inquiry, and therefore statistics provides an excellent opportunity for interdisciplinary planning. You can begin by asking students to design experiments to answer a question you have selected, such as one of these: What is the width of maple leaves that fall to the ground? Is leaf size related to tree height? How many times do different types of balls bounce when each type is dropped from the same height? How many days does it take for different types of bean, squash, and pea seeds to germinate when kept in moist paper towels? Students should next be able to generate their own questions (related to a particular science focus).

As noted earlier, a distinguishing feature of statistics is that the context is front and center. Therefore, it is particularly important that the context be culturally meaningful. Culturally meaningful contexts create a supportive classroom environment (McGlone, 2008). This can be as simple as asking about a favorite family meal or game, or it can include an exploration

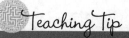

Ask students to turn in a note card with three statistical questions they would like to investigate during the year. This provides an anonymous or confidential way in which students can share interests and curiosities that can then be connected to statistics.

of family customs. The key to having such questions lead to a supportive classroom environment is sharing the results in a way that helps others in the class appreciate the unique features of the lives of their classmates.

The Internet is a vital resource, making data on almost any topic readily available. Students may have interests in various sports, nature, or international events. Whatever their interests, data can be located on the Web. For example, students may wonder how athletes are chosen for the Olympics.

Students will need help in designing questions that can be answered with statistics. These are questions that include variability and for which data can be gathered. Providing examples and non-examples can help students, in particular students with disabilities, focus on the elements of an appropriate statistical question. For example, some of the questions below can be answered with statistics, and some cannot.

1. How much change do I have in my pocket?
2. What is the typical amount of loose change a person carries in his or her pocket?
3. What cereal is most healthy?
4. What reasons do people use in selecting gum (e.g., taste, cost, bubble-making quality, long-lasting flavor, good breath)?
5. How long do different kinds of gum keep their flavor?
6. Which store has the best prices?
7. Where will you buy shampoo?

Did you identify the questions that are not statistical in nature? They are questions 1, 3, and 7. Question 3 could be adapted to a statistical question with a more specific focus on what is meant by "healthy." Similarly, question 6 is very broad and would have to be focused in order to collect the data needed to answer it. Facilitating discussions with students about examples and non-examples, as well as the questions they develop, will help improve their ability to generate appropriate statistical questions.

Collecting Data

How to collect good data is an important (and sometimes skipped) part of the discussion as students learn how to do statistics. Students may start by just raising their hands or counting events, then move to using ballots with limited (a narrowed range of) possible answers, and finally unlimited response options (Hudson, Shupe, Vasquez, & Miller, 2008).

If you do not gather representative data, then you cannot draw valid inferences about the population. For example, if you wonder what movie will be the most popular for a Friday night school event and poll just the sixth graders or ask several groups of girls at lunch, the data gathered may not represent what the response from the whole school would be.

There are two types of data that can be collected—categorical and numeric. Categorical data (as the name implies) are data grouped by labels (categories), such as favorite vacations, colors of cars in the school parking lot, and the most popular suggestion for a mascot for the middle-school team. The mode is often used to describe categorical data, telling what happened most often. (Mode is not mentioned in the *Common Core State Standards*.)

Have students look at several sets of data, some categorical and some numeric. Ask them to select one of the measures of central tendency (mode, median, or mean) that they think best describes the center of the data. Students may start to try to find median or mean of categorical data and realize that it is impossible!

Numeric data, on the other hand, count things or measures on a continuous scale. Numeric data are ordered numerically, like a number line, and can include fractions and decimals. Data of this type include how many miles to school, the temperature in your town over a one-week period, and the weight of students' backpacks. Students need to explore explicitly the idea that statistical measures such as mean and median involve numeric data (Leavy, Friel, & Mamer, 2009).

Oftentimes, we think of data collection as a survey, but data can be collected through observation. This creates a shared context for students in that they will all be a part of observing phenomena. For example, you can explore the question, "What kinds of birds live near our school?" You can set up a bird feeder outside the classroom window and collect data at different times during the day (e.g., each period, students can record data at the beginning, middle, and end of class) to count either the number or types of birds. Students can also conduct observational data collection events on field trips (Mokros & Wright, 2009) and during evening or weekend activities with their families.

◆ Sampling

When a question about a small population, like your class, is asked, data can be gathered on everyone. But statistics generally does not involve gathering data from the whole population; instead, a representative sample is used. The *Common Core State Standards* identify learning how to sample populations in order to make inferences as a critical area for seventh graders (CCSSO, 2010).

Sampling must take variability into consideration. For example, a poll on favorite TV shows will obtain different answers from a survey of seventh graders than from a group of teachers or third graders. And the results may vary for girls and boys or may vary culturally. Answers also may vary based on the day the question is asked or on whether a particular show has been recently discussed. To help students determine whether they have identified a representative sample, ask these questions:

- "What is the population for your question?"
- "Who or what is the subject of your question?"

Then ask students to consider how they will gather data that will include representatives across that population. For example, if they are hoping to learn the movie choice for a seventh-grade movie night at your school, they need to poll girls and boys across the seventh-grade classes within the middle school.

Even when it appears that a sample is representative, it may not be. Unintentional biases can occur, and we cannot always know what subsets might exist within a population. Therefore, *random sampling* is used in statistics. It increases the validity of the results and therefore allows more confidence in being able to make inferences about the population. When seventh graders begin informal work with random sampling, they consider the importance of representative samples for drawing inferences (CCSSO, 2010). Activity 15.2 can help students develop an awareness of the importance of sampling.

◣ *Activity* 15.2 **DO WE FIT IN?**

Using Scholastic's *Book of Lists: Fun Facts, Weird Trivia, and Amazing Lists on Nearly Everything You Need to Know!* by James Buckley and Robert Stremme, or a similar book or online resource, find a list based on sampling a group of people. Read the question to the students and gather data by using the class as the sample. Ask students, "Do you think our class will be a representative sample of the population targeted in this question?"

Ask students to offer why the class might or might not be a representative sample. Gather data from the class. Compare the two data sets. If appropriate, create a stem-and-leaf plot or other data display to compare the two data sets. After displaying the two sets, ask students what technique they think the authors might have used to sample the population.

Although this activity involves people, the term *population* in statistics is used broadly to mean "group" or "subjects of a study." So, the population could be plants of a certain species, insects, or cars of a certain type. The activity above can be replicated with other data. For example, you can look up favorite car colors online and then see if cars that pass by the school form a representative sample of all cars.

◆ Using Existing Data Sources

Data do not have to be collected by a survey or by observation; existing data abound in various places, such as the following print and Web sources.

Print Resources

Newspapers, almanacs, sports record books, maps, and various government publications are possible sources of data that may be used to answer student questions.

Nonfiction literature can be a source of data for middle-school students. The Scholastic *Book of Lists* was mentioned in Activity 15.2. Books on sports, such as *A Negro League Scrapbook* by Carole Boston Weatherford, can have very interesting statistics about historical periods that students can explore and compare.

Web Resources

The Internet provides seemingly limitless data that are often accessed simply by typing the related question into a search. Students may be interested in facts about another country as a result of a social studies unit or a country in the news. Records in various Olympic events over the years or data related to environmental issues are other examples of topics around which student questions may be formulated. For these and hundreds of other questions, data can be found on the Internet. Below are several Web sites with a lot of interesting data.

- The USDA Economic Research Service (www.ers.usda.gov/data/foodconsumption) offers wonderful data sets on the availability and consumption of hundreds of foods. Annual per capita estimates often go back to 1909.

- Google Public Data (www.google.com/publicdata/home) makes large data sets available to explore, visualize, and interpret.

- IMDb (Internet Movie Database at www.imdb.com) offers information about movies of all genres.

- The NCTM Illuminations State Data Map (http://illuminations.nctm.org/Activity Detail.aspx?ID=151) is a source that displays state data on population, land area, political representation, gasoline use, and so on.

- The CIA World Factbook (www.cia.gov/library/publications/the-world-factbook /index.html) provides demographic information for every nation in the world (population, age distributions, death and birth rates) as well as information on the economy, government, transportation, and geography.

- The U.S. Census Bureau (www.census.gov) has copious statistical information organized by state, county, or voting district.

Analyzing Data: Graphs

Graphs summarize data that have been collected. How data are organized should be directly related to the question that caused you to collect the data in the first place. For example, suppose students want to know how many songs their friends listen to in one day. The question is, "How many songs do the students in our class listen to in one day?" For data collection, you decide to have each student keep track on a school day (e.g., Tuesday) and come to class on Wednesday with his or her own total. Each student records the number on a sticky note that is placed on the board.

Stop and Reflect

If your sixth-grade class had collected these data, what methods might you have suggested that the students use for organizing and graphing them? Is one of your ideas better than others for answering the question about how many songs? ■

A dot plot (also called a *line plot*) can be created to illustrate the spread and shape of the data. Or a histogram can be created to capture how many students fall within a range of songs listened to (between 0 and 10, 11 and 20, etc.). Or a box plot can be created to box in the middle 50 percent, focusing attention on the center of the data as well as the range. Each of these displays gives a different snapshot of the data and provides different insights into the question posed.

Students should be involved in deciding how they want to represent their data, but they will need to be introduced to what the options are and when each display can and cannot be used. The value of having students construct their own graphs is not so much that they learn the techniques but that they are personally invested in the data and learn how a graph conveys information. Once a graph is constructed, the most important activity is discussing what it tells the people who see it. Discussions about graphs the students have created help them analyze and interpret other graphs and charts that they see in newspapers and on TV.

Creating graphs does require care, including a determination of appropriate scales and labels. But the reason for the precision is so that an audience is able to see at a glance the summary of the data gathered for a particular question. Questioning and assessment should focus on how effectively the graph communicates the findings of the data gathered, which includes, but goes beyond, using appropriate labels.

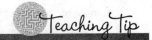

Standards for Mathematical Practice

◄ **5 Use appropriate tools strategically**

Teaching Tip

Select graphs from newspapers or websites and ask students, "What can you learn from this graph? What do you not know that you wish you knew?" These questions help students focus on what different graphs can and cannot illustrate.

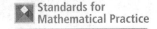

Standards for Mathematical Practice

◄ **6 Attend to precision**

technology note

Computer programs and graphing calculators can provide a variety of graphic displays. Use the time saved by technology to focus on the discussions about the information that each display provides. Students can make their own selections from among different graphs and justify their choice based on their own intended purposes. The graphing calculator puts data analysis technology in the hands of every student. The TI-73 calculator is designed for middle-grade students. It will produce eight different kinds of plots or graphs, including circle graphs, bar graphs, and picture graphs, and it will compute and graph lines of best fit.

The Internet also offers opportunities to explore different graphs. The NCES Kids' Zone "Create a Graph" (http://nces.ed.gov/nceskids/createagraph) provides tools for creating five different graphic displays.

Standards for Mathematical Practice

◄ **5 Use appropriate tools strategically**

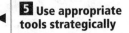

The NCTM Illuminations "Data Grapher" (http://illuminations.nctm.org/ActivityDetail.aspx?ID=204) and "Advanced Data Grapher" (http://illuminations.nctm.org/ActivityDetail.aspx?ID=220) allow you to enter data, select which set(s) to display, and choose the type of representation (e.g., bar graph, pie chart, line graph).

Once a graph has been constructed, engage the class in a discussion of what information the graph tells or conveys—the analysis. "What can you tell by looking at this graph about the number of songs our class listens to in one day?" Graphs convey factual information (e.g., there is a wide variability in the number of songs sixth graders listen to in one day), and they also provide opportunities to make inferences that are not directly observable in the graph (e.g., most sixth graders listen to between 20 and 30 songs in a day).

The difference between *actual facts* and *inferences that go beyond the data* is an important idea in data analysis. Students can examine graphs found in newspapers or magazines and discuss the facts in the graphs and the message that may have been intended by the person who made the graph. Students' conceptual ability to analyze data, draw conclusions, and make interpretations is often weak (Tarr & Shaughnessy, 2007), so be sure to work on emphasizing this higher-level thinking skill.

In the sections that follow, we share options for data displays, with less attention given to the displays that students explore in elementary school (e.g., bar graphs and pie charts) and more to the displays that are the focus of middle school (e.g., displays on a number line).

 **Standards for Mathematical Practice**

2 Reason abstractly and quantitatively ▶

Figure 15.2

Pie charts show ratios of part to whole and can be used to compare ratios.

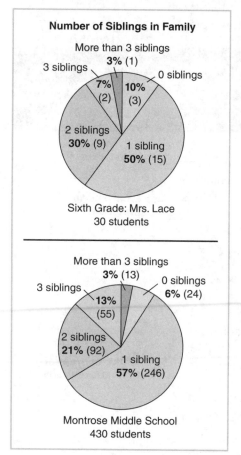

Number of Siblings in Family

Sixth Grade: Mrs. Lace
30 students

Montrose Middle School
430 students

◆ Categorical Data

If students have asked questions such as "What is your favorite ice-cream flavor?" and "What city would you most like to visit?" the data are categorical. In this case, bar graphs and circle graphs are good choices for summarizing the data. Bar graphs and pie charts can also be used for numeric data, but they are the only graphs that can be used for non-numeric data.

Bar Graphs

Bar graphs are learned and used throughout elementary school. The category of bar graphs includes "real" graphs (real objects used in the graph) and picture graphs. In middle school, bar graphs can be used to collect data quickly; as students come into class and see a question posted on the board, they can pull a sticky note and place it on the bar that is their personal response to the question posed.

Recall that analyzing data in this way is step 3 of the process of doing statistics. A question is posed (step 1), and data are collected based on the categories that will be graphed (step 2). A class of 25 to 30 students can make a graph in less than 10 minutes. Then the graph can be used as a community builder in a discussion of what is known about the class. Also, the sticky notes can be rearranged in other ways in order to discuss the varying ways data can be summarized in a graph, comparing the pros and cons of different graphs and displays.

Pie Charts

Pie charts (also called *circle graphs*) show information that is not as easily available from the other graphs. Pie charts are commonly found in newspapers. They are less often used in statistics because it can be more difficult to make comparisons (angle measures are harder to compare than lengths of bars). Pie charts do, however, lend themselves to a comparison of two different-size data sets. The two graphs in Figure 15.2 show the percentages of students with different numbers of siblings. One graph is based on classroom data, and the other on data for the whole school. Because pie charts display ratios rather than quantities, the small set of class data can be compared with the large set of school data, which cannot be done with bar graphs. There are several fun and simple ways to make a pie chart, one of which is the focus of Activity 15.3.

Activity 15.3 HUMAN BARS TO PIES

Determine a question that lends itself to preset categories and is of interest to students, such as a question about their favorite basketball team in the NCAA Tournament's "Elite 8" (or "Final Four"). Post a sign for each team. Ask students to line up in front of the name of the team they like the best. Ask, "About what percent of our class likes [team name]?" Have students estimate the percent for each team (verbally to a partner, or on a note card). Explain that you are going to look at your data again. Ask students to stay in their "row" but to curve their line to form a circle with the rest of the students. Tape the ends of eight (or four) long strings to the floor in the center of the circle, and extend them to the circle at each point where the teams change. Voilà! You now have a life-size circle graph! Ask students if they want to revise their estimates for the percent of the class that supports each team. If you then place a rational number wheel (see Blackline Master 10) on the center of the circle, the strings will show the approximate percentages for each part of your graph (Figure 15.3). Note the approximate percentages for each team. Discuss with students the pros and cons of the bar and pie graphs.

Figure 15.3

A human pie chart: Students are arranged in a circle, with string stretched from the center to show the divisions.

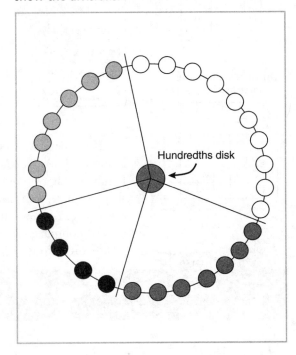

Activity 15.3 can be done on a smaller scale with different colored sticky notes or paper clips. Each category is represented by a different color. Then, tape the sticky notes into strips or hook the paperclips, and attach each same-colored strip together end to end. Next, tape (hook) the two ends together to form a circle. Estimate where the center of the circle is, draw lines to the points where the different bars meet, and trace around the full loop.

Creating pie charts can be a good connection to percents and proportional reasoning. The numbers of data in each category are added to form the total or whole. Then students find the percent of each part. It is an interesting proportional problem for students to convert between percents and degrees because the one is out of 100 and the other is out of 360. It is helpful to start students with obvious values like 50 percent, 25 percent, and 10 percent before moving to more difficult values. A ratio table with one row for percent and one row for degrees can serve as an important tool to help students reason.

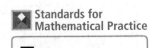

Standards for
Mathematical Practice

1 Make sense
of problems and
persevere in
solving them

◆ Numeric Data

When data are grouped on a continuous scale, they should be ordered along a number line (e.g., temperatures that occur over time, height or weight over age, and percentages of test takers scoring in different intervals).

Figure 15.4

Constructing a stem-and-leaf plot for baseball team wins.

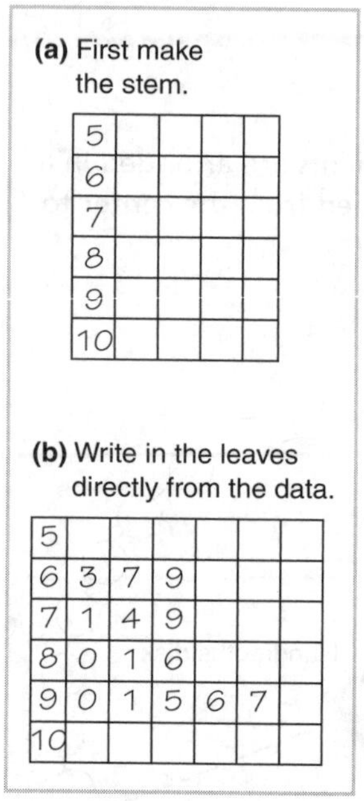

(a) First make the stem.

| 5 |
| 6 |
| 7 |
| 8 |
| 9 |
| 10 |

(b) Write in the leaves directly from the data.

5				
6	3	7	9	
7	1	4	9	
8	0	1	6	
9	0	1	5	6	7
10

Stem-and-Leaf Plots

Stem-and-leaf plots (sometimes called *stem plots*) are a form of bar graph in which numeric data are graphed and displayed as a list. By way of example, consider the American League baseball teams' total wins for 2012:

Team	Number of Wins	Team	Number of Wins
Baltimore Orioles	93	Chicago White Sox	85
Tampa Bay Rays	90	Cleveland Indians	68
Boston Red Sox	69	Detroit Tigers	88
Toronto Blue Jays	73	Oakland Athletics	94
New York Yankees	95	Los Angeles Angels	89
Minnesota Twins	66	Texas Rangers	93
Kansas City Royals	72	Seattle Mariners	75

If the data are to be grouped by tens, list the tens digits to form the "stem," as shown in Figure 15.4a. Next, write the ones digits next to the appropriate tens digits, as shown in Figure 15.4b, ordered from smallest to largest, to form the "leaves." The result shows the shape of data, indicating where the data cluster and where the outliers are. Furthermore, every piece of data can be retrieved from the graph.

To compare two sets of data, create a common stem and extend the leaves in opposite directions (Figure 15.5). The stem in this illustration is grouped by fives instead of tens. Using rows grouped by fives instead of by tens illustrates the spread of the data, perhaps particular grades (e.g., B and B+). Determining how to set up the stem-and-leaf plot depends on the context and on the question being asked. In addition, students can find the range, median, and outliers from the plot.

Stem-and-leaf plots are also effective for large numbers in data sets. For example, if the data range from 600 to 1300, the stem can be the numerals from 6 to 13, and the leaves can be made of two-digit numbers separated by commas.

Teaching Tip

Stem-and-leaf plots are best made on graph paper so that each digit takes up the same amount of space.

Figure 15.5

Stem-and-leaf plots can be used to compare two sets of data.

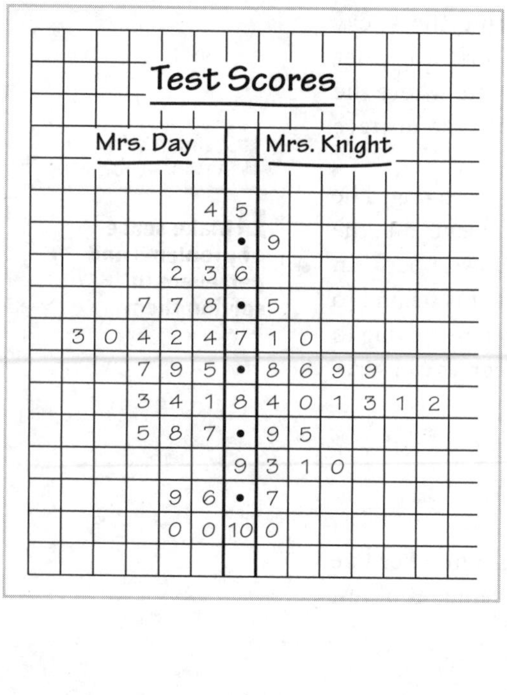

Test Scores

Mrs. Day				Mrs. Knight					
			4	5					
				•	9				
		2	3	6					
	7	7	8	•	5				
3	0	4	2	4	7	1	0		
	7	9	5	•	8	6	9	9	
	3	4	1	8	4	0	1	3	1	2
		5	8	7	•	9	5		
			9	3	1	0			
		9	6	•	7				
		0	0	10	0				

Line Plots and Dot Plots

Line plots and dot plots are among the data displays on a number line, which are emphasized in middle-school data analysis in the *Common Core State Standards*. Both terms are used in the CCSS; line plots are introduced in grade 2 with whole-number units and progress to the display of data in fractions of a unit in grade 5 (CCSSO, 2010, p. 37). Line plots and dot plots are counts of things along a numeric scale on a number line. Line plots use Xs to represent each data point, and dot plots use dots. To make a dot plot, a number line is drawn, and a dot is made above the corresponding value on the line for every corresponding data element. One advantage of line and dot plots is that every piece of data is shown on the graph. It is also a very easy type of graph for students to make. An example with temperatures is shown in Figure 15.6.

These plots also lend themselves to comparisons. For example, if data are gathered from two different groups, separate dot plots can be created, providing a great visual to see the difference in the shapes of the data.

Histograms

Line plots and dot plots are widely used for small data sets, but many real data sets include a large amount of data and many different numbers. A dot plot would be too tedious to create and would not illustrate the spread of data as effectively. In this case, a histogram is an excellent choice because data are grouped in appropriate intervals.

A histogram is a form of bar graph in which the categories are consecutive equal intervals along a numeric scale. The number of data elements falling into a particular interval determines the height or length of that bar. Histograms differ from bar graphs in that bar graphs can be used for categorical data and the bars can be placed in any order without changing the results (Metz, 2010).

Histograms are not difficult in concept but can be challenging to construct: What is the appropriate interval to use for the bar width? What is a good scale to use for the length of the bars? The need for all of the data to be grouped and counted within each interval causes further difficulty. Figure 15.7 shows a histogram for the same temperature data used in Figure 15.6. Notice how similar the two displays are in illustrating the spread and clustering of data.

Figure 15.6
Dot plot summarizing June temperatures.

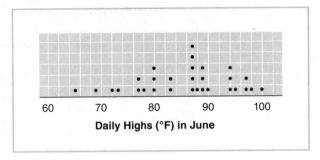

Figure 15.7
Histogram of June high temperatures.

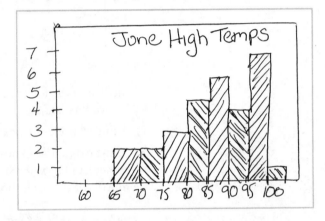

technology note

Histograms can be created with graphing calculators and computer software, or online with the NCTM Illuminations "Histogram Tool" (http://illuminations.nctm.org/ActivityDetail.aspx?ID=78).

Box Plots

Box plots (also called *box-and-whisker plots*) are used for visually displaying not only the center (median) but also the range and spread of data. Sixth graders should be able to create and analyze box plots (CCSSO, 2010). In Figure 15.8, the ages in months for 27 sixth-grade students are given, along with stem-and-leaf plots for the full class and the boys and girls separately. The stem-and-leaf plot is a good way to prepare for creating a box plot. To find the two quartiles, find the medians of the upper and lower halves of the data. Mark the two extremes, the quartiles, and the median. Then create the box plot on a number line. Box plots for the same data are shown in Figure 15.9.

Each box plot has three features:

1. A box contains the "middle half" of the data, with one-fourth to the left and one-fourth to the right of the median. The ends of the box are at the *lower quartile* (the

Figure 15.8

Ordered stem-and-leaf plots grouped by fives. Medians and quartiles are circled or are represented by a vertical bar if they fall between two elements.

The following numbers represent the ages in months of a class of sixth-grade students.

Boys		Girls	
132	122	140	131
140	130	129	128
133	134	141	131
142	125	134	132
134 *Joe B.*	147	124	130
(137)	131	129 *Whitney*	127
139	129	(125)	

All students

```
12 | 2, 4
 • | 5, 5, 7, 8, (9) 9, 9,
13 | 0, 0, 1, 1, (1) 2, 2, 3, 4, 4, 4
 • | (7) 9
14 | 0, 0, 1, 2
 • | 7
```

Boys

```
12 | 2
 • | 5, 9
13 | (0) 1, 2, 3, | 4, 4
 • | 7, (9)
14 | 0, 2
 • | 7
```

Girls

```
12 | 4
 • | 5, 7, | 8, 9, 9
13 | (0) 1, 1, 2, | 4
 • |
14 | 0, 1
 • |
```

median of the lower half of the data) and the *upper quartile* (the median of the upper half of the data).

2. A line is inside the box at the median of the data.

3. A line (sometimes known as the *whisker*) extends from the end of each box to the *lower extreme* and *upper extreme* of the data. Each line, therefore, covers the upper and lower fourths of the data, showing the *interquartile range*.

Stop and Reflect

Notice that in Figure 15.9, the box for the boys is actually a bit longer than the box for the whole class. How can that be, when there are clearly more students in the full class than there are boys? How would you explain this apparent discrepancy to a class of seventh graders? ■

Figure 15.9

Box plots show a lot of information. In addition to the distribution of data, data points of particular interest can be shown.

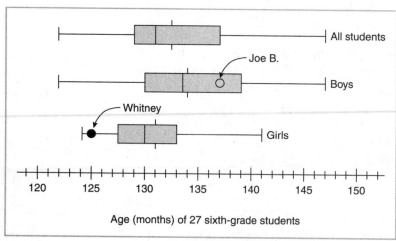

Age (months) of 27 sixth-grade students

Look at the information these box plots provide at a glance! The box and the lengths of the lines provide a quick indication of how the data are spread out or bunched together. Because the median is shown, this spreading or bunching can be determined for each quarter of the data. The entire class in this example is much more spread out in the upper half than in the lower half. The girls are much more closely grouped in age than either the boys or the class as a whole. The range of the data (the difference between the upper and lower extremes) is represented by the length of the plot, and the extreme values can be read directly. The mean is indicated by the small marks above and below each box. A box plot provides useful visual information to help understand the shape of a data set.

Because box plots contain so much information and require proportional thinking, students may find it difficult to interpret them (Bakker, Biehler, & Konol, 2004). Support for students' making these connections can be provided by using contexts that are meaningful and by having them ask questions about the various statistics that are shown on the plot. An understanding of the proportional relationships can be supported through the use of percent strips or ratio tables. (See Chapter 11 for more on the use of models to support proportional thinking.)

Remember that a box plot, like any graph, is a tool for learning about the question posed, not an end in itself (McClain, Leckman, Schmitt, & Regis, 2006). Because a box plot offers so much information on the spread and center of the data, much can be learned from careful examination, and particularly from a comparison of two box plots with related data.

Graphing calculators and several computer programs draw box plots, making this process even more accessible. The TI-73, TI-84, and TI-Nspire calculators can draw box plots for up to three sets of data on the same axis. See also http://illuminations.nctm.org/ActivityDetail.aspx?ID=77 for the NCTM Illuminations applet "Box Plotter."

Formative Assessment Note

Students should write about their graphs in a *journal*, explaining what each graph tells and why they selected that type of graph to illustrate the data they have. As you evaluate students' responses, it is important to focus on whether they chose an appropriate representation and have provided a good rationale for its selection that connects back to the context of the data gathered.

◆ Bivariate Graphs

Standards for Mathematical Practice

◀ **4 Model with mathematics**

In eighth grade, the focus of statistics is to analyze bivariate data (CCSSO, 2010). The term *bivariate data* may be new to the eighth-grade curriculum, but the topic is not. Stated simply, *bivariate* describes two things that vary together (e.g., as the number of bikes increases, the number of wheels increases). Concepts and activities related to covariation are addressed in Chapter 11 ("Proportional Reasoning") and Chapter 12 ("Exploring Algebraic Thinking, Expressions, and Equations"). In this chapter, the focus is on graphing such situations as a way to display and analyze the data collected.

Line Graphs

A coordinate axis allows bivariate data to be plotted. When the data are continuous, a line connects the data points and illustrates the trend in the data. For example, a line graph might be used to show how the length of a flagpole shadow changed from one hour to the next during the day. The horizontal scale would be time, and the vertical scale would be the length of the shadow. Data can be gathered at specific points in time (e.g., every 15 minutes), and these points can be plotted. A straight line can be drawn to connect the points because time is continuous, and data points do exist between the plotted points. See Figure 15.10 for a line graph on temperature change.

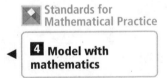

Students tend to connect the dots any time they are plotting points. Instead, they should ask, "Does it make sense to connect the points plotted based on this situation?"

Scatter Plots

Scatter plots are an emphasis in grade 8 (CCSSO, 2010; NCTM, 2006). Bivariate data can be plotted on a scatter plot, a graph of points on a coordinate grid with each axis representing one of the two variables (see Blackline Master 42). Each pair of numbers from the two sets of data, when plotted, produces a visual image of the data as well as a hint concerning any possible relationships. Ask, "What are the relationships, if any, between time spent watching television and overall grades?"

Figure 15.10

Line graph of one day's temperatures.

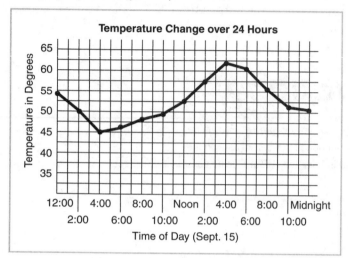

For example, suppose the following data have been gathered from 25 eighth-grade boys: height in inches, weight in pounds, and number of letters in last name. If the data are graphed on a scatter plot, you can ask, "Is there a relationship between height and weight?" and "Is there a relationship between name length and weight?" See the respective scatter plots in Figure 15.11.

The scatter plots indicate that there is a relationship in the boys' weights and heights, although there is some variation. But there is no relationship between name length and weight. Encourage students to plot many data sets, including data sets that suggest linear relationships as well as data sets that indicate no apparent relationship between the variables, and to look for relationships in the scatter plots. Activity 15.4 provides engaging ways to explore the relationship between bivariate data.

Activity 15.4 IS THERE A RELATIONSHIP?

Prepare cards with different questions on them about bivariate situations. For example, Is there a relationship between any of these?

- Distance a toy car rolls and its weight
- Distance a toy car rolls and height of ramp on which it rolls
- Distance a toy car rolls and its height on the ramp when it starts to roll
- Foot length and height
- Shoulder width and height
- Nose length and hand span
- Months of age and height
- Head circumference and wrist circumference
- Minutes watching TV and minutes doing homework

Distribute cards to groups of four students. Ask students to (1) predict whether there is a relationship and (2) determine how they will gather data. Have students gather data and create a scatter plot on paper that they will display to the class (see Blackline Master 42). English language learners (ELLs) may be more familiar with metric measures and will benefit from seeing what is being measured through gestures or demonstration. The students in each group report on their findings and explain whether they think there is a relationship or not. Other groups listen and determine whether they agree that there is a relationship, and what that relationship is. As an extended experience, have students generate their own questions in which they wonder, "Is there a relationship between x and y?"

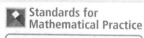
Standards for Mathematical Practice

3 Construct viable arguments and critique the reasoning of others

Figure 15.11   Scatter plots show potential relationships or lack of relationships.

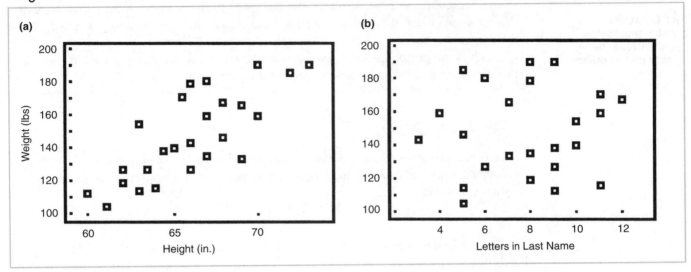

Best-Fit Lines

If your scatter plot indicates a relationship, it can be simply described in words: "As boys get taller, they get heavier." This may be correct but is not particularly useful. What exactly is the relationship? If I knew the height of a boy, could I predict what his weight might be? As in much of statistical analysis, the value of a statistic is to create a model that can predict what has not yet been observed. (For example, we poll a small sample of voters before an election to predict how the population will vote.)

   The relationship in this case is a ratio between the two measures. If the scatter plot seems to indicate a steadily increasing (as in the height–weight graph) or steadily decreasing relationship, you can find the ratio between the variables by drawing a straight line through the data points that "best" represent the pattern or shape of all of the dots.

   What determines best fit? From a strictly visual stand-point, the line you select defines the observed relationship and can be used to predict other values not in the data set. The more closely the dots in the scatter plot cluster around the line you select, the greater the confidence you will have in the predictive value of the line. Certainly, you can try to draw a straight line somewhere in the name length–weight graph, but you will not have much confidence in its predictive capability because the dots will be quite dispersed from the line.

◆ Standards for
Mathematical Practice

4 **Model with
mathematics**

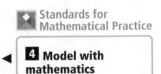

Teaching Tip

Give students pieces of uncooked spaghetti (for use with graphs on notebook paper) or a quarter-inch dowel rod (for use with graphs on posters or chart paper) to help them find the line of best fit.

▶ *Activity* 15.5   **BEST-FIT LINE**

BLM

Pick a topic of interest to the class. For example, does one's shoe size relate to one's height? Or does a person's name length relate to how many times they can say their name in one minute? Gather class data on a coordinate axis on $8\frac{1}{2}$ by 11-inch paper (see Blackline Master 42). Once students have collected data and recorded it on the coordinate axis (making a scatter plot), make dupli-cates of the plot for each group of students. Provide groups with one piece of uncooked

**Standards for
Mathematical Practice**

**3 Construct
viable arguments
and critique the
reasoning of others**

▶

spaghetti to use as a line. Students tape the spaghetti on the plot so that it is the "best" line to represent the relationship in the dots. Ask students to write the equation that describes their line (estimates are fine!) and develop a rationale for why they positioned the line as they did.

Using a projection device, compare the lines chosen by various groups and their rationales. Use the different choices to predict the data for a new value.

Stop and Reflect

Before reading further, return to the height–weight plot in Figure 15.11a and draw a straight line that you think will make a good line of best fit. Why did you draw the line where you did? ◼

Encourage students to use a "mathematical" reason for why a line might be best. A good line is one around which most dots cluster—that is, one from which the distances of all of the points are minimal. This general notion of least distance to the line for all points is the basis for an algorithm, which is introduced in high school, that will always produce a unique line for a given set of points.

Graphing calculators can be directed to locate the best-fit line. Students can enter their data into the table feature, plot it on the graph, and then find the line of best fit. If students have already drawn a line by hand, then the calculator provides a good opportunity to compare equations to see whether they are both reasonable.

Analyzing Data: Measures of Center and Variability

Although graphs provide visual images of data, measures of center and variability of the data are also important ways to summarize, analyze, and describe the data. Measures of center include *mean, median,* and *mode,* and measures of variability include *range* and *mean absolute deviation.* This is a sixth-grade critical area of the *Common Core State Standards,* and a review of the CCSS summary reveals that the emphasis in teaching mean, median, and mode is *not* on how to find each (or which one is which) but on how to select the appropriate measure based on the context and the population. Students can get an idea of the importance of these statistics by exploring the ideas informally.

◆ Measures of Center

The term *average* is heard quite frequently in everyday usage. Sometimes, it refers to an exact arithmetic average, as in "average daily rainfall." Other times, it is used quite loosely, as in "about average height." In either situation, an average is a measure that describes a set of numbers. Students' understanding of average may be any of the following: average as mode (what is there most of?), average as something reasonable, average as the standard algorithm for finding the mean, and average as mathematical equilibrium (Garcia & Garret, 2006).

Mode

The mode is the most frequently occurring value in the data set. The mode is the least frequently used as a measure of center because data sets may not have a mode or may have more than one mode, or the mode may not be descriptive of the data set.

Median

The median is the middle value in an ordered set of data. Half of all values lie at or above the median, and half at or below. The median is easier to understand and to compute, and it is not affected, as the mean is, by one or two extremely large or extremely small values outside the range of the rest of the data. The most common misconception in using the median emerges when students neglect to order the numbers in the data set from least to greatest.

Mean

Ask adults what the mean is, and they are likely to tell you something like this: "You get the mean when you add up all the numbers in the set and divide the sum by the number of numbers in the set." This is not what the mean *is*; this is how you calculate the mean. This is a reminder of the procedurally driven curriculum in our history and the need to shift to a more conceptually focused approach. Another limited conception about the mean is that students think it is *the* way to find a measure of center regardless of the context (not considering median as a viable option) (McGatha, Cobb, & McClain, 1998). In fact, in the *Common Core State Standards*, sixth graders are expected to determine when the mean is appropriate and when another measure of center (e.g., the median) is more appropriate: "Students recognize that a data distribution may not have a definite center and that different ways to measure center yield different values" (CCSSO, 2010, p. 39). The next section focuses on developing the concept of the mean.

● Understanding the Mean: Two Interpretations

There are actually two different ways to think about the mean. First, it is a number that represents what all of the data items would be if they were *leveled*. In this sense, the mean represents all of the data items. Statisticians prefer to think of the mean as a *central balance point*. This concept of the mean is more in keeping with the notion of a measure of the "center" of the data or a measure of central tendency. Both concepts are discussed in the following sections.

Leveling Interpretation

Suppose that the average number of family members for the students in your class is 5. One way to interpret this is to think about distributing the entire collection of moms, dads, sisters, and brothers to each of the students so that each has a "family" of the same size. To say that you have an average score of 93 for the four tests in your class is like spreading the total of all of your points evenly across the four tests. It is as if each student had a family of the same size and all the test scores were the same, but the totals matched the actual distributions. An added benefit of this explanation of the mean is that it connects to the algorithm for computing the mean.

◀ *Activity* 15.6 **LEVELING THE BARS**

Have students make a bar graph of some data with connecting cubes (one cube per dollar). Choose a situation with five or six values. For example, Figure 15.12 shows bars for the price of six games. The task for students is to use the stacks of cubes (bars) to determine what the price would be if all of the games were the same price. Encourage students to use various techniques to rearrange the cubes to "level" the prices, or make the price the same for each item. Be sure that ELLs understand the meaning of "leveling" the bars.

Figure 15.12

Understanding the mean as a leveling of the data.

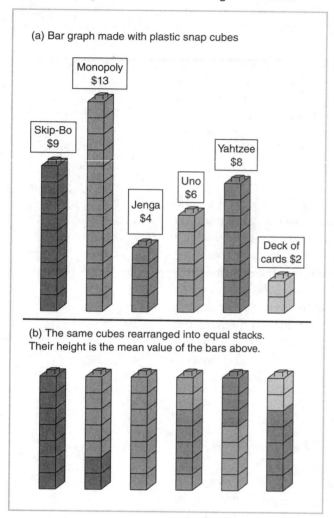

(a) Bar graph made with plastic snap cubes

Monopoly
$13

Skip-Bo
$9

Jenga
$4

Uno
$6

Yahtzee
$8

Deck of
cards $2

(b) The same cubes rearranged into equal stacks.
Their height is the mean value of the bars above.

Explain to students that the size of the leveled bars is the mean of the data—the amount that each item would cost if all items cost the same amount but the total of the prices remained fixed. The next activity is a good follow-up to this activity and begins to conceptually develop an algorithm for finding the mean.

Activity 15.7 THE MEAN FOOT

Pose the following question: "What is the mean length of our feet in inches?" This context needs to be clear to ELLs because *foot* is not being used as a measurement unit, but as an object to measure. Also, consider measuring in centimeters rather than inches. Have each student cut a strip of cash register tape that matches the length of his or her foot. Students record their names and the length of their feet in inches on the strips. Suggest that before finding a mean for the class, you first get means for smaller groups. Put students into groups of four, six, or eight. (Some students will realize that they can fold the combined strip to find equal lengths. Placing them into groups of even numbers makes it easier to find the equal lengths by folding.) In each group, have the students tape their foot strips end to end. The task for each group is to come up with a method of finding the mean without using any of the lengths written on the strips. They can use only the combined strip. Each group will share its method with the class. From this work, the groups will devise a method for determining the mean for the whole class. For students with disabilities, help them fold the cash register strip to see how to divide it into equal lengths.

To distribute the inches for each student's foot evenly among the members of the group, the students can fold the strip into equal parts so that there are as many sections as students in the group. Then they can measure the length of any one part.

How can you find the mean for the whole class? Suppose there are 23 students in the class. Using the strips that are already taped together, make one very long strip for the whole class. It is not reasonable to fold this long strip into 23 equal sections. But if you wanted to know how long the resulting strip would be, how could that be done? The total length of the strip is the sum of the lengths of the 23 individual foot strips. To find the length of one section if the strip were actually folded in 23 parts, simply divide by 23. In fact, students can mark off "mean feet" along the strip. There should be very close to 23 "feet" of equal length. This dramatically illustrates the algorithm for finding the mean.

Balance Point Interpretation

Statisticians think about the mean as a point on a number line where the data on either side of the point are balanced. To help think about the mean in this way, it is useful to think about the data placed on a line plot. Notice that the important points include how many pieces of data are on either side of the mean *and* their distances from the mean.

Figure 15.13

(a) If all data points are the same, the mean is that value. (b) By moving data points away from the mean in a balanced manner, different distributions can be found that have the same mean.

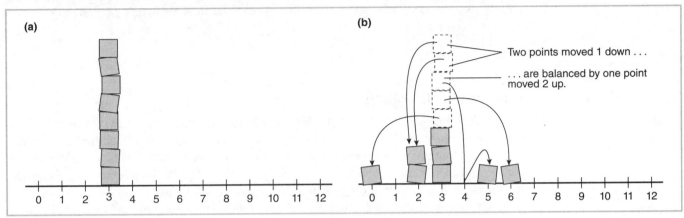

To illustrate, draw a number line on the board, and arrange eight sticky notes above the number 3, as shown in Figure 15.13a. Each sticky note represents one family. The notes are positioned on the line to indicate how many pets each family owns. Stacked like this, the notes indicate that all families have the same number of pets. The mean is three pets. But different families are likely to have different numbers of pets. So, we could think of eight families with a range of numbers of pets. Some may have zero pets, and some may have ten pets or even more. How could you change the number of pets for these eight families so that the mean remains at 3? Students will suggest moving the sticky notes in opposite directions, probably in pairs. This will result in a symmetric arrangement. But what if one of the families has eight pets, a move of five spaces from the 3? This might be balanced by moving two families to the left—one family three spaces to the 0 and one family two spaces to the 1. Figure 15.13b shows one way the families could be rearranged to maintain a mean of 3. Can you find at least two other distributions of the families, each having a mean of 3?

Use the next activity to find the mean or balance point given the data.

Activity 15.8 FINDING THE BALANCE POINT

Have students draw a number line from 0 to 12 with about 2 inches between the numbers. Use six small sticky notes to represent the prices of six games, as shown in Figure 15.14. Have the students place a light pencil mark on the line where they think the mean might be. For the moment, avoid the add-up-and-divide computation. Ask students to determine the mean by moving the sticky notes in toward the "center." That is, the students are to find out what price (point on the number line) balances the six prices. For each move of a sticky one space to the left, a different sticky must be moved one space to the right. Eventually, all sticky notes should be stacked above the same number, the balance point or mean.

Figure 15.14

Move data points in toward the center or balance point without changing the balance around that point. When you have all points at the same value, that is the balance, or the mean.

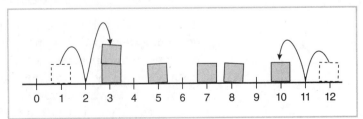

Stop and Reflect

> **Stop and try this exercise yourself. Notice that after any pair of moves that keeps the distribution balanced, you actually have a new distribution of prices with the same mean. The same was true as you moved the sticky notes out from the mean when they were all stacked on the same point. ■**

Changes in the Mean

The balance approach to finding the mean clearly illustrates that different data distributions can have the same mean. Especially for small sets of data, the mean is significantly affected by extreme values. For example, suppose another game with a price of $20 is added to the six in Figure 15.12. How will the mean change? If the $2 game were removed, how would the mean be affected? Suppose that one new game is added that increases the mean from $7 to $8. How much does the new game cost? Small sets of data and either the balance or the leveling concept should be used to challenge students with questions such as these.

In the NCTM e-Examples from *Principles and Standards for School Mathematics*, Applet 6.6, "Comparing Properties of the Mean and the Median" (www.nctm.org/standards/content.aspx?id=26777), shows seven data points that can be dragged back and forth along a number line with the mean and median updated instantly. The applet allows students to see how stable the median is and how changing one point can affect the mean.

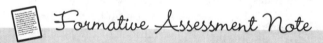

Formative Assessment Note

Consider using a *diagnostic interview* to assess whether students are able to determine the best measure of center to use in a given situation, such as the average height of students in the class. You can begin with general questions such as these: "What is an average? What does the mean represent? What does the median represent? What is the difference between the mean and the median? What is each useful for?" Then move to more analytical questions: "Which should we use for this set of data? Might we use a different measure of center for another class? When you've found the average height of the students in our class, is it possible that no one is that height? Why?"

⬦ Choosing a Measure of Center

As mentioned earlier, the context in statistics is important. The context of a situation will determine whether the mean or median is the measure you want to use. For example, in reporting home prices (see p. 325), the median is quite different from the mean, with the mean higher. Which better portrays the cost of housing? Very expensive homes can drive the mean up, so typically the median is a more common measure for describing average housing costs. Activities 15.8 and 15.9 provide strategies for engaging students in selecting a measure of center.

Activity 15.9 WHERE'S THE CENTER?

 Prepare topics of possible data sets, like the ones listed here.

- Sizes of shoes sold in a shoe store
- Salaries in a large company
- Salaries in a small company
- Prices of houses in your local area
- Test scores for a student
- Sizes of cereal boxes in a grocery store
- Costs of hotel rooms at a particular hotel
- A person's monthly telephone bills for a year

The students' task is to decide which measure of center makes the most sense, and to be able to justify their decision. There are several interactive ways to design this lesson. One is to have each topic written on a card and give one card to each of the small groups. The students in each group do the following: (1) select which measure of center they think makes the most sense for their topic, (2) prepare a data set that illustrates their point, and (3) prepare a justification of why they picked their measure. Results can be shared through a jigsaw of students, an interactive exchange in which students from one group find a student from another group and share, or through whole-class reports. Students with special needs may benefit from being given several sets of data for their topic as a way to consider which measure might be best.

Activity 15.10 YOU BE THE JUDGE

The gymnastics coach can send only one person to the all-star state competition. She wants to select the student with the best average for the season. The table below gives overall scores for the eight most recent competitions. Whom should she pick?

Meet	Jenna	Miah	Leah
1	9	9	5
2	3	9	6
3	10	7	7
4	9	8	6
5	7	7	9
6	5	9	8
7	10	9	10
8	9	8	10

Ask students questions such as the following: "Which measure of center seems to be the fairest way to judge the competition? What else might influence a coach's decision? Which person would you pick and why?"

Students can investigate an NCTM Illuminations applet, "Mean and Median," at http://illuminations.nctm.org/ActivityDetail.aspx?ID=160 to find the mean and median for a set of data that they create.

◆ Measures of Variability

Measures of center are a long-standing topic, but measures of variability also need explicit attention in the curriculum (Franklin & Garfield, 2006; Franklin et al., 2005; Rossman, Chance, & Medina, 2006; Scheaffer, 2006). Increased attention to variability is needed, and variability may not be adequately addressed in textbooks that have tended to focus on measures of center. In the *Common Core State Standards*, variability is introduced in grade 6 and is a major focus of seventh grade (CCSSO, 2010). Sixth graders should "recognize that a measure of variability (interquartile range or mean absolute deviation) can also be useful for summarizing data because two very different sets of data can have the same mean and median yet be distinguished by their variability" (CCSSO, 2010, p. 39–40). Shaughnessy (2006) summarized the findings on what students should know about variability in the following list, starting with basic notions and progressing to more sophisticated ideas:

1. Focusing only on outliers or extremes (but not on the full distribution of the data)

2. Considering change over time (which can lead into discussions of other types of variation)

3. Examining variability as the full range of data (Range is everything that occurs, but it doesn't reveal the frequency of different events within the range.)

4. Considering variability as the likely range or expected value

5. Looking at how far data points are from the center (e.g., the mean)

6. Looking at how far a set of data is from some fixed value

In order to be prepared to teach students variability beyond outliers and extremes, it is important to know about the way that variability occurs in statistics.

In the *Guidelines for Assessment and Instruction in Statistics Education (GAISE) Report* (Franklin et al., 2005), three levels of statistical thinking are discussed that, although developmental in nature, can be roughly mapped to elementary, middle, and high school curriculum. At the first level, the focus is on variability within a group—for example, the varying lengths of students' names, varying family sizes, and so on. When students create a bar graph of class data and compare the data collected, they are discussing the variability within a group.

At the second level, variability within a group continues, but groups of data are also considered. Students might compare the variability of fifth graders' favorite music choices with eighth graders' music choices, an example of variability between groups. In addition, middle-school students study how the change in one variable relates to change in another variable—yes, algebra! Students analyze two variables to see whether there is a relationship (as discussed in the section on scatter plots).

One way to help students understand variability is to ask questions about variability in the discussion of data. Friel, O'Conner, and Mamer (2006), using the context of heart rates, suggest the following questions as examples of how to get students to focus on variability:

- If the average heart rate for 9- to 11-year-olds is 88 beats per minute, does this mean every student this age has a heart rate of 88 beats per minute? (Note that the range is actually quite large—from 60 to 110 beats per minute.)

- If we found the heart rates for all students in the class (of 30), what might the distribution of data look like?

- If the heart rates of students in another class (of 30) were measured, would the distribution look like the one for our class? What if they had just come in from the gym?

- Would the distribution of data from 200 students look like the distribution of data from the two classes?

Comparing different data sets or playing a game repeatedly also provides the opportunity for students to analyze the spread of data and think about variability in data (Franklin & Mewborn, 2008; Kader & Mamer, 2008).

Range

Range is a *measure* of variability. The range of a data set is the difference between the highest and lowest data points, or range can be expressed simply by stating the minimum and maximum values. The *interquartile range* of the data is connected to the box plot previously described. It is the difference between the lower and upper quartiles (Q3 – Q1), or the range of the middle 50 percent of the data. A small interquartile range means that there is a lot of clustering around the median.

Let's look at an example.

The data set below is the number of hours seventh graders spent playing sports or playing outside over the weekend (the data have already been placed in order).

0 0 0 1 3 4 4 4 5 5 5 5 6 6 7 8 8 9 10 10

Find the interquartile range. What does the result tell you about the variation in the data set?

In this case, the median is 5 (because the tenth and eleventh values of the 20 values are both 5). This is also referred to as quartile 2 (Q2). Quartile 1 (Q1) is the median of the lower half of the data. This median is the average of the fifth and sixth values in the data set, which is 3.5. Quartile 3 (Q3) is the median of the upper half of the data set; in this case, it falls between 7 and 8, so it is 7.5. The interquartile range is 7.5 – 3.5, or 4. For hours spent exercising, the interquartile range is fairly small, showing that there is a lot of clustering around the center of the data.

Mean Absolute Deviation

Whereas the range relates to the median, the mean absolute value relates to the mean, describing how far away data is from the mean. In the *Common Core State Standards, mean absolute deviation* is introduced in sixth grade, with the intent that it be explored in an informal manner to develop a deeper understanding of variability. Let's use the data set above to explore mean absolute variation.

Use the data set below to find the mean absolute deviation:

0 0 0 1 3 4 4 4 5 5 5 5 6 6 7 8 8 9 10 10

What does the result tell you about the variation in the data set?

Figure 15.15 places the data in a dot plot. The mean of the data set is 5 hours.

The first step in finding the mean absolute deviation is to find the *deviation* (difference) of each data point from the mean. Figure 15.16a illustrates these differences in a dot plot. The *absolute deviation* is the distance from the mean, which means the positive difference (Figure 15.16b). Finally, the *mean of the absolute deviation* is the mean of all these differences (Figure 15.16c)—in this case, 2.4. Did you notice that you started with the end of the phrase *mean absolute deviation*, finding first the deviation, then the absolute deviation, and finally the mean absolute deviation? Pointing this out can help

Figure 15.15

A dot plot illustrates the data on hours spent exercising over the weekend.

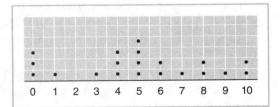

Figure 15.16

Dot plots illustrate the difference from the mean of each data point for hours spent exercising over the weekend.

(a) Deviation (from the mean)

					0					
−5				−1	0					
−5				−1	0	1		3		5
−5	−4		−2	−1	0	1	2	3	4	5
0	**1**	**2**	**3**	**4**	**5**	**6**	**7**	**8**	**9**	**10**

(b) Absolute deviation (from the mean)

					0					
5				1	0					
5				1	0	1		3		5
5	4		2	1	0	1	2	3	4	5
0	**1**	**2**	**3**	**4**	**5**	**6**	**7**	**8**	**9**	**10**

(c) Mean absolute deviation (from the mean)

$$\frac{5+5+5+4+2+1+1+1+0+0+0+0+1+1+2+3+3+4+5+5}{20} = \frac{48}{20} = 2.4$$

Teaching Tip

A good way to have students focus on variability is to have two data sets, one with a very small absolute mean deviation and one with a large one. Focus attention on how this measure helps interpret the data set.

students, in particular students with disabilities, focus on the meaning of what they are doing, and why.

In context, this value indicates that the average distance from the mean hours of exercise is about two and a half hours.

 Interpreting Results

Interpreting results is the fourth step in the process of doing statistics. Although it is helpful to ask mathematical questions, it is essential to ask questions that are statistical in nature. That means focusing the questions on the context of the situation and seeing what can be learned or inferred from the data. In addition, the questions should focus on the key ideas of statistics, such as variability, center of the data, and shape of the data. As stated in the introduction to the *Common Core State Standards* for sixth grade, students "learn to describe and summarize numerical data sets, identifying clusters, peaks, gaps, and symmetry, considering the context in which the data were collected" (CCSSO, 2010, p. 39-40). During interpretation, students might want to loop back and create a different data display to get a different perspective of the data, or gather data from a different population to see whether their results are representative.

Different researchers have recommended questions that focus on statistical thinking (Franklin et al., 2005; Friel et al., 2006; Russell, 2006; Shaughnessy, 2006). Here are some ideas from their lists to get you started on having meaningful discussions interpreting data:

- What do the numbers (symbols) tell us about our class (or another population)?
- If we gathered the same kind of data from another class (population), how would those data look? If we asked a larger group, how would the data look?
- How do the numbers in this graph (population) *compare* with this graph (population)?
- Where are the data "clustering"? How many of the data are in the cluster? How many are *not* in the cluster? About what percent of the data are or are not in the cluster?
- What kinds of variability might need to be considered in interpreting these data?
- Would the results be different if . . . [change of sample/population or setting]? (Example: Would gathered data on word length in a third-grade book be different from those in a fifth-grade book? Would a science book give different results from a novel?)
- How strong is the association between two variables (scatter plot)? How do you know? What does that mean if you know *x*? If you know *y*?
- What does the graph *not* tell us? What might we infer?
- What new questions arise from these data?
- What is the maker of the graph trying to tell us?

These prompts apply across many data displays. It certainly should be a major focus of your instruction. Consider it the *After* phase of your lesson, although some of these questions will be integrated in the *During* phase as well. The emphasis of the questions in this phase is on getting students to notice differences in the data and provide possible reasons for those differences (Franklin & Mewborn, 2008).

Students should also become good consumers of data from print and online sources. They should be able to determine flaws or biases in data they read. There are various resources on misleading graphs. The book *200% of Nothing: An Eye-Opening Tour through the Twists and Turns of Math Abuse and Innumeracy* (Dewdney, 1993) includes explanations of the many ways in which "statistics are turned" to mislead people. Because the examples are *real* (provided by readers of *Scientific American*), this book is an excellent tool for showing how important it is to be statistically literate in today's society. Reading the examples can launch a mathematics project into looking for errors in advertisements. (See Bay-Williams and Martinie, 2009, for more ways to use this book.)

Our world is inundated with data, from descriptive statistics to various graphs. It is essential that we prepare students to be literate about what can be interpreted from data and what cannot, about what should receive attention and what can be discarded as misleading or poorly designed statistics. This is important for success in school and for being a mathematically literate citizen.

Expanded Lesson

Playing with Measures of Central Tendency

Content and Task Decisions

Grade Level: 6–8

Mathematics Goals

- To develop an understanding of how the characteristics of a data set (e.g., distribution of data, outliers) affect the mean, median, and mode

Grade Level Guide

NCTM Curriculum Focal Points	Common Core State Standards
In eighth grade, students use the mean, median, and mode to summarize data sets. They explore how changes in data values cause changes in the mean, median, and mode.	Students in the sixth grade use measures of center (mean and median) to describe data. They understand how the mean is a balance point.

Consider Your Students' Needs

Students know how to find the mean, median, and mode of a data set.

For English Language Learners

- If these terms are not already known, *mean, median,* and *mode* will need explicit attention before the lesson, which may include visuals and translations.
- All students, but particularly ELLs, will benefit from a focus on what *prediction* and *estimation* mean as they participate in the *Before* phase of the lesson.

For Students with Disabilities

- Students with disabilities may find that working with a partner on the "Playing with Measures" recording sheet will help them support their thinking.
- By using a set of play dollar bills to represent the total game purchases and putting the money in six "piles," students can see how the mean can play out as a balance point in more concrete ways.

Materials

Each student will need:

- Blackline Master 38 ("Playing with Measures of Central Tendency")

The teacher will need:

- A way to display "Game Purchases"(Blackline Master 39)

Lesson

Before

Begin with a simpler version of the task:

- Give the students the following data set: 3, 3, 3, 3, 3. Ask them to determine the mean, median, and mode. After verifying that the mean, median, and mode for this set are 3, ask the students to predict what, if any, changes in these statistics will occur if the number 15 is added to the set. Elicit students' ideas and rationales, asking others to comment on or question the ideas.

- Students should be able to compute the new statistics mentally. Clearly, the median and mode for this new data set remain unchanged. The mean changes from 3 to 5. For each of these statistics, discuss why changes occurred or did not occur.

Present the focus task to the class:

- On the display of "Game Purchases," show students the six games that they have purchased and their prices. Have students calculate the mean, median, and mode for this data set and share those values to ensure that all students have found the correct values.

- The task is to make a series of changes to this original data set of six prices (see the following five suggestions). For each change, first predict—without *computation*—the mean, median, and mode for the new data set, and give a reason for the predictions. Second, for each change, compute the actual statistics for the changed set and compare these with the predictions. Each of the following changes is made to the original set of six game prices:

1. You decide to buy a seventh game, which costs $20.
2. You return the $2 game to the store (leaving only five games).
3. If you buy six games, the store gives you a free game.
4. You decide to buy a second game of Monopoly for $13.
5. Make a change you think will be interesting.

- Present the recording sheet "Playing with Measures of Central Tendency" to the class. Students first record their predictions of the new mean, median, and mode, along with their reason for the prediction for each of the five changes. Be sure students understand that each change is to the original set of six games. The fifth change is one that they think might make an interesting change in the statistics.

- After sharing predictions and reasons with a partner, students should calculate the statistics and compare those with their predictions. If a prediction is very different from the calculation, they should try to find an error in their reasoning.

Provide clear expectations:

- Students work in pairs, but each student completes "Playing with Measures of Central Tendency."

During

Initially:

- Be sure students understand that each change is to the original set of six games.

Ongoing:

- Listen to individual students' predictions and justifications for their predictions. Is there evidence in students' explanations that they understand the meaning of the different statistics?

- How are students incorporating the free game into the set? Do they believe it will affect the mean, median, and mode? (The free game adds a seventh data point of $0. The mean and median will change.)

- Be sure students do not change their predictions after doing the calculations. They want to talk about the differences between their predictions and the actual results.

- For a challenge, ask the following question: "Suppose that one new game is added that increases the mean from $7 to $8. How much did the new game cost?"

After

Bring the class together to share and discuss the task:

- Have students share their predictions and reasoning and discuss how their predictions compared with the actual statistics.

- Discuss what effect outliers (data that are much greater or smaller than the rest of the data in the set) seem to have on the mean, median, and mode, and which statistic(s) are affected more by an outlier.

- Based on their findings, which measure of central tendency do they think will be a better representation of a data set that contains one or more outliers? Students should realize that the mean is significantly affected by extreme values, especially for small sets of data.

- Discuss the fact that these have been very small data sets. How would similar changes affect the mean and median if there were about 100 items in the data set?

Assessment

Observe

- How are students using current values for mean, median, and mode to make predictions? Are their predictions reasonable?

- Do students seem dependent on procedures to determine mean, median, and mode?

Ask

- Which statistic is affected most by an outlier? Why?

- Which statistic is unaffected or barely affected by an outlier? Why?

- Can you determine the change in the mean (median) without completely redoing the process of finding the mean (median) for the data set? How?

16

Investigating Concepts of Probability

BigIDEAS

1 Chance has no memory. The chance occurrence of six heads in a row has no effect on whether another head will occur on the next toss of the coin. That chance remains 50–50.

2 The probability that a future event will occur can be characterized along a continuum from impossible (0) to certain (1). A probability of $\frac{1}{2}$ indicates an even chance of the event occurring.

3 The relative frequency of outcomes (of *experiments*) can be used as an estimate of the probability of an event. The larger the number of trials, the better the estimate will be. The results for a small number of trials may be quite different from those obtained in the long run.

4 For some events, the exact probability can be determined by an analysis of the event itself. A probability determined in this manner is called a *theoretical probability*.

5 *Simulation* is a technique used for answering real-world questions or making decisions in complex situations in which an element of chance is involved. To see what is likely to happen in the real event, a model must be designed that has the same probabilities as the real situation.

References to probability are all around us: The weather forecaster predicts a 60 percent chance of snow, medical researchers predict that people with certain diets have a high chance of heart disease, investors calculate the risks of specific investments, and so on. Simulations of complex situations are frequently based on probabilities and then used in making decisions about such situations as airplane safety under different weather circumstances, highway traffic patterns after new housing has been built, and disaster plans.

Realistic concepts of chance require considerable development before students are ready to construct formal ideas about the probability of an event. Optimally, this

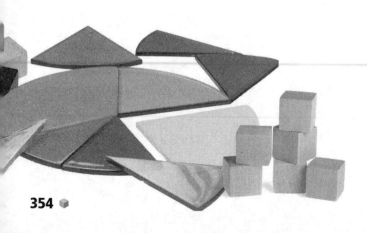

development occurs as students consider and discuss with their peers the outcomes of a wide variety of probabilistic situations. The emphasis should be on exploration rather than on rules and formal definitions. These informal experiences will provide a useful background from which more formal ideas can be developed in middle and high school.

In the NCTM *Curriculum Focal Points* (NCTM, 2006) and the *Common Core State Standards for Mathematics* (CCSSO, 2010), probability is one of the major concepts developed in seventh grade, and all of the big ideas listed above are addressed.

 ## Introducing Probability

Probability does not appear in the *Common Core State Standards* expectations until seventh grade. Notions of chance and fairness, however, should be developed early in school and through playing games, and students should have developed some intuition about how likely an outcome might be. Although such intuition can be a positive thing, in probability it can also be a preconception that works against understanding the randomness of events (Abu-Bakare, 2008). Because middle school is the first time probability is addressed in the standards, we begin this chapter with some introductory-level experiences.

◆ Likely or Not Likely?

Probability is about how likely an event is. Therefore, a good place to begin is with a focus on *impossible*, *possible*, and *certain*. This can be as easy as listing events, as in Activity 16.1, or having students give examples that fall in each category.

◆ Activity 16.1 IS IT LIKELY?

Ask students to judge various events as *impossible*, *possible*, or *certain*. Consider these examples:

- It will rain tomorrow.
- Drop a rock in water, and it will sink.
- The sun will rise tomorrow morning.
- A hurricane/tornado will hit our town.
- In an election, candidate A will be elected.
- If you ask people who the first U.S. president was, they will know.
- You will have two birthdays this year.
- You will be in bed by 11:00 p.m.

For each event, students should justify their choice of how likely they think it is. Notice that the last two ideas are about the students. This is an opportunity to bring in students' identities and cultures. Ask students to work with their families to write down family events that are certain, impossible, or possible. Encourage native language use, as appropriate, for English language learners (ELLs). For students with disabilities, use a strip of cash register tape, and label the ends with the words *impossible* and *certain* to assist them in organizing their thinking. Write the events listed above on cards so that students can place them along the strip.

The use of random devices (tools) that can be analyzed (e.g., spinners, number cubes, coins to toss, colored cubes drawn from a bag) can help students make predictions about how likely a particular occurrence is. Begin with random devices that students can use to count the outcomes. Colored dots can be stuck on the sides of a wooden cube to create different color

Standards for Mathematical Practice

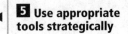
5 Use appropriate tools strategically

Figure 16.1

A recording sheet for "1-2-3 How Likely?" and "1-2-3 How Likely Are Sums?"

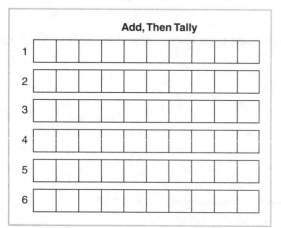

Add, Then Tally

1
2
3
4
5
6

probabilities. Colored tiles (e.g., eight red and two blue) can be placed in opaque bags. Students draw a tile from the bag and then return it after each draw. The following two activities are games of chance with unequal outcomes. However, students may not initially connect that having more of something means it is more likely. A common initial misconception is that there is a one-in-three chance of each of the values because each one is possible.

Activity 16.2 1-2-3 HOW LIKELY?

Make number cubes with sides labeled as follows: 1, 1, 2, 3, 3, 3. Ask students to predict what number they might get when they roll the cube. What is likely? What is impossible? Have students roll the cube and record the results in a bar graph (as in Figure 16.1, but with just the first three rows). Students should mark an X in the column for 1, 2, or 3 each time the cube shows that value and stop when one row is full.

Activity 16.3 1-2-3 HOW LIKELY ARE SUMS?

This game requires two cubes labeled as above. It is a more difficult task because it considers the probability of two events (two dice rolls). Students take turns rolling the two cubes and recording the sums of the two numbers. Before the game begins, ask students to predict which row will fill the fastest or if the rows will fill at equal rates. Ask students to keep track of their data on a recording sheet (as illustrated in Figure 16.1, with rows labeled 1 through 6). Students roll the cubes until one of the rows is full.

Area models, such as spinners, are more challenging because students cannot simply count the possible outcomes (Abu-Bakare, 2008). It is therefore important to connect counting to area, as in the following spinner activity.

Activity 16.4 RACE TO TEN

 Provide a spinner for students (see options in Figure 16.2). Ask, "Which color option will be the first one to happen 10 times?" Have students work in pairs, taking turns spinning the spinner and creating a tally for each result. Repeat three times. Switch to other spinners. For virtual spinners, try the NCTM Illuminations "Adjustable Spinner" (http://illuminations.nctm.org/activitydetail.aspx?ID=79). This spinner can be adjusted to have any number of sections of any size and can be spun any number of times.

Figure 16.2

Spinners for "Race to Ten."

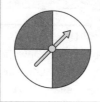   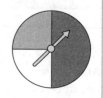

 Teaching Tip

A two-color spinner or probability wheel can be constructed easily by cutting out two circles of different colors, cutting a radius in each, and sliding one into the other. Then use a paperclip as the spinner.

Figure 16.3 The probability continuum. Use these spinner faces to help students see how chance can be at different places on a continuum between impossible and certain.

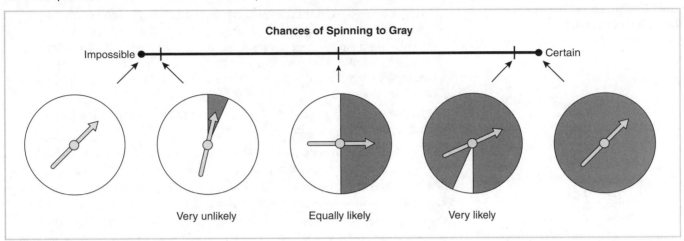

Chances of Spinning to Gray

Impossible ●————|————————————|————————|———● Certain

Very unlikely Equally likely Very likely

This activity provides an opportunity to explore how likely an event is with an area model, but because 10, the total goal, is a small number, students may have surprising results. This issue is addressed in the section "The Law of Large Numbers."

◆ The Probability Continuum

The number line is an important model across mathematical concepts, and it is emphasized across the content strands in the *Common Core State Standards*. Probability is no exception. Presenting probability on a number line from 0 to 1 provides a visual model of how likely an event can be. The number line can be connected to spinners, as illustrated in Figure 16.3. Post the probability continuum in the classroom, where it can be used as a reference for other opportunities to talk about how likely something is.

In order to deepen students' understanding of the probability continuum, select a particular mark along the continuum—for example, $\frac{1}{4}$—and have them create a spinner with a color that is about that likely to occur. This can also be done with counters, as in Activity 16.5.

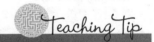

Teaching Tip

The probability continuum also serves to estimate the relative size of fractions and therefore strengthens rational number sense. Ask students comparison questions related to probability, such as "Which is more likely?" Connect to the comparison of fraction strategies.

Activity 16.5 **DESIGN AND TRADE BAGS**

Provide students with a copy of the "Design a Bag" recording sheet shown in Figure 16.4 (see Blackline Master 40). Place students in groups and give each group a value on the probability continuum (e.g., $\frac{1}{3}$, $\frac{3}{4}$, $\frac{1}{6}$). Give students markers of two colors, and have them color the tiles a designated color (e.g., red) so that the probability of selecting a red tile is the probability they have been assigned. Once they have colored the tiles on the "Design a Bag" Blackline Master to match their fraction (e.g., $\frac{1}{3}$ are red, for example), the students trade papers. Each group now has another group's bag. With the new bag, students do the following:

BLM

Figure 16.4

A possible recording sheet for the "Design a Bag" activity (see Blackline Master 40).

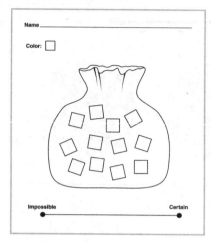

1. They mark the probability line at the point they think matches the number of tiles colored red.

2. They use actual colored tiles and brown paper bags based on what is colored on the "Design a Bag" Blackline Master they received. They draw a tile from the bag (with replacement) 50 times and determine the fraction of times they have drawn a red tile. Remind students to shake their bag each time to ensure random sampling. Students can revise their mark on the probability continuum if they choose to do so.

3. They return the papers to the group that colored the Design a Bag and find out what the original probability was.

Remember, the purpose of this activity is simply to determine approximately where on the continuum the probability might be—not to actually calculate it. At the end of the activity, have students explain (on the back of the handout or in their journals) how they decided where to place their mark on the probability line. ELLs and students with disabilities can benefit from sentence starters, such as, "In the bag we received, there were _____ red and _____ blue tiles. We first thought _____. After we did our experiment, we thought _____. We picked this probability because _____."

Standards for Mathematical Practice

3 Construct viable arguments and critique the reasoning of others

▶ This activity engages students in conjecturing about how likely an event is, experimenting, and comparing their predictions with experimental outcomes as they continue to explore and refine their conjectures about theoretical probability. This builds a strong foundation for the more advanced probability techniques they will develop in seventh grade and beyond.

As a fun twist on Activity 16.5, have a group select a probability, design a bag, and then trade bags with another group. Rather than see the tiles, the second group just conducts 50 draws and then predicts what is in the bag. The students can check their guess by pouring the tiles out of the bag.

"Marble Mania!" (www.sciencenetlinks.com/interactives/marble/marblemania.html) offers virtual activities like "Design and Trade a Bag." You control how many marbles and of what colors to place in a virtual marble bag. An advantage of this resource is that you can run a large number of different trials in a short time.

 Formative Assessment Note

As students work, *observe* whether they see the connection between the count of the colored tiles and the probability, or if they rely on the experiment. In their *writing*, see whether their explanations are based on what they saw in the bag (4 reds out of 12 would be about $\frac{1}{3}$ the way along the continuum) or on what they learned from drawing tiles out of the bag (we drew red 20 out of 50 times, so that is a little less than halfway along the continuum).

Theoretical Probability and Experiments

The *probability* of an event is a measure of the chance that the event will occur (Franklin, Kader, Mewborn, Moreno, Peck, Perry, & Scheaffer, 2005). So, how do you measure the chance of an event? The answer to this depends on the event itself. Events fall into two different categories. The first category includes events whose probability of occurrence is known or can be determined through an analysis of the situation, as in the following example.

What is the probability of rolling a six with a fair die?

When the probability of an event is known, probability can be established theoretically by examining all the possibilities.

The second category includes events whose probability of the occurrence is *not* observable. In this case, probability can be established only through empirical data or evidence from past experiments or data collection (Colgan, 2006; Nicolson, 2005).

What is the probability that Jon V. will make his free throws (based on his previous record)?

What is the chance of rain (based on how often it has rained under similar conditions)?

Although this type of probability is less common in the school curriculum, it is the most applicable to fields that use probability and therefore important to include in your teaching (Franklin et al., 2005).

In both cases, experiments or simulations can be designed to explore the phenomena being examined. (Sometimes, textbooks refer to experiments as *experimental probability*, but this terminology is not used by statisticians and therefore is not used here.) Some experiments have outcomes that are equally likely, whereas other experiments do not. With coin flips, there are two possible outcomes that are equally likely, so each has a probability of $\frac{1}{2}$. Hence, the theoretical probability of obtaining a head is $\frac{1}{2}$. When all possible outcomes of a simple experiment are equally likely, the probability of an event can be expressed as follows:

$$\frac{\text{Number of Outcomes in the Event}}{\text{Number of Possible Outcomes}}$$

Consider the shift in meaning of the question, "Is this coin fair?" This is a statistics problem that can be answered only by doing an experiment and establishing the frequency of heads and tails over the long run (Franklin et al., 2005). The answer requires empirical data, and the probability will be as follows:

$$\frac{\text{Number of Observed Occurrences of the Event}}{\text{Total Number of Trials}}$$

Because it is impossible to conduct an infinite number of trials, we can only consider the relative frequency for a very large number of trials as an approximation of the theoretical probability. This emphasizes the notion that probability is more about predictions over the long term than about predictions of individual events.

◆ Theoretical Probability

A problem-based way to introduce theoretical probability is to engage students in an activity that involves an unfair game or one in which the outcomes are not equally likely. In the following activity, the results of the game will likely be contrary to students' intuitive ideas. This, in turn, will provide a real reason to analyze the game in a logical manner and find out why things happened as they did, which leads to the development of the theoretical probability.

Figure 16.5   A student's correct conclusion but incomplete reasoning for "Fair or Unfair?"

I think, that player C will win because a coin flips a 50-50 chance and he's guessing a 50-50 change. He's guessing that it will be one then, the other witch is 50-50. The game is unfair for player B and B. Player C had the advantage.

Activity 16.6   FAIR OR UNFAIR?

Three students toss two like coins (e.g., two pennies or two nickels), and they record points according to the following rules: Player A gets 1 point if the coin toss result is "two heads"; player B gets 1 point if the toss result is "two tails"; and player C gets 1 point if the toss result is "mixed" (one head, one tail). The game is over after 20 tosses. The player who has the most points wins. Have students play the game at least two or three times. After each game, the players are to stop and discuss if they think the game is fair and make predictions about who will win the next game.

When the full class has played the game several times, conduct a discussion on the fairness of the game. Challenge students to make an argument *not* based on the data as to whether the game is fair, and why. For ELLs, discuss the meaning of *fair* before beginning the game, and review the term when asking students to create an argument.

A common analysis of the game in Activity 16.6 might go something like this: At first, students think that because there are three possible outcomes—two tails, one head and one tail, and two heads—each player has an equal chance, so the game should be fair. However, after playing "Fair or Unfair?" students find that player C (who gets a point for a mixed result) appears to have an unfair advantage (especially if several games have been played or the class has pooled its data). This observation seems to contradict the notion that all the outcomes are equally likely.

Figure 16.6

Four possible outcomes of flipping two coins.

First Coin	Second Coin
Head	Head
Head	Tail
Tail	Head
Tail	Tail

When students from fifth through eleventh grades performed a similar two-coin task and were asked for the probability of getting a head and a tail with two coins, similar misconceptions were found (Rubel, 2006, 2007). About 25 percent of the students said the probability was $\frac{1}{3}$ because one of three things could happen: two heads, one of each, or two tails. Although about half answered correctly, many of these students used faulty reasoning, explaining that they picked that answer because there is a 50–50 chance in any experiment. See, for example, Figure 16.5.

In order to help students connect how likely an event is to the possible outcomes, encourage them to analyze the situation and generate all the possible outcomes—for example, by using a table such the one in Figure 16.6. A player gets a head and a tail in two of the four possible outcomes. Figure 16.7 provides an example of a student's correct explanation for "Fair or Unfair." This theoretical probability is based on a logical analysis of the experiment, not on experimental results.

Figure 16.7 A student's reasoning for "Fair or Unfair?" that connects outcomes to probability.

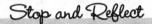

> I think this game is unfair because it is more likley to get a mix than two of the same sides. This is true because there are more possibilitys for a mix Such as heads tails, and tails heads, but the only possibility for player A is two heads, and the only possibility for player B is a tails. So for playerC they have a 1/2 chance for geting a point, but for the other two they only have a 1/4 chance of geting a point,

"Rock-paper-scissors" is another great context for exploring fair games and possible outcomes. It can be played in the normal way or adapted so that "same" scores 1 point for one player and "different" scores 1 point for the other player. Decide whether this is a fair game (Ellis, Yeh, & Stump, 2007–2008).

Figuring out the probability of hitting a target is an excellent way to explore probability, and it also applies knowledge of area formulas. For example, students can develop models for geometric probability, as in the dartboard task below.

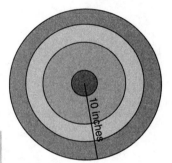

The radii of the circles on the dartboard are 2 inches, 6 inches, 8 inches, and 10 inches. What is the probability of landing in each section? How many points would you assign to each section?

Stop and Reflect

Use the target pictured and determine the probability of landing in each section. What might students suggest as dartboard points for each section, and what rationale might they give? ∎

Students may assign values in various ways. For example, they may think the skinny outer circle is harder to land on and give it more points than other sections, even though the area of that region may be more. Allow them time to share their reasoning and to critique others' ways of assigning points.

◆ Experiments

As noted previously, some probabilities cannot be determined by the analysis of possible outcomes of an event; instead, they can be determined only through gathering empirical data. The data may be preexisting or may need to be established through an experiment, with a sufficiently large number of trials conducted to become confident that the resulting relative frequency is an approximation of the theoretical probability. For example, the probability of a hurricane is based on historical data. (See http://landfalldisplay.geolabvirtualmaps.com for an interesting look at the probability of hurricanes.) The following activities are examples of situations in which the only way to establish how likely an outcome is to do an experiment and use the results of a large number of trials.

Activity 16.7 DROP IT!

1. *Cup toss.* Provide a small plastic cup to each pair of students. Ask them to list the possible ways that the cup could land if they tossed it in the air and let it fall on the floor. Which of the possibilities (upside down, right side up, or on the side) do they think is most likely and which least likely? Why? Have students toss the cup 20 times, each time recording how it lands. Students should agree on a uniform method of tossing the cups to ensure unbiased data (e.g., dropping the cups from the same height). Record each pair's data in a class chart. Discuss the differences, and generate reasons for them. Have students predict what will happen if they pool their data. Pool the data and compute three ratios: one for each type of landing (upside down, right side up, or on the side) to the total number of tosses. The relative frequency of the combined data should approximate the actual probability.

2. *Toy animal drop.* Bring in small plastic toys that can land in different ways. Repeat the first activity. (See Nelson and Williams, 2009, for an exploration with toy pigs.)

3. *Falling kisses.* Using Hershey Kisses, conduct an experiment to see how often they land directly on the base (Gallego, Saldamando, Tapia-Beltran, Williams, & Hoopingarner, 2009). Alternative foods include Hershey's Rolo Caramels, or for more healthy options, consider fish crackers (direction in which they face).

◆ Standards for Mathematical Practice

8 Look for and express regularity in repeated reasoning ▶

In these experiments, there is no practical way to determine the results before you start. However, once you have results for 200 tosses (empirical data), you will undoubtedly feel more confident in predicting the results of the next 100 tosses. After gathering data for 1000 trials, you will feel even more confident. In other words, the more tosses that are made, the more confident you become. For example, in dropping the cup, after 100 or so trials, you may have determined a probability of $\frac{4}{5}$, or 80 percent, for the cup to land on its side.

The Law of Large Numbers

The phenomenon in which the relative frequency of an event becomes a closer approximation of the actual probability or the theoretical probability as the size of the data set (sample) increases is referred to as *the law of large numbers.* The larger the size of the data set, the more representative the sample is of the population. In thinking about statistics, a survey of 1000 people provides more reliable and convincing data about the larger population than does a survey of 5 people. The larger the number of trials (people surveyed), the more confident you can be that the data reflect the larger population. The same is true when you are attempting to determine the probability of an event through data collection.

Although critical to understanding probability, this concept is difficult for students to grasp. Students commonly think that a probability should play out in the short term, a misconception sometimes referred to as *the law of small numbers* (Flores, 2006; Tarr, Lee, & Rider, 2006). The next two activities are designed to address students' emerging understanding (or misunderstanding) of probability and the number of trials needed to approximate a probability.

Teaching Tip

Comparing small data sets with large data sets is one way to help students think more deeply about the fact that the size of the trial matters.

Activity 16.8 GET ALL SIX!

Ask students to list the numbers 1 through 6 at the bottom of a frequency table. Ask students to roll a die and to mark an X over each number until they have rolled each number at least once. Repeat five or six times. Discuss how different students' frequency charts compare for each number. Students will see that in some cases there were many fours, for example, or that it took 25 rolls before all numbers were rolled, while in other cases, they got all the numbers in only 10 rolls. Now, pool all the data and discuss the relative frequencies for the numbers that emerge. Focus discussion on the fact that in the short run, data vary a lot—it is over the long run that data "even out." This activity can also be done on a graphing calculator (Flores, 2006).

Truly random events often occur in unexpected groups; a fair coin may turn up heads five times in a row. A 100-year flood may hit a town twice in 10 years. Drawing random devices such as spinners, dice, or cubes from a bag gives students an intuitive feel for the imperfect distribution of randomness. The next activity is designed to help students with this difficult idea.

Activity 16.9 WHAT ARE THE CHANCES?

Use a copy of Blackline Master 41, shown in Figure 16.8. Provide each pair of students with a spinner having a face that is half red and half blue. Discuss the chances of spinning to blue. Mark the $\frac{1}{2}$ point on the continuum of impossible to certain, and draw a vertical line down through all of the lines below this point. Then have the students in each pair spin their spinner 10 times, tallying the number of red and blue spins. Mark the number of blue spins on the second line. For example, if there are 3 blue and 7 red spins, place a mark at about 7 on the 0-to-10 number line. If the result of the 10 spins is not exactly 5 and 5, discuss possible reasons why this may be so.

Repeat 10 more times. Add the count from the first 10 spins, and again mark the total (i.e., out of 20) in the right-hand box of the third line. Repeat at least two more times, continuing to add the results of new spins to the previous results. If a graphing calculator or applet is used, even 1000 trials are possible in a short amount of time. Ask students to reflect on what they notice in each number line.

Figure 16.8

Activity to explore probability in the short run and in the long run (see Blackline Master 41).

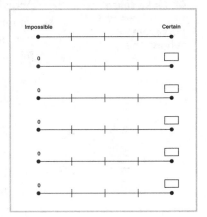

The successive number lines used in "What Are the Chances?" all have the same length, and each represents the total number of trials. When the results are plotted on any one number line, the position shows the fraction of the total spins as a visual portion of the whole line. With more trials, the marks will get closer and closer to the $\frac{1}{2}$ mark. Note that 240 blue spins out of 500 is 48 percent, or very close to one-half. This is so even though there are 20 more red spins (260) than blue.

The same Blackline Master and the same process of accumulating data in stages can and should be used for other experiments. For example, try using this approach with the cup toss experiment. Rather than draw a vertical line before collecting data, decide on the best guess at the actual probability after the numbers have become large, and then draw the vertical line in the appropriate position. Observe and record on the number lines 10 additional trials, 20 additional trials, and 50 additional trials. Compare these smaller data sets with the larger data set. Write the probabilities as percents and as fractions to show the connection between these representations.

Formative Assessment Note

Use the following *performance assessment* to assess students' ideas about long-run results versus short-run results. Have students write about their ideas.

> Margaret spins the spinner 10 times. Blue turns up on 3 spins. Red turns up on 7 spins. Margaret says that there is a 3-in-10 chance of spinning to blue. Carla then spins the same spinner 100 times. Carla records 53 spins to blue and 47 spins to red. Carla says that the chance of spinning to blue on this spinner is about even. Who do you think is correct—Margaret or Carla? Explain. Draw a spinner that you think they may have been using.

Look for evidence that students understand that the result of 10 spins is not very good evidence of the probability, and that the result of 100 spins tells us more about the chances. Also, to assess whether students understand the big idea that chance has no memory (e.g., each toss of a coin is independent of prior tosses), have students write in their *journals* about the following:

> Duane has a lucky coin that he has tossed many, many times. He is sure that it is a fair coin with an even chance of heads or tails. Duane tosses his coin six times, and heads come up six times in a row. Duane is sure that the next toss will be tails because he has never been able to toss heads seven times in a row. What do you think the chances are of Duane tossing heads on the next toss? Explain your answer.

Standards for Mathematical Practice

1 Make sense of problems and persevere in solving them

Why Use Experiments?

Actually conducting experiments and examining outcomes in teaching probability are important in helping students address common misconceptions and build a deeper understanding of why certain things are more likely than others. Specifically, experiments do the following:

- Model real-world problems that are actually solved by conducting experiments (doing simulations). See, for example, "Undersea Treasure" at The Futures Channel website (www.thefutureschannel.com/dockets/hands-on_math/undersea_treasure). A probability map is used to locate sunken ships that contain gold treasure.

- Provide a connection to counting strategies (lists, tree diagrams) to increase confidence that the probability is accurate.

- Provide an experiential background for examining the theoretical model. When you begin to sense that the probability of two heads is $\frac{1}{4}$ instead of $\frac{1}{3}$, the analysis in Figure 16.6 seems more reasonable.

- Help students see how the ratio of a particular outcome to the total number of trials begins to converge toward a fixed number. For an infinite number of trials, the relative frequency and theoretical probability would be the same.

- Help students learn more than students who are not doing experiments (Gurbuz, Erdem, Catlioglu, & Birgin, 2010).

Try to use an experimental approach whenever possible, posing interesting problems to investigate. If a theoretical analysis is possible (e.g., as in the two-coin experiment in "Fair or Unfair?"), it should also be examined and the results compared with the expected outcome.

Use of Technology in Experiments

Many simple calculators and graphing calculators are able to produce random outcomes at the press of a button. These random numbers can be related to the possible outcomes in an experiment. For example, if the final digit is odd, you can assign it to represent one outcome, and if it is even to represent a second outcome. If there are four outcomes, you can look at the remainder when the last two digits are divided by 4 (i.e., the remainder will be 0, 1, 2, or 3) and assign a remainder to each outcome. In addition, some calculators, like the TI-73, TI-83, and TI-84, can run the free Probability Simulation App, an interactive tool that simulates tossing coins, rolling number cubes, spinning spinners, and generating random numbers. (Visit the Texas Instruments website Education Technology at http://education.ti.com.)

Also, computer applets can be used to flip coins, spin spinners, or draw numbers from a hat virtually. NCTM Illuminations has a series of lessons, "Probability Explorations" (http://illuminations.nctm.org/LessonDetail.aspx?ID=U190), in which students explore probability through virtual experiments and can also graph the results. As long as students accept the results generated by the technology as truly random or equivalent to those of hands-on devices, virtual devices have the advantage of being quick, motivating, and accessible. Web-based tools, such as "Spinners" at the National Library of Virtual Manipulatives (http://nlvm.usu.edu), have the advantage of generating many more trials in much less time. Because of the speed at which an experiment can be done, virtual devices afford the opportunity to explore probability across a variety of tools (virtual dice, coins, cards, etc.), and they provide graphic displays of the trials. Also, in a virtual world, dice can be "loaded" and used to challenge students' thinking (Beck & Huse, 2007; Phillips-Bey, 2004): "Are these fair dice? How can you find out?"

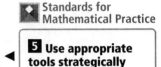

◄ **Standards for Mathematical Practice**

5 Use appropriate tools strategically

Sample Spaces and the Probability of Two Events

Understanding the concepts of *sample space* and *event* is central to understanding probability. The *sample space* for an experiment or chance situation is the set of all possible outcomes for that experiment. For example, if a bag contains two red, three yellow, and five blue tiles, the sample space consists of all ten tiles. An *event* is a subset of the sample space. The event of drawing a yellow tile has three elements or outcomes in the sample space, and the event of drawing a blue tile has five elements in the sample space. For rolling a single common die, the sample space consists of the numbers 1 through 6. A two-event experiment requires two (or more) actions to determine an outcome. Examples include rolling two dice, drawing two tiles from a bag, and the combination of the occurrence of rain and forgetting your umbrella.

When two-event experiments are explored, there is another factor to consider: Does the occurrence of the event in one stage have an effect on the occurrence of the event in the other? In the following sections, we will consider two-event experiments of both types—those with independent events and those with dependent events.

Independent Events

In Activity 16.6, "Fair or Unfair?," students explored the results of tossing two coins. The toss of one coin had no effect on the toss of the other. Tossing a coin twice is an example of *independent events*; the occurrence or nonoccurrence of one event has no effect on the other.

Let's explore rolling two dice and adding the results. Suppose that your students gather data on the sums that they get for two dice. The results might be recorded in a dot plot, as in Figure 16.9a. These events (sums) do not appear to be equally likely, and in fact the sum of 7 appears to be the most likely outcome. To explain this, students might look for the combinations that make 7: 1 and 6, 2 and 5, and 3 and 4. But there are also three combinations for 6 and for 8. It seems as though 6 and 8 should be just as likely as 7, and yet they are not.

Now suppose that the experiment is repeated. This time, for the sake of clarity, suggest that the students roll two dice of different colors and that they keep the tallies in a chart like the one in Figure 16.9b.

Teaching Tip

Using dice (or counters) of different colors can help students focus on each event separately and therefore more clearly see the different possible outcomes.

Figure 16.9 Exploring the probabilities for the sum of two dice. A dot plot is used to record sums, then a matrix is used to document the possible outcomes.

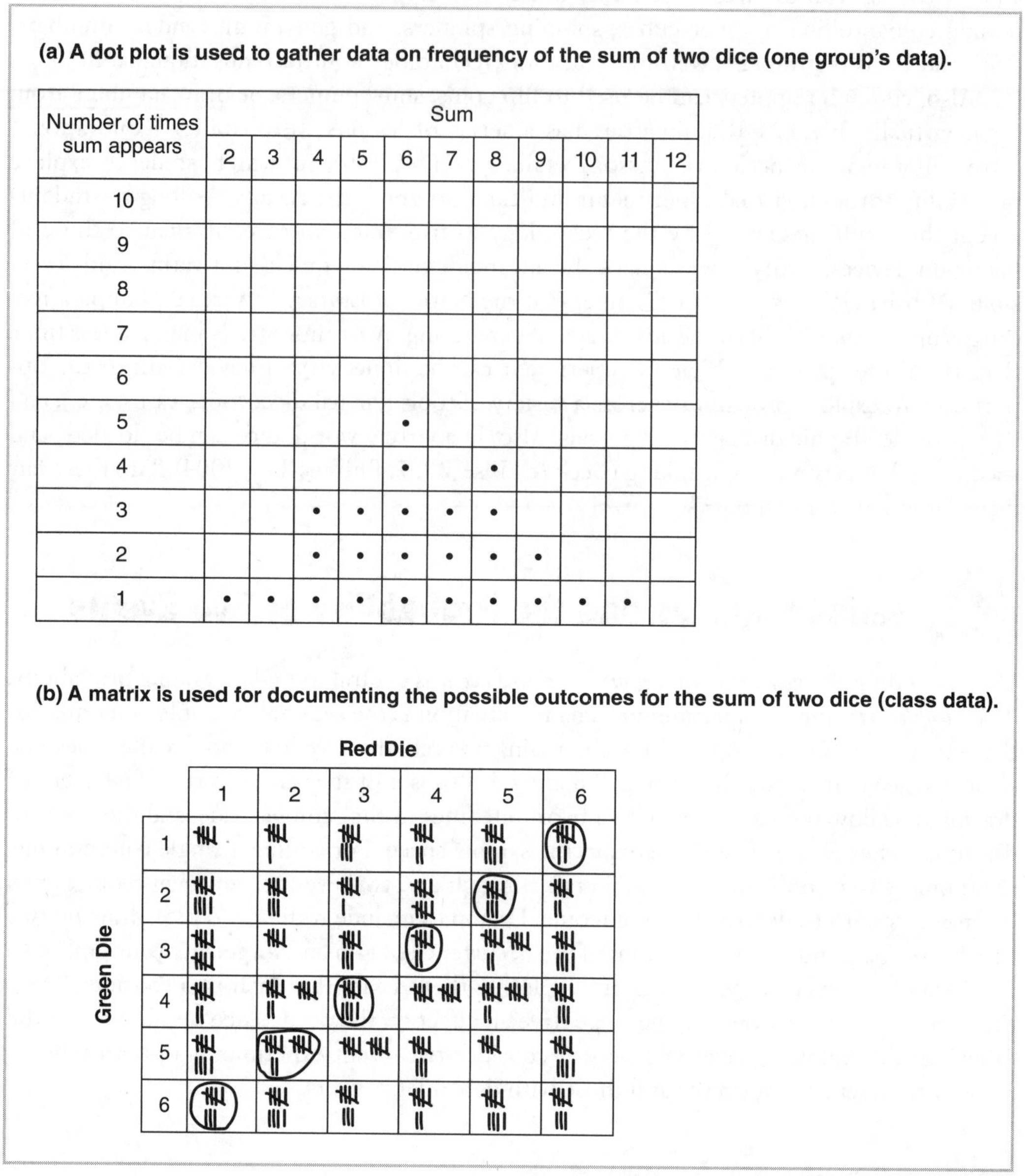

(a) A dot plot is used to gather data on frequency of the sum of two dice (one group's data).

Number of times sum appears	Sum										
	2	3	4	5	6	7	8	9	10	11	12
10											
9											
8											
7											
6											
5					•						
4					•		•				
3			•	•	•	•	•				
2			•	•	•	•	•	•			
1	•	•	•	•	•	•	•	•	•	•	

(b) A matrix is used for documenting the possible outcomes for the sum of two dice (class data).

The results of a large number of dice rolls indicate what one would expect—namely, that all 36 cells of this chart are equally likely (However, the sums are not equally likely. Why?). Comparing the sums of 6, 7, and 8 reveals that for 7, 3 red, 4 green is different from 4 red, 3 green. There are six outcomes in the desired event (getting a 7) out of a total of the sample space (36), for a probability of $\frac{6}{36}$, or $\frac{1}{6}$. Both 6 and 8 have doubles, and therefore only five outcomes, for a probability of $\frac{5}{36}$.

To create the sample space for two independent events, use a chart or diagram that keeps the two events separate and illustrates all possible combinations. The matrix in Figure 16.9b is effective when there are only two events. A tree diagram (Figure 16.10) can be used to determine sample spaces with any number of events. For example, consider the context of creating an ice-cream cone. You can choose a waffle cone or a regular cone, ice cream that is dipped or not dipped, and any of three single flavors. This can be simulated with coins and a spinner, as illustrated in Figure 16.10.

Stop and Reflect

Use a chart and/or a tree diagram to analyze the sum of two number cubes, each with sides 1, 1, 2, 3, 3, and 3. (These were the cubes used in Activity 16.5.) What is the probability of each sum, 1 through 6? How might these tools support student understanding of sample space and the probability of independent events? ■

A common process to help students connect sample space with probability is to ask them first to make a prediction of the probability of the event, then conduct an experiment with a large number of trials, and finally compare the prediction with what happened. Then ask students to create the sample space and see how it compares with the prediction and the results of the experiment. Games provide an excellent context for such explorations, as described in Activity 16.10.

Activity 16.10 **LU-LU**

This Hawaiian game involves taking turns tossing four stones (illustrated below) and calculating the resulting score. (You can get glass stones from a craft store and mark dots on one side.) The first player to reach 50 wins. (See McCoy, Buckner, and Munley, 2007, for more on this game.) Invite students to play the game with a partner.

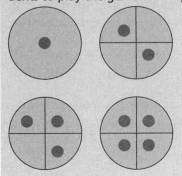

After they have played, ask what they notice about the sums they are getting. Ask questions about probability: "What sums are possible? What sums were common?" Also ask students these questions: "What scores are possible in a single turn? What are all the outcomes (possible combinations of stones)? What is the probability of each score?"

ELLs may have games from their native countries. These can be used to explore probability; ask questions like the ones posed here.

Figure 16.10

A tree diagram showing all possible outcomes for ice-cream cone options. Coins are used for choice of cone and choice of dipping, and spinner is used for choice of three flavors.

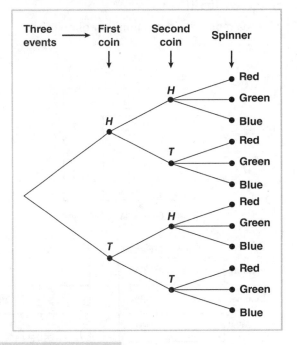

The following are additional examples of probabilities of independent events. Any one of these could be explored as part of a full lesson.

- Rolling an even sum with two dice
- Spinning "blue" twice on a spinner
- Having a tack *or* a cup land up when each is tossed once
- Getting *at least* two heads from tossing four coins
- Rolling two dice and getting a difference that is *no more than* 3

◆ Area Representation

One way to determine the probability of a multistage event is to list all possible outcomes and count the number of outcomes that make up the event. This is effective but has some limitations. First, a list implies that all outcomes are equally likely. Second, lists can get tedious

Teaching Tip

Words and phrases such as *and, or, at least,* and *no more than* may cause students some confusion and therefore require explicit attention. Of special note is the word *or* because its meaning in everyday usage is generally not the same as its strict logical meaning in mathematics. In mathematics, *or* includes the case of *both*. For example, in the tack-and-cup experiment, the event includes tack up, cup up, and *both* tack *and* cup up.

when there are many possibilities. Third, students can lose track of which possibilities they have included in the list and may leave off some of the possibilities. For all of these reasons, an area representation is a good option for determining probability, the focus of Activity 16.11.

Figure 16.11

An area model for determining probabilities.

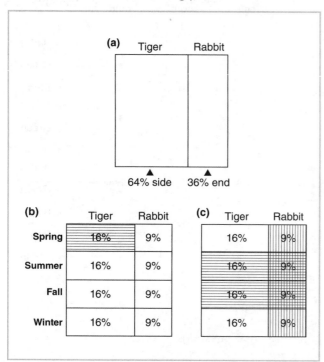

Activity 16.11 ARE YOU A SPRING TIGER?

Before doing this activity, determine which Chinese birth year animals are likely to be represented in the classroom (e.g., the tiger and the rabbit). Spend some time discussing the Chinese birth year animals with students. (This would be particularly timely at the Chinese New Year!) Begin by finding out what percentage of the class is represented by each animal. Ask, "If I name one of the Chinese birth year animals, what is the probability it will be *your* birth year animal?" Illustrate this percentage by partitioning a rectangle, as in Figure 16.11a. (This particular illustration finds that 64 percent of the students in the class were born in the year of the tiger, and 36 percent were born in the year of the rabbit.) Ask, "If I name one of the seasons, what is the probability it will be *your* season?" Ask students to illustrate their response by partitioning and shading a rectangle (Figure 16.11b). Then ask, "What is the probability of being both a spring and a tiger?"

Teaching Tip

The area representation is accessible to a range of learners because it is less abstract than equations or tree diagrams.

In Figure 16.11b, you can visually see that students in the year-of-the-tiger and spring groups make up $\frac{1}{4}$ of 64 percent, or 16 percent, of the population. This should look very familiar because the same process is used for multiplying fractions.

The area representation is also effective in solving "or" situations. Consider the question, "What is the probability you were born in fall or summer, or that you are a rabbit?" The shading for this example is illustrated in Figure 16.11c. Half of the students are born in summer or fall, and 36 percent are born in the year of the rabbit. Students can add the percentages in the boxes, or they can think about the two situations separately: 50 percent are born in summer or fall and 36 percent are born in the year of the rabbit. The combination of these results is 86 percent, but some students are both and have therefore been double-counted (see overlap in diagram). In this example, the overlap is 18 percent. Therefore, the population that is born in summer or fall or born in the year of the rabbit is $50 + 36 - 18 = 68$ percent of the population. This can be generalized to the following model for the probability of two independent events:

$$P(A \text{ or } B) = P(A) + P(B) - P(A \text{ and } B)$$

Standards for Mathematical Practice

2 Reason abstractly and quantitatively ▶

The following activity is a challenging and engaging way for students to think about the probability of independent events, but this time students design the random device (Ely & Cohen, 2010).

Activity 16.12 **DESIGN A WINNING SPINNER**

Explain that each student is going to create a winning spinner, which means that when it is spun twice, the sum will be on a number strip with values 2, 3, 4, 5, 6, 7, and 8. Students create their own spinner, partitioning the circle however they like and writing a number in each sector. Once students have their spinner, they pair with someone else and play the game with their own spinner. Student A spins twice and adds the two values. If the sum is 5, student A covers 5 on his or her number strip. Student B takes a turn. The first partner to cover all numbers on his or her strip wins. Play three rounds. Next, ask students to re-design their spinner, find a new partner, and play three more rounds. If possible, repeat a third time. Afterward, discuss how they designed a winning spinner.

In going backward (from the desired outcome to the spinner), students can build a deeper understanding of how to determine the probability of independent events.

Dependent Events

A dependent event is a second event whose result depends on the result of a first event. For example, suppose that there are two identical boxes. One box contains one genuine dollar bill and two counterfeit bills, and the other box contains one genuine and one counterfeit bill (you do not know which box is which). You may choose one box and from that box select one bill without looking. What are your chances of getting a genuine dollar bill? Here, there are two events: selecting a box and selecting a bill. The probability of getting a dollar in the second event depends on which box is chosen in the first event. The next activity engages students in a dependent events task.

Figure 16.12
Should you place your key in Room A or Room B to have the best chance at winning?

 Activity 16.13 **KEYS TO A NEW CAR**

Pose the following problem: In a game show, you can win a car—if you make it through the maze to the room where you have placed the car key. You can place the key in either Room A or Room B (see maze in Figure 16.12). At the start and at each fork in the path, you must spin the indicated spinner and follow the path it points to. In which room should you place the key to have the best chance of winning the car?

You can also use the area approach to determine the probability for dependent events. Figure 16.13 illustrates the "Keys to a New Car" task.

Stop and Reflect

How would the area representation for the car problem be different if the spinners at Fork I and Fork II were $\frac{1}{3}$ A and $\frac{2}{3}$ B spinners? What questions like this one can you ask students in order to help them think about how one event depends on the next? ■

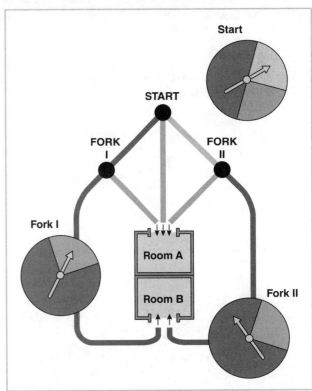

Figure 16.13

Using the area approach to solve the "Keys to a New Car" task.

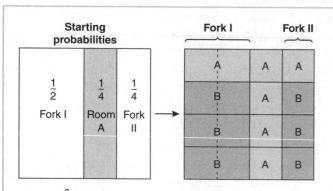

At Fork I, $\frac{3}{4}$ of the time you will go to Room B.

(Note: Not $\frac{3}{4}$ of the square but $\frac{3}{4}$ of the times you go to Fork I.)

At Fork II, $\frac{3}{4}$ of these times (or $\frac{3}{16}$ of total time) you will go to Room B.

Therefore, you will end up in Room A $\frac{7}{16}$ of the time and Room B $\frac{9}{16}$ of the time.

Teaching Tip

Having students describe the connection between the area representation and the tree diagram can help build meaning for the tree diagram approach, which can be used in any multiple-events probability task.

Figure 16.14

A tree diagram is another way to model the outcomes of two or more dependent events.

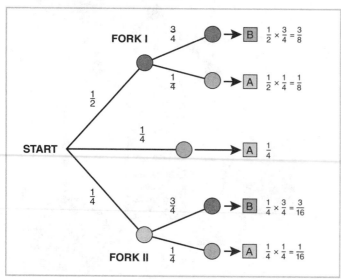

Figure 16.14 shows a tree diagram for the "Keys to a New Car" problem, with the probability of each path in the maze written on the "branch" of the tree. The tree diagram is more abstract than the area approach, but it applies to a wider range of situations. Each branch of the tree diagram in Figure 16.14 matches with a section of the square in Figure 16.13. Use the area approach to explain why the probability for each complete branch of the tree is determined by multiplying the probabilities along the branch.

 Simulations

Simulation is a technique used for answering real-world questions or making decisions in complex situations in which an element of chance is involved. Many times, simulations are conducted because it is too dangerous, complex, or expensive to manipulate the real situation. To see what is likely to happen in the real event, a model must be designed that has the same probabilities as the real situation. For example, in the design of a rocket, a large number of related systems all have some chance of failure that might cause serious problems with the rocket. Knowing the probability of serious failures will help determine whether redesign or backup systems are required. It is not reasonable to make repeated tests of the actual rocket. Instead, a model that simulates all of the chance situations is designed and run repeatedly with the help of a computer. The computer model can simulate thousands of flights, and an estimate of the chance of failure can be made.

For example, water must be pumped from A to B within a system (Figure 16.15). The five pumps that connect A and B are aging, and it is estimated that at any given time, the probability of pump failure is $\frac{1}{2}$. If a pump fails, water cannot pass that station. For example, if pumps 1, 2, and 5 fail, water flows only through pumps 4 and 3. Consider the following questions, which might well be asked about such a system (Gnanadesikan, Schaeffer, & Swift, 1987):

- What is the probability that water will flow at any time?

- On average, about how many stations need repair at any time?

For any simulation, the following steps can serve as a useful guide.

1. Identify key components and assumptions of the problem. The key component in the water problem is the condition of a pump. Each pump is either working or not working. In this problem, the assumption is that the probability that a pump is working is $\frac{1}{2}$.

2. *Select a random device for the key components.* Any random device can be selected that has outcomes with the same probability as those of the key component—in this case, the pumps. Here, a simple choice might be tossing a coin, with heads representing a working pump.

3. *Define a trial.* A *trial* consists of simulating a series of key components until the situation has been completely modeled one time. In this problem, a trial could consist of tossing a coin five times, each toss representing a different pump (heads for pump is working and tails for pump is not working).

4. *Conduct a large number of trials and record the information.* For this problem, it would be useful to record the number of heads and tails in groups of five because each set of five is one trial and represents all of the pumps.

5. *Use the data to draw conclusions.* There are four possible paths for the water, each flowing through two of the five pumps. As they are numbered in the drawing, if any one of the pairs 1–2, 5–2, 5–3, and 4–3 is open, it makes no difference whether the other pumps are working. By counting the number of trials in which both coins in at least one of the four pairs come up heads, we can estimate the probability of water flowing. To answer the second question, the number of tails (pumps not working) per trial can be averaged.

Here are a few more examples of problems for which a simulation can be used to gather empirical data.

Figure 16.15

Each of these five pumps has a 50 percent chance of failure. What is the probability that some path from A to B is working?

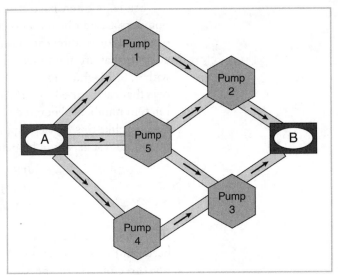

In a true-or-false test, what is the probability of getting 7 out of 10 questions correct by guessing alone? (*Key component:* Answering a question. *Assumption:* Chance of getting the correct answer is $\frac{1}{2}$.)

Simulation option: Flip a coin 10 times for one trial.

In a group of five people, what is the chance that two were born in the same month? (*Key component:* Month of birth. *Assumption:* All 12 months are equally likely.)

Simulation option: Use 12-sided dice or 12 cards. Draw/roll one, replace, and draw/roll again.

Casey's batting average is .350. What is the chance he will go hitless in a complete, nine-inning game? (*Key component:* Getting a hit. *Assumptions:* The probability of a hit for each at-bat is .35. Casey will get to bat four times in the average game.)

Simulation option: Use a spinner that is 35 percent shaded. Spin four times for one trial.

Krunch-a-Munch cereal packs one of five games in each box. About how many boxes should you expect to buy before you get a complete set? (*Key component:* Getting one game. *Assumption:* Each game has a $\frac{1}{5}$ chance.)

Simulation option: Use a spinner with five equal sections. Spin until all sections occur at least once. Record how many spins it took (this is one trial). Repeat. The average length of a trial answers the question. *Extension:* What is the chance of getting a set in eight or fewer boxes?

Students often have trouble selecting an appropriate random device for simulations. Spinners are an obvious choice because areas can be adjusted to match probabilities. Coins or two-color counters are useful for probabilities of $\frac{1}{2}$. A standard die can be used for probabilities that are multiples of $\frac{1}{6}$. There are also dice available online and on smart phones with 4, 8, 12, and 20 sides. Many calculators include a key that will produce random numbers that can be used to simulate experiments (e.g., 1 means true, 2 means false). Usually, the random numbers generated are between 0 and 1, such as 0.8904433368. How could a list of decimals like this replace flipping a coin or spinning a spinner? Suppose each was multiplied by 2. The results would be between 0 and 2, as shown here:

$$0.8904433368 \times 2 = 1.7808866736$$
$$0.0232028877 \times 2 = 0.0464057754$$
$$0.1669322714 \times 2 = 0.3338645428$$

If you focus on the ones column, you have a series of zeros and ones that could represent heads and tails, boys and girls, true and false, or any other pair of equally likely outcomes. For three outcomes, the same as a $\frac{1}{4} - \frac{1}{4} - \frac{1}{2}$ spinner, you might decide to look at the first two digits of the number and assign values from 0 to 24 and from 25 to 49 to the two one-quarter portions and values from 50 to 99 to the one-half portion. Alternatively, each randomly generated number could be multiplied by 4 and the decimal part ignored, resulting in random numbers 0, 1, 2, and 3. These could then be assigned to the desired outcomes.

In this activity, consider how you would design a simulation.

 Activity 16.14 **CHANCE OF TRIPLET GIRLS**

Ask students, "What is the chance that a woman having triplets will end up with all girls?" Record estimates. Ask students to create a simulation to model this problem, using the five steps previously described. Encourage students to use various tools to simulate (flipping three coins, using a random number generator, spinning a two-color spinner three times, etc.). After examining the results, ask questions to relate the predictions to the results. This may lead to creating a tree diagram of the options to make sense of the results.

Explore "A Better Fire!" at Shodor "Interactivate" (www.shodor.org/interactivate/activities/AbetterFire). This is an excellent simulation focused on actual forest fires, with controls for wind speed and direction to add more realism and interaction. A virtual "die" is rolled to see whether a tree should be planted for each square. Then the fire is set and allowed to burn.

 ## Common Misconceptions about Probability

Tasks like "Chance of Triplet Girls" can lead to interesting follow-up questions (Tillema, 2010): "Are three girls less likely or more likely than two girls and a boy? If a family already has two girls, what do you think they will have for their third child?" The questions connect to two of the common misconceptions students have related to probability: commutativity confusion and gambler's fallacy. These misconceptions, and one shared earlier, are discussed briefly here.

1. *Commutativity confusion.* Students may think that two girls and one boy is one possible outcome. But notice that if you list the eight possible combinations for three children, you have three girls only once (GGG) but two girls and one boy three times (GGB, GBG, BGG). The combination of two girls and one boy is three times as likely. We refer to this as *commutativity confusion* because students, knowing that 3 + 4 is the same as 4 + 3, think that that one boy and two girls is one event, not three. Students need to think about all the ways an event can occur when they try to determine how likely an event is.

2. *Gambler's fallacy.* The gambler's fallacy is the notion that what has already happened (two girls) influences the event. Students will argue a boy is more likely because there are already two girls. Similarly, students think that if a tossed coin has had a series of four heads, it is more likely on the fifth toss to be tails (Ryan & Williams, 2007). But a coin has no memory, and the probability of heads or tails is still 50–50, just as the probability of a girl is still 50–50.

3. *Law of small numbers.* This misconception is like the gambler's fallacy in that it relates to small samples, but with this misconception, students expect small samples to be like the greater population (Flores, 2006; Tarr et al., 2006). This was discussed in the section "The Law of Large Numbers" (see Activities 16.8 and 16.9). So, in the case of the three girls, it is not so unusual—it is just a very small data set, so it is not likely to resemble the larger population.

Whether doing simulations, experiments, or theoretical probability, it is important for students to use many models (lists, area, tree diagrams) and to explicitly discuss developing conceptions and misconceptions. In addition to being more interesting, teaching probability in this way allows students to understand important concepts that have many real-world implications.

Expanded Lesson

Design a Fair Game

Content and Task Decisions

Grade Level: 7

Mathematics Goals

- To explore informally the probability of an event with equally likely outcomes through an experiment
- To consider what equally likely events (fair games) look like
- To explore the concept of variation and the law of large numbers

Grade Level Guide

NCTM Curriculum Focal Points	Common Core State Standards
Probability, in particular being able to explore equally likely outcomes and establish theoretical probabilities, is one of the four grade 7 connections.	Seventh graders are expected to be able to "investigate chance processes and develop, use, and evaluate probability models" (CCSSO, 2010, p. 50). In particular, students "begin informal work with random sampling to generate data sets and learn about the importance of representative samples for drawing inferences" (CCSSO, 2010, p. 46).

Consider Your Students' Needs

Although students need not have a firm understanding of probability, they should have been exposed to the basic idea that the outcome of an experiment can lie at different points along the probability continuum from impossible (0) to certain (1).

For English Language Learners

- The instructions are complicated in this lesson, so providing them in writing and/or adding illustrations will help ELLs understand the focus task.
- The mathematical terms *fair, equally likely, probability,* and *variability* are key words to develop in the lesson,

with the word *variability* better addressed in the *After* phase, when students are describing what happened in their games.

For Students with Disabilities

- Students who struggle may be challenged to create their own game. Instead, have cards for games that use different combinations of tiles. Have students try the games, sorting the cards into "fair games" and "unfair games."

Materials

Each pair of students will need:

- Small paper bag (opaque)
- Colored tiles, connecting cubes, or any similarly shaped object that comes in four colors
- Note card (one per pair)

Lesson

Before

Begin with a simpler version of the task:

- Discuss students' favorite games. Ask, "Have you ever wondered how games are created? Today, we are going to make up our own games and decide whether they are fair games." Explain that the game will consist of putting tiles (or whatever is to be used) in a bag and taking turns drawing out a tile. Each player will be given a color (or two). The person whose color is drawn gets a point. After 10 draws, the game is over.

- Say, "Suppose we wanted to put in tiles of two colors—red and blue. We want four tiles in the bag. How many tiles of each color should we put in?" Play the game quickly between two halves of the class. Be sure to return the tile to the bag after each draw. Ask if they think this is a good game or not. Is it fair? Why?

- Now suggest putting in five red tiles and seven blue tiles. Play the game quickly between two halves of the class. Be sure to return the tile to the bag after each draw. Ask if they think this is a fair game. Why or why not?

Present the focus task to the class:

- In pairs, have students design a game of their own. In the design of the game, each player gets points for two colors. The number of each color has to be different (so if there are five reds, there cannot be five of the other color). Of the two colors for each player, one of the colors is worth 2 points and one is worth only 1 point. The tiles are drawn one at a time and returned to the bag.

Provide clear expectations:

- Students work with partners.
- Students must prepare the game, placing the appropriately colored tiles/cubes in the bag and writing on a note card the colors that are worth 2 points and 1 point for player 1 and player 2.

During

Initially:

- Be sure that students understand the directions and are applying them correctly in designing their game.

Ongoing:

- Watch for when students are getting close to having their games prepared. Give a time limit for preparing a bag for play. The team must also prepare the note card telling the players which colors score what points.
- Have each pair of students trade bags and note cards with another pair of students.
- Play the game to 10 points. Repeat three times. Ask, "Is the game fair? Why or why not?"
- Then have the students empty their bags (prepared by another group) and see if they think the game was designed to be fair. Tell students to be ready to report to the group whether their game was fair or not.
- Listen to the ideas that students use in deciding whether the game is fair. With only 10 points in a game, the winner may continue to be the same person, even if the game is designed fairly. This notion of variation (and the need for large samples—law of large numbers) is

a core concept in probability. Listening to these discussions will give you insights into students' understanding of variability and fairness.

After

Bring the class together to share and discuss the task:

- Have groups share their reports on whether the game they played was fair or not, and their justification. Ask students who won the three games.
- Ask students why a game might be fair and yet the same person wins all the games. "You thought the game was fair, but Sandra won every time. Why do you think that happened? If you play a lot of times, who do you think will win the most times?"
- Engage the class in this discussion of game designs, probability, and short- and long-term results.

Assessment

Observe

- Pay attention to students who seem to believe more in chance or luck than in observable probabilities. This is a main idea in their understanding of probability that you want to develop at this point.
- Try to decide how well your students are able to determine the probabilities of the outcomes in these games. Students who correctly analyze these games— who can tell whether a game is fair or not and who can design fair and unfair games—are ready to progress further.

Ask

- What are the possible outcomes—what could you draw out of the bag?
- Is it as likely that you will draw a red tile as a green one (or whatever colors you are using)? Why?
- If a game is fair, if you won the last game, will I win the next one? Why or why not?

Common Core State Standards

Standards for Mathematical Practice

The Standards for Mathematical Practice describe varieties of expertise that mathematics educators at all levels should seek to develop in their students. These practices rest on important "processes and proficiencies" with longstanding importance in mathematics education. The first of these are the NCTM process standards of problem solving, reasoning and proof, communication, representation, and connections. The second are the strands of mathematical proficiency specified in the National Research Council's report *Adding It Up*: adaptive reasoning, strategic competence, conceptual understanding (comprehension of mathematical concepts, operations and relations), procedural fluency (skill in carrying out procedures flexibly, accurately, efficiently and appropriately), and productive disposition (habitual inclination to see mathematics as sensible, useful, and worthwhile, coupled with a belief in diligence and one's own efficacy).

1 Make sense of problems and persevere in solving them.

Mathematically proficient students start by explaining to themselves the meaning of a problem and looking for entry points to its solution. They analyze givens, constraints, relationships, and goals. They make conjectures about the form and meaning of the solution and plan a solution pathway rather than simply jumping into a solution attempt. They consider analogous problems, and try special cases and simpler forms of the original problem in order to gain insight into its solution. They monitor and evaluate their progress and change course if necessary. Older students might, depending on the context of the problem, transform algebraic expressions or change the viewing window on their graphing calculator to get the information they need. Mathematically proficient students can explain correspondences between equations, verbal descriptions, tables, and graphs or draw diagrams of important features and relationships, graph data, and search for regularity or trends. Younger students might rely on using concrete objects or pictures to help conceptualize and solve a problem. Mathematically proficient students check their answers to problems using a different method, and they continually ask themselves, "Does this make sense?" They can understand the approaches of others to solving complex problems and identify correspondences between different approaches.

2 Reason abstractly and quantitatively.

Mathematically proficient students make sense of quantities and their relationships in problem situations. They bring two complementary abilities to bear on problems involving quantitative relationships: the ability to *decontextualize*—to abstract a given situation and represent it symbolically and manipulate the representing symbols as if they have a life of their own, without necessarily attending to their referents—and the ability to *contextualize*, to pause as needed during the manipulation process in order to probe into the referents for the symbols involved. Quantitative reasoning entails habits of creating a coherent representation of the problem at hand; considering the units involved; attending to the meaning of quantities, not just how to compute them; and knowing and flexibly using different properties of operations and objects.

3 Construct viable arguments and critique the reasoning of others.

Mathematically proficient students understand and use stated assumptions, definitions, and previously established results in constructing arguments. They make conjectures and build a logical progression of statements to explore the truth of their conjectures. They are able to analyze situations by breaking them into cases, and can recognize and use counterexamples. They justify their conclusions, communicate them to others, and respond to the arguments of others. They reason inductively about data, making plausible arguments that take into account the context from which the data arose. Mathematically proficient students are also able to compare the effectiveness of two plausible arguments, distinguish correct logic or reasoning from that which is flawed, and—if there is a flaw in an argument—explain what it is. Elementary students can construct arguments using concrete referents such as objects, drawings, diagrams, and actions. Such arguments can make sense and be correct, even though they are not generalized or made formal until later grades. Later, students learn to determine domains to which an argument applies. Students at all grades can listen or read the arguments of others, decide whether they make sense, and ask useful questions to clarify or improve the arguments.

4 Model with mathematics.

Mathematically proficient students can apply the mathematics they know to solve problems arising in everyday life, society, and the workplace. In early grades, this might be as simple as writing an addition equation to describe a situation. In middle grades, a student might apply proportional reasoning to plan a school event or analyze a problem in the community. By high school, a student might use geometry to solve a design problem or use a function to describe how one quantity of interest depends on another. Mathematically proficient students who can apply what they know are comfortable making assumptions and approximations to simplify a complicated situation, realizing that these may need revision later. They are able to identify important quantities in a practical situation and map their relationships using such tools as diagrams, two-way tables, graphs, flowcharts and formulas. They can analyze those relationships mathematically to draw conclusions. They routinely interpret their mathematical results in the context of the situation and reflect on whether the results make sense, possibly improving the model if it has not served its purpose.

5 Use appropriate tools strategically.

Mathematically proficient students consider the available tools when solving a mathematical problem. These tools might include pencil and paper, concrete models, a ruler, a protractor, a calculator, a spreadsheet, a computer algebra system, a statistical package, or dynamic geometry software. Proficient students are sufficiently familiar with tools appropriate for their grade or course to make sound decisions about when each of these tools might be helpful, recognizing both the insight to be gained and their limitations. For example, mathematically proficient high school students analyze graphs of functions and solutions generated using a graphing calculator. They detect possible errors by strategically using estimation and other mathematical knowledge. When making mathematical models, they know that technology can enable them to visualize the results of varying assumptions, explore consequences, and compare predictions with data. Mathematically proficient students at various grade levels are able to identify relevant external mathematical resources, such as digital content located on a website, and use them to pose or solve problems. They are able to use technological tools to explore and deepen their understanding of concepts.

6 Attend to precision.

Mathematically proficient students try to communicate precisely to others. They try to use clear definitions in discussion with others and in their own reasoning. They state the meaning of the symbols they choose, including using the equal sign consistently and appropriately. They are careful about specifying units of measure, and labeling axes to clarify the correspondence with quantities in a problem. They calculate accurately and efficiently, express numerical answers with a degree of precision appropriate for the problem context. In the elementary grades, students give carefully formulated explanations to each other. By the time they reach high school they have learned to examine claims and make explicit use of definitions.

7 Look for and make use of structure.

Mathematically proficient students look closely to discern a pattern or structure. Young students, for example, might notice that three and seven more is the same amount as seven and three more, or they may sort a collection of shapes according to how many sides the shapes have. Later, students will see 7×8 equals the well remembered $7 \times 5 + 7 \times 3$, in preparation for learning about the distributive property. In the expression $x^2 + 9x + 14$, older students can see the 14 as 2×7 and the 9 as $2 + 7$. They recognize the significance of an existing line in a geometric figure and can use the strategy of drawing an auxiliary line for solving problems. They also can step back for an overview and shift perspective. They can see complicated things, such as some algebraic expressions, as single objects or as being composed of several objects. For example, they can see $5 - 3(x - y)^2$ as 5 minus a positive number times a square and use that to realize that its value cannot be more than 5 for any real numbers x and y.

8 Look for and express regularity in repeated reasoning.

Mathematically proficient students notice if calculations are repeated, and look both for general methods and for shortcuts. Upper elementary students might notice when dividing 25 by 11 that they are repeating the same calculations over and over again, and conclude they have a repeating decimal. By paying attention to the calculation of slope as they repeatedly check whether points are on the line through $(1, 2)$ with slope 3, middle school students might abstract the equation $(y - 2)/(x - 1) = 3$. Noticing the regularity in the way terms cancel when expanding $(x - 1)(x + 1)$, $(x - 1)(x^2 + x + 1)$, and $(x - 1)(x^3 + x^2 + x + 1)$ might lead them to the general formula for the sum of a geometric series. As they work to solve a problem, mathematically proficient students maintain oversight of the process, while attending to the details. They continually evaluate the reasonableness of their intermediate results.

Connecting the Standards for Mathematical Practice to the Standards for Mathematical Content

The Standards for Mathematical Practice describe ways in which developing student practitioners of the discipline of mathematics increasingly ought to engage with the subject matter as they grow in mathematical maturity and expertise throughout the elementary, middle, and high school years. Designers of curricula, assessments, and professional development should all attend to the need to connect the mathematical practices to mathematical content in mathematics instruction.

The Standards for Mathematical Content are a balanced combination of procedure and understanding. Expectations that begin with the word "understand" are often especially good opportunities to connect the practices to the content. Students who lack understanding of a topic may rely on procedures too heavily. Without a flexible base from which to work, they may be less likely to consider analogous problems, represent problems coherently, justify conclusions, apply the mathematics to practical situations, use technology mindfully to work with the mathematics, explain the mathematics accurately to other students, step back for an overview, or deviate from a known procedure to find a shortcut. In short, a lack of understanding effectively prevents a student from engaging in the mathematical practices.

In this respect, those content standards which set an expectation of understanding are potential "points of intersection" between the Standards for Mathematical Content and the Standards for Mathematical Practice. These points of intersection are intended to be weighted toward central and generative concepts in the school mathematics curriculum that most merit the time, resources, innovative energies, and focus necessary to qualitatively improve the curriculum, instruction, assessment, professional development, and student achievement in mathematics.

Common Core State Standards

Grades 6–8 Critical Content Areas and Overviews

CCSS Mathematics | Grade 6 Critical Areas

In Grade 6, instructional time should focus on four critical areas:

1. connecting ratio and rate to whole number multiplication and division and using concepts of ratio and rate to solve problems;

2. completing understanding of division of fractions and extending the notion of number to the system of rational numbers, which includes negative numbers;

3. writing, interpreting, and using expressions and equations; and

4. developing understanding of statistical thinking.

1. *Students use reasoning about multiplication and division to solve ratio and rate problems about quantities.* By viewing equivalent ratios and rates as deriving from, and extending, pairs of rows (or columns) in the multiplication table, and by analyzing simple drawings that indicate the relative size of quantities, students connect their understanding of multiplication and division with ratios and rates. Thus students expand the scope of problems for which they can use multiplication and division to solve problems, and they connect ratios and fractions. Students solve a wide variety of problems involving ratios and rates.

2. *Students use the meaning of fractions, the meanings of multiplication and division, and the relationship between multiplication and division to understand and explain why the procedures for dividing fractions make sense.* Students use these operations to solve problems. Students extend their previous understandings of number and the ordering of numbers to the full system of rational numbers, which includes negative rational numbers, and in particular negative integers. They reason about the order and absolute value of rational numbers and about the location of points in all four quadrants of the coordinate plane.

3. *Students understand the use of variables in mathematical expressions.* They write expressions and equations that correspond to given situations, evaluate expressions, and use expressions and formulas to solve problems. Students understand that expressions in different forms can be equivalent, and they use the properties of operations to rewrite expressions

in equivalent forms. Students know that the solutions of an equation are the values of the variables that make the equation true. Students use properties of operations and the idea of maintaining the equality of both sides of an equation to solve simple one-step equations. Students construct and analyze tables, such as tables of quantities that are in equivalent ratios, and they use equations (such as $3x = y$) to describe relationships between quantities.

4. ***Building on and reinforcing their understanding of number, students begin to develop their ability to think statistically.*** Students recognize that a data distribution may not have a definite center and that different ways to measure center yield different values. The median measures center in the sense that it is roughly the middle value. The mean measures center in the sense that it is the value that each data point would take on if the total of the data values were redistributed equally, and also in the sense that it is a balance point. Students recognize that a measure of variability (interquartile range or mean absolute deviation) can also be useful for summarizing data because two very different sets of data can have the same mean and median yet be distinguished by their variability. Students learn to describe and summarize numerical data sets, identifying clusters, peaks, gaps, and symmetry, considering the context in which the data were collected.

Students in Grade 6 also build on their work with area in elementary school by reasoning about relationships among shapes to determine area, surface area, and volume. They find areas of right triangles, other triangles, and special quadrilaterals by decomposing these shapes, rearranging or removing pieces, and relating the shapes to rectangles. Using these methods, students discuss, develop, and justify formulas for areas of triangles and parallelograms. Students find areas of polygons and surface areas of prisms and pyramids by decomposing them into pieces whose area they can determine. They reason about right rectangular prisms with fractional side lengths to extend formulas for the volume of a right rectangular prism to fractional side lengths. They prepare for work on scale drawings and constructions in Grade 7 by drawing polygons in the coordinate plane.

Grade 6 Overview

Ratios and Proportional Relationships

- Understand ratio concepts and use ratio reasoning to solve problems.

The Number System

- Apply and extend previous understandings of multiplication and division to divide fractions by fractions.
- Compute fluently with multi-digit numbers and find common factors and multiples.
- Apply and extend previous understandings of numbers to the system of rational numbers.

Expressions and Equations

- Apply and extend previous understandings of arithmetic to algebraic expressions.
- Reason about and solve one-variable equations and inequalities.
- Represent and analyze quantitative relationships between dependent and independent variables.

Geometry

- Solve real-world and mathematical problems involving area, surface area, and volume.

Statistics and Probability

- Develop understanding of statistical variability.
- Summarize and describe distributions.

CCSS Mathematics | Grade 7 Critical Areas

In Grade 7, instructional time should focus on four critical areas:

1. developing understanding of and applying proportional relationships;
2. developing understanding of operations with rational numbers and working with expressions and linear equations;
3. solving problems involving scale drawings and informal geometric constructions, and working with two- and three-dimensional shapes to solve problems involving area, surface area, and volume; and
4. drawing inferences about populations based on samples.

1. *Students extend their understanding of ratios and develop understanding of proportionality to solve single- and multi-step problems.* Students use their understanding of ratios and proportionality to solve a wide variety of percent problems, including those involving discounts, interest, taxes, tips, and percent increase or decrease. Students solve problems about scale drawings by relating corresponding lengths between the objects or by using the fact that relationships of lengths within an object are preserved in similar objects. Students graph proportional relationships and understand the unit rate informally as a measure of the steepness of the related line, called the slope. They distinguish proportional relationships from other relationships.

2. *Students develop a unified understanding of number, recognizing fractions, decimals (that have a finite or a repeating decimal representation), and percents as different representations of rational numbers.* Students extend addition, subtraction, multiplication, and division to all rational numbers, maintaining the properties of operations and the relationships between addition and subtraction, and multiplication and division. By applying these properties, and by viewing negative numbers in terms of everyday contexts (e.g., amounts owed or temperatures below zero), students explain and interpret the rules for adding, subtracting, multiplying, and dividing with negative numbers. They use the arithmetic of rational numbers as they formulate expressions and equations in one variable and use these equations to solve problems.

3. *Students continue their work with area from Grade 6, solving problems involving the area and circumference of a circle and surface area of three-dimensional objects.* In preparation for work on congruence and similarity in Grade 8 they reason about relationships among two-dimensional figures using scale drawings and informal geometric constructions, and they gain familiarity with the relationships between angles formed by intersecting lines. Students work with three-dimensional figures, relating them to two-dimensional figures by examining cross-sections. They solve real-world and mathematical problems involving area, surface area, and volume of two- and three-dimensional objects composed of triangles, quadrilaterals, polygons, cubes and right prisms.

4. *Students build on their previous work with single data distributions to compare two data distributions and address questions about differences between populations.* They begin informal work with random sampling to generate data sets and learn about the importance of representative samples for drawing inferences.

Grade 7 Overview

Ratios and Proportional Relationships

- Analyze proportional relationships and use them to solve real-world and mathematical problems.

The Number System

- Apply and extend previous understandings of operations with fractions to add, subtract, multiply, and divide rational numbers.

Expressions and Equations

- Use properties of operations to generate equivalent expressions.
- Solve real-life and mathematical problems using numerical and algebraic expressions and equations.

Geometry

- Draw, construct and describe geometrical figures and describe the relationships between them.
- Solve real-life and mathematical problems involving angle measure, area, surface area, and volume.

Statistics and Probability

- Use random sampling to draw inferences about a population.
- Draw informal comparative inferences about two populations.
- Investigate chance processes and develop, use, and evaluate probability models.

CCSS Mathematics | Grade 8 Critical Areas

In Grade 8, instructional time should focus on three critical areas:

1. formulating and reasoning about expressions and equations, including modeling an association in bivariate data with a linear equation, and solving linear equations and systems of linear equations;

2. grasping the concept of a function and using functions to describe quantitative relationships;

3. analyzing two- and three-dimensional space and figures using distance, angle, similarity, and congruence, and understanding and applying the Pythagorean Theorem.

1. ***Students use linear equations and systems of linear equations to represent, analyze, and solve a variety of problems.*** Students recognize equations for proportions ($y/x = m$ or $y = mx$) as special linear equations ($y = mx + b$), understanding that the constant of proportionality (m) is the slope, and the graphs are lines through the origin. They understand

that the slope (m) of a line is a constant rate of change, so that if the input or x-coordinate changes by an amount A, the output or y-coordinate changes by the amount $m \cdot A$. Students also use a linear equation to describe the association between two quantities in bivariate data (such as arm span vs. height for students in a classroom). At this grade, fitting the model, and assessing its fit to the data are done informally. Interpreting the model in the context of the data requires students to express a relationship between the two quantities in question and to interpret components of the relationship (such as slope and y-intercept) in terms of the situation.

Students strategically choose and efficiently implement procedures to solve linear equations in one variable, understanding that when they use the properties of equality and the concept of logical equivalence, they maintain the solutions of the original equation. Students solve systems of two linear equations in two variables and relate the systems to pairs of lines in the plane; these intersect, are parallel, or are the same line. Students use linear equations, systems of linear equations, linear functions, and their understanding of slope of a line to analyze situations and solve problems.

2. ***Students grasp the concept of a function as a rule that assigns to each input exactly one output.*** They understand that functions describe situations where one quantity determines another. They can translate among representations and partial representations of functions (noting that tabular and graphical representations may be partial representations), and they describe how aspects of the function are reflected in the different representations.

3. ***Students use ideas about distance and angles, how they behave under translations, rotations, reflections, and dilations, and ideas about congruence and similarity to describe and analyze two-dimensional figures and to solve problems.*** Students show that the sum of the angles in a triangle is the angle formed by a straight line, and that various configurations of lines give rise to similar triangles because of the angles created when a transversal cuts parallel lines. Students understand the statement of the Pythagorean Theorem and its converse, and can explain why the Pythagorean Theorem holds, for example, by decomposing a square in two different ways. They apply the Pythagorean Theorem to find distances between points on the coordinate plane, to find lengths, and to analyze polygons. Students complete their work on volume by solving problems involving cones, cylinders, and spheres.

Grade 8 Overview

The Number System

- Know that there are numbers that are not rational, and approximate them by rational numbers.

Expressions and Equations

- Work with radicals and integer exponents.
- Understand the connections between proportional relationships, lines, and linear equations.
- Analyze and solve linear equations and pairs of simultaneous linear equations.

Functions

- Define, evaluate, and compare functions.
- Use functions to model relationships between quantities.

Geometry

- Understand congruence and similarity using physical models, transparencies, or geometry software.
- Understand and apply the Pythagorean Theorem.
- Solve real-world and mathematical problems involving volume of cylinders, cones and spheres.

Statistics and Probability

- Investigate patterns of association in bivariate data.

A Guide to the Blackline Masters

This appendix contains thumbnails of all of the Blackline Masters that are referenced throughout the book. Each full-size master can easily be downloaded from the PDToolkit at http://pdtoolkit.pearson.com. Once downloaded, you may print as many copies as you need. Keep the files on your computer.

Tips for Use of the Blackline Masters

When a Blackline Master is either to be used as a work mat for students or to be cut apart into smaller pieces, the best advice is to duplicate the master on card stock. Card stock (also known as index stock) is heavy paper that comes in a variety of colors and can be found at copy or office supply stores.

With materials that require cutting into smaller pieces, we suggest that you laminate the card stock before you cut out the pieces. This will preserve the materials for several years and save valuable time in the future. For the Assorted Shapes (BLMs 12–18), make each set of seven pages a different color. Otherwise, it is very difficult to tell to which set a stray shape belongs to.

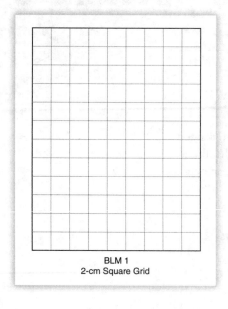

BLM 1
2-cm Square Grid

BLM 2
2-cm Isometric Grid

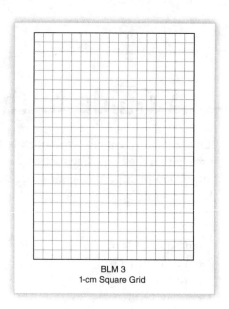

BLM 3
1-cm Square Grid

BLM 4
1-cm Square Dot Grid

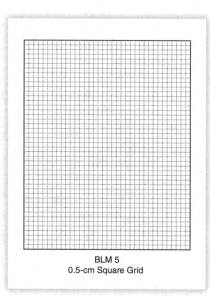

BLM 5
0.5-cm Square Grid

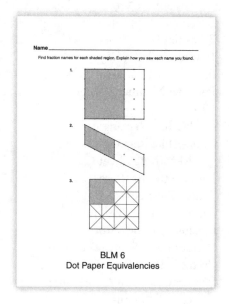

BLM 6
Dot Paper Equivalencies

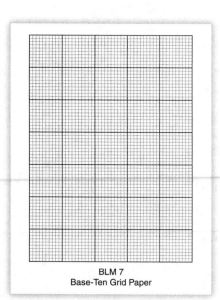

BLM 7
Base-Ten Grid Paper

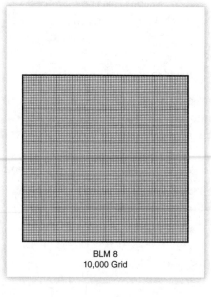

BLM 8
10,000 Grid

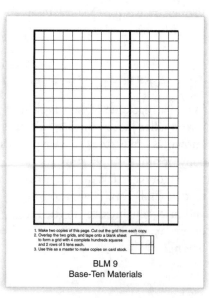

BLM 9
Base-Ten Materials

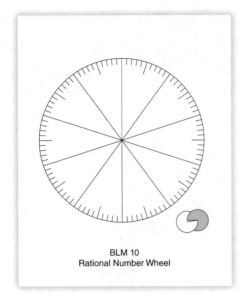

BLM 10
Rational Number Wheel

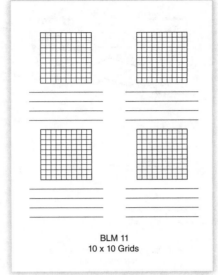

BLM 11
10 x 10 Grids

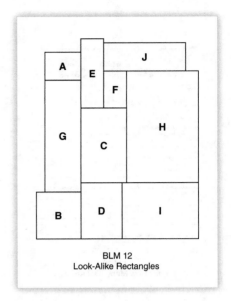

BLM 12
Look-Alike Rectangles

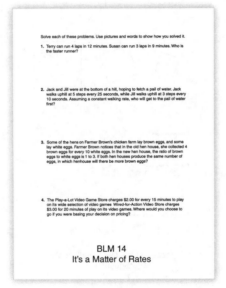

Three Groups and an Odd Ball

Rectangles Group 1 (Letter of rect.) | Measures in cm Long side | Short side | Ratio of sides Short/Long

Rectangles Group 2 (Letter of rect.) | Measures in cm Long side | Short side | Ratio of sides Short/Long

Rectangles Group 3 (Letter of rect.) | Measures in cm Long side | Short side | Ratio of sides Short/Long

Odd Ball (Letter of rect.) | Measures in cm Long side | Short side | Ratio of sides Short/Long

BLM 13
Look-Alike Rectangles Recording Sheet

Solve each of these problems. Use pictures and words to show how you solved it.

1. Terry can run 4 laps in 12 minutes. Susan can run 3 laps in 9 minutes. Who is the faster runner?

2. Jack and Jill were at the bottom of a hill, hoping to fetch a pail of water. Jack walks uphill at 5 steps every 25 seconds, while Jill walks uphill at 3 steps every 10 seconds. Assuming a constant walking rate, who will get to the pail of water first?

3. Some of the hens on Farmer Brown's chicken farm lay brown eggs, and some lay white eggs. Farmer Brown notices that in the old hen house, she collected 4 brown eggs for every 10 white eggs. In the new hen house, the ratio of brown eggs to white eggs is 1 to 3. If both hen houses produce the same number of eggs, in which henhouse will there be more brown eggs?

4. The Play-a-Lot Video Game Store charges $2.00 for every 15 minutes to play on its wide selection of video games. Wired-for-Action Video Store charges $3.00 for 20 minutes of play on its video games. Where would you choose to go if you were basing your decision on pricing?

BLM 14
It's a Matter of Rates

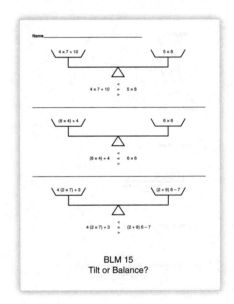

BLM 15
Tilt or Balance?

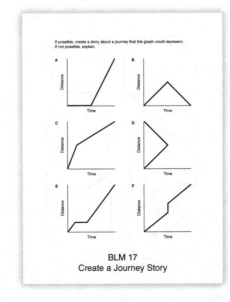

BLM 16
Tilt or Balance? Extended

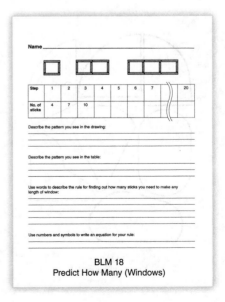

BLM 17
Create a Journey Story

Predict How Many (Windows)

BLM 18
Predict How Many (Windows)

Name_____

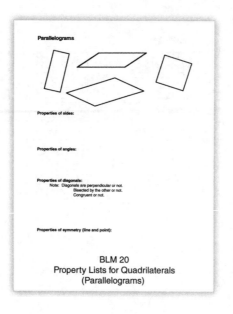

Describe the pattern you see in the drawing:
_____
_____

Describe the pattern you see in the table:
_____
_____

Use words to describe the rule for finding out how many dots you need to make any dot array:
_____
_____
_____
_____

Use numbers and symbols to write an equation for your rule:
_____
_____

BLM 19
Predict How Many (Dot Arrays)

Parallelograms

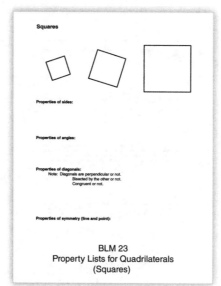

Properties of sides:

Properties of angles:

Properties of diagonals:
Note: Diagonals are perpendicular or not.
Bisected by the other or not.
Congruent or not.

Properties of symmetry (line and point):

BLM 20
Property Lists for Quadrilaterals
(Parallelograms)

Rhombi

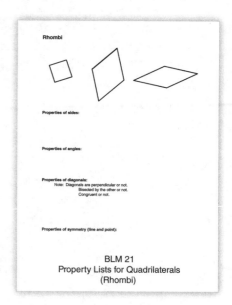

Properties of sides:

Properties of angles:

Properties of diagonals:
Note: Diagonals are perpendicular or not.
Bisected by the other or not.
Congruent or not.

Properties of symmetry (line and point):

BLM 21
Property Lists for Quadrilaterals
(Rhombi)

Rectangles

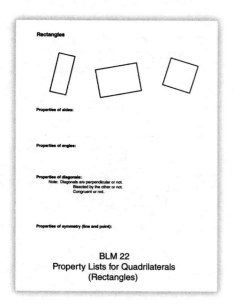

Properties of sides:

Properties of angles:

Properties of diagonals:
Note: Diagonals are perpendicular or not.
Bisected by the other or not.
Congruent or not.

Properties of symmetry (line and point):

BLM 22
Property Lists for Quadrilaterals
(Rectangles)

Squares

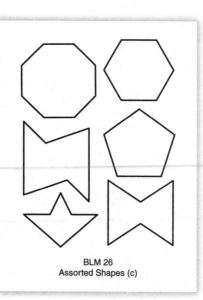

Properties of sides:

Properties of angles:

Properties of diagonals:
Note: Diagonals are perpendicular or not.
Bisected by the other or not.
Congruent or not.

Properties of symmetry (line and point):

BLM 23
Property Lists for Quadrilaterals
(Squares)

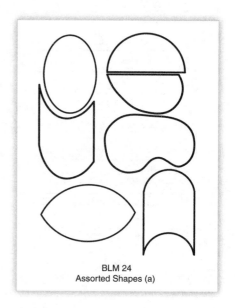

BLM 24
Assorted Shapes (a)

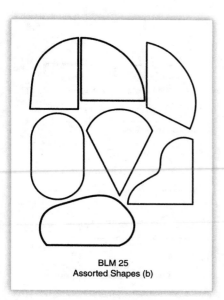

BLM 25
Assorted Shapes (b)

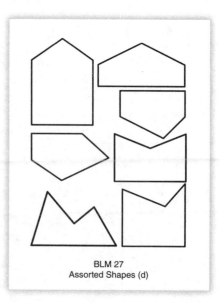

BLM 26
Assorted Shapes (c)

BLM 27
Assorted Shapes (d)

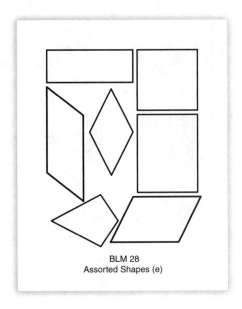

BLM 28
Assorted Shapes (e)

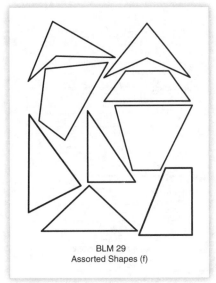

BLM 29
Assorted Shapes (f)

BLM 30
Assorted Shapes (g)

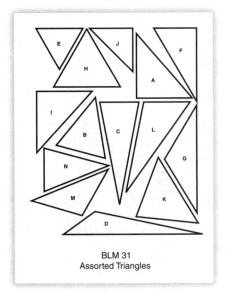

BLM 31
Assorted Triangles

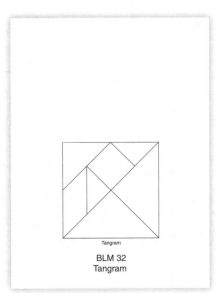

Tangram

BLM 32
Tangram

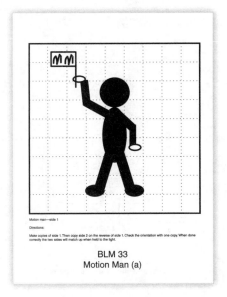

BLM 33
Motion Man (a)

BLM 34
Motion Man (b)

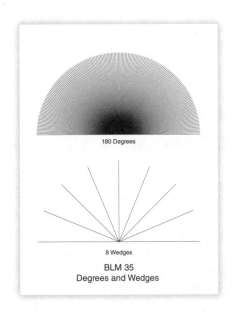

180 Degrees

8 Wedges

BLM 35
Degrees and Wedges

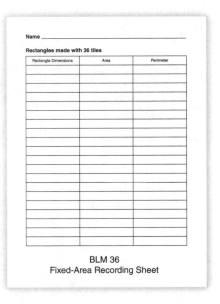

Name _____

Rectangles made with 36 tiles

Rectangle Dimensions	Area	Perimeter

BLM 36
Fixed-Area Recording Sheet

Name: _____

Base of Rectangular Prism		Height of Rectangular Prism	Volume of Rectangular Prism	Surface Area of Net (illustrated on grid paper)
Length	Width			

How do you know whether you found all the possible whole number dimensions for this rectangular prism?

BLM 37
Fixed-Volume Recording Sheet

Name _____

	Mean	Median	Mode
Original			

Make predictions based on these changes. Give reasons for your predictions.

Add a $20 game			
Reasons			
Return the $2 game			
Reasons			
Get a free game			
Reasons			
Buy a second $13 game			
Reasons			
Your change:			
Reasons			

Calculate the actual statistics for each of the changes.

Add a $20 game			
Return the $2 game			
Get a free game			
Buy a second $13 game			
Your change:			

BLM 38
Playing with Measures of
Central Tendency

BLM 39
Game Purchases

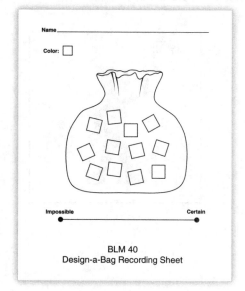

Name _____

Color: ☐

Impossible ●————————————● Certain

BLM 40
Design-a-Bag Recording Sheet

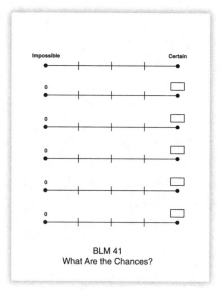

BLM 41
What Are the Chances?

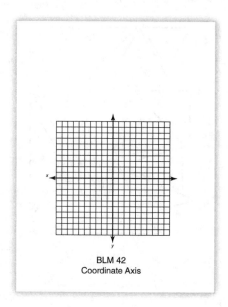

BLM 42
Coordinate Axis

Abu-Bakare, V. (2008). *Investigating students' understandings of probability: A study of a grade 7 classroom* (Master's thesis). Retrieved from http://hdl.handle.net/2429/4073

Ambrose, R. (2002). Are we overemphasizing manipulatives in the primary grades to the detriment of girls? *Teaching Children Mathematics, 9*(1), 16–21.

Arizona Department of Education. (2010). *Arizona's common core standards—mathematics.* Retrieved from www.azed.gov/standards -practices/mathematics-standards

Aspiazu, G. G., Bauer, S. C., & Spillett, M. D. (1998). Improving the academic performance of Hispanic youth: A community education model. *Bilingual Research Journal, 22*(2), 1–20.

Assouline, S. G., & Lupkowski-Shoplik, A. (2011). *Developing math talent: A comprehensive guide to math education for gifted students in elementary and middle school* (2nd ed.). Waco, TX: Prufrock Press.

Averill, R., Anderson, D., Easton, H., Te Maro, P., Smith, D., & Hynds, A. (2009). Culturally responsive teaching of mathematics: Three models from linked studies. *Journal for Research in Mathematics Education, 40*(2), 157–186.

Baek, J. M. (2008). Developing algebraic thinking through exploration in multiplication. In C. E. Greenes & R. Rubenstein (Eds.), *Algebra and algebraic thinking in school mathematics: 70th NCTM yearbook* (pp. 141–154). Reston, VA: NCTM.

Bakker, A., Biehler, R., & Konold, C. (2004). Should young students learn about box plots? In G. Burrill & M. Camden (Eds.), *Curricular development in statistics education* (pp. 163–173). Lund, Sweden: International Association for Statistical Education (IASE) Roundtable.

Ball, D. L. (2003). Mathematical proficiency for all students: Toward a strategic research and development program in mathematics education. Santa Monica, CA: RAND Corporation, MR-1643-OERI. Retrieved from www.rand.org/pubs/monograph_ reports/MR1643

Ball, D. L., & Bass, H. (2003). Making mathematics reasonable in school. In J. Kilpatrick, W. G. Martin, & D. Schifter (Eds.), *A research companion to Principles and Standards for School Mathematics* (pp. 27–44). Reston, VA: NCTM.

Bamberger, H. J., Oberdorf, C., & Schultz-Ferrell, K. (2010). *Math misconceptions: From misunderstanding to deep understanding.* Portsmouth, NH: Heinemann.

Baroody, A. J. (2011). Learning: A framework. In F. Fennell (Ed.), *Achieving fluency in special education and mathematics* (pp.15–58). Reston, VA: NCTM.

Battista, M. T. (2003). Understanding students' thinking about area and volume measurement. In D. H. Clements (Ed.), *Learning and teaching measurement* (pp. 122–142). Reston, VA: NCTM.

Battista, M. T. (2007). The development of geometric and spatial thinking. In F. Lester (Ed.), *Second handbook of research on mathematics teaching and learning* (pp. 843–908). Reston, VA: NCTM.

Bay, J., & Ragan, G. (2000). Improving students' mathematical communication and connections using the classic game of telephone. *Mathematics Teaching in the Middle School, 5*(8), 486–489.

Bay, J. M., Reys, B. J., & Reys, R. E. (1999). The top 10 elements that must be in place to implement standards-based mathematics curricula. *Phi Delta Kappan, 80*(7), 503–506.

Bay-Williams, J. (2010). Influences on student outcomes: Teachers' classroom practices. In D. Lambdin (Ed.), *Teaching and learning mathematics: Translating research for elementary school teachers* (pp. 31–36). Reston, VA: NCTM.

Bay-Williams, J. M., & Martinie, S. L. (2003). Thinking rationally about number in the middle school. *Mathematics Teaching in the Middle School, 8*(6), 282–287.

Bay-Williams, J. M., & Martinie, S. L. (2004). What does algebraic thinking look like? *Mathematics Teaching in the Middle School, 10*(4), 198–199.

Bay-Williams, J. M., & Martinie, S. L. (2009). *Math and non-fiction: Grades 6–8.* Sausalito, CA: Math Solutions.

Bay-Williams, J. M., & Meyer, M. R. (2003). What parents want to know about standards-based mathematics curricula. *Principal Leadership, 3*(7), 54–60.

Bay-Williams, J. M., Reys, B. J., & Reys, R. E. (2003). How do middle schools effectively implement standards-based mathematics curricula? Strategies from schools who have. *Middle School Journal, 34*(4), 36–41.

Beck, S. A., & Huse, V. E. (2007). A virtual spin on probability. *Teaching Children Mathematics, 13*(9), 482–486.

Beckman, C. E., Thompson, D., & Austin, R. A. (2004). Exploring proportional reasoning through movies and literature. *Mathematics Teaching in the Middle School, 9*(5), 256–262.

Behr, M. J., Lesh, R., Post, T. R., & Silver, E. A. (1983). Rational number concepts. In R. Lesh & M. Landau (Eds.), *Acquisition of mathematics concepts and processes* (pp. 91–126). New York, NY: Academic Press.

Berk, D., Taber, S., Gorowara, C. C., & Poetzl, C. (2009). Developing prospective elementary teachers' flexibility in the domain of proportional reasoning. *Mathematical Thinking and Learning, 11*(3), 113–135.

Bezuszka, S. J., & Kenney, M. J. (2008). The three R's: Recursive thinking, recursion, and recursive formulas. In C. E. Greenes & R. Rubenstein (Eds.), *Algebra and algebraic thinking in school mathematics: 70th NCTM yearbook* (pp. 81–97). Reston, VA: NCTM.

Blanton, M. L. (2008). *Algebra in the elementary classroom: Transforming thinking, transforming practice.* Portsmouth, NH: Heinemann.

Blume, G., Galindo, E., & Walcott, C. (2007). Performance in measurement and geometry from the viewpoint of *Principles and Standards for School Mathematics.* In P. Kloosterman & F. Lester, Jr. (Eds.), *Results and interpretations of the 2003 mathematics assessment of the National Assessment of Educational Progress* (pp. 95–138). Reston, VA: NCTM.

Boaler, J. (2006). Promoting respectful learning. *Educational Leadership, 63*(5), 74–78.

Bray, W. S. (2009). The power of choice. *Teaching Children Mathematics, 16*(3), 178–184.

Breyfogle, M., & Williams, L. (2008–2009). Designing and implementing worthwhile tasks. *Teaching Children Mathematics, 15*(5), 276–280.

Bright, G. W., Behr, M. J., Post, T. R., & Wachsmuth, I. (1988). Identifying fractions on number lines. *Journal for Research in Mathematics Education, 19*(3), 215–232.

Bright, G. W., Joyner, J. M., & Wallis, C. (2003). Assessing proportional thinking. *Mathematics Teaching in the Middle School, 9*(3), 166–172.

Brown, G., & Quinn, R. J. (2007). Investigating the relationship between fraction proficiency and success in algebra. *Australian Mathematics Teacher, 63*(4), 8–15.

Brown, S. A., & Mehilos, M. (2010). Using tables to bridge arithmetic and algebra. *Mathematics Teaching in the Middle School, 15*(9), 532–538.

Bruner, J. (1966). *Toward a theory of instruction.* Cambridge, MA: Harvard University Press.

Buerman, M. (2007). The algebra of the arches. *Mathematics Teaching in the Middle School, 12*(7), 360–365.

Burrill, G. F., & Elliot, P. C. (Eds.). (2006). *Thinking and reasoning with data and chance, 68th yearbook.* Reston, VA: NCTM.

Cai, J., & Sun, W. (2002). Developing students' proportional reasoning: A Chinese perspective. In B. Litwiller (Ed.), *Making sense of fractions, ratios, and proportions* (pp. 195–205). Reston, VA: NCTM.

Carpenter, T. P., Franke, M. L., & Levi, L. (2003). *Thinking mathematically: Integrating arithmetic and algebra in elementary school.* Portsmouth, NH: Heinemann.

Carr, J., Carroll, C., Cremer, S., Gale, M., Lagunoff, R., & Sexton, U. (2009). *Making mathematics accessible to English learners, grades 6–12.* San Francisco, CA: WestEd.

Carter, S. (2008). Disequilibrium & questioning in the primary classroom: Establishing routines that help students learn. *Teaching Children Mathematics, 15*(3), 134–137.

Cassone, J. D. (2009). Differentiating mathematics by using task difficulty. In D. Y. White & J. S. Spitzer (Eds.), *Mathematics for every student: Responding to diversity in grades PK–5* (pp. 89–98). Reston, VA: NCTM.

CCSSO (Council of Chief State School Officers). (2010). *Common core state standards.* Retrieved from www.corestandards.org /the-standards/mathematics

CCSSO (Council of Chief State School Officers). (2011). *Application of common core state standards for English learners.* Retrieved from www.corestandards.org/assets/application-for -english-learners.pdf

Celedón-Pattichis, S. (2009). What does that mean? Drawing on Latino and Latina students' language and culture to make mathematical meaning. In M. W. Ellis (Ed.), *Responding to diversity: grades 6–8* (pp. 59–74). Reston, VA: NCTM.

Celedón-Pattichis, S., & Ramirez, N. G. (2012). *Beyond good teaching: Advancing mathematics education for ELLs.* Reston, VA: NCTM.

Chapin, S., O'Connor, C., & Anderson, N. (2009). *Classroom discussions: Using math talk to help students learn* (2nd ed.). Sausalito, CA: Math Solutions.

Che, S. M. (2009). Giant pencils: Developing proportional reasoning. *Mathematics Teaching in the Middle School, 14*(7), 404–408.

Cheng, I. (2010). Fractions: A new slant on slope. *Mathematics Teaching in the Middle School, 16*(1), 35–41.

Civil, M., & Menendez, J. M. (2010). *NCTM research brief: Involving Latino and Latina parents in their children's mathematics education.* Retrieved from www.nctm.org/uploadedFiles/Research_News_and_ Advocacy/Research/Clips_and_Briefs/Research_brief_17-civil.pdf

Civil, M., & Planas, N. (2010). Latino/a immigrant parents' voices in mathematics education. In E. L. Grigorenko & R. Takanishi (Eds.), *Immigration, diversity, and education* (pp. 130–50). New York, NY: Routledge.

Clarke, D., Roche, A., & Mitchell, A. (2008). 10 practical tips for making fractions come alive and make sense. *Mathematics Teaching in the Middle School, 13*(7), 373–380.

Clements, D., & Sarama, J. (2009). *Learning and teaching early math: The learning trajectories approach.* New York, NY: Routledge.

Coates, G. D., & Mayfield, K. (2009). Families ask: Cooperative learning. *Mathematics Teaching in the Middle School, 15*(4), 244–245.

Colgan, M. D. (2006). March math madness: The mathematics of the NCAA basketball tournament. *Mathematics Teaching in the Middle School, 11*(7), 334–342.

Cooper, H. (2007). *The battle over homework: Common ground for administrators, teachers, and parents* (3rd ed.). Thousand Oaks, CA: Corwin Press.

Coughlin, H. A. (2010/2011). Dividing fractions: What is the divisor's role? *Mathematics Teaching in the Middle School, 16*(5), 280–287.

Cramer, K., & Henry, A. (2002). Using manipulative models to build number sense for addition of fractions. In B. Litwiller (Ed.), *Making sense of fractions, ratios, and proportions* (pp. 41–48). Reston, VA: NCTM.

Cramer, K., Monson, D., Whitney, S., Leavitt, S., & Wyberg, T. (2010). Dividing fractions and problem solving. *Mathematics Teaching in the Middle School, 15*(6), 338–346.

Cramer, K., & Whitney, S. (2010). Learning rational number concepts and skills in elementary school classrooms. In D. V. Lambdin & F. K. Lester, Jr. (Eds.), *Teaching and learning mathematics: Translating research for elementary school teachers* (pp. 15–22). Reston, VA: NCTM.

Cramer, K., Wyberg, T., & Leavitt, S. (2008). The role of representations in fraction addition and subtraction. *Mathematics Teaching in the Middle School, 13*(8), 490–496.

Cummins, J. (1994). Primary language instruction and the education of language minority students. In C. F. Leyba (Ed.), *Schooling and language minority students: A theoretical framework* (pp. 3–46). Los Angeles, CA: California State University, Evaluation, Dissemination and Assessment Center.

Darley, J. W. (2009). Traveling from arithmetic to algebra. *Mathematics Teaching in the Middle School, 14*(8), 458–464.

Daro, P., Mosher, F., & Corcoran, T. (2011). *Learning trajectories in mathematics: A foundation for standards, curriculum assessment, and instruction.* Philadelphia, PA: Consortium for Policy Research in Education.

Desmet, L., Gregoire, J., & Mussolin, C. (2010). Developmental changes in the comparison of decimal fractions. *Learning and Instruction, 20,* 521–532.

Dewdney, A. K. (1993). *200% of nothing: An eye-opening tour through the twists and turns of math abuse and innumeracy.* Hoboken, NJ: John Wiley and Sons.

DeYoung, M. J. (2009). Math in the box. *Mathematics Teaching in the Middle School, 15*(3), 134–141.

Dole, S. (2008). Ratio tables to promote proportional reasonings in the primary classroom. *Australian Primary Mathematics Classroom, 13*(2), 18–22.

Earnest, D., & Balti, A. A. (2008). Instructional strategies for teaching algebra in elementary school: Findings from a research-practice partnership. *Teaching Children Mathematics, 14*(9), 518–522.

Echevarria, J., Vogt, M. E., & Short, D. (2008). *Making content comprehensible for English learners: The SIOP model* (3rd ed.). Boston, MA: Allyn & Bacon.

Ellis, M., Yeh, C., & Stump, S. (2007–2008). Rock-paper-scissors and solutions to the broken calculator problem. *Teaching Children Mathematics, 14*(5), 309–314.

Else-Quest, N. M., Hyde, J. S., & Hejmadi, A. (2008). Mother and child emotions during mathematics homework. *Mathematical Thinking and Learning, 10*, 5–35.

Ely, R. E., & Cohen, J. S. (2010). Put the right spin on student work. *Mathematics Teaching in the Middle School, 16*(4), 208–215.

Englard, L. (2010). Raise the bar on problem solving. *Teaching Children Mathematics, 17*(3), 156–165.

Ercole, L. K., Frantz, M., & Ashline, G. (2011). Multiple ways to solve proportions. *Mathematics Teaching in the Middle School, 16*(8), 482–490.

Falkner, K. P., Levi, L., & Carpenter, T. P. (1999). Children's understanding of equality: A foundation for algebra. *Teaching Children Mathematics, 6*(4), 232–236.

Farmer, J. D., & Powers, R. A. (2005). Exploring Mayan numerals. *Teaching Children Mathematics, 12*(2), 69–79.

Fernandez, A., Anhalt, C., & Civil, M. (2009). Mathematical interviews to assess Latino students. *Teaching Children Mathematics, 16*(3), 162–169.

Fernandez, M. L., & Schoen, R. C. (2008). Teaching and learning mathematics through hurricane tracking. *Mathematics Teaching in the Middle School, 13*(9), 500–512.

Flores, A. (2006). Using graphing calculators to redress beliefs in the "law of small numbers." In G. F. Burrill & P. C. Elliott (Eds.), *Thinking and reasoning with data and chance, 68th yearbook* (pp. 139–149). Reston, VA: NCTM.

Flores, A., & Regis, T.P. (2003). How many times does a radius square fit into the circle? *Mathematics Teaching in the Middle School, 8*(7), 363–368.

Flores, A., Samson, J., & Yanik, H. B. (2006). Quotient and measurement interpretations of rational numbers. *Teaching Children Mathematics, 13*(1), 34–39.

Fosnot, C., & Dolk, M. (2001). *Young mathematicians at work: Constructing number sense, addition, and subtraction.* Portsmouth, NH: Heinemann.

Fosnot, C. T., & Jacob, B. (2010). *Young mathematicians at work: Constructing algebra.* Portsmouth, NH: Heinemann.

Foster, T. E. (2007). *The legend of the tangram prince.* Charleston, SC: BookSurge.

Franklin, C. A., & Garfield, J. B. (2006). The GAISE project: Developing statistics education guidelines for grades PreK–12 and college courses. In G. F. Burrill & P. C. Elliott (Eds.), *Thinking and reasoning with data and chance, 68th yearbook* (pp. 345–376). Reston, VA: NCTM.

Franklin, C. A., Kader, G., Mewborn, D., Moreno, J., Peck, R., Perry, M., & Scheaffer, R. (2005). *Guidelines for assessment and instruction in statistics education (GAISE) report: A pre-K–12 curriculum framework.* Alexandria, VA: American Statistical Association.

Franklin, C. A., & Mewborn, D. S. (2008). Statistics in the elementary grades: Exploring distribution of data. *Teaching Children Mathematics, 15*(1), 10–16.

Frayer, D. A., Fredrick, W. C., & Klausmeier, H. J., (1969, April). *A schema for testing the level of concept mastery* (Working Paper No. 16), University of Wisconsin Center for Educational Research.

Friedmann, P. (2008). The zero box. *Mathematics Teaching in the Middle School, 14*(4), 222–223.

Friel, S. N., & Markworth, K. A. (2009). A framework for analyzing geometric pattern tasks. *Mathematics Teaching in the Middle School, 15*(1), 24–33.

Friel, S. N., O'Conner, W., & Mamer, J. D. (2006). More than "mean median mode" and a bar graph: What's needed to have a statistical conversation? In G. F. Burrill & P. C. Elliott (Eds.), *Thinking and reasoning with data and chance, 68th yearbook* (pp. 117–138). Reston, VA: NCTM.

Fuchs, L. S., & Fuchs, D. (2001). Principles for the prevention and intervention of mathematics difficulties. *Learning Disabilities Research and Practice, 16*(2), 85–95.

Fuchs, L. S., Fuchs, D., Yazdian, L., & Powell, S. R. (2002). Enhancing first-grade children's mathematics development with peer-assisted learning strategies. *School Psychology Review, 31*(4), 569–583.

Fung, M. G., & Latulippe, C. L. (2010). Computational estimation. *Teaching Children Mathematics, 17*(3), 170–176.

Fuson, K. (2003). Developing mathematical power in whole number operations. In J. Kilpatrick, W. G. Martin, & D. Schifter (Eds.), *A research companion to principles and standards in school mathematics* (pp. 68–94). Reston, VA: NCTM.

Gagnon, J., & Maccini, P. (2001). Preparing students with disabilities for algebra. *Teaching Exceptional Children, 34*(1), 8–15.

Gallagher, J., & Gallagher, S. (1994). *Teaching the gifted child.* Boston, MA: Allyn & Bacon.

Gallego, C., Saldamando, D., Tapia-Beltran, G., Williams, K., & Hoopingarner, T. C. (2009). Math by the month: Probability. *Teaching Children Mathematics, 15*(7), 416.

Garcia, C., & Garret, A. (2006). On average and open-end questions. In A. Rossman & B. Chance (Eds.), *Proceedings of the Seventh International Conference on Teaching Statistics.* Salvador, Brazil: International Statistical Institute.

Garrison, L. (1997). Making the NCTM's Standards work for emergent English speakers. *Teaching Children Mathematics, 4*(3), 132–138.

Gavin, M. K., & Sheffield, L. J. (2010). Using curriculum to develop mathematical promise in the middle grades. In M. Saul, S. Assouline, & L. J. Sheffield (Eds.), *The peak in the middle: Developing mathematically gifted students in the middle grades* (pp. 51–76). Reston, VA: National Council of Teachers of Mathematics, National Association of Gifted Children, and National Middle School Association.

Gersten, R., Beckmann, S., Clarke, B., Foegen, A., Marsh, L., Star, J. R., & Witzel, B. (2009). *Assisting students struggling with mathematics: Response to Intervention (RtI) for elementary and middle* schools (NCEE 2009–4060). Washington, DC: National Center for Education Evaluation and Regional Assistance, Institute of Education Sciences, U.S. Department of Education. Retrieved from http://ies.ed.gov/ncee/wwc/publications/practiceguides

Gilbert, M. C., & Musu, L. E. (2008). Using TARGETTS to create learning environments that support mathematical understanding and adaptive motivation. *Teaching Children Mathematics, 15*(3), 138–143.

Gnanadesikan, M., Schaeffer, R. L., & Swift, J. (1987). *The art and techniques of simulation: Quantitative literacy series.* Palo Alto, CA: Dale Seymour Publications.

Goldenberg, E. P., Mark, J., & Cuoco, A. (2010). An algebraic-habits-of-mind perspective on elementary school. *Teaching Children Mathematics, 16*(9), 548–556.

Gómez, C. L. (2010). Teaching with cognates. *Teaching Children Mathematics, 16*(8), 470–474.

González, N., Moll, L.C., & Amanti, C. (Eds.). (2005). *Funds of knowledge: Theorizing practices in households and classrooms.* Mahwah, NJ: Lawrence Erlbaum Associates.

Goral, M. B., & Wiest, L. R. (2007). An arts-based approach to teaching fractions. *Teaching Children Mathematics, 14*(2), 74–80.

Gray, S. S., Loud, B. J., & Sokolowski, C. P. (2005). *Undergraduates' errors in using and interpreting algebraic variables: A comparative study.* In G. M. Lloyd, M. R. Wilson, J. L. Wilkins, & S. L. Behm (Eds.), *Proceedings of the 27th Annual Meeting of the North American Chapter of the International Group for the Psychology of Mathematics Education* [CD-ROM]. Eugene, OR: All Academic.

Greenes, C., Teuscher, D., & Regis, T. (2010). Preparing teachers for mathematically talented middle school students. In M. Saul, S. Assouline, & L. J. Sheffield (Eds.), *The peak in the middle: Developing mathematically gifted students in the middle grades* (pp. 77–91). Reston, VA: National Council of Teachers of Mathematics, National Association of Gifted Children, and National Middle School Association.

Gregg, J., & Gregg, D. U. (2007). Measurement and fair-sharing models for dividing fractions. *Mathematics Teaching in the Middle School, 12*(9), 490–496.

Griffin, L., & Lavelle, L. (2010). *Assessing mathematical understanding: Using one-on-one mathematics interviews with K–2 students.* Presented at the Annual Conference of the National Council of Supervisors of Mathematics, San Diego, CA.

Gurbuz, R., Erdem, H., Catlioglu, O., & Birgin, E. (2010). An investigation of fifth grade students' conceptual development of probability through activity-based instruction: A quasi-experimental design. *Educational Sciences: Theory and Practice, 10*(2), 1053–1068.

Gutiérrez, R. (2009). Embracing the inherent tensions in teaching mathematics from an equity stance. *Democracy and Education, 18*(3), 9–16.

Haas, E., & Gort, M. (2009). Demanding more: Legal standards and best practices for English language learners. *Bilingual Research Journal, 32*, 115–135.

Hackbarth, A. J., & Wilsman, M. J. (2008). 1P + 4R = 5D: An equation for deepening mathematical understanding. *Mathematics Teaching in the Middle School, 14*(2), 122–126.

Hattie, J. (2009). *Visible learning: A synthesis of over 800 meta-analyses relating to achievement.* New York, NY: Routledge.

Hawes, K. (2007). Using error analysis to teach equation solving. *Mathematics Teaching in the Middle School, 12*(5), 238–242.

Heddens, J. (1964). *Today's mathematics: A guide to concepts and methods in elementary school mathematics.* Chicago, IL: Science Research Associates.

Heinz, K., & Sterba-Boatwright, B. (2008). The when and why of using proportions. *Mathematics Teacher, 101*(7), 528–533.

Henderson, A. T., Mapp, K. L., Jordan, C., Orozco, E., Averett, A., Donnelly, D., Buttram, J., Wood, L., Fowler, M., & Myers, M. (2002). *A new wave of evidence: The impact of school, family, and community connections on student achievement.* Austin, TX: Southwest Educational Development Laboratory.

Herbel-Eisenmann, B. A., & Phillips, E. D. (2005). Using student work to develop teachers' knowledge of algebra. *Mathematics Teaching in the Middle School, 11*(2), 62–66.

Heritage, M., Kim, J., Vendlinski, T., & Herman, J. (2009). From evidence to action: a seamless process in formative assessment? *Education Measurement: Issues and Practice, 28*, 24–31.

Hiebert, J., Carpenter, T. P., Fennema, E., Fuson, K., Wearne, D., Murray, H., Olivier, A., & Human, P. (1997). *Making sense: Teaching and learning mathematics with understanding.* Portsmouth, NH: Heinemann.

Hiebert, J., & Grouws, D. A. (2007). The effects of classroom mathematics teaching on students' learning. In F. K. Lester (Ed.), *Second handbook of research on mathematics teaching and learning* (pp. 371–404). Charlotte, NC: Information Age Publishing.

Hodges, T. E., Cady, J., & Collins, R. L. (2008). Fraction representation: The not-so-common denominator among textbooks. *Mathematics Teaching in the Middle School, 14*(2), 78–84.

Hoffman, B. L., Breyfogle, M. L., & Dressler, J. A. (2009). The power of incorrect answers. *Mathematics Teaching in the Middle School, 15*(4), 232–238.

Hong, L. T. (1993). *Two of everything: A Chinese folktale.* New York, NY: Albert Whitman.

Hudson, P. J., Shupe, M., Vasquez, E., & Miller, S. P. (2008). Teaching data analysis to elementary students with mild disabilities. *TEACHING Exceptional Children Plus, 4*(3), Article 5. Retrieved from http://escholarship.bc.edu/education/tecplus/vol4/iss3/art5

Huff, K., & Goodman, D. P. (2007). The demand for cognitive diagnostic assessment. In J. P. Leighton & M. J. Gierl (Eds.), *Cognitive diagnostic assessment for education: Theory and applications* (pp. 19–60). New York, NY: Cambridge University Press.

Hyde, A., George, K., Mynard, S., Hull, C., Watson, S., & Watson, P. (2006). Creating multiple representations in algebra: All chocolate, no change. *Mathematics Teaching in the Middle School, 11*(6), 262–268.

Hynes, M. C. (Ed.). (1996). *Ideas: NCTM standards-based instruction, grades 5–8.* Reston, VA: NCTM.

Imm, K. L., Stylianou, D. A., & Chae, N. (2008). Student representations at the center: Promoting classroom equity. *Mathematics Teaching in the Middle School, 13*(8), 458–463.

Izsák, A., Tillema, E., & Tunc-Pekkam, Z. (2008). Teaching and learning fraction addition on number lines. *Journal for Research in Mathematics Education, 39*(1), 33–62.

Jacobs, V. R., & Ambrose, R. C. (2008). Making the most of story problems. *Teaching Children Mathematics, 15*(5), 260–266.

Janzen, J. (2008). Teaching English language learners in the content areas. *Review of Educational Research, 78*(4), 1010–1038.

Johanning, D. J. (2008). Learning to use fractions: Examining middle school students' emerging fraction literacy. *Journal for Research in Mathematics Education, 39*(3), 281–310.

Johnson, G., & Thompson, D. R. (2009). Reasoning with algebraic contexts. *Mathematics Teaching in the Middle School, 14*(8), 504–513.

Joram, E. (2003). Benchmarks as tools for developing measurement sense. In D. H. Clements (Ed.), *Learning and teaching measurement* (pp. 57–67). Reston, VA: NCTM.

Kader, G., & Mamer, J. (2008). Statistics in the middle grades: Understanding center and spread. *Mathematics Teaching in the Middle School, 14*(1), 38–43.

Kaput, J. J. (2008). What is algebra? What is algebraic reasoning? In J. J. Kaput, D. W. Carraher, & M. L. Blanton (Eds.), *Algebra in the early grades.* Reston, VA: NCTM.

Karp, K., & Howell, P. (2004). Building responsibility for learning in students with special needs. *Teaching Children Mathematics, 11*(3), 118–126.

Kersaint, G., Thompson, D. R., & Petkova, M. (2009). *Teaching mathematics to English language learners.* New York, NY: Routledge.

Khisty, L. L. (1997). Making mathematics accessible to Latino students: Rethinking instructional practice. In M. Kenney & J. Trentacosta (Eds.), *Multicultural and gender equity in the mathematics classroom: The gift of diversity* (pp. 92–101). Reston, VA: NCTM.

Kieran, C. (2007). *What do students struggle with when first introduced to algebra symbols? Brief.* Reston, VA: NCTM.

Kilic, H., Cross, D. I., Ersoz, F. A., Mewborn, D. S., Swanagan, D., & Kim, J. (2010). Techniques for small-group discourse. *Teaching Children Mathematics, 16*(6), 350–357.

Kingore, B. (2006, Winter). Tiered instruction: Beginning the process. *Teaching for High Potential,* 5–6.

Kliman, M. (1999). Beyond helping with homework: Parents and children doing mathematics at home. *Teaching Children Mathematics, 6*(3), 140–146.

Kloosterman, P., Rutledge, Z., & Kenney, P. (2009). Exploring the results of the NAEP: 1980s to the present. *Mathematics Teaching in the Middle School, 14*(6), 357–365.

Knuth, E. J., Stephens, A. C., McNeil, N. M., & Alibali, M. W. (2006). Does understanding the equal sign matter? Evidence from solving equations. *Journal for Research in Mathematics Education, 37*(4), 297–312.

Kouba, V. L., Brown, C. A., Carpenter, T. P., Lindquist, M. M., Silver, E. A., & Swafford, J. O. (1988). Results of the fourth NAEP assessment of mathematics: Number, operations and word problems. *Arithmetic Teacher, 35*(8), 14–19.

Kouba, V. L., Zawojewski, J. S., & Strutchens, M. E. (1997). What do students know about numbers and operations? In P. A. Kenney & E. Silver (Eds.), *Results from the sixth mathematics assessment of the National Assessment of Educational Progress* (pp. 87–140). Reston, VA: NCTM.

Kribs-Zaleta, C. (2008). Oranges, posters, ribbons, and lemonade: Concrete computational strategies for dividing fractions. *Mathematics Teaching in the Middle School, 13*(8), 453–457.

Kulm, G. (1994). *Mathematics and assessment: What works in the classroom.* San Francisco, CA: Jossey-Bass.

Lambdin, D. V., & Lynch, K. (2005). Examining mathematics tasks from the National Assessment of Educational Progress. *Mathematics Teaching in the Middle School, 10*(6), 314–318.

Lamon, S. J. (1999). *More: In-depth discussion of the reasoning activities in "Teaching fractions and ratios for understanding."* Mahwah, NJ: Lawrence Erlbaum Associates.

Lamon, S. J. (2002). Part-whole comparisons with unitizing. In B. Litwiller (Ed.), *Making sense of fractions, ratios, and proportions* (pp. 79–86). Reston, VA: NCTM.

Lamon, S. J. (2006). *Teaching fractions and ratios for understanding: Essential content knowledge and instructional strategies for teachers* (2nd ed.). Mahwah, NJ: Lawrence Erlbaum Associates.

Lamon, S. J. (2007). Rational numbers and proportional reasoning: Toward a theoretical framework for research. In F. Lester (Ed.), *Second handbook of research on mathematics teaching and learning* (pp. 629–666). Reston, VA: NCTM.

Langrall, C., Nisbet, S., Mooney, E., & Jansem, S. (2011). The role of context expertise when comparing data. *Mathematical Thinking and Learning, 13* (1–2), 47–67.

Lannin, J. K., Arbaugh, F., Barker, D. D., & Townsend, B. E. (2006). Making the most of student errors. *Teaching Children Mathematics, 13*(3), 182–186.

Lannin, J. K., Townsend, B. E., Armer, N., Green, S., & Schneider, J. (2008). Developing meaning for algebraic symbols: Possibilities and pitfalls. *Mathematics Teaching in the Middle School, 13*(8), 478–483.

Lappan, G., Fey, J. T., Fitzgerald, W. M., Friel, S. N., & Phillips, E. D. (2006a). *Connected mathematics: Comparing and scaling ratio, proportion, and percent.* Upper Saddle River, NJ: Pearson Prentice Hall.

Leavy, A., Friel, S., & Mamer, J. (2009). It's a fird! Can you compute a median of categorical data? *Mathematics Teaching in the Middle School, 14*(6), 344–351.

Lesh, R., Post, T., & Behr, M. (1987). Representations and translations among representations in mathematics learning and problem solving. In C. Janvier (Ed.), *Problems of representation in the teaching and learning of mathematics* (pp. 33–40). Hillsdale, NJ: Lawrence Erlbaum Associates.

Lim, K. H. (2009). Burning the candle at just one end. *Mathematics Teaching in the Middle School, 14*(8), 492–500.

Lobato, J., Ellis, A. B., Charles, R. I., & Zbiek, R. M. (2010). *Developing essential understanding of ratios, proportions, and proportional reasoning: Grades 6–8.* Reston, VA: NCTM.

Mack, N. K. (2004). Connecting to develop computational fluency with fractions. *Teaching Children Mathematics, 11* (4), 226–232.

Mack, N. (2011). Enriching number knowledge. *Teaching Children Mathematics, 18*(2), 101–109.

Maida, P. (2004). Using algebra without realizing it. *Mathematics Teaching in the Middle School, 9*(9), 484–488.

Maldonado, L. A., Turner, E. E., Dominguez, H., & Empson, S. B. (2009). English language learning from, and contributing to, mathematical discussions. In D. Y. White & J. S. Spitzer (Eds.), *Mathematics for every student: Responding to diversity in grades PK–5* (pp. 7–22). Reston, VA: NCTM.

Mark, J., Cuoco, A., Goldenberg, E. P., & Sword, S. (2010). Developing mathematical habits of mind. *Mathematics Teaching in the Middle School, 15*(9), 505–509.

Martinie, S. L. (2007). *Middle school rational number knowledge* (Unpublished doctoral dissertation). Manhattan, KS: Kansas State University.

Martinie, S. L., & Bay-Williams, J. M. (2003). Investigating students' conceptual understanding of decimal fractions using multiple representations. *Mathematics Teaching in the Middle School, 8*(5), 244–247.

Mathis, S. B. (1986). *The hundred penny box.* New York, NY: Puffin Books.

Mazzocco, M. M. M., Devlin, K. T., & McKenney, S. J. (2008). Is it a fact? Timed arithmetic performance of children with mathematical learning disabilities (MLD) varies as a function of how MLD is defined. *Developmental Neuropsychology, 33*(3), 318–344.

McCallum, W. (2011). Illustrative mathematics project. Retrieved from http://illustrativemathematics.org/standards

McClain, K., Leckman, J., Schmitt, P., & Regis, T. (2006). Changing the face of statistical data analysis in the middle grades: Learning by doing. In G. F. Burrill & P. C. Elliott (Eds.), *Thinking and reasoning with data and chance, 68th yearbook* (pp. 229–240). Reston, VA: NCTM.

McCoy, L. P., Buckner, S., & Munley, J. (2007). Probability games from diverse cultures. *Mathematics Teaching in the Middle School, 12*(7), 394–402.

McGatha, M., Cobb, P., & McClain, K. (1998). *An analysis of students' statistical understandings.* Paper presented at the annual meeting of the American Educational Research Association, San Diego, CA.

McGlone, C. (2008, July). *The role of culturally-based mathematics in the general mathematics curriculum.* Paper presented at the Eleventh International Congress on Mathematics Education, Monterrey, Mexico.

McNamara, J., & Shaughnessy, M. M. (2010). *Beyond pizzas & pies: Ten essential strategies for supporting fraction sense (grades 3–5).* Sausalito, CA: Math Solutions.

McNamara, J. C. (2010). Two of everything. *Teaching Children Mathematics, 17*(3), 132–136.

McNeil, N. M., & Alibali, M. W. (2005). Knowledge change as a function of mathematics experience: All contexts are not created equal. *Journal of Cognition and Development, 6,* 285–306.

McNeil, N. M., Grandau, L., Knuth, E. J., Alibali, M. W., Stephens, A. C., Hattikudur, S., & Krill, D. E. (2006). Middle-school students' understanding of the equal sign: The books they read can't help. *Cognition & Instruction, 24*(3), 367–385.

Metz, M. L. (2010). Using GAISE and NCTM standards as framework for teaching probability and statistics to pre-service elementary and middle school mathematics teachers. *Journal of Statistics Education, 18*(3), 1–27.

Meyer, M., & Arbaugh, F. (2008). Professional development for administrators: What they need to know to support curriculum adoption and implementation. In M. Meyer, C. Langrall, F. Arbaugh, D. Webb, & M. Hoover (Eds.), *A decade of middle school mathematics curriculum implementation: Lessons learned from the Show-Me Project* (pp. 201–210). Charlotte, NC: Information Age Publishing.

Mokros, J., & Wright, T. (2009). Zoos, aquariums and expanding students' data literacy. *Teaching Children Mathematics, 15*(9), 524–530.

Molina, M., & Ambrose, R. C. (2006). Fostering relational thinking while negotiating the meaning of the equals sign. *Teaching Children Mathematics, 13*(2), 111–117.

Moschkovich, J. (2011). *Mathematics, the common core, and language: Recommendations for mathematics instruction for ELs aligned with the common core.* Retrieved from http://ell.stanford.edu/sites/default/files/pdf/academic-papers/02-JMoschkovich%20Math%20FINAL.pdf

Moschkovich, J. (2009). *Using two languages when learning mathematics: How can research help us understand mathematics learners who use two languages?* NCTM Research Brief, Reston, VA: NCTM.

Mukhopadhyah, S. (1997). Storytelling as sense-making: Children's ideas about negative numbers. *Hiroshima Journal of Mathematics Education, 5,* 35–50.

Munier, V., Devichi, C., & Merle, H. (2008). A physical situation as a way to teach angle. *Teaching Children Mathematics, 14*(7), 402–407.

Murray, M., & Jorgensen, J. (2007). *The differentiated math classroom: A guide for teachers, K–8.* Portsmouth, NH: Heinemann.

Murrey, D. L. (2008). Differentiating instruction in mathematics for the English language learner. *Mathematics Teaching in the Middle School, 14*(3), 146–153.

National Mathematics Advisory Panel. (2008). *Foundations for success.* Jessup, MD: U.S. Department of Education. (Also available online at www.ed.gov/MathPanel)

National Research Council, Committee on Early Childhood Mathematics. Cross, C. T., Woods, T. A., & Schweingruber, H. (Eds.). (2009). *Mathematics learning in early childhood: Paths toward excellence and equity.* Washington, DC: The National Academies Press.

National Research Council, Mathematics Learning Study Committee. Kilpatrick, J., Swafford, J., & Findell, B. (Eds.). (2001). *Adding it up: Helping children learn mathematics.* Washington, DC: The National Academies Press.

NCES (National Center for Education Statistics). (2011). *The condition of education 2011 (NCES 2011-033).* Washington, DC: U.S. Department of Education.

NCTM (National Council of Teachers of Mathematics). (2000). *Principles and standards for school mathematics.* Reston, VA: NCTM.

NCTM (National Council of Teachers of Mathematics). (2006). *Curriculum focal points for prekindergarten through grade 8 mathematics: A quest for coherence.* Reston, VA: NCTM.

NCTM (National Council of Teachers of Mathematics). (2007). *Research brief: Effective strategies for teaching students with difficulties in mathematics.* Retrieved from www.nctm.org/news/content.aspx?id=8452

NCTM (National Council of Teachers of Mathematics). (2008). *Equity in mathematics education.* Retrieved from www.nctm.org/about

NCTM (National Council of Teachers of Mathematics). (2011). *Position statement on interventions.* Retrieved from www.nctm.org/about/content.aspx?id=30506

Neagoy, M. (2012). *Planting the seeds of algebra: Explorations for the early grades.* Thousand Oaks, CA: Corwin.

Nebesniak, A. L., & Heaton, R. M. (2010). Student confidence and student involvement. *Mathematics Teaching in the Middle School, 16*(2), 97–103.

Nelson, C. Q., & Williams, N. L. (2009). Mathematical explorations: Exploring unknown probabilities with miniature toy pigs. *Mathematics Teaching in the Middle School, 14*(9), 557–565.

Nelson, R. (2001). *Proofs without words II: More exercises in visual thinking.* Washington, DC: Mathematical Association of America.

Neumann, M. D. (2005). Freedom quilts: Mathematics on the underground railroad. *Teaching Children Mathematics, 11*(6), 316–321.

Nicolson, C. P. (2005). Is chance fair? One student's thoughts on probability. *Teaching Children Mathematics, 12*(2), 83–89.

Norton, A., & D'Ambrosio, B. S. (2008). ZPC and ZPD: Zones of teaching and learning. *Journal for research in mathematics education 39*, 220–246.

Parker, M. (2004). Reasoning and working proportionally with percent. *Mathematics Teaching in the Middle School, 9*(6), 326–330.

Parker, R., & Breyfogle, L. (2011). Learning to write about mathematics. *Teaching Children Mathematics, 18*(2), 90–99.

Patall, E. A., Cooper, H., & Robinson, J. C. (2008). Parent involvement in homework: A research synthesis. *Review of Educational Research, 78*(4), 1039–1101.

Perie, M., Moran, R., & Lutkus, A. (2005). NAEP 2004 trends in academic progress: Three decades of student performance in reading and mathematics. Washington, DC: National Center for Education Statistics.

Perkins, I., & Flores, A. (2002). Mathematical notations and procedures of recent immigrant students. *Teaching Children Mathematics, 7*(6), 346–351.

Pesek, D., & Kirshner, D. (2002). Interfereence of instrumental instruction in subsequent relational learning. In J. Sowder & B.P. Schappelle (Eds.), *Lessons learned from research* (pp. 101–107). Reston, VA: NCTM.

Petit, M., & Zawojewski, J. (2010). Formative assessment in elementary school mathematics. In D. Lambdin & F. K. Lester, Jr. (Eds.), *Teaching and learning mathematics: Translating research for elementary school teachers* (pp. 73–79). Reston, VA: NCTM.

Petit, M. M., Laird, R. E., & Marsden, E. L. (2010). *A focus on fractions: Bringing research to the classroom (Studies in mathematical thinking and learning series)*. New York, NY: Taylor & Francis.

Philipp, R., & Vincent, C. (2003). Reflecting on learning fractions without understanding. *OnMath, 2*(2) Available to NCTM members at http://my.nctm.org/eresources/view_article .asp?article_id=6430

Phillips-Bey, C. K. (2004). TI-73 calculator activities. *Mathematics Teaching in the Middle School, 9*(9), 500–508.

Piaget, J. (1976). *The child's conception of the world*. Totowa, NJ: Littlefield, Adams.

Post, T. R. (1981). Fractions: Results and implications from the national assessment. *Arithmetic Teacher, 28*(9), 26–31.

Post, T. R., Wachsmuth, I., Lesh, R. A., & Behr, M. J. (1985). Order and equivalence of rational numbers: A cognitive analysis. *Journal for Research in Mathematics Education, 16*(1), 18–36.

Preston, R., & Thompson, T. (2004). Integrating measurement across the curriculum. *Mathematics Teaching in the Middle School, 9*(8), 436–441.

Pugalee, D. K., Arbaugh, F., Bay-Williams, J. M., Farrell, A., Mathews, S., &. Royster, D. (2008). *Navigating through mathematical connections in grades 6–8*. Reston, VA: NCTM.

Rasmussen, C., Yackel, E., & King, K. (2003). Social and sociomathematical norms in the mathematics classroom. In H. L. Schoen & R. I. Charles (Eds.), *Teaching mathematics through problem solving: Grades 6–12* (pp. 143–154). Reston, VA: NCTM.

Rathouz, M. M. (2011). Making sense of decimal multiplication. *Mathematics Teaching in the Middle School, 16*(7), 430–437.

Ravenna, G. (2008). *Factors influencing gifted students' preferences for models of teaching* (Dissertation). Los Angeles, CA: University of Southern California.

Reis, S., & Renzulli, J. S. (2005). *Curriculum compacting: An easy start to differentiating for high potential students*. Waco, TX: Prufrock Press.

Renzulli, J. S., Gubbins, E. J., McMillen, K. S., Eckert, R. D., & Little, C. A. (Eds.). (2009). *Systems and models for developing programs for the gifted and talented* (2nd ed.). Mansfield Center, CT: Creative Learning Press.

Riskowski, J. L., Olbricht, G., & Wilson, J. (2010). 100 students. *Mathematics Teaching in the Middle School, 15*(6), 320–327.

Roberge, M. C., & Cooper, L. L. (2010). Map scale, proportion, and Google™ Earth. *Mathematics Teaching in the Middle School, 15*(8), 448–457.

Robinson, J. P. (2010). The effects of test translation on young English learners' mathematics performance. *Educational Researcher, 39*(8), 582–590.

Rodríguez-Brown, F. V. (2010). Latino families: culture and schooling. In E. G. Murillo, Jr., S. A. Villenas, R. T. Galván, J. S. Muñoz, C. Martínez, & M. Machado-Casas (Eds.), *Handbook of Latinos and education: Theory, research, and practice* (pp. 350–360). New York, NY: Routledge.

Rossman, A., Chance, B., & Medina, E. (2006). Some important comparisons between statistics and mathematics, and why teachers should care. In G. F. Burrill & P. C. Elliott (Eds.), *Thinking and reasoning with data and chance, 68th yearbook* (pp. 323–334). Reston, VA: NCTM.

Rotigel, J., & Fellow, S. (2005). Mathematically gifted students: How can we meet their needs? *Gifted Child Today, 27*(4), 46–65.

Rubel, L. (2006). Students' probabilistic thinking revealed: The case of coin tosses. In G. Burrill & P. C. Elliott (Eds.), *Thinking and reasoning with data and chance, 68th yearbook* (pp. 49–60). Reston, VA: NCTM.

Rubel, L. (2007). Middle school and high school students' probabilistic reasoning on coin tasks. *Journal for Research in Mathematics Education, 38*(5), 531–557.

Russell, S. J. (2006). What does it mean that ì5 has a lotî? From the world to data and back. In G. F. Burrill & P. C. Elliott (Eds.), *Thinking and reasoning with data and chance, 68th yearbook* (pp. 17–30). Reston VA: NCTM.

Ryan, J., & Williams, J. (2007). *Children's mathematics 4–15: Learning from errors and misconceptions*. New York, NY: McGraw-Hill/Open University Press.

Sadler, P., & Tai, R. (2007). The two pillars supporting college science. *Science, 317*(5837), 457–458.

Saul, M., Assouline, S., & Sheffield, L. J. (Eds.). (2010). *The peak in the middle: Developing mathematically gifted students in the middle grades*. Reston, VA: National Council of Teachers of Mathematics, National Association of Gifted Children, and National Middle School Association.

Scheaffer, R. L. (2006). Statistics and mathematics: On making a happy marriage. In G. F. Burrill & P. C. Elliott (Eds.), *Thinking and reasoning with data and chance, 68th yearbook* (pp. 309–322). Reston, VA: NCTM.

Schifter, D. (1999). Reasoning about operations: Early algebraic thinking, grades K through 6. In L. Stiff & F. Curcio (Eds.), *Developing mathematical reasoning in grades K–12* (pp. 62–81). Reston, VA: NCTM.

Schifter, D., Bastable, V., & Russell, S. J. (1999). *Developing mathematical understanding: Numbers and operations, Part 2, Making meaning for operations (Casebook)*. Parsippany, NJ: Dale Seymour Publications.

Schifter, D., Monk, G. S., Russell, S. J., & Bastable, V. (2007). Early algebra: What does understanding the laws of arithmetic mean in the elementary grades? In J. Kaput, D. Carraher, & M. Blanton (Eds.), *Algebra in the early grades.* Mahwah, NJ: Lawrence Erlbaum Associates.

Schifter, D., Russell, S. J., & Bastable, V. (2009). Early algebra to reach the range of learners. *Teaching Children Mathematics, 16*(4), 230–237.

Sconyers, J. M. (1995). Proof and the middle school mathematics student. *Mathematics Teaching in the Middle School, 1*(7), 516–518.

Scott, T. & Lane, H. (2001). *Multi-tiered interventions in academic and social contexts.* Unpublished manuscript, University of Florida, Gainesville.

Secada, W. G. (1983). *The educational background of limited-English-proficient students: Implications for the arithmetic classroom.* Arlington Heights, IL: Bilingual Education Service Center (ERIC Document Reproduction Service No. ED 237318).

Seeley, C., & Schielack, J. F. (2007). A look at the development of ratios, rates, and proportionality. *Mathematics Teaching in the Middle School, 13*(3), 140–142.

Seeley, C. L. (2009). *Faster isn't smarter: Messages about math, teaching, and learning in the 21st century.* Sausalito, CA: Math Solutions.

Setati, M. (2005). Teaching mathematics in a primary multilingual classroom. *Journal for Research in Mathematics Education, 36*(5), 447–466.

Shaughnessy, J. M. (2003). Research on students' understanding of probability. In J. Kilpatrick, W. G. Martin, & D. Schifter (Eds.), *A research companion to Principles and Standards for School Mathematics* (pp. 216–226). Reston, VA: NCTM.

Shaughnessy, J. M. (2006). Research on students' understanding of some big concepts in statistics. In G. F. Burrill & P. C. Elliott (Eds.), *Thinking and reasoning with data and chance, 68th yearbook* (pp. 77–98). Reston, VA: NCTM.

Shaughnessy, J. M. (2007). Research on statistics learning and reasoning. In F. Lester, Jr. (Ed.), *Second handbook of research on mathematics teaching and learning* (pp. 957–1010). Reston, VA: NCTM.

Sheffield, L. J. (Ed.). (1999). *Developing mathematically promising students.* Reston, VA: National Council of Teachers of Mathematics.

Siebert, D., & Gaskin, N. (2006). Creating, naming, and justifying fractions. *Teaching Children Mathematics, 12*(8), 394–400.

Siegler, R., Carpenter, T., Fennell, F., Geary, D., Lewis, J., Okamoto, Y., & Wray, J. (2010). *Developing effective fractions instruction for kindergarten through 8th grade: A practice guide* (NCEE #2010-4039). Washington, DC: National Center for Education Evaluation and Regional Assistance, Institute of Education Sciences, U.S. Department of Education. Retrieved from www.whatworks.ed.gov/publications/practiceguides

Skemp, R. (1978). Relational understanding and instrumental understanding. *Arithmetic Teacher, 26*(3), 9–15.

Small, M. (2009). *Good questions: Great ways to differentiate mathematics instruction.* Reston, VA: NCTM.

Smith, D. (2011) *If the world were a village: A book about the world's people* (2nd ed.). Tonawanda, NY: Kids Can Press.

Smith, J. P., III. (2002). The development of students' knowledge of fractions and ratios. In B. Litwiller (Ed.), *Making sense of fractions, ratios, and proportions* (pp. 3–17). Reston, VA: NCTM.

Smith, M., Hughes, E., Engle, R., & Stein, M. (2009). Orchestrating discussions. *Mathematics Teaching in the Middle School, 14*(9), 548–556.

Sousa, D., & Tomlinson, C. (2011). *Differentiation and the brain: How neuroscience supports the learner-friendly classroom.* Bloomington, IN: Solution Tree Press.

Sowder, J. T., & Wearne, D. (2006). What do we know about eighth-grade student achievement? *Mathematics Teaching in the Middle School, 11*(6), 285–293.

Steele, D. F. (2005). Using schemas to develop algebraic thinking. *Mathematics Teaching in the Middle School, 11*(1), 40–46.

Stein, M., Smith, M., Henningsen, E., & Silver, E. (2009). *Implementing standards-based mathematics instruction: A case for professional development* (2nd ed.). New York, NY: Teachers College Press.

Steinle, V., & Stacey, K. (2004a). Persistence of decimal misconceptions and readiness to move to expertise. *Proceedings of the 28th conference of the International Groups for the Psychology of Mathematics Education, 4,* 225–232.

Steinle, V., & Stacey, K. (2004b). A longitudinal study of students' understanding of decimal notation: An overview and refined results. In I. Putt, R. Faragher, & M. McLean (Eds.), *Mathematics education for the third millennium: Towards 2010. Proceedings of the 27th annual conference of the Mathematics Education Research Group of Australasia, 2,* 541–548. Townsville: Mathematics Education Research Group of Australasia.

Stemn, B. S. (2008). Building middle school students' understanding of proportional reasoning through mathematical investigation. *Education, 36*(4), 3–13.

Stephan, M., & Akyuz, D. (2012). A proposed instructional theory for integer addition and subtraction. *Journal for Research in Mathematics Education, 43*(4), 428–464.

Stephan, M., & Whitenack, J. (2003). Establishing classroom social and sociomathematical norms for problem solving. In F. K. Lester, Jr. & R. I. Charles (Eds.), *Teaching mathematics through problem solving: Prekindergarten-grade 6* (pp. 149–162). Reston, VA: NCTM.

Stephan, M. L. (2009). What are you worth? *Mathematics Teaching in the Middle School, 15*(1), 16–24.

Stephens, A. C. (2005). Developing students' understanding of variable. *Mathematics Teaching in the Middle School, 11*(2), 96–100.

Stiggins, R. (2009). Assessment for learning in upper elementary grades. *Phi Delta Kappan, 90*(6), 419–421.

Storeygard, J. (2010). *My kids can: Making math accessible to all learners, K–5.* Portsmouth, NH: Heinemann.

Sullivan, P., & Lilburn, P. (2002). *Good questions for math teaching: Why ask them and what to ask, K–6.* Sausalito, CA: Math Solutions.

Swanson, P. E. (2010). The intersection of language and mathematics. *Mathematics Teaching in the Middle School, 15*(9), 516–523.

Taber, S. B. (2005). The mathematics of *Alice's Adventures in Wonderland. Mathematics Teaching in the Middle School, 11*(4), 165–171.

Taber, S. B. (2009). Capitalizing on the unexpected. *Mathematics Teaching in the Middle School, 15*(3), 149–155.

Tarr, J. E., Lee, H. S., & Rider, R. L. (2006). When data and chance collide: Drawing inferences from empirical data. In G. Burrill & P. C. Elliott (Eds.), *Thinking and reasoning with data and chance, 68th yearbook* (pp. 139–149). Reston, VA: NCTM.

Tarr, J. E., & Shaughnessy, J. M. (2007). Data analysis, statistics, and probability. In F. Lester & P. Kloosterman (Eds.), *Results from the 2003 National Assessment of Educational Progress.* Reston, VA: NCTM.

Thompson, P. W. (1995). Notation, convention, and quantity in elementary mathematics. In J. T. Sowder & B. P. Schappelle (Eds.), *Providing a foundation for teaching mathematics in the middle grades* (pp. 199–221). Albany, NY: State University of New York Press.

Thompson, T. D., & Preston, R. V. (2004). Measurement in the middle grades: Insights from NAEP and TIMSS. *Mathematics Teaching in the Middle School, 9*(9), 514–519.

Tillema, E. (2012). What's the difference: Using contextualized problems. *Mathematics Teaching in the Middle School, 17*(8), 472–478.

Tillema, E. S. (2010). Math for real: A three-girl family. *Mathematics Teaching in the Middle School, 48*(5), 304.

Tirosh, D. (2000). Enhancing prospective teachers' knowledge of children's conceptions: The case of division of fractions. *Journal for Research in Mathematics Education, 31*(1), 5–25.

Tobias, S. (1995). *Overcoming math anxiety.* New York, NY: W. W. Norton & Company.

Tomlinson, C. (1999). Mapping a route towards differentiated instruction. *Educational Leadership, 57*(1), 12–16.

Tomlinson, C. (2003). *Fulfilling the promise of the differentiated classroom: Strategies and tools for responsive teaching.* Alexandria. VA: Association for Supervision and Curriculum Development.

Tompert, A. (1997). *Grandfather Tang's story.* New York, NY: Dragonfly Books.

Torgesen, J. K. (2002). The prevention of reading difficulties. *Journal of School Psychology, 40*(1), 7–26.

Towers, J., & Hunter, K. (2010). An ecological reading of mathematical language in a grade 3 classroom: A case of learning and teaching measurement estimation. *The Journal of Mathematical Behavior, 29*(1), 25–40.

Tsankova, J. K., & Pjanic, K. (2009/2010). The area model of multiplication of fractions. *Mathematics Teaching in the Middle School, 15*(5), 281–285.

Turner, E. E., Celedón-Pattichis, S., Marshall, M., & Tennison, A. (2009). "Fijense amorcitos, les voy a contra una historia": The power of story to support solving and discussing mathematical problems among Latino and Latina kindergarten students. In D. Y. White & J. S. Spitzer (Eds.), *Mathematics for every student: Responding to diversity in grades PK–5* (pp. 23–42). Reston, VA: NCTM.

Tzur, R. (1999). An integrated study of children's construction of improper fractions and the teacher's role in promoting learning. *Journal for Research in Mathematics Education, 30*(4), 390–416.

U.S. Census Bureau. (n.d.). *Population clocks.* Retrieved from www.census.gov/population/international

Usiskin, Z. (2007). Some thoughts about fractions. *Mathematics Teaching in the Middle School, 12*(7), 370–373.

Van Dooren, W., De Bock, D., Vleugels, K., & Verschaffel, L. (2010). Just answering . . . or thinking? Contrasting pupils' solutions and classifications of missing-value word problems. *Mathematical Thinking and Learning, 12*(1), 20–35.

Van Hiele, P. M. (1999). Developing geometric thinking through activities that begin with play. *Teaching Children Mathematics, 5*(6), 310–316.

VanTassel-Baska, J., & Brown, E. F. (2007). Toward best practice: An analysis of the efficacy of curriculum models in gifted education. *Gifted Child Quarterly, 51*(4), 342–358.

Vlassis, J. (2004). Making sense of the minus sign or becoming flexible in "negativity." *Learning and Instruction. Special Issue: The*

Conceptual Change Approach to Mathematics Learning and Teaching, *14*(5), 469–484.

Vygotsky, L. S. (1978). *Mind and society.* Cambridge, MA: Harvard University Press.

Wallace, A. (2007). Anticipating student responses to improve problem solving. *Mathematics Teaching in the Middle School, 12*(9), 504–511.

Watson, J. M., & Shaughnessy, J. M. (2004). Proportional reasoning: Lessons learned from research in data and chance. *Mathematics Teaching in the Middle School, 10*(2), 104–109.

Wearne, D., & Kouba, V. L. (2000). Rational numbers. In E. A. Silver & P. A. Kenney (Eds.), *Results from the seventh mathematics assessment of the National Assessment of Educational Progress* (pp. 163–191). Reston, VA: NCTM.

Weidemann, W., Mikovch, A. K., & Hunt, J. B. (2001). Using a lifeline to give rational numbers a personal touch. *Mathematics Teaching in the Middle School, 7*(4), 210–215.

Whiteford, T. (2009/2010). Is mathematics a universal language? *Teaching Children Mathematics, 16*(5), 276–283.

Wiggins, G., & McTighe, J. (2005). *Understanding by design* (2nd ed.). Alexandria, VA: Association for Supervision and Curriculum Development.

Wiliam, D. (2010). *Practical techniques for formative assessment.* Presented at Boras, Sweden. Retrieved from www.slideshare.net/BLoPP/dylan-wiliam-bors-2010

Williams, M., Forrest, K., & Schnabel, D. (2006). Water wonders (math by the month). *Teaching Children Mathematics, 12*(5), 248–249.

Witzel, B. S. (2005). Using CRA to teach algebra to students with math difficulties in inclusive settings. *Learning Disabilities—A Contemporary Journal, 3*(2), 49–60.

Wood, T. & Turner-Vorbeck, T. (2001). Extending the conception of mathematics teaching. In T. Wood, B. S. Nelson, & J. Warfield (Eds.), *Beyond classical pedagogy: Teaching elementary school mathematics* (pp. 185–208). Mahwah, NJ: Lawrence Erlbaum Associates.

Wood, T., Williams, G., & McNeal, B. (2006). Children's mathematical thinking in different classroom cultures. *Journal for Research in Mathematics Education, 37*(3), 222–255.

Woodward, J. (2006). Developing automaticity in multiplication facts: Integrating strategy instruction with timed practice drills. *Learning Disability Quarterly, 29*(4), 269–289.

Yackel, E., & Cobb, P. (1996). Sociomathematical norms, argumentation, and autonomy in mathematics. *Journal for Research in Mathematics Education, 27*(4), 458–477.

Ysseldyke, J. (2002). Response to "Learning disabilities: historical perspectives." In R. Bradley, L. Danielson, & D. Hallahan (Eds.), *Identification of learning disabilities: Research to practice* (pp. 89–98). Mahwah, NJ: Lawrence Erlbaum Associates.

Yu, P., Barrett, J., & Presmeg, N. (2009). Prototypes and categorical reasoning: A perspective to explain how children learn about interactive geometry objects. In T. Craine & R. Rubenstein (Eds.), *Understanding geometry for a changing world.* Reston, VA: NCTM.

Zambo, R. (2011). Percents can make sense. *Mathematics Teaching in the Middle School, 13*(7), 418–422.

Zwillinger, D. (Ed.) (2011). *Standard mathematical tables and formulae* (32nd ed.). Boca Raton, FL: CRC Press.

Index